Children's Encounters With Death, Bereavement, and Coping

Charles A. Corr, PhD, CT, is a Professor Emeritus at Southern Illinois University Edwardsville and is a member of the Association for Death Education and Counseling (1978–present; Board of Directors, 1980–1983); the International Work Group on Death, Dying, and Bereavement (1979–present; chairperson, 1989–1993); the ChiPPS (Children's Project on Palliative/Hospice Services) Leadership Advisory Council of the National Hospice and Palliative Care Organization (1998–present); the Board of Directors of the Suncoast Institute, an affiliate of the Suncoast Hospice (2000–present); and the Executive Committee of the National Donor Family Council of the National Kidney Foundation (1992–2001, 2006–present). Dr. Corr's publications include more than 30 books and booklets, together with more than 100 chapters and articles in professional journals, on subjects such as death education, death-related issues involving children and adolescents, hospice principles and practice, and organ and tissue donation. His most recent books are the sixth edition of *Death and Dying, Life and Living* (2009), coauthored with Clyde M. Nabe and Donna M. Corr, and *Adolescent Encounters With Death, Bereavement, and Coping* (Springer Publishing, 2009), coedited with David E. Balk.

David E. Balk, PhD, FT, is a Professor in the Department of Health and Nutrition Sciences at Brooklyn College of the City University of New York, where he directs graduate studies in thanatology. He is an Associate Editor of *Death Studies* and serves as that journal's Book Review Editor. His work in thanatology has focused primarily on adolescent bereavement. He is the author of *Adolescent Development: Early Through Late Adolescence* (1995), and with Carol Wogrin, Gordon Thornton, and David Meagher, he edited *Handbook of Thanatology: The Essential Body of Knowledge for the Study of Death, Dying, and Bereavement* (2007). With Charles Corr, he coedited *Handbook of Adolescent Death and Bereavement* (Springer Publishing, 1996) and *Adolescent Encounters With Death, Bereavement, and Coping* (Springer Publishing, 2009). Dr. Balk serves on the Mental Health Advisory Board for National Students of AMF, a program begun by bereaved college students to assist one another.

Children's Encounters With Death, Bereavement, and Coping

CHARLES A. CORR, PhD, CT
DAVID E. BALK, PhD, FT

Editors

SPRINGER PUBLISHING COMPANY

New York

Springer Publishing Company, LLC
11 West 42nd Street
New York, NY 10036
www.springerpub.com

Acquisitions Editor: Sheri W. Sussman
Project Manager: Mark Frazier
Cover Design: Mimi Flow
Composition: Apex CoVantage, LLC

E-book ISBN: 978-0-8261-3423-3
09 10 11 12/ 5 4 3 2 1

The authors and the publisher of this work have made every effort to use sources believed to be reliable to provide information that is accurate and compatible with the standards generally accepted at the time of publication. Because medical science is continually advancing, our knowledge base continues to expand. Therefore, as new information becomes available, changes in procedures become necessary. We recommend that the reader always consult current research and specific institutional policies before performing any clinical procedure. The authors and publisher shall not be liable for any special, consequential, or exemplary damages resulting, in whole or in part, from the readers' use of, or reliance on, the information contained in this book. The publisher has no responsibility for the persistence or accuracy of URLs for external or third-party Internet Web sites referred to in this publication and does not guarantee that any content on such Web sites is, or will remain, accurate or appropriate.

Library of Congress Cataloging-in-Publication Data
Children's encounters with death, bereavement, and coping / Charles A. Corr, David E. Balk, editors.
       p. cm.
   Includes bibliographical references and index.
   ISBN 978-0-8261-3422-6 (alk. paper)
  1. Children and death.   2. Grief in children.   3. Bereavement in children.
4. Adjustment (Psychology) in children.   I. Corr, Charles A.   II. Balk, David E., 1943–
      BF723.D3C555 2009
      155.9'37083—dc22   2009037535

Printed in the United States of America by Hamilton Printing.

*This book is dedicated to
Dr. Richard J. Blackwell,
teacher, scholar, mentor,
and long-time family friend,
with respect, admiration, and gratitude*

*And to
Janet Renee Balk,
My daughter, my child,
Whose joy for life,
Sense of humor, steadfast loyalty,
Desire for social justice,
Courage in the face of wrong,
And loving heart
Fill her parents with pride and admiration*

Contents

Contributors

Patricia Bolster, RSM, DHCE, MEd, MTh, is Chaplain in the oncology unit of the Children's Hospital at Westmead, Sydney, Australia.

Michelle R. Brown, PhD, is a Clinical Assistant Professor in the Division of Child Psychiatry, Stanford University School of Medicine, and a Pediatric Psychologist with the Pediatric Psychiatry Consultation-Liaison Service at Lucile Packard Children's Hospital at Stanford in Stanford, California.

Grace Christ, DSW, is a Professor in the School of Social Work, Columbia University, New York City.

Diane Snyder Cowan, MA, MT-BC, is Director of the Elisabeth Severance Prentiss Bereavement Center, Hospice of the Western Reserve, in Cleveland, Ohio.

Edith Crumb, LCSW, was Grief Intake Counselor at Alive Hospice and Emergency Department Social Worker at Monroe Carell Jr. Children's Hospital at Vanderbilt in Nashville, Tennessee, at the time of her contribution to this book. She is currently a teaching assistant in the bachelor's of social work program while pursuing her doctorate in social work at the University of Louisville.

Jana DeCristofaro, MSW, is the Coordinator of Children's Grief Services at the Dougy Center for Grieving Children in Portland, Oregon.

Craig Demmer, EdD, PhD, is a Professor in the Department of Health Sciences, Lehman College of the City University of New York.

Ann M. Fitzsimons, MBA, is a bereaved aunt and the Cofounder/Associate Director of Compassionate Passages, Inc. She lives in Farmington Hills, Michigan.

Melissa J. Hagan, MPH, MA, is a Prevention Research Fellow at Arizona State University, Tempe, Arizona.

John H. Hoover, PhD, is Associate Dean of the College of Education, St. Cloud State University, St. Cloud, Minnesota.

Susan M. Huff, RN, MSN, is the Director of Pediatrics at Home, a company of Johns Hopkins Home Care Group and Johns Hopkins Medicine in Baltimore, Maryland.

Katrina Koehler, BA, is the Executive Director at Gerard's House, in Santa Fe, New Mexico.

Kathryn A. Markell, PhD, teaches at Anoka-Ramsey Community College in Coon Rapids, Minnesota.

Marc A. Markell, PhD, CT, is a Professor of Special Education at St. Cloud State University, St. Cloud, Minnesota.

Clint Moore III, MDiv, PhD, BCC, FT, is an ordained Episcopal priest in the Diocese of Chicago and a Clinical Ethicist at Advocate Lutheran General and Advocate Lutheran General Children's Hospitals, Park Ridge, Illinois. He is also a part-time faculty member in the Philosophy Department at Loyola University Chicago.

Jane Moore, EdD, FT, is an Associate Professor at National-Louis University, Chicago, Illinois, and a part-time faculty member in the Thanatology Program at King's University College, the University of Western Ontario, London, Ontario, Canada.

Rebekah Lancto Near, CAGS, MS, LCAT, is a consulting licensed expressive arts therapist for Friends of Karen, Inc., in Brooklyn, New York.

Stacy F. Orloff, EdD, LCSW, is Vice President of Palliative Care and Community Programs at Suncoast Hospice in Clearwater, Florida.

Marie-Thérèse Proctor, BA Psych and Rel Studies, BA Psych Hons, PhD, is a Psychologist and Project Research Officer with the Life-Limiting Conditions Project in the Oncology Unit of the Children's Hospital at Westmead, Sydney, Australia.

Rhondda J. Rytmeister, BA (Hons), MClinPsych, is Senior Clinical Psychologist in the Oncology Unit at the Children's Hospital at Westmead, Sydney, Australia.

Irwin N. Sandler, PhD, is Regents' Professor and Director of the Prevention Research Center, Arizona State University, Tempe, Arizona.

Donna L. Schuurman, EdD, FT, is Executive Director of the Dougy Center for Grieving Children in Portland, Oregon.

Heather L. Servaty-Seib, PhD, HSPP, is an Associate Professor of Counseling and Development in the Department of Educational Studies, Purdue University, West Lafayette, Indiana.

Beth A. Seyda, BS, is a bereaved parent, Board Past-President of the Pregnancy Loss and Infant Death Alliance, and cofounder and Executive Director of Compassionate Passages, Inc. She lives in Chapel Hill, North Carolina.

Barbara Sourkes, PhD, is an Associate Professor of Pediatrics and Psychiatry at Stanford University School of Medicine and the Kriewall-Haehl Director of the Pediatric Palliative Care Program at Lucile Packard Children's Hospital at Stanford in Stanford, California.

Michael M. Stevens, AM, FRACP, is Senior Staff Specialist in the Oncology Unit of the Children's Hospital at Westmead, Sydney, New South Wales, Australia.

Amy Griffith Taylor, LMSW, is the Counseling Supervisor at the Victim Intervention Program (VIP) of the Metropolitan Police Department of Nashville and Davidson County in Nashville, Tennessee.

Sara J. Tedrick, BA, is a graduate student in the Counseling Psychology Doctoral Program in the Department of Educational Studies, Purdue University, West Lafayette, Indiana.

Tamina Toray, PhD, is a Professor in the Psychology Division at Western Oregon University, Monmouth, Oregon, and Adjunct Faculty at Oregon State University College of Veterinary Medicine, Corvallis, Oregon.

Andrea C. Walker, PhD, LADC, is an Associate Professor of Psychology at Oral Roberts University, Tulsa, Oklahoma.

Nancy Boyd Webb, DSW, BCD, RPT-S, is Distinguished Professor Emerita of Fordham University's Graduate School of Social Service, where she served as the founding director of the Post-Master's Certificate Program in Child and Adolescent Therapy in Westchester County, New York.

Dayna D. Wood, EdS, NCC, LMHC, is a bereavement counselor for the Visiting Nurse Service of New York Hospice Care program in New York City.

Foreword

All adults know that everyone will die sooner or later, but until confronted with an actual death, or with a situation of a serious health condition, most of us prefer to push the idea of death for ourselves and our loved ones into the distant future. It is the ultimate loss experience, and it is an event over which we have no control. When someone close to us becomes terminally ill or dies, we feel devastated, and this may be one of the most powerful emotions we have ever known. Even the strongest and the mightiest bow down to the power and finality of death. Some people never "get over" their loss. In view of this reality, it is no wonder that adults have great difficulty talking with children about death and in trying to help bereaved youth with their questions and confused emotions. Adults who themselves feel helpless and overwhelmed when confronted with death are ill-equipped to answer children's questions and to help them process their feelings about it.

Thankfully, the field of death education has stepped in to offer assistance in the form of guide books and manuals intended to help professionals assist bereaved individuals of all ages. In the past decade a virtual flood of bereavement books has been published, and these have been eagerly welcomed by the broad range of helpers who find themselves in a situation of having to comfort a bereaved child or young person. No longer can the topic of death be ignored as the general public in this country watches daily television or news accounts about homicides, terrorist attacks, and wartime deaths. The media give extensive exposure to this subject, and all professionals who interact with children, whether pastoral counselors, medical personnel, nurses, school counselors, social workers, teachers, or parents, must be prepared to encounter children who are trying to deal with their emotions related to deaths in their families, in their schools, and in their communities.

I learned this many years ago in my own experience as a child therapist counseling children and families who were dealing with a variety of problematic situations. The death of a grandmother in a family that was trying to adapt to a boy with severe attention deficit problems taught me that stresses between the generations over the management of a terminally ill elderly woman can seriously complicate and negatively impact the family's ability to focus on their child, who was struggling with other problems (see Webb, 1993). Because of this case, and several others in which death emerged as a complicating factor in a child's therapy, I realized that it was necessary to acknowledge and focus on the child's and family's reaction to a significant death, in addition to helping with other troublesome issues. Over time I have worked with children who have experienced a variety of death experiences, including the loss of a close friend in a car accident, a mother who had terminal AIDS, a father who died suddenly in a house fire, and a father who perished in the attacks of September 11, 2001, to mention a few. Because there was a paucity of professional literature covering traumatic events such as these, I decided to edit a book about helping bereaved children in order to share my clinical experience with other therapists, counselors, and students. Over the course of 15 years, that book (*Helping Bereaved Children*) has been published in two updated and distinct editions with a third edition currently in press, thereby confirming my original impression that the subject was one that was greatly needed.

The invitation to write the foreword to the present book, *Children's Encounters With Death, Bereavement, and Coping,* provided me with another welcome opportunity to express my own commitment to help the helpers who are helping bereaved children. Charles Corr and David Balk have assembled a very comprehensive group of topics and authors in this volume that can serve as exemplars for assisting in a variety of bereavement circumstances. The extensive coverage includes a review of children's reactions to various types of deaths and chapters that present a variety of helping interventions. These include chapters focused on death education, on the use of expressive arts therapies, on peer groups, and on the role of hospice and palliative care, as well as on family and individual psychotherapy. The appendix, containing a rich selection of books for children about loss and grief, will serve as a wonderful resource for professionals and parents who will welcome having this annotated listing of books to read with bereaved children.

We know that death comes in many forms, from the anticipated decline and eventual demise of an elderly grandmother, to the sudden, completely unexpected accidental death of a sibling in a skiing accident. Deaths may be peaceful and quiet or violent and mutilating. They may occur singly or in groups. They may involve close family members, school friends, or unknown, but famous, rock stars such as Michael Jackson. Several factors will determine children's bereavement responses. I have grouped these into an assessment formulation that I refer to as the "Tripartite Assessment of the Bereaved Child" (Webb, 2002). These include Individual Factors such as the child's age, past experience with death, and ability to comprehend the meaning of the loss. Another important factor is the nature of the child's relationship with the person who died. It seems understandable that the closer the relationship, the deeper will be the pain of the loss, and the more complicated will be the child's bereavement. Corr's two opening chapters cover many of these issues. A second group of factors that I refer to as "Death-Related Factors" includes what the child has been told about death in general terms and also what has been communicated to the child about the current death event.

Family, Social, Religious, and Cultural Factors constitute the third part of the tripartite assessment of the bereaved child. It is important to know the degree to which the child has been included in the family rituals surrounding the death, including the funeral. Children benefit from having the opportunity to say goodbye in an age-appropriate manner, if the culture approves of this. We know that religious beliefs, which can be such a comfort to adults, sometimes confuse and anger the young child who does not comprehend the abstract distinction between the body and the soul and whose literal thinking may wonder why God chose to take away his or her mother or father. Children need repeated and patient explanations, given in small doses in simple terms. Readers will find some very helpful suggestions about doing this in several chapters in part 4 of this book.

This book is a wonderful resource that can be consulted repeatedly by professionals and used as a text in thanatology courses. Unfortunately, none of us can take away the pain of bereaved children that will come and go at significant milestones in the child's growing life when he or she misses the absent loved person. However, it is possible to keep that grief from becoming disabling and to foster children's resilience so that they can incorporate their bereavement and carry on with their lives. The concept of the "transformative" power of grief (Peterson, Park, D'Andrea, & Seligman, 1995; Tedeschi & Calhoun, 1995) refers to the ability of some individuals not only to move beyond the pain of their loss, but also to use it in a positive way. One might think that this would be an unrealistic expectation for young children, but I cite several examples of children's positive experiences with death in my latest book, *Helping*

Children and Adolescents With Chronic and Serious Health Conditions. Readers who want an inspiring example should check out the autobiographical account of Mattie Stepanek, who at age 12 had experienced the deaths of several siblings from a rare disease and who, himself, had a terminal condition (Stepanek, 2001). This boy's young life is a beautiful demonstration of the power of resiliency and hope that transformed a situation of sadness and doom to one of possibility and positive thinking. In a similar manner, Corr and Balk's book will help adults find many ways to lead bereaved children to a hopeful belief in their future, despite their considerable losses. This book is a real contribution to the growing literature in this field.

Nancy Boyd Webb, DSW, LICSW, RPT-S
Distinguished Professor of Social Work Emerita,
Graduate School of Social Service,
Fordham University

REFERENCES

Peterson, C., Park, N., D'Andrea, W., & Seligman, M. E. (2008). Strengths of character and posttraumatic growth. *Journal of Traumatic Stress, 21*(2), 214–217.

Stepanek, M. J. T. (2001). *Journey through heartsongs.* New York: Hyperion.

Tedeschi, R. G., & Calhoun, L. G. (1995). *Trauma and transformation: Growing in the aftermath of suffering.* Thousand Oaks, CA: Sage.

Webb, N. B. (Ed.). (1993). *Helping bereaved children: A handbook for practitioners* (2nd ed., 2002; 3rd ed., in press). New York: Guilford Press.

Webb, N. B. (Ed.). (2009). *Helping children and adolescents with chronic and serious medical conditions.* Hoboken, NJ: Wiley.

Preface

Children who are struggling with death-related issues deserve caring and competent assistance from the adults around them. These are issues that have staggered many adults. When provided with timely and appropriate support, children are resilient in many ways, but encounters with loss, death, and bereavement challenge their abilities to cope.

Unfortunately, children's experiences and endeavors in this field have not always received the full-scale, in-depth exploration they deserve. There are many reasons for this deficiency. All too often, issues involving children and adolescents are run together as if there were no important differences between these two developmental groups. In addition, on their own, children are diverse in many ways, and it has often seemed to many adults that children's encounters with death and bereavement are few in number, with perhaps little impact on their lives in the long run.

We disagree. On the contrary, we believe there is need for a robust and ongoing focus on issues related to death, bereavement, and coping during childhood. Such a focus needs to include, but go beyond, investigations of familiar topics, such as parental or sibling bereavement as experienced by children. We offer this book as part of a new effort to provide a broad resource to guide care providers, such as nurses, counselors, social workers, educators, and clergy, as well as parents, family members, and other concerned persons, who seek to understand and help children as they attempt to cope with death-related issues.

Writing separately and together, we have attempted over the years to contribute to the literature on death-related topics as they involve children. One of us has coedited three prior books in this subject area. Those books included *Helping Children Cope With Death: Guidelines and Resources* (1982; 2nd ed., 1984), coedited with Hannelore Wass; *Childhood and Death* (1984), also coedited with Hannelore Wass; and *Handbook of Childhood Death and Bereavement* (Springer Publishing, 1996), coedited with Donna M. Corr.

Together, the two editors of the present volume coedited *Handbook of Adolescent Death and Bereavement* (Springer Publishing, 1996) and *Adolescent Encounters With Death, Bereavement, and Coping* (Springer Publishing, 2009).

We agreed to undertake a new book on death-related issues and children, the one you now hold in your hands, because we recognized that a great deal has transpired since the 1980s and 1990s in terms of theoretical understandings, research advances, and clinical management. For example, our knowledge of the development of children's understandings of death has been increasing and becoming more sophisticated, sensitivity to both cultural differences and the individual voices of children has been enhanced, appreciation of diverse populations around the world has grown, new insights have been gained about children's resilience following bereavement, and multiple attempts have been made to bridge the gaps that often separate researchers and practitioners. At the same time, the availability of pediatric palliative and hospice care has expanded greatly, as have grief support programs for bereaved children and their families. In addition, we have learned a great deal in recent years about effective ways to talk to and teach children about death-related issues, and the resources available to help us in these endeavors have greatly expanded, as shown by the 125 titles that are identified and described in the appendix to this book.

In developing this book, we approached individuals who could draw on a wide variety of expertise and invited them to contribute. We asked them to make every effort to synthesize contemporary scholarship, to link practice and current research, and to examine topics with more than mainstream American culture in mind, insofar as that was possible. We greatly appreciate the generosity with which so many fine authors took time from their busy schedules to join in this project. The contributors to this book come from multiple professional backgrounds and disciplinary perspectives, including psychology, education, counseling, health sciences, nursing, social work, medicine, philosophy, and pastoral care. Several contributors work in pediatric palliative care and hospice programs, as well as in children's bereavement support programs.

As we received initial manuscripts from these contributors, we were continually impressed by the quality of the information, insights, and lessons they contained. We also appreciated the willingness of contributors to work with us to sharpen and polish their chapters so as to make them as instructive and as useful as possible for readers of this book. New evidence, scholarly research, practical wisdom, and exciting interpretations came together in important ways. As a result, we believe *Children's Encounters With Death, Bereavement, and Coping* provides an overarching framework for understanding these topics, offers persuasive syntheses of specific areas of inquiry, initiates scholarly discussion on subjects not previously examined, and offers practical guidance for helping children. We trust you will share our judgment once you have had an opportunity to examine the contents of this book.

Charles A. Corr
David E. Balk

Children's Encounters With Death, Bereavement, and Coping

Background

The four chapters in part 1 provide essential background for understanding and helping children in their encounters with death, bereavement, and coping. Chapter 1 addresses a series of topics related to childhood development and typical encounters with death and bereavement in both the United States and other countries around the world. The goal of this chapter is to provide a broad overview of both child development and death-related encounters during childhood, while also suggesting some of the many ways in which the two interact. Many of the topics introduced in this chapter, such as leading causes of death both in the United States and elsewhere around the globe, and typical patterns in children's grief and mourning, will be developed in greater detail in later chapters in this book.

Chapter 2 explores children's emerging awareness and understandings of death. The journey from early inklings about separation and loss to full-blown concepts of death is a complex one, navigated in different ways by different children. Chapter 2 describes the typical journey of well children from a young child's first awareness of themes and events related to separation and loss through direct encounters with death during childhood. The chapter also explains a well-known, stage-based theory of the development of children's understandings of death, offers some critical remarks about such stage-based schemas, and points out the complexity of the concept of death. In conclusion, the chapter offers advice about listening actively and carefully to children's concerns about loss and death, and sets forth 17 guidelines for adults who are interacting with or seeking to help children cope with sadness, loss, and death-related events.

Chapters 3 and 4 explore ethical principles and issues that are likely to arise when adults engage in counseling or research with seriously ill, dying, or bereaved children. Both chapters stress the importance of professional competence, whether in counseling children or in the design and implementation of child-related research projects. In each case, the chapters emphasize the need to respect autonomy, informed consent or child assent, confidentiality, and the legitimate role of parents and other family members.

A basic lesson that reappears throughout these and subsequent chapters in this book is the need to listen actively and carefully to each child as he or she shares descriptions and accounts of his or her death-related experiences. It is also important to realize that adults who read this book are not immune to encounters with death, loss, and bereavement. For that reason alone, while we seek to help children who are coping with similar death-related encounters, we can also learn from them at the same time.

Children, Development, and Encounters With Death, Bereavement, and Coping

CHARLES A. CORR

This chapter addresses four fundamental subjects that underlie every-thing else that appears in this book: (1) typical developmental processes in childhood; (2) broad patterns of encounters with death during child-hood in the United States and in selected examples from other parts of the world; (3) typical patterns of encounters with bereavement during childhood; and (4) children's coping with death-related challenges. Spe-cific topics examined include (1) the meaning of the terms "child" and "childhood"; (2) the difference between normative and non-normative life events and transitions within childhood; (3) developmental tasks that are likely to confront children during four distinct eras in child-hood; (4) some complications in childhood development; (5) numbers of deaths, death rates, and leading causes of death in three age group-ings during childhood in the United States, along with the key variable of race; (6) distinctive encounters with death during childhood in some other areas of the world; and (7) examples of loss and death during childhood, what we currently know about children's grief and mourn-ing, and some suggestions about needs of bereaved children. The goal of this chapter is to introduce these topics as important in their own right and as preparation for more detailed explorations in the chapters that follow.

CHILDHOOD DEVELOPMENT

Childhood and Its Four Principal Eras

Ever since medieval times, the term *child* has designated the offspring of human parents, that is, the unborn or newly born human being, "originally always used in relation to the mother as the 'fruit of the womb'" (Simpson & Weiner, 1989, vol. 3, p. 113). Such offspring may be young children, adolescents, or even the adult children of their parents, but the word "child" most properly refers to an individual below the age of puberty. The related term *childhood* normally identifies the portion of the life span from birth to puberty or the beginning of adolescence.

Within childhood as it is typically experienced in most developed societies in the world today, an interval including approximately the first 10–12 years of life, it has become customary to think of four basic developmental eras (sometimes called "ages," "periods," or "stages"): infancy, toddlerhood, early childhood or the preschool years, and middle childhood or the school-age years (see Table 1.1). Although the justifications for these divisions are generally obvious, there may be some arbitrariness

Table 1.1

PRINCIPAL DEVELOPMENTAL ERAS DURING CHILDHOOD

ERA	AGE[a]	PREDOMINANT ISSUE	VIRTUE
Infancy	Birth through 12–18 months	Basic trust vs. mistrust	Hope
Toddlerhood	Infancy to 3 years of age	Autonomy vs. shame and doubt	Will or self-control
Early childhood; sometimes called play age or the pre-school period	3–6 years of age	Initiative vs. guilt	Purpose or direction
Middle childhood; sometimes called school age or the latency period	6 years to puberty	Industry vs. inferiority	Competency or skill

[a]All chronological ages are approximate.
Source: Adapted from Erikson (1963).

in the number of eras identified during childhood and in their precise boundaries. For example, some might wish to draw a further distinction between children in the early primary school years and pre-teenagers. In addition, some authors (e.g., Newman & Newman, 2005; Papalia, Olds, & Feldman, 2005) advocate the prenatal period, extending from conception to birth, as being the very first era in the human life course. For our purposes here, it is enough to consider the standard division of four basic developmental eras in childhood.

Clearly, children differ among themselves in many ways. In addition to differences arising from their developmental status, children differ as unique individuals; as males and females; as members of different racial, cultural, religious, or economic communities; as a result of divergent life experiences; and in other salient ways. When generalizations about children are offered, it is helpful to keep these many variables in mind and to be extremely cautious (as suggested in the footnote in Table 1.1) about linking developmental eras with chronological ages or confounding the two as if there were no real distinction between them.

Normative and Non-Normative Transitions and Life Events

Throughout the human life span, it has become commonplace to distinguish between normative and non-normative life events and transitions (e.g., Baltes, Reese, & Lipsitt, 1980). A normative life event is one that is expected to occur at a certain time, in a certain relationship to other life events, with predictability, and to most if not all of the members of a developmental group or cohort. Because normative life events follow familiar patterns or standards, they lead to expected transitions or turning points in individual development. Entering the primary school system around the age of six is a familiar example of a normative life transition in the United States and many other developed countries. This transition is the basis for the previously noted distinction between preschool and school-age children or early and middle childhood.

As the language itself indicates, non-normative life events are those that are unexpected or unforeseen. Unlike normative life transitions, these events occur atypically or unpredictably, with apparently random relationship to other life events and to some but not all members of a developmental cohort. Because non-normative life events are characteristically unanticipated, they usually catch children and adults unprepared.

A child's discovery that he or she is a musical prodigy who has the ability to play an advanced piece of classical music or a child experiencing the accidental death of a pet during childhood are both examples of non-normative or distinctively personal life events. Such events obviously do occur from time to time in the lives of some children, but there is no reliable basis for predicting if, and much less when, they will happen in the life of a specific child.

Most of the death-related events discussed in this book are, or involve, situational occurrences or non-normative life experiences. Events such as the death of a youngster during childhood or a child's encounter with the death of a parent, sibling, other relative, or friend are best thought of as unanticipated life crises. These events do not rise to the frequency or predictability of normative life transitions during childhood.

Normative life transitions and unanticipated or situational life events do share some common characteristics. Both may confront the children who experience them with life crises, and both may evoke coping processes from such children. Events that are properly described as life crises or turning points in a child's life present "dangerous opportunities." That is, they offer opportunities for growth and maturation if a child copes with them effectively, but they also represent danger in the form of possible psychological harm to the child and distorted or unsatisfactory development if the coping response is inappropriate or inadequate. As a result, it is useful to understand both the nature of normative life transitions in childhood and the potential implications for children of unanticipated life events—especially those that may be distressing in character. In the case of events related to death and bereavement, it is also helpful for adults to learn how to foster constructive coping processes in childhood, how to minimize unproductive or counterproductive coping, and how to support children while they are engaged in the work of coping.

Developmental Tasks Within Four Principal Eras in Childhood

Throughout the human life span, normative life transitions are usually described in association with developmental tasks. Within childhood, these tasks represent the work children need to undertake in order to navigate successfully the developmental challenges that confront them. In his well-known analysis of life-span development within childhood (summarized in Table 1.1), Erikson (1963, 1968) described each era within childhood in terms of a predominant psychosocial issue or central conflict and in terms of a leading virtue that would be achieved through the normal and healthy development of an individual ego. Erikson meant that in each era of their development, children (and other human beings) are confronted by a pair of opposed tendencies or orientations toward life, the self, and other people. The way in which each of these basic tensions or conflicts is resolved successfully has its outcome in a transformed quality of ego functioning that Erikson calls a "virtue," such as the virtue of hope or the virtue of self-control. Successful resolution or integration results in growth or maturation; unsuccessful responses to developmental challenges may stunt or harm maturation and leave unfinished work for later in life.

In his account of infancy, Erikson depicted the central conflict as one between basic trust and mistrust. The developmental task in this era of childhood is to develop a sense of basic trust upon which the virtue of hope can be founded. In this context, trust and hope mean that children believe they can rely on people and the world to fulfill their needs and satisfy their desires. A view of the world as unfriendly or unpredictable might lead to mistrust in children and a self-protective withdrawal.

In toddlerhood, Erikson described the central conflict as being autonomy versus shame and doubt. This conflict is a tension between self-regulation and external control. According to Erikson, the primary developmental task for toddlers is to establish their own legitimate autonomy or independence in making decisions and to develop the virtue of will or self-control.

During early childhood, Erikson identified the central conflict as one between initiative and guilt. The developmental task for children in this era is to cultivate their own initiative or desire to take action and pursue goals and to balance that with the healthy moral reservations that they may have about their plans—a combination of spontaneity and responsibility. Developing this sort of self-regulation promotes the virtue of purpose or direction in a child's life.

Finally, for Erikson, children in middle childhood are confronted with a developmental conflict between industry and inferiority. These children face the challenge of developing their capacities to do productive work. The virtue that results from successful resolution of this crisis is competence, which reflects the child's sense of self-esteem rooted in a view of the self as able to master skills and carry out tasks.

Complexities in Childhood Development

It needs to be kept in mind that human development is complex and multifaceted and that it extends over a relatively long period of time.

Beginning from the successful fertilization of an ovum by a sperm, child development characteristically proceeds through a fairly well-recognized set of physical processes related to biological (or anatomical and physiological) development. After birth, physical development includes mastery of large motor and other skills. For example, normally-developing children learn to reach out to toys and other objects; to hold their bottles; to roll over, crawl, and walk; and eventually to perform other activities that involve complex coordination skills.

At the same time, most children also experience psychological, social, and spiritual development. In these areas, greatest attention has been given to personality and social development in childhood (represented by the work of Erikson and many others), to intellectual development (represented by the work of Piaget & Inhelder [1958] and others), and to spiritual development (represented by the work of Coles, 1990). However, no aspect of child development is a simple process occurring in isolation. For example, in some children development is delayed, obstructed, or even prevented for various reasons. An infant may not start walking as expected, or a child may be handicapped by a range of disabilities. Perhaps that is why Erikson (1963) spoke of the need for "triple bookkeeping," by which he meant that one must take into account social context, ego process or identity, and somatic process or constitution in any satisfactory explication of human development. Elsewhere, Erikson (1975, p. 228) described these variables as the "history, personality, and anatomy" of a developing individual.

The full scope of human development during childhood and all of the variables that might affect it cannot and need not be explored here in all of its complexities. For example, whereas most non-normative events occur to some but not all members of a developmental cohort, others seem to be different in their character and implications. Thus, singular events that are relatively limited in the timing of their occurrence, such as the bombing of Hiroshima, the terrorist attack on the World Trade Center and the Pentagon on September 11, 2001, or Hurricane Katrina in the New Orleans area, had a momentous quality, with a wide and enduring impact both on persons who were directly affected and on others across populations. Other powerful events, such as the Holocaust or the situation of children and families forced to live in great poverty or situations of violent conflict for year after year, have lasting, perhaps permanent, influence on human development.

These few examples—and there must be many more—remind us of the complexities of human development during childhood in relationship to both normative and non-normative life events and transitions. With that in mind, this chapter focuses on ways in which developmental processes (and other factors) can play important roles in affecting encounters with death during childhood and how encounters with bereavement arising from the deaths of significant others may influence a child's subsequent development.

ENCOUNTERS WITH DEATH DURING CHILDHOOD

Children do die. This section offers a broad overview of the frequency of children's encounters with death and an analysis of the principal features of those encounters to heighten appreciation of the general patterns of childhood deaths. This examination includes numbers of deaths, death rates, and leading causes of death during different eras of childhood in the United States, as well as some comments on the important variables of race. These patterns of childhood encounters with death are reasonably typical of those in many developed areas of the world. (Note that the mortality figures for 2005 cited in this chapter are the most recent final data available from the National Center for Health Statistics [NCHS] as this chapter is being written; also, because the presentation of those data follows NCHS terminology [e.g., for racial and cultural groupings] and format, it may not always be identical with our earlier usage and our discussion of four eras during childhood.)

Numbers of Deaths and Death Rates Among Children in the United States

For several years, numbers of deaths and death rates during childhood in the United States have remained relatively stable with a slight downward trend. General patterns can be summarized in the following ways (Kung, Hoyert, Xu, & Murphy, 2008):

- A total of 36,033 children between birth and 9 years of age died in our society in 2005.
- The largest number of child deaths (18,514) occurred among White Americans (who represent the largest portion of the total population).
- More male children died than females in every age grouping during childhood.

- More deaths (28,440) occurred during infancy (children less than 1 year of age) than in any other segment of childhood.
- The highest death rates during childhood occurred among Black Americans for children under 1 year of age (1,311.2 deaths per 100,000 children) and for children from 5 to 9 years of age (21.1 deaths per 100,000); highest deaths rates for children 1–4 years of age occurred among American Indians and Alaskan Natives (59.2 deaths per 100,000).
- The highest infant mortality rates in our society occurred among Black Americans (13.7 per 1,000 live births versus 5.7 for White Americans and 8.1 for Hispanic Americans).

Leading Causes of Death During Childhood in the United States

This section describes the five leading causes of death for all races and both sexes in the United States in 2005, according to three age groups: infants; children between the ages of 1 and 4; and children between the ages of 5 and 9. It is useful to examine these data with special attention to causes of death that are associated with developmental problems.

Infants

The leading causes of death among infants in the United States have remained basically stable for many years (see chapter 5 in this book for a more detailed analysis of infant deaths). Approximately 54% of all infant deaths in 2005 resulted from five principal causes: congenital anomalies; disorders relating to short gestation and unspecified low birth weight; Sudden Infant Death Syndrome (SIDS); newborns affected by maternal complications of pregnancy; and newborns affected by complications of placenta, cord, and membranes (Kung et al., 2008). (The sixth-ranking cause of death in this age group in 2005 was accidents or unintentional injuries.) An unfortunate portion of these deaths are associated with an absence of effective prenatal health care, injurious maternal behavior (e.g., smoking, using alcohol, or taking illicit drugs during pregnancy), and lack of adequate health care for all segments of American society. Congenital anomalies, an increasing population of low birth-weight infants, and SIDS all point to problems associated with a child's development before birth, during the birth process, or not long after birth.

The prominence of Sudden Infant Death Syndrome—typically involving the sudden death of an apparently healthy infant less than 1 year of age with no advance warning—as the leading cause of death among infants from 1 month to 1 year of age across all economic, ethnic, and cultural groupings is particularly relevant to our interest in child development. Although its underlying cause is unknown, SIDS is a recognizable constellation of events that can often be diagnosed with some precision by a thorough postmortem and circumstantial investigation. Recent research has pointed to brainstem abnormalities and preliminary neurochemical evidence as possibly helping to understand some infants' vulnerability to SIDS (Paterson et al., 2006). Even without definitive information on this point, during the early 1990s, new research (e.g., Dwyer, Ponsonby, Blizzard, Newman, & Cochrane, 1995) led the health systems in the United States and many other countries to recommend that infants might be at less risk for SIDS if they were placed on their backs for sleep, rather than on their stomachs (e.g., American Academy of Pediatrics, 1992, 2005). Then in June 1994 the U.S. federal government initiated a "Back to Sleep" campaign that has led to dramatic and sustained reductions in SIDS deaths—numbers fell from approximately 5,400 deaths in 1990 to 2,230 in 2005, a reduction of nearly 59%.

Children 1–4 Years of Age

As children move from infancy to toddlerhood, they typically become more mobile and more independent of their parents and other caretakers, both within and outside the family home. This growing autonomy results in accidents becoming the leading cause of death among children 1–4 years of age and accounts for approximately 40% of all deaths in this age group in 2005 (Kung et al., 2008). Unintentional injuries of this type involve such causes as motor vehicle accidents, drowning, burning, ingesting harmful substances, choking, falling, and misadventures with firearms (see chapter 6 in this book for a more detailed discussion of unintentional injuries during childhood).

Other leading causes of death for this cohort of children include so-called natural causes of death, such as congenital anomalies, cancer (malignant neoplasms), and heart disease, as well as homicide (called "assault" in the international classification system).

Children 5–9 Years of Age

In this age group, the leading cause of death—accidents—is again by far the most critical. Accidents—in or near motor vehicles, on playgrounds, or in activities such as cycling—caused nearly 38% of all deaths among school-age children in the United States in 2005 (Centers for Disease Control and Prevention [CDC], 2008).

Other leading causes of death for children between 5 and 9 years of age include cancer (malignant neoplasms), congenital anomalies, assault (homicide), and heart disease.

Race as a Key Variable in Deaths of Children in the United States

The realities of death during childhood are not the same for all children in the United States. Race is the most notable variable.

As previously noted, there are obvious differences in numbers of deaths and death rates for White and Black children in the United States. This disparity applies to all three age groups that we are considering during childhood. For example, among infants problems with disorders related to short gestation and low birth weight are the principal cause of death for Black infants (versus its ranking as the third leading cause of death for White infants). In fact, more Black infants died from this cause in 2005 (2,025) than did White infants (1,926) (Kung et al., 2008). This inequality likely reflects a number of contributing factors, such as a higher incidence of early pregnancy, inadequate prenatal care, and premature birth among Blacks than Whites.

For children 1–4 years of age, variances in death rates between White children and Black children are a bit less dramatic than those for infants, but still substantial (27.0 deaths versus 41.8 per 100,000 in the population), and disadvantages for American Indians and Alaskan Natives are even more dramatic, with a death rate of 59.2 per 100,000 in this age group (Kung et al., 2008). Homicide also ranks higher as a leading cause of death for Black children versus White children in this age group.

Among children 5–9 years of age, death rates are again markedly different: 13.3 deaths per 100,000 for White children, 21.1 for Black children, and 17.4 for American Indian and Alaskan Native children (CDC, 2008).

Some Examples of Encounters With Child Death Elsewhere in the World

Infant mortality is often regarded as an important benchmark in evaluating quality of life and the health care and social services systems in societies. Here, more than two dozen countries around the world have lower infant mortality rates than those in the United States. This poor record is a notable black mark against our society. There are, however, other ways in which the United States and other developed countries such as Canada, France, Germany, Italy, Japan, and the United Kingdom are far more fortunate in encounters with child death than countries elsewhere in the world.

Developing countries are generally thought of as those that have relatively low standards of living and a limited degree of industrialization relative to their populations. It is in these countries that the highest numbers of child deaths are typically found. For example, the World Health Organization (WHO, 2004) has reported that 75% of all child deaths under the age of 5 years occur in the African and Southeast Asian regions of the world. In terms of causality, WHO reports, "Six causes of death account for 73% of the 10.4 million deaths among children under the age of five years worldwide" (p. 14). These causes are acute respiratory infections (mainly pneumonia), diarrheal diseases, prematurity and low birth weight, neonatal infections such as sepsis, birth asphyxia and trauma, and malaria. Among these six causes, WHO adds that "the four communicable disease categories above account for one half (50%) of all child deaths. Undernutrition is an underlying cause in an estimated 30% of all deaths among children under five" (p. 14; see chapter 7 in this book for a more detailed analysis of infectious diseases during childhood). Some of these causes of child death, such as malaria, have been virtually eradicated in developed countries. Poverty and malnutrition are often widespread in countries where infectious diseases are prominent. One striking example is a cholera epidemic in Zimbabwe in 2009, a country that once was a leading exporter of food, but has more recently been plagued by a breakdown in government services, rampant inflation, and shortages of food.

In contexts such as these, as well as areas marked by ongoing acts of genocide, violent conflict, and disruption of populations, encounters with child death are all too typical, and child development is harmed. Indeed, simple survival is often at risk.

ENCOUNTERS WITH BEREAVEMENT DURING CHILDHOOD

Losses and Deaths Experienced by Children

Losses of all types are an unavoidable part of children's lives. Many, perhaps most, of these losses have nothing to do with death. For example, a child's favorite toy may be broken, misplaced, or stolen; parents may divorce; the family may need to move to a new city or location resulting in a loss of familiar routines, school settings, or playmates. These and other types of losses can bring sadness and grief into a child's life.

Deaths of significant others are also a reality in the lives of children. For example, grandparents, parents, and other important adults—such as a beloved aunt or uncle, a dear neighbor, a favorite teacher or coach, or even a familiar school janitor who brightens a dark, scary room by changing a light bulb—may die (see chapter 9 in this book). Sisters and brothers also sometimes die (see chapter 10 in this book), especially during the first year of their lives, when more than 28,000 babies and infants die each year in our society (see chapter 5 in this book). The death of a friend or classmate during childhood can also be an important event, though its impact on a child may not always be properly appreciated by adults (see chapter 11 in this book). And the deaths of some animals—pets, companion animals, or service animals, sometimes even a favorite figure in a zoo—can have an important effect on a child who had become attached to them (see chapter 12 in this book).

Grief in Childhood

Encountering any significant loss or death can be an important experience for a child. It is likely to generate a *grief reaction,* one that is typically distinctive for each individual child and may have special meaning for that child's subsequent development. Children experience and express grief in many ways, some of which are distinctive of their developmental situations. They may experience a roller coaster of emotions, including such feelings as numbness, sadness, anger, confusion, fear, worry, regret, loneliness, guilt, and self-blame. Sometimes, children's grief involves fatigue and turning within themselves, whereas at other times it can lead to agitation, irritability, lashing out, or getting into trouble. Young children may regress to thumb sucking, bed wetting, and attention-seeking behaviors. Difficulties in sleeping are common. Many bereaved children lose interest in favorite activities or experience a decline in school performance, whereas others strive to be the so-called perfect child, suppressing their grief and trying to take care of others in their families. Quite often, bereaved children have a sense of themselves as being different or alienated from other children, thinking that no one understands how they feel. In short, children's grief may have psychological (emotional or cognitive), physical, behavioral, social, and spiritual dimensions and may be expressed in a variety of ways.

In their grief, children frequently ask questions like the following: Did I cause this to happen? Is it going to happen to me? And very importantly, Who is going to take care of me? The egocentricity associated with such questions is obvious. When a child does not correctly understand the causality involved in a loss, perhaps because of ignorance or magical thinking, it is not surprising that issues of origin and endangerment should present themselves. Children who do not understand that death is final may want to know what sort of activities are undertaken by the deceased, who is thought to be somehow alive in a different way or place, and children who do realize that death is irreversible may ask concrete questions about what happens to a dead body when it stops working. (See chapter 2 in this book for further discussion of these subjects.)

However, it should be kept in mind that children do not always articulate their grief in words. Many bereaved children express their grief through physical activities, such as crying, play, sports, or art. It is also common to cling to sources of comfort and security, for example seeking nurturance and reassurance by cuddling with stuffed animals or pets or wanting to be hugged and held by someone a child loves.

Generally, children's grief comes in waves or recurs at different times, often in relationship to new events or developmental milestones in their lives. Also, children are likely to grieve not only the primary loss, but also secondary losses that follow, such as changes in routines, schedules, and family dynamics, alterations in family finances, and having to move house or change schools. Each of these and other implications of a significant death can be important to a bereaved child.

Mourning in Childhood

There once was a scholarly debate about whether children are able to mourn after a death (see, e.g., Furman, 1973). Partly, this debate depended on claims about children's inability to understand the concept of death, but it also arose from theoretical models of mourning drawn almost wholly from studies of bereaved adults. These models assumed that mourning involved universal patterns (e.g., a group of normative stages or phases) that were thought to lead to goals such as resolution or completion (Doka, 2007). In recent years, this way of thinking about mourning has been challenged, both for adults and for children.

Worden (2009) proposed, instead, that mourning involves active processes in the form of tasks in coping with loss and grief. Worden (1996) identified four tasks of mourning for bereaved children: (1) to accept the reality of the loss; (2) to experience the pain or emotional aspects of the loss; (3) to adjust to an environment in which the deceased is missing; and (4) to relocate the dead person within one's life and find ways to memorialize that person. Worden was careful to note that these tasks "can only be understood in terms of the cognitive, emotional, and social development of the child" (1996, p. 12). As a result, mourning tasks may need to be addressed throughout childhood again and again in appropriate ways at different developmental points in a child's life and in different contexts. For example, a child might mourn the death of his or her mother at the time of the event, her absence in the months and years that follow, what that may mean afterward for being different from schoolmates who have a living mother, and the child's inability to draw on the absent mother's support or to share achievements with her in later school years. Reworking losses and grief reactions through shifts in the focus and significance of mourning tasks is quite consistent with maturational processes.

As they try to cope with their losses and their grief reactions, bereaved children typically find themselves looking both backward, to the death event itself and what they have lost, and forward, to what all these events will mean for their present and future lives. Each child is likely to cope in his or her own ways and in different ways at different times in his or her life. Quite often these coping processes will be aided by efforts to maintain an ongoing connection to the individual who has died (Klass, Silverman, & Nickman, 1996). These connections involve continuing bonds with an internal representation of that individual. Such bonds depend on new, altered relationships with the deceased, who remains a transformed, but ongoing presence in the life of a bereaved child. At their best, dynamic bonds of this type can provide comfort, solace, and support, a kind of enriched remembrance that helps a child move on in constructive living. Continuing bonds are often supported by linking objects, such as photographs or other mementoes, through which children keep alive the memory and the legacy of the person who died.

In the Harvard Child Bereavement Study (see Worden, 1996), the most extensive research project on child bereavement that we have (in this case, involving the death of a parent), two things became evident. First, instead of simply withdrawing and becoming preoccupied with thoughts about the person who died, many bereaved children immerse themselves in activities of everyday life, such as play and school. This behavior pattern appears to reflect a temporary defense against being overwhelmed by the implications of the loss. In so doing, children seem to engage in a kind of dosing themselves with grief and mourning, allowing themselves to experience their grief reactions and their efforts to cope for a while, but then turning away when that becomes overwhelming or when other concerns attract their attention. As a result, children's grief reactions are often more intermittent in character than those of many adults, and their overall bereavement may be longer in duration.

Second, in the Harvard Child Bereavement Study, Worden (1996) also noted a late effect of bereavement in which a significant minority of the school-age children being studied were found to be encountering more difficulties at 2 years after the death of a parent than they were at 4 months or 1 year after the death. This fact about the bereavement of many children suggests that it is important to be sensitive to the possibility of both ongoing issues for a bereaved child and those that may arise only at a later point in the child's life. Of course, much of a child's coping depends on the family context of the child and especially on the functioning of a surviving parent or other adult care provider.

From his research, Worden (1996) offered a list of lessons about the needs of bereaved children. They need:

- Adequate information—clear and comprehensible information about an impending death (whenever that is possible) and certainly after a death has occurred
- Fears and anxieties addressed—to know that they will be cared for and to experience consistent discipline
- Reassurance that they are not to blame
- Careful listening—in the form of someone who will hear them out and not minimize their concerns
- Validation of their feelings—including respect for and safe ways to express individual reactions in their own ways
- Help with overwhelming feelings—especially when sadness, anger, anxiety, and guilt are intense
- Involvement and inclusion—both before and after a death, with preparation and without being forced to join in
- Continued routine activities—in the form of age-appropriate activities, such as play and school
- Modeled grief behaviors—through adults who can share their own grief and mourning and show how to experience and express these in constructive ways
- Opportunities to remember—both after a death and throughout life

CONCLUSION

Children have important work to do as they face the many challenges of life. For some, problems in development arise that can threaten a child's life and cause his or her death. For others, the death of an important person or loss of a significant relationship can have a powerful impact on a child's subsequent development. Although not predictable in their specifics, it is inevitable that many children will be confronted by these events and by challenges related to loss and death. Such challenges are grounded in the very human and personal contexts within which children live their lives.

To ignore or turn a blind eye to these challenges is to abandon children and put them at risk of much harsher futures than they need experience. This essentially leaves children alone without help and support just when they most need assistance from the adults around them. As Katzenbach (1986, p. 322) has written, "Children can adapt wonderfully to specific fears, like a pain, a sickness, or a death. It is the unknown which is truly terrifying for them. They have no fund of knowledge in how the world operates, and so they feel completely vulnerable."

That is the positive message of this book: adults can bring experience, insight, skill, and caring presence to the aid of children who may feel vulnerable and alone in the terrifying face of the unknown. In some cases, skilled adults can eliminate or minimize challenges that confront children. In many cases, thoughtful adults can guide children and help them cope more effectively with challenges arising in their lives. In all cases, wise adults can offer support while children are addressing meaningful events in their lives.

In order to be available to children in these ways, it is essential for adults to be aware of the realities of death-related events in the lives of children and to appreciate the many ways in which coping with tasks arising from death and bereavement can interact with coping with normative developmental tasks.

REFERENCES

American Academy of Pediatrics (AAP), Task Force on Infant Positioning and SIDS. (1992). Positioning and SIDS. *Pediatrics, 89,* 1120–1126.
American Academy of Pediatrics (AAP), Task Force on Sudden Infant Death Syndrome. (2005). The changing concept of sudden infant death syndrome: Diagnostic coding

shifts, controversies regarding the sleeping environment, and new variables to consider in reducing risk. *Pediatrics, 116,* 1245–1255.

Baltes, P. B., Reese, H. W., & Lipsitt, L. P. (1980). Life-span developmental psychology. *Annual Review of Psychology, 31,* 65–110.

Centers for Disease Control and Prevention (CDC). (2008, June 16). Unpublished data from the National Vital Statistics System, National Center for Health Statistics, Mortality Statistics Branch. Retrieved on February 6, 2009, from http://www.cdc.gov/nchs/data/dvs/LCWK1_2005.pdf

Coles, R. (1990). *The spiritual life of children.* Boston: Houghton Mifflin.

Doka, K. J. (2007). Challenging the paradigm: New understandings of grief. In K. J. Doka (Ed.), *Living with grief: Before and after the death* (pp. 87–102). Washington, DC: Hospice Foundation of America.

Dwyer, T., Ponsonby, A.-L., Blizzard, L., Newman, N. M., & Cochrane, J. A. (1995). The contribution of changes in the prevalence of prone sleeping position to the decline in sudden infant death syndrome in Tasmania. *Journal of the American Medical Association, 273,* 783–789.

Erikson, E. H. (1963). *Childhood and society* (2nd ed.). New York: Norton. (Original edition published 1950)

Erikson, E. H. (1968). *Identity: Youth and crisis.* New York: Norton.

Erikson, E. H. (1975). *Life history and the historical moment.* New York: Norton.

Furman, R. A. (1973). The child's capacity for mourning. In E. J. Anthony & C. Koupernik (Eds.), *The child in his family: Vol. 2, The impact of disease and death* (pp. 225–231). New York: Wiley.

Katzenbach, J. (1986). *The traveler.* New York: Putnam.

Klass, D., Silverman, P. R., & Nickman, S. L. (Eds.). (1996). *Continuing bonds: New understandings of grief.* Washington, DC: Taylor & Francis.

Kung, H-C., Hoyert, D. L., Xu, J. Q., & Murphy, S. L. (2008). Deaths: Final data for 2005. *National Vital Statistics Reports, 56*(10). Hyattsville, MD: National Center for Health Statistics.

Newman, B. M., & Newman, P. R. (2005). *Development through life: A psychosocial approach* (9th ed.). Belmont, CA: Thomson Wadsworth.

Papalia, D. E., Olds, S. W., & Feldman, R. D. (2005). *A child's world: Infancy through adolescence with LifeMAP CD-ROM and PowerWeb* (10th ed.). Boston: McGraw-Hill.

Paterson, D. S., Trachtenberg, F. L., Thompson, E. G., Belliveau, R. A., Beggs, A. H., Darnall, R., et al. (2006). Multiple serotonergic brainstem abnormalities in sudden infant death syndrome. *Journal of the American Medical Association, 296,* 2124–2132.

Piaget, J., & Inhelder, B. (1958). *The growth of logical thinking from childhood to adolescence* (A. Parsons & S. Milgram, Trans.). New York: Basic Books.

Simpson, J. A., & Weiner, E. S. C. (Eds.). (1989). *The Oxford English dictionary* (2nd ed., 20 vols.). Oxford, England: Clarendon Press.

Worden, J. W. (1996). *Children and grief: When a parent dies.* New York: Guilford.

Worden, J. W. (2009). *Grief counseling and grief therapy: A handbook for the mental health practitioner* (4th ed.). New York: Springer Publishing.

World Health Organization (WHO). (2004). *The global burden of disease: 2004 update.* Retrieved on January 29, 2009, from http://www.who.int/healthinfo/global_burden_disease/2004_report_update/en/index.html

Children's Emerging Awareness and Understandings of Loss and Death

2

CHARLES A. CORR

Adults sometimes seem to believe that young children have no awareness of loss and death. That is incorrect. Not surprisingly, children may not always understand loss and death-related events in the same ways that adults do, given the limited experiences with life events that many young children have. However, we need only to recall what happens when there is an interruption while an infant is feeding from a breast or bottle. Unless the child's hunger has been satisfied, he or she is likely to be aware that something unpleasant has happened and is equally likely to react by expressing displeasure.

Young children perceive or become aware of many events around them before they understand or can explain to themselves or others what has taken place. These early perceptions underlie growing awareness and emerging understandings of events involving loss. From that foundation, more complex understandings of loss and ultimately of death itself arise as a child's cognitive capacities develop.

There is a twofold danger in failing to appreciate the early perceptual basis that underlies children's emerging awareness and understandings of loss and death. First, it blinds us to what is actually going on within a child as he or she engages with the surrounding world. So often parents and other adults realize only in retrospect that children have been aware of what they perceive as important events in their lives. If we were more attentive and more engaged with such children, we might appreciate them better and be able to engage in more effective communications with them.

Second, to believe that young children are simply unaware of all loss and death-related events can only cause problems for adults and is self-serving. This belief is problematic because it raises a series of unanswerable questions, such as the following: If children have no awareness of loss and death when they are young, when does that awareness come into their lives? At what critical age does this awareness magically pop into a child's mind? What will cause that leap in awareness? The same belief on the part of adults is self-serving because it gets us off the hook from having to explain events related to loss and death to a child or to teach a child about coping with such events.

In fact, adults should be prepared to help children, even very young children, understand loss and death-related events in keeping with what they want to know, what they need to know, and what they are able to understand. That is the only constructive way to teach children about such events and to help them learn to cope with such events.

This chapter expands and updates an earlier analysis (Corr, 2008) to describe the current state of our knowledge about children's awareness and understandings of death. The chapter covers six major topics: (1) early inklings, or the beginning of awareness of themes and events related to loss and death; (2) direct encounters with loss and death during childhood; (3) a stage-based theory of the development of children's understandings of death; (4) some critical remarks about stage-based schemas; (5) the complexity of the concept of death; and (6) advice about listening actively and carefully to children's concerns about loss and death. Each section concludes with one or more lessons for parents, care providers, educators, counselors, and other interested adults. The chapter ends with 17 guidelines for adults who are interacting with or seeking to help children cope with sadness, loss, and death-related events.

EARLY INKLINGS

Children typically receive messages from the media, parents, family members, and other adults, as well as other children, that certain topics, such as excretory functioning or sexual organs, are or are not considered suitable for open and frank discussion. They also receive overt or subtle messages about whether death-related topics are acceptable for discussion and, if so, when and how these subjects can be discussed. Unfortunately, these messages can be confusing and contradictory. Adults may talk freely among themselves (often within the hearing of a curious child) about what they think of as "acceptable" death-related events (e.g., the death of an elderly relative or a distant public figure), but may try to suppress mention of "unacceptable" or stigmatized deaths (e.g., those involving suicide or HIV/AIDS). Some adults deny that children have any awareness of death, even though television reports describe in dramatic ways fatalities on the highway, homicides, disasters, and casualties in war-torn countries, and entertainment programs are full of violent events (Diamant, 1994; Slaughter & Lyons, 2003).

For many years, researchers have pointed out that even the supposedly innocent environment of children's play is filled with death-related themes (Opie & Opie, 1969). For example, Maurer (1966) argued that peek-a-boo games involve the sudden disappearance (death) of the external world and its rapid reappearance. Other play activities involve acting out violent crashes and other forms of "killing" under the control of a child-master. From his research on children's play activities, Rochlin (1967) observed that "death is a matter of deep consideration to the very young child . . . thoughts of dying are commonplace" (p. 54) and concluded that "at a very early age well-developed mental faculties are functioning to defend oneself against the realization that life may end" (p. 61). It is not necessary to claim that children are conceptualizing these events as directly related to what adults understand as death in order to notice how children may be perceiving them. In addition, it is advisable not to dismiss these activities too quickly, given that play is the main work of a child's life, and especially because in recent years various types of video games and other entertainment forms have increasingly come to include violent and warlike situations.

Death-related themes are also prominent in children's rhymes and songs, which have a long history in many cultures. For example, most are familiar with the creepy song "the worms crawl in, the worms crawl out," but what about "Ring Around the Rosie"? This seemingly innocuous tune originated during a plague in England and describes the roseate skin pustules of the disease, as a result of which "we all fall down." The familiar lullaby "Rock-a-Bye, Baby" has a falling-cradle theme (Achté, Fagerström, Pentikäinen, & Farberow, 1990), and the child's prayer "Now I lay me down to sleep" is essentially a petition for safekeeping against death and other hazards of the night.

Many fairy tales, with their long and diverse cultural backgrounds, also contain references to death (Lamers, 1995). For example, in the original version of the story, Little Red Riding Hood and her grandmother are eaten by the wicked wolf, not saved by a passing woodsman or hunter. In "The Three Little Pigs," the big bad wolf dies in a scalding pot of hot water when he falls down the chimney of the third pig's house. And Hansel and Gretel (who had been left to die in the forest by their parents because there was not enough food to feed them) ultimately shut the wicked witch up in her own hot oven. The wicked stepmother orders the death of Snow White and demands her heart as proof. "The Goose Girl" has perhaps the most gruesome outcome—the false bride is put into a barrel lined with sharp nails and rolled until she is dead. The obvious conclusion is that death is not absent from the fantasy world of childhood (Bettelheim, 1977); the real issue is whether it is presented in healthy or unhealthy ways. Many of the examples noted here can actually allow children to work through fears and anxieties related to loss and death in safe and distanced ways. Two lessons emerge from these early involvements of children with death: (1) most children are curious about death and death-related events, even when adults try to "protect" them from pursuing their curiosity; and (2) adults have the responsibility of helping children to engage with these early inklings of loss and death in constructive ways.

DIRECT ENCOUNTERS WITH LOSS AND DEATH DURING CHILDHOOD

Experiences of separation and loss during early childhood foreshadow later, more direct encounters with death-related events. Children are often surprisingly well tuned in to the events that take place around them. Even quite young babies are able to notice when significant others leave their immediate surroundings. Their awareness is likely to increase as their cognitive abilities develop and as life events increasingly impinge on everyday activities. They may not always interpret the separations correctly, but understanding is grounded in early awareness.

Children also notice disruptions in the emotional currents of their families, so it is not unusual for them to sense that something important is happening when the adults around them are grieving. Children may not completely understand such emotional disruptions, but they are not likely to be wholly oblivious. If they do not receive accurate information to guide their understandings of such events, they most often will attempt to develop their own explanations about what is going on. The danger is that the demons of their imaginations may be far scarier than the truth about what is really happening.

Beginnings and endings, as well as separations and losses, are aspects of children's daily lives. Children are naturally curious about these and other events that seem new or puzzling. In connection with death-related events, a child might ask, "Where did Grandpa go? Will he be here to read me a story at bedtime?" or "What happened to Fluffy? When will she come back?" Questions such as these are part of a child's taking notice of life events and seeking to make sense of them. Recent research has shown that helping to improve children's understandings of death-related events is associated with decreases in their fears about what is happening or has happened (Slaughter & Griffiths, 2007).

Children encounter death in many ways. Grandparents, parents, and other important adults may die (see chapter 9 in this book). Siblings may also die (see chapter 10 in this book), particularly during the first year of life—more than 28,000 infants under 1 year of age die each year in our society (see chapters 1 and 5 in this book). And the death of a friend during childhood can be an important, but not always properly appreciated, event (see chapter 11 in this book).

In addition, pets are important sources of unconditional love for children. Their presence in the lives of children can help them learn about the responsibilities involved in caring for a living creature. But pets typically have shorter—often much shorter—life spans than those of the children who love and care for them. An attachment to a childhood pet almost guarantees an eventual encounter with that pet's death (see chapter 12 in this book).

The lesson in this section is that normal, healthy children do have thoughts, feelings, and encounters with death in various forms.

UNDERSTANDING DEATH: DEVELOPMENTAL STAGES

Children's understandings of death arise out of early inklings and direct encounters. The systematic study of the development of children's understandings of death began many years ago in the 1930s (Anthony, 1939, 1940; see also Anthony, 1972; Schilder & Wechsler, 1934). Since that time, numerous research reports on this subject have been published in English alone (Stambrook & Parker, 1987). The best-known and most frequently mentioned theory in this field is that of Maria Nagy, a Hungarian psychologist who examined 378 children living in Budapest just before World War II (Corr, 1996). Nagy (1948/1959) published an account of her study shortly after the war and a slightly revised version later.

In Nagy's study, children in the 7- to 10-year-old range were asked to "write down everything that comes into your mind about death" (1948, p. 4), and children in the overlapping 6- to 10-year-old range were asked to make drawings about death (many of the older children also wrote explanations of what they had drawn). Discussions were held with all the children, either about their compositions and drawings or (in the case of 3- to 5-year-olds) to encourage them to talk about their ideas and feelings about death.

According to Nagy, the children's understandings of death developed in three stages:

1. *There is no definitive death.* In this first stage, "the child does not know death as such" (Nagy, 1948, p. 7). The reason may be that the child has not fully distinguished the concept of death from other concepts or has not grasped its full implications. For example, a child may think of death in terms of departure or sleep. If death is thought of as departure, it involves some sort of continued life elsewhere; if death is like sleep, it involves a diminished form of life. In either case, life is not completely over, and death is not seen as final.

2. *Death = a person.* In the second stage in their understandings of death, children may imagine death as a separate person (e.g., the grim reaper, a skeleton, a ghost, or a death angel). Or they may identify death with dead persons. Nagy referred to these representations as reflecting the personification of death. If death is some sort of person external to the child, then those caught by that person die, but those who are sufficiently clever or quick can escape and need not die. Children with this understanding acknowledge the finality of death but still believe it can be avoided.

3. *The cessation of corporal life.* According to Nagy, children reach a third stage in their understandings of death when they recognize that death is a process that operates within us, a process in which bodily life ends. In this view, death is both final and universal.

In brief, Nagy saw a progression that moved from the idea that death is not final to death is final but avoidable, to death is final and inevitable. She described her results as involving a developmental process, one that advances from an unrealistic to an ever more realistic and mature understanding of death.

Many later descriptions of children's understandings of death have followed this broad three-stage model, although some writers have argued that avoidability, not personification, is the key concept in stage 2 (e.g., Gartley & Bernasconi, 1967; Kane, 1979; Koocher, 1973, 1974). Perhaps using the device of an external figure is a child's concrete way of representing a being that can be avoided. Nagy's methods (asking children to make drawings of death) and her cultural context no doubt influenced her results. For example, her study involved pre–World War II Hungarian children who were familiar with oral traditions about death. These children differ in many ways from children in our society today who are saturated with television and other media.

Nagy and other writers attached ages to the three developmental stages. She wrote, "The child of less than five years does not recognize death as an irreversible fact. In death, it sees life. . . . Between the ages of five and nine, death is most often personified and thought of as a contingency. . . . In general, only after the age of nine is it recognized that death is a process happening in us according to certain laws" (1948, p. 7). In a later publication, Nagy added, "It should be kept in mind that neither the stages nor the above-mentioned ages at which they occur are watertight compartment. . . . Overlapping does exist" (1959, p. 81). The lesson in this section is that many adults approach children with a stage-based schema of their understandings of death at different ages in their development.

"STAGING" CHILDREN AND THEIR UNDERSTANDINGS OF DEATH IS NOT DESIRABLE

Research in the field of children's understanding of death has been plagued by methodological problems, such as lack of precision and agreement about the terms and definitions used for various components of the concept of death, as well as lack of reliable and valid standardized measures for these components. As a result, the literature on this subject offers a "confusing array of results" (Stambrook & Parker, 1987, p. 154). Also, commentators have often applied their results uncritically, made them more rigid than they should be, and oversimplified their conclusions. Each of these ways of misusing stage-based theories of the development of children's understandings of death risks creating undesirable problems.

In terms of how *critically* these schemas are applied, the most important point is that there are undeniable differences between individual children. Adults should not expect children who have encountered war and genocide to think about death in ways identical to children who live in more peaceful areas of the world. Much the same is true of differences between children who have suffered multiple, tragic losses from epidemics such as AIDS or natural disasters and children who have not had such experiences. Life experiences, cultural or ethnic contexts, and messages from the adults and societies around them clearly influence how children do or do not think about death (e.g., Wass & Towry, 1980).

In terms of how *rigidly* these schemas are employed, it is curious to think about the theoretical boundaries between Nagy's cognitive stages. For example, an inflexible application of this stage-based theory would seem to suggest that a child who is 4 years and 11 months old will have a different concept of death than a child who is 5 years and 1 month old simply because of the 2 months' difference in their ages. Indeed, it might suggest that the same child somehow inexplicably changes his or her understanding of death by simply crossing some arbitrary age boundary. The point is that the chronological boundaries given for these stages are neither absolute nor inviolable. Children are not like elevators that jump from one level of understanding loss and death to another in some mysterious, mechanical fashion. In fact, children's cognitive development is only one part of their overall maturation, and every aspect of that maturation is complex and organic, influenced by many internal and external factors and moving at its own pace.

In terms of *oversimplifying* how we view children, it is important to keep in mind that stage-based theories of cognitive development are appealing precisely because they put forward clear and undemanding progressions toward relatively well-defined goals. The danger is that the broad generalizations they depend on may, and very likely will, gloss over the unique differences that differentiate children as distinct individuals. The stage-based portrait of the development of children's understandings of death is attractive because it assumes a single, straightforward path toward a "mature" concept. The portrait is highly seductive because it asks little of us beyond memorizing a few age ranges.

Instead of thinking about children's cognitive development (much less their overall developmental processes) in a mechanical, step-by-step way—and then confounding that with their chronological age—we would do far better to respect the complexity of their cognitive development and to recognize its close relationships to other aspects of their lives, such as their feelings, the social contexts in which they find themselves, and their spirituality. And we should always keep in mind how each individual child and the distinctive features of his or her personality influence how he or she thinks about difficult subjects such as separation, loss, and death. In brief, all children at the same age (even in similar social and cultural contexts) do not think in the same ways about death, any given child is likely to think about death in different ways at different points in his or her development, and age alone is not an accurate indicator of cognitive development.

The lesson in this section is twofold: (1) we should be cautious in broadly applying a stage-based theory of the development of children's understandings of death; and (2) we should distinguish between a child's cognitive development and his or her chronological age.

THINKING ABOUT DEATH IS A COMPLEX MATTER

Stage-based accounts of the development of children's understandings of death assume that it is a relatively straightforward process of working toward a mature concept of death. What is understood as a "mature" concept of death is not necessarily unproblematic, although some researchers (e.g., Slaughter & Griffiths, 2007) have suggested that it involves accepting death as fundamentally a biological event. Still, it is clear that the concept of death is neither a simple nor an uncomplicated notion. Many adults repeatedly return to ponder this concept at various points in their lives, perhaps in an ongoing effort to come to understand it adequately. Here we can try to draw out some of the components or aspects of a mature concept of death.

To begin, it is clear that the two central components of most stage-based accounts of the concept of death—finality and universality—are neither simple nor uncomplicated in themselves (Corr, 1995; Speece & Brent, 1984, 1996). For example, *finality* embraces at least two elements: irreversibility and nonfunctionality.

Irreversibility as a subconcept within the concept of death means that the natural processes involved in the transition from being alive to being dead, as well as the state that results from those processes, cannot be overturned or undone (Brent & Speece, 1993). Once the physical body of a living thing is dead, it can never be alive again. Apart from miracles or magical events, life is permanently and irrevocably absent from a dead body. (Medical resuscitation is not an exception here; it stimulates life in a body that is not yet fully dead, but rather is located in a kind of boundary region between being alive and being dead.)

The other key element of finality is *nonfunctionality*. Children are often curious about what dead people might be doing in heaven or wherever else they might be, treating the dead as inhabiting a kind of altered state of life (Barrett & Behne, 2005). But if death is truly final, that means the complete and absolute cessation of all the life-defining or functional capabilities (whether external and observable or internal and inferred) that are typically attributed to a living physical body. So nonfunctionality is another important subcomponent within the overall concept of death.

Universality reveals even more complex dimensions of the concept of death. It brings together three closely related subconcepts: all-inclusiveness, inevitability, and unpredictability. *All-inclusiveness* has to do with how broadly death applies to the group of living things. It responds to a familiar question: "Does everyone die?" The answer is yes, at least for all living things (non-living things do not die because they have never been alive; dead things are no longer alive and thus cannot die). Again apart from miracles or supernatural intervention, no living thing is exempt from death.

Inevitability carries this understanding of death one step further. To say that death is inevitable means that death is unavoidable for all living things. This attribute relates not merely to the extent or number of those who will die, but to the fact that none of them can escape their deaths. A person may avoid this or that death-related event, but not death itself. Every living thing must and will eventually die (again, barring miraculous events).

If death is all-inclusive and inevitable, one might think its timing would be certain and predictable, but that is not the case. In fact, death is *unpredictable*—any living person or thing might die at any time. These three components or subconcepts of the concept of death are challenging to acknowledge and accept; they bear directly on our own personal mortality and on the mortality of those we love.

Each of these aspects of the finality and universality of death is important, but taken together, they are not the only subjects of concern to children, who often ask additional questions about death. One type of question has to do with the events or conditions that bring about the death of a living thing: "Why do living things die?" or "What makes living things die?" Questions such as these are about what causes death. Children (and others) try to understand the external and internal events or forces that can bring about death. For children, it is important to learn to distinguish real causes from magical thinking, in which bad behavior or merely wishing could cause someone to die (Fogarty, 2000).

These three aspects of the concept of death—finality, universality, and causality—apply to the physical body, but they do not exhaust the death-related concerns of many children and adults. Those concerns lead to efforts to try to grasp or articulate what might be involved in some type of continued life apart from the physical body (Brent & Speece, 1993). For example, children often ask, "What happens after death?" and "Where does your soul or spirit go when you die?" These questions indicate a conviction that some type of continued life exists after the death of the physical body. That conviction may be expressed in various ways, such as a belief in the ongoing life of a soul in heaven without the body or the reincarnation of a soul in a new and different body or the resurrection and rebirth or restoration to life of one's former body. Although many persons believe an afterlife is implausible, it is important not to insist on that point of view in our research, impose it on studies of children's concerns, and thus bias claims about children's understandings of death. In fact, the great majority of persons in this world uphold some version of continued existence after death as fundamental to human existence, and various religious, philosophical, and spiritual systems have attempted to provide frameworks for these convictions and for children's questions on this topic (see, e.g., Gignoux, 1998). The important point here is that many children try to carry their understandings beyond the death of the physical body.

The lesson in this section is that death is not a simple and uncomplicated notion. It has many dimensions and implications. Children are not likely to grasp all of these dimensions simultaneously or all at once. In fact, individual children may have many different understandings of death at the same time, and they are likely to hold different understandings of death at different times throughout their lives. Adults who are aware of the complexity of the concept of death will be able to approach children and their understandings of death with a more sensitive ear than if they merely focus on undifferentiated concepts of finality and universality.

LISTEN TO THE INDIVIDUAL CHILD

Researchers who have studied the development of children's under-standings of death have disagreed on two key points: (1) at what age does a child attain a "mature" concept of death, and (2) do children first apply their concepts of death to other people or to themselves? For the first point, we have already noted that Nagy seems to think this concept is achieved after the age of 9. By contrast, Speece and Brent (1996) con-cluded, "Most studies have found that *by seven years of age* most chil-dren understand each of the key bioscientific components—Universality, Irreversibility, Nonfunctionality, and Causality" (p. 43; emphasis added). We have already noted that both of these claims are broad generaliza-tions that tend to conflate developmental processes and age in ways that are not reliable. Thus Speece and Brent added the following caution: "Age by itself explains nothing. It is rather a convenient general, omni-bus index of a wide range of loosely correlated biological and environ-mental variables" (p. 43).

For the second point, some researchers have maintained that chil-dren recognize that death is possible for other people before they apply it to themselves (e.g., Lonetto, 1980; Schilder & Wechsler, 1934). By contrast, Speece and Brent think it more likely that most children under-stand their own personal mortality before they understand that all other people die. Disagreement on this and the previous point suggest that we should be wary of wide-ranging generalizations of this type. They may be quite imperfect and unsound. Furthermore, they may be unhelpful if they lead us to rely on sweeping statements that oversimplify reality and our involvements with individual children. What we need is: (1) to heed calls for better research that distinguishes, standardizes, and operation-alizes key subconcepts within the concept of death (Kenyon, 2001; Lazar & Torney-Purta, 1991); and (2) to combine more nuanced appreciation and application of the results of currently available research with careful listening to individual children,

It is perhaps obvious to anyone who has interacted with a young child that children usually do not think about death in the same ways that adults do. Nevertheless, it would be wrong to conclude from these different ways of thinking that children have no concept of death what-soever. Even when children incorrectly think of death as sleep, they are exhibiting *an understanding* of death. Trying to understand death as a type of sleep is an effort to explain something that is unknown or only partially grasped (death) through something else (sleep) that is a familiar part of a child's life.

Confusing death with sleep indicates that the two concepts have not been properly differentiated, but it also shows that a child is trying to make sense of his or her experience. As Kastenbaum and Aisenberg (1972, p. 9) noted, "between the extremes of 'no understanding' and explicit, integrated abstract thought, there are many ways by which the young mind can enter into relationship with death."

In fact, cognitive development is not the only relevant variable in the story of how children come to their understandings of death, though it is an important and perhaps a critical aspect of the multidimensional processes involved in children's maturation. Other pertinent variables include life experiences, each child's individual personality, and the ways in which children are able and willing to communicate their death-related thoughts with others, together with the support and comfort they receive from those others (Kastenbaum, 1977).

That leads us to a larger lesson about theories that seek to explain the development of children's understandings of death. Carl Jung, one of our greatest theoretical psychologists, said, "Theories in psychology are the very devil. It is true that we need certain points of view for their orienting and heuristic value; but they should always be regarded as mere auxiliary concepts that can be laid aside at any time" (1954, p. 17). Jung certainly does not advocate abandoning all theoretical frameworks. We need guidance from theoretical insights such as those set forth in this chapter. As long as we subject theories to critical analysis, appreciate their limits, and draw judicious lessons from them, they can help identify what we might otherwise have missed and point us in useful directions.

At the same time, Jung wanted us to recognize the limitations of psychological theories and insights. They are auxiliary concepts or tools meant to assist our comprehension and appreciation—in this case, of children's emerging awareness and understandings death. Any tool has its own strengths and limitations. We should value it for its strengths and the help it can provide, but at the same time, we should recognize its limitations and the ways in which it may become a hindrance. Jung advised us to set the tool aside when we touch the miracle of a living soul.

Nagy concluded her original article with these words of advice: "To conceal death from the child is not possible and is also not permissible.

Natural behavior in the child's surroundings can greatly diminish the shock of its acquaintance with death" (1948, p. 27). Natural behavior involves active and sympathetic listening. We can learn the causes of a child's shock and concern, as well as the nature of his or her acquaintance with death, only by listening. Active listening allows us to appreciate the child's concerns and questions and helps us respond in effective ways (Corr, 1995, 1996). More important, by allowing the child to become our teacher in this way, we can enrich each other's appreciation of death in life.

The basic lesson in this section is twofold: (1) children do make an effort to grasp or understand death when it comes into their lives, and (2) a good way—perhaps the only effective way—to gain insight into a child's understandings of death is to establish a relationship of confidence and trust with the child and to listen carefully to the child's comments, questions, and concerns about loss and death.

SOME GUIDELINES FOR HELPING CHILDREN COPE WITH THEIR EMERGING AWARENESS AND UNDERSTANDINGS OF DEATH

The lessons at the end of each of the six main sections of this chapter suggest some useful guidelines for interacting with children and helping them cope with their emerging awareness and understandings of death.

- Do not assume that children, even young children, have no awareness of death.
- Accept that most children are curious about many aspects of life and death.
- Acknowledge that death and loss are not absent from the fantasy lives of children.
- Recognize that death-related themes and events are part of the ordinary environment of children's lives, as in play activities and fairy tales.
- Grant that healthy, normal children are likely to encounter death-related events in their own lives, as well as through the media and in the world around them.
- Appreciate that most children have thoughts and feelings about death and that they make an effort to grasp or understand death when it comes into their lives.

- Be aware that many adults approach children with a stage-based schema in mind regarding the child's understanding of death at various ages.
- Acknowledge that stage-based theories of the development of children's understandings of death are not undesirable in themselves, but they can lead us astray when we apply them uncritically, too rigidly, or in oversimplified ways.
- Concede that any sound theory of the development of children's understandings of death is likely to be valid in a broad, general way.
- Know that any sound theory of the development of children's understandings of death must be applied in a careful and sensitive way to match the realities of a particular child's life.
- Recognize that chronological age is only a crude indicator of cognitive development; it may not be a precise guide for many individual children.
- Be conscious of the fact that the concept of death is not a simple and uncomplicated notion; it has many dimensions and implications.
- Understand that children are not likely to grasp each of the central dimensions of the concept of death or all of its implications at once. That is one reason they repeat their questions about death or ask them again in different ways.
- Appreciate that adults who are aware of the complexity of the concept of death will be able to approach children with a more sensitive ear than if they merely focus on undifferentiated concepts of finality and universality.
- Realize that one good way—perhaps the only effective way—to gain insight into a child's understanding of death is to establish a relationship of trust and confidence with the child and to listen carefully to the child's comments, questions, and concerns about death.
- Make an effort to answer a child's questions about death and to respond to the concerns that underlie such questions in an honest, accurate, and helpful way.
- Frame your answers and responses in ways that are suitable to the child's capacities and needs. Don't be afraid to say, "I don't know."

Additional guidance for talking to children and educating them about loss and death can be found in chapters 14 and 15 in this book.

REFERENCES

Achté, K., Fagerström, R., Pentikäinen, J., & Farberow, N. L. (1990). Themes of death and violence in lullabies of different countries. *Omega, Journal of Death and Dying, 20,* 193–204.

Anthony, S. (1939). A study of the development of the concept of death [Abstract]. *British Journal of Educational Psychology, 9,* 267–277.

Anthony, S. (1940). *The child's discovery of death.* New York: Harcourt Brace.

Anthony, S. (1972). *The discovery of death in childhood and after.* New York: Basic Books. [Revised edition of *The child's discovery of death*]

Barrett, H. C., & Behne, T. (2005). Children's understanding of death as the cessation of agency: A test using sleep versus death. *Cognition, 96,* 93–108.

Bettelheim, B. (1977). *The uses of enchantment—The meaning and importance of fairy tales.* New York: Vintage.

Brent, S. B., & Speece, M. W. (1993). "Adult" conceptualizations of irreversibility: Implications for the development of the concept of death. *Death Studies, 17,* 203–224.

Corr, C. A. (1995). Children's understandings of death: Striving to understand death. In K. J. Doka (Ed.), *Children mourning, mourning children* (pp. 3–16). Washington, DC: Hospice Foundation of America.

Corr, C. A. (1996). Children and questions about death. In S. Strack (Ed.), *Death and the quest for meaning: Essays in honor of Herman Feifel* (pp. 217–238). Northvale, NJ: Jason Aronson.

Corr, C. A. (2008). Children's emerging awareness of death. In K. J. Doka & A. S. Tucci (Eds.), *Living with grief: Children and adolescents* (pp. 5–17). Washington, DC: Hospice Foundation of America.

Diamant, A. (1994, October). Special report: Media violence. *Parents Magazine,* 40–41, 45.

Fogarty, J. A. (2000). *The magical thoughts of grieving children: Treating children with complicated mourning and advice for parents.* Amityville, NY: Baywood.

Gartley, W., & Bernasconi, M. (1967). The concept of death in children. *Journal of Genetic Psychology, 110,* 71–85.

Gignoux, J. H. (1998). *Some folk say: Stories of life, death, and beyond.* New York: FoulkeTale.

Jung, C. (1954). *The development of personality.* In H. Read, M. Fordham, & G. Adler (Eds.), *The collected works of Carl G. Jung* (2nd ed., Vol. 17). Princeton, NJ: Princeton University Press.

Kane, B. (1979). Children's concepts of death. *Journal of Genetic Psychology, 134,* 141–153.

Kastenbaum, R. (1977). Death and development through the lifespan. In H. Feifel (Ed.), *New meanings of death* (pp. 17–45). New York: McGraw-Hill.

Kastenbaum, R., & Aisenberg, R. (1972). *The psychology of death.* New York: Springer Publishing.

Kenyon, B. L. (2001). Current research in children's conceptions of death: A critical review. *Omega, Journal of Death and Dying, 43,* 63–91.

Koocher, G. P. (1973). Childhood, death, and cognitive development. *Developmental Psychology, 9,* 369–375.

Koocher, G. P. (1974). Talking with children about death. *American Journal of Orthopsychiatry, 44,* 404–411.

Lamers, E. P. (1995). Children, death, and fairy tales. *Omega, Journal of Death and Dying, 31,* 151–167.

Lazar, A., & Torney-Purta, J. (1991). The development of the subconcepts of death in young children: A short-term longitudinal study. *Child Development, 62,* 1321–1333.

Lonetto, R. (1980). *Children's conceptions of death.* New York: Springer Publishing.

Maurer, A. (1966). Maturation of the conception of death. *Journal of Medical Psychology, 39,* 35–41.

Nagy, M. A. (1948/1959). The child's theories concerning death. *Journal of Genetic Psychology, 73,* 3–27. Reprinted with some editorial changes as "The child's view of death," in H. Feifel (Ed.), *The meaning of death* (pp. 79–98). New York: McGraw-Hill.

Opie, I., & Opie, P. (1969). *Children's games in street and playground: Chasing, catching, seeking, hunting, racing, dueling, exerting, daring, guessing, acting, and pretending.* Oxford, England: Oxford University Press.

Rochlin, G. (1967). How younger children view death and themselves. In E. A. Grollman (Ed.), *Explaining death to children* (pp. 51–85). Boston: Beacon Press.

Schilder, P., & Wechsler, D. (1934). The attitudes of children toward death. *Journal of Genetic Psychology, 45,* 406–451.

Slaughter, V., & Griffiths, M. (2007). Death understanding and fear of death in young children. *Clinical Child Psychology and Psychiatry, 12,* 525–535.

Slaughter, V., & Lyons, M. (2003). Learning about life and death in early childhood. *Cognitive Psychology, 46,* 1–30.

Speece, M. W., & Brent, S. B. (1984). Children's understanding of death: A review of three components of a death concept. *Child Development, 55,* 1671–1686.

Speece, M. W., & Brent, S. B. (1996). The development of children's understanding of death. In C. A. Corr & D. M. Corr (Eds.), *Handbook of childhood death and bereavement* (pp. 29–50). New York: Springer Publishing.

Stambrook, M., & Parker, K. C. (1987). The development of the concept of death in childhood: A review of the literature. *Merrill Palmer Quarterly, 33,* 133–157.

Wass, H., & Towry, B. (1980). Children's death concepts and ethnicity. *Death Education, 4,* 83–87.

Ethical Issues in Counseling Bereaved and Seriously Ill Children

3

HEATHER L. SERVATY-SEIB AND SARA J. TEDRICK

This chapter provides an overview of common ethical issues involved when counseling bereaved and seriously ill children. In general, ethical decision making is a dynamic process, whether for mental health practitioners or for volunteers who serve bereaved or seriously ill children in family-based support programs and camps for children. Clinicians cannot anticipate every potential ethical issue that may arise and cannot access definitive direction regarding how to proceed in each specific situation. Rather, even from a legal standpoint, the focus is on the idea of the "reasonable practitioner" model and the fact that clinicians will be held accountable by the courts for acting in a manner that is consistent with what a "reasonable" professional would do (Henkelman & Everall, 2001). In addition, Schmidt (2003) emphasized that the clinicians who most often encounter difficulties are not those who act in a reasonable way that can be justified by ethical standards and legal precedent, but those who choose *not* to act out of a concern about making a mistake. Practitioners and their clients are well served when practitioners access and make use of a sound ethical decision-making model when they are faced with difficult ethical dilemmas. Although a review of such models is beyond the scope of the present chapter, readers are directed to general models (e.g., Corey, Corey, & Callanan, 2006; Hartsell, 2006), as well as to works by scholars who have made specific application of models to the field of thanatology (e.g., Gamino & Ritter, 2009).

Surprisingly, the ethical codes of major mental health–related organizations provide limited guidance to clinicians engaged in counseling with children (Sori & Hecker, 2006). More specifically, the American Counseling Association (ACA, 2005) code uses the term *child* or the term *children* only three times, two instances related to the issue of consent and one related to clearly distinguishing roles and relationships with parents of child clients. In parallel fashion, the American Psychological Association (APA, 2002) code offers standards related to consent issues when individuals are "legally incapable of giving consent" (p. 7) and the need for clarification of roles and responsibilities when more than one family member is involved in treatment.

Adding a focus on death and dying to the already multifaceted process of engaging in ethical clinical practice with children requires particular coverage of issues of professional competence, autonomy, and confidentiality. These general ethical arenas are highlighted in this chapter, and specific relevance to death and dying issues is addressed throughout each section. In addition, the topically relevant ethical issue of touch in counseling is addressed at the end of the chapter.

PROFESSIONAL COMPETENCE

Professional competence is the lens through which all other ethical issues related to counseling bereaved and seriously ill children must be viewed. Practitioners cannot be ethical in their practice unless they are competent in key areas associated with working with a particular client population. The present discussion of competence in working with bereaved and seriously ill children is structured around the domains of knowledge, skills, and dispositions, a common framework for addressing the issue of competence within mental health–related fields (e.g., Association for Specialists in Group Work, 2000; Sue, Arredondo, & McDavis, 1992).

Knowledge

Clinicians who seek to provide ethical care to bereaved and seriously ill children must be knowledgeable about child development in general, as well as about issues specific to the topic of children and death. Working with children requires solid understanding of the physical, emotional, cognitive, and social developmental challenges faced by children

(Lawrence & Kurpius, 2000; Webb, 2002). Practitioners working with bereaved and seriously ill children need to be aware of concepts such as children's unique conceptualization of death (see chapter 2 in this book), the differences between adult and child expressions of grief and the dying process (e.g., Bluebond-Langner, 1995; Mitchell et al., 2006), and the interplay between trauma and grief (e.g., Layne et al., 2001) and need to remain current on the scholarly literature related to these areas. To work effectively with children facing life-threatening illness, clinicians must be aware of the physical, cognitive, and emotional symptoms of the relevant illnesses as well as children's medications; this area of competence has been particularly addressed for HIV issues (e.g., Brewer & Parish, 1998; Walker, 2003). More in-depth information regarding specific children and death/dying situations is readily available through academic database (e.g., PSYCINFO) and/or Internet searches.

Practitioners working with bereaved and seriously ill children must be knowledgeable about and sensitive to issues of diversity. More specifically, if clinicians seek to provide adequate care, they must be prepared, regardless of their personal values, to discuss spiritual issues with grieving and dying children (Fosarelli, 2006). Religious and cultural differences are often most salient in times of great stress or transition such as prior to and following death (cf. Gallup & Lindsay, 1999). Practitioners working with bereaved and seriously ill children must be culturally competent and mindful of the fact that models of grief and/or dying based on Western ideas and values may not be applicable to other cultural groups (De Baets, Sifovo, Parsons, & Pazvakavambwa, 2008; Rosenblatt, 2008).

Skills

The skills required to engage in the ethical treatment of children (in general) must be acquired through experiential and supervised training that goes beyond minimum coursework. Skills most particularly relevant to the treatment of bereaved and seriously ill children include those in the areas of assessment, working as a member of a multidisciplinary team, and advocacy.

Assessment

Clinicians working with bereaved and seriously ill children must make ethical decisions regarding whether treatment is appropriate or necessary and, if so, what modality of treatment is most suitable. Clinicians must be skilled at determining which bereaved and seriously ill children will likely benefit from treatment and which are experiencing expected reactions and are coping adequately. It can be difficult to distinguish between those who are experiencing normative reactions and those suffering from significant adjustment disorders (Worden, 1996) and diagnosable conditions such as PTSD (Webb, 2002). However, screening, assessment, and early intervention are critical, given that a recent meta-analysis by Currier, Holland, and Neimeyer (2007) calls into question the general effectiveness of interventions for bereaved children. They emphasized that interventions appeared most beneficial when they were provided in a timely way to children who were already exhibiting signs of difficulty. Although similar literature was not found on the need for assessing and screening the counseling needs of seriously ill children, a similar process is recommended. Greene (1998) highlighted the need for a focus on meeting the concrete needs of children with cancer, including continuing assessment and contact.

To guide clinicians in making professional assessments, Webb (2002) outlined a tripartite assessment approach for *disabling grief,* or grief that "has become all-encompassing and detrimental, instead of helping free the child to proceed with his/her life" (p. 22). This approach includes individual factors, factors related specifically to the death, and family, social, and religious/cultural factors. Although all of these areas are necessary for assessment prior to engaging in the treatment process with bereaved children, they also guide the clinician in determining "the extent to which a child can carry out his/her usual activities and proceed with his/her developmental tasks despite the presence of grief reactions" (p. 21).

Complementing Webb's focus on professionals, Worden's (1996) approach emphasizes helping support-group volunteers identify bereaved children who may need to be referred for a professional assessment. His list of "red flags" include persistent difficulty talking about the death, aggressive behavior, anxiety, somatic complaints, sleeping difficulties, eating disturbances, marked social withdrawal, school difficulties or serious academic reversal, persistent self-blame or guilt, and self-destructive behavior or a desire to die. In contrast to Webb, Worden emphasized the duration of a reaction (i.e., a child should be professionally evaluated if the behavior lasts for several months) rather than its intrusiveness. An additional point to consider is the assessment and screening process when forming a support group for bereaved children. It is important to avoid allowing one child's complicated grief to negatively affect the entire group (Samide & Stockton, 2002).

If a clinician determines that treatment is in fact indicated, the next ethical questions to be addressed include the following: Who is the client? And what treatment modality matches best with the needs of the identified client? When counseling bereaved and seriously ill children, it is quite difficult to separate a focus on the child from a focus on the entire family. Individual counseling may be important for children who need a safe and secure place to have their experiences validated. However, death and dying issues are not processed in isolation, but rather are social and familial experiences (Steen, Helm, & Johnson, 2007). Identifying the family system as the client can decrease the risk of potential ethical dilemmas (e.g., related to confidentiality of material within the family) and allows for direct as well as indirect benefits to the child because the functioning of the child has been consistently shown to be associated with the functioning of the parents of bereaved and seriously ill children (Haine, Wolchik, Sandler, Millsap, & Ayers, 2006; Hope & Hodge, 2006; Thastum, Johansen, Gubba, Olesen, & Romer, 2008).

A combination model, incorporating psychoeducation and support for caregivers and therapy for children, may be particularly useful (Worden, 1996). For example, in the case of seriously ill children, this combination could take many forms but may include individual child interventions such as behavior modification to help manage pain, peer groups and parental/family interventions focused on education about illness, parent mentoring, and/or couples counseling (Cloutier, Manion, Walker, & Johnson, 2002; Kenny & Frager, 1996; Morison, Bromfield, & Cameron, 2003; Rowland, Pfefferbaum, Adams-Greenly, & Redd, 1989). Maintaining a dialectical balance between the needs of the child and the family may be addressed through the relational ethic approach (see Wall, Needham, Browning, & James, 1999).

Ability to Work With a Team

Competent work with children (and families) experiencing bereavement and illness requires that professionals understand the roles of other professionals (e.g., medical practitioners, therapists, social workers, funeral home staff, school nurses, school counselors, teachers, school staff, and support-program staff and volunteers) and maintain the skill of effectively working with these professionals in order to best serve clients and utilize local services (Brewer & Parish, 1998; Etemad, 1995). It is critical that professionals work together cohesively so that children and their families feel confident about the care received. Minimal or disorganized communication will lead to fragmented and subpar treatment (Curnick, 1990). For example, school counselors, nurses, and teachers need to keep updated on a seriously ill child's prognosis, and medical practitioners need to be notified when ill children experience novel symptoms during school hours.

Advocacy

Grieving and seriously ill children are vulnerable with regard to both their developmental level and their particular life circumstances. Practitioners working with these populations must often advocate for the needs of their clients in order to fulfill their ethical responsibilities. The need for advocacy most often arises in schools and hospitals.

Practitioners who interact with or work from within school systems must be prepared to advocate for clients through the provision of staff training and through conversations with administration regarding school policies. Clinicians knowledgeable about the needs of bereaved and seriously ill children have an obligation to share that knowledge with those who do not have such knowledge. The group in need of training is not bound by discipline; rather, individuals from all of the following professions could be in a position of trainer or trainee: school counselors, social workers, nurses, teachers, and administrators. Such training may need to include information on how to recognize and respond to children's medical emergencies, red flags for referring students for a professional psychological assessment, children's unique psychological reactions to death and dying, and strategies for best supporting students who experience excessive discrimination or stigma (e.g., HIV status, family suicide) (Brewer & Parish, 1998; Goldman, 2001; Worden, 1996). With regard to policy-related advocacy, practitioners must work to persuade those in positions of power to adopt policies in line with legal and clinical standards. For example, children with HIV/AIDS have the legal right to an education, and exclusion is prohibited by the Americans With Disability Act (Brewer & Parish; Etemad, 1995). Grieving and seriously ill children also need assurance and structure that allows them to take breaks from academic demands if their psychological or physical functioning requires such allowances.

In hospital settings, advocacy often may be needed to ensure that seriously ill children and their families receive appropriate and accurate education regarding all available care-related options (Curnick, 1990; Weithorn & McCabe, 1988). The clinician's goal should be to provide education that will allow the family to make informed and non-pressured decisions based on their family situation, functioning, and resources. Those working with seriously ill children are clearly *not* in a position of imposing or defining what constitutes quality of life or implying what specific decisions will lead to a greater or lesser level of quality of life. Kenny and Frager (1996) provided a thorough overview of difficult decisions faced when children are seriously ill (e.g., palliative care, refractory symptoms, terminal sedation). They argued that mental health professionals have a role to play in facilitating conversation regarding these difficult issues. Another area where families may need added information regarding potential benefits and drawbacks is the choice between hospital and home care (Baum, Dominica, & Woodward, 1990; Buckingham, 1989).

Dispositions

Working with bereaved and dying children is a personally and professionally challenging process. Practitioners who engage in such work must be committed to self-awareness and self-care.

In order to work competently with bereaved or seriously ill children, clinicians need to develop and maintain comfort with their own mortality and with issues related to death and dying (Samide & Stockton, 2002; Walker, 2003). Without such awareness, the services provided will suffer. The onus on the practitioner working with bereaved and seriously ill children is much higher than it is in general clinical situations. Not only are children more dependent than adolescents and adults, and thus more likely to suffer from poor clinical care; they are also less likely to realize when they are receiving poor care (Koocher & Keith-Spiegel, 1990).

Self-care is a critical dispositional issue for practitioners working with bereaved and seriously ill children because dealing with death and dying on a daily basis takes a heavy toll on mental health practitioners, and there is a risk for burnout (Brewer & Parish, 1998; Webb, 2002). Practitioners need to be vigilant to issues of self-care, making intentional decisions regarding their practice such as varying their caseloads and scheduling time for engaging in outside activities that bolster their coping resources (Walker, 2003; Wolgrin, 2007). Part of self-care also involves being open to the possible need to grieve and mourn the deaths that are experienced in the course of professional work and taking the necessary public or personal actions appropriate to process these experiences.

AUTONOMY, INFORMED CONSENT, AND CHILD ASSENT

The principle of autonomy is commonly included as an ethical principle in the codes of professional organizations for mental health practitioners in the West (Wall et al., 1999; see ACA & APA codes as examples). The goals of counseling regularly include the fostering of independence and self-reliance (Crowhurst & Dobson, 1993). However, determining the appropriate level of child involvement in death and dying situations is not simple. In addition, the extent to which children are involved in decisions regarding their own treatment requires the consideration of legal and ethical issues as well as the potential consequences of such involvement (Jacob & Hartshorne, 2003).

In clinical situations involving children and death, autonomy, informed consent, and assent are particularly critical issues. There is no greater time when individuals feel out of control than when they are faced with the realities of death. This fact is intensified with grieving and seriously ill *children* because children are not recognized to possess the cognitive and emotional or legal capacity to make their own decisions (Kenny & Frager, 1996; Lawrence & Kurpius, 2000). Clinicians must work to assist family members in balancing the limits of grieving and ill children's capabilities with their right to be involved and included.

Talking With Children About Death and Dying

Is it appropriate to talk with children about death and dying issues? Are children capable of such discussions? Do children have a right to be included in death and dying conversations? Is it harmful for children to engage in such discussions, or is it harmful to avoid engaging in such conversations with children? The accumulated experience of medical and mental health professional alike suggests that children have a need to be included in open, honest, and concrete discussions about death and dying (Brewer & Parish, 1998; Buckingham, 1989; see chapter 14). As noted by Monroe (1995), "it is impossible not to communicate with children" (p. 87). Children know when there is something challenging occurring within the family system. Scholars who advocate for open communication do so in reference to situations when a family member has died, a stigmatized family death (e.g., suicide) has occurred, a family member has a life-threatening illness, the family member has a stigmatized illness (e.g., HIV), or the child has a stigmatized or non-stigmatized illness (Anderson, 1995; Curnick, 1990; Elder & Knowles, 2002; Grollman, 1995; Trozzi, 1999). The primary rationale offered in the literature for the inclusion of children in death-related conversations is the fact that children experience less isolation and function better when they are included (DeMaso, Meyer, & Beasley, 1997; Etemad, 1995; Hope & Hodge, 2006; Nickman, Silverman, & Normand, 1998; Siegel & Gorey, 1994).

An ethical dilemma for mental health practitioners working with seriously ill children arises when the parents have decided against open, honest communication with their children about the seriousness of the child's condition. Although parents have the ultimate responsibility and control, mental health practitioners have a role in encouraging them to be open and honest with their children. This clinical obligation could present an ethical dilemma between autonomy (i.e., parent's desire to not talk with their child) and beneficence (i.e., professional understanding of the benefits of open communication) (Garcia, Forrester, & Jacob, 1998). What if parents refuse to tell a child that the child has HIV? Mental health practitioners are faced with the following ethical questions: "How much should children know about their condition?" "What are the potential consequences of this disclosure?" (Garcia et al., p. 169). Such questions are not easy to answer, and respecting children's autonomy to know the truth in this situation could actually result in harm when others learn of their diagnosis. However, not informing children of their HIV status would not provide them with the opportunity to take precautions to safeguard the health of others.

Professionals have an ethical responsibility to know the literature such that they can accurately inform and guide those with whom they work (see chapter 14). They should encourage open communication about death, serve as effective role models for discussing death and dying, and support parents in their discussions about death with children. However, clinicians must also remain informed regarding the ethnic and cultural overlays that may affect the process of communicating with children about death (e.g., De Baets et al., 2008; Murphy, Roberts, & Hoffman, 2003). Monroe (1995) argued that it is not enough for clinicians to recommend to parents that they be open with their children but that they must provide them with resources that help guide them through the process. She offers an elegant outline including steps such as treating parents as colleagues, offering them information so that the process is more manageable, anticipating difficulties, and encouraging them to be gentle with themselves (see Monroe, pp. 89–96).

Informed Consent

Although the necessity for immediately obtaining parents' consent may vary slightly by the setting in which services are provided (e.g., school setting), counselors who obtain signed informed consent from parents during the first session of working with a child are engaging in legal and ethical practice and are decreasing their risk of being sued (Myers, 1982; Sori & Hecker, 2006). In the United States, parents have the legal authority to consent or deny the provision of psychological services to their minor children (Gumaer, 1984; Jacob & Hartshorne, 2003; Lawrence & Kurpius, 2000). By definition "informed consent is the formal permission given by a client that signals the beginning of the legal, contractual agreement that allows treatment to be initiated" (Lawrence & Kurpius, p. 133). Lawmakers and courts operate based on the assumption that minor children are not developmentally competent to independently make decisions regarding their own treatment (Gamino & Ritter, 2009). Although parents have the legal authority to make health- and mental health–related decisions for their children, parents can involve children in the consent process as much or as little as they chose (Weithorn & McCabe, 1988).

Clinicians working with grieving and seriously ill children need to be particularly mindful of who possesses legal guardianship of the child being presented for treatment. In situations where a parent has died, for example, the legal custody of the child may be held by the surviving parent, but it is also possible that guardianship has been awarded to a grandparent, aunt/uncle, or older sibling. It is also possible that children may become wards of the state if the surviving parent is not capable of parenting or if the child's illness presents a challenge that the parents do not have the resources to manage. In short, clinicians must determine who holds legal guardianship of children and must know state laws regarding the rights of noncustodial parents over issues such as the need to consent to treatment and access to client records (Lawrence & Kurpius, 2000; Sori & Hecker, 2006).

Child Assent

Beyond the legal requirement for parental consent, clinicians have an ethical responsibility to involve children in decisions related to their care (Corey et al., 2006; Prout, DeMartino, & Prout, 1998). The concept of assent has been developed as the means to obtain minors' permission for treatment and involves "the same elements as consent but with a lower standard" (Kenny & Frager, 1996, pp. 40–41). Although children under the age of 6 are likely not capable of providing assent for treatment, children ages 6–12 years appear to have the capacity to make competent decisions regarding treatment (Kenny & Frager; Lawrence & Kurpius, 2000). Children should be informed of the "scope and nature of the proposed intervention" (Jacob & Hartshorne, 2003, p. 56), "involved in the process of treatment goal setting" (Corey et al., p. 134), allowed the opportunity to express any concerns they may have about the process (Towbin, 1995), and asked questions that will elicit and encourage their active participation in the therapeutic process—for example, "What do you expect to have happen here?" (Henkelman & Everall, 2001, p. 116).

The rights identified in the literature related to mental health treatment appear to be quite parallel to those offered in connection with children's involvement in their own health care decisions and treatment. More specifically, Weithorn and McCabe (1988) argued that the rationale for involving children in their own treatment process is based on ethics, but that this decision is also understood as best practice in the literature. In fact a number of models exist that are specifically directed at promoting children's involvement in their care (e.g., Rushton, 2005).

With regard to the general care of grieving and seriously ill children, clinicians must be mindful of the need to offer choice points throughout the process of treatment. However, such choices should be offered only if the child's refusal can reasonably be accommodated (e.g., their decision either way will not place them at risk) (Koocher, 2005; Walker, 2003).

Autonomy-Related Dilemmas

Ethical dilemmas arise when the parental legal right to provide or deny consent for a child's treatment conflicts with what the *counselor* perceives to be in the child's best interest or what the *child* desires. For example, a parent may report a therapy goal for a child based on a behavior that the child does not believe is a problem (Prout et al., 1998). If the child refuses to engage in the treatment, and the therapist accepts the refusal, what obligation does the therapist have to the parent or parents (Ross, 1980)? Factors to consider include the child's age and cognitive level, the extent of impairment in the child and/or the parents, and the extent to which the therapist perceives the treatment to be necessary (Johnson, Rasbury, & Siegel, 1986). For example, the surviving mother of a grieving child may present the child for therapy because she is concerned that the child is not engaging socially with her peers. The child reports that she has a best friend in whom she confides and that beyond this friend she does not feel the need for more friends. The counselor will likely need to build rapport with both child and parent to the point that candid conversations can be facilitated around the differences in the mother's and daughter's perceptions of the child's grief and the need for treatment.

Dilemmas also arise in medical situations involving autonomy versus beneficence and/or nonmaleficence. Perhaps the most controversial issue related to this ethical area is who should have the right to decide against potential life-sustaining treatment when the patient is either an infant or a child who is not competent to consent (Weithorn & McCabe, 1988). There is actually not agreement on what criteria should be used in this situation. A related situation is one in which a seriously ill child may be engaging in behavior that will likely put his or her health at even greater risk (Garcia et al., 1998). Such behavior could include noncompliance with a medication regimen or even active risky behavior such as playing in the rain when immune functioning is known to be at a decreased level.

CONFIDENTIALITY

Although confidentiality is a critical issue when working with any client population, it becomes an even more challenging consideration when counseling children as questions arise regarding who the client is. Confidentiality is the base upon which the counseling relationship is built because trust is central to the process of sharing, and "all codes in the mental health professions address confidentiality" (Sori & Hecker, 2006, p. 160). However, "there is no clear-cut rule that guides professional counselors in working with minor children when issues of confidentiality arise" (McCurdy & Murray, 2003, p. 394).

Factors to Be Considered

Determining how much information to share with the parents of child clients requires sound clinical and professional judgment. Although research suggests counselors rely most on their intuition and judgment about potential harm when making decisions about confidentiality, several domains must be considered when working with children

(Zingaro, 1983). These domains include legal requirements, severity of client behavior, ethical guidelines, and unique child characteristics.

Federal and state statutes offer guidance regarding how to handle confidentiality issues when working with children; however, care must be taken because laws are open to interpretation. Legally, parents have the right to access their children's assessment, psychotherapy, and general treatment records. As a general rule, scholars and clinicians contend that parents have a legal right to know what happens in counseling sessions and about the child's progress in counseling (Corey et al., 2006; Lawrence & Kurpius, 2000). Even beyond parental notification, there are, of course, more general legal limitations to confidentiality, including when the child indicates a plan to harm self or harm another and in situations where the child reports abuse. It is worth noting that *harm* is a difficult term to define. Although statements about suicidal and homicidal thoughts and plans are clear regarding the need to notify and warn, there are many other situations where the indication of risk to the welfare of the client is much less clear. The law may not require a clinician to notify parents of a behavior, but the severity of any specific behavior must be considered by clinicians as they weigh whether to disclose certain information to parents (Isaacs & Stone, 2001; Milne, 1995). Clinicians must also be aware that although there are general federal limits to confidentiality, state laws vary. For example, states may differ on the threshold for abuse reporting and on the specifics related to privileged communication and duty to warn (for example, some states do not require an identifiable victim). With regard to setting, state education codes include specific legal guidelines for credentialed school counselors with regard to confidentiality of counseling interactions. In addition, hospital personnel must follow HIPAA regulations.

Although confidentiality is invariably discussed in the ethical codes of mental health professions, the codes actually offer little if any guidance regarding how to negotiate the issue when working with child clients. With this lack of guidance, unique child characteristics are important to consider when addressing issues of confidentiality with children and their parents (Isaacs & Stone, 2001; McCurdy & Murray, 2003). For example, Koocher and Keith-Spiegel (1990) offered an excellent question regarding the interaction between developmental level and the issue of confidentiality: "Can the child at the preoperational stage of cognitive development, who assumes that her parents are omnipotent and omniscient, conceive of another adult's withholding any information from her parent?" (p. 81). They go on to argue that in such a situation, the concept of confidentiality has little if any meaning.

Clinical Recommendations

The scholarly literature focused on ethical issues when working with children offers confidentiality-related recommendations for clinicians. Suggestions are offered with regard to establishing trust, determining a general clinical approach, clarifying the clinical approach with children and parents at the start of treatment, and considering the limits and consequences of material to be disclosed.

Trust and the issue of confidentiality go hand in hand. Although it is often assumed that clients need to believe that counselors will keep material private in order to trust them, an argument can also be made that "treating children and adolescents with truthfulness, personal respect, serious consideration, and involvement in goal setting goes a lot further in establishing a trusting relationship than does any absolute promise of confidentiality" (Koocher & Keith-Spiegel, 1990, p. 81). Children are not likely to need a complete assurance that all of what they say will be kept private. In fact, clinicians take quite a risk regarding potential rupture in the therapeutic relationship if they make such a promise because it is impossible to predict whether they will in fact be able to keep that promise.

Hendrix (1991) offered a solid overview of the general approaches to confidentiality when working with children. He suggested that there are four options, including complete confidentiality, limited confidentiality, informed forced confidentiality, and no guarantee of confidentiality. Hendrix detailed the strengths and weaknesses of each approach and provided clinicians with information they can use to determine their own general approach such that they are prepared to discuss that approach with child clients and their parents. Hendrix argued for closest consideration of the informed forced confidentiality approach because he contended that it is the one of the four approaches that most closely fits with Kitchener's (1984) five ethical principles. According to Hendrix,

> this stance is one in which the mental health counselor is unlikely to make a promise he or she might feel compelled to breach (fidelity). The mental health counselor reveals only what, in his or her opinion, is likely to further the cause of therapy (beneficence). The client is told what will be revealed and has an opportunity to voice any objections (autonomy), and the mental

health counselor can then reevaluate the plan to avoid any unforeseen problems (nonmaleficence). Finally, children and adults are not treated as having equal decision-making ability; instead, allowances are made for the inequalities (justice). Furthermore, it would seem that the fact that the child is at least informed of information to be revealed increases the probability that the child's best interest will be served and that the therapeutic relationship will not be damaged. (pp. 328–329)

Again, regardless of the approach chosen, it is imperative that those working with children have a clear sense of their approach to handling confidentiality issues. Two points to emphasize in this area include letting children and parents know that the clinicians will attempt to seek permission from the client prior to forced disclosure and encouraging clients to be the discloser of material if at all possible (Koocher & Keith-Spiegel, 1990; Lawrence & Kurpius, 2000).

Clinicians who have a clear approach to confidentiality can share that approach from the start of the therapeutic interaction. When parents, children, and clinicians all have the same understanding of how issues of confidentiality will be handled, a "three-way bond of trust" (Lawrence & Kurpius, 2000, p. 134) is established, and much prevention work has been done. Documenting such understanding in the session note, in the informed consent, or in a "special client-therapist contract" is also recommended (Sori & Hecker, 2006).

Clinicians and their child clients are best served when the least necessary amount of material is shared with only those who need to be made aware of the information and when disclosure consequences are fully considered (Jacob & Hartshorne, 2003; Koocher & Keith-Spiegel, 1990). Even when there is a signed release of information, clinicians must make decisions about how much information or what type is best released to certain audiences. It is critical that clinicians discuss the potential consequences with both child clients and their parents so that all can prepare as much as possible for what may occur.

Confidentiality-Related Dilemmas

The professional literature reflects several confidentiality-related ethical dilemmas that are common to working with grieving or seriously ill children. Three of these dilemmas include group work with children, children sharing family secrets related to death and dying, and disclosure of a child's HIV/AIDS status.

Working with children in groups presents unique confidentiality challenges. Children in groups must understand the limits of confidentiality because confidentiality is harder to maintain in a group format (McCarthy & Sorenson, 1993). Another relevant issue is the privacy of the setting where the group meets (see Samide & Stockton, 2002). These challenges are particularly relevant to the current conversation given that groups are a common form of intervention for grieving children and, to a lesser extent, for children with serious illness.

According to McCurdy and Murray (2003), the ethical literature offers little direction for clinicians in situations where a child shares a family secret with a clinician within a family counseling context. Such disclosure is a particular issue when the child shares the secret during an individual session with the family therapist. Although prevention is preferred to avoid such dilemmas (i.e., being clear about limits/boundaries at the start), clinicians who find themselves in this situation must tread lightly. In the case of a bereaved family, a child may spontaneously describe the suicidal nature of the family death, a factor that no other family members had disclosed. The child may describe immediate feelings of anxiety after sharing with the clinician because he has been told to tell no one. How will the clinician handle this issue? Will he or she keep the child's secret or discuss the discrepancy with all family members? Keeping this secret would likely limit the effectiveness of the treatment offered to the family. Determining the best way to talk with the family about the secret requires consideration of issues such as recalling the conversations about the limits/boundaries that did take place, the level of rapport built with the family, the age of the child, and the general level of familial pathology (e.g., parental personality disorder).

Confidentiality is a key issue for any child with HIV/AIDS. Professionals are legally bound to keep a child's HIV status confidential, and clinicians are also compelled to keep the information confidential in connection to the potential negative consequences for the family following disclosure of the condition. However, it is also critical to consider that the stress associated with keeping the HIV status a secret can be significant for children and their families (Wiener, Battles, & Heilman, 1998). Those working with children with HIV and their families may consider recommending an approach of "selective disclosure" (Walker, 2003, p. 216) to persons that the family trusts, to decrease the burden of not disclosing and to increase the opportunity for others to offer help and support.

TOUCH

Touch is a sensitive topic within the therapeutic literature. Concerns raised about touch are far from unfounded, considering that the most common ethical violations resulting in expulsion from professional organizations are dual relationships, particularly those with a sexual component (Phelan, 2007). However, avoiding touch in counseling work with children is almost impossible (McNeil-Haber, 2004). For young children, touch is a developmental part of how they function in the world. They are tactile in their experience of the world, and touch is one of the primary avenues through which they learn about their environment.

Rather than a hindrance to treatment, touch has actually been specifically used in treating adults facing death and dying issues. For example, therapeutic touch has been shown to positively affect the grief and immunological and psychological functioning of bereaved adults (Quinn & Strelkauskas, 1993; Robinson, 1996). In addition, touch appears to enhance the immunological functioning of adults with HIV and to decrease pain and anxiety in cancer patients (Ironson et al., 1996; Jackson et al., 2008).

Counselors need to be mindful of the ethical issues that do arise because touch is often a part of the therapeutic work with grieving and seriously ill children. McNeil-Haber (2004) provided practical guidelines for use by practitioners as they consider the use of touch in working with children. More specifically, she offered questions such as "Whose needs are being met by the touch, the child's or the clinician's?" (p. 137) and highlights considerations such "the child's diagnosis, abuse history, and the family's history of abuse" (p. 138).

CONCLUSION

Practitioners working with bereaved and seriously ill children must be aware of the common ethical issues that arise when working with children in general (e.g., informed consent and confidentiality). Particular attention is warranted in the areas of competence, autonomy regarding child inclusion in death-related conversations, and unique issues that arise in connection with suicide, HIV, and touch in therapy.

REFERENCES

American Counseling Association (ACA). (2005). *ACA code of ethics.* Retrieved April 5, 2009, from http://www.counseling.org/Resources/CodeOfEthics/TP/ Home/CT2.aspx

American Psychological Association (APA). (2002). *APA ethical principles of psychologists and code of conduct.* Retrieved April 5, 2009, from http://www.apa.org/ethics/code2002.html

Anderson, B. (1995). Children and HIV: Orphans and victims. In K. J. Doka (Ed.), *Children mourning, mourning children* (pp. 57–65). Washington, DC: Hospice Foundation of America.

Association for Specialists in Group Work (ASGW). (2000). *ASGW professional standards for the training of group workers.* Retrieved April 5, 2009, from http://www.asgw.org/training_standards.htm

Baum, J. D., Dominica, S. F., & Woodward, R. N. (1990). *Listen. My child has a lot of living to do.* New York: Oxford University Press.

Bluebond-Langner, M. (1995). Worlds of dying children and their well siblings. In K. J. Doka (Ed.), *Children mourning, mourning children* (pp. 115–130). Washington, DC: Hospice Foundation of America.

Brewer, L. K., & Parish, M. T. (1998). Children and HIV: Concepts and strategies for teachers and counselors. In L. L. Palmatier (Ed.), *Crisis counseling for a quality school community: Applying Wm. Glasser's choice theory* (pp. 269–303). Philadelphia: Accelerated Development.

Buckingham, R. W. (1989). *Care of the dying child: A practical guide for those who help others.* New York: Continuum.

Cloutier, P. F., Manion, I. G., Walker, J. G., & Johnson, S. M. (2002). Emotionally focused interventions for couples with chronically ill children: A 2-year follow-up. *Journal of Marital & Family Therapy, 28,* 391–398.

Corey, G., Corey, M. S., & Callanan, P. (2006). *Issues and ethics in the helping profession* (7th ed.). Pacific Grove, CA: Brooks/Cole.

Crowhurst, B., & Dobson, K. S. (1993). Informed consent: Legal issues and applications to clinical practice. *Canadian Psychology, 34,* 329–346.

Curnick, S. (1990). Domiciliary nursing care. In J. D. Baum, S. F. Dominica, & R. N. Woodward (Eds.), *Listen. My child has a lot of living to do* (pp. 28–33). New York: Oxford University Press.

Currier, J. M., Holland, J. M., & Neimeyer, R. A. (2007). The effectiveness of bereavement interventions with children: A meta-analytic review of controlled outcome research. *Journal of Clinical Child & Adolescent Psychology, 36,* 253–259.

De Baets, A. J., Sifovo, S., Parsons, R., & Pazvakavambwa, I. E. (2008). HIV disclosure and discussions about grief with Shona children: A comparison between health care workers and community members in eastern Zimbabwe. *Social Science & Medicine, 66,* 479–491.

DeMaso, D. R., Meyer, E. C., & Beasley, P. J. (1997). What do I say to my surviving children? *Journal of the American Academy of Child & Adolescent Psychiatry, 36,* 1299–1302.

Elder, S. L., & Knowles, D. (2002). Suicide in the family. In N. B. Webb (Ed.), *Helping bereaved children: A handbook for practitioners* (pp. 128–148). New York: Guilford.

Etemad, J. G. (1995). Children, adolescents, and HIV: Ethical issues. *Child and Adolescent Psychiatric Clinics of North America, 4,* 823–835.

Fosarelli, P. (2006). The spiritual issues faced by children and adolescents at the end of life. In C. M. Puchalski (Ed.), *A time for listening and caring* (pp. 83–100). New York: Oxford University Press.

Gallup, G., & Lindsay, D. M. (1999). *Surveying the religious landscape: Trends in the U.S. beliefs.* Harrisburg, PA: Morehouse.

Gamino, L. A., & Ritter, R. H. (2009). *Ethical practice in grief counseling.* New York: Springer Publishing.

Garcia, J. G., Forrester, L. E., & Jacob, A. V. (1998). Ethical dilemma resolution in HIV/AIDS counseling: Why an integrative model? *International Journal of Rehabilitation and Health, 4,* 167–181.

Goldman, L. (2001). *Breaking the silence: A guide to help children with complicated grief-suicide, homicide, AIDS, violence and abuse* (2nd ed.). New York: Brunner/Routledge.

Greene, P. (1988). Responsibilities of the medical community to children with cancer. In R. E. Dowell Jr., D. R. Copeland, & J. van Eys (Eds.), *The child with cancer in the community: Proceedings of the Twelfth Annual Mental Health Conference* (pp. 57–67). Springfield, IL: Charles C Thomas.

Grollman, E. A. (1995). Can you answer children's questions? In D. W. Adams & E. J. Deveau (Eds.), *Beyond the innocence of children* (Vol. 1, pp. 9–14). Amityville, NY: Baywood.

Gumaer, J. (1984). *Counseling and therapy for children.* New York: Free Press.

Haine, R. A., Wolchik, S. A., Sandler, I. N., Millsap, R. M., & Ayers, T. S. (2006). Positive parenting as protective resource for parentally bereaved children. *Death Studies, 30,* 1–28.

Hartsell, B. D. (2006). A model for ethical decision-making: The contexts of ethics. *Journal of Social Work Values and Ethics, 3.* Retrieved February 12, 2009, from http://www.socialworker.com/jswve/content/view/26/44/

Hendrix, D. H. (1991). Ethics and intrafamily confidentiality in counseling with children. *Journal of Mental Health Counseling, 13,* 323–333.

Henkelman, J. J., & Everall, R. D. (2001). Informed consent with children: Ethical and practical implications. *Canadian Journal of Counseling, 35,* 109–121.

Hope, R. M., & Hodge, D. M. (2006). Factors affecting children's adjustment to the death of a parent: The social work professional's viewpoint. *Child & Adolescent Social Work Journal, 23,* 107–126.

Ironson, G., Field, T., Kumar, M., Patarca, R., Price, A., et al. (1996). Massage therapy is associated with enhancement of the immune systems of cytotoxic capacity. *International Journal of Neuroscience, 84,* 205–218.

Isaacs, M. L., & Stone, C. (2001). Confidentiality with minors: Mental health counselors' attitudes toward breaching or preserving confidentiality. *Journal of Mental Health Counseling, 23,* 342–357.

Jackson, E., Kelley, M., McNeil, P., Meyer, E., Schlegel, L., & Eaton, M. (2008). Does therapeutic touch help reduce pain and anxiety in patients with cancer? *Clinical Journal of Oncology Nursing, 12,* 113–120.

Jacob, S., & Hartshorne, T. S. (2003). *Ethics and law for school psychologists.* Hoboken, NJ: John Wiley & Sons.

Johnson, J. H., Rasbury, W. C., & Siegel, L. J. (1986). *Approaches to child treatment: Introduction to theory, research, and practice.* New York: Pergamon.

Kenny, N. P., & Frager, G. (1996). Refractory symptoms and terminal sedation of children: Ethical issues and practical management. *Journal of Palliative Care, 12,* 40–45.

Kitchener, K. S. (1984). Intuition, critical evaluation and ethical principle: The foundation for ethical decisions in counseling psychology. *Counseling Psychologist, 12,* 43–56.

Koocher, G. P. (2005). Behavioral research with children: The fenfluramine challenge. In E. Kodesh (Ed.), *Learning from cases: Ethics and research with children* (pp. 179–193). New York: Oxford University Press.

Koocher, G. P., & Keith-Spiegel, P. C. (1990). *Children, ethics, & the law: Professional issues and cases.* Lincoln: University of Nebraska Press.

Lawrence, G., & Kurpius, S. E. R. (2000). Legal and ethical issues involved when counseling minors in nonschool settings. *Journal of Counseling & Development, 78,* 130–136.

Layne, C. M., Pynoos, R. S., Saltzman, W. R., Arslanagic, B., Black, M., Savjak, N., et al. (2001). Trauma/grief-focused group psychotherapy: School-based postwar intervention with traumatized Bosnian adolescents. *Group Dynamics: Theory, Research, and Practice, 5,* 277–290.

McCarthy, M. M., & Sorenson, G. P. (1993). School counselors and consultants: Legal duties and liabilities. *Journal of Counseling & Development, 72,* 159–167.

McCurdy, K. G., & Murray, K. C. (2003). Confidentiality issues when minor children disclose family secrets in family counseling. *The Family Journal: Counseling and Therapy for Couples and Families, 11,* 393–398.

McNeil-Haber, F. M. (2004). Ethical considerations in the use of nonerotic touch in psychotherapy with children. *Ethics & Behavior, 14,* 123–140.

Milne, J. (1995). An analysis of the law of confidentiality with special reference to the counselling of minors. *Australian Psychologist, 30,* 169–174.

Mitchell, A. M., Wesner, S., Brownson, L., Dysart-Gale, D., Garand, L., & Havill, A. (2006). Effective communication with bereaved child survivors of suicide. *Journal of Child and Adolescent Psychiatric Nursing, 19,* 130–136.

Monroe, B. (1995). It is impossible not to communicate—Helping the family grieve. In S. C. Smith & S. M. Pennells (Eds.), *Interventions with bereaved children* (pp. 87–106). Philadelphia: Jessica Kingsley Publishers.

Morison, J. E., Bromfield, L. M., & Cameron, H. J. (2003). A therapeutic model for supporting families of children with a chronic illness or disability. *Child and Adolescent Mental Health, 8,* 125–130.

Murphy, D. A., Roberts, K. J., & Hoffman, D. (2003). Regrets and advice from mothers who have disclosed their HIV+ serostatus to their young children. *Journal of Child and Family Studies, 12,* 307–318.

Myers, J. E. B. (1982). Legal issues surrounding psychotherapy with minor clients. *Clinical Social Work Journal, 10,* 303–314.

Nickman, S. L., Silverman, P. R., & Normand, C. (1998). Children's construction of a deceased parent: The surviving parent's contribution. *American Journal of Orthopsychiatry, 68,* 126–134.

Phelan, J. E. (2007). Membership expulsions for ethical violations from major counseling, psychology, and social work organizations in the United States: A 10-year analysis. *Psychological Reports, 101,* 145–152.

Prout, S. M., DeMartino, R. A., & Prout, H. T. (1998). Ethical and legal issues in psychological interventions with children and adolescents. In H. T. Prout & D. T. Brown

(Eds.), *Counseling and psychotherapy with children and adolescents: Theory and practice for school and clinical settings* (pp. 26–48). Hoboken, NJ: John Wiley & Sons.

Quinn, J. F., & Strelkauskas, A. J. (1993). Psychoimmunologic effects of Therapeutic Touch on practitioners and recently bereaved recipients: A pilot study. *Advances in Nursing Science, 15,* 13–26.

Robinson, L. S. (1996). The effects of Therapeutic Touch on the grief experience. Retrieved April 7, 2009, from ProQuest Digital Dissertations. (AAT 9607297)

Rosenblatt, P. C. (2008). Grief across cultures: A review and research agenda. In M. S. Stroebe, R. O. Hansson, H. Schut, & W. Stroebe (Eds.) *Handbook of bereavement research and practice: Advances in theory and intervention* (pp. 207–222). Washington, DC: American Psychological Association.

Ross, A. O. (1980). *Psychological disorders of children: A behavioral approach to theory, research, and therapy* (2nd ed.). New York: McGraw-Hill.

Rowland, J. H., Pfefferbaum, B., Adams-Greenly, M., & Redd, W. H. (1989). Childhood cancer: Psychological issues and their management. In J. C. Holland & J. H. Rowland (Eds.), *Handbook of psychooncology: Psychological care of the patient with cancer* (pp. 517–581). New York: Oxford University Press.

Rushton, C. H. (2005). A framework for integrated pediatric palliative care: Being with dying. *Journal of Pediatric Nursing, 20,* 311–325.

Samide, L. L., & Stockton, R. (2002). Letting go of grief: Bereavement groups for children in the school setting. *Journal for Specialists in Group Work, 27,* 192–204.

Schmidt, J. J. (2003). *Counseling in schools: Essential services and comprehensive programs* (4th ed.). Boston: Allyn & Bacon.

Siegel, K., & Gorey, E. (1994). Childhood bereavement due to parental death from acquired immunodeficiency syndrome. *Journal of Developmental & Behavioral Pediatrics, 15,* S66–S70.

Sori, C. F., & Hecker, L. L. (2006). Ethical and legal considerations when counseling children and families. In C. F. Sori (Ed.), *Engaging children in family therapy: Creative approaches to integrating theory and research in clinical practice* (pp. 159–174). New York: Routledge/Taylor & Francis.

Steen, L., Helm, H. M., & Johnson, L. S. (2007). "But he needs me": Responding to a child's catastrophic illness. In S. M. Dugger & L. Carlson (Eds.), *Critical incidents in counseling children* (pp. 278–291). Alexandria, VA: American Counseling Association.

Sue, D. W., Arredondo, P., & McDavis, R. J. (1992). Multicultural counseling competencies and standards: A call to the profession. *Journal of Counseling and Development, 70,* 477–486.

Thastum, M., Johansen, M. B., Gubba, L., Olesen, L. B., & Romer, G. (2008). Coping, social relations, and communication: A qualitative exploratory study of children of parents with cancer. *Clinical Child Psychology and Psychiatry, 13,* 123–138.

Towbin, K. E. (1995). Evaluation, establishing the treatment alliance, and informed consent. *Pediatric Psychopharmacology I, 4,* 1–14.

Trozzi, M. (1999). *Talking with children about loss: Words, strategies, and wisdom to help children cope with death, divorce, and other difficult times.* New York: Berkley Publishing.

Walker, J. (2003). HIV and sexuality. In L. D. Burlew & D. Capuzzi (Eds.), *Sexuality counseling* (pp. 209–230). Hauppauge, NY: Nova Science.

Wall, J., Needham, T., Browning, D. S., & James, S. (1999). The ethics of relationality: The moral views of therapists engaged in marital and family therapy. *Family Relations, 48,* 139–149.

Webb, N. B. (Ed.). (2002). *Helping bereaved children* (2nd ed.). New York: Guilford.

Weithorn, L. A., & McCabe, M. A. (1988). Emerging ethical and legal issues in pediatric psychology. In D. K. Routh (Ed.), *Handbook of pediatric psychology* (pp. 567–606). New York: Guilford.

Wiener, L., Battles, H. B., & Heilman, N. E. (1998). Factors associated with parents' decision to disclose their HIV diagnosis to their children. *Child Welfare, 77,* 115–135.

Wolgrin, C. (2007). Professional issues and thanatology. In D. Balk, C. Wogrin, G. Thornton, & D. Meagher (Eds.), *Handbook of thanatology: The essential body of knowledge for the study of death, dying, and bereavement* (pp. 371–386). Northbrook, IL: ADEC & New York: Routledge.

Worden, J. W. (1996). *Children and grief: When a parent dies.* New York: Guilford.

Zingaro, J. C. (1983). Confidentiality: To tell or not to tell. *Elementary School Guidance and Counseling, 17,* 261–267.

4

Ethics, Research, and Dying or Bereaved Children

ANDREA C. WALKER

Vulnerable populations include those that are exposed to the possible threat of wrongdoing in specific ways. This exposure arises because members of the population may be unable to defend themselves in certain settings, especially when they face an imbalance of power. The definition of vulnerability holds special significance for dying and bereaved children, in that not only is their cognitive development immature because of their young age, but also they are forced to confront death and mortality, an issue in relation to which even adults may be vulnerable. Literature has suggested that infants and young children through adolescence whose parents die are more likely than older individuals to experience the loss as traumatic (Freudenberger & Gallagher, 1995). Additionally, many children are facing the death of a parent to a terminal illness such as HIV/AIDS, the stigma of which can compound the degree of vulnerability children experience. The increase in recent decades of research being conducted with pediatric AIDS victims themselves (Ackerman, 1990) further exacerbates the risk of exploitation of this group. As a result, the issue of conducting ethical research with dying and bereaved children demands our attention.

CHILDREN IN RESEARCH

General Issues

A major source of this population's vulnerability involves the separation of dying and bereaved children from those conducting research. Because researchers are adults, they are never able to enter the world of children except in terms of their own memories, which are likely to distort their current perceptions of child participants' experiences. The power differential between child and researcher is evident in differences of physical stature and strength, as well as in social rights (Morrow & Richards, 1996). For this reason, as well as the current social images of children as either competent or vulnerable, children may be considered to be "always othered" (Lahman, 2008, p. 281). Lahman suggested that children are actually both vulnerable and competent in that they are smaller people and less capable of meeting their own physical and emotional needs, but also resilient and adaptive. The risks described here highlight the need to protect children in research by empowering them, including them in the process, and developing more flexible designs.

Recent literature has underscored the importance of *empowering children* and *inviting their participation in research* to avoid the potential negative outcomes of overprotection (Ireland & Holloway, 1996). In many cases children are able to act as their own agents, and they should be encouraged to do so, especially in the decision of whether to participate in the project. Full understanding of a study's purposes will be mediated by the child's developmental position, and researchers should carefully consider this constraint because it varies with the individual child. Younger children are the least able to demonstrate voluntariness based on full understanding of a study, but children approximately ages 7–12, developing concrete operations according to Piaget (1930), may be able to understand a study as it relates to their own experiences. Adolescents usually are able to act with complete autonomy. The child's assent, a requirement in addition to parental consent, should be viewed in terms of proactive agreement based on understanding, rather than a passive lack of refusal to participate (Ireland & Holloway).

To further empower children in the research process, some researchers recommend that children be given a more ongoing proactive role (Hill, Laybourn, & Borland, 1996). Strengthening the children's presence involves incorporating their input into the data collection process by identifying those methods that will result in the most useful information.

In addition, children should have a role in analysis and interpretation to verify that the data obtained are valid and accurately represent their experiences.

Including children in the research process leads to a third general issue in the research of children: *a need for flexibility in the process* to adapt to changing needs of participants. Researchers should act in concert with children's wishes, utilizing methods that are most congruent with the children's communication habits, which may vary according to development and family environment. This issue of flexibility means that members of the sample of any given study may utilize multiple data collection techniques, measurements, and settings in which collection takes place. The very nature of the dynamic environment of the dying or bereaved child promotes the necessity of incorporating a design that is usually at least partially qualitative. Other types of methods, such as conducting a sensitive interview using a survey-type instrument, leading to quantitative analysis may also provide the needed flexibility.

Children's Concepts of Death

A brief exploration of children's cognitive development in terms of the death concept provides important context to the discussion of ethics and the resulting design issues in the research with this population. Slaughter and Griffiths (2007) identified five major components of the death concept, command of which typically occurs with children in the following specified order: (1) inevitability: everything dies at some point; (2) universality: nothing is exempt from death; (3) irreversibility or finality: the dead will never be alive again; (4) cessation or nonfunctionality: the body ceases to work; and (5) causality: something in the body prevents it from functioning properly (see also chapter 2 in this book). Children approach understanding of these concepts at different rates but typically do so between the ages of 5 and 10 years.

As expected, the ability of a child to understand an abstract concept such as death or illness parallels the child's general cognitive development. Young children, ages 5–7, have been found to associate non-physiological reasons, such as punishment or being near a sick person, with development of an illness, and as age increases, so does the ability to distinguish between cancer and colds (Bares & Gelman, 2008). By age 9, children often conceptualize illness as a set of symptoms and are progressing toward understanding the finality of death (Murphy, 2008). Even very young children, however, were shown to observe the internal disposition of illnesses, confirming prior suggestions that in some cases abstraction can occur before concrete thought (Bares & Gelman; Simons & Keil, 1995).

Most of the time, however, very young children do not think abstractly. Those ages 2–4 years generally think about death in concrete, egocentric, present terms (Oltjenbruns, 2007) without understanding any of Slaughter and Griffiths's death concept components. After mastering Piaget's object concept—awareness of the continual existence of a person or object after it leaves the child's sensory field, which typically occurs around 2 years—a child can be confused when an individual he or she remembers does, in fact, permanently disappear. Children ages 4–6 years begin to understand the nonfunctionality of the dead person and the irreversibility and universality of death, though still thinking primarily with concrete operations. By 7–11 years of age, children typically grasp that death is final and unavoidable and has a cause. The bereaved child at this age has an improved ability to comprehend life without the person who died (Oltjenbruns). When faced with their own death, children at this age are likely to want to explore thoughts of their lives after death.

ETHICAL ISSUES IN RESEARCH

General issues of empowerment, involving children as collaborators, and design flexibility should be discussed specifically through the lens of ethical standards in child research. *Nonmaleficence,* or the avoidance of harm, requires deeper understanding of the emotional implications of discussing experiences with death and dying for both the participant and the researcher. *Beneficence,* or the doing of good, involves developing a primary research goal that will specifically benefit the participant (Normand, Meyer, & Bentley, 2003); if interviews, observations, surveys, or other methods benefit a bereaved or dying child, even in terms of helping others like him or her, those studies are worthy of conducting. Empowering children to exercise their competency through proactive choice regarding such issues, with guidance and support from significant adults, may help diminish the risk of harm to this population.

The principle of *autonomy* involves deliberate intention of the participant to be involved in the research, incorporating the use of voluntary consent (Normand et al., 2003). Informed consent of parents or legal guardians is usually required, coupled with the child's assent. Balen and colleagues (2006) described children as "human becomings" and "active agents" (p. 29) capable of consenting to their own participation in research, as opposed to merely depending on an adult for such determination. In some cases, requiring parental consent challenges the validity of research findings and disempowers developing children who are capable and competent. Obtaining consent from both child and parent is an ongoing process, particularly in the fluid environment of a dying or bereaved child, and should continually be discussed and confirmed. The balance between protection and subversion of vulnerable children must be delicately sought.

The final principle of *justice* involves "right" treatment of participants according to moral codes of confidentiality, privacy, and anonymity if relevant. Dying or bereaved children, who are already dealing with a sense of "unfairness" in their circumstances, need assurance that they have power in the relationship with the researcher and are free to share only what they wish and with whom they wish and to stop if desired. Other child researchers have also emphasized the importance of involving children in making decisions regarding research, challenging the popular view of children as incompetent, vulnerable, and powerless (Hill et al., 1996; Ireland & Holloway, 1996; Morrow & Richards, 1996).

Research in death and dying with a developing child can involve multiple dimensions as death approaches or as a child progresses through the aftermath of a loss. Increasing participant involvement in the research process adds further complexity. Research needs to be able to respond sensitively to the participant and adapt to the fluidity of the process, highlighting the need to operate within ethical guidelines rather than under strict, unmalleable criteria (Normand et al., 2003). Flexibility from the Institutional Review Board (IRB) enables the researcher to incorporate ethical standards in a more comprehensive manner.

Dying Children

Research in dying children has been under the scrutiny of ethical review boards for numerous reasons. Researchers may demonstrate a lack of comprehensive understanding of relevant ethical principles, a tendency to consider children incapable of deciding their own preferences regarding research, or a propensity to assume children operate just as adults do (Levetown, 1996). Children's wishes and desires are sometimes ignored or disregarded in exchange for parental involvement in research-related decisions. Adults' centralized understanding of children's experiences has sometimes resulted in inappropriate or inaccurate protection of children in research. Principles of beneficence and nonmaleficence have been casually disregarded as a result of failure to recognize children's competence.

Consequently, research on life-limiting diseases, such as HIV/AIDS, with children has frequently been conducted without the child's assent to participate (Levetown, 1996). Child assent involves deliberate choice to comply with the research process, rather than merely a passive lack of resistance. Parental informed consent and child assent indicate that the participant has received the following information:

> explanation of the purposes of the study, expected duration of participation, procedures to be followed, foreseeable risks and benefits to the participant or to others, alternative procedures or courses of treatment, extent to which confidentiality will be maintained, participant's rights, and a contact person for questions about the study. (Carnevale, MacDonald, Bluebond-Langner, & McKeever, 2008, p. 25)

Informed consent also includes clearly understanding that participation is voluntary and that the participant may withdraw at any time without suffering any penalties, for instance, being refused access to treatment because of discontinuing participation in the research study.

Informed consent of the parent should be sought only in combination with the child's assent; it should never replace a child's refusal. Some children are not able to fully understand the gravity of health-related matters but should be given as much autonomy as possible in this decision, according to level of competence rather than simple chronological age. Notions of informed consent/assent should continually be assessed, and if a child does not want to engage in the tasks required of participants, his or her request should be respected. One adolescent in particular was found to regress from the role of an independent, autonomous decision maker early in her illness to relying increasingly on her mother to make difficult decisions as the illness progressed (Penson et al., 2002). Such changes require that the researcher be allowed to react quickly to continue to maintain ethical standards.

Some unfortunate situations have demonstrated that even with full communication about the study, as required for informed consent, outcomes are not always optimal. Mothers of children participating in randomized treatment options for acute lymphoblastic leukemia were found to have confused understanding of treatment effects as well as of randomization, even though they were given both oral and written explanations (Eiser, Davies, Jenney, & Glaser, 2005). When solicited for research involving a new drug, children may misunderstand and believe that the drug will certainly help them get better, but that may not be the case. In a study where children were, in fact, fully informed of all of the potential side effects of a new drug as well as other treatment options for their life-threatening illnesses, voluntary participation in the study dropped dramatically (Nitschke et al., 1982). This finding highlights the importance of voluntary consent in ensuring the ethical standard of autonomy of the dying child and his or her parents.

Furthermore, consent may be required of both parents, rather than only one, depending on the degree of risk involved in the research as well as the benefit to the participant and/or greater community. Parental consent may be waived altogether if in such cases harm could be brought to the children and benefit minimized. Other situations, such as with cultural groups who view requiring a signature as a lack of trust, may command forgoing the use of written consent altogether, lest completion of the study be compromised (Carnevale et al., 2008). Such decisions are typically made by the IRB beforehand, but again these variations highlight the fluid nature of research with dying children.

The potential ramifications of misunderstanding treatment options and outcomes point to how important it is that research benefit the dying child and that those benefits outweigh the risks. The principle of justice embedded in this ethical standard demands that very ill children not be involved in multiple demanding or tiring treatments unless it is expressly in the children's best interest to do so, and this prospect should be evaluated holistically. Medical research should not be conducted with children if adult participants could provide the same information (Carnevale et al., 2008), particularly when data involving complex, not-fully-understood diseases such as HIV/AIDS are sought (Ackerman, 1990). Finally, a multidimensional approach should be taken to evaluate the risks of a dying child's participation in social or medical research. Although illnesses such as cancer hold no prejudices, those such as HIV/AIDS are unfairly represented among minorities, families with low socioeconomic status (SES), and families dealing with the illness or death of a parent. Such stressors should be taken into account when evaluating the risk/benefit ratio; perhaps child participants with numerous social stressors (McCubbin & Patterson, 1983) should not be considered for research, unless doing so provides needed help and resources.

Bereaved Children

Bereaved individuals embody a qualitatively unique experience, and researchers have an ethical responsibility to proceed delicately at the pace established by the beckoning of the participant (Stroebe, Stroebe, & Schut, 2003). Adults experiencing grief may be considered vulnerable because judgment and reason may be compromised through emotionality; so children with less experience, social skill, and cognitive capacity to understand the loss of their loved one are more likely to be a vulnerable population. (IRB procedures already group children and minors as a vulnerable population; bereavement can be seen to increase their vulnerability). Bereaved children may grapple to comprehend their own mortality through the death concept, just as the dying child does, but perhaps with less emphasis on the factor of time.

Promoting nonmaleficence and beneficence in research with bereaved children requires that the process of gathering data, whether through survey, interview, observation, or other methods, be not harmful and benefit the child. Benefits oftentimes transcend the experience of the bereaved child to others like him or her, but studies have indicated that discussing one's loss and sharing one's experience is also beneficial to the currently bereaved child, provided that the child is comfortable doing so (Bohanek, Marin, & Fivush, 2008; Mitchell et al., 2006). Children may, in fact, need help in understanding death, saying goodbye, and handling their emotions (Oltjenbruns, 2007). Discussing their loss with the researcher can help them to understand the finality of death and move on with their lives after their loved one has died. The most beneficial interviews are conducted by an empathic listener demonstrating support and positive regard for the bereaved child and with researchers who are prepared to respond to a distressed participant (Stroebe et al., 2003). In all studies, especially those not involving interviews, professional therapeutic and counseling sources should be provided to the participants for further help in handling their losses.

Because of the sensitivity of the issue of bereavement, researchers should evaluate cautiously the most appropriate time to request children's participation. Timing is an important factor in whether discussing a loss proves therapeutic. If too little time has passed since the loss, participating can be distressing. Stroebe and her coauthors (2003) have recommended conducting a pilot study with individuals who have been bereaved for longer periods, perhaps a minimum of 2 years, and asking those participants how soon after their loss they would have welcomed solicitation from a researcher. When using this method with children, special attention should be paid to the range of ages of children in the pilot study as compared to those composing the actual study, given that "readiness" at a particular time frame since the loss may vary with development. Bereaved children, like their parents, need full information and encouragement to make autonomous decisions to participate in any study; if it is too soon for a child, he or she should feel comfortable and supported in refusing.

The benefits of the research must outweigh the risks for the bereaved, as with the dying child, and the selection of the sample must reflect thoughtful attention to this requirement. Children from higher-risk families and lower SES and those experiencing multiple deaths may be embedded in a pileup of losses that outweighs the child's resources (McCubbin & Patterson, 1983). Only if the proposed research provides additional support and assistance should children with these experiences be approached. Those from lower-risk situations embody more ideal candidates for studies that could potentially be emotionally distressing.

Families of Dying and Bereaved Children

Demi and Warren (1995) defined vulnerable families as being "susceptible to harm because of their socioeconomic, minority, or other stigmatizing status, such as having a family member with HIV infection or a family member who uses illicit drugs" (p. 188). Regardless of whether a family as a whole is vulnerable, if one of its members is a dying or bereaved child, the family becomes acquainted with closely associated issues. In either case, the family members are likely to be bereaved themselves and reassessing their own concepts of mortality while assisting the child to do the same. Researchers need to consider the whole family during analysis of adherence to ethical principles. These simultaneous processes have complex implications for researchers of dying and bereaved children.

Families of dying or bereaved children are facing trauma that accompanies the pain of being unable to rescue the child or fix his or her physical or mental health. Although the needs and desires of the dying or bereaved child take precedence, the family should be considered throughout the entire research process. Because of the nature of the family's interdependence, nonmaleficence and beneficence are likely to be relevant for the whole family if also for the child. In certain cases such as abuse and neglect, however, what is beneficial for a child may, in fact, not be beneficial for others in the family, in which case the child's needs take precedence.

In most cases, at least one family member, a parent, must be involved in giving informed consent for his or her child's participation. The difficult emotions of the parent(s) of dying or bereaved children must be addressed sensitively and empathically when approaching the family about the research study. Confidentiality should be discussed and monitored appropriately. Information provided by the child should not be reported to his or her parents without explicit permission from the child; exception to this rule is made if the child presents a danger to self or others, or in situations of abuse and/or neglect (Demi & Warren, 1995). Maintaining confidentiality can be a delicate walk in ensuring autonomy and justice for the child while including the family in the process. Finally, justice is ensured by choosing appropriate families for research who have not disproportionately endured stressors and with whom the benefits of the research outweigh the risks.

DESIGN ISSUES IN RESEARCH

Though death is a normal part of everyone's life, empirical studies can help to increase understanding of who is at the highest risk for maladjustment and how to assist those individuals. Research on dying children primarily focuses on health issues; bereavement research focuses on processes of coping and adapting to losses. Adult researchers attempting to understand the worlds of children often are subject to influence from society's stereotypes and their own subjective experiences as children. Consequently, children are easily misunderstood and incorrectly reported and interpreted in research. To maximize validity of data collected, researchers should embody roles of "varieties of adult" (Lahman, 2008, p. 290) so that they can present themselves to children in a variety of ways as the environments of dying or bereaved children inevitably change. For instance, adults in such environments may be seen as visitors, helpers, authority figures, family support, or even as friends. More recent views of child research indicate that ethical principles are highlighted and accuracy of findings maximized by viewing the child participant as a collaborator in the research process (Lahman). It has been imperative that methods focus on ethical standards because of the heightened vulnerability of this group while incorporating general issues of empowerment, involvement of children in methods, and flexibility of the design.

Dying Children

Few studies have focused on dying children, and those that have usually have not involved direct reports from the children (Hinds, Brandon, et al., 2007). Recent literature has highlighted the importance of employing more qualitative methods in the research of dying children (Aoun & Kristjanson, 2005; Carnevale et al., 2008; Hinds, Burghen, & Pritchard, 2007; Lahman, 2008), although some recommend quantitative or mixed methods (Boyle, Miller, & Forbes-Thompson, 2005). Research involving dying children is often for medical, as opposed to psychological or sociological, reasons and is thus typically conducted in a health care setting. The passage of the Health Insurance Portability and Accountability Act (HIPAA) in 1996, intended to help increase patients' trust in hospitals and other health care settings, demands that practitioners focus on maintaining appropriate standards of confidentiality in dealing with client records and communicating with family members and other practitioners (Benefield, Ashkanazi, & Rozenski, 2006). Because of the potential to breach important ethical standards such as confidentiality in busy hospital units, studies involving in-depth, qualitative analysis of a child's situation have often been avoided.

Carnevale and colleagues (2008) have recommended using participant observation, but with careful, intentional focus on upholding ethical standards. Consistently, Lahman (2008) also suggested the importance of natural observation to prevent polarization of the power differential between researcher and child participant. Alternative methods of data collection, such as focus groups led by the participant, art, play, and Web-based activities, might also be utilized to enhance richness of the findings. Observation of these activities is less intrusive to the child, incorporates more trust-building with the researcher, and presents possibilities of understanding the child's interactions with family members (Carnevale et al.). Such methods incorporate various data sources, relieving stress on the dying child.

Though there have been opposing opinions on the types of methods that yield the best data, Hinds, Burghen, and Pritchard (2007) recommended flexibility to change as needed amid data collection to better meet the needs of the dying children. For instance, if participants prefer to engage in an interview over the telephone rather than in person, the researcher should adapt the study to make that change. In such cases, the researcher may be able to compare findings between in-person and telephone interviews for differences. This type of flexibility requires more trust in the researcher from the ethical review board (Normand et al., 2003) but empowers the researcher to integrate the ethical standards more comprehensively within the design of the study.

Bereaved Children

Stroebe and her colleagues (2003) discussed the importance of survey versus in-depth interview data collection, as well as quantitative versus qualitative instruments for measuring bereaved individuals. Surveys provide objective data from participants who are not as likely to answer questions in ways that they believe the researcher expects. However, often only cross-sectional information is provided, preventing deeper analysis, and the format of the closed-ended, self-report questionnaires prevents follow-up questions for clarification. In-depth interviews present possibilities for longitudinal research but are time-consuming and expensive. A mixed-methods approach, involving initial interview with subsequent individual questionnaires, may be the most effective approach.

Quantitative measurements can be used to assess children's grief experiences and allow for statistical analyses to describe and compare populations. Qualitative measures explore the experience on a deeper level without confinement to specific categorical responses. Stroebe and her colleagues (2003) recommended methodological pluralism, beginning with deeper, qualitative assessment and moving into utilization of established reliable and valid grief scales. Also, incorporation of both quantitative and qualitative data collection processes constructs an option within the research design for flexibility should the bereaved child indicate a preference for an alternate method.

Implementation of recommended methods requires incorporation of the ethical standards already discussed, which can add complexity to the study. For instance, optimizing participant autonomy involves making the decision whether to participate throughout the process. Using multiple methods and data collection periods increases chances that bereaved children may decide they do not wish to participate, complicating the analysis with missing data. The suggestion for more flexibility by adopting different methods of collecting data to accommodate participants' needs can also complicate the analysis and interpretation. These complexities point to the need for more open designs, again highlighting the importance of qualitative research that can be developed and conducted to adapt quickly to a changing environment. This openness is required to derive the most accurate data regarding bereaved children while holding ethics to the highest standards.

Families of Dying and Bereaved Children

The nature of a child's vulnerability and the consent required from the parent or legal guardian of a dying or bereaved child to participate in a study dictates that research ultimately involve not only the child but also parents and family. It is necessary for researchers to approach a study with an inclusive attitude, making deliberate efforts to build trust with participant and family. This concern requires that particular attention be made to sampling, measurement, data collection, and analysis/interpretation issues.

Researchers may clarify any ambiguity regarding who family members are by defining "family" in consideration of culture. Definitions may vary with participants, so the child and parent(s) should help the researcher in this process. Participants may be sought through hospitals, counseling centers, schools, and so forth, though each avenue presents potential limits to the generalizability of the sample. Deriving random samples of dying or bereaved children is difficult at best and, as discussed, may not yield the most helpful information anyway. As participants and families are approached, they must be informed of the nature of the study to give full consent; deception in a study of this type, as with families of dying children, should be minimized because of the potential vulnerability of the population.

All data collection methods, particularly interviews, should include everyone defined to be part of the family, and the process should thus be multidimensional and flexible. Quantitative instruments measuring family members' experiences should be valid and reliable (Demi & Warren, 1995) and are recommended to be used along with qualitative methods. In one study, parents of 37 families who had lost a child through suicide were measured in terms of their experience of the research process (Dyregrov, 2004). Most reported that discussing the loss was a painful albeit positive experience because of the opportunity to explain the entire event, utilizing the interview data collection method, and the possibility of assisting other families in similar situations. Cook and Bosley (1995) conducted a follow-up survey to a study interviewing participants on their experiences with loss, and of the 32 participants taking the survey, the majority indicated that the experience of the research was very positive. About a third indicated that the research had had a powerful effect on them, a result that was particularly strong for men. Participants described the most helpful qualities of the researcher using terms such as "empathy, warmth, caring, kind, gentle, human, understanding, sincere, non-judgmental, and interested" (p. 166). These studies underscore the benefits that the research process itself, particularly interviews, can have for participants. Qualitative interview questions should thus be sensitively conveyed and carefully constructed so that they can be altered as needed to remove evidence of expectation based on researchers' perceived notions, biases, and personal perspectives.

Though it may also be impossible to completely remove a researcher's personal perspective from analysis and interpretation of results, self-reflection is an important tool in identifying what influence that personal perspective may have on the study. Having an outside researcher review the results and the process for consistency and unseen confounding factors may help identify potential problems. In the case of qualitative data, member checking—or having a member of the family review the results for correctness—also improves the accuracy of the study. The sensitivity of the data, however, demands consideration, in that participants and/or family members may not want their thoughts, opinions, and experiences shared with others in the family. In such cases, member checking should be utilized with caution, and confidentiality should be upheld at every step in the process to ensure autonomy of participants and families. Conclusions drawn should be accurate and represent an effort to benefit and not harm participants in the study. Giving family members the opportunity to review, explain, or interpret data correctly will minimize inaccuracy and misunderstandings, as well as provide further protection to this vulnerable population.

CONCLUSIONS AND RECOMMENDATIONS FOR RESEARCH

Ethical conduct of research with dying or bereaved children commands attention to child empowerment, involvement in research, and flexibility of the design. To pervasively integrate the ethical standards of beneficence, nonmaleficence, autonomy, and justice in the research with dying and bereaved children and their families, I will provide recommendations regarding (a) the roles of child and researcher in empowering participants, (b) the interaction between child and researcher to increase participant involvement, and (c) resulting methodological issues. Embedded within each component is deliberate, thoughtful incorporation of each of the ethical principles. These topics are summarized in Table 4.1.

Table 4.1

GENERAL ISSUES, ETHICAL PRINCIPLES, AND DESIGN RECOMMENDATIONS FOR RESEARCHING DYING OR BEREAVED CHILDREN

GENERAL ISSUES	ETHICAL PRINCIPLES	DESIGN RECOMMENDATIONS
Empowerment/ protection	Beneficence	Design research to benefit child and family directly or indirectly (e.g., providing or developing end-of-life treatment methods).
	Nonmaleficence	Pay careful attention to ensure that the design does not directly or indirectly bring harm to child or family (e.g., soliciting discussion about grief too soon after the loss).
		Minimize deception, use of which could easily make risks outweigh benefits with this vulnerable population.
		Fully understand and adhere to the boundaries of confidentiality of family and among family members.
Child involvement	Autonomy	Allow child to choose his or her own participation status.
		Invite child to collaborate and provide input into data collection, analysis, and interpretation.
Innovative methods	Justice	Use alternate techniques appropriate for child's developmental level as needed (e.g., art, play, Internet, etc.).
		Incorporate qualitative data collection, such as participant observation and interviews, and analysis wherever appropriate to increase flexibility.
		Maintain researcher reflexivity to minimize bias and inaccurate conclusions.
		Conduct ongoing, open communication with IRB to foster collaborative relationship and build trust needed to ensure flexibility in the design.

The researcher is seen differently by members of the family being researched. The dying or bereaved child, in particular, is in a very different position than parents or the adult researcher. Consistent with societal authority structures, adults are always in socially more powerful positions than children, having more general privileges and decisions (Lahman, 2008). This power differential can charge the researcher–child relationship instantly, with the child feeling powerless, submissive, and expected to do as instructed by the adult. It is imperative that adults, in order to develop significant researcher–child relationships, engage in heedful regard for children, with conscious refusal to encroach on children's freedom to make choices and express themselves. The researcher's critical analysis of self on an ongoing basis will increase levels of personal awareness and congruency to improve interaction with the child, resulting in the child feeling more comfortable and relaxed. The researcher's role should thus be that of an empathic and caring listener and observer who holds the trust of the participant and family and promotes their needs above the research objectives. To remove the usual stigmatized position of the dying or bereaved child as incompetent, incapable of understanding his or her own experiences, and dependent on an adult for protection, the researcher should actively empower children to be agents of their own actions, maximizing their autonomy. Balen and colleagues (2006) warned that "the laudable effort to protect potentially vulnerable participants avoids overprotection, paternalism, and the further disenfranchisement of already marginalized young people" (p. 29). These researchers argue that in many cases children are capable of providing their own informed consent, and parental consent should be forgone. Lahman indicated that children should be seen as "experts" and given a collaborative role in the research process.

IRBs should thus employ the following. First, although all the family members, especially child and parent, are seen as participants, consider the child's assent as central, and parental consent as peripheral, to fulfilling the principle of autonomy. In the case of conflicting positions of parent and child, the researcher should encourage and facilitate further discussion between the two for the purpose of arriving at consensus. If consensus cannot be reached, participation should be abandoned; specifically, the law currently requires parental approval, even if a child assents, but it should never override a child's dissent. Second, the IRB should increase its trust in researchers who are professionals in child development and family dynamics to understand the level of comprehension a child has regarding the study's purposes, trust that is developed through ongoing communication between researcher and IRB extending beyond the IRB's original approval of the project. Such empowerment of participants will result in greater openness of the dying or bereaved child and more comprehensive understanding of his or her world.

Sufficient time is needed to develop a relationship of trust and acceptance between child and researcher. Children's thoughts and experiences are not typically sought by strangers, so children need to adjust to this new type of interaction (Morrow & Richards, 1996). Researcher self-reflexivity and empowerment of the child leads to an enhanced, richer interaction between researcher and child. The relationship will be characterized by greater trust, more authentic exchange, and significant mutual understanding. Lahman (2008) named this interaction "intersubjectivity" (p. 292) and suggested that the improved communication will deepen the meaning created from the relationship and improve overall accuracy of the findings. Lahman's ideas emerged from inferences grounded in developmental theory and signal important areas for empirical researchers to test hypotheses about critical decision making with children. This more interactive relationship between child and researcher leads to increasing influence from the child on the research process. The child may be involved in choosing data collection methods, interpreting results, and verifying conclusions. Approaching the dying or bereaved child according to more traditional perspectives of the researcher as separate and objective may not result in the most effective way to measure the topic or yield accurate results.

Finally, methods should reflect the unique challenges of researching this potentially vulnerable population. When dealing with dynamic environments, such as those experienced by a dying or bereaved child, more flexibility is needed in the research process to accommodate the changing needs of the child and his or her family. This flexibility requires that researchers have more general adaptability and more trust and communication with the IRB (Normand et al., 2003). Initial research questions requiring "positivist, adult-framed answers" (Morrow & Richards, 1996, p. 101) should be replaced by more open-ended, informed questions. Informed consent should be sought to the degree of comprehension possible from both child and parent. Multiple methods should be utilized to provide opportunity for all children to express themselves comfortably, reducing the likelihood of further marginalization of children. Researchers should be familiar and comfortable with utilizing creative methods for collecting data, such as art, play, and other expressive modes. Designs utilizing qualitative (Lahman, 2008; Normand et al.)

or mixed methods (Stroebe et al., 2003) are recommended in studies with dying or bereaved children. In addition, children are not usually able to impugn results presented in literature, so researchers should interpret their findings cautiously. Conclusions should thus be reviewed and verified by child participants before publishing.

Dying or bereaved children make up a potentially vulnerable population that calls for full employment of the ethical principles of social and health research. Despite the risks and challenges, we as researchers are under an ethical obligation to empower these participants to act as autonomously as possible. In many cases, children may have the capacity to make more decisions than they are typically allowed, and we must take intentional steps to prevent their marginalization. Flexible and alternate methods will accommodate the needs of dying or bereaved children and keep the objective of maximizing fulfillment of ethical principles central to our research goals.

REFERENCES

Ackerman, T. F. (1990). Protectionism and the new research imperative in pediatric AIDS. *IRB: A Review of Human Subjects Research, 12,* 1–5.

Aoun, S. M., & Kristjanson, L. J. (2005). Evidence in palliative care research: How should it be gathered? *Medical Journal of Australia, 183,* 264–266.

Balen, R., Blyth, E., Calabretto, H., Fraser, C., Horrocks, C., & Manby, M. (2006). Involving children in health and social research. *Childhood, 13,* 29–48.

Bares, C. B., & Gelman, S. A. (2008). Knowledge of illness during childhood: Making distinctions between cancer and colds. *International Journal of Behavioral Development, 32,* 443–450.

Benefield, H., Ashkanazi, G., & Rozenski, R. H. (2006). Communication and records: HIPAA issues when working in health care settings. *Professional Psychology: Research and Practice, 37,* 273–277.

Bohanek, J. G., Marin, K. A., & Fivush, R. (2008). Family narratives, self, and gender in early adolescence. *Journal of Early Adolescence, 28,* 153–176.

Boyle, D. K., Miller, P. A., & Forbes-Thompson, S. A. (2005). Communication and end-of-life care in the intensive care unit: Patient, family, and clinician outcomes. *Critical Care Nursing Quarterly, 28,* 302–316.

Carnevale, F. A., MacDonald, M. E., Bluebond-Langner, M., & McKeever, P. (2008). Using participant observation in pediatric health care settings: Ethical challenges and solutions. *Journal of Child Health Care, 12,* 18–32.

Cook, A. S., & Bosley, G. (1995). The experience of participating in bereavement research: Stressful or therapeutic? *Death Studies, 19,* 157–170.

Demi, A. S., & Warren, N. A. (1995). Issues in conducting research with vulnerable families. *Western Journal of Nursing Research, 17,* 188–202.

Dyregrov, K. (2004). Bereaved parents' experience of research participation. *Social Science & Medicine, 58,* 391–400.

Eiser, C., Davies, H., Jenney, M., & Glaser, A. (2005). Mothers' attitudes to the randomized controlled trial (RCT): The case of acute lymphoblastic leukaemia (ALL) in children. *Child: Care, Health & Development, 31,* 517–523.

Freudenberger, H. J., & Gallagher, K. M. (1995). Emotional consequences of loss for our adolescents. *Psychotherapy: Theory, Research, Practice, Training, 32,* 150–153.

Hill, M., Laybourn, A., & Borland, M. (1996). Engaging with primary-aged children about their emotions and well-being: Methodological considerations. *Children & Society, 10,* 129–144.

Hinds, P. S., Brandon, J., Allen, C., Hijiya, N., Newsome, R., & Kane, J. (2007). Patient-reported outcomes in end-of-life research in pediatric oncology. *Journal of Pediatric Psychology, 32,* 1079–1088.

Hinds, P. S., Burghen, E. A., & Pritchard, M. (2007). Conducting end-of-life studies in pediatric oncology. *Western Journal of Nursing Research, 29,* 448–465.

Ireland, L., & Holloway, I. (1996). Qualitative health research with children. *Children & Society, 10,* 155–164.

Lahman, M. K. E. (2008). Always othered: Ethical research with children. *Journal of Early Childhood Research, 6,* 281–300.

Levetown, M. (1996). Ethical aspects of pediatric palliative care. *Journal of Palliative Care, 12,* 35–39.

McCubbin, H. I., & Patterson, J. M. (1983). The family stress process: The Double ABC-X Model of adjustment and adaptation. *Marriage and Family Review, 6,* 7–37.

Mitchell, A. M., Wesner, S., Brownson, L., Dysart-Gale, D., Barand, L., & Havill, A. (2006). Effective communication with bereaved child survivors of suicide. *Journal of Child and Adolescent Psychiatric Nursing, 19,* 130–136.

Morrow, V., & Richards, M. (1996). The ethics of social research with children: An overview. *Children & Society, 10,* 90–105.

Murphy, D. A. (2008). HIV-positive mothers' disclosure of their serostatus to their young children: A review. *Clinical Child Psychology and Psychiatry, 13,* 105–122.

Nitschke, R., Humphrey, G. B., Sexauer, C. L., Catron, B., Wunder, S., & Jay, S. (1982). Therapeutic choices made by patients with end-stage cancer. *Journal of Pediatrics, 101,* 471–476.

Normand, C., Meyer, J., & Bentley, J. (2003). Research ethics and complex studies. *NT Research, 8,* 17–26.

Oltjenbruns, K. A. (2007). Lifespan issues and loss, grief, and mourning, part 1: The importance of a developmental context: Childhood and adolescence as an example. In D. Balk, C. Wogrin, G. Thornton, & D. Meagher (Eds.). *Handbook of thanatology: The essential body of knowledge for the study of death, dying, and bereavement* (pp. 143–150). Northbrook, IL: Association for Death Education and Counseling.

Penson, R. T., Rauch, P. K., McAfee, S. L., Cashavelly, B. J., Clair-Hayes, K., Dahlin, C., et al. (2002). Between parent and child: Negotiating cancer treatment in adolescents. *The Oncologist, 7,* 154–162.

Piaget, J. (1930). *The child's conception of physical causality.* London: Kegan Paul.

Simons, D. J., & Keil, F. C. (1995). An abstract to concrete shift in the development of biological thought: The inside story. *Cognition, 56,* 129–163.

Slaughter, V., & Griffiths, M. (2007). Death understanding and fear of death in young children. *Clinical Child Psychology and Psychiatry, 12,* 525–535.

Stroebe, M., Stroebe, W., & Schut, H. (2003). Bereavement research: Methodological issues and ethical concerns. *Palliative Medicine, 17,* 235–240.

Death

In part 2, four chapters explore the leading causes of death and loss during childhood. Because deaths during the first year of life represent more than half of all child deaths in the United States and other developed countries, and an even larger percentage in many other parts of the world, a separate chapter is devoted to the special problems of infant death (chapter 5). Thereafter, three additional chapters investigate the principal causes of deaths during the remainder of childhood: accidents or unintentional injuries and homicide (chapter 6), infectious diseases (chapter 7), and life-threatening or life-limiting illnesses (chapter 8).

The effects of these leading causes and the child deaths that result from them are seen both in the United States and around the world. Some are more lethal in particular parts of the globe; others have been all but eradicated or at least greatly reduced in their danger in some societies. Some causes of child deaths are preventable; all can be curtailed. Each of the four chapters in this part explains how these causes are influential during childhood, what can be done to minimize the numbers of deaths that result from them, and what can be done to decrease their impacts on children, their families, and their communities.

5 Infant Deaths

BETH A. SEYDA AND ANN M. FITZSIMONS

I don't think we ever really get over losing a child, but we do somehow get through it.

—Ginger, bereaved mother of an infant
(in Davis, 1996, p. 82)

The death of a child is one of the, if not the, most devastating losses that a family can suffer. Everyone is affected—parents, surviving siblings, future siblings, grandparents, extended family, friends, the community, and even the health care professionals who cared for the child. Unfortunately, more children die in the first year of life, and particularly in the first month of life, than at any other time during childhood. The death of babies and infants, whether sudden or expected, deeply impacts the very fabric of society. Although many of these deaths cannot be prevented, the care and support, or lack thereof, that grieving families receive during and after an infant's death can either facilitate or hinder their journey toward a "new normal" and healing as a family unit.

In this chapter, infant death, the death of a child less than 1 year of age, is examined from a variety of perspectives, including the types and causes of infant deaths, efforts to help prevent or mitigate such deaths, and the impact they have on a family. Practical support and interventions are also identified that can help a family's transition through grief and bereavement.

INFANT DEATH DEFINED

The National Center for Health Statistics defines an infant death as that of a child less than 1 year of age. This definition includes neonatal deaths of an infant less than 28 days old. Fetal death is the intrauterine death of a fetus at any gestational age and excludes data for induced terminations of pregnancy (MacDorman & Kirmeyer, 2009; Mathews & Mac-Dorman, 2008).

INFANT DEATHS AND DEATH RATES IN THE UNITED STATES

In 2005 there were 28,384 infant deaths in the United States. This statistic translates to an infant mortality rate of 6.86 per 1,000 live births. This 2005 infant mortality rate is statistically unchanged from 6.78 in 2004, but is significantly lower than the 7.57 rate in 1995. Two-thirds of infant deaths occur in the neonatal period (18,782 of 28,384 deaths), and more than one-half of neonatal deaths happen during the first week after birth (for these data and U.S. data in the following two sections of this chapter, see MacDorman & Kirmeyer, 2009; Mathews & MacDorman, 2008).

More infant deaths occur in the first year of life than all other children's deaths combined. For instance, in the United States in 2005, there was an overall total of 28,440 infant deaths compared to 25,061 deaths of children ages 1 to 19 years (see Table 5.1; as the note in that table indicates, the overall total of 28,440 infant deaths differs slightly from the alternative figure of 28,384 deaths under 1 year of age, which is derived from linked data based on live births). In addition, when considering pregnancy losses in this country, there were almost as many fetal deaths of 20+ weeks gestation as infant deaths (25,894 vs. 28,384). The National Survey of Family Growth estimates about 1 million total fetal losses per year in the United States, with the vast majority of these deaths occurring *before* 20 weeks gestation (Ventura, Abma, Mosher, & Henshaw, 2008).

LEADING CAUSES OF INFANT DEATH

The five leading causes of infant death on a combined basis accounted for more than 50% of all infant deaths in the United States in 2005. The lead-

Table 5.1

NUMBER AND PERCENTAGE OF TOTAL CHILDHOOD DEATHS BY AGE GROUP IN THE UNITED STATES, 2005

AGE (YEARS)	NUMBER OF DEATHS	% OF TOTAL
<1	28,440	53
1–4	4,756	9
5–9	2,837	5
10–14	3,765	7
15–19	13,703	26
	53,501	100

Note: Deaths for under 1 year differ from linked data based on live births.
Adapted from Kung et al. (2008).

ing cause was congenital malformations, deformations, and chromosomal abnormalities, which resulted in 20% of all infant deaths. This large classification includes a wide range of malformations such as Trisomy 13/18, spina bifida, hypoplastic left heart syndrome, fetal alcohol syndrome, and conjoined twins (International Classification of Diseases, 1992). The second leading cause of infant deaths was disorders related to short gestation and low birth rate (17%), which included extremely low birth weight (999 grams or less; 2.20 pounds) and extreme prematurity (less than 28 completed weeks of gestation). The third leading cause of infant death was Sudden Infant Death Syndrome (SIDS; 8%), followed by newborns affected by maternal complications of pregnancy (6%) and newborns affected by complications of placenta, cord, and membranes (4%). The order of the four leading causes in 2005 was the same as in 2004.

When considering early infant deaths globally, the World Health Organization (WHO) estimates there were 3,910,000 neonatal deaths in 2003 (Van Lerberghe, Manuel, Matthews, & Wolfheim, 2005). The WHO suggests that almost three-fourths of all global neonatal deaths could be prevented if mothers were properly nourished and received care during pregnancy, childbirth, and the postnatal period. Not surprisingly, the highly populated and less developed regions of Southeast Asia and Africa have the highest numbers of neonatal deaths (1,362,000 and 1,148,000, respectively). The more developed regions of the Americas (including the United States) and Europe have the lowest levels of neonatal deaths (195,000 and 116,000, respectively). The causes of neonatal deaths can differ dramatically by region. For example, severe infection (27%) and birth asphyxia (24%) are the top causes of neonatal deaths in the African region. These statistics are in contrast to the top two causes of neonatal deaths in the United States and Canada, which are preterm birth (45%) and congenital anomalies (29%) (see Table 5.2).

TRENDS IN INFANT MORTALITY

Race and Hispanic Origin of Mother

There continues to be a wide variation in U.S. infant mortality rates by race and Hispanic origin of mother. The highest mortality rate in 2005 was for infants of non-Hispanic Black mothers (13.63), which was more than three times the lowest rate of 4.42 for infants of Cuban mothers. Rates were also fairly high for infants of Puerto Rican (8.30) and American Indian/Alaska Native (8.06) mothers. Infant mortality rates lower than the U.S. average (6.86) include non-Hispanic Whites (5.76), Mexicans (5.53), Asian/Pacific Islanders (4.89), and Central/South Americans (4.68).

Sex of Infant

The overall infant mortality rate for female infants in 2005 was 6.12 per 1,000 live births, 19% lower than the rate for male infants (7.56). Higher mortality rates for infant males are consistently found across all races.

Multiple Births

The infant mortality rate for multiple births (31.50) was more than five times the rate of single births (6.0) in 2005. As might be expected, the risk of infant death increases with each additional infant in the pregnancy: single (6.0), twins (29.84), triplets (59.60), and quadruplets (105.26). Multiple pregnancy increases the risk that births will be preterm and at low birth weight, which have a considerable impact on overall infant mortality. As a result, in 2005 multiples accounted for only 3% of all live births, but 15% of all infant deaths in the United States.

Table 5.2

ANNUAL NUMBERS OF DEATHS BY CAUSE FOR NEONATES IN WHO REGIONS, ESTIMATES FOR 2000–2003

CAUSE	ALL MEMBER STATES (N)	% TOTAL	AFRICA (N)	%	THE AMERICAS ALL (N)	%	U.S./CANADA (N)	%	SOUTHEAST ASIA (N)	%	EUROPE (N)	%	EASTERN MEDITERRANEAN (N)	%	WESTERN PACIFIC (N)	%
Preterm birth	1083	28	265	23	78	40	13	45	413	30	44	38	132	22	152	32
Severe infection	1016	26	313	27	34	17	2	6	374	27	21	18	174	28	101	21
Birth asphyxia	894	23	274	24	36	19	4	14	314	23	21	18	122	20	127	26
Congenital anomalies	294	8	70	6	31	16	8	29	77	6	21	19	54	9	40	8
Neonatal tetanus	257	7	108	9	2	1	0	0	58	4	1	1	72	12	16	3
Diarrheal diseases	108	3	40	3	1	1	0	0	37	3	1	1	22	4	7	1
Others	258	7	78	7	13	7	2	7	89	7	7	6	35	6	36	8
Total neonatal deaths	3910	100	1148	100	195	100	29	100	1362	100	116	100	610	100	480	100

Notes: Preterm birth causes include only deaths directly attributed to prematurity and to specific complications of preterm birth such as surfactant deficiency, but not all deaths in preterm infants. Severe infection causes include pneumonia, meningitis, sepsis/septicaemia, and other infections during the neonatal period.
Source: Adapted from Van Lerberghe et al. (2005).

Birth Weight and Period of Gestation

Birth weight and period of gestation are the two key predictors of an infant's health and survival. Infants born with extremely low birth weight (e.g., under 1,500 grams; 3.31 pounds) or premature (e.g., less than 32 weeks gestation) have a significantly greater risk of death than those born at term (37–41 weeks) or those weighing 2,500 grams or more at birth (5.51 pounds). Infants with low birth weight and premature infants born to black mothers have the highest mortality rate compared to mothers of other races.

Prenatal Care

A mother who receives prenatal care during her pregnancy improves the chances of her infant being healthy and surviving. Although data were reported from only seven states, those mothers starting prenatal care after the first trimester (8.42) or not at all (34.78) have higher infant mortality rates compared to those who began care in the first trimester (5.35).

Maternal Age

Infant mortality rates vary with maternal age. The highest death rates are for infants among teenage mothers (10.28), and the lowest are for infants of mothers in their early thirties (5.47). The higher mortality risk for infants of younger mothers may be correlated with the mother's socioeconomic status and less mature, less developed bodies (Kirchengast & Hartman, 2003). Infants of older mothers (age 40+ years), especially first-time moms, have an increased risk of prematurity and low birth weight, which result in higher infant mortality (Nabukera, Wingate, Alexander, & Salihu, 2006).

Maternal Education

Infant mortality rates decrease as education levels increase. Mothers with a college degree (3.6) have a significantly lower infant mortality rate than those with less than a high school diploma (9.84).

Marital Status

In 2005 infants of mothers who were married had an infant mortality rate (5.25 per 1,000 live births) that was 45% lower than the rate for unmarried mothers (9.61). Across all races this relationship held true, that infants of unmarried mothers had significantly higher mortality rates.

Maternal Smoking

Smoking during pregnancy causes substances (e.g., nicotine) to transfer from the placenta into the fetal blood supply, which in turn restricts the infant's access to oxygen. This consequence can contribute to low birth weight, preterm delivery, and infant mortality. The infant mortality rate for infants of mothers who smoked was 10.69 in 2005, which was 79% higher than the rate for nonsmokers (5.96).

EFFORTS TO PREVENT OR MITIGATE INFANT DEATHS

Although many of the infant deaths that occur are unexplainable (e.g., SIDS), several risk factors are thought to contribute to infant mortality. Various research-based organizations (e.g., Centers for Disease Control and Prevention [CDC], 2006; First Candle/SIDS Alliance, 2007a; March of Dimes, 2007) have identified specific factors that potentially increase the occurrence of infant deaths. These high-risk factors include preterm or low birth weight, exposure to cigarette smoke before or after birth, stomach or side sleep positions, being between the ages of 2 and 6 months, being bottle-fed, being a multiple-birth infant, and being born to a mother with little or no prenatal care during pregnancy, among others. Higher infant mortality rates associated with some of these factors were mentioned previously.

The March of Dimes (2008) has also identified a number of measures to follow for women who are considering becoming or who are pregnant to help reduce or prevent the occurrence of some of these high risk factors. These measures include regularly visiting a health care provider for preconception care and during pregnancy; avoiding alcohol, illicit drugs, and smoking; eating a balanced diet; limiting exposure to hazardous substances and chemicals; avoiding stress; and learning about family history to identify any genetic factors that may put the baby at risk. If a mother has had a previous baby with a birth defect, or if there is a family history of birth defects, a consultation with a genetic counselor is generally recommended.

Regular prenatal care of a pregnant woman may also lead to early detection and monitoring of certain medical conditions that could increase the likelihood of preterm labor (e.g., infections, high blood pressure, diabetes, clotting disorders). If identified during routine prenatal care appointments, appropriate treatments can be undertaken to help reduce any risks to the baby and mother. This prenatal care is especially critical when these conditions are present in the late stages of pregnancy.

The American Colleges of Obstetricians and Gynecologists also recommends that women wait until 39 weeks gestation to have elective C-sections. This recommendation is based on new research showing that babies born at 37–39 weeks gestation are up to two times more likely to have serious complications requiring medical intervention such as ventilation and admission to the neonatal intensive care unit (NICU) (*Medical News Today,* 2009). Educating pregnant women and the health care professionals who care for them (e.g., OB/gyn, labor and delivery nurses, high-risk maternal fetal physicians) about the signs and symptoms of preterm labor and what to do if it occurs is also identified as important for helping to prevent poor pregnancy outcomes.

Sudden Infant Death Syndrome (SIDS), the third leading cause of all infant deaths, "is the sudden, unexpected death of an apparently healthy infant under one year of age that remains unexplained after the performance of a complete postmortem investigation, including an autopsy, an examination of the scene of the death, and a review of the medical history" (First Candle/SIDS Alliance, 2007a). Importantly, SIDS continues to be the leading cause of death of infants 1 month to 1 year of age, claiming the lives of more than 2,100 babies each year. Three of the most recommended steps to help prevent SIDS deaths include always placing the baby on his or her back at nap and nighttime, using safety-approved cribs with tight-fitting sheets and no extra toys or blankets in the crib, and not having the baby sleep in an adult's bed (First Candle/SIDS Alliance, 2007a).

Unfortunately, in many of the infant deaths that occur, like those from congenital malformations, deformations, and chromosomal abnormalities, there is little, if anything, that can be done to prevent the death. In these cases, the option of perinatal hospice can be suggested to the family for consideration. "Perinatal hospice is an innovative and compassionate model of support that can be offered to parents who find out during pregnancy that their baby has a fatal condition" (PerinatalHospice.org, 2005). It is a new and emerging extension of traditional hospice, with a multidisciplinary team of health care professionals including obstetricians, perinatologists, labor and delivery nurses, NICU staff, spiritual care, social workers, genetic counselors, therapists, and other hospice professionals collaborating with the family before, during, and after the baby's birth. Perinatal hospice care includes support in terms of birth planning, medical decision making, and care of the baby from the time of the fatal diagnosis through the baby's death, and into bereavement support for the family.

IMPACT OF INFANT DEATHS ON THE FAMILY

The Parents

Parental grief from the death of a child is life-changing, regardless of the years since the death, the child's age at the time of death, or the cause of the child's death. Although difficult to describe, the majority of bereaved parents liken it to an image of "a hollow or empty space inside" (Arnold & Gemma, 2008, p. 664). This outcome is especially true when the child is an infant because the parents have had such a short time to be with the child and create memories that will have to last a lifetime. Importantly, grieving for an infant is different from grieving for an adult. With the death of an adult, one grieves their past, but with the death of an infant, one grieves their future.

Although every parent's grief experience after the loss of an infant is unique, bereaved parents generally experience some commonly shared emotional and somatic effects. Parents' initial reactions to the death of their infant are usually ones of overwhelming numbness and intense shock, disbelief, and confusion, especially if the death was unexpected, as with an infant death from SIDS. The parents are overcome with many emotions, but often so low on energy and resources that they are unable to seek out help or support, presuming they even know where to access it.

Other emotions or feelings experienced by bereaved parents of an infant might include anger (e.g., at themselves, the infant's physician, or God), frustration, irritability, sadness or depression, withdrawal, disappointment, remorse, and regret. Common themes of their grief may fall into three categories: (1) guilt that they did something to cause the death; (2) blame (oftentimes misplaced) that someone else did something to cause the death; and (3) a compelling need to find out the cause and details of the death because these facts often are not absorbed at the actual time of death (First Candle/SIDS Alliance, 2004a). Their life has been turned upside down, and fear, instability, and insecurity abound.

Bereaved parents may experience emotional outbursts and be unable to normalize their day-to-day routines. Holidays (e.g., first Christmas, Mother's Day) or anniversaries (e.g., of the infant's birth, death, milestones he or she will not obtain like graduation or a wedding) can also can serve as triggers and cause setbacks in the bereaved parents' grief work.

Mothers and fathers will likely experience the grief of their infant differently. The mothers' responses may be more intense and extreme (presumably as a result of their physical bond with the baby that the fathers did not have) and include sadness, guilt, suicidal ideation, and feelings of emptiness, isolation, irritability, and anger (Kavanaugh, 1997; McCreight, 2004). In contrast, fathers' feelings may range from isolation, restlessness, anger, sadness, and powerlessness to concerns about the mothers' emotional and physical well-being (Puddifoot & Johnson, 1997). Mothers may be more open to talking about their infant and the death, whereas fathers often may "suffer in silence." Fathers may return to work quickly after the baby's death either because they must do so or as an escape from their own grief or that of their spouse or other family members (First Candle/SIDS Alliance, 2007b; Kavanaugh, 1997; McCreight, 2004).

Some bereaved parents have reported life changes that they can attribute to the impact of their child's death, including a strain in their marital relationship, decreased communication between spouses, and feelings of being less competent and less in control. In contrast, others cite feeling stronger, bolder, more sensitive, and with a renewed sense of faith (Arnold & Gemma, 2008). Contrary to a commonly cited myth that there is a high divorce rate among bereaved parents, a study conducted by the Compassionate Friends (1999) found that "72% of parents who were married at the time of their child's death were still married to the same person (at the time of the study)"; only 12% of these marriages between bereaved parents had ended in divorce. In the remainder of the marriages (16%), the spouse had died following the death of the child; in these cases, it should be remembered that some of these child deaths could have included adult children.

Bereaved parents are often worried about becoming pregnant again after the death of an infant, and when they do, the actual birth may be an overwhelming emotional experience. They also report a wide range of feelings and emotions about their relationships with children born or adopted after the death of their child. Some parents develop a stronger sense of love and attachment to the surviving children. Other bereaved parents find it difficult to love their remaining children and may shun their responsibility of caring for them. Still others live in fear for the safety of the other children in the family, experiencing high levels of anxiety and the need to protect them at all costs (Arnold & Gemma, 2008).

The Siblings

When a family experiences the death of an infant, the surviving children often become the "forgotten or invisible mourners" who receive cues from those around them to hold in and deny their own grief (Devita-Raeburn, 2004; Rosen, 1985). Older children internalize messages from significant adults in their life to deny or repress their grief and "remain strong" for their parents (Horsley & Patterson, 2006). Yet the impact of losing their baby brother or sister can be profound and stay with them for a lifetime as they revisit this loss at key events in their own lives (e.g., going away to summer camp, graduation, marriage, the birth of their own children). This lack of acknowledgement and validation of the surviving siblings' feelings can be attributed to much of the support being focused on the parents and their grief, with little regard to the surviving siblings. Unfortunately, even when the siblings are attended to, they may often be asked about how their parents are doing and not how they, themselves, are.

The loss of a sibling is sometimes referred to as a "double loss" for the surviving children because they experience both the loss of their infant brother or sister and the loss of parental support from parents reeling from the death of their baby. The siblings' grief may be further complicated by witnessing their parents' distress and vulnerability upon the death of the infant, in addition to the intense nature of their parents' feelings during this loss (Horsley & Patterson, 2006). However, the importance of parental support should not be underestimated in helping the surviving children navigate through their grief; parental involvement is key to helping the siblings cope and adapt from this death in their family (McCown & Pratt, 1985).

The effect of a child's death on the surviving siblings is often expressed in four general responses, which, according to Davies (1999, p. 199), are "best characterized in the words of siblings themselves." They include the following: (1) "I hurt inside," (2) "I don't understand," (3) "I don't belong," and (4) "I'm not enough." Some of these responses may be acted out in the form of tears, withdrawal, misbehavior, complaints of aches and pains, nightmares, and picking fights, among others. Others may be internalized in feelings of being puzzled and confused about the death and the events surrounding it, feelings of being different from peers, and feelings of inadequacy when compared to the deceased sibling.

Two common themes bereaved siblings express during their grief include taking responsibility or questioning their role in the death (i.e., "Did I cause the baby to die?") and questioning their own immortality and that of their parents (i.e., "Will I die?" "Are Mommy and Daddy going to die too?") (First Candle/SIDS Alliance, 2004b).

Although the feelings that bereaved siblings may experience upon the death of an infant brother or sister are dependent on their age and cognitive development, there are many grief-related feelings that are likely shared among children school-age and older. These feelings include anger, sadness, confusion, an empty feeling inside, fears of abandonment or death, insecurity, rejection from parents if the parents are distracted or inattentive, guilt, and anxiety (Compassionate Friends, 2008). Sensitivity to differences in how children of various ages grieve will help to tailor bereavement interventions that are developmentally and age-appropriate. Importantly, the actions of children in grief may often speak louder than words because children will act out how they are feeling when they cannot articulate it. They are all grieving the loss of the infant; it is just being expressed in different ways and therefore needs to be attended to in different ways.

Key factors influencing the surviving siblings' reaction to the infant's death include personal characteristics of the sibling themselves (e.g., their physical traits and gender, as well as their coping style, temperament, and other experiences with death and loss), the circumstances surrounding the death (e.g., cause/place/time of death, duration of illness, participation in events and rituals surrounding the death, etc.), and environmental factors such as parent–child communication, sharing of a room with the deceased infant, and so forth. However, what can often help a sibling work through his or her tasks of mourning after the death of an infant brother or sister is finding ways to preserve and maintain the connection to the brother or sister that existed before the death (Packman, Horsley, Davies, & Kramer, 2006).

The Grandparents

The grandparents of a deceased infant experience a wide variety of emotions, many similar to the bereaved parents' emotions, but others unique to grandparents alone. These emotions often include feelings of helplessness, frustration, grief, guilt, and anger. Grandparents' grief is also different in that they have suffered two losses, the loss of their grandchild, in addition to the loss of a part of their son or daughter who will never be the same as a result of losing their baby. Like the surviving siblings, grandparents are often seen as "forgotten grievers" (First Candle/SIDS Alliance, 2007c), given that all the focus is directed toward the parents of the infant. However, their grief is no less complicated or painful.

As parents of bereaved parents, grandparents feel the pain of their child who has had a child die. They are frustrated and angry that they cannot "fix"' this pain and make it better so that their own child does not have to experience this kind of anguish. Unfortunately, they cannot take away their bereaved son or daughter's heartache, so they feel that they have been rendered helpless, which further complicates their own grief. Their grief may also be long-lasting because their offers to help their son or daughter are sometimes rebuffed as he or she closes ranks around his or her own immediate family to get through this death, shutting out the grandparents, who are grieving too (First Candle/SIDS Alliance, 2007c). It is important for grandparents to acknowledge their own grief and loss with the death of their grandchild and not subvert their feelings in order to help their bereaved son or daughter.

GRIEF AND BEREAVEMENT SUPPORT AFTER AN INFANT DEATH

For the Parents

A family that has experienced the death of an infant is fragile and in need of support. Research indicates that interactions with health care providers have a profound effect on parents with perinatal and neonatal losses (Gold, 2007). How the grieving parents perceive the actions and words of the health care professionals caring for them and their infant can influence how well they cope with their loss. If the grieving parents' impression is that the physicians' or nurses' behaviors were thoughtless and insensitive, this will be remembered and may further complicate their grief reaction. Conversely, if the health care team is perceived to be compassionate and empathetic, healing may be facilitated more positively (Gold).

Grieving parents will recall for years, or even a lifetime, not only small acts of kindness, but also insensitive comments, actions, or avoidance of the family. Research studies often conclude that physicians and nurses may benefit from increased training about grief and bereavement (Gold, 2007). There is significant room for improvement in the end-of-life care provided to infants, children, and youth and their families. Specific priorities identified for improvement include communication of the care plan and the eventual death to all those providing care for, or who are in contact with, the family; providing parents more information about the autopsy results and the details surrounding the actual death; sensitivity and empathy on the part of health care professionals; and physical care, including pain management, for the baby and mother (if she has just given birth) (Contro, Larson, Scofield, Sourkes, & Cohen, 2002; Seecharan, Anderson, Norris, & Toce, 2004; Widger & Picot, 2008).

The Institute of Medicine's report *When Children Die* (Field & Behrman, 2003, p. 348), suggests that "healthcare professionals who care for children should be trained to have a basic competence of understanding in palliative, end-of-life, and bereavement care as part of their residency training, continuing education, and model curricula."

In light of this recommendation, several national health care and community-based organizations have developed standards and practice guidelines for the care of infants and their families through the illness to death to bereavement trajectory. These standards and guidelines may be useful for hospitals and other health care centers dealing with seriously ill children and their families, including those who care for dying or deceased babies and infants. Through review of the standards and practice guidelines for care from the Pregnancy Loss and Infant Death Alliance (PLIDA, 2005, 2007), the MISS Foundation (2009), and the U.S. Department of Health and Human Services and First Candle/SIDS Alliance (2002), the following suggestions emerge for professionals interacting with these families:

- Work to cultivate an empathic relationship with both parents, the mother and the father, and other family members, including siblings. Know that an empathic relationship with these parents can aid in their adjustment to the grief that will follow and the letting go.
- Work to individualize care for each family.
- Follow the parents' lead and encourage the parents to do what is meaningful to them.
- Elicit, listen to, and respect parents' needs and wishes.
- Practice cultural and religious/spiritual sensitivity.
- Reassure parents by addressing their fears and concerns.

- Be available to give anticipatory guidance by understanding and accepting parents' wide range of emotions and offer appropriate grief support and interventions.
- Call the infant by name when referring to him or her to the family; show the *infant* respect and dignity in life and death.
- Honor the infant–parent bond and the parents' role as parents; let them be parents by participating in decision making about the infant's care and in the actual care and feeding of the infant, where possible.
- Utilize caution in the language used when speaking to parents and about the infant; balance hope with reality and communicate in terms they can understand.
- Be supportive by sitting quietly next to the parents if they do not want to talk. Nonverbal support can be communicated through eye contact, attentive listening, and concerned facial expressions.
- Avoid making statements that minimize the parents' loss; do not impose personal, moral, or religious values on them; do not judge them or increase their guilt in any way.

During and after an infant death, other suggestions for supportive grief and bereavement care from these and other perinatal and neonatal practice guidelines include the following:

- Provide opportunities for the parents and extended family to spend time with the infant.
- Ask if they want to hold, bathe, or dress their infant. Many parents and families benefit from opportunities to have close contact with and care for their infant and from seeing others gently touch and hold their infant after death.
- Ask permission to take pictures of the infant and collect mementoes of the infant (e.g., lock of hair, ID bracelet, footprints, plaster casts of hands or feet).
- Express sorrow for the loss of their infant and for their pain.
- Ask the parents about their infant and encourage them to share memories of their child.
- Inquire as to whether the family wants to honor the infant with any special religious or spiritual rituals of meaning to them, and whether they need any assistance.
- Encourage the entire family to participate in the funeral or memorial service planning and at the actual service itself.

- Pre-screen local funeral directors who have experience with and can be compassionate in accommodating the cremation or burial of an infant.

Parents will continue to grieve for some time, perhaps for the remainder of their lives; incorporating this loss into their daily lives will take time and patience on their part. When they seem to be experiencing prolonged depression subsequent to the death of the infant, it could be suggested that they do the following:

- Talk to another bereaved parent one-on-one, through an online chat room or forum, or through an in-person support group.
- Obtain support from friends and relatives.
- Seek out counseling (religious, spiritual, or grief/bereavement-related).

Research has shown that bereaved parents' sources of support come overwhelmingly from family, friends, and their faith. Other helpful support comes from knowing or having contact with other bereaved parents and participation in bereaved-parent support groups, which helps to make them feel less isolated and alone (Arnold & Gemma, 2008).

Many bereaved parents feel abandoned after the death of their child; to them, it seems like everyone else has disappeared, including the health care team, which often becomes a "surrogate family" while the child is hospitalized or in and out of the hospital. Bereaved families indicate they feel the need for a follow-up phone call and information on where to go for counseling after the child's death (Gold, 2007). The majority of parents whose children have died also want to meet with a critical care doctor for support (59%) and to get more information on their child's death. Unfortunately, only 13% claim to have actually met with any physician to discuss their child's death (Huff, 2007). The family's need for ongoing contact with their child's health care professionals after the child's death has been identified as important in several studies and often found to be lacking (Davies & Connaughty, 2002; Woodgate, 2006).

The majority of negative experiences bereaved families have encountered with their health care team center around issues of miscommunication, relationships, care of the child, and a lack of bereavement care (Widger & Picot, 2008). Specifically, avoidance, insensitivity, and poor staff communications are often cited as the most distressing behaviors parents of fetal and early infant loss experience in their interactions with their health care providers (Kavanaugh & Moro, 2006).

Even when all this bereavement support is made available and utilized, Woodgate (2006) has suggested that it is not reasonable to expect parents to achieve closure after their child's death. Research has found that parents who had experienced the death of a child did not want to experience "closure" on the death, but instead wanted to (1) keep the memories alive so as to maintain some sense of connection to the child; (2) receive validation and acknowledgement that they were good parents and that they had done everything they could to keep the child alive; (3) be present for the child's death and have the health care providers caring for their child present; and (4) have family and friends there for them after the child's death for support. This study and other current bereavement and grief literature support parental grief and bereavement as a transition that has no closure, suggesting that keeping the parent–child bonds strong and not detaching may be more helpful ways for parents to deal with their loss (Attig, 2001). This is not to say, however, that bereaved parents should not work through processing their grief; but instead, they should find healthy ways to keep their infant alive via memories, linking objects, rituals, and the creation of legacies, all of which are thought to have value in helping to maintain parental bonds with the deceased child (Woodgate).

Bereaved parents need to be reminded to take care of their physical needs, as well as their emotional and spiritual health. Maintaining a balanced diet, staying hydrated, and getting adequate rest will be important to their grief work, which is exhausting and long-term. This self-care is particularly important when the loss was a baby, and the mother has just given birth.

Parents also need to be educated before leaving the hospital about the impact of this grief on them or, minimally, given contact information for grief support groups or a bereavement coordinator at the hospital should they need this resource later. One mother wrote,

> It would have helped if somebody had educated us and told us what it was going to be like and said, "You're going to feel these things. Don't think you're going crazy, because it's normal." I didn't know what was going on. So I thought I was going crazy and I didn't want to tell anybody about the feelings. (Davis, 1996, p. 9)

Physicians who offered medical information as well as counseling about what to expect in the grieving process were rated as highly competent by bereaved parents, supporting that this communication is valued by bereaved families (Harper & Wisian, 1994). It is recommended that bereavement follow-up be conducted with the family via a phone call one week after the infant's death, and then again several weeks later (Kavanaugh & Moro, 2006). This follow-up should also include longer-term support such as remembering the family on key anniversary dates (e.g., the infant's birth, death, first holiday without the infant) with a phone call or card to show the baby is being remembered. Bereaved parents should also be given the opportunity to meet with the physician for a postpartum appointment to ask questions, to clear up any questions on the details of the infant's death and how it could impact subsequent pregnancies, and to have their feelings of grief and loss validated. Resource materials such as Web sites, books, and national and local support organizations can also be given to the parents at this time (Kavanaugh & Moro).

Given the similarities in their expressions of grief at the loss of an infant, the interventions identified to help bereaved parents would also be appropriate for the bereaved grandparents. Additionally, grandparents may find it useful to talk to or join a discussion forum or support group (including Web or online groups) specifically composed of other grieving grandparents who have experienced similar grandbaby losses.

Last, and importantly, if anyone in the family is experiencing symptoms of severe depression or extreme symptoms other than those previously identified, it is recommended they seek professional medical help or counseling.

For the Siblings

Parents may dismiss the significance of the siblings' relationship with the deceased child, particularly when the child died before or at birth, died a short time after birth, or never came home from the hospital. It is important to recognize that the surviving siblings need help with their grief work and, when they are at risk for complicated grief, may require professional counseling.

Open communication within the family is critical after an infant has died. Most bereaved siblings can benefit from opportunities to talk about their reactions not only at the time of death but also for many years to come, as they reach new developmental levels of understanding of death. Bereaved siblings want to share their grief experiences with adults and may need to be encouraged to bring up and talk about the infant who has died (Davies & Connaughty, 2002; Horsley & Patterson, 2006; McCown & Pratt, 1985).

Children need honesty when learning sad news. Explain the infant's death using the "d" words of "death" and "died." Use of such euphemisms as "the baby is sleeping in heaven" or "the baby went away" cause younger children to think the child may return or that the separation is only temporary. Avoid telling them that God has taken their loved one. Avoid associating death with "sleep" or "something lost." Use concrete and understandable statements such as these: "The baby died." "His heart stopped beating, and his body doesn't work anymore." "He is not with us now like he used to be, but we will always remember him and love him very much" (SHARE, 2009, n.p.).

The literature emphasizes that it is very important to include surviving siblings in the events surrounding the death (in the hospital and at home) and in the memorial and funeral planning and service so that they can feel a part of what is going on. Parents may also want to talk to them about their own beliefs around death and dying to help guide them to a better understanding of this loss experience. Surviving siblings should be reminded that their grief is theirs and not that of their parents or other family members and that it is unique because of the special bond they had as brother or sister to the infant who died (Packman et al., 2006).

Although bereaved siblings cannot control what they feel, they can control how they process their feelings. If they need to talk to someone, and their parents are unavailable to them, suggest they talk to a teacher, minister or counselor, friend, or some other adult they trust. Bereaved children should be told that it is okay to cry and feel sad and to live in the past and reminisce about what life was like with the infant alive. However, they also need to be told that it is also all right to have fun and enjoy life again, to go on living. In addition, it should be emphasized that it is not acceptable to ease or numb the pain of the loss through destructive behaviors such as using drugs or alcohol, acting out feelings with reckless behaviors, or doing things to hurt themselves or others (Compassionate Friends, 2008).

Other grief-related interventions that may be helpful to the bereaved siblings of a deceased infant include the following:

- Offering them the opportunity to say goodbye in the hospital or at the funeral.
- Reassuring them that they did not cause the infant's death.
- Normalizing their day-to-day activities at school and play.
- Respecting their individual coping styles, even if they may not appear to grieve at all.

- Preparing them for experiences that may trigger their grief when they may not expect it.
- Having them avail themselves of bereavement groups, online forums, or other similar resources through which they can interact with other siblings who have lost a brother or sister.

Surviving children should be monitored for signs of stress after an infant death. Ongoing regressive behaviors, such as bedwetting, loss of appetite, nightmares, or problems in school, that cause problems in daily life may be indicators of a child's need for medical or psychological care.

A variety of resources for health care professionals and the family of dying or deceased infants have been identified and are included in the appendix to this chapter.

CONCLUSION

As has been underscored throughout this chapter, more children die in the first year of life, and particularly in the first month of life, than at any other time in childhood. The sheer magnitude of the number of families bereaved by infant deaths calls out to the need for immediate and compassionate care for the infants and families before, during, and after death. Also, even though these deaths know no boundaries, the wide disparity in infant mortality rates across race, education, and age suggests that certain population segments may be more at-risk for these deaths than others. Communication and education about preventative measures that can be taken to help reduce a poor pregnancy outcome or about perinatal hospice when the baby's prenatal diagnosis is fatal are two key ways these families can be served, from their infant's illness to death to bereavement trajectory.

The impact on the family from the death of an infant is life-changing because they are left with a "hollow or empty space" inside. They will carry this grief with them through a lifetime, but with the right interventions (e.g., bereaved parent, sibling, or grandparent support groups; online chat rooms; grief and bereavement pamphlets and books; or counseling) and support from family, friends, and their faith or spiritual communities, they can begin to transition through their grief with the goal of keeping the family unit intact for the future. Each family's grief will be unique, as will be the grief of each member within the family, so tolerance of each others' coping styles and open communication both within and outside the family will be critical for survival of the family in the aftermath of this infant death.

Health care professionals have an opportunity to significantly and positively affect a family's healing from grief after an infant's death by being cognizant of their interactions with the families before, during, and after the death. For example, health care professionals can cultivate an empathic relationship with these families, while also being present with and providing anticipatory guidance through the infant's birth and death and into bereavement. Supportive interventions of this type can help families in their grief work both now and later. Bereaved parents want continued and ongoing contact with their health care professionals after the death to have their loss validated, to clarify any questions or issues they have surrounding the death, and to just be supported through their bereavement by people intimately involved in the short life, and death, of their infant. However, these health care professionals may need to be better trained in palliative care, end-of-life care, and bereavement care if they are to be able to competently and compassionately support these grieving families. Specific practice guidelines for the care of critically ill infants and their families have been developed for health care professionals, as have infant loss, grief, and bereavement training programs. Health care professionals, and the hospitals and acute care centers that have contact with dying or deceased infants and their families, need to be made aware of these resources and be given opportunities to avail themselves of the training.

ADDITIONAL RESOURCES FOR HEALTH CARE PROFESSIONALS AND/OR PATIENT/FAMILY

Centering Corporation, http://www.centering.org. With over 500 resources for grief and loss, provides education for professionals and the families they serve. Has specific resources for infant loss.

Compassionate Passages, Inc., http://www.compassionatepassages.org. Promotes the family voice for supportive pediatric end-of-life care through advocacy and research on behalf of all seriously ill or dying children, with a special emphasis on babies and infants.

First Candle/SIDS Alliance, http://www.firstcandle.org. Mission is to advance infant health and survival. Provides resources for both grieving families and health care professionals. Has a 24/7 crisis hotline for grieving families.

Gundersen Lutheran Bereavement Services, http://www.bereavementprograms.com. Offers a comprehensive, clinically based professional training program for health care providers who care for families whose babies died during pregnancy or shortly after birth.

March of Dimes, http://www.marchofdimes.com. Focuses on prevention of birth defects, premature births, and infant mortality. Offers continuing education for health care professionals on preterm labor and delivery and patient information sheets.

MISS Foundation, http://www.missfoundation.org. Provides education and support to grieving families and the health care professionals caring for them, including through support groups; online bereaved parent forums; and workshops, articles, and conferences for professionals.

Now I Lay Me Down to Sleep, http://www.nowilaymedowntosleep.org. A network of almost 6,000 volunteer photographers in the United States and 25 international countries that offers beautiful bereavement photography services in a compassionate and sensitive manner that allows families to honor their babies and their short lives.

Perinatal Hospice, http://www.perinatalhospice.org. Clearinghouse of parental and professional resources for perinatal hospice support when a baby is given a fatal diagnosis during pregnancy.

Pregnancy Loss and Infant Death Alliance, http://www.plida.org. A nationwide, collective community of parents and health care professionals working to ensure that all families experiencing the death of a baby during pregnancy, birth, or infancy will receive comprehensive and compassionate care from diagnosis through the reproductive years. Publishes position statements and care guidelines for health care professionals.

Share Pregnancy Loss & Infant Support, Inc., http://www.nationalshare.org. Offers resources and local support groups to bereaved parents who have experienced the death of a baby as a result of early pregnancy loss or stillbirth or in the first few months of life. Also offers professional health care resources for downloading and linking.

REFERENCES

Arnold, J., & Gemma, P. B. (2008). The continuing process of parental grief. *Death Studies, 32,* 658–673.

Attig, T. (2001). Relearning the world: Making and finding meanings. In R. A. Neimeyer (Ed.), *Meaning construction and the experience of loss* (pp. 33–53). Washington, DC: American Psychological Association.

Centers for Disease Control and Prevention (CDC). (2006). Recommendations to improve preconception health and health care, United States. A report of the CDC/ ATSDR Preconception Care Work Group and the Select Panel on Preconception Care. *Morbidity and Mortality Weekly Report, 55*(6), 1–23.

The Compassionate Friends. (1999). *A survey of bereaved parents.* Conducted by NFO Research, on behalf of the Compassionate Friends.

The Compassionate Friends. (2008). *When a brother or sister dies.* Retrieved on January 9, 2009, from http://www.compassionatefriends.org/Other_Pages/When_a_Brother_or_ Sister_Dies.aspx

Contro, N., Larson, J., Scofield, S., Sourkes, B., & Cohen, H. (2002). Family perspectives on the quality of pediatric palliative care. *Archives of Pediatrics & Adolescent Medicine, 156,* 14–19.

Davies, B. (1999). *Shadows in the sun: The experiences of sibling bereavement in childhood.* Philadelphia: Brunner/Mazel.

Davies, B., & Connaughty, S. (2002). Pediatric end-of-life care: Lessons learned from parents. *Journal of Nursing Administration, 32*(1), 5–6.

Davis, D. (1996). *Empty cradle, broken heart: Surviving the death of your baby.* Golden, CO: Fulcrum.

Devita-Raeburn, E. (2004). *The empty room: Surviving the loss of a brother or sister at any age.* New York: Scribner.

Field, M. J., & Behrman, R. E. (Eds.). (2003). *When children die: Improving palliative and end-of-life care for children and their families.* Washington, DC: National Academie Press.

First Candle/SIDS Alliance. (2004a). *Surviving the death of your baby.* Retrieved on January 9, 2009, from http://www.firstcandle.org/FC-PDF3/surviving.pdf

First Candle/SIDS Alliance. (2004b). *When a baby has died, coping with grief: Children.* Retrieved on January 9, 2009, from http://www.firstcandle.org/whenababy/when_cop_child.html

First Candle/SIDS Alliance. (2007a). *Facts on SIDS.* Retrieved on January 9, 2009, from http://www.firstcandle.org/FC-PDF4/Expectant%20Parents/facts%20on%20sids.pdf

First Candle/SIDS Alliance. (2007b). *When a baby has died, coping with grief: Parents.* Retrieved on January 9, 2009, from http://www.firstcandle.org/whenababy/when_cop_par.html

First Candle/SIDS Alliance. (2007c). *When a baby has died, coping with grief: Grandparents.* Retrieved on January 9, 2009, from http://www.firstcandle.org/whenababy/when_cop_grpar.html

Gold, K. J. (2007). Navigating care after a baby dies: A systematic review of parent experiences with health providers. *Journal of Perinatology, 27*(4), 230–237.

Harper, M. B., & Wisian, N. B. (1994). Care of bereaved parents. A study of patient satisfaction. *Journal of Reproductive Medicine, 39*(2), 80–86.

Horsley, H., & Patterson, T. (2006). The effects of a parent guidance intervention on communication among adolescents who have experienced the sudden death of a sibling. *American Journal of Family Therapy, 34*(2), 119–137.

Huff, C. (2007). Study: Grieving parents want to connect with clinicians; few do. *Hospitals & Health Networks, 81*(6), 17.

International Classification of Diseases (10th rev.). (1992). WHO Web site. Retrieved on January 9, 2009, from http://www.who.int/classifications/apps/icd/icd10online

Kavanaugh, K. (1997). Gender differences among parents who experience the death of an infant weighing less than 500 grams at birth. *Omega, Journal of Death and Dying, 35,* 281–296.

Kavanaugh, K., & Moro, T. (2006). Supporting parents after stillbirth or newborn death: There is much that nurses can do. *American Journal of Nursing, 106*(9), 74–79.

Kirchengast, S., & Hartman, B. (2003). Impact of maternal age and maternal somatic characteristics on newborn size. *American Journal of Human Biology, 15,* 220–228.

Kung, H.-C., Hoyert, D. L., Xu, J. Q., & Murphy, S. L. (2008). Deaths: Final data for 2005. *National Vital Statistics Reports, 56*(10). Hyattsville, MD: National Center for Health Statistics.

MacDorman, M., & Kirmeyer, S. (2009). Fetal and perinatal mortality, United States, 2005. *National Vital Statistics Reports, 57*(8). Hyattsville, MD: National Center for Health Statistics.

March of Dimes. (2007). *Pre-term birth fact sheet.* Retrieved on January 9, 2009, from http://www.marchofdimes.com/printableArticles/21326_1157.asp

March of Dimes. (2008). *10 steps to getting healthy before pregnancy.* Retrieved on January 9, 2009, from http://www.marchofdimes.com/pnhec/173_14005.asp

Mathews, T. J., & MacDorman, M. (2008). Infant mortality statistics from the 2005 period linked birth/infant death data set. *National Vital Statistics Reports, 57*(2). Hyattsville, MD: National Center for Health Statistics.

McCown, D. E., & Pratt, C. (1985). Impact of sibling death on children's behavior. *Death Studies, 9,* 323–335.

McCreight, B. S. (2004). A grief ignored: Narratives of pregnancy loss from a male perspective. *Social Health and Illness, 26*(3), 326–350.

Medical News Today. (2009). Elective C-sections before 39 weeks associated with increased risks to infants, study says. Retrieved on January 9, 2009, from http://www.medicalnewstoday.com/printerfriendlynews.php?newsid=134874

MISS Foundation. (2009). *The do's and don'ts of grief support.* Retrieved on January 9, 2009, from http://www.missfoundation.org/pro/articles/Doanddont.pdf

Nabukera, S., Wingate, M. S., Alexander, G. R., & Salihu, H. M. (2006). First-time births among women 30 years and older in the United States: Patterns and risk of adverse outcomes. *Journal of Reproductive Medicine, 51*(9), 676–82.

Packman, W., Horsley, H., Davies, B., & Kramer, R. (2006). Sibling bereavement and continuing bonds. *Death Studies, 30,* 817–841.

PerinatalHospice.Org. (2005). *Frequently asked questions about perinatal hospice.* Retrieved on January 9, 2009, from http://www.perinatalhospice.org/FAQs.html

Pregnancy Loss and Infant Death Alliance (PLIDA). (2005). *PLIDA position statement: Infection risks are insignificant.* Retrieved on January 9, 2009, from http://www.plida.org/pdf/infectionRisks.pdf

Pregnancy Loss and Infant Death Alliance (PLIDA). (2007). *PLIDA practice guidelines.* Retrieved on January 9, 2009, from http://www.plida.org/pdf/PLIDA_Guidelines_Offering_Baby.pdf

Puddifoot, J. E., & Johnson, J. P. (1997). The legitimacy of grieving: The partner's experience at miscarriage. *Social Science and Medicine, 45*(6), 837–845.

Rosen, H. (1985). Prohibitions against mourning in childhood and sibling loss. *Omega, Journal of Death and Dying, 15,* 307–316.

Seecharan, G. A., Anderson, E. M., Norris, K., & Toce, S. S. (2004). Parents' assessment of quality of care and grief following a child's death. *Archives of Pediatrics & Adolescent Medicine, 158,* 515–520.

Share Pregnancy & Infant Loss Support (SHARE). (2009). *Questions about grief: How will I know if my child needs more help than I can give?* Retrieved September 10, 2009, from http://www.nationalshare.org/parents.html

U.S. Department of Health and Human Services, Health Resources and Services Administration, & First Candle/SIDS Alliance. (2002). *Guidelines for medical professionals: Providing care to the family experiencing perinatal loss, neonatal death, SIDS or other infant death.* Retrieved January 9, 2009, from http://www.firstcandle.org/FC-PDF2/HHS&P/guidelines_for_medical_professionals-final.pdf

Van Lerberghe, W., Manuel, A., Matthews, Z., & Wolfheim, C. (2005). *The world health report 2005: Make every mother and child count.* Geneva, Switzerland: World Health Organization.

Ventura, S. J., Abma, J. C., Mosher, W. D., & Henshaw, S. (2008). Estimated pregnancy rates by outcome for the United States, 1990–2004. *National Vital Statistics Reports, 56*(15). Hyattsville, MD: National Center for Health Statistics.

Widger, K., & Picot, C. (2008). Parents' perceptions of the quality of pediatric and perinatal end-of-life care. *Pediatric Nursing, 34*(1), 53–59.

Woodgate, R. L. (2006). Living in a world without closure: Reality for parents who have experienced the death of a child. *Journal of Palliative Care, 22*(2), 75–83.

6 Children, Unintentional Injuries, and Homicide

EDITH CRUMB AND AMY GRIFFITH TAYLOR

Unintentional injury deaths and homicides are the two leading causes of childhood deaths in developed or high-income countries. Although in many ways on the opposite ends of a spectrum, these deaths have several similarities. First, they are preventable; second, both cut across all boundaries of geography, race, religion, and culture. No country is immune to these tragic and often violent deaths. Note that this chapter follows the international system for classifying causes of death that now uses "unintentional injuries" rather than "accidents." Health professionals believe until we can name the behavior in terms that provide a structure identifying modifications in behavior or equipment safety, we will not be able to reduce effectively the number and severity of unintentional injuries and deaths. This chapter focuses on various types of unintentional injury deaths and homicides of children from birth to 12 years of age. Additionally, we explore prevention strategies and how theories of human development provide explanations and insight to prevent similar deaths in the future.

UNINTENTIONAL DEATHS: EPIDEMIOLOGY AND TYPES

Unintentional injuries kill more than 830,000 children a year worldwide (Picard, 2008). In addition, millions of children who are not killed suffer non-fatal injuries leaving them physically or mentally disabled or both. The highest overall rates of unintentional injury deaths are found in Africa, whereas high-income countries in Europe and the Western Pacific, such as Australia, the Netherlands, New Zealand, Sweden, and the United Kingdom, have the lowest rates, 10 times lower than rates in Africa (UNICEF, 2001). Nevertheless, unintentional injuries are the primary cause of child deaths in all developed nations, accounting for nearly 40% of these deaths.

In the United States, unintentional injuries are the most important cause of death during infancy or the first year of life after congenital malformations, SIDS, and various pregnancy-related causes described in chapter 5 and are the leading cause of death for children from 1 to 12 years of age.

In all areas of the world, the most common unintentional childhood injuries involve motor vehicles, drowning, burns, falls, and poisoning.

Road Traffic Deaths

Motor vehicle accidents account for 41% of childhood deaths. Most children who are killed are pedestrians or cyclists, not passengers in a vehicle. About two-thirds of child road-traffic deaths occur in the Southeast Asia and Western Pacific regions. Africa and Eastern Mediterranean regions have the highest rate of traffic fatalities. In European countries the fatality rate is not as high, but still accounts for 1 in 5 child deaths. Low-income and middle-income countries account for 93% of all child-related road traffic deaths. Children who survive road traffic crashes often sustain injuries or are left disabled. Boys are twice as likely to be involved in a road traffic crash as girls. The overall death rate from this cause in the United States is 13.8 per 100,000 for boys and 7.5 per 100,000 for girls (UNICEF, 2008a).

The most effective interventions to reduce deaths among children associated with road traffic accidents are those that involve adapting child behaviors and that take into consideration children's needs when designing and managing the entire road system. In its *World Report on Child Injury Prevention*, UNICEF (2008b) recommended six interventions that target the safety of children:

1. Engineering measures—creating and adapting road environments to be safe for motor vehicles as well as walkers and bicycle riders as a forethought, not an afterthought.

2. Vehicle design—encouraging features specifically designed to improve the safety of children as passengers, walkers, or cyclists.
3. Safety equipment—advocating that children traveling in motor vehicles always be strapped into approved child restraints including car seats, booster seats, or seatbelts depending on the child's height and weight, not age; ensuring that all children riding a bicycle, motorbike, or ATV wear properly fitting headgear; and encouraging children to wear clothes that are white, bright colored, or reflective whenever cycling or walking close to traffic areas.
4. Legislation and standards—promoting laws and standards that increase the overall road safety for individuals as well as those designed to specifically increase the safety of children.
5. Developing education and skills—proposing educational programs that take an ecological approach to improving children's road safety skills, behaviors, and attitudes, such as teaching children to stop, look, and listen before crossing a road as well as how to determine where it is safest to cross a street.
6. Emergency and trauma care—improving and strengthening emergency medical services to decrease the number of road traffic deaths and permanent injuries.

Drowning

Drowning is the second leading cause of unintentional injury-related deaths among children. The majority of drownings or near-drownings occur in residential swimming pools or open water sites. Over 98% of child deaths from drowning occur in low- or middle-income countries. In high-income countries, most child drowning deaths occur in swimming pools. Children under the age of five are at the greatest risk globally of drowning and can drown in as little as an inch of water (UNICEF, 2008a).

The following interventions can help to prevent or minimize child drowning deaths (UNICEF, 2008b):

1. Engineering measures—creating safe bridges and installing piped water systems, both of which have been proven to reduce drowning rates in developing countries.
2. Environmental measures—covering or removing all water hazards and creating barriers to protect wandering children, such

as fencing materials around swimming pools and wells and near open bodies of water.

3. Legislation and standards—upgrading laws and policies regarding fencing around pools, use of personal floatation devices, and the use of alcohol in water recreational facilities.
4. Developing education and skills—teaching swimming and always providing active adult supervision (lifeguards and caretakers) when children are in or around water.
5. Managing drowning—training in resuscitation techniques.
6. Adapting interventions—adjusting interventions and strategies to coincide with a child's developmental stage and to make them effective in different environments or countries, as in use of barrier fencing in regions where irrigation systems or canals are utilized extensively.

Burns

Burns are the third leading cause of child deaths. Burn injuries make up about 10% of all child abuse cases as well as hospital admissions (Peltier, Purdue, & Shepherd, 2001). Death rates caused by burns are 11 times higher in low- and middle-income countries by comparison with high-income countries. Babies and young children are especially susceptible to burns because they are inquisitive. Although many burns are caused by contact with scalding hot objects, hazardous chemicals, and electricity, the majority of burn-related deaths result from fires and smoke inhalation (Peltier et al.).

Children who are intentionally burned are likely to be under 2 years of age. Immediate identification is crucial with this age group because they are typically unable to speak for themselves. Children who receive intentional burns, by contrast with children who receive accidental burns, are usually younger, have significantly longer hospital stays, and have a higher mortality rate. Accidental burns typically do not have a distinct pattern because the child quickly moves away from the heat. In addition, accidental burns are usually shallower, irregular, and less defined than non-accidental burns. Multiple burns that obviously could not have been caused from the same accident are strong indicators of abuse.

Burns occur in various ways. *Immersion burns* involve immersing a child in scalding water for cleaning or for punishment. In deliberate immersion burns, the burn will be uniform. The wound borders are distinct with sharply defined waterlines. *Inflicted burns* leave characteristic patterns of injury and cannot be concealed. *Scald burns* are the most common type and are caused by any type of hot liquid, which may be splashed or spilled on the child. It is difficult for a child to be accidentally scalded on his or her back. *Contact burns* leave an identifying mark from the object that caused the burn such as a cigarette lighter.

UNICEF (2008b) has offered the following recommendations for interventions to reduce the rate of child burn injuries and deaths:

1. Engineering measures—designing safer lamps and stoves, placing smoke detectors on each floor of homes and encouraging monthly testing to ensure they are working properly, installing residential sprinklers, and using fire-retardant household materials.
2. Environmental measures—mandating stricter building codes, improving construction materials, and improving home heating and lighting equipment.
3. Laws and regulations—regulating the water temperature in preset home water heaters, establishing standards for child-resistant lighters, and banning children from purchasing or using fireworks.
4. Educational approaches—offering education to support legislation, safety standards, and product modification.
5. Managing burns—providing access to treatment, immediate first aid, and availability of acute management of burns.

Falls

Falls are the fourth leading cause of unintentional injury–related deaths among children. The greatest risk for death or serious injury is likely to occur at school or recreational activities in children 5–12 years old. The most common types of these injuries include fractures, head and neck injuries, contusions, or lacerations. Children ages 5–9 are often adventuresome and therefore are not likely to see the dangers in the activities they attempt such as jumping, climbing, or riding a skateboard or bike (UNICEF, 2008b).

Adults often minimize falls as a normal part of children learning to walk, and in fact, when the falls are not from heights, they may not be serious. Nevertheless, falls can result in serious injury or death when they occur from a second- or upper-story window, balcony, or stairs or even when a child falls from a changing table or bed, down stairs, or off playground equipment. Many of these falls are preventable.

UNICEF (2008b) has recommended the following interventions to reduce children's deaths from falls:

1. Engineering measures—redesigning nursery furniture, playgrounds, and sports or recreational equipment.
2. Environmental measures—creating and maintaining safety-conscious playground areas and encouraging the use of window guards and stair gates.
3. Laws and regulations—encouraging standards such as those that decrease structural failures in baby walkers and the likelihood that such child equipment would tip over.

Poisoning

Poisoning is a common event among children in the United States and the fifth leading cause of child deaths worldwide (UNICEF, 2008b). Common types of poison exposure include cosmetics, personal care products, cleaning substances, medications, and plants (Vroman, 2008). According to the American Association of Poison Control Centers (2000), 53% of poison exposure occurs in children under the age of 6, and the greatest danger is for children under 3 years of age. Ingesting poisons during early childhood is largely associated with developmental milestones, such as increased mobility, curiosity, oral exploration, and attraction to bright colors, as well as children mistaking medication for candy or adults accidentally administering an incorrect drug or dose.

UNICEF (2008b) has recommended the following interventions to prevent or minimize child poisoning:

1. Engineering measures—reducing toxicity in poisonous substances and making use of safer packaging and storage.
2. Environmental measures—keeping all medications and poisons such as household cleaning products out of the reach of children.
3. Laws and legislation—requiring child-resistant caps and packaging.
4. Educational approaches—developing prevention programs that incorporate increasing knowledge and skills related to poison prevention, raising awareness, changing attitudes and behaviors, and influencing policy and legislation.
5. Managing poisoning—ensuring that caregivers are able to receive help from a poison center or professional medical worker if a poisoning is suspected.

UNINTENTIONAL INJURY PREVENTION SUMMARY

Although all educational programs do not eliminate or reduce the rate of unintentional child injury deaths, many are successful. A model program is the UNICEF and World Health Organization prevention booklet titled *Have Fun, Be Safe* for children ages 7–11 (UNICEF/WHO, 2008). It is a child-oriented companion guide to the UNICEF's *World Report on Child Injury Prevention* and provides information on various types of injuries and prevention interventions. This information is conveyed through illustrations, quizzes, and visual activities using child-friendly language to convey tips and lifesaving advice to children to protect them and reduce their risks from unintentional injuries.

Other innovative educational interventions include the creation of safety stores at children's hospitals. A model hospital is Riley Hospital for Children in Indianapolis. Their safety store (http://www.riley childrenshospital.com/parents-and-patients/wellness-center/commed/ safety-store.jsp) provides low-cost products designed to prevent unintentional injuries including products specifically designed for children with disabilities and special needs as well as written and visual resources. The staff are trained to answer questions and help caregivers identify needs to keep children safe in their home and play environments.

Two additional simple and extremely effective interventions for the prevention of all unintentional injuries/deaths are (1) active adult supervision of children in and outside of the home environment, with an emphasis on active, and (2) providing prevention education/strategies at "teachable moments," defined as the optimal time a person can learn, which is often just after an unintentional injury occurred or could have occurred. Caregivers are in an excellent position to provide this intervention to children as the opportunities arise, as are medical staff when children and their caregivers present to emergency departments for treatment after an unintentional injury.

HOMICIDE

Homicide is the fourth leading cause of death in the United States for children 1–9 years of age (Finkelhor & Ormrod, 2001). Deaths of children resulting from falls, infectious diseases, cancer, and congenital defects are decreasing while homicide rates of children are increasing.

Moreover, the actual homicide statistics for children may be higher than the numbers reported—perhaps as much as double—because many of these fatalities resemble other types of death (U.S. Advisory Board on Child Abuse and Neglect, 1997). For example, it may be difficult to distinguish the death of a child who dies from being thrown or intentionally dropped versus a child who dies from an accidental fall.

Homicides of young children (ages 5 and under) and children in middle childhood (6–11) differ on a number of dimensions, signifying that they should be analyzed separately. Homicides of young children are typically committed by family members through beating and suffocation. Homicides of children in middle childhood often arise from a variety of causes, such as child maltreatment, use or misuse of firearms, sexual abuse, or multiple-victim familial homicide.

Weapons used in child homicides vary with the age, sex, or race of the child victim, as well as the relationship to the offender. Bodily force or a blunt object is often the principal weapon for children under 9 years of age. Guns or knives were used in one-third of the homicides involving victims over 3 years of age. According to the Centers for Disease Control and Prevention (CDC, 1982), guns were used in 40% of child homicides, knives in 15%, strangulation in 6%, and other specified means in 31%. The weapon was not specified in 7% of the cases.

In some countries such as Australia, homicides exceed the number of deaths caused by motor vehicle accidents, poisonings, falls, or drowning for children less than 1 year of age (Strang, 1996). In these young children's deaths most perpetrators used fists, feet, shaking, dropping, or throwing, whereas in older children perpetrators were more likely to use a firearm or knife. This pattern shows that younger children are more likely to be victims of abuse, and older children are more likely to be involved in family violence involving use of weapons. In Australia, girls are more likely to be victims of homicide.

Bowlby's attachment theory (1982) and Mahler's object-relation theory (Mahler, Pine, & Bergman, 1975) provide possible explanations as to why caregivers harm or do not protect their children, ultimately resulting in homicide. These theories emphasize the importance of forming secure relationships between a child and the primary caregiver and how the early relationships children experience affect their feelings, emotions, and expectations of future relationships. When a child does not develop a secure relationship with the primary caregiver, the child's social and emotional development is compromised. Later when the child is an adult and a parent, a secure relationship with his or her child is impeded because he or she did not receive proper guidance to care for and protect that child.

Child death review (CDR) teams were initially created to review the deaths of children to determine if there could be unrecognized causes for these deaths, primarily child abuse and or neglect. Today, nearly all states in the United States, as well as the countries of Australia, the United Kingdom, New Zealand, and Canada, have established CDR teams and have broadened their responsibilities to focus on understanding and responding to many other preventable deaths (Covington, Foster, & Rich, 2005). It is a collaborative process with individuals from multiple disciplines working together to understand the circumstances leading to the death of a child in order to prevent harm to other children in the future. Each team's jurisdiction is different and may convene at a city, county, regional, state, or country level. Their reviews can lead to action to prevent future deaths locally, at a state level, and nationally. The teams are an effective prevention intervention for child homicides as well as other causes of death.

Conflict in South Africa

One example of a country in which the overall child mortality rate is reportedly six times higher than that in the United States is South Africa, said to be the most violent society in the world (Barolsky, 2007). Crimes against children often dominate the news headlines in South Africa (Lockhat & Van Niekerk, 2000). Gender-based violence is a common occurrence at school, in the community, and on the streets. Rape accounts for the highest number of crimes committed against women and children. Dempster (2002) reports that a female born in South Africa has a greater chance of being raped in her lifetime than of learning how to read. Assaulted by family members, teachers, or others in the community, children often feel too intimidated to report the abuse.

Child Abuse and Neglect

Roughly every 10 seconds an incident of child abuse is reported. More than 3 million of these reports were made in 2003 (Gurian, 2006). The Australian Institute of Criminology (Strang, 1996) reported that a quarter of all homicides were the result of fatal child abuse. The caregiver was usually the offender and appeared to be expressing frustration and rage through severe punishment or discipline of the child, shaking (resulting in shaken baby syndrome), assault, burns, poisoning, and strangulation.

Instability and poverty are often key factors leading to child abuse. Mothers are usually very young and living in uncertain relationships with the fathers. At least one of the offenders was usually unemployed at the time the abuse occurred.

Child maltreatment is typically committed by a person in charge of the care of a child. Deaths caused by negligence are situations in which the caretaker fails to provide food or needed medical attention. Providing inadequate supervision that could seriously injure or kill a child is considered negligence. Among child maltreatment fatalities, 42% result from neglect or negligence, 54% are the direct result of abuse, and 4% result from abuse and neglect combined. The majority of child maltreatment fatalities involve children 5 years of age and younger. Two factors that account for very young children's unusually high risk of death in cases of maltreatment are the high demands that young children impose on the adult caretaker and the fact that young children are small and physically vulnerable. A limited amount of physical force inflicted on a small child could potentially cause serious damage due to immaturity of the child's head and neck. Head trauma is the major cause of death in child abuse victims.

Shaken baby syndrome (SBS) is a specific type of child abuse in which permanent brain injury or death is caused by the violent shaking of a young child. At this time, it is difficult to say with confidence how many children have been victims of SBS because it is a new classification for child injury and death. The Shaken Baby Syndrome Web site (http://aboutshakenbaby.com) reports that 15% of all deaths resulting from abuse and neglect are attributable to this syndrome. About 80% of perpetrators are male, as are 60% of victims. Roughly 1,000–3,000 children are diagnosed in the United States every year with SBS, and of those children 100–120 die. Parents who are experiencing extra stress, such as through financial, emotional, or social situations, are at increased risk of engaging in this violent behavior.

Bandura's social learning theory (1977) indicates why caregivers kill or seriously harm the children they have the responsibility to nurture and protect. This theory of human development introduced the concept of observational learning or modeling that accounts for why adults abused as children are more likely to abuse their children and in some instances cause death. Homicide and child abuse experts agree that in many cases involving parents killing children, the violent action is not premeditated, but a part of a lengthy pattern of violent behavior that ends with loss of the child's life.

Child maltreatment is a complex problem with multiple causes in all countries, and it can be successfully addressed and incidents reduced only if the prevention responds to the full range of needs. The *World Report on Violence Against Children* (Pinheiro, 2006) states that "effective responses to violence involve comprehensive efforts, combining long-term investment in prevention, challenging attitudes which condone or support violence, reliable data collection, and improving the functioning of State institutions and ensuring accountability." Within the United States, Prevent Child Abuse America (n.d.) recommends the following prevention interventions: (1) providing support programs for new parents; (2) providing parenting programs to all parents with specific teaching tools focused on reward and punishment, praise, and specific encouragement; (3) providing early and regular child and family screening and treatment; (4) creating child care opportunities; (5) providing age-appropriate treatment programs for abused children to minimize the long-term effect of the abuse and to stop the cycle of abuse; (6) providing life skills training for children and young adults; (7) providing family support services; and (8) educating the public through educational campaigns addressing the seriousness of child abuse, its implications, and how each individual can make a difference. Mandatory reporting laws have also been enacted in all 50 U.S. states requiring even the *suspicion* of child abuse to be reported to the appropriate investigating authorities.

Neonaticide

Neonaticide was defined by Resnick (1970) as the killing of an infant within the first 24 hours of birth. This definition was refined by Bonnet (1993) who suggested there are two distinct types of neonaticide: active neonaticide, the killing of a newborn through violence and typically following panic, and passive neonaticide as the result of negligence. Explanations offered to explain neonaticide include illegitimacy, societal preferences for males, disabilities, population control, religious beliefs, and poverty. Statistical data are difficult to obtain because many neonaticides go undetected, and there is no continuing data collection process for this social problem. The U.S. Advisory Board on Child

Abuse and Neglect (1997) estimated that 33 infants were found dead in 1997, and 105 infants were discarded in that year—an increase of 62% from 1992.

Mothers primarily commit neonaticide; it is extremely rare for fathers to cause these types of death. The majority of women who commit neonaticide are emotionally immature, have psychological disorders, or may feel socially isolated. Research has shown that most women who commit neonaticide are young, unmarried, and usually not involved in a relationship with the father. Most of these women typically live with their parents or in poverty. Women who commit neonaticide are from all different racial/ethnic backgrounds.

The most common reason for neonaticide is an "unwanted child." Research has found that these women typically submit to sexual relations rather than initiate the relationship. According to Drescher-Burke, Krall, and Penick (2004), many of these women would not attempt an abortion because that would require acceptance of the situation and active decision making, which is not a characteristic of neonaticide. Most of these women are in denial about their pregnancy and often avoid making any decisions about it. Further research has shown that many of these women lack good judgment skills, insight into their current situation, or adequate coping skills.

A widely accepted intervention to prevent neonaticide is to increase access to family-planning education and contraceptives. This intervention would reduce the chance of unplanned pregnancies for some women. Others have suggested that until the stigma of becoming pregnant out-of-wedlock is removed, many young unwed mothers will continue to deny their pregnancy and be less likely to seek alternatives to neonaticide such as safe medical abortions, adoption, or raising the child on their own. It is also important to educate professionals—teachers, health care staff, and others in the helping professions—to be alert to changes in moods or dress that could indicate pregnancy and to be willing to compassionately intervene. There have also been "safe haven" laws passed in all 50 U.S. states, as well as in many European countries, that allow newborns and infants to be left in a safe location, without fear of the mother being prosecuted. This intervention will be discussed in greater length in the discussion of prevention of infanticide because it is thought to be less effective in the prevention of neonaticide, given that the panic and fear associated with neonaticide make it less likely a newborn will be dropped off at a designated safe location.

Infanticide

Infanticide is the killing of a child within the first year of life. Milner (1998) reports that anthropologist Laila Williamson summarized the data she collected by stating that infanticide has been practiced on every level of cultural complexity, from hunters to gatherers to high civilization. According to Milner, there is significant evidence to document the tendency of parents to murder their children when faced with a variety of stressful situations. Many countries have limited the number of children allowed to survive to adulthood as a result of concerns about overpopulation and starvation.

Milner (1998) reported that for infants under 1 year of age, the American homicide rate is 11th in the world, but for ages 1–4, it is first, and for ages 5–14, it is fourth. Today infanticide is most commonly seen in areas where poverty is the most severe. Statistically, mothers most often commit infanticide, and the victim is usually a newborn or a very young infant. Research has shown that children over the age of 1 are more likely to be killed by their father (Milner). Black fathers are 50% more likely to murder their child than a Black mother, whereas White fathers are 10% more likely to murder their child than White mothers.

Many risk factors contribute to infanticide, including young maternal age, low level of education, and lack of employment. Mothers who have signs of psychopathology such as alcohol or drug abuse or a criminal history are more likely to murder their children. The most common causes of infanticide are physical punishment, head trauma, strangulation, or drowning.

UNICEF (2008b) has reported that up to 50 million girls and women are missing in India as a result of gender discrimination. In that country, the practice of infanticide seems to be prompted by the existence of the dowry system. Some countries that practice Hinduism have the lowest female-to-male ratio in their populations, which is said to be due to female infanticide. Infanticide has been occurring in the People's Republic of China because of the one-child-per-family policy, although this behavior is not believed to be widespread. In the 1990s the Yangtze River was known to be the common site of infanticide by drowning. However, the local government made access to the river more difficult, thus preventing many infanticides from occurring.

Many reasons have been proposed to explain why infanticide is continuing around the globe in modern society (Milner, 1998). These explanations include economics, population control, customs/taboos, psychology, and/or genetics. Many historians believe that the primary explanation is economics and that families are having more children than they are prepared to support. Infanticide typically occurs as a means to control the population and to keep population in line with the resource base. In many tribal religions, beliefs, taboos, and local customs have led to various forms of infanticide. Postpartum psychosis has also been identified as a cause of infanticide. In cases where childbirth and lactation cause severe stress on new mothers, it has been suggested that infanticide and suicide may result.

Interventions to prevent infanticide include (1) increased availability and access for family planning and birth control; (2) transformation of the cultural, economic, and social practices of societies globally to reject all forms of violence against children, none being seen as justifiable or acceptable; (3) elimination of the underlying social and economic conditions typically present with violence against children; (4) development of consistent registration of births and comprehensive death registration, investigation, and reporting systems in all countries; and (5) publicity of safe haven locations. In the United States, each of the 50 states has passed laws that seek to prevent infanticide by decriminalizing leaving unharmed infants in designated locations, typically at a medical or public safety facility. How old the child is allowed to be varies from state to state and ranges from newborn to 1 year old.

Filicide

Filicide is the deliberate killing of a child (Marleau, Poulin, Webanck, Roy, & LaPorte, 1999). The majority of homicides of young children are committed by family members, mostly by using hands and feet to batter, strangle, or suffocate victims (Finkelhor & Ormrod, 2001). Mothers who commit filicide usually are poor, are socially isolated, are victims of domestic violence, are involved in relational problems, or are full-time caregivers. Persistently crying infants were sometimes precipitants for filicide.

An American study found that older children were more likely to be victims of maternal filicide-suicide (Papapietro, 2005). The average age of the child is 6 years old. Based on perpetrators' motivations, Friedman and Resnick (2007) identified five basic types of filicide: *Altruistic filicide* occurs when a mother kills out of love in the belief that killing her child is in the best interest of the child. *Acutely psychotic filicide* takes place when a psychotic or delirious mother kills her child without any logical motive. *Fatal maltreatment filicide* occurs when there is recurrent child abuse, neglect, or factitious disorder by proxy (i.e., the intentional production of physical or psychological symptoms in another person who is under the individual's care for the purpose of indirectly assuming the sick role). *Unwanted child filicide* occurs when the mother perceives that her child is a hindrance to her needs or wishes. And *spousal revenge filicide,* the rarest motivation, occurs when one parent kills the child in an attempt to emotionally harm the other parent.

Filicide has been on the rise recently in Japan, with more than 100 cases a year reported in that country. The cases feature a wide variety of triggers and involve similar themes, such as young mothers who feel isolated or receive no support from uninvolved or abusive husbands (Norrie, 2008). Many Japanese women feel ashamed to seek treatment for their depression. The Japanese culture seems to put added stress on young mothers as a result of their being full-time mothers and professionals, with little to no support from extended family generations. Women are now depending on the Internet and magazines to learn how to parent their children instead of benefiting from family knowledge and support.

Interventions to prevent filicide include the following: (1) providing additional programs and services to children who are especially vulnerable to different forms of violence, such as children with disabilities, orphans (including those orphaned by AIDS), indigenous children, ethnic minority and other marginalized children, children working or living on the streets, children in detention and institutions, child refugees and other displaced children, and children living in communities with high concentrations of poverty, unemployment, and inequality; (2) making accessible parenting education focused on increasing protective factors, such as encouraging the development of strong attachment bonds between parents and children and eliminating violence in all forms; (3) educating psychiatrists to assess filicide risks systematically, as they do for suicide, and to ask specific questions related to the fate of children when a parent is suicidal; (4) increasing support services for mothers and accessible psychiatric services for at-risk populations; (5) encouraging child protective agencies to accept children into their care, even if prior to abuse or neglect; (6) educating evaluators of child custody disputes on the potential risks of spouse revenge filicide; and (7) educating pediatricians of children at high risk.

School Shootings

School shootings involving child perpetrators are actually quite rare occurrences. In the United States as of August 2009, there have been only two school shootings where the perpetrator was under the age of 13. The first, known as the Jonesboro Massacre, occurred on March 24, 1998, at a middle school in Jonesboro, Arkansas. Andrew Golden (age 11) set off the school fire alarm while Mitchell Johnson (age 13) took weapons to a wooded area near the school. The two boys opened fire on a teacher and students when they came out of the school. Five victims died in this school shooting: two 11-year-old children, two 12-year-olds, and a 32-year-old teacher. Many other students were also injured ("Westside Middle School Massacre," n.d.).

Another school shooting occurred on February 29, 2000, when 6-year-old Dedrick Owen brought a .32 caliber handgun with him to Buell Elementary School in Mount Morris Township, Michigan ("Buell Elementary School," 2002). Later in the day, during a class change, Owen fired one shot that killed 6-year-old Kayla Rolland in the presence of a teacher and 22 students. After firing the handgun, he threw it in a trashcan and fled to a nearby restroom. He was found by a teacher and taken into police custody. Dedrick Owen is the youngest known school shooter, and Kayla Rolland is the youngest known victim in U.S. history.

Experts agree that most youth who are school shooters are emotionally troubled, angry, and depressed (Cornell, 1999). They are often very capable but are not satisfied with their accomplishments and feel as though others treat them unfairly. They are typically loners and are very sensitive to bullying and teasing. As they become more depressed, their perspectives and decision-making abilities become distorted. Unable to see any other way to solve their problems, they decide to kill others.

Recommendations given to the House Judiciary Committee Oversight Hearing to Examine Youth Culture and Violence on May 13, 1999, to address motives for this type of violence included (1) providing education and training for students and their parents on conflict resolution and understanding violence on a monthly basis and (2) having a staff position for one mental health professional per 1,000 students to provide risk assessment, crisis intervention, and short-term mental health counseling to potentially violent students.

Recommendations to address methods by which children engage in violence included (1) making information and tools easily available to help parents supervise their children's exposure to extremely violent entertainment; (2) having straightforward information on extremely violent video games and movies, not obscure codes; and (3) labeling Web sites with extremely violent content (e.g., on making bombs or committing murder) so that parents can lock them out with browser software. In addition, it is important to reduce minors' access to firearms in order to limit means by which youth can engage in homicidal violence.

Parricide

Parricide, or the killing of parents by a child, is rather uncommon under the age of 12. From 1972 to 2005, 62 cases were reported of children 7 or 8 years of age who were arrested on murder charges in the United States. Children who kill their parents are usually White males who most often use a gun that is already in the house (Heide, 1992). Typically, these children have been the victims of severe child abuse and see no other way out of the situation, although mental illness or simple feelings of frustration can also trigger this behavior. Recently, an 8-year-old boy in New York went on a rampage, killing his father and another man with a rifle at close range (Goldman, 2008). Another incident involved a 10-year-old boy in Houston in 1989 who shot and killed his mother and father because they would not let him go outside to play.

Intervention strategies include those stated previously for child abuse, emphasizing early intervention and age-appropriate treatment programs for child abuse victims, given that most of the children who kill their parent(s) have been abused themselves. Intervention strategies for severely mentally ill or antisocial children involve intensive mental health services.

Children as Combatants and Victims of War

Historically, the intentional and strategic involvement of children in armed combat has been minimal. In those instances when children have been involved, the actual number was small, and participation was traditionally peripheral. Roles assigned to children might have included helping with the wounded and other minor or ancillary support roles, but not on the frontline, in the battlefield, as true combatants, or as an essential part of the militaries in which they served. In recent decades, however, the number of children directly involved in combat has dramatically increased throughout the globe, and their roles have become much more dangerous and diverse. Children are serving as active combatants in more than three-fourths of the armed conflicts around the world (Singer, 2006). This complex and escalating global phenomenon is further complicated by the fact that these are not just children on the edge of adulthood, but as young as the age of 6. In 1999, an estimated 450,000 children under the age of 15 were carrying guns in armed conflicts (Boothby, 1999).

Sierra Leone is often thought of as the epicenter of child soldiers because of the prominent role children had in armed combat from 1991 to 2001 during the country's civil war. In the Revolutionary United Front (RUF), the organization that initiated the violence, 80% of the soldiers were between the ages of 7 and 14, and most were forcibly abducted. Unfortunately, however, the phenomenon of the child solider is not limited to one country or one continent. In recent decades every continent except Antarctica has had a significant number of children serving as combatants in organized military as well as in political groups such as rebel and terrorist groups (Singer, 2006). During this time more than 2 million children have been killed in warfare, or one child every 3 minutes for a full 10 years (Singer). It is estimated that more than 6 million children who survived were seriously injured or permanently disabled.

In commenting on this situation, Graca Machel, the former first lady of Mozambique, has said,

> These statistics are shocking enough, but more chilling is the conclusion to be drawn from them: more and more of the world is being sucked into a desolate moral vacuum. This is a space devoid of the most basic human values; a space in which children are slaughtered, raped, and maimed; a space in which children are exploited as soldiers; a space in which children are starved and exposed to extreme brutality. Such unregulated terror and violence speak of deliberate victimization. There are few further depths to which humanity can sink. (Machel, 1996, p. 5)[1]

CONCLUSION

Unintentional injuries and homicide deaths are a tragedy to everyone involved. Interventions should focus on understanding children's developmental milestones and what is needed to promote constructive coping with the situation. Children are resilient if they are given the tools to be successful. Our role as adults should be to protect children and prepare them to face difficult times with resilience by providing a nurturing environment that will allow children to live healthy lives, grow, and adapt to change. It is important to teach children self-sufficiency so that they will feel empowered to conquer life's adversities.

NOTE

1. Although it is not within the scope of this chapter to fully or appropriately address the global phenomenon of children and war, the authors believe it is imperative for more research and education to be carried out in order to plan strategic interventions for this most vulnerable and too often invisible child population.

REFERENCES

American Association of Poison Control Centers. (2000). Retrieved January 21, 2009, from http://www.aapcc.org

Bandura, A. (1977). *Social learning theory.* Englewood Cliffs, NJ: Prentice Hall.

Barolsky, V. (2007). *Violence and non-violence in Africa.* New York: Routledge.

Bonnet, C. (1993). Adoption at birth: Prevention against abandonment or neonaticide. *Child Abuse & Neglect, 17,* 501–513.

Boothby, N. (1999). Child combatants: The road to recovery. *America's defense monitor* [Interview with Glenn Baker]. Public Broadcasting Service, Washington, DC, April 12. Retrieved September 7, 2009, from http://www.cdi.org/ADM/1201/Boothby.html

Bowlby, J. (1982). *Attachment and loss, Vol. 1: Attachment* (2nd. ed.). New York: Basic Books.

Buell Elementary School. (2002). Retrieved December 26, 2008, from http://en.wikipedia.org/wiki/Buell_Elementary_School

Centers for Disease Control and Prevention (CDC). (1982). Perspectives in disease prevention and health promotion child homicide: United States. *Morbidity and Mortality Weekly Report, 31*(22), 292–294. Retrieved January 8, 2009, from http://www.cdc.gov

Cornell, D. (1999). Psychology of school shootings. *American Psychological Association.* Retrieved February 9, 2009, from http://www.apa.org/ppo/issues/pcornell.html

Covington, T., Foster, V., & Rich, S. (2005). *A program for child death review.* Retrieved January 4, 2009, from http://www.childdeathreview.org/cdrprocess.htm

Dempster, C. (2002). Rape: Silent war on South African women. *BBC News.* Retrieved January 5, 2009, from http://news.bbc.co.uk/2/hi/africa/1909220.stm

Drescher-Burke, K., Krall, J., & Penick, A. (2004). *Report on discarded infants and neonaticide: A review of the literature.* Berkeley: National Abandoned Infants Assistance Resource Center, University of California at Berkeley. Retrieved December 30, 2008, from http://aia.berkeley.edu/media/pdf/discarded_infants_literature_review.pdf

Finkelhor, D., & Ormrod, D. (2001, October). Homicides of children and youth. *Office of Juvenile Justice and Delinquency Program. Juvenile Justice Bulletin.* Retrieved December 30, 2008, from http://www.ncjrs.gov/pdffiles1/ojjdp/187239.pdf

Friedman, S., & Resnick, P. (2007). Child murder by mothers: Patterns and prevention. *World Psychiatry, 6*(3), 137–141.

Goldman, R. (2008). Why do kids kill? 8 year old's killing spree raises questions about why children murder. *ABC News.* Retrieved February 9, 2009, from http://abcnews. go.com/print?id=6233064

Gurian, A. (2006). Child abuse and neglect: An overview. Retrieved January 5, 2009, from http://www.aboutourkids.org/articles/child_abuse_neglect_overview

Heide, K. (1992, September). Why kids kill parents. Tragedy in the family: When kids murder their parents. *Psychology Today, 25*(5). Retrieved December 15, 2008, from http://www.psychologytoday.com/articles/index.php?term=pto-19920901-000027&print=1

Lockhat, R. I., & Van Niekerk, A. (2000). South African children: A history of adversity, violence, and trauma. *Ethnicity & Health, 5*(3–4), 291–302.

Machel, G. (1996). *Impact of armed conflict on children: Report of the expert of the Secretary-General, Ms. Graca Machel, August 26, 1996, United Nations, General Assembly, 51st session.* Retrieved September 11, 2009, from www.unicef.org/graca/ a51-306_en.pdf

Mahler, M., Pine, F., & Bergman, A. (1975). *The psychological birth of the human infant.* New York: Basic Books.

Marleau, J., Poulin, B., Webanck, T., Roy, R., & LaPorte, L. (1999). Paternal filicide: A study of 10 men. *Canadian Journal of Psychiatry, 54*(5), 679–687.

Milner, L. (1998). *A brief history of infanticide: General historical evidence.* The Society for the Prevention of Infanticide. Retrieved February 9, 2009, from http://www. infanticide.org/history.htm

Norrie, J. (2008). Why Japan's isolated mothers are killing their children. *The Age.* Retrieved February 9, 2009, from http://www.theage.com.au/world/why-japans-isolated-mothers-are-killing-their-children-20081107-5k7s

Papapietro, D. (2005). Commentary: Toward a psychodynamic understanding of filicide—beyond psychosis and into the heart of darkness. *The Journal of the American Academy of Psychiatry and the Law, 33*(4), 505–508.

Peltier, P., Purdue, G., & Shepherd, J. (2001). *Burn injuries in child abuse.* Retrieved January 22, 2009, from http://www.ncjrs.gov/txtfiles/91190.txt

Picard, A. (2008, December 10). Cutting childhood fatalities: Half of 830,000 annual childhood deaths from injury could be avoided, study says. *The Globe and Mail,* p. A8. Retrieved December 14, 2008, from http://www.theglobeandmail.com/life/ cutting-childhood-fatalities/article727722/

Pinheiro, P. (2006). *World report on violence against children.* Retrieved January 20, 2009, from http://www.crin.org/docs/UNVAC_World_Report_on_Violence_against_ Children.pdf

Prevent Child Abuse America. (n.d.). *An approach to preventing child abuse.* Retrieved January 4, 2009, from http://member.preventchildabuse.org/site/DocServer/an_ approach_to_prevention.pdf?docID=121

Resnick, P. J. (1970). Murder of the newborn: A psychiatric review of neonaticide. *American Journal of Psychiatry, 126,* 1414–1420.

Shaken baby syndrome. Retrieved January 5, 2009, from http://aboutshakenbaby.com/ shaken_baby_statistics.htm

Singer, P. (2006). *Children at war.* Berkeley: University of California Press.

Strang, H. (1996). *Children as victims of homicide.* Canberra: Australian Institute of Criminology. No. 53.

UNICEF. (2001). *A league table of child deaths by injury in rich nations.* Innocenti Report Card, no. 2. Retrieved December 10, 2008, from http://www.unicef-irc.org/publications/pdf/repcard2e.pdf

UNICEF. (2008a). *Children and road traffic injury.* Retrieved September 7, 2009, from http://www.who/int/violence_injury_prevention/child/injury/world_report/Road_Traffic-injuries_english.pdf

UNICEF. (2008b). *First world report on child injury prevention.* Retrieved December 12, 2008, from http://www.unicef.org/health/vietnam_46799.html

UNICEF/WHO. (2008). *Have fun, be safe.* Retrieved January 5, 2009, from http://www.unicef.org/publications/index_46790.html

U.S. Advisory Board on Child Abuse and Neglect. (1997). *A nation's shame: Fatal child abuse and neglect in the United States. A report of the U.S. Advisory Board on Child Abuse and Neglect.* Washington, DC: U.S. Department of Health and Human Services.

Vroman, R. (2008, April). The perils of toxic exposure in the pediatric population. *Emergency Medical Services Magazine.* Retrieved January 23, 2009, from http://www.emsresponder.com/publication/article.jsp?pubId=1&id=7433

Westside Middle School massacre. (n.d.). In *Wikipedia, the free encyclopedia.* Retrieved January 19, 2009, from http://en.wikipedia.org/wiki/Jonesboro_massacre

7 Children and Infectious Diseases

CRAIG DEMMER

Throughout history, infectious diseases have been the main cause of death for adults and children. Currently, infectious diseases account for about one-third of all deaths worldwide. Over the past few decades, there has been a reduction in the prevalence of infectious diseases, depending on which part of the world you live in. This reduction has been achieved mainly through improved knowledge of the importance of proper hygiene practices (such as washing hands and safe handling of food), the development of drugs and vaccines, and investments by governments in sanitation and clean water systems (Kent & Yin, 2006).

Infectious diseases are caused by bacteria, viruses, protozoans, or fungi. The infectious agent enters the body via air or bodily fluids (e.g., blood and sweat), food, or drink; it then reproduces and subsequently infects other people. Infectious diseases can be benign, such as the cold, or they can be deadly and incurable (e.g., HIV).

Scanning the table of contents of the March 2009 issue of *Emerging Infectious Diseases* published by the Centers for Disease Control and Prevention (CDC, 2009) provides a startling snapshot of just a few of the emerging threats within humans and animals: avian influenza in Kenya, Hong Kong, and Cambodia; Rocky Mountain Spotted Fever in Brazil; astrovirus MLB1 in Missouri; Crimean-Congo hemorrhagic fever virus in Turkey; and Extended-spectrum β-lactamase (ESBL)—producing Enterobacteriaceae among children in a state orphanage in Mali. Garrett

(1994), in her critically acclaimed book *The Coming Plague*, meticulously documented an array of new viruses such as HIV and Ebola; old viruses that are resurfacing such as hantavirus, yellow fever, and dengue fever; and mutant strains of cholera and methicillin-resistant staphylococcus aureus (MRSA) and *E. coli* 0157:H7 that the world must deal with. In 2008, there was a massive cholera outbreak in Zimbabwe causing several thousand deaths. This grim news is made worse by the lack of preparedness of the global health system to deal effectively with these threats (Garrett, 2000).

BURDEN ON CHILDREN IN DEVELOPING COUNTRIES

For people living in developing countries, infectious diseases are still a major cause of death, and this danger is particularly prevalent for children. According to the World Health Organization (WHO), in 2004 there were approximately 58.8 million deaths globally, and almost one in five deaths was of a child under the age of 5 years (WHO, 2008). Globally, 98% of all child deaths occur in developing countries. Of the 20 countries in the world with the highest child mortality (deaths under 5 years of age), 19 are in Africa, along with Afghanistan (WHO, 2003). Of the 10.4 million deaths among children under 5 years, infectious diseases account for 50% of all child deaths (WHO, 2008).

Although media attention is often focused on diseases such as Ebola, *E. coli*, avian flu, and most recently in the United States, staph infections, they represent a very small portion of the deaths worldwide associated with infectious disease. The two leading infectious-disease killers among children are diarrheal diseases and respiratory infections. A single continent, Africa, bears the heaviest burden of mortality among children associated with infectious diseases. By contrast with other areas of the world, in Africa are found more than 90% of all deaths of children under 5 years of age attributable to malaria, 90% of all under-5 deaths due to HIV/AIDS, 50% of all under-5 deaths due to pneumonia, and 40% of all under-5 deaths due to diarrheal diseases (WHO, 2008).

The situation in the United States is vastly different. In 2002 there were 2.4 million deaths in the United States; 12,000 of these deaths were among children under 15 years of age. Accidents (unintentional injuries) are the leading cause of death among children under 15 years. Despite periodic news flashes alerting us to some new or resurgent infectious disease, the reality is that infectious diseases represent a very small portion of all child deaths in the United States (Anderson & Smith, 2005).

MAIN TYPES OF INFECTIOUS DISEASES CAUSING CHILD DEATHS

Globally, four types of infectious diseases are the main causes of death in children: pneumonia or respiratory illnesses, diarrheal diseases, malaria, and HIV/AIDS.

Pneumonia

Pneumonia is the most common cause of death in children in the world (Ahmed, 2006). Each year close to 2 million children die of pneumonia, with 5,000 children dying each day, and most of these cases are in developing countries (Russell & Mulholland, 2004). Yet despite these numbers, pneumonia has not received the attention it deserves in terms of funding. For instance, there is no UN agency for pneumonia as there is to combat AIDS, tuberculosis, and malaria (Greenwood, Weber, & Mulholland, 2007). There are still huge gaps in our knowledge about the distribution of pneumonia deaths in developing countries, causes of pneumonia, and most effective ways to treat pneumonia in children (Russell & Mulholland). More widespread and more effective immunization campaigns have enormous potential to reduce the incidence of pneumonia in children in developing countries. In Japan, mass vaccination of schoolchildren was implemented in the 1960s and was associated with a decrease in the overall mortality rate resulting from influenza. But when the program was discontinued in 1994, there was an increase in influenza-associated deaths among young children. With the recent increase in influenza vaccinations among young children in Japan, together with the routine therapeutic use of neuraminidase inhibitors, there has again been a decrease in the influenza-associated mortality (Suqaya & Takeuchi, 2005).

We need to better understand the role that poor access to health care, malnutrition, crowding, and pollution play with respect to pneumonia deaths in children (Scott, Abdullah Brooks, Malik Peiris, Holtzman, & Mulholland, 2008). Strategies such as immunization must be coupled with broader strategies to improve socioeconomic development if significant headway is to be made in reducing child mortality from pneumonia in developing countries (Russell & Mulholland, 2004). A study of children admitted to a rural hospital in central Philippines revealed that young age (2–3 months) and malnutrition were significant independent predictors of death (Lupisan et al., 2007). In a similar type of study, the individual case histories of children who had died of pneumonia in rural Uganda were reviewed to investigate why these children did not survive. Of the deaths, one-third occurred at home. The median duration of pneumonia illness was 7 days, and median time taken to seek care outside the home was 2 days. It was concluded that there were incorrect treatments with anti-malarials at home, delays in seeking care, and low-quality hospital care for children with fatal pneumonia (Källander et al., 2008). The following factors were found to contribute to high mortality caused by pneumonia among children under 5 years of age in Kalabo District, Zambia: lack of consistent and standardized case management of pneumonia, reliability of diagnoses of severe pneumonia by rural clinic health staff, low birth weight, and distance and lack of transport to the clinic. Shortage of drugs was not a factor because most clinics in the area were well stocked with essential drugs (Stekelenburg, Kashumba, & Wolffers, 2002).

Diarrhea

The number of global deaths from diarrhea of children less than 5 years of age is estimated at 1.87 million, which represents approximately 19% of all child deaths. Together, African and Southeast Asian countries have 78% (1.46 million) of all diarrhea deaths among children in the developing world (Boschi-Pinto, Velebit, & Shibuya, 2008). Many of these deaths are due to unsafe drinking water. Efforts need to be directed at improving clean water, sanitation, and hygiene standards and reducing the widespread, indiscriminate use of antimicrobial therapies that appear to be driving up resistance (Steiner, Samie, & Guerrant, 2006).

Numerous studies have examined the impact of improvements in water and sanitation facilities on diarrheal disease. Most of them have reported positive effects, including an intervention in Kabul, Afghanistan, that involved the construction of a new latrine or renovation of an existing latrine. The results of this study indicated that the latrine intervention was a cost-effective method for reducing mortality among children due to diarrhea (Meddings, Ronald, Marion, Pinera, & Oppliger, 2004).

There is a need to identify more simple and cheap ways to treat unsafe water in order to reduce the high mortality from diarrhea among children. For instance, a controlled study of Guatemalan households using a new treatment for drinking water (flocculant-disinfectant) resulted in a significant reduction in the prevalence of diarrhea among children under 5 years, especially infants, who are at most risk of dying from diarrhea (Chiller et al., 2006).

Oral hydration therapy to replace loss of body fluids is a major factor in decreasing diarrhea deaths (Victora, Bryce, Fontaine, & Monasch, 2000). A randomized controlled trial of children younger than 2 years in an urban, low-income population in Bangladesh has also shown that weekly zinc supplements to treat diarrhea can potentially reduce mortality (Brooks et al., 2005).

More effort is needed to educate families and health care workers in developing countries to diagnose and treat diarrhea. In rural Mexico a study of child deaths resulting from diarrheal diseases and acute respiratory infections (ARIs) showed that a substantial proportion of caregivers (mothers) with severely ill children did not appear to recognize the severity of the illness or did not seek health services in time. Furthermore, many children who were taken to a doctor did not benefit from the visit. A large proportion of health care providers gave poor-quality care. Late care-seeking and poor case management likely contributed to 68% of these deaths (Bojalil, Kirkwood, Bobak, & Guiscafre, 2007).

Malaria

Every year, there are up to 3 million deaths worldwide associated with malaria. A large proportion of malaria deaths are in sub-Saharan Africa among children under 5 years of age (Ferreira, Zilversmit, & Wunderlich, 2007; Rowe et al., 2007). Malaria is a parasitic infection that is transmitted by anopheline mosquitoes, and *Plasmodium falciparum* is responsible for most of the morbidity and mortality due to malaria worldwide (Olliaro, 2005). Mortality due to malaria in children in Africa continues to rise, and the single most important cause of this increase is probably resistance to the former "miracle drug" chloroquine. In low-income countries, lack of access to care, poor-quality health care treatment, shortages of drugs, and drug resistance make malaria control very difficult (Olliaro).

Malaria is an entirely preventable disease. However, low-cost interventions such as spraying homes with insecticides, installing screen doors and windows to keep mosquitoes out, and using insecticide-treated bed nets are out of reach for most poor people (Sachs, 2005). In a study in Ghana, where malaria is the most common cause of death in children under 5 years, caregivers in villages reported being unable to afford anti-malarial drugs or treated bed nets to protect themselves and their children from mosquitoes. Besides home remedies and visits to local healers, they resorted to buying anti-malarials from local drug vendors without prescription. The inappropriate use of anti-malaria drugs also complicated treatment outcome (Ahorlu, Koram, & Weiss, 2007). These findings have been echoed in many other studies, and an added concern is that many developing countries have inadequate systems for collecting mortality data, so the exact number of children who die of malaria is uncertain (Iley, 2006).

Until a few years ago, little was being done by the international community to combat the millions of children dying of malaria. It was only in 2002 that the Global Fund to Fight AIDS, Tuberculosis and Malaria was established (see http://www.theglobalfund.org/en/). The Global Fund is a worldwide public/private partnership providing three-quarters of all international financing for malaria. There is no doubt that the Global Fund has been effective in reducing the number of cases of malaria in children. By the end of 2008, the Global Fund had distributed 70 million insecticide-treated bed nets (ITNs). ITNs have been shown to reduce malaria morbidity and mortality in children.

In 2000, member states adopted the United Nations Millennium Declaration that committed nations to a new global partnership to reduce extreme poverty and identified eight time-bound goals that have become known as the Millennium Development Goals (see http://www .un.org/millenniumgoals/bkgd.shtml). Each goal has a series of targets to be met by 2015. They include reducing child mortality by two-thirds and halting the spread of HIV/AIDS, malaria, and other diseases. Unfortunately, it is unclear whether the United Nations' Millennium Development Goals of halting malaria and reducing child mortality by two-thirds by 2015 will be met, given that there have been inequities in the use of ITNs across socioeconomic groups. Of particular concern is the difficulty in ensuring widespread access and use of ITNs among the poorest groups who are most affected by malaria (Binka & Akweongo, 2006).

It should be mentioned that malaria-free countries in Western Europe and the United States are not totally immune to malaria. These countries are exposed to increasing numbers of imported cases of malaria, many of them among children. During 1992–2002, there were

more than 17,000 cases of imported malaria in children in 11 industrialized countries, resulting from travel to visit family and friends in high-
risk malaria-endemic areas such as the Comoros Islands and western and
central African countries (Stäger et al., 2009). Increasing global tourist
and migrant travel, combined with growing proportions of life-threatening
P. falciparum malaria, increased drug resistance, and inexperience with
imported malaria by physicians in industrialized countries, can lead to
delays in diagnosis and treatment of children with clinical malaria in traditionally low-risk countries (Stäger et al.).

HIV/AIDS

In 2005, there were an estimated 380,000 AIDS-related deaths in children under 15 years of age, out of a total of 3.1 million HIV/AIDS-related
deaths worldwide. The majority of these deaths were in children living
in sub-Saharan Africa. Although children represent just 6% of all people infected with HIV/AIDS as of December 2005, they accounted for
14% of the AIDS deaths in 2005. The main reasons behind the higher
childhood mortality associated with HIV/AIDS are the aggressive rate
of disease progression in children with immature immune systems and
the absence of appropriate pediatric medical treatment, in the form of
antiretrovirals and cotrimoxazole prophylaxis, to prevent opportunistic
infections (Dionisio et al., 2007).

 According to the World Health Organization (WHO), 2.5% of
all child deaths are due to HIV/AIDS. In Africa, however, about 5% of all
child deaths are due to HIV/AIDS (WHO, 2008). Although relatively
fewer child deaths occur worldwide from AIDS compared to other infectious diseases, in countries such as Botswana and Zimbabwe, AIDS
causes more than half of child deaths (Black, Morris, & Bryce, 2003).
The amount of attention and, in particular, the proportion of funds allocated to HIV/AIDS has aroused criticism about the level of effort directed at preventing a comparatively small proportion of child deaths
due to AIDS with expensive and complex medical treatments, at the
expense of saving millions of more children each year who succumb to
other diseases (Jones, Steketee, Black, Bhutta, & Morris, 2003).

 Much progress has been made in recent years to reduce child deaths
from AIDS by providing access to antiretroviral therapies in low- and
middle-income countries, but this increased access to treatment has
been counterbalanced by lack of access for many others, and a dispro-
portionate number of children are still not receiving treatment compared

to adults with HIV/AIDS (Dionisio et al., 2007). There are still many children in sub-Saharan Africa, which is most affected by HIV/AIDS, who do not have access to this lifesaving treatment. By mid-2000 in low- and middle-income countries, less than 5% of HIV-positive children in need of treatment received it ("The Devastating Effects of HIV/AIDS on Children," 2006).

There have been few studies of children with AIDS in palliative care settings (Lavy, 2007). One study revealed alarming inadequacies in the provision of terminal care to children with AIDS. At a large hospital in Cape Town, South Africa, more than one-half of the children experienced pain and distress in their last 48 hours that was not treated, under-treated, or treated too late. There were also significant problems with medical providers adhering to documented comfort care plans that focused on comfort and pain relief rather than providing lifesaving medical treatment (Henley, 2002). A study of children receiving palliative care in Malawi indicated that children with HIV/AIDS presented with a larger variety of symptoms (e.g., weight loss, cough, fever, sores in the mouth, poor appetite, and diarrhea) than those with cancer or other diagnoses, reflecting the multi-organ nature of advanced HIV (Lavy). Children dying of HIV/AIDS are likely to have the additional stress of a mother who died of AIDS or a mother who is sick, unlike the other infectious diseases mentioned in this chapter (Lavy). Also, children who are HIV-positive, either through mother-to-child transmission or following sexual abuse, are often not told what could happen to them and may be frightened when they experience symptoms ("The Devastating Effects," 2006). A study of HIV-infected children in Romania indicated that knowledge of one's own HIV infection status is associated with a delay in the progression of the disease. Children who know their status are likely to be more closely monitored and to receive better medical care (Ferris et al., 2007).

In terms of research on the psychological impact of child deaths due to AIDS, like the other infectious diseases mentioned, little is known. Despite the amount of attention AIDS has received worldwide, there has been hardly any research to date on the bereavement experiences of parents who have lost a child to AIDS or on children who have lost siblings to this disease. Most of the research (and there is not much) has focused on the experiences of children who have lost one or both parents to AIDS (Cluver & Gardner, 2007; see also chapter 17 in this book). It should not, therefore, be surprising that there is even less research on interventions to help families cope with the loss of a child to AIDS.

So far, there have been no documented studies of bereavement interventions for children who have lost a sibling to AIDS or for parents who have lost a child to AIDS.

LACK OF RESEARCH ON BEREAVEMENT ASSOCIATED WITH INFECTIOUS DISEASE DEATHS IN CHILDREN

There is a paucity of bereavement research with children (Bonanno & Mancini, 2008). The research that has been conducted is based mostly in the Western context and deals primarily with deaths from cancer, birth defects, and to a lesser extent, homicides and accidents (or unintentional injury). On a broader level, we know little about the bereavement experiences of people in developing countries who have experienced the loss of a child from *any* cause. Not surprisingly, research on bereavement associated with child deaths due to infectious diseases is almost impossible to locate.

Although bereavement interventions with children are relatively commonplace in the West, there are very few studies of these interventions. A recent systematic review of 13 bereavement interventions with children concluded that they had limited overall psychotherapeutic effectiveness and that current methods are inadequate for assessing children at high risk, for identifying who would most benefit from professional help, and what types of assistance—professional or otherwise—would be most appropriate (Currier, Holland, & Neimeyer, 2007).

The majority of bereavement research in general has centered on psychological processes and individual pathology. Insufficient attention has been given to resilience and exploring alternate ways of promoting adaptation to grief among community members beyond individual counseling and support groups (Bonanno & Mancini, 2008). Duplicating Western bereavement interventions in contexts in developing countries that are vastly different in so many ways is not an option. In fact, I would urge caution in even *adapting* interventions to these contexts. A better approach in my opinion is to start fresh by asking researchers and practitioners (indigenous and foreign) in these local contexts to establish an agenda for research and practice relating to experiences surrounding child deaths from infectious diseases (and other causes) that identifies ways to promote resilience and adaptation in extremely difficult environments. Strategies and interventions could subsequently be developed that are responsive to whatever the needs are within these communities, while also being mindful of the limited availability of resources. I challenge bereavement researchers from all disciplines, from high-income as well as low-income countries, to work together on this endeavor. We have a unique opportunity to demonstrate the value of interdisciplinary research in promoting a more holistic and relevant understanding of bereavement related to the loss of a child from infectious disease (and other causes) in resource-limited settings. We can work together to develop informal or formal strategies and interventions that are truly needed by the communities, that are compatible with the local context, and that are effective.

It would be inappropriate for me to offer clinical guidelines or even suggestions on how to help families as well as children cope with the death of a child from an infectious disease in developing countries, based on the little amount of information we have. But I would like to suggest Bronfenbrenner's (1979) social ecology model as a potentially useful theoretical framework for understanding and addressing bereavement for this type of death and in these contexts. The social ecology model focuses on the person, the environment, and the interaction between the two. According to this model, four major factors could influence the well-being of the individual bereaved by a child's death from an infectious disease in resource-poor countries:

- *Person factors,* which include the biological, personality, and intellectual characteristics of the individual.
- *Process factors,* which include the types of interaction that occur among individuals.
- *Contextual factors,* which include families, communities, cultures, and so forth.
- *Time variables,* meaning the changes that occur over time with regard to person, process, and context variables.

The way in which a bereaved individual is influenced by these factors is dependent on the way these factors interact with each other. Contextual factors in developing countries are likely to be extremely important in determining the bereavement experience of individuals who have lost a child to an infectious disease, whether it is pneumonia, malaria, diarrheal diseases, or HIV/AIDS. Bronfenbrenner (1979) postulated that "the ecological environment is conceived as a set of nested structures, each inside the next, like a set of Russian dolls" (p. 3). If the loss of a child from an infectious disease is viewed as the central focus of influence on the bereaved individual's life, the mesosystem, exosystem, macrosystem, and chronosystem can be viewed as concentric circles surrounding the loss. A microsystem involves the behaviors and interactions of the bereaved individual in his or her immediate environment (e.g., home). A mesosystem involves interrelationships between the bereaved individual and other settings such as the extended family, neighbors, friends, the community, and religious institutions (e.g., church, mosque, synagogue). The exosystem includes those settings that influence bereavement but do not play an active role. Examples are the health and social welfare system. The macrosystem involves traditional and cultural beliefs about death, mourning, and how to grieve. It also includes political and economic policies of the government regarding certain infectious diseases among children and the care and support of people affected by these types of deaths. Finally, the chronosystem includes political, cultural, and social changes as well as medical advances relating to infectious diseases over time that may influence the bereavement experience.

Stokols (1992) described several core assumptions underlying the social ecological perspective that I believe can be applied to the study of bereavement associated with child deaths from infectious diseases in developing countries. First, the well-being of the bereaved individual is influenced by various factors in the physical environment (e.g., geography, technology) and social environment (e.g., culture, economics, politics). In addition, the well-being of the individual is influenced by a variety of personal attributes (e.g., behavioral patterns, psychological predispositions). Thus, bereavement associated with deaths from infectious diseases should explore the dynamic interplay among diverse environmental factors (e.g., poverty, stigma, lack of services, government response) and personal factors (coping capacity, history of loss, relationship to the deceased), rather than focusing only on environmental or personal factors.

Second, a study of bereavement in this area should address the multidimensional and complex nature of human environments. Environments can be described in terms of their physical and social components as well as their actual or perceived qualities and their scale of immediacy to individuals. Studies need to examine factors in the bereaved individual's home, village, and community that influence his or her bereavement (e.g., lack of privacy, friendship network, relationship with spouse/family members as well as others in the community, perceptions of the availability of support in the community).

Third, the social ecological perspective incorporates multiple levels of analysis (e.g., individuals, small groups, organizations) and diverse methodologies (e.g., medical exams, questionnaires, behavioral observations, epidemiological analyses) for assessing the well-being of individuals and groups who are grieving child deaths from infectious diseases. Studies need to explore the influence of factors in groups and communities (e.g., attitudes toward these types of deaths in children among community members) as well as formal structures such as nonprofit and governmental organizations (e.g., access to support services, outreach, welfare policies) on bereavement.

Fourth, the social ecological perspective incorporates a variety of concepts from systems theory (e.g., interdependence, homeostasis, negative feedback) to understand the dynamic interrelations between people and their environments. Thus, people–environment transactions are characterized by cycles of mutual influence, whereby the physical and social features of settings directly influence individuals' well-being and bereavement, and individuals in these settings modify the healthfulness and supportiveness of their surroundings through their individual and collective actions. Strategies should be proposed to address bereavement at various levels (e.g., individual, community, government) and through various means.

I wish to reiterate the importance of contextual factors in trying to understand bereavement resulting from the death of a child from an infectious disease in developing countries. There is consensus in the bereavement literature that the context plays an important role in influencing the bereaved individual's response to loss (Stroebe & Schut, 1999). In reality, there have been relatively few empirical studies exploring the interaction of contextual factors on bereavement. Cultural factors have not been adequately understood, particularly in relation to complicated grief. We need more systematic, scientific studies of different patterns of reactions to loss across cultures (Stroebe, Hansson, & Stroebe, 1993). This call for more careful attention to the cultural aspects of reactions to loss includes infectious disease deaths in children in both high-income and low-income countries. Bereavement interventions will be effective only if they incorporate the influence of culture on grieving and the bereaved individual's cultural understanding of death. We need to consider how political and economic interests influence the individual's bereavement experience. Furthermore, we need to pay more attention to involving those who have little voice in the formulation of bereavement models and the development of strategies to promote healing (Klass, 1999).

CONCLUSION

Most child deaths due to infectious diseases are preventable and occur in poor countries. A common misperception is that the primary causes of death among children around the world are HIV/AIDS and malnutrition. Malnutrition is an underlying cause of 53% of child deaths because it renders children vulnerable to disease, and HIV/AIDS—though a serious problem—is not the worst threat facing children in developing countries. Pneumonia and diarrhea are the leading causes of child deaths in the world (Black et al., 2003). Experts agree that the interventions needed to achieve the Millennium Development Goal of reducing child mortality by two-thirds by 2015 are available, but that they are not being as effectively and as widely delivered as they need to be (Jones et al., 2003). They need to be greatly improved and scaled up (Bryce et al., 2003). We also need to reduce malnutrition in children and address the root causes of poverty, lack of education, and sex inequality (Edejer et al., 2006). It is estimated that in order to meet the Millennium Development Goal of reducing child mortality by two-thirds by 2015, an additional $52.4 billion will be required between 2006 and 2015 (Stenberg, Johns, Scherpbier, & Tan-Torres Edejer, 2007). With the worsening global economic situation, it is hard to feel confident at this point that we will be able to achieve this goal.

From a public health perspective, for too long we have turned a blind eye to the suffering and needless deaths of children in developing countries of the world. The priority must be to immediately find ways to provide financing and other support to reduce child deaths from infectious diseases and other causes in poor countries. But on another level, for those of us who work in the bereavement field, the question needs to be asked, "Where have we been?" Why has there been so little published on bereavement relating to infectious diseases in children, and on a more general level, why have child deaths in developing countries received so little of our scholarly attention? Although reports reveal that bereavement interventions and services are widely available yet underutilized in the United States and the West (Cherlin et al., 2007; Steiner, 2006), we have the opposite situation in developing countries where mental health services and bereavement support services are few and far between, and we have little knowledge of how much interest there is for these types of services if and when they are offered. Granted, factors such as securing funding for this type of research, access to research participants, cultural issues, and ethical challenges make this undertaking daunting, but this does not let us off the hook. We need to marshal our resources and work together globally to acknowledge, understand, and address the situation of these children as well as their survivors. The challenge now awaits us.

REFERENCES

Ahmed, K. (2006). Pneumonia and child mortality. *Lancet, 368*(9548), 1646–1647.

Ahorlu, C. K., Koram, K. A., & Weiss, M. G. (2007). Children, pregnant women and the culture of malaria in two rural communities of Ghana. *Anthropology & Medicine, 14*(2), 167–181.

Anderson, R. N., & Smith, B. L. (2005). Deaths: Leading causes for 2002. *National Vital Statistics Reports, 53*(17). Hyattsville, MD: National Center for Health Statistics.

Binka, F., & Akweongo, P. (2006). Prevention of malaria using ITNs: Potential for achieving the Millennium Development Goals. *Current Molecular Medicine, 6*(2), 261–267.

Black, R. E., Morris, S. S., & Bryce, J. (2003). Where and why are 10 million children dying every year? *Lancet, 361*(9376), 2226.

Bojalil, R., Kirkwood, B. R., Bobak, M., & Guiscafre, H. (2007). The relative contribution of case management and inadequate care-seeking behaviour to childhood deaths from diarrhoea and acute respiratory infections in Hidalgo, Mexico. *Tropical Medicine & International Health, 12*(12), 1545–1552.

Bonanno, G. A., & Mancini, A. D. (2008). The human capacity to thrive in the face of potential trauma. *Pediatrics, 121*(2), 369–375.

Boschi-Pinto, C., Velebit, L., & Shibuya, K. (2008). Estimating child mortality due to diarrhoea in developing countries. *Bulletin of the World Health Organization, 86*(9), 710-B.

Bronfenbrenner, U. (1979). *The ecology of human development: Experiments by nature and design.* Cambridge, MA: Harvard University Press.

Brooks, W. A., Santosham, M., Naheed, A., Goswami, D., Wahed, M. A., Diener-West, M., et al. (2005). Effect of weekly zinc supplements on incidence of pneumonia and diarrhoea in children younger than 2 years in an urban, low-income population in Bangladesh: Randomised controlled trial. *Lancet, 366*(9490), 999–1004.

Bryce J., el Arifeen, S., Pariyo, G., Lanata, C. F., Gwatkin, D., Habicht, J-P. (2003). The multi-country evaluation of IMCI study group. *Lancet, 362,*159–164.

Centers for Disease Control and Prevention (CDC). (2009, March). *Emerging Infectious Diseases, 15*(3). Atlanta, GA: Author.

Cherlin, E. J., Barry, C. L., Prigerson, H. G., Schulman-Green, D., Johnson-Hurzeler, R., Kasl, S. V., & Bradley, E. H. (2007). Bereavement services for family caregivers: How often used, why, and why not. *Journal of Palliative Medicine, 10*(1), 148–158.

Chiller, T. M., Mendoza, C. E., Lopez, M. B., Alvarez, M., Hoekstra, R. M., Keswick, B. H., et al. (2006). Reducing diarrhoea in Guatemalan children: Randomized controlled trial of flocculant-disinfectant for drinking-water. *Bulletin of the World Health Organization, 84*(1), 28–35.

Cluver, L., & Gardner, F. (2007). The mental health of children orphaned by AIDS: A review of international and Southern African research. *Journal of Child and Adolescent Mental Health, 19*(1), 1–17.

Currier, J. M., Holland, J. M., & Neimeyer, R. A. (2007). The effectiveness of bereavement interventions with children: A meta-analytic review of controlled outcome research. *Journal of Clinical Child and Adolescent Psychology, 36*(2), 253–259.

The devastating effects of HIV/AIDS on children. (2006). *Lancet, 368*(9534), 424.

Dionisio, D., Gass, R., McDermott, P., Racalbuto, V., Madeo, M., Braghieri, G., et al. (2007). What strategies to boost production of affordable fixed-dose anti-retroviral drug combinations for children in the developing world? *Current HIV Research, 5*(2), 155–187.

Edejer, T. T., Aikins, M., Black, R., Wolfson, L., Hutubessy, R., Evans, D. B. et al. (2006). Cost effectiveness analysis of strategies for child health in developing countries. *British Medical Journal, 331*(7526), 1177–1180.

Ferreira, M. U., Zilversmit, M., & Wunderlich, G. (2007). Origins and evolution of antigenic diversity in malaria parasites. *Current Molecular Medicine, 7*(6), 588–602.

Ferris, M., Burau, K., Schweitzer, A. M., Mihale, S., Murray, N., Preda, A., et al. (2007). The influence of disclosure of HIV diagnosis on time to disease progression in a cohort of Romanian children and teens. *AIDS Care, 19*(9), 1088–1094.

Garrett, L. (1994). *The coming plague.* New York: Farrar, Straus and Giroux.

Garrett, L. (2000). *The betrayal of trust.* New York: Hyperion.

Greenwood, B. M., Weber, M. W., & Mulholland, K. (2007). Childhood pneumonia—preventing the world's biggest killer of children. *Bulletin of the World Health Organization, 85*(7), 502–503.

Henley, L. D. (2002). End of life care in HIV-infected children who died in hospital. *Developing World Bioethics, 2*(1), 38–54.

Iley, K. (2006). Malaria deaths are the hardest to count. *Bulletin of the World Health Organization, 84*(3), 165–166.

Jones, G., Steketee, R. W., Black, R. E., Bhutta, Z. A., & Morris, S. S. (2003). How many child deaths can we prevent this year? *Lancet, 362*(9377), 65.

Källander, K., Hildenwall, H., Waiswa, P., Galiwango, E., Petersona, S., & Pariyob, G. (2008). Delayed care seeking for fatal pneumonia in children aged under five years in Uganda: A case-series study. *Bulletin of the World Health Organization, 86*(5), 332–338.

Kent, M. M., & Yin, S. (2006). Controlling infectious diseases. *Population Bulletin, 61*(2), 1–24.

Klass, D. (1999). Developing a cross-cultural model of grief: The state of the field. *Omega, Journal of Death and Dying, 39*(3), 153–178.

Lavy, V. (2007). Presenting symptoms and signs in children referred for palliative care in Malawi. *Palliative Medicine, 21*(4), 333–339.

Lupisan, S. P., Ruutu, P., Abucejo-Ladesma, P. E., Quiambao, B. P., Gozum, L., Sombrero, L. T., et al. (2007). Predictors of death from severe pneumonia among children 2–59 months old hospitalized in Bohol, Philippines: Implications for referral criteria at a first-level health facility. *Tropical Medicine & International Health, 12*(8), 962–971.

Meddings, D. R., Ronald, L. A., Marion, S., Pinera, J. F., & Oppliger, A. (2004). Cost effectiveness of a latrine revision programme in Kabul, Afghanistan. *Bulletin of the World Health Organization, 82*(4), 281–289.

Olliaro, P. (2005). Drug resistance hampers our capacity to roll back malaria. *Clinical Infectious Diseases, 41*, S247–S257.

Rowe, A. K., Steketee, R. W., Arnold, F., Wardlaw, T., Basu, S., Bakyaita, N., et al. (2007). Viewpoint: Evaluating the impact of malaria control efforts on mortality in sub-Saharan Africa. *Tropical Medicine & International Health, 12*(12), 1524–1539.

Russell, F., & Mulholland, E. K. (2004). Recent advances in pneumococcal vaccination of children. *Annals of Tropical Paediatrics, 24*(4), 283–294.

Sachs, J. S. (2005). *The end of poverty.* New York: Penguin Books.

Scott, J. A. G., Abdullah Brooks, W., Malik Peiris, J., Holtzman, D., & Mulholland, E. K. (2008). Pneumonia research to reduce childhood mortality in the developing world. *Journal of Clinical Investigation, 118*(4), 1291–1300.

Stäger, K., Legros, F., Krause, G., Low, N., Bradley, D., Desai, M., et al. (2009). Imported malaria in children in industrialized countries, 1992–2002. *Emerging Infectious Diseases, 15*(2), 185–191.

Steiner, C. S. (2006). Grief support groups used by few: Are bereavement needs being met? *Journal of Social Work in End-of-Life and Palliative Care, 2*(1), 29–53.

Steiner, T. S., Samie, A., & Guerrant, R. L. (2006). Infectious diarrhea: New pathogens and new challenges in developed and developing areas. *Clinical Infectious Diseases, 43*(4), 408–410.

Stekelenburg, J., Kashumba, E., & Wolffers, I. (2002). Factors contributing to high mortality due to pneumonia among under-fives in Kalabo District, Zambia. *Tropical Medicine & International Health, 7*(10), 886–893.

Stenberg, K., Johns, B., Scherpbier, R. W., & Tan-Torres Edejer, T. (2007). A financial road map to scaling up essential child health interventions in 75 countries. *Bulletin of the World Health Organization, 85*(4), 305-B.

Stokols, D. (1992). Establishing and maintaining healthy environments toward a social ecology of health promotion. *American Psychologist, 47*(1), 6–22.

Stroebe, M., & Schut, H. (1999). The dual process model of coping with bereavement: Rationale and description. *Death Studies, 23*(3), 197–225.

Stroebe, M. S., Hansson, R. O., & Stroebe, W. (1993). Contemporary themes and controversies in bereavement research. In M. S. Stroebe, W. Stroebe, & R. O. Hansson (Eds.), *Handbook of bereavement: Theory, research, and intervention* (pp. 457–475). Cambridge, England: Cambridge University Press.

Suqaya, N., & Takeuchi, Y. (2005). Mass vaccination of schoolchildren against influenza and its impact on the influenza-associated mortality rate among children in Japan. *Clinical Infectious Diseases, 41*(7), 939–947.

Victora, C. G., Bryce, J., Fontaine, O., & Monasch, R. (2000). Reducing deaths from diarrhea through oral rehydration therapy. *Bulletin of World Health Organization, 78*, 1246–1255.

World Health Organization (WHO). (2003). *The world health report 2003: Shaping the future.* Switzerland: World Health Organization.

World Health Organization (WHO). (2008). *The global burden of disease: 2004 update.* Switzerland: World Health Organization.

Children Living With Life-Threatening or Life-Limiting Illnesses: A Dispatch From the Front Lines

8

MICHAEL M. STEVENS, RHONDDA J. RYTMEISTER,
MARIE-THÉRÈSE PROCTOR, AND PATRICIA BOLSTER

We work as members of a multidisciplinary team of health care professionals caring for infants, children, and young people with life-threatening forms of cancer, including leukemias, cerebral tumors, and solid tumors. Our department, the Oncology Unit at The Children's Hospital at Westmead in Sydney, Australia, was established in 1975. Over the ensuing 35 years, more than 3,600 young patients have attended for care, of whom more than 2,600 have survived. Some of these survivors are now in their fourth or even fifth decade. Over the same period, 997 other patients have died, in most cases from progression of their underlying disease, in spite of our attempts at curative therapy. Some of these deaths have occurred within weeks or even days of diagnosis, others many years after diagnosis and completion of therapy.

Two of us (MS, RR) have worked continuously in our department for 35 and 20 years, respectively. In addition to these clinical responsibilities, two of us (MS, M-TP), along with three other health care professionals, recently conducted a qualitative study in which 91 members of 29 families caring for one or more children with life-limiting illnesses were interviewed about their experiences of day-to-day life and about their encounters with the health care system and health care professionals.

We define *life-threatening illnesses* (as in the case of all of our Oncology Unit patients) to be illnesses that are potentially curable, but that will

147

prove fatal if treatment fails or if fatal complications of treatment occur, and *life-limiting illnesses* (as encountered in our life-limiting families research) as serious illnesses of childhood of a progressive and ultimately life-threatening nature, for which curative therapy is not yet available, and for which there is an expectation by the health care team that the patient will not survive past early adulthood.

There is general acceptance now of information about awareness of death in both well and ill children that is no longer controversial and that informs current practice. Emerging awareness of death in well children is described in chapter 2 in this book. In this chapter, we describe awareness of death in seriously ill and dying children.

We believe there may be considerable value in experiences gained "at the front lines," and we will draw on these experiences to provide information gained while caring for our patients and their families, while drawing also from interviews of members of families with children with life-limiting illnesses. We hope this information may serve as corroboration and authentication of readers' own observations and experiences.

We consider many of the psychosocial and spiritual issues discussed here to be central issues that arise for children when they are living with life-threatening or life-limiting illnesses, issues that are important for their family members and care providers as well. We hope that the advice we provide toward the end of each section will be considered in good faith and will assist others in their care of seriously ill children and their families and that some of our observations and comments may suggest directions for new research.

THE WALKING WOUNDED: FAMILIES OF SERIOUSLY ILL CHILDREN

Much of our working time is dedicated to communicating with the families of the patients for whom we are responsible, particularly parents, and the young patients themselves. This triangular arrangement (child, parent, health care professional) confers on pediatric medicine its distinctive feel and its appeal to those who work with sick children and their families. Parents, siblings, grandparents, and the extended family are all caught up in the unfolding drama of the onset of a serious illness in one of their children.

Effective Communication With Parents as a Foundation for Successful Care

Much of the time we are informing, supporting, and encouraging parents who, as a result, feel more confident about informing, supporting, and encouraging their sick child. The quality of the family's experience in the first few weeks after diagnosis, which in life-threatening illnesses is usually the earliest phase of the child's illness, is particularly important in determining the family's adjustment to their new circumstances.

On receiving the diagnosis, parents always assume the worst: that their child will certainly die, and soon. One goal of the initial consultations with the child's pediatrician and other members of the care team is to readjust the parents' expectations to a more hopeful level, in keeping with the child's actual outlook. Effective communication with the child's parents in the days after diagnosis also lays the foundation for successful palliative care later, should that become necessary (see chapter 21 in this book). When information, friendly encouragement, practical support, and hope have been made freely available to the family by the treatment team, parents will be more likely to cope successfully with later challenges, including the possible death of their child, than when they are left feeling uninformed, misunderstood, and unsupported.

Parents will usually be stunned and disbelieving at the outset, and there will be an initial period of shock, confusion, and numbness. Parents will describe a feeling of being overwhelmed by the situation or of feeling unable to function. There may be doubt about or denial of the diagnosis, or intellectual acceptance without any emotional release.

As initial shock declines, a progressive testing of reality occurs, usually accompanied by feelings of anger, guilt, sadness, and depression. There is often guilt over a perceived delay in diagnosis and a sentiment that the illness might not have occurred had attention been sought earlier. There is a similarity between these early reactions at diagnosis and those experienced in the early phases of bereavement.

Pointers to Good Communication Early in Therapy

- Ensure that both parents are present for the initial consultation, thereby acknowledging the importance of both parents and lowering the possibility of one partner misinterpreting or filtering information.

With single-parent families, encourage the parent to allow another trusted person to sit in on the consultation with him or her.

■ Use a quiet comfortable room, with everyone seated.

■ During important discussions, permit parents to include a close friend or relative, who may recall information that parents forget.

■ Have one or two other members of the caregiving team present, to help identify areas for discussion.

■ Give parents a clear description of their child's illness; identify the illness as cancer; avoid medical terminology and use plain English. Provide the full name of the disease in writing.

■ Emphasize that the parents did not cause the disease and could not have prevented it, that the diagnosis has been made promptly, and that effective therapy is available that has cured patients similar to their child.

■ Seek feedback about what parents have understood from each consultation, avoid creating a perception of being rushed, and permit parents adequate time for questions.

■ Parents will be shocked and even disbelieving and then guilty, depressed, and occasionally angry. These reactions are expected, but limit parents' ability to absorb and retain information. Repeat information patiently over several consultations. At the outset, avoid overly technical information that parents may misunderstand or forget.

■ In the longer term, always allow parents hope, no matter how poor the outlook. Support the family in their current hope and help them maintain a realistic outlook on what their child can still do.

Considerable research has been conducted on how to break bad news, and useful information on this topic to guide health care professionals is available (Buckman, 1992). A helpful protocol by Buckman (paraphrased for a pediatric setting) includes six steps: (1) getting started, (2) finding out how much the patient or parents know, (3) finding out how much the patient or parents want to know, (4) sharing the information (aligning and educating), (5) responding to the patient's or parents' feelings, and (6) planning and follow-through.

Effective communication with parents in the circumstances of a patient's diagnosis, or at the time of a recurrence of a previously controlled disease, is always difficult and may fail even in skilled hands. One of us (MS), along with another pediatrician training in pediatric oncology, was called to the orthopedic ward to see a 10-year-old boy who was being investigated for suspected osteomyelitis and who had been found to have multiple lesions in a bone scan and an abnormal blood film, suggestive of leukemia. "And what section of the hospital are you from?" inquired the parents, who were sitting on either side of the boy's bed. Evidently our orthopedic colleagues had not mentioned the possibility of cancer, saying that they were consulting some colleagues from another part of the hospital to help with the diagnosis. "We work in the cancer unit," I replied, deciding that honesty would be the best policy, going on to explain that a bone marrow aspirate was required because of concerns that the boy may have leukemia. This information understandably upset the parents and patient, despite the fact that it would not have been possible to conceal our subspecialty, nor the purpose of the bone marrow aspirate.

Soon afterward, we met the parents without the patient, in a quiet interview room, adhering to all the principles of effective communication. Both parents became distressed when the diagnosis of leukemia was confirmed. The expectation of a favorable prognosis was emphasized appropriately. Provision of any additional information was then curtailed, and instead, we sat in silence with the parents, seeking to share their shock and distress. On the next day, information came back from the laboratory that the patient's leukemia was a rare but particularly adverse subtype that had a much poorer prognosis and that would require a bone marrow transplant in first remission. This possibility had been mentioned in passing in the initial interview, with emphasis that it was most unlikely.

When the parents were invited to return to the same interview room for further discussion, the mother became agitated and distressed, saying she did not want to hear any more bad news. As the parents sat down in the room, she became even more agitated, and her husband actually struck her on the back in an attempt to calm her down. The discussion ended abruptly as soon as the information about subtype and poorer outlook was conveyed. Soon afterward, the mother requested a second opinion at another hospital and subsequently requested that another physician in the author's department take over the supervision of their son's treatment. (Happily, this young man remains well and is in his fourth year of follow-up after completing treatment.)

Siblings of Seriously Ill Children

In the absence of a known cause, siblings of pediatric cancer patients may have their own private version of the causation of the patient's illness. There may be misconceptions about the nature of the illness because of lack of a visible focus of disease. There may be misconceptions about the treatment program and about what happens when the patient visits the hospital. There may be a fear about developing the same illness. There may be guilt and shame coupled with relief for *not* having developed the illness, ambivalent feelings about the patient (envy, resentment over the family's preoccupation with the patient, embarrassment and shame occasioned by having a disfigured or bald brother or sister), and compromised academic and social functioning because of preoccupation with the stress of illness. These emotions may lead the sibling to exhibit irritability, social or emotional withdrawal, academic underachievement, and acting-out behavior.

Siblings should be given a clear and unambiguous description of their ill brother or sister's medical condition, emphasizing that although the cause is not known, nothing the sibling or any other family member has thought, said, done, or failed to do has caused the illness. Siblings need encouragement to dispense with any erroneous concepts about the cause of the illness and reassurance they are not going to get the illness. Siblings benefit by being allowed to visit the hospital, meet staff, and witness the patient's treatment program and by being given opportunities to ventilate any feelings of resentment toward parents or the patient. Meetings with other well siblings facilitated by staff can be helpful.

Parents may assist the siblings of the ill child by treating the children equally, taking into account the special needs of each, keeping in contact with the siblings during the ill child's admissions to hospital, spending some one-on-one time with each sibling, and permitting the siblings to live their lives as normally as possible.

There may be issues of concern to siblings that parents can discern by "reading between the lines" of siblings' questions. For example, one of our patients, a 12-year-old boy seriously ill with recurrent adrenal carcinoma, was receiving chemotherapy to try to prevent further recurrence. His mother complained that his 15-year-old sister was dwelling on issues that the mother deemed unimportant. "She asked me," the mother said, "have I bought his school uniform for next year?" Our suggestion that the sister was really asking, "Will my brother be alive next year?" changed the mother's perception of her daughter.

If the patient's condition eventually deteriorates, and his or her death is drawing near, siblings should be provided with an opportunity to say goodbye. Siblings should be allowed to view the patient's body after death and attend the patient's funeral if they wish to, but not forced to do so if they do not. They need the freedom to participate to the degree they feel comfortable and to express grief in their own way. Siblings commonly grieve in spurts and then go out to play. They may revisit their grief as they grow older, understanding death with a more mature perspective.

The Grandparents and Extended Family

The ill child's grandparents, relatives, family friends, and school will all be deeply disturbed by news of the diagnosis. Grandparents feel doubly concerned—about their son or daughter and their child's partner, as well as their sick grandchild. Some grandparents worry about a genetic vulnerability or flaw that may have been passed on to their grandchild to cause the illness. Others worry that it might have been something they did that caused it, for example, the head lice shampoo that was used to wash the child's hair. With the parents' approval, grandparents benefit considerably from a consultation with the child's physician soon after diagnosis. This consultation allows any misconceptions or irrational guilt to be dispelled. Grandparents may subsequently become closely involved in the day-to-day care of their grandchild and thus provide practical assistance to the parents. Grandparents who cope well during the child's illness will also cope more successfully with bereavement after the child's death.

Extended family members worry about and grieve for all the members of the family. They seek information about the ill child's condition, about how they can best support the child and family, and about measures available to help them cope.

AWARENESS OF DEATH IN WELL CHILDREN

The development of children's concept of death is influenced by a number of variables, including age and, of particular importance when considering children with life-threatening illnesses, health status. Most children understand universality, irreversibility, nonfunctionality, and causality by 7 years of age. Helpful advice about children's emerging awareness of death has been provided by Corr (2008; see also chapter 2 in this book).

AWARENESS OF DEATH IN SERIOUSLY ILL
AND DYING CHILDREN

Up until the 1970s, it was thought widely that, irrespective of their health status, children under the age of 10 could not conceptualize death and so did not experience anxiety about the prospect of their own death. In the late 1960s and early 1970s, observations by several investigators (Binger et al., 1969; Solnit & Green, 1963; Vernick & Karon, 1965), a definitive study by Waechter (1971), and research by Bluebond-Langner (1978) showed conclusively that gravely ill children much younger than 10 were indeed aware they were dying, in spite of well-intentioned efforts by their families and caregivers to shield them from this information, and that such children frequently experienced loneliness, anxiety, and fear as a consequence.

In a key article published in mid-1971, prepared from research conducted for her doctoral dissertation on anxiety about death in terminally ill children, Waechter reported on 64 children between ages 6 and 10, divided into four equally sized groups: those with a fatal disorder, those with a chronic non-fatal disease, those with a brief illness, and a group of well elementary school children who were not hospitalized (Waechter, 1971). A general anxiety scale for children measuring concerns in many areas of living was administered to each child. A set of pictures depicting ill hospitalized children and their families and caregivers was also shown individually to each child, and stories were requested in order to elicit fantasy expression of the child's concerns regarding present and future body integrity and functioning. Parents of children in the first three groups were interviewed to assess how the quality and quantity of their children's concerns about death were influenced by their previous experience with death, the religious devoutness within the family, the quality of maternal warmth toward them, and the opportunity the children had had to discuss their concerns or the nature of their illness with their parents, caregivers, or other meaningful adults.

Although only 2 of the 16 fatally ill children had been informed of their prognosis, generalized anxiety was high in all 16 cases, almost double that of the two comparison groups of hospitalized children and three times that of the well children. In their fantasy stories, the children threatened with death discussed loneliness, separation, and death much more frequently. Waechter's most striking finding was the

dichotomy between the children's degree of awareness of their prognosis, as inferred from their imaginative stories, and the parents' beliefs
about their child's awareness. Only 2 of the 16 fatally ill children had
discussed their concerns about death with their parents, yet 63% of
stories told by these 16 children related to death. The children often
gave the characters in the stories their own diagnoses and symptoms;
they frequently depicted death in their drawings, and occasionally they
would express awareness of their prognoses to persons outside their
immediate family.

In the early 1970s, Bluebond-Langner, an anthropologist, confirmed
Waechter's findings by conducting detailed long-term observations of
and conversations with children with leukemia, other severe hemato-
logic disorders, or cystic fibrosis; their parents; and many of the health
care professionals caring for them. She conducted the research over a
9-month period in the department of pediatrics of a large Midwestern
teaching hospital in the United States (Bluebond-Langner, 1978).

Although parents and staff provided little or no information to the
child about any aspect of the illness, in the hope of lessening the child's
anxiety, it was shown that over time children acquired information about
their disease and that particular experiences during the progression of
the illness prompted the ill child to revise his or her concept of the illness and of self. This awareness commenced with early information that
"it was a serious illness"—"I was previously well but am now seriously
ill." With progressive relapses, it was revised to a concept of the disease
as a seemingly endless series of relapses and remissions—"I am always
ill and will never get better"—and lastly, after learning of the death of
an ill peer, to an understanding that the disease was to end in death:
"I am dying."

The children's personal experiences were a much more significant
determinant than age or intellectual ability in determining concepts of
sickness. Thus a 3- or 4-year-old child might know more about his or her
prognosis than a very intelligent 9-year-old.

Not only did terminally ill children know they were dying before
death became imminent; they also kept such knowledge a secret to avoid
causing their parents further upset and to reduce the likelihood of being
abandoned by loved ones or caregivers because of anxieties such dis-
closures might cause. Instead, the children, together with their parents
and the caregivers, practiced an elaborate ritual of mutual pretense, in
which all parties defined the patient as dying, but acted as if the patient
was going to live.

THE SICK CHILD'S WORLD

Perhaps surprisingly, little has changed in encounters with these children and their families—at least in our experience—in the ensuing 30 years. However, there has been an encouraging improvement in the overall cure rate for childhood malignancy, now approaching 75%. This medical advance means that contemporary ill children, at least those with leukemia or other malignant diseases, and their families, are now encountering a protracted chronic illness with a good prospect of cure, rather than a catastrophic and short illness with little or no prospect of cure. Greater attention is paid today to preventing or controlling pain, including routine provision of semi-permanent indwelling central venous catheters for intravenous access, anesthesia for painful procedures such as bone marrow aspirates and lumbar punctures, and patient-controlled analgesia during recovery from painful surgical procedures. More of the required treatment today is administered on an outpatient basis, admission to hospital is minimized, and early return to school while treatment is continuing is encouraged. These developments, and the more open style of communication with the child that is presently recommended, will have undoubtedly altered the perceptions of our seriously ill patients about what is wrong with them, why they have become sick, and why unpleasant or painful things are being done to them apparently with their parents' assent.

The Effect of a Life-Threatening Illness on a Child's Attachment to Loved Ones

We frequently see infants and very young children being wheeled into our clinic's treatment room for yet another unpleasant procedure who turn to their parent with a bewildered look, as if asking, "Why are you letting them do this to me?" and clinging anxiously to the parent, with distress or withdrawal on separation.

According to Bowlby's theory of attachment (1987), affectional bonds are conceived as the consequence of preprogrammed patterns of so-called "attachment behavior" becoming focused on another individual, usually the mother. Their goal is to bring the first individual close to the other, to maintain proximity, and to ensure safety. The attachments are specific, enduring, accompanied by positive emotions when secure, and by negative emotions such as anxiety, sorrow, and anger if threatened. Attachment behaviors include crying and calling, which elicit care, and strong protest should a child be left alone with strangers. With age, the frequency and intensity with which all these forms of behavior are exhibited diminish steadily, but they become evident again when a person is stressed, ill, or afraid (Bowlby, 1973, 1987).

Evidence suggests there is a strong causal relationship between an individual's experiences with his or her parents and later capacity to cope with adversity. We wonder what effect, if any, traumatic experiences such as those encountered unavoidably during treatment have on children and on their personalities later as long-term survivors. It becomes important to provide both the child and his or her parents additional and compassionate support at these trying times.

What Dying Children Say to Their Families and to Us

Those of our patients who have progressive disease and who are considered to be in the terminal phase of their illness do not necessarily discuss their situation either with their parents or with us. It is generally accepted now that it is not appropriate to assume they are unaware of their situation because they are not discussing the matter. Rather, it is wiser in the long run if we remember to make the opposite assumption—that the child has full knowledge of the situation—and we must seek to maintain whatever professional relationship we share with the child on that basis.

There have been occasions when patients in our department have not understood the import of the advice that there has been a serious change in their condition and treatment has failed. An 11-year-old girl with acute myeloid leukemia in second remission relapsed again 2 months after receiving a stem cell transplant. Her oncologist met with her and her parents to explain that her leukemia had returned and that nothing more could be done. The mother reported that the doctor said, "The medicines we've been giving you haven't worked, so we're going to stop them." According to the mother, the patient's initial understanding of the implications of this conversation was, "Oh, so I'll always be sick then." We have learned not to assume that our patients "read between the lines" and understand that death is now inevitable. The implications of "nothing more can be done" may not necessarily be decoded by patients accustomed to setbacks in their treatment course, who are aware of their parents' distress but think it is because they will always be a "sick child."

However, from other accounts related to us by parents, teachers, and others who have had contact with our patients, and our own occasional experiences, we would say that most, if not all, of our seriously ill children who are not expected to live much longer or whose deaths are imminent are well aware of their situation, even in cases where the parents are adamant the child is unaware. Occasionally we too fall into the oversight of talking with the child as if he or she has a future when he or she actually does not.

One of our patients received treatment for cancer as an infant, including a stem cell transplant, only to develop a second cancer at 7 years old. He received further intensive chemotherapy and a second transplant but relapsed again 2 years after this treatment had been completed and died a year later, when he was halfway through his first year of high school. His parents, who were loving and sensitive people, were convinced he was unaware of his impending death and for that reason chose not to raise this topic with him.

After his funeral service, one of his teachers spoke in private to one of us (RR), revealing that shortly before his death, he had brought her an article he had prepared for the school magazine, featuring interviews with his peers about their hoped-for future careers. As he was leaving her room, she called to him, saying, "But you haven't done one for yourself." He turned, looked at her, and said, "No...I won't be here." She said she had felt unable to speak, profoundly moved by her sudden realization of this boy's unassuming courage and grace. "It's all right," he said quietly, and left the room.

A 9-year-old boy died suddenly, shortly after the abrupt onset of severe interstitial pneumonitis 8 months after stem cell transplant. His family owned one of a number of shops clustered in a marina, and their son was well known to the other tenants. After he died, the parents learned that he had visited and spent time with each and every tenant in the marina on the day before his death.

A 12-year-old boy terminally ill with Ewing's tumor who was confined to a wheelchair, and whose parents had already discussed his situation with him, confided in his doctor one day in the clinic, saying, "I'm worried my parents won't be able to afford my funeral." The doctor replied, "Why don't you go to the funeral people and see what they can sort out?" When he returned home, his parents took him to the funeral director. The next time the doctor saw him, the patient was pleased to report he had made a successful visit to the funeral director. "Guess what!" he said. "I went to the funeral place and I've organized my funeral—I've picked a white coffin—and they gave me a discount." He had not only chosen his coffin, but also arranged for a Harley Davidson guard of honor—details that his parents told us they would not have considered.

One of our patients, a 9-year-old boy, was terminally ill. His mother reported that he called to his parents soon after midnight one night, asking them to wake his brothers and sisters because he was dying and wanted to say goodbye to them. The mother said they almost laughed because he was so insistent and because they did not expect his death for some time. He said that his friend, naming another patient who had died some time earlier, was waiting with some friends, and they were going to play cricket. To humor him, the parents woke his siblings, and he said goodbye to them. Shortly afterward, within about an hour, he died. His mother reported that as he died, he smiled, naming the deceased friend, saying, "Hello—I'm coming."

Another patient, a 5-year-old boy with terminal acute lymphoblastic leukemia, died at home. On the night he died, he came into his parents' bedroom. He explained that he did not know quite what to say to them and instead sang a familiar children's song, "Sing A Rainbow."

The emotional needs of the dying child are those of all children regardless of their health, those arising from the child's reaction to illness and admission to hospital, and those arising from the child's concept of death. To assist such children to communicate inner experiences related to their illness, we should at the outset ascertain the child's own perception of the situation, taking into account his or her developmental level and experience. We should also be alert to understanding the child's symbolic language. Children often experience emotions without being able to describe them, and young children can use symbolic language to communicate their worries. Children often have difficulty distinguishing between reality and fantasy and between actions and thoughts. We should aim to clarify reality and dispel fantasy. A common fantasy of sick children is that of being responsible for the illness. Thus, admission to hospital and medical procedures are interpreted as punishment. We should dispel such misinterpretations vigorously and encourage the expression of feelings. When children are permitted to express their anger, sadness, and anxiety, they are able to examine these feelings, place them in perspective, and gain control over them. Art therapy and music therapy are both forms of expressive therapy that can be used for effective communication with the child (see chapter 19 in this book).

The self-esteem of the child with cancer is threatened by pain, frustration, deprivation, changes in body image, and the possibility of death. As a result, school attendance and relationships with peers may both suffer. School is the ideal setting in which to encourage the child to communicate about his or her illness in a way that will promote self-esteem through mastery. We should not underestimate the child's ability to master life's challenges creatively and with humor and dignity. A child who asks, "Am I going to die?" has already chosen the person being asked, and so the wisest and best response is to be honest, confirm that such is the case, and stay with the child to address whatever specific concerns he or she may mention next. Like adults, dying children are concerned that they will be comfortable, safe, and not alone.

Children sometimes may wait to die until they are alone, in spite of their family's comforting presence during their last days, perhaps out of a desire for privacy or as a courtesy to their families. This distressing development causes the family additional grief, but an explanation by the care team of the aforementioned possible reasons can help provide some comfort.

Children and young people who are dying may linger close to death for prolonged periods. They may simply need permission from their loved ones to die and will die promptly when such permission is given. One of our patients, an 11-year-old boy with osteogenic sarcoma, was dying at home after a 5-year illness. Throughout his illness, he had demonstrated a notable tenacity to survive and willingness to endure continuing and painful treatment as long as it entailed some hope for further quality survival. After his death, his father reported that as the boy's death drew close, he lingered on in a coma for more than 7 days. An Aboriginal community nurse who was caring for him spoke with his father, informing him that the boy needed his parents' permission to die. The parents ushered the boy's grandmother and other relatives out of his room, sat down alone by the boy's bed, spoke to him of their love for him, and gave him their permission to die. The boy died peacefully a few hours later.

LOOKING TO THE ILL CHILD'S SPIRITUAL WELFARE

The care that can be offered by a team of health care professionals, including pastoral care workers, to children with cancer is summarized by the World Health Organization as that in which control of pain, of other symptoms, and of psychological, social, and spiritual problems is paramount (WHO, 1998).

We must remember to look to the child's spiritual welfare as an essential component of the care we offer the child and family. The ability of young children to communicate about spiritual issues may still be in development. However, absence of expression does not equate to absence of spirituality. We need to be attentive to assist children in finding ways of expressing themselves. We must not press our own convictions on the child or on the family, even unwittingly. Rather, we should become informed about and respect the family's convictions, and if possible, seek to work with the child always within the framework provided by his or her family's beliefs. This professional obligation may become more difficult for staff at times when a particular family's beliefs come into direct conflict with essential or even lifesaving treatment such as transfusion of blood products for life-threatening anemia or thrombocytopenia.

The family's faith tradition is an important influence on the child's spirituality, but religion does not equal spirituality, and families may manifest a strong spirituality without necessarily following any particular faith tradition. In some cases, the family's faith tradition may intrude unhelpfully. For instance, there may be difficulty if the family's belief system is narrow and judgmental.

At times, other members of the care team may not well understand the potential value of pastoral care staff's contribution to the child and family's care. There may be a reluctance to invite the pastoral care team's input into support being provided to a particular family, based on misunderstandings about a perceived connection between the pastoral care worker's own faith tradition and the type of support deemed likely to be offered to the family. The attitude of staff members may, understandably, be influenced by adverse experiences they themselves may have had in the past.

These difficulties can be overcome by regular communication between staff about patients, families, and their needs for support and by the sharing of information about what support is being provided. Our agenda should not intrude on the patient and family's agenda. Instead, we should acknowledge that what is most important will always be the best interests of the child. Our priority must be to aim always to facilitate the child's coping with the illness, with treatment, and with whatever challenges arise for the child and family along the way.

CHILDREN'S FUNERALS AND BEYOND:
WE WILL REMEMBER THEM

For those patients whose death is drawing near, parents may welcome encouragement to give some thought to the child's funeral, although some refuse to give any thought to funeral arrangements until the child has died. They will be required to decide whether the child's body is to be buried or cremated and will need to be in touch with a funeral director who will make the necessary arrangements when the time comes. Although seemingly difficult subjects, a small amount of planning in advance will later be regarded by the parents as valuable.

After the child dies, the family may benefit from a quiet time with the child's body. Hasty attempts by staff or relatives to have the child's body removed from the ward and transferred to the hospital mortuary, or moved from the family's home to the funeral home, are not to be encouraged. Brothers and sisters should be asked if they wish to see the child's body and allowed to do so, but not forced to if they decide they do not want to. Young family members who are excluded may harbor distressing fantasies of how the deceased looked after death and may be deprived of an important opportunity to "say goodbye." Issues such as these may lead to additional emotional disturbance in bereavement. In essence, it may be necessary to relearn practices that were considered perfectly familiar and desirable by earlier generations.

The family should be encouraged to be fully involved in planning the funeral, including in the choice of readings; in the inclusion of particular rites, rituals, and music; in choosing who is to speak; and in selecting the content of audiovisual presentations. The presider's knowledge of the child and ability to establish rapport with mourners at the ceremony will be assisted by information about the deceased child that the family can share while the funeral is being planned. Such measures assist not only the family but also all who attend the funeral to accept the reality of the child's death, to begin expressing their grief and sense of loss, and to comfort one another.

Attitudes of staff to attending patients' funerals will vary, and each member of the care team is entitled to be guided by his or her own point of view. Staff may simply find the thought too difficult or upsetting or have concerns about going to a particular patient's funeral as establishing a precedent for subsequently being expected to go to them all. Our department generally tries to have at least one representative attend the funeral. We find attending patients' funerals a useful way of honoring the child and saying goodbye and, from a medical perspective, of bringing clinical closure, but we do not feel obliged to attend every deceased patient's funeral. Occasionally, one of our pastoral care team members is invited by the family to preside at the ceremony. We have frequently been informed afterward by families that they felt touched and comforted by knowing that members of their child's care team attended the funeral.

Valuable information and advice about supporting parents and families through the days surrounding the ill child's death, and helping them plan a meaningful funeral, has been provided by Dominica (1997). In our experiences and contacts with bereaved parents, the pain reported by our patients' parents appears frighteningly severe, diminishing only somewhat with time, and persisting indefinitely. One mother attending an annual memorial service organized by our hospital's pastoral care department confided that this was the first occasion on which she had openly grieved for the stillborn daughter she had lost 40 years earlier. Parents report to us that the pain of loss and separation does not go away, but that over time, they learn better to live on with it.

COPING WITH RECOVERY: REFLECTIONS FROM LONG-TERM SURVIVORS

In their conversations with us, long-term survivors frequently include recollections of earlier diagnosis and treatment and reflections on their experiences, which offer interesting insights into living with, and surviving, childhood cancer.

One of our patients had received 2 years of treatment for non-Hodgkin's lymphoma as a 10-year-old. As a young man of 18, he reported frequent depressive feelings and symptoms of posttraumatic stress, including engagement in high-risk behaviors. He described feeling a sense of excitement during the time of treatment, of "living on the edge—there's an edge to it. When you're on treatment, you're in danger, and it's sort of exciting. When you stop treatment, it's all a bit flat, a bit downhill."

A woman aged 24 recalled being diagnosed at age 13 years with acute lymphoblastic leukemia and saying sadly to her parents when she and they were told she had leukemia, "And you've just spent all that money on my teeth."

A woman aged 28 recalled her diagnosis of acute lymphoblastic leukemia 18 years earlier in the early 1970s. Her parents had insisted she not be told the diagnosis, telling her only that she had sick blood. She recalled hearing "snippets of conversation" and noting the way people spoke to her and looked at her. She looked up blood diseases at the local library; read about leukemia, which few patients survived at that time; and concluded that she was going to die:

> I became very afraid and withdrawn, too scared to tell anyone how I felt, as I thought then I'd be told "the truth!" I thought that if I expected to die, I wouldn't be disappointed when I found out. The hospital scared me, as I thought I'd get the "bad news" there one day, and it always meant pain, with needles and blood tests. I never wanted to be seen as different—very few people, teachers or friends, knew what I was going through then. Years passed and I went into remission. My intense year of fear turned into an incredible will to live. I can remember walking home from school one day, and I was suddenly filled with absolute certainty that I wasn't going to die. I can't tell you how strong and clear that feeling was.

At another time, the same long-term survivor said, "I fought so hard to survive, and when I did, I didn't know what to do with my life, or how to live it."

It is common to hear stories from long-term survivors of how they have worked through their memories and experiences of diagnosis and treatment and feelings of fear, pain, anger and frustration, sorrow, hope, disappointment, resentment—the list goes on—until they have truly integrated them. They also acknowledge positive aspects of their experience that they say enrich them and contribute to their sense of calm and joy in life, such as the resourcefulness and courage they now recognize and appreciate in themselves and in others who supported them and saw them through. They describe how they have been able to move on with confidence and purpose, the importance of close relationships, and how much they now value and enjoy life. It is clear that coping with recovery can be a long process, not at all orderly, but with many stops and starts. It seems that at every major life stage, the experiences of the past may need to be reassessed and reintegrated in the light of changed circumstances.

THE TEMPERAMENT OF FAMILIES

It should be recognized by the care team that families have differing temperaments. Being confronted by the onset of a life-threatening or life-limiting illness in any member of the family, particularly one of the children, is a drama for any family. Some families add to the drama; others do not. As caregivers, we need to be able to accommodate a variety of styles of coping utilized by families. Some styles of coping, despite being different from those we ourselves might imagine we would use, are effective nevertheless and, provided they are not bizarre or potentially damaging to family members, deserve our nonjudgmental acceptance and support.

CARING FOR ONESELF AND FOR ONE'S COLLEAGUES: TOURS OF DUTY

Health care workers caring for seriously ill children face the prospect of repeated losses occasioned by the deaths of many of their patients. Staff caring for terminally ill children face stresses similar to those confronting the families. Because the family's outlook will be influenced by the personality and reactions of the staff, a special degree of maturity and caring is required. Caregivers under these circumstances should recognize their limitations and the importance of the support that a multidisciplinary team can and should offer. Staff must guard against becoming desensitized to the plight of patients and families, against making erroneous judgments about families, and against feeling more sympathy for some families than others. Staff should be realistic in the goals they set for themselves and use supports available to them. The vicarious trauma of repeated exposure to distressing situations can have an adverse effect on well-being and can increase the risk of burnout. Regular periods of leave and interests and commitments outside the workplace will all help to ensure a continuing effective level of care to those in need. Mindful of the number of professionals who have become exhausted and burned out in their work, and of the importance for health care workers of coming into right relationship with their colleagues and with those for whom they care, others have already emphasized the value of acknowledging and embracing a spiritual dimension to our work (Wright & Sayre-Adams, 2000).

We should bear in mind that no amount of research, study, or reading on our part will produce a solution enabling us to "fix things up and make it all better" for families of children with life-threatening or life-limiting illnesses. The meaning and effects of illnesses such as these on parents and families, and particularly of the death of a child, have been part of the human story since time immemorial. We will not be able to change reality or shield such families from the tragedy that may unfold for them. We can, however, offer kindness and compassion as we care for them, and they will find that comforting. Hopefully, we will not inadvertently wound them even more as they make their way through the experience.

We are occasionally asked by people how it is that we can work in such an emotionally charged field. The response, as others who work in this field will know, is that we mostly enjoy our work and find working with children such as these and their families rewarding, fascinating, frequently unpredictable, never boring, and always a privilege.

REFERENCES

Binger, C. M., Ablin, A. R., Feuerstein, R. C., Kushner, J. H., Zoger, S., & Mikkelsen, C. (1969). Childhood leukemia: Emotional impact on patient and family. *New England Journal of Medicine, 280,* 414–418.

Bluebond-Langner, M. (1978). *The private worlds of dying children.* Princeton, NJ: Princeton University Press.

Bowlby, J. (1973). *Attachment and loss: Vol 2. Separation, anxiety and anger.* London: Hogarth Press & the Institute of Psycho-analysis.

Bowlby, J. (1987). Attachment. In R. L. Gregory (Ed.), *The Oxford companion to the mind* (pp. 57–58). Oxford, England: Oxford University Press.

Buckman, R. (1992). *How to break bad news: A guide for healthcare professionals.* Baltimore: Johns Hopkins University Press.

Corr, C. A. (2008). Children's emerging awareness of death. In K. J. Doka & A. S. Tucci (Eds.), *Living with grief: Children and adolescents* (pp. 5–17). Washington, DC: Hospice Foundation of America.

Dominica, F. (1997). *Just my reflection: Helping parents to do things their way when their child dies.* London: Darton, Longman & Todd.

Solnit, A., & Green, M. P. (1963). The pediatric management of the dying child, Part II. The child's reaction to the fear of dying. In A. Solnit & S. Provence (Eds.). *Modern perspectives in child development* (pp. 217–228). New York: International Universities Press.

Vernick, J., & Karon, M. (1965). Who's afraid of death on a leukemia ward? *American Journal of Disease of Children, 109,* 393–397.

Waechter, E. H. (1971). Children's awareness of fatal illness. *American Journal of Nursing, 71,* 1168–1172.

World Health Organization. (1998). *Cancer pain relief and palliative care for children* (p. 8). Geneva, Switzerland: Author.

Wright, S. G., & Sayre-Adams, J. (2000). *Sacred space: Right relationship and spirituality in healthcare.* Edinburgh: Churchill Livingston.

Bereavement

As we have seen in part 2, there are all too many ways in which children both in the United States and elsewhere around the world encounter death and loss. In part 3, five chapters focus on some of the most frequent and most prominent types of bereavements in the lives of children as a result of death-related losses: what life is like for a child when a parent has died (chapter 9); the impact of the death of a brother or sister (chapter 10); the importance of the death of a child's friend (chapter 11); children's encounters with the deaths of pets (chapter 12); and distinctive problems for children arising from traumatic deaths (chapter 13).

Each of these bereavement experiences is unique, with its own characteristics and qualities, but all are linked insofar as they involve losses that can have a significant impression on the life of a child. Some of these bereavement situations are generally well recognized (e.g., the death of a parent or sibling), whereas others are not always properly appreciated and may even be disenfranchised (e.g., the death of a friend or pet). Traumatic deaths during childhood, in particular, are the subject of much current discussion and debate.

Each chapter in this part explores reactions that children are likely to have to these specific types of losses, coping strategies typically used by children to manage these bereavements, factors that can help or hinder such coping, and the role of family and other potential helping resources.

All of these bereavements can be daunting, not only when they involve some type of violent, stigmatized, or traumatic death, but also because any of them may involve a child's first encounter with the loss and death of a significant other. We need better research and better appreciation of the nature and significance of these losses for developing children, both for their own sake and in order to be able to work out effective intervention strategies. In the end, it will be the capacity of individual children over time to construct a coherent and confident meaning to their narratives of living with these losses that will enable them to build resilient futures.

9

Children Bereaved by the Death of a Parent

GRACE H. CHRIST

Current demographic data suggest that approximately 3.5% of children in the United States who are under 18 years of age have experienced the death of a parent, and 4% of children in all Western countries have confronted this highly stressful experience (Harrison & Harrington, 2001; Yamamoto, Davis, Dylak, Whittaker, Marsh, & van der Westhuizen, 1996). Although many bereaved children demonstrate resilience and stress-related growth after loss of a parent, multiple studies have found that parentally bereaved children are at risk for adverse mental health outcomes in both the near and the long term (Cerel, Fristad, Verducci, Weller, & Weller, 2006; Melhem, Walker, Moritz, & Brent, 2008). Recent studies have provided evidence that a parent's sudden death creates additional risk of adverse mental health outcomes for both the surviving caregiver and the children (Melhem et al., 2008).

Professional experience and research evidence have advanced the field of child bereavement considerably in the last two decades. Three factors contributed to advances in the knowledge base in this area: the completion of clinical trials of several interventions with bereaved children and families (Christ, Raveis, Siegel, Karus, & Christ, 2005; Rotheram-Borus, Stein, & Lin, 2001; Sandler et al., 2003), the identification of risk and protective factors, and the emergence of both symptom- and multisystem-focused care in the literature (Cohen, Mannarino, & Deblinger, 2006; Haine, Wolchik, Sandler, Millsap, & Ayers, 2006; Monroe & Krause, in press).

This chapter reviews some of the important stresses confronted by bereaved families and the factors that need to be integrated into effective biopsychosocial assessments and interventions. It draws on findings from two interventions with children who lost a parent. The first intervention, the Parent Guidance Program developed at Memorial Sloan-Kettering Cancer Center in New York City, focused on children before and after one parent died of cancer. The second, a long-term intervention (up to 7 years) provided evaluations and services to a cohort of 50 families of firefighters from the New York City Fire Department (FDNY) who died in the World Trade Center disaster on September 11, 2001. This program was called the FDNY–Counseling Service Unit (CSU)/Columbia University Family Program. Four clinically relevant topics associated with the two interventions are reviewed here:

- The impact of developmental level on children's grief responses.
- The relevance of type of death (anticipated or sudden).
- Risk and protective factors that impede or facilitate reconstitution over time.
- Families' needs and preferences regarding interventions with bereaved children.

IMPACT OF DEVELOPMENTAL LEVEL ON CHILDREN'S MANIFESTATIONS OF GRIEF

Although all children grieve after a parent's death, all children do not grieve in the same way. Our study of children confronting a parent's terminal illness and death from cancer clarified the importance of developmental level on children's expression and experience of loss and their loss-related needs (Christ & Christ, 2006). Information from our later intervention with bereaved families of firefighters added knowledge about how the sudden, unexpected loss of a parent affects children's capacity to cope in these circumstances (Christ, 2006). Because the FDNY families were followed for up to 7 years, we were able to observe the ways in which school-age children revisit the parent's death at times of cognitive and emotional progression and in response to changed circumstances such as family moves from one home to another, changes in school, parent dating and remarriage, mental or physical illness, or deaths of other family members or friends.

The influences of cognitive and emotional development have long been neglected in the child literature because of the difficulty of controlling enough variables to clarify differences when using traditional quantitative statistical methods. Yet the first questions that surviving parents or caregivers ask professionals often relate to how their children's age or developmental level may affect their grief experience and to which approaches are best in helping children cope. Using qualitative analytic methods with one sample of 157 children ranging in age from 3 to 17 years who had lost a parent to cancer, we were able to identify five developmentally different age groups: 3 to 5, 6 to 8, 9 to 11, 12 to 14, and 15 to 17 years. Although these age categories may vary to a degree in other populations, using emotional, cognitive, and social developmental attributes allowed us to group children whose reactions were similar to each other in important ways and clearly different from the older and younger cohorts.

Differences in Expressions and Experiences of Grief

This section focuses on the significant differences between 6- to 8-year-olds (late preoperational) and 9- to 11-year-olds (concrete operational) to exemplify the distinctiveness of the developmental variations in each group. In contrast to their younger preschool peers, 6- to 8-year-olds generally understand the finality of the parent's death after an illness and are appropriately sad and upset when informed about the death. However, because late preoperational thinking includes both magical and logical attributes, these children have difficulty fully understanding the many impacts of such a loss. As a result, they often make logical errors, such as misunderstanding cause and effect, and may be afraid that aggressive thoughts, words, or wishes will be harmful. As one 7-year-old girl said, "I prayed my mother would be out of pain the night before she died. I think I killed her." Unlike 9- to 11-year-olds, children in the 6- to 8-year-old age group cannot retrace opinions or ideas to their origin to correct these erroneous opinions, thoughts, or ideas. However, they do understand that the parent will not return and that death is universal (it could happen to me). This knowledge makes them more anxious than their younger peers. In fact, they often appear to be highly emotional and have difficulty containing their emotions. Because they blame themselves when bad things happen, their self-esteem can be adversely affected. Thus, parental support of their self-esteem is as essential for them as it is for younger children.

Because the self-esteem of late preoperational children also is affected by important adults and children outside the home, these outside influences can either be a significant buffer and open important avenues for therapeutic intervention or be an additional source of stress. For example, a 7-year-old girl cried because a classmate said, "You can't go to the father–daughter dance because your daddy is dead." When her mother explained that all her uncles wanted to take her to the dance, the girl was very relieved.

A major change occurs in the cognitive ability of 9- to 11-year-old concrete operational children. These children can use logical thinking, understand cause and effect, and retrace memories to aid in correcting erroneous opinions, thoughts, and conclusions. However, unlike their 12- to 14-year-old peers, they cannot draw inferences from insufficient information because their ability to deal with abstract concepts is limited. For example, they need detailed, concrete explanations to understand the parent's illness and course of treatment and to feel a sense of control. One 10-year-old boy eavesdropped on family conversations and routinely listened in on telephone calls, especially those from the hospital. His behavior changed radically when his well parent was encouraged to have regular updating conversations with him and after he and the parent met with the physician, who answered all his questions. Therefore, professionals and parents are instructed to provide children with information in small doses over time.

In the study of families of cancer patients, children ages 9 to 11 years seemed, on the whole, to be more resilient than their older and younger peers and were relatively easy for parents to manage in the first year after the parent's death when adequately and appropriately informed about the ill parent's current illness (Siegel, Mesagno, & Christ, 1990). In contrast to younger children, children in this concrete operational group are able to use compartmentalization and distraction to contain strong emotions. Consequently, they generally appear to be less emotional. However, they often have outbursts of emotion, followed by embarrassment and avoidance. During the parent's terminal illness, children this age often want to help with the parent's care. However, leaving the child alone and in charge of a seriously ill parent carries with it a psychological risk. If an adverse medical event occurs, and the parent dies, the child may feel responsible. Nevertheless, in families with inadequate financial resources, children ages 9–11 and older are often an ill parent's primary caregiver.

Following sudden death of a parent, however, such as child bereavement after 9/11/01, children 7–11 years showed greater anxiety and symptoms of traumatic stress than found in previous samples of bereaved children who experienced parental death from all causes. However, they also reported less depression than has been reported for bereaved children this age in samples that included all causes (Pfeffer, Altemus, Heo, & Jiang, 2007).

Re-Experiencing Grief Over Time

Because most bereavement studies follow children for 18 to 24 months after the parent's death, knowledge about longer-term outcomes is limited (Christ, 2000; Worden, 1996). Worden did report that children's symptoms began to increase 2 years after the death, their final evaluation point. In clinical practice families also sometimes report that although their children had a relatively mild initial reaction to the parent's death from cancer, they experienced significant problems 3 years later.

The follow-up of a cohort of 50 bereaved FDNY families and their 125 children for up to 7 years after the fathers' sudden violent deaths on 9/11 provided additional evidence that the intensity of children's grief process undergoes exacerbations and remissions as they mature and as their life circumstances change (Christ, 2006). Because all these families were affected by the same loss at the same time and in a similar social context, differences related to developmental progression became more apparent. The mothers in these families reported that children and adolescents at all levels of development continued to describe an exacerbation or "revisiting" of grief responses as they went through cognitive and emotional maturation.

Preschool children demonstrated some of the most vivid and unexpected reactions illustrating this progression. Children who were in the 3- to 5-year age group when their firefighter father died were angry because he did not return, and they constantly asked where he had gone. Being unable to understand that death is permanent, asking repeated questions helped them have some feeling of mastery. Their questions gradually declined until they entered the 6- to 8-year age group, when their bereaved mothers reported that their children were suddenly expressing grief about the father's death and wanted to know more about why he had died and why "it" could not have been "fixed"—that is, why their father could not be rescued. One 6-year-old said, "I was thinking maybe they could build the towers up, take Dad out, and then let them fall down again." The children this age now also wanted to express their grief. In addition to cognitive advances, they became more aware of their loss as they compared themselves to their school peers. Discussing the intense grief with young children was difficult for the widows, who were beginning to feel grief more intermittently and were reluctant to return to the intense grief they felt while listening as their children expressed their grief. At times, parents used children's bereavement groups supported by the FDNY CSU after the 9/11 disaster or existing hospice program services to give their children additional opportunities to express their new sense of loss. This often helped the widow to remain focused on her emerging emotional stability.

Both the children and their mothers in the FDNY cohort found that the reminders of the sudden, totally unexpected loss also changed over time. Initially, the reminders were birthdays, anniversaries, holidays, and marker events, such as graduation, confirmations, or other events in which the deceased father probably would have played an important role. Other reminders of the disaster, such as the beginning of the war in Afghanistan, terrorist threats, and school lock-downs, became familiar and therefore easier to manage over time. However, later reminders that often were unexpected sometimes overwhelmed them with waves of grief. Consider the following example:

> Five years after 9/11, one 10-year-old boy reported that the reminders on our standardized questionnaire were no longer relevant. Instead, he said he became sad whenever he noticed cars lining the street outside his house because it reminded him of the day shortly after the disaster when he came home from school and found that cars were lining his street. He had been excited because he thought his father had come home and was having a party like he usually did. Then he realized that the cars belonged to fire department officials, who had come to inform his mother that his father's body had been found.

Helping these children learn to cope with unexpected reminders in ways that limited disruption of their functioning was an important focus of the FDNY intervention. For example, mothers were encouraged to suggest to school teachers that it would be helpful to inform children ahead of time that events related to the World Trade Center disaster would be discussed in class. Some children, especially during the first 3 years after the event, accepted the option of sitting with the school nurse or a school administrator in his or her office during these discussions.

Implications of the Interventions

Profound differences in how children express and experience their loss, depending on their developmental level, can lead to misunderstandings. For example, surviving parents mistakenly believe that their children are not grieving at all, are unaffected by the parent's death, or are callous and unfeeling (Christ, 2000). Often adults find it disconcerting when a child intermittently exhibits brief sadness and then returns to playing normally. However, the capacity to move away from sad or angry emotions and back to normative activities is primarily protective and integrative. A clear understanding and interpretation of children's grief reactions and their specific needs for support and guidance helped to rebuild empathy between parent and child.

In our studies, parental recognition of the value of revisiting the loss and grief during subsequent developmental phases also helped children integrate the loss into their emerging self-concept and life story. Through this process, children learned how to cope with the intensity of their feelings and ongoing reminders of their loss. Their parents were able to be supportive when they understood that their child's apparent regression actually represented progression and that they had not failed to support the child's grief adequately during an earlier phase of development.

TYPE OF DEATH: ANTICIPATED VERSUS TRAUMATIC LOSS

Anticipatory Loss

In the case of cancer, children experience the highest levels of anxiety and depression during the parent's terminal illness. The children's symptoms decrease after the death when the children's ongoing care is adequate (Siegel, Karus, & Raveis, 1996). This finding highlights the importance of interventions before the parent's death, even though the terminal phase of disease is an especially difficult time for professionals to work with young families because of their intense anxiety, sadness, and fear. Interventions focused on communication and preparation when the death is inevitable have been shown to be effective in helping caregivers prepare children for the loss. Interventions with the same focus also were effective in improving communication between the child and the surviving caregiver in both the short and the longer term, a critical variable in children's outcomes (Raveis, Siegel, & Karus, 1999).

Children's ability to anticipate the death before it actually occurred also varied. Children ages 3 to 5 years could not really anticipate the permanence of death no matter how rigorous the efforts were to prepare them. They learned the words, which gave them some sense of control, but not the concept. Only gradually, as they experienced the parent's failure to return after the death and repeatedly asked, "Why can't he [or she] come back?" did these preschool-age children begin to grasp what had happened.

Unlike the younger group, the 6- to 8-year-olds experienced what we termed anticipatory anxiety, rather than anticipatory grief, when the parent's death was expected. They knew something bad was going to happen and could not imagine how the family would survive such a catastrophe. Some expressed their fears in statements such as "The whole world will end, and nothing will be here." As a consequence, after the parent's death, these early school-age children often felt some relief that "the worst is over" and that they and the rest of the family had survived.

Children in the older group (ages 9 to 11 years) were among the first with the ability to articulate the reality of the death before it occurred and to report the sad feelings connected to their thoughts about that reality. Receiving information incrementally in small doses helped the children in all age groups to feel prepared and less traumatized and to have a greater sense of control when the death occurred.

In the cancer program Parent Guidance Intervention, which emphasized preparative communication between parent and child, children often said, "I was shocked, but I was prepared. Mom told me it could happen." Enhancing this type of communication seemed to reduce some of the anxiety children experienced during the pre-death phase. In the follow-up period, 9 and 14 months after the death, children reported more improvement in communication with their surviving parent over time than did the children participating in the comparative supportive intervention conducted by telephone (Christ, 2006). More recent research suggests that with the increasing length of terminal illness resulting from medical advances, other traumatic aspects associated with the process of treatment and care during later phases of illnesses may expose children to traumatic levels of stress and require intervention (Saldinger, Cain, & Porterfield, 2003).

Traumatic Loss

For a child, the loss of a parent or sibling is extremely stressful, in part because such deaths have become untimely in developed countries. Even when death can be anticipated—from an illness, for example—conditions the ill parent experiences during the advanced stages of disease may be particularly stressful for a child: for instance, if the parent loses the ability to function, becomes disfigured or disabled, exhibits radical changes in mental state, or experiences sudden exacerbation of symptoms. Consequently, research is needed on the ramifications of these new, longer trajectories of illness to identify traumatic stress reactions in children, test the efficacy of ongoing but less frequent professional contacts, and possibly determine when exposure to a parent's illness impedes, rather than facilitates, healthy grieving.

Increasingly, the particular circumstances of the parent's death are found to shape children's as well as adults' responses to loss, especially during the immediate aftermath. A recent well-conducted study provided evidence that a parent's sudden death from suicide, accident, or illness increases the risk of depression and severe stress over and above other vulnerability factors for both children and surviving caregivers (Melhem et al., 2008). Although none of these three causes of sudden parental death contributed more than the other two to longer-term mental health problems among children, the authors did find that sudden loss from any of the three causes increased mental health problems among the surviving caregivers, which resulted in impaired functioning that had a negative impact on the children's functioning.

Four conditions involving traumatic stress responses in children have been the subject of research and require ongoing study: (1) posttraumatic stress disorder (PTSD); (2) traumatic bereavement; (3) subclinical levels of symptoms, such as anxiety; and (4) no current symptomatology.

Posttraumatic Stress Disorder

PTSD is the most severe and least frequent of the four conditions. The symptoms of the disorder—re-experiencing, numbing, and increased arousal—often occur in combination with symptoms of depression and anxiety. Because PTSD is likely to interfere with normal grieving, intervening to reduce the symptoms of trauma is recommended by trauma specialists (Cohen, Mannarino, Greenburg, Padlo, & Shipley,

2002; Pynoos, 1992). An intervention to separate treatment of trauma from a grief-focused intervention is currently being studied (Cohen et al., 2006).

The standard assessment for PTSD in children includes the PTSD component of the Anxiety and Depression Interview Schedule for Children (ADIS-C) (Silverman & Albano, 1996). Treatments are being evaluated for this diagnosis in children with cognitive behavioral therapies and eye movement desensitization and reprocessing (EMDR) (Cohen et al., 2001; Cohen et al., 2006; Yule & Smith, in press).

Traumatic Bereavement

Traumatic bereavement in children sometimes occurs in addition to symptoms of PTSD, depression, and anxiety after a major loss. In these circumstances, the child's preoccupation with thoughts about the dead person, anger about the death, and feelings that the dead person is still around also interfere with an adaptive grief process (Yule & Smith, in press). Efforts to develop consensus on this condition are ongoing. Three measures are currently under development to assess children for traumatic grief: the Traumatic Grief Inventory for Children (Dillen, Fontaine, & Verhofstadt-Denève, 2009; Dyregrov et al., 2001), the Inventory of Complicated Grief (Melhem, Moritz, Walker, Shear, & Brent, 2007), and the Extended Grief Inventory (Layne, Savjak, Saltzman, & Pynoos, 2001). Risk factors for traumatic bereavement include a previous loss or multiple losses, sudden death, violent death, and the child's perception that his or her own life was threatened (Brown et al., 2008).

Subclinical Traumatic Stress Reaction, Anxiety, or Depression

Although this manifestation includes a much larger group of children than do either of the first two conditions, few studies have addressed this population. Children with this condition also may have traumatic grief reactions with greater emphasis on the loss of the person, rather than on the details surrounding the loss. However, the symptoms of traumatic grief do not reach what is considered to be a clinical level. Current evidence supports the efficacy of parent guidance, psychoeducation, and supportive interventions with the child and the surviving caregiver in these situations (Christ et al., 2005; Sandler et al., 2003).

Further research needs to address whether the symptoms of trauma are most effectively treated separately from the grief in these subclinical conditions or whether the two are best treated simultaneously. Additional research also is needed concerning the frequency and intensity of interventions.

No Current Symptomatology

This is the least severe but a frequent manifestation in children following traumatic loss. Although children may fail to exhibit symptoms, in situations where the particular event and its aftermath was highly traumatic, it seems advisable to offer the family crisis intervention and thereby create safety for child and parent, promote appropriate acceptance and closure, and provide psychoeducation with regard to the possibility of delayed reactions. In addition, Yule and Smith (in press) recommend linking a child to a treatment program that provides ongoing surveillance and assessment.

Implications for Intervention

Anticipatory Loss

Parents with a terminal illness vary greatly in their ability to help with their children's responses while fighting to prolong their own lives. Some of these parents need to withdraw completely for medical reasons or because dealing with their children's emotions is too difficult for them in their debilitated state (Christ, 2000). Others are remarkably motivated to be involved in preparing their children emotionally as well as materially. For example, one mother with advanced cancer who had two school-age daughters was attending a community workshop on problems confronting families of cancer patients. Halfway through the workshop, she said, "I have been sick for a couple years, and I think I am dying now. I think it is time for me to tell my children that. What do you all think about this? I don't want to make them more anxious." Some group members shared examples of losses in their own lives and described how helpful it had been to feel prepared and to hear from the person who subsequently died how much they were loved. Others members pointed to evidence that the girls were already anxious and might feel less frightened if they knew how they would be cared for when their mother died.

Most parents who participated in the Parental Guidance Intervention were unaware of how much their children knew about the impending loss of one parent and were afraid that discussing the loss with their children, even when the loss was indeed imminent, would make them even more anxious. When we talked with the children separately, we usually found that even some of the 6- to 8-year-old children were well aware of the parent's illness and probable death, but they were not asking questions or revealing their knowledge for fear of upsetting the surviving parent even more or causing the ill parent's condition to worsen. They were extremely anxious and frightened and felt alone with their fears. Thus, they were greatly relieved when their parents began talking openly about what might happen, how the family would cope, and how the children would be cared for.

Traumatic Loss

A variety of approaches to intervention regarding traumatic loss are currently being evaluated. Some professionals who work with children who have experienced a traumatic loss view their responses from a trauma perspective and emphasize the importance of traumatic memories, which interfere with the tasks of grief (Cohen et al., 2006). They suggest that the symptoms of trauma should be treated before the grief is treated. However, those who emphasize the importance of the person–environment transactions after the death as the cause of adaptational problems view traumatic memories as only one of many factors influencing children's adaptation (Sandler, Wolchik, & Ayers, 2008). Consistent with other systems approaches, they focus on intervening more broadly in the post-bereavement environment: for example, by improving parenting competence and communication. For example, the approach used in our FDNY study includes both a person–environment contextual model and a multisystem approach—intervention at the individual, family, school, and community level.

FACTORS THAT IMPEDE OR FACILITATE RECONSTITUTION OVER TIME

Beneficial Outcomes of Bereavement

Some controversy has emerged in the literature over the terms used to define beneficial outcomes of child bereavement. Sandler and his colleagues (2008) used the term "resilient adaptation" when describing a positive mix of risk and protective factors that can buffer or alleviate children's distress and foster their growth. By contrast, Balk (2004) used "recovery," meaning "redefining and reintegrating ourselves into life" (p. 362), to describe the beneficial adaptive outcomes of bereavement.

In our studies, we have used the term "reconstitution" to describe what we view as later tasks of the bereavement process, whereas earlier tasks focus more on managing the loss, trauma, and grief (Christ, 2000). In the FDNY intervention, managing grief responses was the predominant preoccupation during family interviews in the first several years after the parent's death. In subsequent years, the predominant preoccupation was redefinition of self and integration with ongoing life. Although both grieving and reconstitution were stressful processes, some family members were especially challenged by one or the other.

Because all the FDNY families experienced the same loss at the same time in a similar post-death environment, we were able to observe changes in their process over time as they discussed their grief and reconstitution in groups and individual family sessions. Immediately after the loss, the widows and children engaged in both grief-focused and "restoration"-focused processes, as described in Stroebe and Schut's dual process model (1999) and in Rubin and Malkinson's two-track bereavement model (2001). Both widows and children had to assume the tasks formerly performed by the firefighter father at a time when they were dealing with intense grief and trauma. In the face of ongoing trauma, they eventually experienced numbness, which permitted them to plan and organize. This phase was followed by one of more intense mourning in the second year. During the interviews in the third year, however, many widows exhibited a subtle downward shift in the amount of content devoted to grief issues. Gradually, they devoted more content to the task of redefining and reintegrating their new selves into ongoing life. Among the children, this shift tended to occur earlier, and it differed somewhat from that of the mother. The children's normative task was to integrate the loss of their father into their ongoing developmental progression.

The amount of time the reintegration process takes was further clarified by a survey we conducted with 115 FDNY widows shortly before the fifth anniversary of the World Trade Center disaster. Only 15% of these young women had remarried at the time of the survey. In individual and group interviews conducted in the FDNY–Columbia University Family Program with the CSU, many widows indicated that restructuring their identity, which included redefining themselves and going forward, was extremely stressful. Those women were relieved when their distress was defined as another step in the adaptation, recovery, or reconstitution process, not as an indication they were stuck in their grief or were experiencing pathologically prolonged or complicated grief. In fact, fewer social or cultural guidelines exist for this later process (especially for young widows) than exist for coping with loss. Therefore, we began to view reconstitution as a later process characterized by emphasis more on redefining the self and reintegrating it into life than on managing the grief.

One caveat: The numbness-mourning-reconstitution processes in the real-life experiences of the firefighters' widows were messier than the "clarifying" sequences all of us struggle to define. After all, most of us do not "get over" profound losses, such as the death of a young spouse or a child. We learn to live with them.

Empirically Supported Risk and Protective Factors

Over the past two decades, studies in child bereavement have clarified risk and protective factors that make it more or less likely that parents and children will experience clinical symptoms and other adverse psychological consequences following a loss as well as undergo positive growth. It is important for practitioners to incorporate an understanding of each client's risk and protective factors into their assessment process. Because these factors are considered to be "malleable"—that is, they can be altered—they often become the focus of interventions. These factors and related evidence-based treatments have been summarized by Haine, Ayers, Sandler, and Wolchik (2008); Haine et al. (2006); Kwok, Haine, Sandler, Ayers, Wolchik, and Tein (2005); Lutzke, Ayers, Sandler, and Barr (1997); and Raveis et al. (1999). Haine and colleagues have also described evidence-based practices designed for empirically supported risk and protective factors (Haine et al., 2008). The protective factors for children include increasing their self-esteem and self-worth, improving their perceptions of their ability to control events, developing their coping skills, and having opportunities to express necessary emotions. The parenting factors associated with better child outcomes include a positive parent–child relationship, parental warmth, good parent–child communication, effective discipline, reduced parental distress and mental health problems, and a minimal number of negative life events that can follow a major loss.

Another group of factors having an impact on outcome are often referred to as "nonmalleable" attributes. Although such attributes predate the parent's death and cannot be changed, they may be related to outcome. (For a discussion of the importance of pre-crisis factors on one's ability to cope with life crises, see Moos & Schaefer, 1986.) Among the nonmalleable attributes are genetic, developmental, gender-related, and sociocultural factors. Understanding children's cognitive, emotional, and social needs and the gender and cultural contexts of those needs can be crucial when attempting to engage children and implement effective therapeutic interventions for them. Reviewed in the discussion of developmental attributes are the specific needs of children related to their developmental level and the differences in approaches to intervention those differences suggest (Christ & Christ, 2006).

Clinicians also use knowledge of culture and gender to assess the adaptiveness of children's behavior and to provide an optimal level of intensity in the intervention and the surveillance plan. For example, evidence suggests that in some cultures, expression of intense emotion is not beyond the norm, whereas expression of intense emotions may be frowned on in cultures where emotional restraint is the norm. The results of studies by Raveis and colleagues (1999) and Sandler and colleagues (2003) suggest that girls are more reactive than boys to the loss of a parent or to other family stresses and therefore may require more ongoing monitoring and intervention.

Although specific risk and protective factors are used as a focus for preventive interventions, evidence suggests that the outcomes of children's bereavement are more likely to be predicted by the cumulative effect of multiple risk and protective factors, rather than by any single stressor (Sandler et al., 2008). Consequently, understanding the importance of the cumulative impact of multiple stresses and diminished resources occurring over a relatively short time after a loss is important when assessing children's level of risk and determining the frequency and intensity of surveillance and intervention.

About a year before 9/11, the eldest child in one FDNY family of three children was injured in a life-threatening accident resulting in residual disability in the child and depression in the mother, who had also recently experienced the death of her own father. After the firefighter's death, the loss of income through a fraudulent investor (the income was later recovered) and the mother's diagnosis with a life-threatening but treatable illness resulted in psychological symptoms in the two younger early adolescent children. As one early adolescent boy explained to his mother, "When you were diagnosed with this disease, we thought it was all over after everything else that has happened, even though you told us you would be OK."

Risk Factors Over Time

In this section, two risk factors—preexisting mental health and personality problems and uneven parenting competence—are discussed from the perspective of their impact over time (up to 7 years after the event) on the outcomes of the FDNY widows and children.

Preexisting Mental Health and Personality Problems

The presence of mental health and personality problems in either the surviving parent or the child places both at risk for more complicated bereavement and exacerbation of existing conditions, such as depression or anxiety disorder in both the short and the long term (Haine et al., 2006; Kwok et al., 2005; Lin, Sandler, Ayers, Wolchik, & Luecken, 2004).

The FDNY mothers with personality problems often experienced difficulty maintaining consistency in their parenting over time as they sought to avoid the intensity of grief or anger by making impulsive decisions and changes. They also had difficulty addressing their own needs versus their children's needs. Despite mental health problems, some of these mothers were able to manage their caretaking tasks well during the acute phase of early bereavement. However, they often had greater difficulty in the later stages of reconstitution (years 4 to 7 after 9/11), which required restructuring of identity and finding a new way forward for themselves, including separation from their children, building a new support network, and forming new intimate relationships. Risk factors, such as dependency, lack of autonomy, and weaknesses in the formation of their identity before the loss, tended to increase the mother's anxiety and impulsiveness and made this phase of reconstitution especially challenging. Parents' mental health problems could also be exacerbated after making a major change, such as moving the family to a different part of the country or remarrying.

The challenges of the parenting task also change over time: for example, when symptoms of pathology appear in a child during early or middle adolescence. The child's difficulties may be attributed to the loss, whether or not they actually are related to it. Some mothers hoped the child's symptoms were caused by the trauma, rather than by a predisposition to depression, anxiety, or a mental illness that was present in other family members. We also found that soon after the loss, some children exhibited symptoms and conditions that not only predated the loss but also may have been unrelated to it as well. For example, a child in one family was diagnosed with anorexia nervosa, and one child in a second family had a psychoneurological condition. Both children received treatment, improved their functioning over time, and moved into adolescence and beyond with satisfactory success both academically and socially.

Because of this complexity of the impact of preexisting mental health factors in child or parent on the adaptive process over time, the presence of mental health problems required careful assessment and monitoring and longer-term surveillance with routine follow-up two or three times per year after the first 2 years of more intensive intervention. We concluded that planned follow-up represented best practices under these conditions, and we would make it routine in any subsequent programs.

Uneven Parenting Competence

In most studies (e.g., Raveis et al., 1999), parenting competence (consistency, warmth, effective discipline, open communication) is associated with better outcomes among children with regard to mental health. For this reason, interventions generally include some form of parent guidance, education, and training. Our studies along with others used an independent measure of the parent's competence—an assessment by the children themselves—as an important component of the process of assessing and formulating the problem (Sandler et al., 2003; Siegel, Raveis, & Karus, 1996).

Although most of the mothers who participated in the FDNY-CSU intervention had difficulty empathizing with their children early in the course of their own bereavement, usually related to their own overwhelming grief and distress, their empathic connection improved remarkably over time. In the second and third years, the widows began to struggle with feelings of abandonment by their children, who rather than wanting to "grieve" or be "9/11 kids" any longer, wanted to be like other kids, catch up in school, and be with their peers. Although being a "9/11 kid" initially felt special, later the children began to feel different and stigmatized. The mothers' learning to understand and accept these differences in the timing and intensity of the grief experienced by children and adults also contributed to their improved relationships with children.

Over time, the women were confronted with new challenges to their parenting abilities. These included difficulty deciding whether and when to date, selecting a mate, sometimes marrying again (though at 5 years only 15% of the 115 FDNY widows surveyed reported having remarried, and a few had divorced), managing their children's feelings about change of any kind, coping with separation as children matured, and recalibrating relationships within the family as the mothers became stronger, and the children were able to be more open with them. The mothers also had to learn how to manage the ubiquitous reminders of this catastrophic event, recognizing that if properly managed, the waves of grief and reminders could advance the children's integration of the loss into their new sense of themselves.

ISSUES REGARDING DEVELOPMENT AND IMPLEMENTATION OF INTERVENTIONS

Interventions with bereaved children include those focused on symptoms, such as PTSD, anxiety, and depression (Christ et al., 2005; Sandler et al., 2003), and more recently, those focused on multisystem interventions that aim to provide multiple services and intervention at the individual, family, and community level (Christ, 2006; Monroe & Krause, in press).

Dyregrov and Dyregrov (in press) ask the following relevant question: How do families in which one member died by suicide define their needs and what they want from an intervention? This question is important because recruiting families into child bereavement programs has often been difficult, especially after a sudden or traumatic loss. For example, the families that had participated in the Dyregrovs' study after a family member's death from suicide recommended the following:

- Be organized—develop or instigate routines for response.
- Be proactive; don't wait for us to come to you.
- Don't swamp us with help initially and then leave us with nothing.
- Be there when the reality of the death sets in.
- Be flexible—listen to what we need. Provide us with information (What will happen? Where and from whom will we get help? What are "normal" grief reactions?).
- Help our children and help us to help them.
- Do not forget the extended family.

■ Help us get in contact with others who have experienced the same bereavement.
■ Be available to us for at least a year.

These recommendations were similar to the recommendations we received from families that had completed our Parent Guidance Intervention in the context of anticipated loss from cancer (Christ, 2005). Although the families were pleased with the focus on parent guidance and how the intervention had been implemented, they recommended a longer term of engagement with professionals, greater flexibility with regard to the intensity of services, and more direct work with children.

A recent quantitative analysis of existing controlled intervention studies on child bereavement recommended that researchers pay more attention to the type and context of the death and intervene in a timely way, that is, as close to the time of the death as possible (Currier, Holland, & Neimeyer, 2007). The authors found that, in general, children responded more favorably to grief therapy the closer the treatment was to the actual death. Furthermore, the authors encouraged efforts to identify high-risk individuals for intervention. How does one go about developing such an intervention within a given population?

Characteristics of the Intervention Developed for Families in the FDNY/CSU-Columbia University Program

This section describes how an intervention was developed for families of firefighters killed in the World Trade Center disaster. In some ways, the intervention incorporated the risk factors identified earlier. However, it also incorporated a new element: It was developed in collaboration with the affected families to reflect their requests and preferences.

Working with acutely bereaved parents and children presents special problems but also offers special rewards to clinicians. One problem is a countertransference issue related to an acute and devastating trauma visited on a psychologically normal family. Clinicians are especially at risk for countertransference when interviews are conducted in the family home, which is virtually essential when several young children are involved. And the risk is even greater when the interviews are stretched out over several years with decreasing frequency, a situation that presents unusual boundary-related problems for both family and practitioner. The following describes approaches that team members found effective in helping them with their reactions in this emotionally complex and intense environment.

By the second year after 9/11, the dead firefighters' preschool and school-age children spoke of the clinicians as "one of the family." Issues of reconstitution are, after all, psychologically normal issues precipitated by an unexpected event that fits the idea of "there but for the grace of God go I." The surviving parents' problems are not the usual psychopathological problems that clinicians are familiar with. Instead, the surviving parents' problems represent troublesome life issues all of us encounter in daily life. Thus, families involved in an intervention are more like close friends or acquaintances and our own families that struggle with an overwhelming life catastrophe.

When negotiating our roles with the FDNY families, we found that it was extremely helpful to conduct home visits with a co-practitioner, each seeing different family members. With the families' permission, all interviews were audiotaped and transcribed. Another practice that proved to be extremely helpful was having each two-person team of practitioners discuss their interviews with family members on audiotape after each session. They summarized the content of their interviews, along with their current understanding of the individual and family dynamics. Clinicians found this mutually supportive peer supervision, which included the free give-and-take of thoughts, ideas, and suggestions that develops over time with competent colleagues, informative and helpful. Finally, all the clinicians attended weekly supervisory meetings, during which they discussed emerging problems and emergency issues first and then discussed one family in depth. These meetings also were audiotaped. All data gathered in the family interviews, the discussions between co-practitioners, and the supervisory meetings were entered into N-Vivo software for future analysis.

Implementation of the Intervention

The need to provide services to the widows and children of the 343 firefighters who died and to the severely stressed surviving firefighters and their families forced the FDNY-CSU to grow exponentially almost immediately after the World Trade Center disaster. Within a month of the disaster, I was contacted by CSU's associate director, who had begun to receive many requests from the firefighters' widows for help with their children. By February 2002, I submitted a final draft describing our proposed intervention. A month later, we signed a contract for the FDNY to pay for clinical interviews through FEMA recovery funds that were allocated to them. The CSU sent letters to all 343 widows describing this new service. In April, we scheduled our first interview.

Our experience with the randomized clinical trial at Memorial Sloan-Kettering Cancer Center consisting of the telephone intervention versus the Parent Guidance Intervention was invaluable in addressing the FDNY widows' initial requests for help with their children. The women feared that their children would be harmed for life by such a traumatic loss. When we began working with these families, we learned the following early on:

- The modified version of the original parent guidance model was appropriate for work with these families.
- The traumatic impact of the father's death on the widows and children would require careful assessment and exploration over time.
- The grief counseling component of the intervention would need to provide parent guidance, deal with traumatic grief, and find and arrange for assessment treatment of more severe responses, including prescription for medications.
- We would need to work with the CSU regarding the provision of activities for children and group meetings for widows that would complement our own more individual and family approach.

In short, we suspect that each major event that affects large populations may require services outlined in manual form regarding evidence-based components of an intervention, such as parent guidance, medication for depression, grief counseling, and traumatic grief intervention. In addition, however, the intervention must include approaches dictated by the specific characteristics of each catastrophic event. Finally, the following resources are part of a successful intervention's armamentarium: familiar and trusted support networks (e.g., the FDNY and its CSU), excellent public schools, mental health clinics competent in brief work with children and parents, pro bono legal services, legal aid–related services, and so forth.

Our own roles over the 7 years shifted in response to the FDNY families' changing needs. The intensity of the contacts also gradually changed from initial sessions every 2 weeks for the first 2 months, to one session each month, to three sessions per year, and contact every 2 years after the fifth year. The biyearly contacts did not necessarily mean a reduction in intensity. At times, however, they involved a brief series of telephone and face-to-face contacts as well as specialized referrals.

CONCLUSION

Much has been learned about the grief of children over the past two decades: about risk and protective factors, about mediating and moderating forces, and about contextual and symptom- and system-focused approaches to intervention. Childhood bereavement is an exciting new area of study that promises to increase our knowledge of the impact of a broad range of stresses on children, their coping processes, and the interventions that can help them. This expansion of scientific knowledge has been welcomed in an area often dominated by emotionality and ideological perspectives. It has engaged the interest of many researchers as well as clinicians and opened exciting new opportunities for better dissemination of both clinical and research findings. More recently, knowledge of the impact of sudden loss, trauma, developmental variations, and longer-term outcomes has suggested new directions and questions that still need to be addressed. How can a clinician best integrate these more recent findings into ongoing assessment processes with children and families? What kinds of interventions with what intensity and duration yield best results with bereaved children? Does this differ with children who have a high exposure to a traumatic situation yet remain asympomatic? Does it differ with children who evidence subclinical responses as well as those whose responses are severe enough to warrant a clinical diagnosis in either child or parent? What are optimal and yet cost-effective surveillance systems for these high-risk bereaved children over longer periods of time?

REFERENCES

Balk, D. (2004). Recovery following bereavement: An examination of the concept. *Death Studies, 28,* 361–374.
Brown, E. J., Amaya-Jackson, L., Cohen, J., Handel, S., De Bocanegra, H. T., Zatta, E., et al. (2008). Childhood traumatic grief: A multi-site empirical examination of the construct and its correlates. *Death Studies, 32,* 899–923.
Cerel, J., Fristad, M., Verducci, J., Weller, R., & Weller, E. (2006). Childhood bereavement: Psychopathology in the 2 years postparental death. *Journal of the American Academy of Child and Adolescent Psychiatry, 45,* 681–690.

Christ, G. H. (2000). *Healing children's grief: Surviving a parent's death from cancer.* New York: Oxford University Press.

Christ, G. H. (2006). Providing a home-based therapeutic program for widows and children. In P. Greene, D. Kane, G. H. Christ, S. Lynch, & M. P. Corrigan (Eds.), *FDNY crisis counseling: Innovative responses to 9/11 fire fighters, families and communities* (pp. 180–211). New York: John Wiley & Sons.

Christ, G. H., & Christ, A. E. (2006). Current approaches to helping children cope with a parent's terminal illness. *CA: A Cancer Journal for Clinicians, 56,* 197–212.

Christ, G. H., Raveis, V. A., Siegel, K., Karus, D., & Christ, A. E. (2005). Evaluation of a preventive intervention for bereaved children. *Journal of Social Work in End-of-Life and Palliative Care, 1,* 57–81.

Cohen, J., Greenberg, T., Padlo, S., Shipley, C., Mannarino, A. Deblinger, E., & Subenbort, K. (2001). *Cognitive behavioral therapy for traumatic bereavement in children: Treatment manual.* Pittsburgh, PA: Center for Traumatic Stress in Children and Adolescents, Department of Psychiatry, Allegheny General Hospital.

Cohen, J. A., Mannarino, A. P., & Deblinger, E. (2006). *Treating traumatic grief in children and adolescents.* New York: Guilford.

Cohen, J. A., Mannarino, A. P., Greenburg, T., Padlo, S., & Shipley, C. (2002). Childhood traumatic grief: Concepts and controversies. *Trauma, Violence, and Abuse* 3(4), 307–327.

Currier, J. M., Holland, J. M., & Neimeyer, R. A. (2007). The effectiveness of bereavement interventions with children: A meta-analytic review of controlled outcome research. *Journal of Clinical Child and Adolescent Psychology, 36,* 253–259.

Dillen, L., Fontaine, J. R. J., & Verhofstadt-Denève, L. (2009). Confirming the distinctiveness of complicated grief from depression and anxiety among adolescents. *Death Studies, 33,* 437–461.

Dyregrov, A., Yule, W., Smith, P., Perrin, S., Gjestad, R., & Prigerson, H. (2001). *Traumatic Grief Inventory for Children (TGIC).* Bergen, Norway: Children and War Foundation (cf. http://www.childrenandwar.org).

Dyregrov, K., & Dyregrov, A. (in press). Helping the family following suicide. In B. Monroe & F. Krause (Eds.), *Brief interventions with bereaved children* (2nd ed.). New York: Oxford University Press.

Haine, R. A., Ayers, T. S., Sandler, I. N., & Wolchik, S. A. (2008). Evidence-based practices for parentally bereaved children and their families. *Professional Psychology: Research and Practice, 39,* 113–121.

Haine, R. A., Wolchik, S. A., Sandler, I. N., Millsap, R. M., & Ayers, T. S. (2006). Positive parenting as a protective resource for parentally bereaved children. *Death Studies, 30,* 1–28.

Harrison, L., & Harrington, R. (2001). Adolescent bereavement experiences: Prevalence, association with depressive symptoms, and use of services. *Journal of Adolescence, 24,* 159–169.

Kwok, O., Haine, R. A., Sandler, I. N., Ayers, T. S., Wolchik, S. A., & Tein, J-Y. (2005). Positive parenting as a mediator of the relations between parental psychological distress and mental health problems of parentally bereaved children. *Journal of Clinical Child and Adolescent Psychology, 34,* 260–271.

Layne, C. M., Savjak, N., Saltzman, W. R., & Pynoos, R. S. (2001). *UCLA/BYU Extended Grief Inventory.* Los Angeles: University of California. Available from Christopher. Layne@byui.edu.

Lin, K. K., Sandler, I. N., Ayers, T. S., Wolchik, S. A., & Luecken, L. J. (2004). Resilience in parentally bereaved children and adolescents seeking preventive services. *Journal of Clinical Child and Adolescent Psychology, 33,* 673–683.

Lutzke, J., Ayers, T., Sandler, I., & Barr, A. (1997). Risks and interventions for the parentally bereaved child. In S. Wolchik & I. N. Sandler (Eds.), *Handbook of children's coping: Linking theory and intervention* (pp. 215–243). New York: Plenum Press.

Melhem, N. M., Moritz, G., Walker, M., Shear, M. K., & Brent, D. (2007). Phenomenology and correlates of complicated grief in children and adolescents. *Journal of the American Academy of Child & Adolescent Psychiatry, 46*(4), 493–499.

Melhem, N. M., Walker, M., Moritz, G., & Brent, D. (2008). Antecedents and sequelae of sudden parental death in offspring and surviving caregivers. *Archives of Pediatric Adolescent Medicine, 162,* 403–410.

Monroe, B., & Krause, F. (Eds.). (in press). *Brief interventions with bereaved children* (2nd ed.). New York: Oxford University Press.

Moos, R. H., & Schaefer, J. A. (1986). Life transitions and crises: A conceptual overview. In R. H. Moos (Ed.), *Coping with life crises: An integrated approach* (pp. 3–28). New York: Plenum Press.

Pfeffer, C., Altemus, M., Heo, M., & Jiang, H. (2007). Salivary cortisol and psychopathology in children bereaved by the September 11, 2001, terror attacks. *Biological Psychiatry, 61,* 957–965.

Pynoos, R. (1992). Grief and trauma in children and adolescents. *Bereavement Care, 11,* 2–10.

Raveis, V. H., Siegel, K., & Karus, D. (1999). Children's psychological distress following the death of a parent. *Journal of Youth and Adolescence, 28,* 165–180.

Rotheram-Borus, M. J., Stein, J. A., & Lin, Y-Y. (2001). Impact of parent death and an intervention on the adjustment of adolescents whose parents have HIV/AIDS. *Journal of Consulting and Clinical Psychology, 69,* 763–773.

Rubin, S., & Malkinson, R. (2001). Parental response to child loss across the life cycle: Clinical and research perspectives. In M. R. Stroebe, O. Hansson, W. Stroebe, & H. Schut (Eds.), *Handbook of bereavement research: Consequences, coping, and care* (pp. 219–240). Washington, DC: American Psychological Association.

Saldinger, A., Cain, A., & Porterfield, K. (2003). Managing traumatic stress in children anticipating parental death. *Psychiatry: Interpersonal and Biological Processes, 66*(2), 168–181.

Sandler, I. N., Ayers, T. S., Wolchik, S. A., Tein, J-Y., Kwok, O-M., Haine, R. A., et al. (2003). The Family Bereavement Program: Efficacy evaluation of a theory-based prevention program for parentally-bereaved children and adolescents. *Journal of Consulting and Clinical Psychology, 71,* 587–600.

Sandler, I. N., Wolchik, S. A., & Ayers, T. S. (2008). Resilience rather than recovery: A contextual framework on adaptation following bereavement. *Death Studies, 32,* 59–73.

Siegel, K., Karus, D., & Raveis, V. H. (1996). Adjustment of children facing the death of a parent due to cancer. *Journal of the American Academy of Child & Adolescent Psychiatry, 35,* 442–450.

Siegel, K., Mesagno, F. P., & Christ, G. (1990). A prevention program for bereaved children. *American Journal of Orthopsychiatry, 60,* 168–175.

Siegel, K., Raveis, V. H., & Karus, D. (1996). Patterns of communication with children when a parent has cancer. In L. Baider (Ed.), *Cancer and the family* (pp. 109–126). New York: John Wiley & Sons.

Silverman, W. K., & Albano, A. M. (1996). *Anxiety disorders interview schedule for DSM-IV: Child version.* San Antonio, TX: Psychological Corporation.

Stroebe, M., & Schut, H. (1999). The dual process model of coping with bereavement: Rationale and description. *Death Studies, 23,* 1–28.

Worden, J. (1996). *Children and grief: When a parent dies.* New York: Guilford Press.

Yamamoto, K., Davis, O. L., Dylak, S., Whittaker, J., Marsh, C., & van der Westhuizen, P. C. (1996). Across six nations: Stressful events in the lives of children. *Child Psychiatry and Human Development, 26,* 139–149.

Yule, W., & Smith, P. (in press). Working with traumatically bereaved children. In B. Monroe & F. Krause (Eds.), *Brief interventions with bereaved children* (2nd ed.). New York: Oxford University Press.

10

Sibling Bereavement in Childhood

KATRINA KOEHLER

We were distant, yet close. He did his own thing. And he picked on me a lot. But whenever people were hurting me, Isaiah was the only one that would stick up for me . . . After he died, I didn't really have anybody anymore.

—Johnny, age 20, 11 years after his brother
Isaiah's death by suicide

Nat was my best friend . . . probably the best friend I will ever have . . . I miss her every day and night. I hope I always will. I don't ever want to stop missing her.

—Kimmy, age 10, 2 years after her sister
Natalie died of cancer

My brother and I didn't always get along. He could make my life hell, and he did. But we were there together for all the screwed up stuff that happened in our family. Now I'm the only one who knows how bad it really was.

—Caitlin, age 20, 10 years after her brother's death
by an apparently accidental overdose

Max was my hero for sure. I didn't really know him until he came to visit me when he was 18. It seems like we were just getting close when he passed away.

—Alex, age 17, 9 years after his 19-year-old
half-brother was hit by a car

195

We knew we might not have her for very long, so I tried to love her as
much as I could. I miss holding her and playing with her.
                          —Angelica, age 7, 2 months after the death
                                          of her infant sister Lupita

The quotes at the start of this chapter, taken together, offer a small, precious glimpse into the world of childhood sibling bereavement, a world that is hard to define, partly because of the bewildering complexity of the sibling grief experience, but also because one child's grief experience can be so dramatically different from another's—even within the same family.

This chapter explores both the common features of sibling bereavement and the singular journeys of the children who are confronted with the death of a brother or sister. The chapter begins with some comments on the sibling relationship. It then turns to an account of a roller coaster of emotions in sibling-bereaved children, other common reactions to sibling bereavement, reasons that this type of bereavement may stretch out, intensify, or come in waves over time, and factors that may complicate a child's bereavement experiences. In addition to relevant literature, this chapter is based on my personal experience being with and listening to grieving children and their families for the last 8 years, enlarged by interviews with children, teenagers, and adults who experienced the death of a brother or sister during childhood.

THE SIBLING RELATIONSHIP

What is unique about relationships between siblings? If you have at least one brother or sister, reflect for a moment on your childhood relationship. Was it "distant, yet close," like Johnny and Isaiah's (see opening quotes), or were you best friends like Kimmy and Natalie? Was he or she your tormentor (like Caitlin's big brother), your hero (like Alex's much-older half-brother), or someone you comforted and cared for (like Angelica's baby sister)? Perhaps you identify with some combination of these experiences.

It is difficult to lump all sibling relationships together, partly because they are so varied and partly because they are so complicated (Cicirelli, 1995). The phrase *universal ambivalence* has been coined to describe the multilayered, conflicted, and intense quality of most childhood sibling relationships (Stahlman, 1996, p. 150). When the death of one sibling interrupts this complex relationship midstream, the surviving sibling is left alone to resolve this quandary. This ambivalence often factors heavily into the surviving sibling's experience of grief and mourning. And yet this is not always the case.

Between some childhood siblings there is so little conflict that the term *ambivalence* does not seem apt. Similarly, what we uniquely share with most childhood siblings is the experience of growing up together, but in some multiple-household families or blended families, children have grown up only partly—or not at all—together. Sometimes a child's relationship to a half- or step-sibling or adopted or foster sibling may resemble the relationship to a new acquaintance or to a distant relation. But still there is a connection, a sibling connection, even if it is only in the knowledge that another child is out there, somewhere, to whom one is inexplicably linked.

As these examples illustrate, there may not be any single statement that applies without qualification to all sibling-bereaved children or that captures everyone's experience, but there are a host of themes and difficulties that many children who are grieving the death of a brother or sister experience in one way or another (Robinson & Mahon, 1997). Many of those themes appear in the following sections that describe a roller coaster of emotions and other common reactions found in sibling-bereaved children.

A ROLLER COASTER OF EMOTIONS

> When a child dies and when siblings do not understand what has happened, is happening, or is going to happen, they become more anxious in a situation where they already feel overwhelmed . . . Their own feelings are also confusing to them; it is puzzling and frightening, for example, to feel very sad because one's brother has died and, at the same time, feel very angry with him for leaving. (Davies, 1999, p. 200)

Most grieving children I meet do not know what the word "grief" means until I begin to talk to them about it. They know that most people are sad after someone dies and that people may cry and miss the person. They are usually surprised to learn that anger and fear are two of the main feelings children feel after the death of a family member. Many nod emphatically when I recount the kinds of scared and mad feelings grieving children usually experience, recognizing themselves in these descriptions.

Fear, anger, and sadness are only part of the emotional equation. Though grief is different for each child, it is very common for bereaved siblings to feel confused, guilty, worried and anxious, numb, over-amped with nervous energy, lonely, silly, happy, and more—an unpredictable, tumultuous cycle of feelings. During grief, these emotions can be stronger than children are prepared for as they cycle through, often coming in quick succession, as if competing for time on stage. For example, a child does not know in advance that he or she will be hit with a wave of extreme sadness and longing for the deceased sister while walking to school or experience a jolt of anger when asked to do a routine chore. This internal storm of emotions can be very disorienting. It is likely to be compounded by the instability a child may feel because of other life changes wrought by the sibling's death and the difficulties of navigating the unfamiliar waters of a newly-bereaved family.

Feeling Alone and Feeling Different

All kinds of memories bind most siblings together, from the wonderful and magical to the painful and bizarre. After a child's death, the surviving brother or sister is left holding this entire legacy alone. It can be scary, painful, bewildering. Parents, relatives, friends, and other siblings are also grieving the loss of the child who died, but that's different because it was a different relationship. Even in the closest and most supportive families, feeling alone is a normal part of grief.

Most bereaved siblings do not know other children who have experienced the death of a brother or sister. Research findings indicate that bereaved children feel different from their peers and because of this do not feel they belong with their friends as they did before the death (Davies, 1995). Being different in this way is one of the toughest aspects of grief for people of every age. As anyone can tell you who has experienced a devastating loss, it is emotionally bewildering to have one's personal world rocked to the core while business goes on as usual for most of the rest of the world. The discomfort for grieving *children* in this respect is particularly acute, both because of their especially strong need to belong and because of the way groups of children tend to withdraw from anyone who is different.

Children sometimes do not have the perspective to understand that they feel alone and different because they are grieving. When feelings of abandonment and isolation come over the sibling-bereaved child, that child may not associate the feelings with the death or the grief.

Feeling Awkward, Embarrassed, Ashamed, or Weird

> The main thing I remember right after JD got shot is that I couldn't talk
> to anyone about it. People kept asking me, "How *are* you? How do you
> *feel?*" I hated that! At the funeral they were all saying that stuff to me. I just
> wanted to get out of there.
>
> —Amanda, age 10, 3 years after her stepbrother JD was murdered
> at a party

Grieving children often report that no one knows what to say to
them, how to talk to them, or even how to be around them after the
death. Children feel that the burden is on them to figure out how to act,
and even to help others with their own awkwardness. It is embarrassing
for kids to be different. Having their peers, and even adults, know of
their misfortune can make them feel ashamed. It is awkward for children not knowing what to say or how to act around others after the death
or how to answer their questions or reply to their attempts to console or
reassure the child.

When the circumstances of the sibling's death are violent, rumors
often spring up, fueled by the curiosity and imaginations of other children and even adults. A grieving child already feels vulnerable. Being
at the center of a rumor mill while at a low point in one's life is a mis-
erable experience that can leave a young person feeling wounded and
alienated.

When a young person dies by suicide, there are added troubles for
the surviving sibling: the child's family, school, and faith community
are left to make sense of the death and wonder what went wrong. The
family often feels ashamed or defensive, with segments of the community taking part in finger-pointing, assigning of blame, or worse. After
Isaiah's suicide, 9-year-old Johnny remembers a classmate telling him
that his brother would burn in hell. Later, at Isaiah's funeral recep-
tion, he overheard someone say, "The priest they wanted to do the
funeral refused because suicide is a mortal sin. And the idiot is in hell
for that."

When 10-year-old Caitlin returned to school after her brother died
of an apparently accidental overdose, she arrived nervous and not sure
how to act. Unfortunately, the school administrators did not notify the
students of Rob's death, so rumors and questions were circulating instead of facts. Some students avoided Caitlin, and this response made
her feel like an outcast. When children in her class did interact with her,

they did not know what to say. She remembers them being tongue-tied and asking, "Are you okay?" Questions like this were difficult for her, as she explains:

> What do you say to something like that? I wanted to scream, "Of course I'm not okay! My brother just died! How can you even ask me that?" I couldn't say that, though, or they would think I was a freak, and they were probably trying to be nice. So I just tried to get through it.

But the worst part for Caitlin was that several older children tried to get information from her about the details of her brother's death. Did he die at the party or at the hospital? What did he take? Who was there? To make matters worse, she had not been told the whole story herself and so did not know the answers to some of these questions. Reflecting on these experiences years later, Caitlin recalls feeling pried into, ashamed, and wounded, as if no one cared about her.

Guilt and Regrets

> The death of a sibling can be among the most traumatic events in a child's life. Why? Because not only has a family member died, but a family member for whom the child probably had very strong and ambivalent feelings. As those of us who have brothers and sisters know, sibling relationships are characterized by anger, jealousy, and fierce closeness and love—a highly complex mélange of emotion. This complexity colors the surviving child's grief experience. (Wolfelt, 1996, p. 22)

In most families, it is with their siblings that children most openly express—and feel—anger in childhood. For one thing, it is generally safer than getting mad at parents or other adults. An even bigger issue, though, is that siblings are usually specially positioned to bedevil us. They can trigger frustration, annoyance, jealousy, resentment, righteous indignation, even out-of-control rage. Brothers and sisters are the ones with whom we have to share (or fight over) most of our childhood resources—whether the backseat of the car, mom's attention, dad's approval, control of the TV, or the last piece of cake.

Many children who have no other outlet for their anger act out on a handy sibling when no one else is looking, setting off cycles of yelling, crying, and fighting. In fact, most young siblings fight with the older child, usually initiating aggression (Abramovitch, Corter, & Lando, 1979). Even in families where siblings treat each other with exceptional kindness and respect, some friction comes with the territory. Older brothers get to do things younger brothers cannot yet do, and younger brothers tend to receive special affection and attention.

So when a brother or sister dies, the surviving child is very often haunted by a yearning to take back the fights, the harsh words, the unkind actions, but now—the child feels—it is too late. Besides the things that were said and done, the child may regret thoughts and feelings too—especially feelings of anger. Most of the children I have worked with whose siblings have died have struggled with some kind of remorse. They may have general regrets, saying things like, "I wish I had told her I loved her," "I wish I had been nicer to her," or "I feel bad about all the times we fought." They may also regret something more specific. Interestingly, one study (Hurd, 2002) reported that four bereaved siblings (all sisters) in two families, with the assistance of a supportive adult in each case, contributed to each other's healthy grieving by providing emotional closeness, mutual support, and models for each other of constructive ways to mourn their losses.

One girl wished she had played with her little brother more often. Another girl regretted sneaking into her older sister's room while her sister was in the hospital and borrowing her clothes. Some children have been almost consumed by guilt and regrets before receiving support, especially if the sibling died by suicide. Johnny's story is illustrative of the regret that survivors of a sibling's suicide often feel.

> I had gotten into a fight with him the last time I saw him before he died. He was cussing at my Mom and pushing her, and I said, "Why don't you leave! Why don't you just go to hell! Quit ruining everyone's life!". . . I always thought it was my fault, but nobody in my family knows that. I still haven't told them.

Though a suicide tends to turn the volume up on these thoughts and feelings, in all cases after the death, the opportunity to apologize and make amends (or to be apologized to and have amends made)—the chance to heal the relationship—has seemingly been taken away. In a sense, the child is grieving the loss of the possibility of someday working things out.

Magical Thinking

Children often blame themselves for siblings' deaths in ways that make no logical sense to adults (Fogarty, 2000). Whereas a father may feel guilty about having been angry at his son before he died, a child may believe that his or her anger actually caused a brother or sister to die. With surprising frequency, children also feel and believe that if they had done something differently, they might have prevented the death. Alex recalls how he suffered as a child believing that he had been meant to protect his half-brother, Max, from getting hit by a car while riding his bike. He felt that he was supposed to tell Max about a dream he had had, and that by not telling him, he had let Max die.

> About six months before the accident, I had this dream that Max was riding on his bike, and he was going really fast down a hill. He was riding away from me and then all of a sudden, he was gone. I never told anyone about it, that dream. A little while after he died, I started to wonder if that dream was maybe a premonition, and that if I would have told him about it, he would have been more careful on his bike. I thought I had been given this chance to save my brother from getting killed and that I had completely blown it.

Anger, Irritability, Lashing Out, and Getting in Trouble

> The first year after JD got shot I got sent to the principal's office like every day. I didn't know how to deal with my feelings at the time, so I got in trouble.
>
> —Jeremiah, age 12, 3 years after his brother JD's death

Bereaved siblings have a lot to be angry about (see Table 10.1). Their lives have usually been turned upside down. Not all grieving siblings throw temper tantrums or start getting in trouble at school, but many do if anger is a prominent feature in their roller coaster of emotions. For these kids, the anger associated with their grief often manifests as irritability, a "short fuse," or sudden flares of rage in response to triggers that would not normally have generated such intensity. Anger can also show up as sullen, withdrawn behavior.

Unfortunately for bereaved siblings who experience their grief this way, their impulsive, inconsiderate words and actions may repel their friends and classmates and cause problems in their relationships with

Table 10.1

SPECIFIC ANGERS/GRIEVANCES OF BEREAVED SIBLINGS

- Anger that their brother or sister died.
- Anger at their brother or sister for leaving them, especially if the death was a suicide.
- Anger at whomever they blame for the death, especially in the case of an accidental death or murder, but also sometimes in cases of illness.
- Anger at God or fate.
- Anger about the changes in the family environment.
- Anger that no one understands what they are going through.
- Anger and jealousy because their parents and caregivers are preoccupied with the child who died.

---

parents, teachers, and other adults in their lives—the very ones whose loving attention and support they need (Birenbaum, Robinson, Phillips, Stewart, & McCown, 1990; McCown & Davies, 1995). A vicious cycle can easily develop when the grieving child becomes even more angry in response to the consequences of his or her acting out.

Being Extra Good/Overachieving/Perfectionism

> My parents had already been through so much with Rob. Then he died. I felt like I couldn't put them through one more thing. I tried not to do anything to upset them, and I tried to make up for everything he had done.
> —Caitlin, age 20, 10 years after her brother's death by an apparently accidental overdose

In this flip side of acting out, a child turns inward, assumes unrealistic expectations, and does not let himself or herself be a child. Bereaved siblings are at risk for painting themselves into this kind of emotional corner because they usually have an abundance of inner turmoil and yet are keenly aware of their parents' suffering and vulnerability. It is not uncommon for a bereaved sibling to try to be the good one, the one who cannot stand to create any problems, who works hard to please everyone all the time, and who redeems the family with his or her achievements—the family hero.

A bereaved sister who copes with her grief and her parents' grief through perfectionism will usually try to suppress her grief or hide it from other family members. She is hard on herself, tries too hard not to get in trouble, and strives for perfect grades, athletic achievement, or other markers of success. Striving for perfection helps her to feel less out-of-control, as if by being extra-good she can somehow soothe her parents' pain and compensate for her sibling's death and for all the pain and turmoil the family is experiencing.

In most cases, the sibling-bereaved child with this coping strategy tends to fly under the radar, at least for a while. He is the one about whom teachers, parents, and relatives are likely to remark, "He's handling it so well!" This is exactly the effect he is aiming for, even though he is really hurting inside. He may not feel safe to let himself grieve and needs some kind of support to feel secure enough to surface his feelings. Otherwise, the pressure cooker he is holding is probably going to boil over—even if it happens years later.

When Caitlin's brother died by accidental overdose, she was 10 years old. She made a pact with herself that she would make every attempt to be her parents' version of the perfect child. By the time she was 14, she had developed an eating disorder, was thinking about suicide, and was scraping her arms and legs with pins until she bled, a self-destructive practice called cutting. Caitlin is now 20. "I didn't even know that what was happening to me had anything to do with Rob's death, or that grief could come out like that," she says. "I thought it was my fault, that something was really wrong with me. Now when I think about everything I was holding in . . . it was like I was holding my breath for 4 years without thinking this would hurt me."

Not all children who appear to be coping well are masking their true feelings. If they can openly and comfortably express their grief in some way, and are okay with making mistakes or displeasing an adult, then the "perfectionist" coping strategy probably does not apply to them.

Fear and Anxiety

When a child's brother or sister dies, another young person has died. So, for the child, confronting this reality can mean confronting the possibility of one's own death. Be prepared to honestly but reassuringly answer questions such as, "Will I die, too?" (Wolfelt, 1996, p. 22)

Parallel to the grief process, sibling-bereaved children go through a process of coming to terms with death, usually for the first time. The realization "I could die, too" means that they are facing their own mortality before most of their peers. The fear of losing other family members to death upsets many children once they have experienced the death of a sibling. They may cling to their parents, request constant communication, want to sleep with them, or want to know where they are all the time. Some sibling-bereaved children have an anxious, worried affect, as if they do not feel safe now that their sense of security has been shaken. Because nighttime, for most children, is when the deepest fears surface, a sibling-bereaved child may object to being left alone at bedtime and may cry in terror of nightmares or night terrors.

Sadness/Depression

Sadness is the one emotion bereaved siblings in our society are expected to feel, but that does not mean their sadness is always accepted by adults. Parents and caregivers may not be prepared for the intensity of a child's heartbreak or for how long it goes on, especially when siblings were very close. In some families, parents want their children to be sad when the parents are sad but to snap out of it when the parents are feeling good. Other families do not "do sadness" well at all, and the child is left with no outlet for feeling or expressing pain within the family.

In her research on child-bereaved siblings, Davies (1999) found that half were sad, unhappy, or depressed. Bereaved siblings in our groups at Gerard's House talk about being sad for many reasons: because they miss their brother or sister, because they are upset thinking about their deceased sibling's experience of death, because their parents and other family members are upset, and because they feel alone at school.

The difference between sadness and clinical depression as manifested in grieving children is not easy to sort out because the natural grief process resembles depression in many ways. Two very basic red flags for depression in grieving children are (1) when the child's self-esteem is very low and (2) when the child appears emotionally shutdown. A bereaved sibling who is sad and not depressed can generally accept comfort, work through feelings by playing, and feel that others value and care about him. He or she can experience moments of happiness or laughter. A depressed child loses much of this perspective and emotional flexibility.

Sad people know who or what they have lost and yearn for the return of what is gone. Despite great sadness, hope is still present; sad people are receptive to support and comfort from others, and their sense of competence and personal worth remains intact. When sadness is accompanied by feeling abandoned, unwanted, and unlovable, pathological depression results. (Davies, 1999, p. 54)

Missing the Sister or Brother

For a child who cherished a brother or sister, the longing for the deceased sibling can be powerful and painful. Davies' (1999) research on the correlation between sibling closeness and grief behaviors showed that "bereaved siblings who were closer to their siblings before the death experienced more internalizing behavior problems after the death" (p. 130). Kimmy, whose sister Nat was her best friend, was heartbroken after Nat's death. She cried herself to sleep many nights and felt desolate on and off for more than 2 years. Now in her third year since Nat's death, she still experiences intense moments of grief at times, especially on Nat's birthday, at family gatherings, and when a song by Nat's favorite singer comes on the radio.

Even a child who did not especially like or feel close to a sibling before he or she died will usually miss that brother or sister after the death, though this missing will be mixed with other feelings. Caitlin, whose brother Rob bullied her, explains her conflicted feelings after Rob's death: "It took me a long time to get used to him not being there. Even though it was almost a relief to have him gone, I still miss him. I remember the good times when we were little."

Relief and Mixed Feelings

Relief is an emotion often expressed by children whose brothers or sisters were suffering before they died. When other family members openly share their feelings of relief with the child after the sibling's death, the child can better accept these feelings. When children do not know that others are also relieved, they tend to feel confused and guilty about their feelings of relief and may even deny them.

Bereaved siblings may also experience a sense of relief if they had conflicted relationships with their deceased siblings, if the sibling was abusive, or if there were other major problems associated with the brother or sister who died (e.g., depression, substance abuse, erratic behavior). Sometimes relief is a relatively small feeling compared with missing and cherishing the deceased sibling, but for children like Caitlin, relief and the accompanying guilt are a major part of their grief process. Ten years later, she can talk openly about the relief and mixed feelings she felt after Rob's death, but as a child, she could not. Children need help accepting all these feelings.

Identity Confusion

A period of identity loss or identity confusion is another part of the grief process for many sibling-bereaved children (Martinson, Davies, & McClowry, 1987).

> One eight-year-old girl I counseled after the death of her brother asked me, "Am I still a big sister?" This little girl was obviously struggling with the confusing task of redefining herself, both within the family unit and the world at large. (Wolfelt, 1996, p. 22)

As they grow, develop, and discover themselves, children look to others as mirrors to help give them a sense who they are. When a sibling dies, a child's self-image and sense of self are called into question. If the brother or sister who died was the closest person in the child's life, the child's old identity is likely to feel disrupted. Moreover, the loss of one child from the family can knock the family system off balance and destabilize the other children's roles within the family. The family system is faced—usually subconsciously—with the problem of how to "fill" the empty space left by the child who died. More than one grieving sibling has shared with me, "I feel like I have to be two people now: me and my sister/brother who died." At times grieving siblings take on mannerisms, expressions, and even interests of the one who died.

> Reorganizing the family system requires family members to reconstruct what the family means to them and their sense of identity as a family. In addition, family members must reapportion or abandon activities and roles formerly assigned to the deceased. . . . Open, honest, and supportive communication within the family system is essential to all of these tasks. (Corr, Nabe, & Corr, 2009, p. 240)

Crying and Not Crying

Parents often ask if it is normal that their grieving child is not crying. My experience is that some children cry a lot, and others very little or not at all, and that the "normal" range is very large. In Davies' studies (1999), about one-quarter of sibling-bereaved children cried "a lot." This means that three-quarters of sibling-bereaved children in Davies' research groups did not cry a lot. Most children benefit from being reassured that it is okay to cry. Still, judging a child for not crying is not helpful, nor is pressuring that child to cry. Some children, especially boys, prefer to cry in secret and will deny crying if asked by their parents. Other children are very upset but may have a hard time expressing through tears. For still others, the sadness associated with crying may not be a primary initial response to the sibling's death.

For the first few days after his brother died, Alex was unable to cry:

> I wanted to cry at Max's funeral, but I couldn't, even though I was completely wrecked. I guess I was too much in shock or something. I didn't actually cry until after my uncle talked to me. But before that, I was kind of wondering what was going on with me that I couldn't cry. I wanted to, I even felt like I should, but I couldn't.

Alex's uncle took the boy to the park to shoot baskets. While they played, he told Alex, "I'm here. If you ever need me, I'm here for you. And you can tell me anything, and it will be just between you and me." That conversation was a turning point for Alex. "That was it," he says. "That was all I needed someone to do." Later, when Alex's uncle was driving him to the restaurant where they were going to have dinner, Alex began to weep. "My uncle didn't say anything. He just put his hand on my shoulder. That really helped."

OTHER COMMON GRIEF REACTIONS OF SIBLING-BEREAVED CHILDREN

Physical manifestations. Children often hold unexpressed grief in their bodies. Headaches, stomachaches, loss of appetite, muscular tension, decreased resistance to illness, and increased blood pressure are all ways that held emotions can show up somatically.

Disturbed sleep patterns. The child may not want to sleep alone, may have difficulty falling asleep, and may be gripped with fear, sadness, or persistent troubling thoughts at night. Fear of the dark and fear of ghosts are common. If the child shared a room with the brother or sister who died, it will usually be especially hard for the child to sleep in that room.

Nightmares, night terrors, and sleepwalking. Death becomes a theme in some bereaved siblings' dreams, and sometimes these dreams are frightening. Insomnia may be accompanied by night terrors. Although sleepwalking is not a common grief response, it does happen to certain children during periods of acute grief and may then subside when the child reconciles some grief feelings.

Playing and being happy in the midst of grief. Most bereaved children amaze adults with their ability to laugh, be silly, and run around and play moments after crying or feeling very sad. "In this way, children may be 'dosing' themselves with their grief and mourning" (Corr et al., 2009, p. 340).

Inability to think straight and concentrate; being preoccupied. Periods of not being able to pay attention, focus, or complete tasks often go on for a long time after the death and may come in waves, just as grief does. The child's room may get messy, and chores may go undone as these tasks become more challenging and overwhelming for the bereaved sibling.

Poor school performance. An inability to concentrate and complete tasks can negatively affect grades, as can the roller coaster of emotions. This failure to perform as well academically as before the death can, in turn, increase tensions and frustrations in relationships with teachers, parents, or caregivers.

Numbing the uncomfortable feelings. Sibling-bereaved children may use TV, video games, and other screen time to numb feelings such as pain, sadness, fear, anger, shock, anxiety, guilt, and regrets.

Restlessness; inability to sit still or relax. Being stirred up emotionally can make children agitated, restless, and easily distracted.

Exhaustion and fatigue. The emotional roller coaster associated with grief can also wear children out, especially if their sleep is also disturbed.

Eating patterns. Some sibling-bereaved children experience a loss of appetite. We see this problem especially in children who feel very sad and bereft and who either desperately miss their brother or sister or have been dramatically affected by a parent's grief. Many children's eating patterns, however, remain relatively unchanged, and some children eat more.

Regressing to younger behaviors. Talking baby talk, bed-wetting, and immature behavior are all examples of how children may regress when they are grieving. Not all sibling-bereaved children regress, though. In fact, some act more responsibly and maturely than ever.

Dreaming about the brother or sister who died. Some bereaved siblings have dreams in which the brother or sister who died is still alive.

Survivor's guilt. A sibling-bereaved child may wonder, "Why did my brother or sister die, and not me?" Both the book and the movie *Ordinary People* (Guest, 1976) beautifully illustrate the guilt a teenage boy feels because he survived the boating accident in which his brother died. Feeling relieved to be the one who is still alive can also make children feel guilty.

Re-grieving at the age when the sibling died. If the sibling who died was older, it is a significant milestone when the bereaved child reaches the age at which the sibling died, one that can catalyze a fear of dying or survivor's guilt.

Re-grieving at new developmental stages. As children get older and develop cognitively, emotionally, and spiritually, they are better equipped to understand the implications of the sibling's death—to realize that it is final and irreversible, for example, and what that means for the child's future. With new insight and perspective can come new layers of grief.

Re-grieving at life milestones. When the deceased sibling's class graduates from middle school, for example, the whole family may be hit with a wave of grief. Also, when the bereaved sibling experiences a milestone—an achievement, award, or church confirmation, for example—it is another trigger for missing the brother or sister who died.

Transformation. At some point down the road, the bereaved sibling may feel gratitude for the life-changing experience of having gone through the natural grief process. Teenagers who experienced significant deaths during childhood, when asked how they are different because of the grief they lived through, talk about increased empathy, emotional depth, and a greater appreciation for life and how precious it is (Balk, 1983; Oltjenbruns, 2001).

Continuing bonds. An important lesson from recent research has been that children who are bereaved by the death of a sibling (and by other significant deaths in their lives) often find it important to maintain some sort of ongoing connection with the person who died (Klass, Silverman, & Nickman, 1996; Worden, 2009). In cases such as this, death ends a life but not necessarily a relationship. The surviving sibling often finds comfort in a continuing bond with a sense of presence or representation of the brother or sister who died (Packman, Horsley, Davies, & Kramer, 2006). This bond is likely to be dynamic, changing over time, and influenced by many factors as part of the child's adaptation to the new world in which his or her sibling is no longer physically present.

OVER TIME CHILDREN'S GRIEF CAN STRETCH OUT, INTENSIFY, OR COME IN WAVES

> Why did everyone tell me I'd be feeling better by now? I wish they hadn't said that, because it's been a year and I feel worse than ever!
> —An older child 1 year after the death of her close cousin, who was like her brother

Some sibling-bereaved children seem to be doing fine right after the death. Then, several months later, they begin to show more signs of grieving. What is hard for these children is that their grief is intensifying at a time when most parents and teachers think the child should be getting over it. There are several reasons for this seemingly delayed response.

First, children usually do not take in the finality of a death and its full implications all at once. It takes time to process this. This is especially true for very young children. In the meantime, children tend to re-experience grief each time the loved person is not there. As painful as this is, children can often tolerate missing the person who died for a little while, but the "goneness" of the person builds up over time. As this "goneness" is getting harder and harder to bear, the fact that the person is not coming back is sinking in deeper over time as a physical and emotional reality for them.

Another reason for a time lag in the grief response is that some children try to "hold it together" during the initial crisis period after a death because their family lives feel unstable and in flux. Many children later reflect on the first several weeks after the death, saying that they were in shock or felt numb at first, that the first few months were all a blur, or that they knew in their minds that the person was dead, but it hadn't really "hit" them yet, not until 2 or 6 or 10 months later.

This seemingly postponed grief is made more difficult for children when parents and teachers expect the child to grieve for a little while (a few days or weeks) and then go back to "normal." The truth is, it is actually quite common for grief to intensify over the first few months as the shock wears off and the finality of the death sinks in. Eventually, almost all sibling-bereaved children do feel better if they have an opportunity to move through their grief, but feeling better may not happen within the first year. Caitlin (age 20), 10 years after her brother's death by an apparently accidental overdose, said, "Most people want you to get over it. They don't understand that you need to grieve. The 'getting over it' is really for them, not for you."

Once a child does start to feel some relief from the grief, it usually comes back in waves or cycles that go on for years, many say for a lifetime. How long a bereaved sibling grieves varies for each child and with each death, but sometimes the pain of loss hits hardest many years after death, especially if the bereaved sibling's natural grief process was somehow blocked or undermined at the time of the death (which happens all too often, for reasons discussed in the next section). Then a trigger many years later may activate the grief process.

FACTORS THAT CAN COMPLICATE CHILDREN'S GRIEF RESPONSES TO SIBLING BEREAVEMENT

The ways children experience their own grief are shaped by many variables, including the child's age and developmental level, the quality of the relationship between grieving parent and grieving child, how the parents cope with their grief (and whether they have sufficient support), the family configuration and family dynamics, the cause and circumstances of the death and relationship to the sibling who died, and the surviving child's personality, temperament, and coping mechanisms. Some of the most prominent of these factors are discussed in the following subsections:

The Child Prior to the Death of a Sibling

In evaluating some of the common feelings, experiences, and behaviors of sibling-bereaved children, it is useful to consider children's preexisting behavior patterns and the extent to which they foreshadow individual children's grieving styles. In most cases, the coping mechanisms a child employs for smaller stresses and losses will be the ones that child relies on when grieving—a normally shy and introspective child tends to withdraw in grief, whereas a child who struggles with anger is likely to act out while grieving. The overachiever may cross the line into harsh perfectionism, whereas the underachiever's grades are likely to dip, if not plummet. But sometimes the bereaved sibling will reach a breaking point, a place where familiar coping mechanisms break down, and dormant or latent behaviors emerge.

One normally even-tempered young girl began to engage in angry outbursts that her mother said were completely out of character. Her mother was shocked when her formally sweet and compliant little girl began to scream at her over seemingly trivial matters. A boy who used to like to play outside with friends began hanging out more and more in front of the TV or in his room with his door closed. Like these bereaved siblings, most children do behave differently when grieving and undergo noticeable behavior changes (though not all do).

Emotional Distress at the Magnitude of Parents' and Caregivers' Grief

> I know my stepdad is really hurt, but he's one of those macho guys who can't cry. You can just see it eating him up. He takes it out on my brother more than me. He's always been hard on Jeremiah, but now it's like [Jeremiah] can't do anything right.
>
> —Amanda, age 13, 3 years after her stepbrother JD was murdered at a party (her stepbrother Jeremiah is 12)

My mom's baby died. My mom is very, very sad. She cries every night.
        —Matteo, age 4, 2 months after the death of his infant sister Lupita

It is hard to think of an event in any adult's life more dreaded, or more catastrophic, than the death of a daughter or son. For surviving siblings, their parents' devastation can have as great an impact on the grieving child as the sibling's death itself. Many children feel deprived of parental attention after the death, even though they need it more than ever. In other families, grieving parents dote on or even cling to their children who are still alive. But whether the grieving child is getting more attention or less attention, if even one parent is incapacitated by grief, or less responsive to the family (e.g., slides into depression, overworking, partying and heavy drinking, or lashing out at other family members), the child is likely to feel insecure and frightened, and depending on the child, he or she may eventually be angry.

Some children respond to these changes in their grieving parents by taking great pains not to do anything to upset them; other children strike out at their parents (or at other people); still others cling to their parents and want to be around them all the time.

Children Becoming Their Parents' Caregivers

My family was kind of stupid in the way they decided to handle it. They asked me to support them. They asked me to hold everybody up. I was 9 years old, I had just lost the only friend I ever had, and I was supposed to hold them up.
        —Johnny, age 20, 11 years after his brother Isaiah's death by suicide

In some families, at least one surviving child becomes an emotional caretaker for the bereaved parent(s). In my experience working with grieving families, this assignment of roles is all right for everyone involved if the child still feels parented, nurtured, and loved, and if the parent is not dependent on the child. It becomes extremely problematic for the child, however, if the caregiving is not reciprocated enough or if the child views himself as the main one responsible for the parent's emotional support and well-being. In those cases, the child's primary grief is largely subverted, and his or her secondary grief (for example, feelings about mother and/or father being incapacitated in whatever ways that happens) is also not given enough room to surface.

Some children naturally gravitate toward the role of caregiver (Mahon & Page, 1995). They put their arms around Mommy when she is crying, or they crawl into Dad's lap when he looks sad. It is natural for a child to be attuned to his or her parents' feelings, as long as space is made for the child's feelings as well, and the child is also able to disengage from the parent when he or she needs to go play or do other things, knowing the parent will be okay. But sometimes grieving parents lean on their children in inappropriate ways.

For 9-year-old Johnny, the adults in his life tasked him with the care of his parents in the wake of his brother's suicide. "Someone took me aside at the funeral and said, 'You need to support your mom. You need to help them [your parents].' I was the one going around in the middle of the night at my house to see who was crying. If they were, I would walk in and give them a hug until they stopped."

Other relatives, including Johnny's father, gave him similar instructions. Even though Johnny was reeling in shock and devastation after his brother's suicide, he was not aware of thinking anything was wrong with being asked to "hold up" everyone in his family. He felt that someone needed to take care of his mom and other family members and that he was the only one there to do it. Only recently has Johnny begun to realize that an excessive burden was placed on him at too young an age. After many years, he is now able to witness himself as a child who was in crisis and whose emotional needs were ignored in favor of everyone else's.

> The worst thing was that no one was bothering to help me. Everyone was too sad in their own right. I can understand people being sad about it, but what I can't understand is that even 3 years later, no one even wanted to talk to me about it. . . . They just sent me off to therapy . . . Nobody was there to comfort me at night, and I couldn't comfort myself.

Children Blocking, Hiding, or Suppressing Their Own Grief

Most children's adult role models have difficulty allowing their own natural grief process to surface. Children tend to learn and emulate this behavior, censoring themselves when grieving unless they are given special acknowledgment and emotional support. The sibling-bereaved child may feel, even with people outside his or her family, "It's my job to hide this so no one else has to deal with it." Another reason children tend to restrain their grief response is because their parents' grief is so intense. The surviving brother or sister may decide, often subconsciously, that the parents cannot handle the child's grief in addition to theirs. They may also get the message from other adults that their parents' grief comes first.

> Because the death of a child is such a traumatic family event, much of the attention from typical sources of support is given to the grieving parents. This may tend to reduce or minimize the importance of the child's grief. (Stahlman, 1996, p. 153)

Children's Concerns About Their Parents' Preoccupation With the Child Who Died

Sibling-bereaved children often have a hard time accepting their own feelings of jealousy and resentment over their parents' emotional fixation on the child who died. Several teens whose siblings died when they were children reported having thought, "What about me? I'm still here! Why am I not important, too?" or "All they care about is my sister!"

Cultural Factors

The significance of cultural factors as influences in the grief of sibling-bereaved children can be seen in the area where I live and work. In Santa Fe, New Mexico, four main cultures dominate the region: Hispanic, Mexican American, Native American (primarily Pueblo and Navajo), and "Anglo" or European American. Each culture has its distinct rituals, beliefs, and traditions around death and grief—some explicit and others unspoken. Yet, within each group, there is huge variation in terms of how individuals actually mourn and grieve. For people who grew up in one of the eight northern pueblos, for example, there is a traditional prohibition against mentioning the person who died more than four days after the death. As explained to me, this restriction is meant to respect the person who died and help the spirit of the person move on to the next world. In reality, however, there is a large spectrum of ways Native Americans from the pueblos interact with this tradition. Some observe it strictly, whereas others completely ignore it, and most Pueblo people I have met end up doing something in between: for example, they may avoid saying the name of the person who died after four days, if possible, but talk freely *about* the person, especially as part of their grief process.

Though there is no such formal restriction against speaking of the dead in either the Catholic or the Hispanic tradition, Johnny, a child who is part Native American and part Hispanic, reports that in terms of the pressure not to talk about his brother who died, the suicide, or his own grief, "the Catholic side was worse than the Native American side" in both his family and his community. "The Hispanic side was not open to my grief," he remembers. "It was, 'Don't talk about it. Don't bring other people into your problems.'"

Ironically, Johnny's Native American grandmother was the person *most* willing to talk to Johnny about Isaiah and his death. "Because my grandma is Native, the four-day rule was built in to the family structure," he says, "but she was more open about it than they were. She was willing to talk about things, and even more so now that she is older."

Though Johnny's experience in his Catholic Hispanic community was that grief was shunted aside, the way Kimmy's Catholic Hispanic mother and family responded to her sister's death was radically different. Her mother was extremely open to both her grief and her daughter's grief, always willing to talk about it and to listen. Kimmy and her mother have become closer since Nat's death, and all the sharing has helped.

CONCLUSION

The effects of early losses in life, such as those that are typically associated with the death of a child's brother or sister, can have a profound and long-term impact on a surviving sibling (Porterfield, Cain, & Saldinger, 2003). Many aspects of this impact are normal manifestations of grief and mourning; some can be disruptive to the sibling-bereaved child's well-being; others can be positive in nature. Davies (1999) identified four general responses found in surviving siblings: (1) "I hurt inside," (2) "I don't understand," (3) "I don't belong," and (4) "I'm not enough." When adults can acknowledge the bereaved child sibling's loss and support his or her natural grief process, with caring attention and understanding, their efforts can help the child cope with each of these responses in constructive ways, along with the various emotional and other reactions described in this chapter.

REFERENCES

Abramovitch, R., Corter, C., & Lando, B. (1979). Sibling interaction in the home. *Child development, 50,* 997–1003.

Balk, D. E. (1983). Adolescents' grief reactions and self-concept perceptions following sibling death: A case study of 33 teenagers. *Journal of Youth and Adolescence, 12,* 137–163.

Birenbaum, L. K., Robinson, M. A., Phillips, D. S., Stewart, B. J., & McCown, D. E. (1990). The response of children to the dying and death of a sibling. *Omega, Journal of Death and Dying, 20,* 213–228.

Cicirelli, V. G. (1995). *Sibling relationships across the lifespan.* New York: Plenum.

Corr, C. A., Nabe, C. M., & Corr, D. M. (2009). *Death and dying, live and living* (6th ed.). Belmont, CA: Wadsworth.

Davies, B. (1995). Long term effects of sibling death in childhood. In D. Adams & E. Deveau (Eds.), *Beyond the innocence of childhood: Vol. 3. Helping children and adolescents cope with death and bereavement* (pp. 89–98). Amityville, NY: Baywood.

Davies, B. (1999). *Shadows in the sun: The experiences of sibling bereavement in childhood.* Washington, DC: Taylor & Francis.

Fogarty, J. A. (2000). *The magical thoughts of grieving children: Treating children with complicated mourning and advice for parents.* Amityville, NY: Baywood.

Guest, J. (1976). *Ordinary people.* New York: Viking.

Hurd, R. C. (2002), Sibling support systems in childhood after a parent dies. *Omega, Journal of Death and Dying, 45,* 299–320.

Klass, D., Silverman, P., & Nickman, S. L. (Eds.). (1996). *Continuing bonds: New understandings of grief.* Philadelphia: Taylor & Francis.

Mahon, M. M., & Page, M. L. (1995). Childhood bereavement after the death of a sibling. *Holistic Nursing Practice, 9,* 15–26.

Martinson, I. M., Davies, E. B., & McClowry, S. G. (1987). The long-term effects of sibling death on self-concept. *Journal of Pediatric Nursing, 2,* 227–235.

McCown, D. E., & Davies, B. (1995). Patterns of grief in young children following the death of a sibling. *Death Studies, 19,* 41–53.

Oltjenbruns, K. A. (2001). Developmental context of childhood: Grief and regrief phenomena. In M. S. Stroebe, R. O. Hansson, E. Stroebe, & H. Schut (Eds.), *Handbook of bereavement research: Consequences, coping, and care* (pp. 169–197). Washington, DC: American Psychological Association.

Packman, W., Horsley, H., Davies, B., & Kramer, R. (2006). Sibling bereavement and continuing bonds. *Death Studies, 30,* 817–841.

Porterfield, K., Cain, A., & Saldinger, A. (2003). The impact of early loss history on parenting of bereaved children. *Omega, Journal of Death and Dying, 47,* 203–220.

Robinson, L., & Mahon, M. M. (1997). Sibling bereavement: A concept analysis. *Death Studies, 21,* 477–499.

Stahlman, S. D. (1996). Children and the death of a sibling. In C. A. Corr & D. M. Corr (Eds.), *Handbook of childhood death and bereavement* (pp. 149–164). New York: Springer Publishing.

Wolfelt, A. (1996). *Healing the bereaved child: Grief gardening, growth through grief and other touchstones for caregivers.* Fort Collins, CO: Companion Press.

Worden, J. W. (2009). *Grief counseling and grief therapy: A handbook for the mental health practitioner* (4th ed.). New York: Springer Publishing.

11

Death of a Friend During Childhood

DIANE SNYDER COWAN

When Mario was in the first grade, his classmate, who had gone home ill, died during the night. He had strep throat. Kayla was 9 when her friend Stacy died after a short time in pediatric hospice care. She had been hospitalized from a scalding at the hands of her abusive father. Roni was 10 when her best friend died after a long battle with cancer. A fifth grader, walking home from school with three friends, was killed during a drive-by shooting. Jake's best friend died playing the choking game. He was 9.

Although it may seem rare, the death of a friend in childhood is more common than many people realize. In our society, for many years the leading cause of death among children 1–9 years of age has been unintentional injuries (i.e., accidents; see chapters 1 and 6 in this book), which account for approximately 40% of all deaths in this age group (Centers for Disease Control and Prevention [CDC], 2008). These unintentional injuries experienced by children involve such causes as accidents in or near motor vehicles, drowning, burning, ingesting harmful substances, choking, falling, misadventures with firearms, and activities like cycling or playing on playgrounds. Other leading causes of death for this cohort of children include so-called "natural causes of death" like congenital anomalies, cancer (malignant neoplasms), and heart disease, as well as homicide (called "assault" in the international classification system).

219

In 2005, there was a total of 11,358 deaths for children between 1 and 14 in the United States. In children ages 1–9, 2,415 died from unintentional injury, and 1,580 from congenital anomalies and malignant neoplasms. The fourth leading cause of death was homicide, with 496 cases reported (Kung, Hoyert, Xu, & Murphy, 2008). In light of these numbers, chances are small that many children will experience the expected or unexpected death of a friend, peer, or classmate. However, deaths of children do occur, and the impact is not alleviated because such deaths are fairly uncommon.

The impact of death on children has been well established. There is a plethora of research related to the death of a parent and sibling, but a paucity of information on the death of a friend (e.g., Noppe & Noppe, 2008; Silverman, 2000). The importance of friendship on childhood and adolescent development is clearly documented (Aboud & Mendelson, 1966; Hartup, 1996). The death of a friend is a life-changing event, and lack of grief resolution can impact the emotional development of children and their relationships throughout their lifetimes.

This chapter focuses on the ways the death of a friend has a prolonged and lingering effect on the lives of children. It describes friendships and their unique characteristics and addresses disenfranchised grief and secondary losses. Finally, the role of the school, sudden death, and helpful strategies are explored.

ON FRIENDSHIP

Definitions of a "friend" in online dictionaries include a person you know well and regard with affection and trust, an ally, an acquaintance, and a supporter. Friendships are voluntary, reciprocal relationships. When a friend dies, a child will grieve the loss of the relationship.

Friendships are a natural part of a child's social learning and growing process. They are fundamental to social development and to emotional and intellectual growth. Friends help one another think things through with more clarity than if one were alone, and they help each other learn about what is right and wrong. Friends teach one another about loyalty and build one another's self-esteem. Children who are able to form strong sustaining friendships where they are valued and accepted are likely to be successful in school and in life.

Sex, age, race, socioeconomic and school factors, and many other demographics play into the selection of friends. The bottom line is that friends pick friends based on "what feels right" (Hartup, 1996). Friends generally select friends who are similar to themselves. They have similar beliefs, attitudes, and interests. In all ages, these similarities seem to be important. Similarity seems more important during the initial phases of friendship development than later, when long-lasting relationships develop (Aboud & Mendelson, 1996). Friends know one another better than non-friends. With friends, expectations are different, a better climate of disagreement occurs, and disagreements are more easily resolved. Social and moral judgments are better supported by friends, and children who have friends are more socially competent than those without (Hartup). Conversely, a friend who gets in trouble may have a serious negative impact on the other's moral development. For example, Megan dabbled in petty theft after becoming friends with Georgia, who had been arrested more than once for shoplifting, and Devon began carrying a weapon after his new friends told him it was required if he wanted to hang out with them.

The positive impact of social interaction, emotional satisfaction, cognitive enhancement, and self-esteem that result from childhood and adolescent friendships sets the stage for mental health and satisfying relationships in adulthood (Noppe & Noppe, 2008). In middle childhood, the amount of time spent with peers steadily increases. Friends help each other on the road toward maturity and in the separation from family by supplying a basis of comparison. Friends present the view that there is a world outside their immediate family and that there are ways of interacting that differ from what is demonstrated at home (Silverman, 2000). Friends provide a different kind of intimacy and loyalty. They define their self-created worlds and learn to keep each others' secrets. Although friendships are often fragile, younger friends frequently make pledges for life. They are "BFFs," best friends forever.

FRIENDSHIP QUALITY

To address grief, it is important to know not only the identity of the friends, but also the quality of the friendship. In writing about the importance of friends on development, Hartup (1996) concluded that friends are a normatively significant condition. Friendships carry developmental advantages and disadvantages, and the identity of a child's friend and the quality of the friendship carry more weight than whether the child has friends (Parker & Asher, 1993).

Friendship quality and perceived friendship impact a peer's grief reaction. The "inner circle" of friends will be more affected than those outside the circle. In addition, there can be several circles; the debate club, the sports team, the homeroom class, the kids on the bus, or church friends. Each constitutes a different "inner circle," and each inner circle needs to be addressed (Cowan & Pompeani, 2007). When looking at friendship quality and perceived friendship, it is important to recognize that close friends will grieve more intensely than those who are more distant or mere acquaintances. However, peers who perceive themselves as friends also grieve, but their grief is often overlooked. For example, Kristen was distraught over the death of Jordon, whom she perceived as a friend when in fact Jordon merely smiled at Kristen every day as she walked down the hallway. Grief workers can easily overlook the grief of a child like Kristen.

DEATH OF A FRIEND

Common reactions that occur when a friend dies include confusion, a sense of disbelief, fear, anger, self-blame, and guilt. Other reactions involve feelings of loneliness, a sense of responsibility or regret, reminders and dreams of the deceased, concentration difficulties, and possible sleeping difficulties and somatic complaints. Indeed, these are the same grief reactions for any type of loss. Like adults, children will grieve in their own unique ways. However, they are often ill-equipped to identify, let alone manage, these feelings and other grief reactions, and the grief may not even manifest itself until months or years later. Additionally, the grief can be intermittent and expressed in a variety of ways.

Preschool Children

The earliest friendships often develop in preschool where children see each other and play together every day. One study found these relationships were stable over a year and provided children the opportunity to experience negotiation skills, positive social orientation, cohesiveness, and control (Park, Lay, & Ramsay, 1993). The death of a peer in preschool is not a common occurrence, but preschoolers do experience losses. When friends move away or transfer to other schools, children left behind may experience a sense of loss and grief reactions (Rubin,

1980). In addition, an adult with whom they were friendly, such as the neighbor who babysat or mom's good friend, may die.

More common is the death of a beloved pet. Children recognize the significance of a loss of this type and often talk repeatedly about deceased companion animals and where they might be. "Skippy, the cat, is in heaven" is a common sentiment. Children often refer to their pet as their best friend, someone who was always there for them. The death of a pet has a profound impact on children who spend a great deal of time alone with their pet and have a strong emotional closeness (Butler & Lagoni, 1996; see also chapter 12 in this book). Young grieving children turn to their parents for support, and the way in which parents acknowledge or deny their children's grief will have a lasting impact on a lifetime of grief responses.

There is a wide variability in the understanding of death at a young age (see chapter 2 in this book). Despite these differences, by age 7 most children understand the key elements of death. Accepted developmental and grief responses of 3- to 5-year-old children include a lack of time/space concepts, belief of death as temporary and reversible, magical thinking, fear of abandonment, and a need for physical comfort, reassurance, and a stable routine. In a preschool where a number of children experienced the death of a loved one, a four-week grief support group was offered. The goals were to facilitate communication between the children and their parents or guardians regarding death, to encourage memories and memory making, to help identity and expression of feelings, and to provide support. Therapeutic interventions focused on individual differences, feelings, being alive versus dead, and memory making. The adults learned to be supportive, and the children developed ways to manage and express their feelings.

Grade School Children

When a friend dies in childhood, a multitude of issues can emerge. Unlike the adolescent who can think abstractly and understand the permanence of death, the younger child, even a toddler, understands mainly that something has changed. There are many secondary losses:

- The adults are sad and may be distant while they confront the realization that "that could have been my child."
- There are no longer play dates at Johnny's.
- Sally is missing at day care.

In a world where children are mastering object permanence (appearance and disappearance), death can be confusing (Noppe & Noppe, 2008). The first challenge for the younger child is to understand the circumstances of death and long-term implications. The death may shake the child's sense of immortality.

Some of the important development issues in elementary school are to take initiative, establish productivity, and establish control over one's life. With death the child's worldview is disrupted. The child's illusion is that the world is out of control. Children often turn to families for support; however, many adults do not recognize their child's grief or are grieving themselves. They are not aware that children respond to death by asking questions repeatedly, and they may inadvertently close the lines of communication by offering euphemisms or by belittling their grief response. Answers such as "the angels came and took her" or "she's at peace now" can be very baffling without further explanation. Children can feel very alone if parents are not supportive or if the school is unable to help. Young children may have no experience with big feelings. They may be reluctant to acknowledge their grief for fear of emotional flooding. Many children think that if they start crying, they will be unable to stop. If the friendship was conflicted, those feelings may be confusing and bewildering. David wondered if he caused Jackson's death because he wished him harm during an altercation. Younger children often lack the resources to express and manage these feelings (Crenshaw, 2002; Smith, 1999).

When Mario was in the first grade his classmate, who had gone home ill, died during the night. He had strep throat, a common ailment in grade school, and many of his classmates had been sick. Despite a valiant effort by the father and emergency responders, the boy died. I was part of the crisis team that responded at the church of the young boy. Some parents stayed as I read the group *When Dinosaurs Die: A Guide to Understanding Death* (Brown & Brown, 1996). The children had many questions that reflected their fears and concerns. A few wanted to know when their classmate would be returning to school. Some wondered if it was safe to go to sleep because they too had had strep throat. Mario wandered around the room very edgy. This death was the first he had experienced. This was his buddy who lived next door, who slept over in the summer, and with whom he rode his bike. Mario was ill-equipped to identify the feelings he was experiencing and to know what to do with them. After reading the book, the children were given the opportunity to create a page for a scrapbook for the deceased's family. Mario made a detailed drawing of adventures with his friend. In sharing the drawing with the group, he was able to talk about his feelings of sadness and loss. This provided an educational opportunity for parents and children. Appropriate responses were modeled, and parental fears were put to rest as the children turned to them for support.

Middle School Children

Preteens have a clearer understanding about the concept and permanence of death than is typically found in younger children. When these preteens are forgotten as mourners, the impact may have far-reaching consequences. Children may begin to question how long they can escape the same fate as their friend. Security disappears. Children are intermittent grievers, and as they move through their developmental stages, grief can resurface (Smith, 1999). Abby died in September, but Emily only started grieving her friend during the school musical that occurred in the spring. Abby and Emily had been in every play together for the past 3 years, and only now did Abby have a greater understanding of death's permanence. This delayed reaction is often confusing to adults who think the child "should be over it" and do not recognize that the child's grief has been triggered by other events. Triggers can include additional losses such as deaths, divorce, relocation, or events associated with the original loss.

Kayla was 9 when her teacher announced to the class that Stacy had died. Stacy was a victim of child abuse and had been hospitalized for complications from burns suffered in an abusive scalding incident. The children knew that she was very ill. The classmates were overwhelmed with the news, and as hospice workers, we were prepared to help. The teachers and school personnel were initially beyond consolation. We provided crisis interventions with Stacy and Kayla's class and then with several other classes. A week later, the teacher called to inform us that her class was having a difficult time. We did an intervention called Treasured Memories that utilizes water, food coloring, bleach, and marbles. The children mention a feeling about the deceased child as they add a drop of food coloring to a vase filled with clear water. The water becomes murky, a metaphor for grief. As they add marbles, the children reveal memories they shared. They are still able to see the marbles despite the murky water. Finally, they each add a coping skill they can use with each droplet of bleach. The water begins to clear but is never the same as it was at the beginning of the activity, another metaphor for grief. This intervention validated feelings, helped students identify grief-relieving activities, and memorialized the deceased.

Two weeks later, we were called by the special education class that Stacy had attended part-time. This group was having an especially hard time accepting the loss. These were friends of Stacy who had not been initially identified. We did the same intervention with them. Subsequently peer support groups were provided for children who were friendly with Stacy and for those who had experienced other deaths. What is impressive about this situation is the prolonged and lingering effect of the loss and the impact on the children's sense of security. Many children were concerned about what would happen if they did something wrong—if their parents became angry. They questioned how something like this could happen.

DISENFRANCHISED GRIEF AND SECONDARY LOSSES

Disenfranchised grief is a phrase developed by Doka (2002) to describe grief that is not publicly acknowledged or socially sanctioned. The grief of children is often disenfranchised, and bereaved children are frequently referred to as the invisible or forgotten mourners. The relationship of a child to the deceased friend is not always adequately recognized (Crenshaw, 2002). After the death, the community rallies around the friend's family. The death may not be acknowledged in the school; if it is, that may be for only a brief period of time. Prolonged and lingering grief is typically not addressed. There is limited support for the grief of friends and few rituals legitimating friends as mourners (Silverman, 2000). The fear of social disapproval, the fear of losing control, and concerns about how peers will perceive the child's grief reaction impact how children will express their grief. Parents create the social norms for the grief experience. Their belief or lack thereof about the impact of the loss can disenfranchise the grief (Rowling, 2002).

Secondary losses occur with the death of a friend. A secondary loss can be a physical or psychosocial loss that develops as a result of the initial loss. These losses include not only the roles that made up the friendship (confidant, companion, soccer buddy) but also intangible losses (dreams, hopes, self-esteem). Each secondary loss results in its own grief reaction and needs to be mourned (Rando, 1993). The death can have an impact on the surviving friend's relationships. If Danielle and Kristen are grieving the death of their close friend Patty, it may be difficult for them to provide each other the mutual support that once occurred during the friendship. A secondary loss can also occur when David and

Matt, longtime buddies, withdraw from one another after Stephen, who had brought them together, dies.

Secondary losses result in incremental grief, a phenomenon that occurs when there are multiple related losses—loss of earlier closeness, comfort, and support and possibly the loss of friendship itself. The primary loss triggers a secondary loss and its own grief reactions, which can trigger another loss and so on. When others do not understand this grief process or reaction, the child often feels unsupported, and if surviving friendships terminate, there is additional pain.

Drawing on a model from Lofland (1982) about the breaking of social bonds, Toray and Oltjenbruns (1996) summed up this discussion of secondary losses by noting that the death of a friend can involve any or all of the following losses for a child:

- Loss of a partner who may have served important roles and functions, such as classmate, neighborhood chum, teammate, comrade, or playmate.
- Loss of help and support in everyday activities.
- Loss of ties to others through the friend as an intermediary to those others.
- Damage to those qualities in one's sense of self that had been brought out or heightened by the companionship of the friend.
- Loss of a buffer from life's hazards in the form of the security and solace provided by the friend.
- Loss of a relationship that helped the child validate his or her own sense of reality.
- Loss of a key element in planning one's goals and future.

Gender differences also play a role in children's grief reactions. Boys seem to be mostly concerned with loyalty and solidarity whereas girls are typically more involved in meeting each other's needs. There are also differences in societal expectations about how children should behave. Early on, children learn their family's scripts and messages about how to react to a death. Girls are frequently given more leniency in expressing their feelings than boys, who may try to be more rational and logical. With traumatic loss, grief can manifest itself in male children in expressions of anger and rage, whereas girls more typically turn their anger inward (Barrett, 1995). Regardless of gender and parental expectations, each child will grieve in his or her own way.

THE ROLE OF THE SCHOOL

As previously noted, there is a sense of shock and disbelief that accompanies the expected death of a friend. Students with life-limiting illnesses often rally from a number of setbacks. Hope is integral in coping with serious illness for both the family and the school community; consequently, when death occurs, it feels unexpected. The shock that accompanies anticipated deaths, combined with the fact that the majority of deaths in childhood are the result of accidents and, to a lesser degree, homicide, requires schools to have crisis plans in place. The grief-sensitive school can identify the inner circles of friends who will be affected by the death, as well as help classmates manage the crisis. Whether the death is due to a critical incident such as a shooting or an expected death from terminal illness, more than one classroom may be affected. The classes of the siblings and other friends, along with the school staff, are all impacted. If the child was in fifth grade and had attended the same school since kindergarten, teachers from grade one through grade five become part of the inner circle. If the student was frequently in the nurse's office, he or she is part of the circle. Although counselors are called on to assist with the crisis response, they too are grieving and need to process the death. That is why it is important to bring in grief workers or crisis counselors from the outside (Johnson, 2000, 2006).

Sudden Deaths

When multiple deaths of friends occur simultaneously, as in motor vehicle accidents, fires, or shootings, the deaths are traumatic. If friends and peers are also grieving past deaths, reactions to those prior deaths can interfere with the current grief response and coping. In addition, children react to the event itself (e.g., the horror of the fire, in addition to the devastation of the loss of friends). It can be difficult to distinguish between "normal" and "traumatic" grief because children grieve intermittently, and any number of triggers (such as school, teachers, and anniversaries) can cause a new burst of grief. In general, however, in normal grief children might dream about their loved one that died, whereas in traumatic grief children may have nightmares and can be more fearful for their own personal safety (for more on this subject, see chapter 13 in this book). Resolving traumatic loss is complicated because it involves dealing both with the trauma and with the loss (Webb, 1993). One pilot study examined the relationship of television exposure to a bombing incident and posttraumatic stress in younger children. It found that children who had a friend die in the bombing reported suffering more symptoms 8 to 10 months after the event than those who only had an acquaintance die (Pfefferbaum et al., 2000). This finding supports the concept of emotional closeness.

A few years ago, a house fire killed seven children in an urban school system. This fire occurred after multiple responses to death-related crises in the school. Some of the students' reactions included the very real fear that the world was going to end. With critical incidents, contagion can occur as the school melts down into a kind of "community grief" where everyone gets caught up in the event regardless of their relationship with the deceased. An opposite extreme reaction happened in another urban school that experienced several sudden deaths. When a teacher died in a house fire, the response of these students was frightening: there was a lack of a response. The grief counselors and school personnel thought the students appeared to be desensitized.

The school, and particularly the classroom, provides a sense of community and "psychological grounding" for students. When trauma happens, security is lost. Crises make students feel powerless and defeated by the event, which can have a lasting effect on their self-esteem and ability to take risks. Trauma can trigger maladaptive behaviors such as substance abuse, running away, or self-destructive behaviors. These reactions support the value of bringing in outside crisis and grief workers (Johnson, 2000, 2006).

A fifth grader, walking home from school with three friends, was killed during a drive-by shooting. After the initial crisis intervention, a support group was provided at the school. Michael was very angry. The group provided a safe venue for him to express himself. He stated that he was so angry because someone else chose when it was time for his friend to die. Another student talked about how the adults did not understand their feelings—that every day, when attendance was called, he remembered his deceased friend as the teacher skipped over the name. Other students revealed experiencing sleep disturbances and problems at home since the death. Feeling-expression activities and appropriate coping strategies were presented in group. The students completed eight sessions with a set of skills and numerous moments of insight. One student said, "I didn't know other students were carrying grieving feelings, too. Now I know that there are people in the school that I can talk to about my feelings."

Anticipated Deaths

Many grade school children know a classmate with a serious illness. Some schools have people from outside come and talk about the illness and what the classmate is going through. The teacher or school nurse may assume the role as a liaison between the school and the family and periodically send home greetings from the school. The illness will sometimes go into remission, and less often, children will survive. Classmates, school staff, and parents and families harbor hope that the child will beat the disease. However, we know that the second two leading causes of death in children ages 1–9 are congenital anomalies and cancer. And so despite knowing and having thoughtful preparation for a child approaching imminent demise, the death often seems sudden and unexpected. Anticipating a death will not negate grief and the deep feelings of sadness at the time of death.

> Roni was 10 when Jill, her neighbor, died after a battle with cancer. Jill had been an active kid. She participated in many sports and excelled in school. After her illness set in, she was in and out of the hospital and in and out of school. Her cancer would go into remission, her hair would grow back, and life would go on. By the fourth grade, the illness had metastasized throughout her body, and Jill was enrolled in hospice. Our school program became involved in working with the students and staff on how to support a seriously ill student. As Jill declined, plans were made for the day of death and the days following. The students and staff were still full of hope that Jill would rally. When Jill did die, the school was overwrought with emotion and panicked as a school in crisis. Although her death was expected and openly discussed, it felt like a sudden death. Roni experienced a myriad of somatic complaints and cried fervently and openly in school. Jill's inner circle of friends ostracized Roni pointedly, asking her why she was so upset—she wasn't Jill's friend. Roni described how she and Jill always played together over the summer and on school breaks. Roni's grief was disenfranchised. Other girls who did not have a close relationship with Jill began crying as contagion took over. Firm direction by the crisis responders enabled all the students to gain control, express their feelings, and have their grief validated. By focusing on memorializing activities, the students put their grief into action and ritual.

Suicide

Schools need to develop a bereavement response plan (Cowan & Pompeani, 2007) and respond with consistency to all student deaths. In their case study, McNeil, Silliman, and Swihart (1991) reported conflict with the way the school responded with great sensitivity and memorial activities to the death of a popular student who died of leukemia, but hardly acknowledged another less popular student's death. Schools often struggle with what to do when there is a suicide. Even elementary school children complete suicide. School administrators fear that if they honor the student with special activities and memorials, at-risk students will copy the act. Thoughtful and careful consideration needs to be made for responding to each death. It is one thing to honor a student no matter how he or she died and quite another to glorify the event or the way the death occurred.

Suicide is underreported in all age groups, especially in children. In children ages 10–14, suicide was the fourth leading cause of death, with 270 reported suicides in the United States, in 2005 (Kung et al., 2008). The numbers increase with the child's age. Children 9 to 10 years old do have an understanding of the finality of death, but it is difficult to ascertain if they have fully comprehended the implications of a suicidal act.

The "choking game" is an activity some children use to achieve a euphoric state. They either choke each other or use a noose to choke themselves. After a short time, they pass out or die. The CDC used news media reports to estimate the deaths from the choking game and calculated that there were 82 probable deaths among children ages 6 to 19 between 1995 and 2007 (Russell, Paulozzi, & Gilchrist, 2008). In fact, there are likely many more unreported deaths of this type. When a child dies from hanging, it is difficult to determine whether it is the result of the choking game or if it is suicide, especially if there is no suicide note. Parents frequently refer to the death as accidental. Parents and schools need to become familiar with warning signs that children are playing this game. In one community, a parent developed a program for the schools after finding his son hanging in the garage days after watching a news report on television about the choking game.

Jake's best friend died playing the choking game. He was 9. Jake experienced extreme guilt. He and Jake had talked the previous week about the choking game and other kids that were playing it. He felt he could have prevented the death. His belief system was shaken. He was irritable and angry and did not think he would ever find another friend as good as Jake. School became a trigger, and he began doing poorly in subjects that were once easy for him. At one point, he expressed that perhaps dying was a good option, that it was easier than experiencing the pain of grief. He felt that although his parents were supportive, they really did not understand and were suddenly overprotective. He found playing video games, art, and shooting hoops helpful. Moreover, individual counseling outside the school environment provided a specific and safe place to talk about his feelings.

THE FUNERAL

A common question raised by parents and other adults is whether a child should go to the funeral after the death of a friend, and should the school support attendance at the funeral? The rule of thumb is that children and their families should make their own personal decisions about attending a wake or funeral. The funeral is an important ritual for the release of grief and can be a valuable educational opportunity. However, children need to be told what to expect. The sight of a friend in a coffin can heighten fears (Noppe & Noppe, 2008). It can be invaluable to have a supportive adult prepare the child ahead of time, accompany the child during the event, and be available for discussion afterward. When friends are invited to participate in a funeral, it helps them feel respected as mourners. Most families welcome participation by friends of their deceased child because friends can provide additional and different memories and tributes (Silverman, 2000).

WHAT CAN HELP

The death of a friend can be the first death a child experiences. Shock, disbelief, sadness, anxiety, fear, and anger are heightened as part of the grief reaction. It is the role of the families, the school, and the community to help these children identify and express these big feelings, empower them with constructive coping strategies, and transform the experience into something positive.

Acknowledging and validating grief reactions is the first step in recovery. When addressing grief, interventions need to be based on developmental grief reactions. The activities should match where the child is in his or her developmental response to grief. For example, an activity that requires abstract thinking will not work well with a 5-year-old child who is experiencing magical thinking. Activities and interventions to help build student self-esteem are paramount. Books, music, art, and play are the language of children; utilizing these media will be helpful. Be sensitive to a child's spirituality and culture; allow the child to teach the adult about what is important. Consider past histories with death, the meaning of the attachment, gender, and socioeconomic factors. The following list identifies a number of general approaches that can help children who have experienced the death of a friend:

- Ongoing assessment: Identify and monitor high-risk individuals, such as those who have experienced multiple deaths and traumatic loss. Because of the prolonged and lingering effects of grief and grief triggers, reactions can manifest at any time.
- Peer support groups: Because peers and friends are so important in development, peer support groups are very valuable. Participants discover that their feelings are normal and they are not going crazy. Hearing from their own peers has more power than hearing from a well-intentioned adult. Activities need to be age-appropriate.
- Education: There is a lack of death education in the school community (see chapter 15 in this book). Age-appropriate presentations and curricula that focus on dying, death, loss, and grief can help normalize this part of the life cycle. In addition, introducing such subject matter often reveals students who are currently grieving or have a terminally ill family member at home.
- Literature: There are a number of children's books that focus on death and dying (for examples, see the appendix in this book). Younger children can often personalize what is happening in the book to their world. Literature used in middle-school classes frequently includes the death of a character. This storyline can be used as an educational opportunity on how to cope with grief and loss. In addition, there are journals specifically designed for grieving preteens.
- Rituals: Participating in a ritual that becomes a focus for the grief is helpful. Children often can be quite imaginative in helping to construct their own rituals for child friends, as in examples involving drawing pictures or writing out cards to send to the parents of their friend. In all cases, rituals should be meaningful and useful to help "say goodbye." Attendance at the funeral or wake can help children accept the reality of the death.
- Memorializing: Planting a tree or garden, assembling a collage of photographs, mounting a plaque, or dedicating a yearbook page

or sports jersey are just a few examples of commemorating that have great meaning for grieving children. Some schools will develop a shrine or wall dedicated to the deceased right after the death. It is important to be time-sensitive and determine when these temporary memorials should come down and what type of lasting memorial might take their place. It is not helpful to enter a building where there is an *ad hoc* tribute to the deceased, but the classmates no longer attend.

- Legacies: Maintaining a relationship with the deceased is valuable. By living a legacy of the deceased, students feel that they not only are remembering the person who died, but also will be remembered themselves. One student who died had made the honor roll during her struggle with cancer. The following year, her classmates did the same as a tribute. Scholarships or charity drives in the deceased's honor are other examples.

- Expressive therapies: Utilizing art, music, poetry, and photography to help express feelings and/or honor the deceased is very effective (see chapter 19 in this book). If available, art and music therapists can offer great insight and consultation for powerful activities. Having markers and drawing paper available during a post-death intervention will enable children to find the means to express their needs.

- Professional counseling: For some grieving friends, professional counseling will be most helpful. Traumatic grief reactions are complicated, and one-to-one assistance in a safe place can foster grief recovery.

- Internet: Using this medium has become a way of life for children and adolescents who like the immediate and instantaneous communication and information. MySpace and Facebook are popular social networking sites for online communication through an interactive network of photos, music, user profiles, and other media. They can be used for grief expression and support. However, caution should be used when accessing the Web. People can misrepresent themselves as professional helpers or credentialed professionals. The level of support expressed may not be appropriate. In fact, a stranger may exploit the Internet relationship at a time when the child is especially vulnerable. It is the parents' or guardians' responsibility to educate their children on the risk of using the Internet for grief support.

CONCLUSION

This chapter has examined the importance of friendships in childhood development, along with the impact that may occur when a friend dies. Children do grieve, and their grief, whether it be sporadic, traumatic, or ongoing, needs to be validated and normalized. The family, school, and community all play a role in teaching children about death, dying, grief, and loss as part of the growing-up experience. When a death does occur, the children will then be better equipped with information and strategies to express their feelings and other grief reactions in healthy ways. There are numerous interventions that can bolster self-esteem and empower children with skills to manage their grief. Children are often described as resilient. When properly supported and guided in constructive directions, their experience becomes transformative, and they incorporate the death event into their identity formation.

REFERENCES

Aboud, F. E., & Mendelson, M. J. (1996). Determinants of friendship selection and quality: Developmental perspectives. In W. M. Bukowski, A. F. Newcomb, & W. W. Hartup (Eds.), *The company they keep: Friendship in childhood and adolescence* (pp. 87–114). New York: Cambridge University Press.

Barrett, R. K. (1995). Children and traumatic grief. In K. J. Doka (Ed.), *Children mourning: Mourning children* (pp. 85–88). Washington, DC: Hospice Foundation of America.

Brown, L. K., & Brown, M. (1996). *When dinosaurs die: A guide to understanding death.* New York: Little, Brown.

Butler, C. L., & Lagoni, L. S. (1996). Children and pet loss. In C. A. Corr & D. M. Corr (Eds.), *Handbook of childhood death and bereavement* (pp. 179–200). New York: Springer Publishing.

Centers for Disease Control and Prevention (CDC). (2008). *10 leading causes of death by age group, United States, 2005.* Retrieved January 18, 2009, from http://www.cdc.gov/injury/images/LC-Charts/10LC_overall_2005b-a.pdf

Cowan, D. S., & Pompeani, M. (2007, April 13). *Partners in grief: Fostering a grief sensitive school.* Paper presented at Association for Death Education and Counseling annual conference, Indianapolis, IN.

Crenshaw, D. A. (2002). The disenfranchised grief of children. In K. J. Doka (Ed.), *Disenfranchised grief: New directions, challenges, and strategies for practice* (pp. 293–306). Champaign, IL: Research Press.

Doka, K. J. (Ed.). (2002). *Disenfranchised grief: New directions, challenges, and strategies for practice.* Champaign, IL: Research Press.

Hartup, W. W. (1996). The company they keep: Friendships and their developmental significance. *Child Development, 67,* 1–13.

Johnson, K. (2000). *School crisis management.* Salt Lake City, UT: Publishers Press.

Johnson, K. (2006). *Trauma in the lives of children: Crisis and stress management techniques for counselors, teachers, and other professionals* (2nd, rev. ed.) Alameda, CA: Hunter House.

Kung, H., Hoyert, D., Xu, J., & Murphy, S. (2008). *Deaths: Final data for 2005.* National Vital Statistics Reports, National Center for Health Statistics, Mortality Statistics Branch, 56(10). Retrieved April 6, 2009, from http://www.cdc.gov/nchs/data/nvsr/nvsr56/nvsr56_10.pdf

Lofland, L. H. (1982). Loss and human connection: An exploration into the nature of the social bond. In W. Ickes & E. S. Knowles (Eds.), *Personality, roles, and social behavior* (pp. 219–242). New York: Springer-Verlag.

McNeil, J. N., Silliman, B., & Swihart, J. J. (1991). Helping adolescents cope with the death of a peer. *Journal of Adolescent Research, 6*(1), 132–145.

Noppe, I. C., & Noppe, L. D. (2008). When a friend dies. In K. J. Doka & A. S. Tucci (Eds.), *Living with grief: Children and adolescents* (pp. 175–192). Washington, DC: Hospice Foundation of America.

Park, K. A., Lay, K., & Ramsay, L. (1993). Individual differences and developmental changes in preschoolers' friendships. *Developmental Psychology, 29*(2), 264–270.

Parker, J. G., & Asher, S. R. (1993). Friendship and friendship quality in middle childhood: Links with peer group acceptance and feelings of loneliness and social dissatisfaction. *Developmental Psychology, 29*(4), 611–621.

Pfefferbaum, B., Gurwitch, R. H., McDonald, N. B., Leftwich, M. J. T., Sconza, G. M., Messenbaugh, A. K., & Schultz, R. A. (2000). Posttraumatic stress among young children after the death of a friend or acquaintance in a terrorist bombing. *Psychiatric Services, 51*(3), 386–388.

Rando, T. A. (1993). *Treatment of complicated mourning.* Champaign, IL: Research Press.

Rowling, L. (2002). Youth and disenfranchised grief. In K. J. Doka (Ed.), *Disenfranchised grief: New directions, challenges, and strategies for practice* (pp. 275–292). Champaign, IL: Research Press.

Rubin, Z. (1980). *Children's friendships.* Cambridge, MA: Harvard University Press.

Russell, P., Paulozzi, L., & Gilchrist, J. (2008). Unintentional strangulation deaths from the "choking game" among youths ages 6–19 years—United States, 1995–2007. *Morbidity and Mortality Weekly Report, 59*(6), 141–144.

Silverman, P. R. (2000). *Never too young to know: Death in children's lives.* New York: Oxford University Press.

Smith, S. S. (1999). *The forgotten mourners.* Philadelphia: Jessica Kingsley.

Toray, T., & Oltjenbruns, K. A. (1996). Children's friendships and the death of a friend. In C. A. Corr & D. M. Corr (Eds.), *Handbook of childhood death and bereavement* (pp. 165–178). New York: Springer Publishing.

Webb, N. B. (1993). Traumatic death of friend/peer: Case of Susan, age 9. In N. B. Webb (Ed.), *Helping bereaved children: A handbook for practitioners* (pp. 189–211). New York: Guilford.

12 Children's Bereavement Over the Deaths of Pets

TAMINA TORAY

To me, you are still nothing more than a little boy who is just like a hundred thousand other little boys. And I have no need of you. And you, on your part, have no need of me. To you, I am nothing more than a fox like a hundred thousand other foxes. But if you tame me, then we shall need each other. To me, you will be unique in all the world. To you, I shall be unique in all the world.

—de Saint-Exupéry (1943, p. 66)

Pets have become an integral part of the American family. In the United States, more than 70% of households in the United States with children under the age of 18 have pets, and nearly half of those families living with pets describe them as family members (American Pet Product Manufacturers Association [APPMA], 2005–2006; American Veterinary Medicine Association [AVMA], 2007). Americans own approximately 73 million dogs, 90 million cats, 139 million freshwater fish, 9 million saltwater fish, 16 million birds, 18 million small animals, and 11 million reptiles (APPMA). Families with pets cut across all racial and ethnic groups with White pet owners representing the highest numbers, followed by Spanish/Hispanic, Asian/Pacific Islanders/American Indian/ Aleut Eskimo, and African American (AVMA, 2007).

Just how does one define a family? The great diversity and variety in family systems is reflected in the changing demographics of our society. Children grow up in a myriad of family systems including but not limited

237

to blended, adoptive, single-parent, and foster families, as well as with both biological parents. Children also live further away from their extended family members than previous generations, creating a need for greater social relationships beyond the family system. Melson (2003) has argued that when looking at child–pet relations, one needs to view such interactions from a family systems perspective given that family dynamics, particularly parent–child relationships, play a strong role in forming children's relationships with pets. The purpose of this chapter is to take a close look at the special relationships children form with companion animals, to provide specific information for caregivers to help support bereaved children grieving the death of their beloved pets, and to better understand the consequences that the illness and the death of companion pets have on the lives of children.

EXPERIENCING PETS OUTSIDE OF THE HOME

Though children form strong bonds with pets within their homes, there are also numerous environments beyond their homes where those contacts are also made. The most common place for children to interact with pets outside their homes is in the classroom setting. Many classrooms have resident pets such as fish, rabbits, gerbils, hamsters, and other "pocket pets." Rudd and Beck (2003) found that over a quarter of public elementary schools in Indiana had resident pets, and an additional 46% had animal visitors. Pets also enter the classroom as helpers. An example of such assistance comes from the R.E.A.D.—Reading Education Assistance Dog—program (Intermountain Therapy Animals, Salt Lake City, http://www.therapyanimals.org/read/). The goal of this unique program is to improve literacy skills in children by having children read to trained therapy dogs in the classroom setting. Children are less intimidated and more relaxed when practicing their reading skills with the help of a furry friend.

Classroom pets are often utilized to teach responsibility to students in an effort to enhance children's psychological well-being (Melson & Fine, 2006). However, because pets have limited life spans, teachers often have to explain the death of a resident pet to their students and help to comfort grieving children as they cope with the death of resident pets. Such "teachable moments" provide tremendous opportunities for teachers and other adults to offer death education to children if they are prepared to do so.

PETS' INFLUENCES ON THE LIVES OF CHILDREN

Pets enhance the social, emotional, and cognitive lives of children. Children who form attachments to their pets exhibit increased social and emotional development. Pet-owning children versus non-pet-owning children demonstrate stronger pro-social skills, including higher levels of empathy toward other children and toward animals (Daly & Morton, 2006; Melson, Peet, & Sparks, 1991; Vidovic, Stetic, & Bratko, 1999). For instance, pets can help shy children more easily make friends using the pet as a focal point for social interaction. Pets of all kinds can help reduce loneliness in children by providing them a mate with whom to share their thoughts and concerns and someone to play with when a human friend is not present.

Pets present children with powerful motivation to learn and thus increase their opportunity to enhance cognitive skills (Melson, 2003). Children learn more when there is an emotional attachment to pets and when such learning occurs within those meaningful relationships. Different pets provide different cognitive influences. For example, fish or birds allow children to focus their attention without too much stimulation (Beck & Meyers, 1996). Clearly, pets provide daily opportunities to stretch their cognitive and perceptual growth.

PETS AND PHYSICAL HEALTH

Having a pet in the family also has a profound impact on physical health. Companion pets have also been found to lower blood pressure, heart rate, and anxiety; decrease depression; assist in coping with stress; and even warn against seizures and low blood sugar levels in their owners (Allen, Shykoff, & Izzo, 2001; Lynch, Thomas, Mills, Malinow, & Katcher, 1984). Children who live with pets in infancy are less likely to develop allergies and asthma and have lower school absences due to illness (Liccardi et al., 2005; Pohlabeln, Jacobs, & Bohmann, 2007). Children who had a dog present during their physical examination showed lower physical and behavioral distress than when the dog was not present (Nagengast, Baun, Megel, & Leibowitz, 1996). And of course because pets encourage children to laugh while playing with or simply watching them, they help decrease children's anxiety and stress.

DEATH OF A PET AND CHILDREN'S GRIEF

The death of a pet can have a significant influence on children's grief. How a child reacts to any death is highly dependent on his or her cognitive capacity (see chapter 2 in this book). How a child copes with a loss, as well as how that loss may affect future development, is highly influenced by numerous developmental processes (Corr, 1996). Although each child moves through cognitive changes at different rates, the following information may be useful for those helping to support children grieving the death of their family pet.

Preschool-Age Children (2–5)

The irony for children in this age group is that they are extremely curious and open about death, and yet they often learn that the adults in their lives are very uncomfortable about the subject. Preschool children tend to be egocentric in their thinking (the world revolves around me) and are very literal in their understanding of events. This age group benefits from simple and direct answers to their questions.

Preschool-age children also tend to be causal thinkers and will commonly blame themselves for the death of a family pet based on something they may have said, thought, or done in reference to their pet. An example of such a lament would be "I got really mad at Patches for breaking my toy and then he died!" When the family pet then becomes ill or is killed in an accident, the child may feel responsible for causing harm. Because of this causal thinking, caregivers, teachers, and other adult helpers need to provide ongoing reassurance to preschool-age children that they were not responsible for the pet's death. It can help to say things like "I know you got mad at Patches for breaking your toy, but she did not die because you got mad. She got sick and died because she was *very* old, and her body wore out."

Preschool-age children will often act out their feelings of grief via their play or art work. These are great modalities for expression. Adults can be supportive to bereaved children by giving them opportunities to express their grief over the death of their companion pets by giving them the means to draw, paint, or be involved in dramatic play. Reading age-appropriate books can also help children better understand the illness or death of a pet (for examples of such literature, see the appendix in this book). All of these activities can help children say goodbye to a treasured friend.

Preschool-age children also lack the cognitive capacity to understand that death is permanent and that dead pets are nonfunctional (i.e., that all organs and systems cease to operate). These children may believe that death can be reversed. Caregivers need to provide direct, honest, developmentally appropriate explanations about illness or death of a pet. The following example illustrates these limitations in thinking:

> Four-year-old Charlie and his family just buried their cat Sammy in their backyard. Each member of Charlie's family said goodbye to Sammy during this ceremony, and Charlie placed his favorite toy on top of Sammy's grave. Later that evening, Charlie's parents found him taking food out, placing a blanket on top of the grave, and poking holes in it. When Charlie's parents asked him why he was doing these things, he replied, "Sammy will get hungry, and he is having trouble breathing. He also might want to come back inside once he is not dead!"

School-Age Children (6–11)

It is typical of school-age children that they slowly gain an understanding that death is final, permanent, universal, and irreversible and that once dead, the body does not function. School-age children (6–12) are concrete thinkers who believe death exists only if they can see the body. They will often be extremely inquisitive about their pet's illness, posing numerous questions. "I know that Benny is really sick with cancer but what causes cancer?" "Can we get some books so I can see what cancer looks like?" Or "I want to look at Sweetie's body for a while longer, wow, she still feels warm." Their questions may also focus on how the disease will affect their pet's organs and systems and what the body will look like after death. It can be helpful for this age child to ask a veterinarian very specific and concrete questions about trauma, disease, or death.

Adults can be very helpful to school-age children by providing honest explanations of disease (even helping them by searching out information on the topic) and by allowing them to be active participants in the euthanasia procedure. School-age children forge strong emotional bonds with family pets. They are often responsible for many of the instrumental tasks in the lives of their pets such as feeding, walking, and grooming and may consider the family pet one of their "best friends." School-age children should be allowed to have input in end-of-life decisions that affect family pets. Leaving children out of such important family decisions will only lead to lack of trust and resentment.

For both of these age groups, adults can make valuable use of "teachable moments." Such moments have been described by Silverman (2000) as opportunities for children to feel free to ask adults questions about death and dying and to be given truthful answers. In the case of pets, goldfish, with their very short life expectancy, often provide parents with their first teachable moments related to pets. Reading children books that describe the life cycle in age-appropriate developmental terms or stories with a pet-specific focus can be a very useful tool in helping children understand pet death (see the appendix to this book for examples of such literature).

EXPLAINING PET SICKNESS AND DEATH TO CHILDREN

Though it is tempting to try to protect grieving children, using vague or inaccurate explanations only leads to anxiety, confusion, and mistrust. Using euphemisms to explain pet death only creates confusion for children. Telling a child that a pet dog was "put to sleep" will likely produce a fear of going to sleep. Telling them that "God has taken" the pet to heaven or to a better place may create conflict in the child, who then could become angry at a higher power for being cruel to the pet and to him or her. Adults who employ such indirect or confusing communication may ultimately undermine the trust the child has in them (Goldman, 2001, 2004).

When talking with a child about pet illness and death, it is helpful to make children feel as comfortable as possible (use a soothing voice, hold their hand, or put an arm around them) and to talk to them in a familiar setting. Start by clarifying that a child understands what illness and dying mean. Illness can be described as when the pet's body is not working well (children get ill, so parallels can be drawn). Death means that the pet's body stops working at all. Using correct and direct terms such as "sick," "dying," "dead," or "died" decreases confusion for children and thus has a direct and beneficial influence on their grief process. For preschool-age children it can be useful to explain death by using words they know and use. Reading a book such as *Lifetimes: A Beautiful Way to Explain Death to Children* (Mellonie & Ingpen, 1983) to this age child can help capture death in terms they understand as part of nature's cycles. Such cycles also include flowers and bugs. For example, saying, "This is a seed; it turns into a flower, and the flower will eventually die," is a simple but direct way of teaching children about death.

The following is an example of how to explain illness and euthanasia to a school-age child:

> Socks is very, very, sick, and no medicines can make her better. We all love Socks so much and don't want her to hurt anymore. We are going to take her to an animal doctor, a veterinarian, and she will give her a drug that helps animals die in peace. When Socks dies, her heart will stop beating, and she won't be able to do any of the things she did when she was alive. She won't be able to talk, walk, see, smell, or be in any pain.

ATTACHMENT AND LOSS: TWO ENDS OF THE SPECTRUM

The dynamic of attachment is remarkable. Human beings are social animals who require attachment for survival. Although one might not readily assume that humans depend on domesticated pets for survival, few would argue that companion animals do not enhance children's everyday lives. Many have written about the strong bonds people form with their companion pets (e.g., Lagoni, Butler, & Hetts, 1994; Ross & Baron-Sorenson, 2007). The strong bonds that children form with their companion pets, coupled with the reality that most pets have a much shorter life span than humans, create a common dynamic where the death of the family pet often becomes the first significant death children face, and an intense one at that. Thus, the joy of forming the attachment to the companion pet leads to the inevitable suffering from the loss that death involves and to the ensuing grief response.

Early experience of bonding with a pet during childhood also has ramifications for encounters with grief later during adulthood. Given that dogs have a life span ranging between 10 and 15 years, and cats 18 and 20 years, a child may continue a strong attachment to a companion pet well into adolescence and even young adulthood. Parents need to keep this long-term bond in mind when making end-of-life decisions about a family pet. It is often the case that such decisions are made without including young adults who may be in college or starting a career. Not including young adults in such decision making can create tremendous resentment and increased intensity of grief given the important role the family pet had played in their lives.

PETS AS MEMBERS OF CHILDREN'S "SECOND FAMILY"

I use the term "second family" to describe anyone children find important in their lives outside their primary family. As an elementary school
counselor, I would often use the following exercise. I would ask children
to draw a picture with two circles. In the first circle I would have them
write the names or draw pictures of the people in their "first" family,
such as relatives. Next, I would have students write or draw pictures
of those in the "second" family to be placed in the second circle. I fully
expected friends and teachers to show up in the second circle; what surprised me was how consistently children placed their family pets in the
second circle, in their "second family."

Children experience significant life stressors such as the separation
and divorce of parents, coping with adjustment to blended families,
moving away from friends and familiar schools and neighborhoods, dealing with peer rejection, living under conditions of poverty or in abusive
families, and the death of loved ones. These conditions create a need for
comfort and solace that human beings in the lives of children may not
always be able to provide.

These members of a child's "second family" serve as confidants, pals,
companions, and friends. Children's pets are there at the end of difficult
school days, are someone to hold when the child is under stress, and are
loyal vigil keepers when children are sick. Companion pets are placed
high in children's ranking of their social networks, even higher than certain kinds of human relationships (McNicholas & Collis, 2001). In the
company of even the smallest of pets, a child's fears can suddenly vanish.
Many of our most vivid childhood memories come from time spent with
our pet pals.

CHILDREN WITH SPECIAL NEEDS

A child with special needs may become deeply attached to a companion
pet or service animal. The roles pets play in the life of these children
often go far beyond the role played by pets in a non–special needs child.
These pets are often a child's eyes or ears or an extension of the child's
body. For these reasons, the death of service animals or helping pets
can result in great tumult and adjustment for a child. After the death of
a working companion animal, a child must establish a new relationship
with another helping pet. Perhaps the biggest adjustment for a disabled

child coping with the death of an animal as a working partner is learning to trust that a new companion can help him or her with daily needs. Making comparisons to the previous companion is quite common: "Jerad used to know exactly how to help me get ready for bed, and Sam isn't as smart!" In the midst of their grief, special needs children may need to make quick adjustments as new helping pets enter their lives.

Caregivers can provide support by allowing bereaved children to fully express their concerns and be very good listeners while children make this important transition. Allowing special needs children time to establish their unique relationship with their new service animal is vital. This type of loss is multifaceted and thus requires great patience on the part of all concerned. Trying to rush the attachment to the new helper pet will not allow the child the necessary time to grieve the losses being currently experienced.

THE TRAUMATIC OR SUDDEN DEATH OF A FAMILY PET

Parents often feel the need to protect children in cases of sudden or accidental death of a pet. Well-meaning caregivers may explain that a pet has run away when in actuality the pet was run over by a car while the child was at school. Such an explanation serves only to increase the worry and concern a child may have. It is not unusual for children, after hearing such an explanation, to wonder day after day whether the pet will return home unharmed. Children may spend inordinate amounts of time searching for such "lost" pets, placing signs in the neighborhood, asking their neighbors if they have seen their pet, and often not even telling their parents what they are doing. Oltjenbruns (2007) suggests that in order for children to cope with death, they "need the opportunity to say good-bye, share feelings, and deal with emotions" (p. 147). Clearly this mourning cannot be accomplished without open, honest communication. When a pet is fatally injured or is found dead from unknown causes, children need to be reassured that the animal is no longer in pain. If some type of veterinary intervention was attempted, it is important to let the child know that sometimes pets do not survive, even when every attempt to save their life was made.

In the veterinary classes I teach, I make it a practice to ask students if they experienced similar situations as a child, with a parent not telling them the truth about the death of a pet. Inevitably, I find numerous students who have had such experiences. Those students consistently tell me they still hold some resentment about the situation, and all wish their parents had been honest with them.

It is always difficult to explain traumatic events to children. Nevertheless, in the case of the sudden death of a pet through accident or acute illness, children do much better short-term and long-term when they are told the truth. The following are some suggestions for helping children cope with traumatic pet death:

- Ask your veterinarian for advice in explaining how the death took place.
- Always tell the truth in developmentally appropriate terms.
- Do *not* use euphemisms.
- Stay calm when talking to children about the death.
- For preschool-age children, books are often a helpful way to explain death (for examples of such literature, see the appendix in this book).
- Allow school-age children a choice in viewing the dead pet, preparing them for what the body will look like and covering parts that have been highly damaged (always prepare children for what they will see).

TERMINAL ILLNESS AND FAMILY-PRESENT EUTHANASIA

Children have special relationships with animals. Excluding or protecting children from this decision-making process because they are thought to be too young to understand may only complicate and prolong their grief process. Children respect straightforward, truthful, and simple answers. If they are prepared adequately, children usually are able to accept an animal's death. (AVMA, 2007, p. 2)

Deciding how and when to talk with children about pets suffering from terminal illness presents a challenge for most parents. Brandt (2001) analyzed calls made to a pet loss and education hotline and found that almost 25% of the callers indicated that the primary reasons for their contact focused on gathering information on how best to talk with their children about the illness, death, or euthanasia decision-making process involving a family pet. A recent trend in veterinary medicine has been the movement toward family-present euthanasia. This movement recognizes that a decision to euthanize a pet has ramifications for the entire family system.

Brant and Grabill (2007, p. 187) have offered several helpful phrases to use when discussing companion animal end-of-life issues with children:

- "Many animals don't live as long as people can."
- "It's okay you got mad at Toby for peeing on your bed. Your thoughts didn't hurt him. Toby is very sick."
- "How about writing a letter, telling a story, or drawing a picture of your favorite memory about your pet?"
- "It's okay to want a new pet."

Including Children in the Euthanasia Procedure

Children should always be included in the euthanasia decision-making process, regardless of whether they attend the procedure itself. Explaining that a pet is terminally ill is the first step toward a family discussion on euthanasia. Caregivers need to explain to children that because their pet is very ill and suffering, the veterinarian can help to end his or her suffering by injecting a very strong drug so that the pet can die peacefully. It is imperative that parents tell children this is a drug that is only given to dying pets so that children do not fear taking medications when they are sick. Using the term *medicine* instead of *drug* may leave children afraid of taking their medicine when they get sick.

If children decide to attend the euthanasia, it is important for caregivers to prepare them for what will take place. Caregivers can turn to veterinarians to assist them in explaining the medical aspects of death, including how the pet will look after it dies: for example, its eyes will not close, it will remain warm for a period of time, and the body will eventually become stiff. If a family chooses to participate in the euthanasia procedure, it is very important to choose a veterinarian who is comfortable having children present at euthanasia. A skilled and compassionate veterinarian can help explain to children what is being done during the euthanasia process, give children opportunities to ask questions, and allow family members to spend time with the pet before or after the procedure.

Many veterinary clinics now have "comfort rooms" that allow for the family to be in a more relaxed environment, perhaps with a mat on the floor, so that they can gather around and provide solace to each other, and non-fluorescent lighting. Children and other family members can lie close to their companion pet and hold, brush, or even give treats prior to the procedure. Caregivers can help facilitate children's grief processes by providing opportunities for emotional expression or storytelling about the pet's life. Brant and Grabill (2007) suggest that allowing children to be present at the time of euthanasia may also help to alleviate their fears of what death looks like. Allowing such involvement clearly has lifetime implications for the way death is understood and coped with.

Developmental Considerations in Including Children in the Euthanasia Procedure

Because of their increased cognitive skills, school-age children are often very curious about the euthanasia procedure. These older children may benefit from time spent alone with the companion pet prior to or after the euthanasia procedure in order to say their goodbyes. During the procedure, school-age children are likely to ask numerous questions and want to be "helpful" to the veterinarian. Finding a veterinarian that is child-friendly is very important in a family-present euthanasia. Such veterinarians should be willing to make a pre-euthanasia appointment where all of the family members' questions can be answered.

Preschool-age children may also benefit from being involved in family-present euthanasia. Given their short attention span, however, it may be useful to bring along a family friend who can be with the child for playing or reading if the child becomes bored or disruptive. Another option is to have children this young say goodbye to the family pet during the sedation portion of the euthanasia and then stay with a family friend or relative during the actual procedure.

After the euthanasia, families can be offered a clay paw, a clay impression of the pet's paw that can be decorated by children and then baked, and they can take a cutting of the pet's fur. These keepsakes can serve as important linking objects allowing children to have a concrete, permanent memento of their beloved companion pet for years to come.

AFTER-DEATH RITUALS AND COMMEMORATING A PET'S LIFE

Balk (2007, p. 216) defines *commemorating* as "formal and informal ways children can remember the person who died." The purpose of commemorization is the same whether it involves a pet or a person. Commemorating a family pet can provide children a valuable means of acknowledging the important role the pet played in the family, as well as serving as a valuable teachable moment, for in every death, memories do continue. This process allows children to honor their relationship with their companion animal and to concretely and uniquely express their feelings of loss. By allowing children to actively participate in mourning rituals, caregivers are showing respect for a child's grief process and are helping children learn valuable coping strategies that will serve them well as they face future losses.

Commemorative activities may take a myriad of forms, and families can be creative in choosing meaningful ways to acknowledge the loss of a pet. Examples of ways to commemorate the life of a pet include creating a painting, planting trees, keeping baby teeth, and engraving a plaque or stone. Other effective ways to commemorate beloved pets include helping children to create a scrapbook or collage that includes photos of the pet throughout its life, videotaping interactions with the pet and the family, or having the child write a story about the pet (including drawings).

Traisman (1996) has created a pet remembrance journal that allows children a great way to remember their pets. Ideas for entries include the child's first memories of the pet, nicknames, times when the pet got in trouble, and what will most be missed about the pet. Keeping a pet's tags, leash, bowls, and so forth in a special place of honor also serves as a wonderful way to remember an important animal friend.

BODY CARE OPTIONS

Body care decisions can create a challenge for a family. There are several possible choices, including burial, cremation, and allowing the veterinarian to dispose of the body. These choices need to be made clear to the child. For example, in the case of a veterinarian disposing of the body, it usually means the pet will be buried in the local landfill in a section for animals (if this is indeed the case) or even turned over to a rendering company. This decision may become confusing for a child if, at a later date, he or she wishes to visit the deceased pet, believing it is still at the veterinarian's office. As with all discussions about death with children, honesty is vital. Veterinarians can be very helpful in explaining the different aftercare options to the family so that caregivers are well informed.

A common choice for disposition is burial on the family's property or in a pet cemetery. For decades, caregivers have helped children bury family pets such as fish, gerbils, mice, cats, dogs, snakes, and many more.

Of course, a family must have access to some land (and weather that allows for burial to take place) in order to bury pets on their own property. People living in apartments or renting homes may not be able to do so. Another increasingly common choice for many families is cremation. Pet crematoriums are now more accessible, and most veterinarians provide their clients with referral information about them. If the death takes place at home, many of these companies will pick up the pet's body and take it to the facility for cremation. After cremation, a child may wish to spread some or all of the pet's ashes in a favorite place where they spent time together or place the ashes in an urn.

SHOULD WE GET ANOTHER PET?

Each family dynamic is different, and thus, there is no single answer to this frequently asked question. What is important in each case, however, is that children do not learn that one can "replace" the deceased pet by bringing another one into the home, that each relationship we have with our companion animals is unique and special. When deciding whether or when to bring a new pet into the family, another point to be carefully considered is whether the child, as well as the rest of the family, has been given adequate time to grieve. In our society, we often move too quickly to assuage our grief. Helping children to understand that loss brings pain is an important lesson. Acting too quickly to get another pet sends the message that after loss we can distract ourselves by "moving on" without acknowledging and addressing the pain that accompanies our attachment to beloved family pets.

It is also important to note that surviving family pets also go through a grieving process. It is not unusual for pets to show grief responses similar to those of humans, such as loss of appetite, change in sleeping habits, restlessness, and depression. These surviving pets often search for their missing playmate and show an increased need for attention from their owners. The best strategy for supporting surviving pets is to maintain as much of a normal routine as possible (feeding times, walks, etc).

SUPPORTING CHILDREN'S GRIEF

Children grieve based on their developmental level. Children, like adults, grieve cyclically—moving in and out of their grief (see chapter 1 in this book). It would not be at all uncommon for a child grieving the death of a pet to manifest typical grieving signs (crying, withdrawing, acting out, regressing to an earlier time in their development, not being interested in usual activities, exhibiting fear of being alone or of going to sleep), and then go back into normative daily activities such as playing with friends or watching videos, only to then return to their grief several minutes or hours later.

Part of the movement in and out of grief for children necessitates that caregivers be available for ongoing questions the child may have. For example, a child may ask a parent, "Mom, can you tell me one more time why Kipper got so sick?" or "Dad, can you tell me again what will happen when Tigger dies?" Keeping lines of communication open for grieving children will allow them to view their caregivers as sources of support and information during a stressful time. It is also important to keep in mind that children respond behaviorally far more often than they do verbally; thus, observation of their behaviors is extremely important.

Disenfranchised Grief

Adults are no more likely to feel at ease discussing the illness or death of a family pet than they would be discussing the death of a human member of the family. Children coping with the illness or death of the pet will often experience the discomfort and isolation of disenfranchised grief (Doka, 2002), a feeling that their loss and grief are minimized and not properly acknowledged. Telling a child, "You can get another dog, cat, or gerbil" sends a message that minimizes their grief and leaves the child less likely to share feelings with adults who seem to lack understanding and sensitivity toward their grief. It is not difficult to understand that how we respond to a child's grief concerning the death of a pet may have lifelong implications for the child's ability to cope with other deaths (Podrazik, Shackford, Becker, & Heckert, 2000).

Caregivers and other adults are primary models for children as they travel through the process of grief. Providing opportunities for children to feel safe asking questions regarding their pet's illness and death, as well as surrounding grieving children with support and nurturance, allows children to be active participants in an important life experience. If this is accomplished, pets can serve as tremendous teachers for children in learning to navigate and understand grief and loss across the life span (Corr, 1996).

Complicated Grief

The vast majority of children grieving the death of a pet require no therapeutic intervention. Special attention, however, may need to be paid to children who have endured other significant losses close to the time of their pet's death. These death-related or non-death-related losses may include divorce, separation or abandonment of parents, death of a family member, frequent moves, or a child's history of mental health issues. Some children in these cases may be at higher risk for experiencing complicated grief. This type of grief involves long and intense periods of grief, inability to return to normative activities even after several months, withdrawal from friends and family, and continual rumination. Children who experience complicated grief may benefit from therapeutic intervention. Caregivers should seek qualified therapists who have a strong background in grief and loss as well as the human–animal bond.

Key Elements to Consider When Assessing the Severity of the Grief Response

The following factors increase the likelihood that a child will have a more intense grief response over the death of a beloved pet (Lagoni, Butler, & Hetts, 1994):

- No previous experience with significant loss, death, or grief.
- Other recent losses.
- A personal history involving multiple losses.
- Little or no support from friends or family.
- Insensitive comments from others about the loss.
- Feelings of guilt or responsibility for a death.
- Being involved in an untimely death like those of children, young adults, or young companion animals.
- Not being present at death.
- Not viewing the body after death.
- Witnessing a painful or traumatic death.
- Deaths that occur in conjunction with other significant life events such as birthdays, holidays, or a divorce.
- Stories in the media that misrepresent or cast doubt on medical treatment procedures.
- Advice based on others' negative experiences with death or on inaccurate information about normal grief.

Fear of Other Deaths

When the death of a loved one occurs, children's fears are often height-ened that another death may be imminent. Children coping with the illness or death of a beloved family pet may fear that another pet, they, or a family member may become ill or die. Though many children may not directly communicate such fears, their behaviors may give important clues. For example, Cathy, age 12, had her cat die suddenly for no appar-ent reason. Since that experience, every time she is away from home, she calls her parents numerous times "just to check in." This behavior had not occurred prior to her cat's sudden death. Her parents decided to ask Cathy if she was concerned about something, and she admitted that she was afraid that her parents would die suddenly. Reassuring children (if this is the case) that other family members and pets are indeed healthy can help to alleviate many of their fears.

Other Specific Suggestions for Supporting Bereaved Children

Children who have experienced the death of a pet may also be supported in the following ways:

1. Provide honest, developmentally appropriate explanations about the illness or death of the family pet.
2. Avoid euphemisms when discussing death (put to sleep, gone, in a better place, ran away). Instead use the words *dying, dead,* and *died.*
3. Allow children to see the pet's body (cover parts that are highly damaged and explain to the child why you are doing this).
4. Have a funeral and include children in burial, cremation, or other body care decisions.
5. Provide routine activities for grieving children. Routine pro-vides children who have experienced the death of a pet with a sense of safety and security. Consistent bedtimes, bath times, and reading of familiar stories all allow children to feel that the rest of their life remains stable in the face of change.
6. Access books focused on pet loss through lending librar-ies at veterinary clinics and through Web sites of veterinary hospitals, such as the one for the Argus Institute at the Colo-rado State University College of Veterinary Medicine (http://www.argusinstitute.colostate.edu). Children's librarians can be

extremely helpful in suggesting age-appropriate books. In his review of literature focusing on children coping with pet loss, Corr (2004) provided detailed descriptions of a wide array of books that examine this important topic, as well as full bibliographic information that allows parents, teachers, or therapists to access important supportive material. When caregivers are often not sure how to approach the topic of death with their children, finding well-written and age-appropriate books can be of tremendous help.

7. If family-present euthanasia is chosen, find a veterinarian who is comfortable having children involved in the process. Make a pre-euthanasia appointment with the veterinarian to discuss how he or she feels about such involvement.

8. Allowing children to see a caregiver grieve can provide a healthy role model for the expression of emotion at difficult times. As parents acknowledge their own sadness, they also need to be in the position of providing ongoing support for their grieving children.

9. Be observant of children's feelings (especially guilt). See if they feel responsible in some way for the pet's illness or death. It is important to discuss how the child treated his or her pet well, but also to acknowledge any regrets the child may have for behaviors he or she would have liked to change.

10. If a child is experiencing a strong grief response, reach out to a school counselor or local therapist with experience in the human–animal bond and loss.

CONCLUSION

Pets have become a ubiquitous part of the American family. The death of a pet is commonly the first significant loss a child faces. Be it a fish, gerbil, cat, dog, or another pet, children attach quickly to their companion animals and often experience significant grief when their companion dies. How these deaths are dealt with within the family or school system can have both immediate and lifelong implications for how the child will understand and cope with this loss and with future losses. Our society often minimizes child–pet relationships and thus fails to adequately support children's bereavement over these important losses. Well-intentioned caregivers or teachers often lack the necessary information and guidance for assisting children as they maneuver through this special type of bereavement. The child–pet bond illustrates a strong social and emotional connection with broad significance. The loss of that bond merits understanding, patience, and support.

REFERENCES

Allen, K. M., Shykoff, B. E., & Izzo, J. L. (2001). Pet ownership and risk factors for cardiovascular disease. *Medical Journal of Australia, 157,* 298–301.

American Pet Product Manufacturers Association (APPMA). (2005–2006). *2005–2006 APPMA National Pet Owners Survey.* Greenwich, CT: Author.

American Veterinary Medicine Association (AVMA). (2007). *U.S. pet ownership and demographic sourcebook.* Schaumburg, IL: Author.

Argus Institute, Colorado State University Veterinary Teaching Hospital. http://www.argusinstitute.colostate.edu

Balk, D. E. (2007). Working with children and adolescents: An overview of theoretical and practical issues. In K. J. Doka (Ed.), *Living with grief: Before and after the death* (pp. 209–227). Washington, DC: Hospice Foundation of America.

Beck, A. M., & Meyers, N. M. (1996). Health enhancement and companion animal ownership. *Annual Review of Public Health, 17,* 247–257.

Brandt, J. (2001). The Ohio State University pet loss support and information line: A summary of calls. *The Hotliner Newsletter,* 1–2.

Brandt, J. C., & Grabill, C. M. (2007). Communicating with special populations: Children and older adults. In K. K. Cornell, J. C. Brant, & K. A. Bonvicini (Eds.), *Veterinary clinics of North America small animal practice: Effective communication in veterinary medicine.* Philadelphia: W. B. Saunders.

Corr, C. A. (1996). Children, development, and encounters with death and bereavement. In C. A. Corr & D. M. Corr (Eds.), *Handbook of childhood death and bereavement* (pp. 3–28). New York: Springer Publishing.

Corr, C. A. (2004). Pet loss in death-related literature for children. *Omega, Journal of Death and Dying, 48,* 399–414.

Daly, B., & Morton, L. L. (2006). An investigation of human–animal interactions and empathy as related to pet preference, ownership, attachment, and attitudes in children. *Anthrozoös, 19,* 113–127.

de Saint-Exupéry, A. (1943). *The little prince.* New York: Harcourt, Brace & World.

Doka, K. J. (Ed.). (2002). *Disenfranchised grief: New directions, strategies, and challenges for practice.* Champaign, IL: Research Press.

Goldman, L. (2001). *Breaking the silence: A guide to helping children with complicated grief—suicide, homicide, AIDS, violence and abuse* (2nd ed.). New York: Brunner-Routledge.

Goldman, L. (2004). *Raising our children to be resilient: A guide to helping children cope with trauma in today's world.* New York: Routledge.

Lagoni, L., Butler, C., & Hetts, S. (1994). *The human–animal bond and grief.* Philadelphia: W. B. Saunders.

Liccardi, G., D'Amato, G., D'Amato, L., Salzillo, A., Piccolo, A., De Napoli, I., et al. (2005). The effect of pet ownership on the risk of allergic sensitization and bronchial asthma. *Respiratory Medicine, 99,* 227–233.

Lynch, J. J., Thomas, S. A., Mills, M. E., Malinow, K. L., & Katcher, A. H. (1984). The effect of human contact on cardiac arrhythmia in coronary care patients. *Journal of Nervous Mental Disorders, 158,* 88–99.

McNicholas, J., & Collis, G. M. (2001). Children's representations of pets in their social networks. *Child Care, Health and Development, 27,* 279–294.

Mellonie, B., & Ingpen, R. (1983). *Lifetimes: A beautiful way to explain death to children.* New York: Bantam.

Melson, G. F. (2003). Child development and the human–companion animal bond. *The American Behavioral Scientist, 47,* 31–39.

Melson, G. F., & Fine, A. H. (2006). Animals in the lives of children. In A. H. Fine (Ed.), *Handbook on animal-assisted therapy: Theoretical foundations and guidelines for practice* (pp. 207–226). San Diego: Academic Press.

Melson, G. F., Peet, S., & Sparks, C. (1991). Children's attachment to their pets: Links to socio-emotional development. *Children's Environments Quarterly, 8,* 55–65.

Nagengast, S. L., Baun, M. M., Megel, M., & Leibowitz, J. M. (1996). The effects of the presence of a companion animal on physiological arousal and behavioral distress in children during a physical examination. *Journal of Pediatric Nursing, 12,* 323–330.

Oltjenbruns, K. A. (1997). Lifespan issues and loss, grief and mourning, Part 1: The importance of a developmental context: Childhood and adolescence as an example. In D. Balk, C. Wogrin, G. Thornton, & D. Meagher (Eds.), *Handbook of thanatology: The essential body of knowledge for the study of death, dying, and bereavement* (pp. 143–149). New York: Routledge.

Podrazik, D., Shackford, S., Becker, L., & Heckert, T. (2000). The death of a pet: Implications for loss and bereavement across the lifespan. *Journal of Personal and Interpersonal Loss, 5,* 361–395.

Pohlabeln, H., Jacobs, S., & Bohmann, J. (2007). Exposure to pets and risk of allergenic symptoms in the first two years of life. *Journal of Investigational Allergology and Clinical Immunology, 17,* 302–308.

Ross, C. B., & Baron-Sorenson, J. (2007). *Pet loss and human emotion: A guide to recovery.* Philadelphia: Brunner-Routledge.

Rudd, A. G., & Beck, A. M. (2003). Companion animals in Indiana elementary schools. *Anthrozoös, 16,* 241–251.

Silverman, P. R. (2000). *Never too young to know: Death in children's lives.* New York: Oxford University Press.

Traisman, E. S. (1996). *My personal pet remembrance journal.* Wenatchee, WA: Direct Book Services.

Vidovic, V. V., Stetic, V. V., & Bratko, D. (1999). Pet ownership, type of pet and socio-emotional development in school children. *Anthrozoös, 14,* 212–217.

13 Children and Traumatic Deaths

DONNA L. SCHUURMAN AND JANA DECRISTOFARO

A discussion of how children are impacted by traumatic death and effective ways to support these children would not be complete without addressing the intersection of two branches of learning: thanatology (the study of death) and traumatology (the study of trauma). The study of the former is as old as Sigmund Freud and his concept of "working through grief" as a theoretical perspective (Freud, 1917/1959). Psychiatrist Erich Lindemann based his description of grief on the concept of "grief work," postulating that grief was an emotional syndrome with outcomes that could be either normal or morbid. He believed the most common form of grief "gone wrong" was that of delayed onset, during which time the person may either behave normally or display symptoms of "distorted grief" (Lindemann, 1944). Since those times multiple terms have evolved in the field to describe grief reactions that were considered outside of the range of "normal," including complicated grief, traumatic grief, and childhood traumatic grief.

The field of traumatology in the psychological sense and not just pertaining to physical trauma took longer to establish as a specific field of inquiry and scholarship. With its rise grew the popularity of terms such as "traumatic death," "traumatic response," and "posttraumatic stress disorder."

Unfortunately, these two related strands of human experience initially developed without much cross-pollination. Rando states that "in

257

general traumatologists know little to nothing about loss and, conversely, thanatologists know about the same amount regarding trauma. This is quite alarming given that, by definition, in all trauma there is loss and in the majority of losses there is significant trauma" (1997, p. xv). It is only recently that contributions from the areas of neurobiology, brain research, body work, and newer therapies have begun to be considered and integrated holistically.

This brief historical overview underscores that the study of trauma is still a young field, operating under a dearth of research on the effects of trauma on children and adolescents (Schwarz & Perry, 2004). In the current *Diagnostic and Statistical Manual of Mental Disorders, DSM-IV-TR*, the official classification system of mental disorders published by the American Psychiatric Association (APA, 1994), there is no diagnosis specifically for children who are traumatized. A group is working to include the category of developmental trauma disorder in the new *DSM-V* to capture the effects of trauma, specifically multiple traumas, on children. There will also be a proposed diagnostic criteria for the next version of the *DSM* from a group that has been working on this concept from its early designation as "complicated grief" to "traumatic grief" and, most recently, "prolonged grief disorder" (Prigerson & Jacobs, 2001).

Even though it was not until 1980, after years of work and lobbying, that the term posttraumatic stress disorder (PTSD) first appeared as a formal diagnosis in the *DSM-III* (APA, 1980), it is not a new phenomenon:

> In the 19th century, doctors who saw something like it in Civil War veterans and survivors of train wrecks nicknamed it "soldier's heart" and "railroad spine"; the psychologists of the 20th century's two World Wars called it "shell shock," "traumatic neurosis," and "battle fatigue." Recently, in victims of sexual assault, it was given the name "rape trauma syndrome." (Butler, 1997, p. 106)

The *DSM-III* specified that the causal event or "essential feature" of the disorder had to be outside the range of "usual human experience (i.e., outside the range of such common experiences as simple bereavement, chronic illness, etc.)" (APA, 1980, p. 247). This qualification was removed in *DSM-IV*. Another significant shift from 1980 to 1994 in the definition is that the earlier version stated that "the stressor producing this syndrome would be markedly distressing to almost anyone" (APA, 1980, p. 247). The 1994 version removes this restriction; the catalytic event no longer required that a universal distress be involved, but rather that the individual experienced it as disturbing and distressing. This focus on the individual is a critical distinction as we look at children and the effect of traumatic deaths in their lives, as the core definitions of trauma and death have shifted.

CORE DEFINITIONS

It is important to define and distinguish betweens terms and concepts such as trauma, traumatic events, traumatic death, and traumatic responses.

Trauma

The word "trauma" is a derivative from the Greek word for "wound." A further expansion is "an emotional wound or shock that creates substantial, lasting damage to the psychological development of a person, often leading to neurosis" (*American Heritage Dictionary*, 2000, p. 1836). Although people have experienced trauma from the beginning of human existence, the notion that someone exposed to a traumatic event "may become traumatized and so be recognized as a victim is in fact quite a recent idea" (Fassin & Rechtman, 2009, p. xi).

Traumatic Event

The *DSM-IV* describes a traumatic event as one in which (a) the child experiences, witnesses, or is confronted with an event(s) that involves actual or threatened death or serious injury, or a threat to physical integrity of oneself or others; and (b) the child's response involves intense fear, helplessness, horror, or disorganized or agitated behavior (APA, 1994). Traumatic events are described as sudden, unexpected, and creating a subjective experience of terror, threat to survival, or helplessness.

Many clinicians are challenging this limited definition, especially insofar as some events that are not sudden may still be experienced by a child as traumatic, including, for example, the physical wasting away of a parent through disease. Given the individual nature of traumatic responses, it is difficult to identify specific events or circumstances that could be deemed "traumatic" to all children. This variation occurs "because children have unique ways of understanding traumatic events, making meaning of these events in relation to themselves...and integrating these events into their larger sense of self" (Cohen, Manna-rino, & Deblinger, 2006, p. 4).

As explained by Marwit (2001),

> Some believe that the DSM-IV definition is still overly restrictive in that it focuses on the objective nature of the event instead of on the individual's subjective reaction to that event. In other words, it does not allow for the fact that some people can be highly traumatized by events which others might consider normal and not of a particularly traumatic nature, such as the death of an aged parent. (p. 365)

PTSD, for example, is viewed as a psychopathological reaction to a trau-matizing event, and the deeper and important philosophical question becomes, What reactions to traumatic events may be considered psycho-pathological, if any? In other words, is it the *event* or the *response* that is abnormal?

At the Dougy Center for Grieving Children and Families (http://www.dougy.org), we have run peer grief support groups since 1982 for children, teens, and their parents or adult caregivers who have experi-enced the death of a parent or sibling. Our largest population served has consistently been children between 6 and 12 years of age who have had a parent die, with about 60% of those being paternal deaths. After 4 years of running these groups, we found that children who had experienced a death from homicide or suicide often had additional factors that compli-cated their grief experience. Sometimes the details of the deaths were disturbing to those who had had a family member die in less graphic cir-cumstances, although that seems to be a bigger issue among the adults than among the children. The intrusion and often inaccuracies of media portrayals of the deceased added to the social stigma and isolation for those left behind after a suicide or homicide. A sense of perceived pre-ventability heightened the normal questions of "why?" and "why me?" that follow most deaths of those who are not aged. Involvement with law enforcement and the court system, which can last for years, fuels an intensity and duration that is often softened by time in deaths that do not involve these systems.

Because of these circumstances, in 1986 and 1988, respectively, we added specific "Healing From a Suicide Death" and "Healing From a Murder or Violent Death" groups to our general groups for parent or sibling deaths. Families who have had a suicide or homicide death choose whether they would prefer to participate in groups specific to these losses or in the more general groups; the majority select the former.

From our perspective, all of the deaths the families in our program have experienced are inherently "traumatic" by definition. We have never referred to our suicide death or homicide death groups as "traumatic death groups." Given that it is difficult to categorize what children will experience as traumatic based solely on the nature of the death, it is important to look at what the term "traumatic death" means.

Traumatic Death

Traumatic deaths have traditionally been defined as those that are sudden and unexpected (vehicle accidents); viewed as preventable (homicide, suicide); premature (the death of a child); or catastrophically horrific (terrorist attacks, war, natural disasters). Others have proposed that a traumatic death is one that occurs within the context of a traumatic event, for example deaths during disasters, war, other violence, suicide, or severe accidents (Nader, 1997). The *DSM* definition also includes the individual child's response of intense fear, helplessness, or agitated behavior.

Some writers explain that deaths involving suddenness, interpersonal violence, trauma, suicide, and most significantly, an act of "human design" (Clements & Burgess, 2002; Doka, 1996) are more likely to create exaggerated, and potentially complicated, grief responses. These deaths are perceived as "untimely" and "unfair," often intensifying the feelings of disbelief, shock, and anger (DeRanieri, Clements, & Henry, 2002).

Others assert that "a traumatic death is one that is sudden, unanticipated, violent, mutilating or destructive, random and/or preventable, involves multiple deaths or one in which the mourner has a personal encounter with death" (Journey of Hearts, n.d.). In these situations, it is noted that the grief reactions look very different than they do in expected or anticipated deaths. The inability to prepare for the death or say goodbye to the person who died is identified as a risk factor for a "traumatic death" and predisposes the grieving person to be at a much greater risk for suffering subsequent complicated mourning (Journey of Hearts).

SOME IMPLICATIONS OF THESE DEFINITIONS

These definitions inherently rule out the possibility that deaths from prolonged illness or disease could be experienced as traumatic. We believe this restriction does an injustice to children. Consider this example: Imagine 12-year-old Casey, whose 16-year-old sister was brutally murdered by her boyfriend. Six months later, their father, distraught at his inability to protect his daughter, shot himself and died. Five months after his death, their mother jumped off a bridge to her death. Casey was left orphaned, with two younger siblings. Most of us would agree that these three events are inherently traumatic.

Twenty years later, Casey, having earned her PhD, is a clinician specializing in pediatric neurobiology. The factors that contributed to her resiliency—her personality traits, the support of significant other adults in her life—turned out to be more influential than the *events* that occurred in her life.

Now imagine 11-year-old Jacob, whose mother was diagnosed with breast cancer. Jacob witnessed his mother's physical decline over a period of 2 years, as the cancer ravaged her body and stole her from him. At the time of her death and for a long period afterward, Jacob was inconsolable, displaying disturbing symptoms of trauma, including disordered sleep and unhealthy behavioral outbursts. His mother's death, under many definitions of traumatic death, would not qualify, and yet his trauma symptoms were far more evident, disturbing, and potentially dangerous than Casey's.

It is time that we look at the child's experience, and not the event, in determining who is traumatized in response to a death *of any kind.* As Jacobs (1999) has pointed out, the word "traumatic" refers to the phenomenology of the disorder, not the etiology, and the disorder can occur in the absence of an objectively traumatic death. That is, traumatic grief may follow "any death that is personally devastating" (p. 17). Additionally, we ought not pathologize the child for *normal reactions to an abnormal event.* At the Dougy Center, we have serious concerns about viewing bereavement as pathological. When 5-year-old Evan watched his father break through the front door of their house and stab and dismember his mother, leaving him alone with her body for a couple of days before someone found them, we believe that whatever Evan does in response to this horrific experience is "normal" and that we should not pathologize *him* for getting into fights with other children or for the ways in which he displays his reaction. His behaviors are his attempts to make sense of a senseless situation and to act out the pain and hurt inside of him. Our task and challenge is to help him through addressing those thoughts and behaviors that may hurt him or others without pathologizing *him.*

Before we explore risk factors, symptoms, and interventions for children traumatized by death, it may be helpful to consider one additional concept, that of "complicated" or "traumatic" grief.

COMPLICATED GRIEF/TRAUMATIC GRIEF/MOURNING

Prigerson and her colleagues have been conducting studies to develop criteria for distinguishing between "normal grief" and "pathological grief," which they have alternately called "complicated grief," "traumatic grief," and more recently, "prolonged grief disorder." The symptoms are "separation distress" (yearning; longing; searching; indicating an intrusive, distressing preoccupation with the deceased) and "traumatic distress" (efforts to avoid reminders of the deceased; feelings of purposelessness and futility about the future; numbness and detachment; feeling shocked, stunned, or dazed; difficulty acknowledging the death; feeling life is empty and unfulfilling without the deceased; experiencing anger over the death; fragmented sense of trust, security, and control) (Prigerson & Jacobs, 2001). Although it is acknowledged that many of the symptoms of "traumatic grief" are similar to the signs of normal grief (Enright & Marwit, 2002), Prigerson and Jacobs have said that the distinguishing factors are the severity of the reactions and their duration.

A team led by Prigerson is proposing that the next *DSM* (currently slated for publication in 2012) include diagnostic criteria for prolonged grief disorder in adults (Prigerson, Vanderwerker, & Maciejewski, 2008). Numerous arguments on both sides of this issue have appeared in the professional press for several years. A full discussion of the pros and cons is beyond the scope of this chapter, but a helpful resource is a special issue of *Omega, Journal of Death and Dying* (Parkes, 2006). The outcome of this endeavor will "have a significant impact on our understanding of grief" (DeSpelder & Strickland, 2005, p. 279).

RISK FACTORS FOR TRAUMATIC REACTIONS

There are a number of circumstances that make children vulnerable to having traumatic reactions. These factors include preexisting family or individual psychopathology, developmental difficulties, and prior trauma. After a trauma, there are factors that contribute to a traumatic response. These include a loss of faith, the support system's inability to tolerate the child's traumatic responses, lack of opportunities to process or talk about the trauma, extreme avoidance, and a sense of aloneness, what Nader refers to as "posttraumatic estrangement" (Nader, 1996, p. 204; see also Cohen et al., 2006).

Traumatic Responses/Symptoms

We will first look at the current *DSM-IV* definition of PTSD, which is assigned when all of four specific criteria are met:

1. The person has to have been exposed to a traumatic event in which he or she "experienced, witnessed, or was confronted with an event that involved actual or threatened death or serious injury, or a threat to the physical integrity of self or others," and the response has to "involve intense fear, helplessness, or horror" (APA, 1994, p. 403).
2. The event must be persistently re-experienced through intrusive images, thoughts, or perceptions; recurrent distressing dreams related to the event; flashbacks; and/or the experience of intense distress or physiological reactivity when faced with the actual or symbolic situations that resemble the traumatizing event.
3. The sufferer must exhibit avoidance responses to stimuli that are reminiscent of the traumatic event and do so through a combination of tactics including avoidance, numbing, reduced interest, lack of recall, and/or detachment.
4. The sufferer has to display at least two signs of increased arousal that can be manifested by such things as increased irritability, hypervigilance, sleep disturbances, exaggerated startle response, and/or concentration difficulties.

The disturbance or symptoms must be clinically significant in contributing to distress or psychological impairment, and the duration of the disturbance must be more than 1 month.

Although PTSD as a diagnostic category first appeared as a formal diagnosis in *DSM-III* (APA, 1980), some writers believe that "while PTSD is a good definition for acute trauma in adults, it doesn't apply well to children, who are often traumatized in the context of relationships," as written by Boston University Medical Center psychiatrist Bessel van der Kolk (DeAngelis, 2007, para. 4). "Because children's brains are still developing, trauma has a much more pervasive and long-range influence on their self-concept, on their sense of the world and on their ability to regulate themselves" (DeAngelis, para. 4). Van der Kolk and colleagues are proposing a diagnosis called "developmental trauma disorder," or DTD, to capture what they see as central realities of life for these children: exposure to multiple, chronic traumas, usually of an interpersonal nature; a unique set of symptoms that differs from those of posttraumatic stress disorder (PTSD); and a variety of other labels often applied to such children, as well as the fact that these traumas affect children differently depending on their stage of development.

For example, "affective disorders" capture the sadness, loss of interest, physical complaints, and social dependency and withdrawal involved in DTD. But they do not include DTD-related anxiety, reactive anger, shame, guilt, dissociation, and disorganized feelings about trust and relationships.

Additionally, the category of anxiety disorders, including PTSD, captures the fearfulness, worry, and avoidance, but not the additional ranges of changeable emotional states, negative self-beliefs, and disorganized attachment feelings and behaviors that DTD does. Anxiety disorders, chronic hyperarousal, and behavioral disturbances have been regularly described in traumatized children (Van der Kolk, 1994). For children who have experienced a death, these symptoms may emerge:

- Intrusive memories about the death: These symptoms can be expressed by nightmares, guilt or self-blame about how the person died, or recurrent or disturbing thoughts about the terrible way someone died.
- Avoidance and numbing: These symptoms can be expressed through withdrawal, acting as if not upset, or avoiding reminders of the person, the way he or she died, or the things that led to the death.
- Physical or emotional symptoms of increased arousal: Children may show this reaction by their irritability, anger, trouble sleeping, decreased concentration, drop in grades, stomachaches, headaches, increased vigilance, and/or fears about safety for oneself or others.

For some children and adolescents, responses to traumatic events can have a profound effect on the way they see themselves and their world. These children may experience important and long-lasting changes in their ability to trust others, their sense of personal safety, their effectiveness in navigating life challenges, and their belief that there is justice or fairness in life. Traumatized children may develop changes in behavior that are often referred to as *externalizing* problems or *acting out*. They may become involved in fights or other conflicts with peers, have difficulty interacting with authority figures, become socially isolated or withdrawn, develop poor school attendance, and begin using illicit substances. They may also experience changes in their emotional and psychological functioning, referred to as *internalizing* problems, such as depression or anxiety. These internal changes may be more difficult for others to detect than external changes but can still cause significant impairment in functioning (National Child Traumatic Stress Network, http://www.nctsn.org).

THE INTERSECTION OF TRAUMA AND DEATH

How does trauma literature inform treatment protocols for traumatized children who have experienced a death? Remembering that this intersection of traumatology and thanatology is a relatively new field of research and practice, we will look at some of the emerging ways of thinking about how trauma and grief may intersect, as well as some of the implications for addressing destructive symptoms.

Van der Kolk (1994) and somatic therapists have proposed that it is important to start with the body because that is where trauma is stored. In their view, talk therapy, in the absence of body modalities, is limited in its ability to alleviate the symptoms of trauma and at times can intensify the reactions as talking reactivates the biological response system. Cohen, Mannarino, Greenberg, Padlo, and Shipley (2002), though not dismissing body-centered treatments, asserted that you can create the same ameliorative effects with psychotherapy, using their trauma-focused cognitive-behavioral therapy.

Body-Centered Treatments

According to the viewpoint behind body-centered treatments, traumatized people tend to be emotionally disconnected or "numbed out" in their day-to-day lives, punctuated by moments of extreme hyperarousal in reaction to trauma stimulus (Van der Kolk, 1994). With trauma, the sympathetic nervous system is on more often than it is in people who have not experienced trauma. With the body regularly on high alert, the endocrine and hormonal systems are taxed, and people report having exaggerated startle responses, acute responses to triggers that may not be directly related to the trauma, and difficulty modulating their emotional responses due to their bodies. Traumatic memories, in effect, stay "stuck" in the brain's nonverbal, nonconscious, subcortical regions (the amygdala, thalamus, hippocampus, hypothalamus, and brain stem), where they are not accessible to the frontal lobes, which are the parts of the brain in charge of understanding, thinking, and reasoning (Wylie, 2004b). When traumatized people attempt to talk about their experiences, the remembering process often triggers a shutdown of the frontal lobes and impairs their ability to speak clearly, coherently, or sometimes even at all. Memories activate the emotional center of the brain—the amygdala and hypothalamus—which results in a kind of overload of physical sensations that leads to either hyperarousal (such as elevated heart rate, shallow breathing, startle responses) or hypoarousal/dissociation (helplessness, freezing, numbing).

In his work with traumatized patients with PTSD, Daniel Siegel noted their inability to construct a coherent story about their past. In his view, "there was clearly some connection between their traumatic past—what was called their 'disorganized attachment'—and something going on in their brains that prevented them from making sense of their own stories. As a clinician, Siegel knew that PTSD was assumed to be related to dissociation, but what did *that* mean? What if trauma shut off the hippocampus, so that horrible sensations and experiences flooded the amygdala and were laid down as implicit memories, but were blocked from becoming explicit memories?" (Wylie, 2004b, pp. 34, 35). What if, as Butler and others have asserted, "moments of overwhelming horror appear to alter the chemistry—perhaps even the structure—of the brain" (Butler, 1997, p. 106)?

Van der Kolk and other proponents of body-centered treatments assert that people are traumatized more by the feeling of powerlessness than by the actual traumatic event. They lose a sense of efficacy in controlling their environment, their bodies, and their reactions. Being active and productive—as in rebuilding a community after a natural disaster—helps to mitigate the impact of the trauma. "When people get close to re-experiencing their trauma, they get so upset that they can no longer speak," Van der Kolk says. "It was pretty obvious that as long as people just sat and moved their tongues around, there wasn't enough real change" (Wylie, 2004a, p. 33). Other therapists, including Edna Foe, have noted that "scientific funding organizations rarely, if ever, support research in new or unproven treatments" (Wylie, 2004a, p. 39).

Childhood Traumatic Grief

Cohen and her colleagues (2006) hypothesize that trauma symptoms interfere with a child's ability to go through the typical process of bereavement. They have termed this phenomenon "childhood traumatic grief" (CTG) and developed a treatment protocol for CTG.

They assert that a child can experience a combination of trauma and grief symptoms so severe that any thoughts or reminders, even happy ones, about the person who died can lead to frightening thoughts, images, and/or memories. Because these thoughts can be so upsetting, a child may try to avoid any reminders of the loss so as not to stir up upsetting thoughts or feelings. A younger child may be afraid to sleep alone at night because of nightmares about a shooting that she witnessed, and an older child may avoid playing on the school baseball team his father used to coach because it brings up painful thoughts about how his father died in a terrible car accident. In this way, the child can get "stuck" on the traumatic aspects of the death and cannot proceed through the normal bereavement process (National Center for Child Traumatic Stress UCLA-Duke University, 2005).

Nader (1996) asserts that "traumatic aspects of the loss may hinder or complicate aspects of grief resolution, such as grief dream work, the child's continued relationship with the deceased, issues of identification, and the processing of anger" (p. 212). She points to traumatic dreams (characterized by fear, horror, and a sense of helplessness) that prevent the child from having grief dreams that help him or her to feel connected to or reassured by the person who died. She goes on to say that the child's identification issues can be negatively impacted by an overidentification with either the perpetrator or the person who died, particularly negative attributes. The child may also fear that he or she will suffer the same fate as the victim or inherit behaviors or motivations similar to the perpetrator. For example, a child may fear that it is her fate to be depressed and suicidal, just like her father.

At a March 1, 2008, presentation at a Los Angeles children's conference, Cohen acknowledged the early and experimental nature of childhood traumatic grief with the statement that "we're not even sure what traumatic grief is or if it even exists." In a publication she appeared to support the older definition, that "traumatic grief . . . is the loss of a loved one under traumatic circumstances" (Cohen et al., 2006, p. 5). Yet in 2002 the description was broadened:

> Traditionally, childhood traumatic grief has been considered to result from the loss of a loved one in a traumatic event, such as interpersonal violence, natural or manmade disaster, severe motor vehicle or other accident, suicide of a loved one, or war conditions. However, we suggest that death from natural causes can also result in traumatic grief if a child's subjective experience of the death is traumatic and trauma symptoms interfere with grieving and resolving the loss of the loved one. (Cohen et al., 2002, p. 308)

WHAT TYPES OF INTERVENTIONS ARE APPROPRIATE FOR CHILDREN WHO ARE EXPERIENCING TRAUMA SYMPTOMS AFTER A DEATH OR DEATHS?

Drawing on work with adults, as well as grief and trauma, it is not surprising that there are different treatment types and protocols for children. Rando (1997, p. xvi) points out that "the reality is that traumatically bereaved individuals need therapists who understand post-traumatic stress, comprehend loss (physical, psychosocial, and secondary) and its consequent grief and mourning, and how to intervene in both areas separately and in conjunction."

Despite differences in treatment *methods*, there is some common ground in treatment *goals*. Practitioners recognize that traumatic symptoms such as those described previously are interfering with the child's ability to live a healthy life. "The goals of treatment include both repair of the injured aspects of the child and recognition of, recovery of, or reconnection with healthy aspects of the child, which may have been hidden by traumatic response and changes" (Nader, 1996, p. 218). Nader and her colleagues (Pynoos et al., 1987) focus on helping children to acknowledge and express all elements of the trauma and their internal reactions.

In the trauma literature, studies have highlighted the importance of helping to establish or reestablish a sense of control in the individual, a concept that seems to run universally through differing trauma theories (Cassels, 2008; Clements, DeRanieri, Vigil, & Benasutti, 2004; Schwarz & Perry, 1994). A logical outcome of experiencing a traumatic event or events is the sense that one was powerless or helpless to prevent what happened, for example, the death of a parent through a car crash, suicide, or cancer. One of the ways the Dougy Center's program addresses this need with children is through open-ended groups that allow the child to determine the length of time he or she wishes to participate in grief support groups. Another way is by encouraging children to choose the activities they wish to participate in during their sessions, thereby empowering them to regain some control over their lives.

Although the overarching goal is to utilize strategies that assist the child in overcoming the barriers the traumatic memories hold, how to accomplish this outcome is where the lines begin to split along theoretical bases. Adherents of body-oriented trauma therapy like Van der Kolk and Peter Levine, who developed somatic experiencing, assert that treatment protocols and interventions must focus on unlocking or unfreezing the trauma trapped in the body. Levine has argued that PTSD is "fundamentally, a highly activated, incomplete, biological response to threat, frozen in time" (in Wylie, 2004a, p. 37). When people face threats or dangers, they have innate responses to run, fight, or freeze. When we are powerless to prevent attacks or traumatic events, these tendencies, he asserts, become blocked and stay held in the body as undischarged energy. Essentially, they remain on "alert" even long after the precipitating event has passed. According to Van der Kolk, "as long as people don't feel their bodies, we're wasting our time and theirs trying to do talking psychotherapy" (Wylie, 2004a, p. 38). "If you really want to help a traumatized person, you have to work with core physiological states and, then, the mind will start changing" (p. 37).

Although he does not go quite as far as Van der Kolk, Siegel's recognition that traumatized people often could not construct a coherent narrative led to his theorizing that "if the hippocampus is blocked during a trauma, you could be vulnerable to flashbacks and dissociation because, while you'd have the implicit memory of the event, you'd have no explicit, declarative memory of it" (Wylie, 2004b, p. 36). Treatment, therefore, needs to include not simply talking or intellectualizing about things, but other techniques such as guided imagery, sensate-body focusing, and practice in picking up cues from others, both verbal and nonverbal. Siegel's pioneering work in interpersonal neurobiology—that is, linking neuroscience (brain science) with relationship research—integrates attachment theories with research in mind, body, and brain connections (see Siegel, 2001, 2002; for a more extensive review of theoretical bases on trauma treatment, see Siegel & Solomon, 2003, for essays by leading practitioners).

Others counter that getting traumatized people to talk about the loss (Clements et al., 2004) is a key component of healing. Cohen and her colleagues (2006) state,

> Some professionals believe that only certain types of therapeutic activities can access pathways for brain changes (e.g., directed eye movements or body therapy techniques), and that "talking" therapies that do not include specified, physical activities cannot create meaningful brain or bodily changes in traumatized children. We suggest that it is possible to restore adaptive psychobiological functioning in a variety of ways, including through the use of psychotherapeutic components incorporated in the TF-CBT model [trauma-focused cognitive-behavioral therapy]. (p. 15)

The treatment approach developed by Cohen and colleagues "integrates trauma- and grief-focused components in a sequential manner, such that once trauma symptoms have abated, the child and parent are able to begin the grieving process" (p. 5).

The assertion that traumatic elements must be treated before loss-related aspects of grief and mourning may be addressed (Cohen et al., 2006; McClatchey, Vonk, & Palardy, 2009) is not universally accepted: Grief symptoms and trauma symptoms may appear similar, and it is virtually impossible to completely separate these overlapping states. At the Dougy Center, we propose that traumatic symptoms *are part of* the grief process, and attempts to differentiate clear-cut lines between the two may be artificial. Harking back to the statement from Cohen and her colleagues noted in the previous paragraph that "it is possible to restore adaptive psychobiological functioning in a variety of ways," we would advocate for further research and empirical evidence before protocols potentially narrow into one-way treatments.

REFERENCES

The American Heritage Dictionary (4th ed.). (2000). Boston, MA: Houghton Mifflin.

American Psychiatric Association. (1980). *Diagnostic and statistical manual of mental disorders* (3rd ed.). Washington, DC: Author.

American Psychiatric Association. (1994). *Diagnostic and statistical manual of mental disorders* (4th ed). Washington, DC: Author.

Butler, K. (1997). After shock. *Health, 11,* 105–110.

Cassels, C. (2008, November 25). Sense of purpose predicts mental health outcomes following severe trauma. *Medscape Medical News.* Retrieved July 1, 2009, from http://www.medscape.com/viewarticle/584181

Clements, P. T., & Burgess, A. W. (2002). Children's responses to family homicide. *Family and Community Health, 25*(1), 1–11.

Clements, P. T., DeRanieri, J. T., Vigil, G. J., & Benasutti, K. N. (2004). Life after death: Grief therapy after the sudden traumatic death of a family member. *Perspectives in Psychiatric Care, 40*(4), 149–154.

Cohen, J. A., Mannarino, A. P., & Deblinger, E. (2006.) *Treating traumatic grief in children and adolescents.* New York: Guilford.

Cohen, J. A., Mannarino, A. P., Greenberg, T., Padlo, S., & Shipley, C. (2002). Childhood traumatic grief: Concepts and controversies, *Trauma, Violence, & Abuse, 3*, 307–327.

DeAngelis, T. (2007). A new diagnosis for childhood trauma? Some push for a new DSM category for children who undergo multiple, complex traumas. *Monitor on Psychology, 38*(3), 32. Retrieved July 1, 2009, from http://www.apa.org/monitor/mar07/diagnosis.html

DeRanieri, J. T., Clements, P. T., & Henry, G. C. (2002). When catastrophe happens: Assessment and intervention after sudden traumatic deaths. *Journal of Psychosocial Nursing and Mental Health Services, 40*(4), 30–37.

DeSpelder, L. A., & Strickland, A. L. (2005). *The last dance: Encountering death and dying* (7th ed.). New York: McGraw-Hill.

Doka, K. J. (Ed.) (1996). *Living with grief after sudden loss: Suicide, homicide, accident, heart attack, stroke.* Washington, DC: Hospice Foundation of America.

Enright, B. P., & Marwit, S. J. (2002). Reliability of diagnosing complicated grief: A closer look. *Journal of Clinical Psychology, 58*(7), 747–757.

Fassin, D., & Rechtman, R. (2009). *The empire of trauma: An inquiry into the condition of victimhood.* Princeton, NJ: Princeton University Press.

Freud, S. (1917/1959). Mourning and melancholia. In J. Strachey (Ed. & Trans.), *The standard edition of the complete psychological works of Sigmund Freud* (Vol. 14, pp. 237–258). London: Hogarth Press.

Jacobs, S. (1999). *Traumatic grief: Diagnosis, treatment, and prevention.* New York: Psychology Press.

Journey of Hearts. (n.d.). *Dealing with sudden, accidental or traumatic death.* Retrieved April 27, 2009, from http://www.journeyofhearts.org/grief/accident2.html.

Lindemann, E. (1944). Symptomology and management of acute grief. *American Journal of Psychiatry, 101*, 141–148.

Marwit, S. G. (2001). Post-traumatic stress disorder. In G. Howarth & O. Leaman (Eds.), *Encyclopedia of death and dying* (pp. 264–266). New York: Routledge.

McClatchey, I. S., Vonk, M. E., & Palardy, G. (2009). Efficacy of a camp-based intervention for childhood traumatic grief. *Research on Social Work Practice, 19*, 19–30.

Nader, K. O. (1996). Children's exposure to traumatic experiences. In C. A. Corr & D. M. Corr (Eds.), *Handbook of childhood death and bereavement* (pp. 201–220). New York: Springer Publishing.

Nader, K. O. (1997). Childhood traumatic loss: The interaction of trauma and grief. In C. R. Figley, B. E. Bride, & N. Mazza (Eds.), *Death and trauma: The traumatology of grieving* (pp. 17–39). New York: Taylor & Francis.

National Center for Child Traumatic Stress UCLA-Duke University. (2005). *Understanding child traumatic stress.* Durham, NC: Author. Retrieved September 7, 2009, from http://www.nctsn.org/nctsn_assets/pdfs/edu_materials/Understanding_Child_Traumatic_Stress_Brochure_9-29-05.pdf

Parkes, C. M. (Ed.). (2006). Symposium on complicated grief [Special issue]. *Omega, Journal of Death and Dying, 52*(1).

Pynoos, R. S., Frederick, C., Nader, K., Arroyo, W., Steinberg, A., Eth, S., et al. (1987). Life threat and posttraumatic stress in school-age children. *Archives of General Psychiatry, 44,* 1057–1063.

Prigerson, H. G., & Jacobs, S. C. (2001). Traumatic grief as a distinct disorder: A rationale, consensus criteria, and a preliminary empirical test. In M. S. Stroebe, R. O. Hansson, W. Stroebe, & H. Schut (Eds.), *Handbook of bereavement research: Consequences, coping and care* (pp. 613–637). Washington, DC: American Psychological Association.

Prigerson, H. G., Vanderwerker, L. C., & Maciejewski, P. K. (2008). A case for inclusion of prolonged grief disorder in DSM-V. In M. S. Stroebe, R. O. Hansson, H. Schut, & W. Stroebe, *Handbook of bereavement research and practice: Advances in theory and intervention* (pp. 165–186). Washington, DC: American Psychological Association.

Rando, T. A. (1997). Foreword. In C. R. Figley, B. E. Bride, & N. Mazza (Eds.), *Death and trauma: The traumatology of grieving* (pp. xv–xix). Washington, DC: Taylor & Francis.

Schwarz, E., & Perry, B. D. (1994). The post-traumatic response in children and adolescents. *Psychiatric Clinics of North America, 17*(2), 311–326. Retrieved July 1, 2009, from http://www.childtrauma.org

Siegel, D. (2001). *The developing mind.* New York: Guilford Press.

Siegel, D. (2002, September/October). The brain in the palm of your hand. *Psychotherapy Networker, 26*(5), 32–33.

Siegel, D., & Solomon, M. (Eds.) (2003). *Healing trauma: Attachment, mind, body, and brain.* New York: Norton.

Van der Kolk, B. (1994). The body keeps score. *Harvard Review of Psychiatry, 1*(5), 253–265. Retrieved July 1, 2009, from http://www.trauma-pages.com/a/vanderk4.php

Wylie, M. S. (2004a). The limits of talk: Bessel Van der Kolk wants to transform the treatment of trauma. *Psychotherapy Networker, 28*(1), 30–41.

Wylie, M. S. (2004b). Mindsight. *Psychotherapy Networker, 28*(5), 29–39.

Interventions

As part of their assigned topics, many of the earlier chapters in this book have suggested various ways to help children who are experiencing a life-threatening as life-limiting illness, a significant death or other loss, or bereavement and grief resulting from such a death or loss. We realize, however, that many adults who read this book will be particularly interested in constructive interventions to help such children. As a result, we have brought together in part 4 nine chapters that explore such interventions in more robust and direct ways. These discussions cover a broad range of topics: talking to children about loss and death (chapter 14); teaching children about death, bereavement, and coping (chapter 15); guidelines for helping families to help bereaved children (chapter 16); supporting resilience in bereaved youth who have lost a parent to HIV/AIDS, using extended examples from sub-Saharan Africa (chapter 17); principles and practices in conducting support groups and camps for bereaved children (chapter 18); using expressive arts therapies in counseling bereaved children (chapter 19); special problems associated with grieving children who have developmental disabilities (chapter 20); pediatric hospice and palliative care (chapter 21); and psychotherapy for ill children (chapter 22).

One final resource to support the work of adults who want to help seriously ill and bereaved children appears in the appendix to this volume. Here you will find brief descriptions and other information about 125 books designed to be read by or with children. This appendix is organized into eight categories that include coloring and activity books, picture books, and storybooks.

There is much that can be done to prepare children in advance to cope in constructive ways with death and bereavement experiences, to offer support when such experiences are encountered, and to intervene when difficulties arise. It is a privilege to be admitted into the life of a child who is trying to cope with death-related experiences and to be able to provide assistance to such children in ways described in the chapters in this part.

Talking to Children About Death-Related Issues

14

JANE MOORE AND CLINT MOORE III

A glance at the local newspaper headlines on any given day will result in stories of motor vehicle accidents, columns of obituaries, and articles about medical research. Each one of those stories impacts the lives of children. They may be sons, daughters, grandchildren, neighbors, or friends of the deceased or those impacted by a medical crisis. Children receive difficult news about diagnoses, treatments, and impending deaths of parents, siblings, relatives, and friends and about miscarriage and stillbirth of siblings and cousins, as well as about unexpected, accidental, and violent deaths.

"Human beings are storytellers by nature" (McAdams, 1993, p. 27). Frank Smith (1990) examined the nature of stories and their pervasive quality in life: "We look at life in terms of stories.... That is the way we make sense of life: by making stories" (p. 64). The power of story is something that begins early in the life of a child. Parents may read storybooks to young children about the addition of a new baby to the family. They may read other books at bedtime as a means of connecting with their child. Many adults grew up learning about community through the stories offered on *Mister Rogers' Neighborhood*. Adults and children have experienced and continue to experience stories of friendship on *Sesame Street*. Children learn about their relationship with the environment through the stories of *Dora the Explorer*.

Obviously, all of these stories also help children count, pronounce words correctly, or identify colors, and yet all this learning is done in the context of stories that assist the child's imagination in meaning-making. Children learn about numbers before they have to add or subtract, and they learn to make the sounds of particular letters before they necessarily are able to pronounce words made up of those letters. Why should death, as such an important topic of learning in life, be any different? Why should we recreate the wheel when story has already proven to be such an effective tool in facilitating the connection between imagination, thinking, and emotion in the learning of children?

With story as the primary vehicle working in the background of childhood grief and bereavement, we have chosen to recognize four general guidelines for working with children in the context of their grief and attempting to facilitate the process of their bereavement. Our guidelines are as follows: (1) be real; (2) use appropriate and simple language; (3) have an open agenda; and (4) listen and observe. These guidelines are not discrete, mutually exclusive entities, but rather constantly interactive tools that can function to assist children in weaving their ongoing story of the loss across developmental stages. Although there is no designated order to these guidelines, we suggest that one listen to children before one speaks. Because death is an event that all of us will face at some point in our lives, it is incumbent upon us as caring adults to make sure that the stories involving death-related issues are part of our children's world.

BE REAL

Often children are excluded from conversations and experiences about loss and death for a variety of reasons:

- Wanting to protect children from sadness and fear.
- Keeping children out of contexts that are frightening (hospitals, funeral homes).
- Fearing to say or to do the wrong thing.

Current research is not clear as to when children understand death completely. "It appears that children understand that death is a changed state by about four years of age, and most children understand most components by about five years of age. Full understanding of all components is not generally seen before about nine or ten years of age" (Kenyon,

2001, p. 70). Yet adults every day find themselves trying to explain death-related situations to children. Many adults do not recognize that children are aware of death. Both research and observation lead us to note that even young children are aware of tension and worry in the environment, especially in an environment in which a death has occurred. There is reason to believe that the contemporary child's mature concept and understanding of death might occur at an earlier age than his or her predecessors. This change in understanding is largely due to the major cultural trends and experiences (e.g., exposure to media violence and images of death and war) to which today's children are subjected (Hunter & Smith, 2008; see also chapter 2 in this book).

No parent or caring adult wants to inflict pain and worry on a child. However, by attempting to protect children, we often fail to give them the opportunity to learn and grow from life events. Many researchers in death education have dealt with the notion of meaning-making in the death process (e.g., Davies, 1999; Nadeau, 2001; Neimeyer, 2001; Neimeyer, Prigerson, & Davies, 2002). These opportunities for growth can be painful for all involved, yet Davies, for example, quoted a 16-year-old who noted, "I have a better outlook on life now; I realize how important life is as a result of my sister's death" (Davies, 1999, p. 90). In avoiding the subject of death and dying with children, we send an unintentional message that they are uninvolved in the family crisis and not an integral part of the family unit. As well, we may lose the trust of our children as they discover the information we have withheld from them, perhaps affecting their ability to trust in the future.

Further, in failing to discuss difficult topics with children, we frequently cause them to imagine the source of our tension and anxiety. In the absence of clear information, they may often imagine such death-related situations in far more frightening terms than they possibly would if others had shared with them honestly from the beginning. Often, without access to clear and honest sharing of information, children's explanations about death-related situations can be confusing, complex, and self-blaming. This is not what we as adults wish for the children in our care.

Timing can be a critical factor in talking with children about death and dying. It is important that information be given in such a way as to prepare children for an unexpected death. Talking with children requires that the adult be honest and caring and respect the child's age and understanding of death. "Being strong," something that adults often take on in these situations, is not what children need. "Being real" is. If we, as adults, are sad or crying, this behavior is evidence of our love for the person who has died or is about to die. Therefore, allowing children to express their feelings in such situations may involve touching the important person, if possible, sharing a story, drawing a picture, or even crying.

It is important to note that although "being real" does not condone attempting to shelter children from the reality or experience of a loss, it does not demand that children participate in recognizing the loss at an adult level or use adult social or religious rituals to process the loss. Nor are we advocating that all children be exposed to their parents' sorrow. Each of us knows our own children and how they handle emotional distress. Children should be allowed to choose whether they want to visit a loved one whose death is imminent or whether to attend a wake, memorial service, funeral, or burial. They may wish to participate by drawing a picture for a dying loved one, with assurances that this picture will be given to that person or placed on the wall of the hospital or hospice room, or even on the ceiling if that person is bed-bound.

Although there may be certain cultural, ethnic, or religious requirements for adults in the context of loss and death, it should be remembered that such practices might not as yet have significant or even helpful meaning for children. For example, organized religions' rituals may be far more abstract than young children can process. "Souls," "heaven," and concepts of a Higher Power are not necessarily part of a child's coping mechanisms. Some cultures find burial of the deceased to be an important part of the grieving process. However, children may be puzzled as to how the person will eat, or if that individual will be cold in the winter months. Therefore, such practices must be used with care and always with attention to the impact they may have on the child's ongoing and developing ability to grieve. "Being real" with children should allow room to make provisions for compromise so as not to stunt the growth of a child's ability to deal with the reality of a loss and its place in their life and the life of their remaining family.

Even in striving to "be real," parents and other caring adults may feel that the context in which the death or imminent death occurs is not appropriate for children. For example, rules in emergency departments or intensive care units may exclude children, yet in many cases when a parent or significant other is dying, rules can be relaxed, and support can be given for children to be present and participate in saying goodbye. Child life workers in hospitals are often trained in ways to help children understand both the machinery and the significance of the hospital setting. Interventions from such knowledgeable professionals can assist children to understand unfamiliar features of the setting, move beyond the technology, and be able to share their feelings about their loved one. Obviously, parents may want to draw the line when an event occurs that results in the mutilation of a loved one or when the patient's personality has been significantly altered in a negative way. Often we fail to ask for help because we assume the answer is "no." More often than not, help is available to allow our children to participate as fully as they wish both in saying goodbye and in important death rituals.

USE APPROPRIATE AND SIMPLE LANGUAGE

It is important to include children in conversations about loss and death using language that they are able to understand. "Notifiers should consider factors such as age and cognitive development in regard to choice of vocabulary and concreteness of language. However, avoiding the use of euphemisms such as 'passed' and 'lost' is critical, regardless of the student's age" (Servaty-Seib, Peterson, & Spang, 2003, p. 176). One of the authors was working as a chaplain in a large metropolitan hospital and was sitting with a young woman and her 5-year-old son. The woman's husband and child's father had been brought to the emergency department following a head-on collision with a cement truck. In speaking with the medical team, I understood that he had sustained massive head injuries and was not expected to survive. I took the family to a nearby waiting room where the young wife alternated between tearfully facing the loss of her husband and giving thanks for the son they had together.

After some time, a physician came into the small waiting room and sat down across from the family. Although I was hoping for an accurate and understandable explanation of what I anticipated was the death of this husband and father, the family and I did not receive either. Instead, the physician, a young woman herself, told the woman and her son that their loved one "had expired." The woman began crying uncontrollably, and her son, sitting beside his mother, put his hand on her shoulder. The young boy, having interpreted the meaning of the physician's words at his developmental level, said to his mother, "Don't worry, Mama—it's okay. If Daddy expired, we can just renew him like I did my library card."

The words you use with a child need to be age-appropriate. As has been mentioned previously, it is essential not to use euphemisms, such as "passed away" or "went to sleep." Other euphemisms to avoid using with children are "God took her because He loved her so much" or one frequently heard in hospitals—"He expired." Rather, use simple, direct language: "His body stopped working. He died." One can be even more concrete with children by saying, "She can't breathe the way that you and I do" or "He can't eat anymore, and you need to eat to be alive."

For young children, helping them understand what is alive and what is not may prove beneficial when attempting to address death-related situations. For instance you may show them that they are alive by having them breathe on a mirror. When they breathe on the mirror it "fogs up" because of their breath. Then hold a small stone or a pencil up to the mirror and show the child that neither one of these objects is able to "fog up" the mirror, and therefore they do not breathe and are not alive.

You might even have the child help you make a list of what is alive and what is not and why they believe that is so. When speaking with the child, pause frequently to see if there are any questions. Answer those questions, giving only the information that is requested. Sometimes we over-explain to children, causing more confusion. Vicki Scalzitti, director of the Good Mourning Program for children and families at Rainbow Hospice in Park Ridge, Illinois, reassures parents and caregivers that they "shouldn't worry whether the child 'gets it.' Understanding is a process, something people grow into" (Scalzitti, 2008). Asking a child "Do you understand?" is not necessarily helpful in terms of tracking this process. Perhaps a better method is saying, "Tell me what you understand about what has happened (or is happening)." This request may give you the opportunity to confirm accurate perceptions on the child's part and correct misconceptions.

Another brief story may assist in confirming differences between adults' and children's comprehension of information. A 6-year-old girl and her mother came to a monthly bereavement group for children. The mother informed the facilitators of the child's group that upon the death of her husband, she had told her daughter, "God loved your father so much that He took him to live in heaven." The mother described herself as a devout Christian and explained that she found some solace in this belief of a loving God and an afterlife. However, the mother also related that she had used the same way of describing the death to her daughter as a way of attempting to instill a belief in a compassionate God and as a way of protecting her from the stark reality of losing her father.

The mother then reported that over the last several months, her daughter had refused to attend church and would actually hide or refuse to get dressed to the point that the mother was at a loss as to what to do. The child shared in her group, "God needs to give me my daddy back. God doesn't love him more than I do." Following encouragement from the facilitators to take a more age-appropriate, concrete approach with her daughter regarding the death of her father, the mother described how her husband's terminal disease had affected his body. She explained to her daughter that he had died because his heart had stopped beating and not because God had taken him. After several weeks of this consistent message and with the mother answering her daughter's questions, the facilitators learned that the young girl was now attending church services with her mother.

Although we do not presume to tell those caring for children from different cultural, ethnic, or religious backgrounds what to say or not to say, we do suggest that one must be aware of a child's developmental level. If a child is not yet able to think conceptually, it does little to facilitate that child's bereavement process to speak in terms of concepts such as God, eternity, Heaven, or soul.

It is helpful, however, to have spoken about death with a child before that child experiences it and to do so in a way that is appropriate to that child's developmental level and capacities. There is a wealth of children's literature that can support you in developing death as a topic that can be freely discussed (see examples in the appendix to this book). Children's literature is a perfect way to develop a dialogue about difficult topics. There are children's books about death, dying, cancer, children and adults who are ill, and other similar topics. As well, talking about current events of which the child is aware, and using these examples to explain illness, death, accidents, and other death-related topics, can provide opportunities to make death and dying a part of everyday conversation. When talking about death and loss with multiple children, it is important to talk on the level of the youngest child to make sure that understanding as much as developmentally possible occurs.

HAVE AN OPEN AGENDA

Anyone caring for a child who experiences the death of a significant loved one wants that child to be able to process that loss in some meaningful way and also wants that to happen as soon as possible. Many adults function under the misconception that their own bereavement process must proceed in some particular way and must be completed within a particular time frame. Much of this expectation comes from the external responses of others to a death event that this person may have experienced as a child or as an adult. For instance, well-meaning family members or friends may tell women who experience a miscarriage that they "can always have another child," and even adult grievers hear the admonition, "Don't cry." Although such remarks may be an attempt to make the adult griever feel supported, they also may be an effort by supporters to prevent or reduce any emotional response by the griever.

Adults may clearly have certain expectations regarding their own or other adults' grief responses and bereavement processes. However, it is important that such expectations not be imposed on children. Therefore, although anyone may come to the assistance of a grieving child with some agenda, that agenda must remain as open as possible if the child is to experience that support in a healthy and productive way.

It is important to find out what the child already knows about the situation and about death in general. Asking questions such as "Can you tell me what's going on with your mom?" or "What's been the hardest thing for you over the past few days?" can help clarify what the child thinks and how accurate it is. You can ask specifically what the child has seen, heard, or figured out. As well, you can determine what the child "knows" from TV or books by questions that elicit the child's understanding (or misunderstanding) of a situation.

One should not presume to tell a child exactly what to think about death or exactly what to feel or the best way to express his or her feelings. Above all, keep your expectations of how the child should react to yourself. Having a quiet private place where you will not be interrupted allows you to observe the child and his or her reactions to the situation and respond appropriately. One of the best times to have such a conversation with a young child is at bedtime. At that point, children's natural defenses are at a low level because they are tired, and they generally see the bedtime environment as a safe place.

Obviously, this bedtime ideal may not be possible for the single mother who works nights or the grieving father whose cultural role identity requires that the child's grandmother tuck in the child. In such cases it may be necessary to identify other significant persons who can assist in this conversation or to identify other times or activities that are appropriate for that family's situation.

Although it may be tempting for an adult grieving the loss of the same person to push the conversation with a grieving child to some preconceived conclusion or resolution, it is important to avoid this forced closure. Giving the child a choice as to whether to extend or curtail the conversation gives the child some control. Because a death or information about an impending death can be disabling emotionally for a child, "the opportunity to respond to small choices may allow the individual to reconnect with some feeling of power" (Servaty-Seib et al., 2003, p. 177).

When you have a death-related conversation with a child, it is important to be on the child's level physically. If it is appropriate, touching the child or cuddling the child can show support. Use a quiet, calming voice, even though the content of your conversation is about something that may cause great tension. Try to keep eye contact with the child, paying close attention to how he or she is reacting. Above all, keep your expectations of how the child should react to yourself.

Despite wanting a child to be free of pain, it is not helpful to say, "Don't cry." What is important is to accept the responses the child may give. Some adults may feel that if their child cries, then they also will "lose it" and begin to cry. In fact, in most cases that is not bad. Allowing a child to see the extent to which the loss affects you does not subject the child to difficult emotions, does not reduce your standing as a parent or adult in the child's eyes, and does not mar the child for life.

With this in mind, it is true that some grieving children may try to avoid saying or doing things to bring up the loss. They do this because when they do bring it up, they see that their surviving loved one cries. For many children, they are simply living into the expectations that are communicated within the family. The signal for these children is that this family does not share their emotions. A child is not able to understand why it is okay for them to share but adults are somehow not sharing for the child's welfare. Such expectations and signals are frequently transmitted in the way that one communicates with a child.

In presenting information to the child, be brief and focused. You are not engaged in a conversation with a friend over coffee. Realize that you may have to repeat the information over and over again until the child has processed it. Frequently, adults believe that children have not heard what they have been told regarding a loss or a death. This perception arises when children return to playing with their dolls or playing basketball with the child next door after hearing that Daddy is not coming home again because he died.

Children are, in fact, children; they use play for many reasons, one of which includes meaning-making. "Play is, in its own way, a preface to an ongoing and vital cultural activity of making and remaking meaning" (Slade & Wolf, 1994, p. viii). Play is a natural coping mechanism children use; it should not always be seen as behavior used to avoid dealing with a difficult issue, topic, or experience. Play can function both as a way to escape briefly from a difficult situation and also as a way to manage that situation.

Depending on the child's age and understanding, he or she may respond with questions that can stop you in your tracks. Be prepared for surprising questions. For instance, a child may have been told that his or her parent has died but might still ask, "When is Daddy coming back home?" Remember that even though you might tell a child that the drive to grandmother's house will take several hours, the child will probably still ask, "Are we there yet?" Although such a question may point to an inability to understand the concept of time expressed in "Daddy is gone forever," it may also point to other concerns. The child could be asking, Who will take on the roles the deceased person filled? Will we still be a family with only one parent? How will our family traditions change or stay the same? Once assurance has been given that the child is loved, follow-up questions can help us determine what is really worrying the child. It may be that the child has heard someone talk at school about being a foster child or is worried that there will not be gifts this year for Hannukah.

Rather than telling children not to feel difficult emotions, it is best to normalize hard feelings for the child—fear, sadness or guilt, worry or anger are normal feelings in such a difficult situation. It is also important to understand that this may be the first time this child has had such feelings. If the child is told not to feel a certain way, he or she may believe that something is wrong with him or her if these feelings are present.

It is obvious that those caring for this child may have the same or similar feelings. These persons must be careful not to have the child become their primary source of support. This admonition might mean that a surviving parent or older child should seek some professional support rather than expecting their younger child to become the adult in this grieving relationship.

Ben, a second grader who had been attending grief groups for the year following the death of his father, was making good progress in the group. He was able to articulate that his father had had an aneurysm and that he had witnessed his father fall from a standing position to the floor. He reported that the paramedics had explained to his mother that his father had "died before he hit the floor." In his own words, the child explained that an aneurysm was like a balloon that popped in his dad's brain, and the result was his father's death. He was able to talk about how much he missed his time with his dad, recalling the games they played, the sports they participated in, and the bedtime stories they sometimes shared. Group facilitators heard him express his emotions, witnessed him discuss the particulars of the death, and saw him participate in the monthly activities the program offered to bereaved children.

One of the annual activities of the group was a visit from a physician, who would answer any questions that the children might pose. It was their opportunity in a safe setting to question the physician about concerns or confusions the children might have regarding the death of their loved one or about death in general. Though the group was quite small, Ben listened attentively but did not ask any questions. Others wanted to know why dead people were cold and why bodies in funeral homes were hard to the touch. Ben kept quiet. When the facilitator announced that there was time for only one more question, Ben said, "My dad died of a brain aneurysm. I was standing right next to him. The paramedics said that he died before he hit the floor. If I had caught him, would he have been okay?"

The physician beautifully explained that Ben could not have prevented his father's death. Ben's shoulders visibly relaxed. He had been carrying that worry for over a year. No one would have imagined that he might be blaming himself for not being able to prevent his father from dying, yet he did. Although Ben's mother had explained the aneurysm and the details of her husband's death, she could not have known that the remark by the paramedic (which she may not have even registered) could have held Ben hostage for that long period of time. Ben might not have been able to ask his mom the question he posed to the doctor for fear that she would realize that he was to blame.

The lesson we can learn from this story is that it is important to reassure children that they are in no way responsible for the death (if that is true) and to do that over and over again. Sometimes our children need a more objective person with whom to discuss the death. It need not be a professional grief counselor. Often a caring and sensitive teacher, aunt, family friend, or school nurse will do just fine.

LISTEN AND OBSERVE

Many adults and others who function in the role of support for a grieving child may live in fear of saying or doing the wrong thing. Therefore, they may assume that there is some magical word or deed by which they can say or do the right thing—this belief cannot be farther from the truth. For those attempting to support a child through the bereavement process, the twin skills of listening and observation prove to be most significant. For parents with a grieving child this assertion might seem counterintuitive. A child receives many instructions throughout the day: "eat your cereal"; "brush your teeth"; "get dressed for school"; "don't hit your sister." Thus, it may seem natural to conclude that grief is simply another life situation in which a child needs particular instruction and direction. Although we have noted instances when children profited from adult instruction and direction (for example, Ben), it is important to recognize the benefit that can be gained from listening to and observing a grieving child.

Listening may be a skill that most adults believe they have mastered at some point. One hears, comprehends, and responds to what another person is saying, and so one might ask, "What more is there to listening?" The problem is that many people do not actually listen when someone else is speaking, perhaps least of all when the person speaking is a child. Because many grieving children use questions as a way to get, process, and confirm information, much of an adult's response will be to offer answers to these questions. However, if in listening to a child's question, we begin to formulate an answer to that question while that child is still talking, we may claim that we heard the child, but we cannot claim that we were listening. To truly listen to another person, one's internal conversation in the form of "Why is he asking that question again?" or "Didn't he understand that his mom is dead?" or "I'm not sure I know how to answer that one" must become silent. One must not only *hear* what the child is saying but also *listen* in a meaningful way.

These conversations may occur periodically or with more regularity but should still be done with some input from the child. Such follow-ups to difficult conversations may assist in building memories with children, identifying support people (not necessarily professional support), and creating ways in which families and friends can tell the story of the person who has died or is dying.

It can be helpful for a grieving child to engage other family members and friends of their loved one, in terms of telling the story of the person who died and also helping the child craft his or her own story. Every person has a different relationship with the person who died. That person was someone's child, perhaps someone's spouse, and even someone's parent. However, though there may be several children or several siblings left behind, each of them had a different relationship with that person. Within the same family, different people are grieving those various relationships. Although it can be helpful for a child to understand that his grandmother is grieving the loss of her son, his mother is grieving the loss of her husband, and his older sister is grieving the loss of her father, it can also be productive to hear the different stories that come out of those relationships. A friend of the authors was widowed with 5- and 10-year-old sons. At the Shiva, she provided paper and pens and asked friends and relatives to write down stories about her husband to share with the children as they grew up. Hearing these stories can assist a child in establishing his or her ever-expanding circles of support with "go to" people at the time of an intense grief event. As well, family and close friends can form the next circle for ongoing support, and extended family and those in the outer circle can provide interaction and support on an intermittent basis.

Observing a grieving child is another pontentially helpful way to assist in his or her grieving process. However, one must be careful to understand that observing a child does not automatically empower us to interpret that child's behavior. For instance, if we observe a child who has experienced a loss sitting quietly, it does not mean we can interpret that this child is withdrawn and unable or unwilling to grieve. It can be useful to ask the child what his or her behavior means. Some children are quite willing to share their interpretations. By the same token, we are claiming that observation is a helpful tool, and it might be best used to evaluate a grieving child's present behavior as compared with the same child's behavior before the loss. Certainly a child's behavior will change over time, perhaps as a result of changes in family dynamics, economic status, change in schools, and ongoing developmental changes. And yet, one can make some observations about significant changes in a child's behavior that may seem intimately connected to the loss. For instance, a sudden lack of interest in school, a drastic change in how the child interacts with friends, or significant changes in a child's daily routine may all indicate that a child is still struggling with issues related to loss, grief, and coping. Remain aware that all changes in a grieving child's behavior cannot usually be connected solely to the death of a loved one, but rather are often multifactorial.

Experiencing the death of a loved one is a challenging event for most adults and can be a life-altering event for most children. The quality and level of support that an adult is able to garner has much to do with the ongoing psychic and emotional health of that adult in dealing with the loss of a loved one. Even more so, the quality and level of support offered a grieving child may have a direct bearing on the manner in which the child is able to engage the bereavement process. Most importantly, though, such support cannot be a carbon copy of that required by adults and simply reduced in scale for the small people we call children. Rather, children require that those who attempt to support them as they grieve understand that they are not just little adults. Helping children cope with a death requires a concerted effort to understand where each child is in terms of his or her cognitive and emotional development. It is also imperative to appreciate the manner in which the child interacts with the death in different situations. Children may act quite differently when the issue of the loss arises in a school situation, in comparison with how they act at home. Similarly, a child's emotional response and language can differ when talking with friends about the loss as contrasted to speaking with family members.

CONCLUSION

Helping children walk through their own bereavement process requires patience. Children will grieve at their own pace and in their own way. Perhaps one of the more important elements in this process is not to impose adult understandings of death, adult preconceptions of grief, or adult expectations of behavior on these children. In an effort to be of help and support, we find it best to (1) be real, (2) use appropriate and simple language, (3) have an open agenda, and (4) listen and observe. In order to "be real" with children, it is necessary for you to be real with yourself, especially in terms of your own feelings. The effort to be strong for grieving children may not be in their best interests in terms of dealing with the loss. The unhelpful lesson children may learn from such an adult response is that people in this family "don't cry" or that "being strong" is the best way to deal with a loss.

It is also important to use appropriate and simple language when speaking with children who have suffered a loss. Euphemisms are far more confusing for children than they are helpful. Indeed, the use of such euphemisms by adults may only be an attempt to avoid touching difficult feelings of their own. Also, concepts will not be productive in communicating with children who are not yet cognitively capable of conceptual thinking. Try to connect language about loss to concrete examples that a child can truly understand and even explain.

Having an open agenda can be very helpful in working with children in the context of loss. There should be no predetermined deadlines for a child's grief to end nor any expectations of exactly what good grief should look like for that child. Such responsiveness requires that you have such an open agenda for your own grieving process as well.

Finally, the ability to listen and observe may be the most important tool in your toolbox. Effective and active listening is not a skill that many of us have successfully honed. The ability to hear, comprehend, and respond does not by itself constitute truly listening. We must be able to silence internal conversations so that we can truly listen to the conversation we are having with a child. Observing a grieving child can also be an informative and productive tool in facilitating the grieving process of a child. However, it is important to remember that observing a child's behavior following a loss does not provide us with the insight or authority to interpret that behavior in a meaningful way. It is possible, though, to compare the child's behavior following the death with that before the death, especially in terms of the child's ability to maintain usual routines. In the final analysis it might be helpful to heed the advice attributed to the Greek philosopher Epictetus when he said, "We have two ears and one mouth so that we can listen twice as much as we speak."

REFERENCES

Davies, B. (1999). *Shadows in the sun: The experiences of sibling bereavement in childhood.* New York: Brunner/Mazel.

Hunter, S. B., & Smith, D. E. (2008). Predictors of children's understanding of death: Age, cognitive ability, experience and maternal communicative competence. *Omega, Journal of Death and Dying, 57*(2), 143–162.

Kenyon, B. L. (2001). Current research in children's conceptions of death: A critical review. *Omega, Journal of Death and Dying, 43*(1), 63–91.

McAdams, D. P. (1993). *Stories we live by: Personal myths and making the self.* New York: William Morrow.

Nadeau, J. W. (2001). *Family construction of meaning.* Washington, DC: American Psychological Association.

Neimeyer, R. A. (2001). Reauthoring life narratives. *Israel Journal of Psychiatry, 38,* 171–183.

Neimeyer, R. A., Prigerson, H. G., & Davies, B. (2002). Mourning and meaning. *The American Behavioral Scientist, 46*(2), 235–251.

Scalzitti, V. (Ed.). (2008). *Talking with children about death and dying.* Park Ridge, IL: Rainbow Hospice, Good Mourning Program.

Servaty-Seib, H. L., Peterson, J., & Spang, D. (2003). Notifying individual students of a death loss: Practical recommendations for schools and school counselors. *Death Studies, 27,* 167–186.

Slade, A., & Wolf, D. (1994). *Children at play: Clinical and developmental approaches to meaning and representation.* New York: Oxford University Press.

Smith, F. (1990). *To think.* New York: Teachers College Press.

15 Educating Children About Death-Related Issues

KATHRYN A. MARKELL

This chapter explores four principal topics associated with educating children about death-related issues: (1) a brief history of the availability of death education for children; (2) objections to death education for children and counterarguments; (3) teacher and parent attitudes toward death and death education; and (4) death education in the schools.

EARLY ADVOCACY AND SUBSEQUENT DEVELOPMENTS

Nearly 40 years after researchers and educators working in the field of death, dying, and bereavement began to advocate that death education be made available to children and began to develop death education goals and curriculum, formal death education for children is still uncommon. Herman Feifel, one of the first modern death educators, defined the goals of death education broadly. According to Wass (2004, p. 290), Feifel believed that those goals should include "both acquisition of knowledge, the development of self-understanding, and clarification of values, meanings, and attitudes toward death" (see, e.g., Feifel, 1977). Although leaders in the field of death education overwhelmingly support the need for children to receive death education, formal death education still appears to be very limited in high schools and middle schools, and almost absent in elementary and preschool education.

293

In an overview of the history of death education, Pine (1986) noted that in the 1980s there already seemed to be fewer death education courses in high schools than there were in the early 1970s. This decline in numbers was attributed partly to the pressures to enhance basic education offerings, which resulted in the decrease of "elective" topic courses. It was also noted that from 1976 to 1985, death education programs in elementary schools remained "virtually non-existent."

Almost two decades have passed since researchers last surveyed the percentage of U.S. schools that offer death, grief, and suicide-prevention education. In 1990, Wass, Miller, and Thornton found that only 11% of schools surveyed offered death education, 17% offered grief-related programs, and 25% had a suicide prevention/intervention program. Death education programs, specifically, were only half as likely at the preschool through 6th grade level (9%) as at the 10th–12th grade level (18%). The majority of death education teachers had prepared to teach the subject through their own studying and reading, with only one-fourth reporting that they had taken a college course on the subject. Most of the programs were offered as part of health education curricula and were 2 weeks or less in duration.

The majority of formal death-education programs have concentrated on adults, focusing on college students or professionals (nurses, physicians, therapists, etc.). Education about loss, bereavement, and coping may be included in these death education courses, and classes and workshops on these issues are often directed at people who have experienced the death of someone close to them or some other significant loss. Although some elementary and high schools do offer innovative death education programs, death education for children is more likely to be instituted after the loss of a school member or a community/national loss than as part of an ongoing basic education program. Death education for children is also more likely to focus on specific topics, such as suicide prevention, than on general education in the field of death, dying, and bereavement. Formal education about loss, bereavement, and coping for children is more likely to be offered as part of grief therapy than as part of an academic program.

Many educators and therapists also emphasize the importance of informal education for children about death, loss, bereavement, and coping. Adults, especially parents and teachers, are encouraged to take advantage of "teachable" moments, such as when a class pet dies, or when a character in a story dies or experiences a loss. Adults could use such moments to talk to children about these issues and to encourage them to ask questions. Unfortunately, many adults do not know how to take advantage of these informal death education opportunities (Wass, 2003).

Most death educators and scholars agree that the question is not whether death education should be offered, but rather when and how (Weeks & Johnson, 1992). For example, a national study of school psychologists in 2002 found that the topics of grief and death were seen as some of the most important issues facing future school psychologists (Allen et al., 2002). Although the majority of parents and teachers support death education for children, some adults still question the need to educate children about death. Even adults who do recognize the importance of educating children about death often report feeling unprepared and uncomfortable in discussing death with children, and that may lead them to avoid the subject.

Encouragingly, there are a number of successful and innovative programs that have been implemented over the past 40 years to teach children about death, dying, and loss. This chapter summarizes several of these programs. However, because there is still disagreement about "whether" to teach children about death and dying issues, it may be helpful first to offer a brief overview of the remaining objections to teaching this topic to children and lay out the counterarguments (supported by most researchers and educators in the field) to these objections.

OBJECTIONS TO DEATH EDUCATION FOR CHILDREN AND COUNTERARGUMENTS

In many ways, the arguments against death education for children are the same as those against sex education for children:

1. Children are too young to be told about this topic. They are not yet aware or curious about this subject matter.

Although children do not fully understand the universality and finality of death until middle childhood (see chapter 2 in this book for more detail), they are very curious about death and are exposed to it in the culture on a daily basis through media and through their own losses, especially the deaths of pets and grandparents. In the United States, everyone, including children, lives in a culture that emphasizes images of death on television, in movies, in computer games, and in the news.

Like images of sex, images of death are everywhere, but are seldom explained or discussed with children. These images of death are frequently violent, and deaths in movies and on television are often not accompanied by grief (Wass, Raup, & Sisler, 1987).

Young children, especially, have trouble discriminating reality from fantasy. Characters in books or on television may be very real and important to children. Everyone, including children, experiences the deaths of people they know, either personally or through the media, on a regular basis. Just because children do not understand death in the same way that adults do does not mean that they are not interested in, or affected by, the topic of death. In fact, misunderstandings abut the irreversibility or universality of death may lead children to have more fears and anxieties than adults have about death-related issues. Children who have not been educated about these issues may be even more confused and anxious than those who have been exposed to such education. For example, young children often show egocentric thinking and erroneously believe that they did something "bad" to cause a person's death (Schonfeld, 1996).

Adults often assume that children do not experience grief or that they are resilient and will recover from loss quickly (Glass, 1991). In fact, early loss can affect a person's development into adulthood (Jimerson & Miller, 2008).

Many scholars note both a "denial of death" and a fascination with death in our society (Durkin, 2003). In some ways, the dying have become isolated from the rest of society, as the majority of people now die in old age, in institutional settings such as hospitals and nursing homes (Wass, 2003). Unfortunately, this denial is reflected in society's reluctance to educate children about death-related issues and in the avoidance of the subject even when the death of a significant person occurs (Wass et al., 1987). This evasion may lead many adolescents, like the adults around them, to avoid the topic of death and to avoid their bereaved peers because they "don't know what to say" (Rosenthal, 1986).

Children are a society's future. As with other issues, if adults want children to be more open to, and aware of, these topics than they themselves have been, death education needs to start early. It needs to be taught by people who are not afraid or uncomfortable discussing the topic. Like all important educational topics, it needs to be delivered at the appropriate developmental level for the child, and it needs to be included in the curriculum across grade levels, not just in infrequent or one-time units.

2. Parents, not schools, should educate children about death and dying, especially because it involves so many cultural and religious differences.

The majority of parents believe that schools should include death education, and many of them assume that the schools will teach this topic (McGovern & Barry, 2000). However, because parents often do not educate their children about this topic, and the media often give children only violent and frightening views of death, the job of death education may need to begin in the schools.

As noted earlier, if children do not have accurate information about death, grief, and loss issues and do not know whom to ask when they have questions, they may be left with anxiety and an inaccurate view of these topics. Loss and grief are among the most difficult topics for anyone to discuss. If children think about or discuss these topics for the first time after an experience of their own loss, the topic may be even more difficult for them to understand (Milton, 1999).

When a child has lost someone to death, his or her parent has often also experienced that same loss. That parent may not be as able to support and educate his or her child through the loss at that time as effectively as another caring adult may be able to do. For example, teachers can provide important support for children after they experience loss. They can help reshape the child's important relationships with the teacher, the child's family members, and the child's classmates (Perry, 2001). Grief can also affect children's academic performance (Stevenson & Stevenson, 1996), and teachers can help children cope with these problems, too.

There are, however, many cultural and religious differences to consider. Elementary and high schools have begun to embrace the importance of a multicultural education for all children. Discussing the different beliefs, traditions, and rituals associated with death can be an important part of understanding any culture. To ignore this aspect of the human experience is to ignore an important part of every culture (Milton, 1999).

Few studies have examined ethnic and gender differences in the way children view death. These studies do not find significant differences, although Wass and Towry (1980) did find that White boys responded in a more abstract manner to questions such as "What is death?" than White girls or African American boys or girls. More research is needed about cultural differences in the way children understand death and learn to express grief. Cultural expectations may inhibit boys from exhibiting emotional reactions, and therefore they may be more likely than girls to express their grief in aggressive and destructive ways (Aspinall, 1996).

Students in American school systems are becoming more and more diverse in terms of ethnicity, culture, and socioeconomic status. A growing percentage of these students are Third Culture Kids (people accompanying their parents to live all or part of their childhood outside of the country for which they hold a passport) (Pollack & Von Reken, 1999). Research on the grief and loss experiences of these people highlight what many children, of all backgrounds, may experience today as they try to understand the loss and grief issues in their lives.

Third Culture Kids' losses of people, places, pets, and possessions are often not acknowledged. Their grief may be disenfranchised, given that adults sometimes ignore or minimize their losses (Crenshaw, 2002). They often report "existential losses" related to who they are, where they are from, and where they belong (Gilbert, 2008; see also Crockett, 2003). These feelings of loss would clearly affect a child's social and academic performance in school.

Although fewer children today may experience the death of a parent than in previous years, parental "losses" related to issues such as divorce and incarceration are very high (Arditti, Lambert-Shute, & Joest, 2003). Death education programs that address the multiple losses that many children feel could help them to make sense of the world and to focus on how to succeed in it.

3. The "standards movement" in education has emphasized teaching basic skills in school. Many supporters of this movement believe that schools do not have room in their curriculum for additional topics and that teachers should teach only subjects that they are certified to teach (Crain, 2003).

In many ways, there may be no more important topic to include in the school's curriculum than death education. When other controversial topics, such as sex and drug use, are included in the curriculum, they are often presented with an "abstinence-only" approach. Although improbable, it is possible to abstain from activities such as sex for a lifetime. By contrast, death is one of the few events that is a certainty for all humans. It is, therefore, not possible to abstain from experiencing losses due to death.

Research by Hasan and Power (2004) assessed children's apprais-als of the most stressful events that they had experienced in the past 9 months. These 9- to 12-year-old children reported that death and sepa-ration from someone they cared about were perceived as more impor-tant, serious, confusing, and complicated than any other events.

An earlier survey on the loss experiences of middle-school children by Glass (1991) found that 41% of the students had personally experi-enced a death within the past year and that over half listed death as the loss that had had the most influence on them, out of all of the losses they had experienced. Clearly, schools need to address the issues of death, grief, and loss, considering that those issues have been shown to have such an important impact on the lives of children.

4. If children learn about death-related issues, they may try it (i.e., suicide).

In the late 1980s, critics of death education, such as the Eagle Forum, led by Phyllis Schlafly (e.g., 1988), claimed that death education under-mined the parent–child relationship, and could cause depression and even suicidal thoughts in young students. Although research has never supported these claims, and benefits of death education to students have been widely shown, these negative views of death education have been popularized in media reports (Stevenson, 1990).

In actuality, one of the reasons for supporting death education pro-grams in schools is the growing rate of suicide attempts among adoles-cents, even among children under 14 years of age (Jones & Hodges, 1995). Some death educators are concerned that inaccurate death con-cepts of young children could contribute to risky, dangerous, and even unintentional life-threatening behavior (Bernhardt & Praeger, 1985).

Also, children and adolescents are likely to experience the death of a peer at some time during their school years. Because the risk of death due to illness and disease is low in childhood and adolescence in de-veloped countries, deaths of peers are more likely to be sudden, high-trauma losses from accidents or homicide (see chapter 6 in this book). For example, according to final mortality statistics for 2005 from the Centers for Disease Control and Prevention (CDC, 2008) children and adolescents were disproportionately affected by violent injury and death. In 2005 there was a total of 7,593 deaths among children 1–9 years of age in the United States; 3,232 of these deaths, or 42.6 percent, were caused by unintentional injuries (accidents) and assault (homicide).

One example of racial disadvantages is shown by the fact that in 2005 there were 185 deaths of Black children 1–9 years of age caused by assault out of a total of 1,760 deaths (10.5%), but only 283 deaths caused by assault out of a total of 5,426 deaths (5.2%) in the same age group of White children.

Further, homicides in American educational settings, especially those involving the use of firearms, have occurred from time to time in recent years, although the most sensational incidents—such as those at Columbine High School in Colorado in 1999 and at Virginia Tech University in Blacksburg, Virginia, in April 2007—have taken place in secondary and postsecondary institutions, rather than in preschool or elementary school settings. By contrast, much attention has been given to these events by the popular media. Fox and Levin (2006, p. 131) offered the following observation: "Despite the school violence hype and panic, schools actually are the safest place for our kids to be." This comment has been supported by annual reports from the U.S. Departments of Education and Justice (e.g., Dinkes, Cataldi, Kena, & Baum, 2006). Still, many parents and children have been frightened by these reports. In addition, numerous studies examining children's media exposure to death have found that, by age 18, they have viewed at least 40,000 murders (Shackford, 2003). Clearly, given that children cannot be sheltered from the topic of death, they need help understanding and coping with it.

TEACHER AND PARENT ATTITUDES TOWARD DEATH AND DEATH EDUCATION

A survey of parents of preschool children and early childhood teachers about their attitudes toward death education for young children found that both parents and teachers agreed that death education should not be done exclusively at home and in church or other religious institutions and that teachers should develop an understanding of death education (Crase & Crase, 1982). However, parents were less supportive than teachers of having teachers communicate and educate young children about death. More teachers than parents agreed that teachers should introduce children to accurate concepts about death, but fewer than 20% of parents or teachers felt that death education should be included in preschool as a separate unit.

Although many teachers believe that death education is important for children, the majority of them feel unprepared to teach the topic. Pratt, Hare, and Wright (1985, 1987) examined the comfort with, and academic preparation for, discussing the topic of death with children of preschool teachers and teachers-in-training. The majority, between 73% and 90% of the respondents, thought that formal instruction about death was important for young children. The majority also agreed that preschool children are moderately to very curious about death (Pratt et al., 1985). However, only 25%–32% felt that they were adequately prepared to educate children about death (Pratt et al., 1985, 1987). Participants with experience discussing death with children reported feeling more comfortable discussing the topic, but having such experience did not make them feel more confident about their ability to deal with the subject of death.

Reid and Dixon (1999) replicated Pratt, Hare, and Wright's 1987 study in a survey of elementary and middle-school employees that found similar, but in some ways less encouraging, results. Reid and Dixon found that only 12% of their participants had enrolled in a class on death and dying, and 51% felt minimally prepared or completely unprepared to handle the subject of death as it naturally arises in the classroom. This study also measured the participant's attitudes toward death using the Death Attitude Profile-Revised Instrument developed by Wong, Reker, and Gesser (1994). Reid and Dixon found that their sample of public school staff showed greater fear of death and death avoidance and less death acceptance than Wong, Reker, and Gesser had found in their more general sample. Children turn to their teachers for general information and for support during times of sadness and loss. If teachers are fearful about death, avoid the topic, and feel unprepared to discuss it, they may not be able to help their students.

Unfortunately, most studies on teachers' abilities to educate children about death show that teachers from preschool through high school feel unprepared. Cullinan (1990) questioned 192 teachers (kindergarten through 12th grade) about their fear of death, experiences with death, and ability to help their students deal with death-related issues. Most teachers (90%) had had classroom experience with death, and most (87%) had had students who had died, although only 19% of the teachers had participated in death education training. Teachers with higher fear-of-death scores reported feeling less able to help bereaved students. This negative correlation suggests that teacher education about death should address personal death and grief issues on both an emotional and a cognitive level.

A study of the beliefs and attitudes of elementary and middle-school teachers and college education students again found that teachers felt unprepared to teach this topic (Mahon, Goldberg, & Washington, 1999). Although more than half of all respondents felt that death education belonged in schools, less than one-third of the teachers surveyed and one-quarter of the education students felt qualified to teach death education. Like past research, this study also found that having more experience interacting with bereaved students did not make teachers feel more qualified to provide death-related interventions. However, an encouraging study by Molnar-Stickels (1985) found that prospective elementary school teachers could show less fear of death and more comfort discussing death with children after only two brief death education units as part of a health education class.

A study to determine the amount of parental support for death education from parents of fifth and sixth grade students found that 80.6% were generally supportive of death education programs in the schools and that parents who were more knowledgeable about death, suicide, and grieving were more likely to support these programs (Jones & Hodges, 1995).

A study of Irish parents and teachers found that attitudes to death education were very similar to those of their North American counterparts (McGovern & Barry, 2000). This study found that 80% of parents and 63% of teachers of 5- to 12-year-old children believed that the concept of death should be discussed with children before they encounter death in their own lives. Over 70% of both parents and teachers felt that death education was an acceptable topic to include in the school's curriculum, although over half of the adults in both groups believed that death education was best carried out in the home. More teachers (40%) than parents (23%) believed that death education in school would interfere with the parental role concerning this topic. Over 90% of both groups agreed that further training for teachers teaching death education would be desirable. Teachers reported that many of their students had needed to cope with the death or loss of someone close to them in the past 5 years. Thirty-five percent of teachers reported dealing with the death of a child's parent, 23% with the death of a student, and 86% with the death of someone close to the child during that time. However, 71% of parents and teachers reported that they did not feel comfortable talking about loss and grief, and over half reported that it is difficult to explain death to children.

Bowie (2000) was one of the few researchers to ask students for their opinion about whether death education should be offered at school. She found that 73% of Scottish primary school children indicated that death and dying was a topic that they thought about (sometimes too frequently), and over one-third of the students indicated that they worried about death and dying and would like to see the topic discussed in class at school.

DEATH EDUCATION IN THE SCHOOLS

Since the 1970s, pioneers in the field of death education have advocated teaching children about death. In his early overview of the scope of death education, Leviton (1977) noted that all of the goals of death education are related to improving the quality of living and dying: "In this sense, death education is an aspect of primary prevention or preventive health education" (p. 45).

The goals outlined by Corr, Nabe, and Corr (2009) to help children cope with death include most of the common goals of death education for children:

1. Preparation: Death education should provide children with basic knowledge about death-related issues and help them to reflect on their thoughts and feelings about death and loss.
2. Responding to real needs of children: Children will have specific questions and concerns about death-related issues, depending on their developmental level and life experiences; they need to learn strategies to help them cope with the grief and loss that they will inevitably experience.
3. Communicating effectively: Death is a difficult topic to discuss and is impossible for anyone to completely understand; children need reassurance that they can ask questions and express their concerns about these issues and guidance in how to effectively communicate with their bereaved peers.
4. Working cooperatively: Children need to learn that they do not have to deal with difficult issues like death alone; they need to learn about the many community resources that they can turn to during times of grief and loss.

A suggested preschool through high school death education curriculum that includes many of these goals was outlined by Aspinall (1996). It included the following ideas:

1. An initial education program for 4- to 6-year-olds that would focus on helping children to understand that living things die and would help children to identify feelings associated with loss.
2. For 7- to 11-year-olds, an expansion on the initial concepts that would include concrete examples of the irreversibility and universality of death and an exploration of what happens to things when they die. Children could be encouraged to identify different feelings that can accompany death and loss, and they could discuss family and cultural influences on their own grief reactions and those of others.
3. Adolescents would continue to build on their earlier understanding of death issues by using writing, drawing, and role-playing to develop strategies to cope with uncomfortable feelings and to communicate their feelings to others.

Edgar and Howard-Hamilton (1994) argued for non-crisis death education to begin in elementary school, after children have developed the cognitive abilities to understand the universality and finality of death at about 10 or 11 years of age. They described a program offered to over 1,000 fifth grade students over a 10-year period of time. The program, taught in seven sessions over a 3-week period, included a variety of topics such as different cultural practices related to death, emotions experienced when someone dies, and anti-suicide messages. An analysis of the program indicated both increased knowledge (i.e., 74% increase in knowledge about the death process and mourning behaviors) and behavioral changes (13% more involvement in later peer counseling and drug abuse campaigns).

A study by Glass (1990) concerning the impact on death anxiety through a death education unit for grades 6–12 found no significant decrease in death anxiety after the unit but did find that 40% of the students had been personally involved with a death during the past year, and over one-third of them had attended a funeral during that time span. Fifty-eight percent of the students said their parents would be the first people they would go to for information related to death and dying. Because parents are often the people that children trust most for information and advice, parents may benefit from programs to help them provide accurate information about these issues and to provide needed support when their children have experienced a loss.

The use of literature and role-playing is often recommended to help children understand and discuss topics related to death and grief. Klingman's study (1985) compared two death education strategies to help ninth-grade students to be more facilitative in their responses to bereaved classmates. Students were randomly assigned to a 60-minute game-like simulation where the helpfulness of various statements to bereaved classmates was compared, or to a 60-minute bibliotherapy exercise, where students heard a story about a bereaved student and then discussed communication strategies that might be helpful to bereaved classmates. A pre/post-test comparison of statements students would make to a bereaved classmate showed that both strategies resulted in more facilitative statements for the post-test. However, the simulation group showed a greater improvement in the facilitative quality of their statements than the bibliotherapy group. Klingman noted that simulation games may be more expensive, in terms of money and time, for schools than the bibliotherapy option. A similar study by Klingman (1987) comparing the effectiveness of the two strategies for 35 elementary teachers found that both strategies were judged by the teachers to be informative, motivating, and enriching.

As noted earlier, the majority of formal death education programs for children are 2 weeks or less in duration (Wass et al., 1990). One creative approach to teaching a brief unit on death education was presented by Davis and Yehieli (1998). They used the story of *Sadako* (Coerr & Young, 1993), the sequel to *Sadako and the Thousand Paper Cranes* (Coerr, 1977) to discuss death and grief with children. They first read the story of Sadako Sasaki, a Japanese girl who died at age 13 from leukemia after exposure to the atomic bomb 10 years earlier, and then they discussed the Hiroshima Peace Park. The children were then taught how to make paper cranes, based on the story, and were encouraged to explore and discuss their feelings after hearing the story and thinking about these issues of grief and loss. The authors reported successful discussions when using this unit with fourth grade students.

Another brief innovative approach designed to educate students about organ and tissue donation after death was reported by Waldrop, Tamburlin, Thompson, and Simon (2004). Their approach provides a model for ways that children can share their experiences with death education in school with their family at home. Middle and high school students with parental consent, ages 11 to 18, were given a 30-minute presentation about organ and tissue donation. The students were then given a guide to help them share their feelings, attitudes, and decisions about organ/tissue donation with their families. The students were also requested to ask their family members to share their feelings, too.

Students later participated in a debriefing session in which they shared their experiences in leading the family discussion on this topic. Over 80% of the students indicated that the discussion went "ok" or "very well." Students indicated that the most difficult part of the discussion process was "getting it started" and that talking about their deaths and the deaths of others was also difficult. Students indicated that the most positive thing to come from the family discussion was the chance to talk about a topic they had never discussed with their family before. Students also indicated they felt good to be able to share information their family did not already know. When asked what advice they would give to other students about leading this discussion with their families, the students in the study gave such mature and practical suggestions as "Stay calm" and "Pick the right time and be positive about the topic." This educational approach allows students to obtain information about death-related issues, share that information with others, and get practice discussing this important topic with their families.

Balk (1989) employed another interesting approach involving two 50-minute sessions to arouse empathy and promote pro-social behavior toward bereaved peers by using a guided fantasy approach for fourth and fifth grade students. During the first session, the instructor told the students about his interest in helping people who had a family member die. The children then shared information about their family members who had died. Then, using the movie *E.T.*, children discussed problems people may have in making final goodbyes to someone. The children were next told about how people can use guided fantasy to help them relax and improve their performance. They were then guided through a fantasy procedure that helped them to imagine walking through a forest and meeting a person there and then saying goodbye to that person. After the guided fantasy, the children were asked, using a questionnaire format, to consider the emotional reactions they might have to the death of a sibling.

During the second session, the student's questionnaire responses were discussed with the students. The students were asked to consider what they might say to a person who had lost a brother or sister. They were then asked to write a letter to a classmate who had lost a sibling. A discussion followed, and then students filled out the same questionnaire again that had been used in session one.

Comparisons of the responses of the two questionnaires showed that even after only two sessions, more students indicated they would talk to someone about their feelings in the first weeks after the loss of a sibling, and fewer students believed they would never get over their feelings about the loss. The majority of the students wrote a letter to their bereaved peers that the researcher believed reflected empathy.

CONCLUSION

Children are the future of any society, but it is adults who shape and guide the education of children. Recognition of the need for death education has to begin with adults, especially parents and teachers. They need to feel motivated to educate children about grief and loss, and they need to be knowledgeable about and comfortable with discussing these issues.

Research indicates that the majority of parents and teachers think that death education should be taught in school. However, most teachers do not have training to teach this topic or training about how to help their students deal with grief and loss. Teachers need to have death education training as part of their college preparation, and they need ongoing in-service death education training to help them address issues that will inevitably arise throughout their teaching careers.

Teachers and parents must advocate for death education in elementary school, as well as in middle and high school. The educational model designed to teach students about organ and tissue donation by Waldrop, Tamburlin, Thompson, and Simon (2004) could be used as an innovative way to educate students and parents about death and grief issues. It could be expanded to have students share their death education experiences with other students, and even with members of the community, such as educating members of senior citizen centers and nursing homes about topics like advance directives. It may be that adults can sometimes listen to difficult information more easily if it comes from children, and children can feel empowered because they are both learning and teaching topics that really are a "matter of life and death."

REFERENCES

Allen, M., Jerome A., White, A., Marston, S., Lamb, S., Pope, D., & Rawlins, C. (2002). Educational practices and problems: The preparation of school psychologists for crisis intervention. *Psychology in the Schools, 39*(4), 427–439.

Arditti, J. A., Lambert-Shute, J., & Joest, K. (2003). Saturday morning at the jail: Implications of incarceration for families and children. *Family Relations, 52*(3), 194–204.

Aspinall, S. Y. (1996). Educating children to cope with death: A preventive model. *Psychology in the Schools, 33*(4), 341–349.

Balk, D. E. (1989). Arousing empathy and promoting prosocial behavior toward bereaved peers: Using guided fantasy with elementary school children. *Death Studies, 13,* 425–442.

Bernhardt, G. R., & Praeger, S. G. (1985). Preventing child suicide: The elementary school death education puppet show. *Journal of Counseling and Development, 63*(5), 311–312.

Bowie, L. (2000). Is there a place for death education in the primary curriculum? *Pastoral Care in Education, 18*(1), 22–26.

Centers for Disease Control and Prevention (CDC). (2008, June 16). Unpublished data from the National Vital Statistics System, National Center for Health Statistics, Mortality Statistics Branch. Retrieved February 6, 2009, from http://www.cdc.gov/nchs/data/dvs/LCWK1_2005.pdf

Coerr, E. (1977). *Sadako and the thousand paper cranes.* New York: Putnam's.

Coerr, E., & Young, E. (1993). *Sadako.* New York: Putnam's.

Corr, C. A., Nabe, C. M., & Corr, D. M. (2009). *Death and dying, life and living* (6th ed.). Belmont, CA: Wadsworth.

Crain, W. (2003). The standards movement: A child-centered response. *Montessori Life, 15*(3), 8–13.

Crase, D. R., & Crase, D. (1982). Parental attitudes toward death education for young children. *Death Education, 6,* 61–73.

Crenshaw, D. A. (2002). The disenfranchised grief of children. In K. J. Doka (Ed.), *Disenfranchised grief: New directions, challenges, and strategies for practice* (pp. 5–22). Champaign, IL: Research Press.

Crockett, D. (2003). Critical issues children face in the 2000s. *School Psychology Quarterly, 18*(4), 446–453.

Cullinan, A. L. (1990). Teachers' death anxiety, ability to cope with death, and perceived ability to aid bereaved students. *Death Studies, 14,* 147–160.

Davis, T. M., & Yehieli, M. (1998). Hiroshima and paper cranes: A technique to deal with death and grief. *Journal of School Health, 68*(9), 384–386.

Dinkes, R., Cataldi, E. F., Kena, G., & Baum, K. (2006). *Indicators of school crime and safety, 2006* (NCES 2007-003/NCJ 214262). Washington, DC: U.S. Departments of Education and Justice.

Durkin, K. F. (2003). Death, dying, and the dead in popular culture. In C. D. Bryant (Ed.), *Handbook of death and dying* (pp. 43–49). Thousand Oaks, CA: Sage.

Edgar, L. V., & Howard-Hamilton, M. (1994). Noncrisis death education in the elementary school. *Elementary School Guidance and Counseling, 29*(1), 38–46.

Feifel, H. (1977). Death and dying in modern America. *Death Education, 1,* 5–14.

Fox, J. A., & Levin, J. (2006). *The will to kill: Explaining senseless murder.* Boston: Pearson/Allyn and Bacon.

Gilbert, K. R. (2008). Loss and grief between and among cultures: The experience of third culture kids. *Illness, Crisis & Loss, 16,* 93–109.

Glass, J. C. (1990). Changing death anxiety through death education in the public schools. *Death Studies, 14,* 31–52.

Glass, J. C. (1991). Death, loss, and grief among middle school children: Implications for the school counselor. *Elementary School Guidance and Counseling, 26*(2), 139–148.

Hasan, N., & Power, T. G. (2004). Children's appraisal of major life events. *American Journal of Orthopsychiatry, 74,* 26–32.

Jimerson, S. R., & Miller, D. N. (2008). Treating the illness: The school practitioner's response to health-related students' death and children's grief. *Journal of Applied School Psychology, 24*(2), 285–302.

Jones, C. H., & Hodges, M. (1995). Parental support for death education programs in the schools. *School Counselor, 42*(5), 370–376.

Klingman, A. (1985). Responding to a bereaved classmate: Comparison of two strategies for death education in the classroom. *Death Studies, 9,* 449–454.

Klingman, A. (1987). Teacher's workshop in death education: The effects of simulation game and bibliotherapy-oriented methods. *Death Studies, 11,* 25–33.

Leviton, D. (1977). The scope of death education. *Death Education, 1,* 41–56.

Mahon, M. M., Goldberg, R. L., & Washington, S. K. (1999). Discussing death in the classroom: Beliefs and experiences of educators and education students. *Omega, Journal of Death and Dying, 39,* 99–121.

McGovern, M., & Barry, M. M. (2000). Death education, knowledge, attitudes, and perspectives of Irish parents and teachers. *Death Studies, 24,* 325–333.

Milton, J. (1999). Providing anticipatory guidance for our children: Loss and grief education. *Primary Educator, 5*(3), 13–16.

Molnar-Stickels, L. A. (1985). Effect of a brief instructional unit in death education on the death attitudes of prospective elementary school teachers. *Journal of School Health, 55*(6), 234–236.

Perry, B. (2001). Children and loss. *Instructor, 110*(6), 36–38.

Pine, V. R. (1986). The age of maturity for death education: A socio-historical portrait of the era 1976–1985. *Death Studies, 10,* 209–231.

Pollack, D. C., & Van Reken, R. (1999). *Third culture kids: The experience of growing up among worlds.* Yarmouth, ME: Intercultural Press.

Pratt, C. C., Hare, J., & Wright, C. (1985). Death anxiety and comfort in teaching about death among preschool teachers. *Death Studies, 9,* 417–425.

Pratt, C. C., Hare, J., & Wright, C. (1987). Death and dying in early childhood education: Are educators prepared? *Education, 107*(4), 279–286.

Reid, J. K., & Dixon, W. A. (1999). Teacher attitudes on coping with grief in the public school classroom. *Psychology in the Schools, 36*(3), 219–229.

Rosenthal, N. R. (1986). Death education: Developing a course of study for adolescents. In C. A. Corr & J. N. McNeil (Eds.), *Adolescence and death* (pp. 202–214). New York: Springer Publishing.

Schlafly, P. (1988, April 13). Death education comes into open. *The Brooklyn Spectator,* p. 21.

Schonfeld, D. J. (1996). Talking with elementary school-age children about AIDS and death: Principles and guidelines for school nurses. *Journal of School Nursing, 12*(1), 26–32.

Shackford, S. (2003). School violence: A stimulus for death education. *Journal of Loss and Trauma, 8,* 35–40.

Stevenson, R. G. (1990). The eye of the beholder: The media look at death education. *Death Studies, 14,* 161–170.

Stevenson, R. G., & Stevenson, E. P. (1996). *Teaching students about death: A comprehensive resource for educators and parents*. Philadelphia: The Charles Press.

Waldrop, D. P., Tamburlin, J. A., Thompson, S. J., & Simon, M. (2004). Life and death decisions: Using school-based health education to facilitate family discussion about organ and tissue donation. *Death Studies, 28*, 643–657.

Wass, H. (2003). Death education for children. In I. Corless, B. B. Germino, & M. Pittman (Eds.), *Dying, death and bereavement: A challenge for living* (2nd ed., pp. 43–60). New York: Springer Publishing.

Wass, H. (2004). A perspective on the current state of death education. *Death Studies, 28*, 289–308.

Wass, H., Miller, M. D., & Thornton, G. (1990). Death education and grief/suicide intervention in the public schools. *Death Studies, 14*, 253–263.

Wass, H., Raup, J. L., & Sisler, H. H. (1987). Adolescents and death on television: A follow-up study. *Death Studies, 13*, 161–173.

Wass, H., & Towry, B. (1980). Children's death concepts and ethnicity. *Death Education, 4*, 83–87.

Weeks, D., & Johnson, C. (1992). A second decade of high school death education. *Death Studies, 16*, 269–279.

Wong, P. T. P., Reker, G. T., & Gesser, G. (1994). Death attitude profile revised: A multidimensional measure of attitudes toward death. In R. A. Neimeyer (Ed.), *Death anxiety handbook: Research, instrumentation, and application* (pp. 121–148). Washington, DC: Taylor & Francis.

16

Helping Families Help Bereaved Children

KATRINA KOEHLER

A MESSAGE FOR PARENTS, CAREGIVERS, AND ADVOCATES OF BEREAVED CHILDREN

If you have a relationship with a child who has experienced the death of a loved one, you probably have some natural fears and worries about how he or she will be affected in a long-term way, especially if the child is angry and acting out, withdrawn and moody, clingy and anxious, or changing in other ways that concern you. Parents and caregivers of bereaved children are also sometimes concerned because the child shows no signs of grieving and seems strangely unaffected by the loss or never talks about the person who died. No matter what expressions of grief a child is exhibiting, I want to reassure you that even the death of a parent, close sibling, or best friend does not have to result in negative consequences for the child's life or emotional well-being. When a child's grief journey is lovingly supported in the ways described in this chapter, he or she can come through the experience transformed in healthy ways and can be restored to wholeness and emotional health. Though it may take time and, occasionally, may appear to get worse before it gets better, the long-term benefits when a child is given the opportunity to grieve fully are worth both the effort and the wait.

This chapter explores guidelines for parents and other caregiving adults who want to help bereaved children. It begins by addressing our cultural legacy of disavowing and blocking the full experience of grief and how children have been affected by that legacy; then it describes the healing power of the natural grief process when it is supported and allowed to take its course. Next, we look at specific ways that parents, caregivers, and other caring adults can help bereaved children experience their journeys of grief, starting with identifying the great value of adults who can model for children constructive grief reactions and mourning processes, then turning to the importance of allowing children to be children, of telling the truth in an age-appropriate way, and of acknowledging the magnitude of the loss and the validity of the child's grief responses, followed by other specific ways to help bereaved children. After that, resources are mentioned that parents and other caring adults can draw upon to help grieving children, such as grief support groups, grief counseling, and teachers and schools. It is also useful for parents and other adults to be aware of special circumstances that can influence childhood bereavement, such as long illness leading up to a death and various types of sudden, unexpected death. A section on how to help children during a family member's life-threatening illness is also included. The chapter concludes by noting the importance of support for parents and primary caregivers who are helping bereaved children.

THE LEGACY OF EQUATING SURVIVING WITH MOVING ON

Many of us who are now adults grew up in a world where children's feelings were not given much space or importance, even in the wake of a tragedy or traumatic experience. If you are an adult who was raised in the Western world, and you experienced a tremendous loss as a child, such as the death of an immediate family member, there is a good chance that your personal response to the loss was barely addressed. In most families, your parents and caregivers either would not have realized you needed anything from them or would not have known what it was. If you began showing signs of distress several months after the death— angry outbursts, plummeting grades, withdrawal from friends—it may not have occurred to them that this behavior was part of your grief process. If it did, you were most likely either expected or actively encouraged (perhaps even admonished) to "put it behind you" or "move on with your life." Perhaps this legacy of emotional repression is the result of generations of ancestors who functioned in survival mode; when my great-grandmother's young husband died of a sudden heart attack during the Great Depression, for example, she was left with four children and believed that there was no time to grieve. The widespread collective suppression of grief may also be a byproduct of a mechanistic, medical model that overemphasized the mind and body and viewed both as rational machines, failing to take into account the whole human being, let alone the importance of addressing spiritual and emotional needs.

Whatever the constellation of reasons for these long-standing misunderstandings, they are starting to shift now; we are gradually undergoing subtle but significant collective changes (International Work Group on Death, Dying, and Bereavement, 1999). As a society, we notice, value, and honor children's feelings more than before, we are also beginning to give more acceptance to the natural grief process for bereaved people of all ages, and there is now available an extensive body of literature for adults to help bereaved children (see Schuurman, 2004). In addition, there are now more than 400 children's grief centers around the world, many based on the pioneering program at the Dougy Center (http://www.dougy.org; see chapter 18 in this book) of helping children primarily through peer grief support groups that honor their natural grief processes and that trust their innate ability to heal themselves (see Chappell, 2008).

Since 2001 I have been working with grieving children, teenagers, and families at one of these centers, a nonprofit in Santa Fe, New Mexico, called Gerard's House. I was lucky enough to receive excellent training at Gerard's House based on the Dougy Center model, which, combined with some remarkable literature on children's bereavement, has given me both a foundation and a framework for my knowledge of children's grief, but I had to road-test all this information to see and understand how it applied to real-life bereaved kids and how families can be guided to help such children.

THE NATURAL GRIEF PROCESS

In spite of many positive changes in our society, we still struggle with a fundamental lack of understanding about grief, and about how people restore themselves after a loss. Children are still undeniably influenced by the societal pressure described earlier: to move on with one's life as quickly as possible after a death, to push through the grief, to push it away, or to push it down. These coping mechanisms have all been founded on the belief that once we have experienced a loss, it is done, and there is nothing we can do about it, so we might as well put it behind us. Children have internalized this pressure to various degrees. Many bereaved children fight off their feelings without noticing that there is an alternative. What they cannot fight off, many children tend to hide, because they do not want to burden anybody; they do not want to seem weird or make anyone feel awkward.

The tragedy of our old collective strategy of emphasizing "moving on" quickly after a significant loss is this: the very thing we have been pushing away—the natural grief process—is the very thing that can restore us after a loss. The good news is that this natural grief process is built-in. In spite of our cultural conditioning, we all innately know how to do it. Children do not need to be taught how to grieve, but they do need adults' modeling, support, validation, encouragement, and love to help them access their own inherent emotional wisdom. When children are able to let their feelings come to the surface and let their natural grief process happen, their lives can transform.

PARENTS (AND OTHER ADULTS) AS ROLE MODELS FOR BEREAVED CHILDREN

The way children experience their grief, and are affected by their parents' grief, is shaped by many variables, including the child's age and developmental level, the quality of relationship between a surviving parent and a grieving child, the family configuration and family dynamics, the cause and circumstances of the death, the relationship to the person who died, and the bereaved child's personality, temperament, and coping mechanisms. Among all of these variables, however, carefully designed research studies have shown that the single most influential variable in a child's bereavement is how his or her parent(s) and other adults who care for that child cope with their own grief (e.g., Haine, Wolchik, Sandler, Millsap, & Ayers, 2006; Sandler et al., 2003; Worden, 1996).

Whether they are aware of it, parents and other caring adults serve as role models for children. When parental figures are able to express their own grief in their children's presence and explain these reactions to their children, they contribute in important ways to their children's well-being. For example, it is normal for many young children to feel anxious when a parent is crying. A worried child may ask, "Why are you crying, Mommy?" or "Are you okay?" Understandably concerned about upsetting the child, the mother may not know how to respond to these questions except to wipe away her tears and reassure the child that she is fine. The child may, in fact, be relieved that Mom has stopped crying but will also likely feel confused by the mother's reaction, and receive the message that something is going on that is not okay to talk about or ask about. In addition, the child in this scenario gets no help understanding his or her own tears or other feelings of grief.

By contrast, if the mother says, "I'm crying because I miss your Dad, and I'm feeling really sad about it," the child receives several helpful messages: that crying is okay; that Mom feels some of the things I am feeling; that if Mom can talk about her feelings and about Dad, so can I; and that it's okay for me to ask questions when I'm worried about Mom or I don't understand what's going on. Later, the mother can address the child's worried feelings, asking, for example, "Were you worried about me when I was crying?" and then listen to the child's response. This openness helps the child reflect on his or her own secondary grief reactions, with the added benefit of letting the child know his mother notices what he or she is feeing and cares. Mom can also explain that when she is crying, she is hurting inside, but that sometimes crying helps her feel better, and that this is what people do sometimes when they miss someone or feel sad.

Similarly, when parental figures engage in healthy mourning rituals and invite children to participate, they show children that it is okay to find ways to cope with loss and grief (Fristad, Cerel, Goldman, Weller, & Weller, 2001). So the first thing for parents who want to help bereaved children to know is the very great value of sharing their own grief and mourning with children in constructive ways.

ALLOWING CHILDREN TO BE CHILDREN

Children find security in familiar routines and patterns in everyday life. They recognize and appreciate consistency in discipline and other aspects of what they accept as normal in their lives. Parents can help maintain comforting boundaries in a child's life. That is particularly important when external events like loss and death have shaken that life. Parents can show and tell children that they are valued and loved just for being who they are, just as they were before the disturbing event took place.

It is important not to call on children to be more than they responsibly can be. Most young children cannot fairly be asked to take on more responsibilities than they can bear. When parents and other caring adults show that children are valued and loved for who they are, not for anything they may be doing, the message conveyed is that the children need only continue to be themselves and to love and value their family members.

If a child's behavior changes in the wake of a significant loss or death, parents and other caring adults can give that child extra attention, avoid reprimanding the child excessively, and talk with the child about those changes in behavior.

Adults can also help bereaved children feel safe to be children by getting grief support outside of the family—perhaps from a caring relative, a clergy person, or a respected teacher or counselor—because children often try to protect their parents and other family members from the depth of grief that they may be experiencing. Parents can also tell the child, "It's not your job to take care of us," and "It's okay for you to be sad or angry or scared or upset—or anything else—about your sister's death, and about how we've changed and how the family has changed. If you ever want to talk to me about this, or anything else you can come to me anytime." It also does not hurt to tell these kids that they can be kids.

OTHER WAYS TO HELP BEREAVED CHILDREN

I have come to realize that the true expert in the counseling relationship is the bereaved child. This seems so obvious to me now, almost too elementary to write down. Yet this simple realization has proved profound to me in my work with kids. Bereaved children are our finest teachers about grief and mourning. They are naturals!

—Alan Wolfelt (1996, p. xi)

Children who are grieving a significant death in their lives have made clear what tends to support them in their grief and coping, and what is not helpful. Here are some guidelines they have taught us.

Tell the Truth in an Age-Appropriate Way

A child can live through anything, so long as he or she is told the truth and is allowed to share with loved ones the natural feelings people have when they are suffering.

—Eda LeShan (1976, p. 3)

One of the most important and helpful things a parent or caregiver can do for a bereaved child is to explain the death in an age-appropriate way. As the title of one book says, children are *Never Too Young to Know* (Silverman, 2000). Honesty from adults is essential. It helps children come to terms with the death and feel honored as grieving members of the family. In grief support groups at Gerard's House, we can see the difference between children who have been told the truth about a family member's death with understanding and acceptance and those who, in addition to everything else they are coping with, feel left in the dark and are still trying to figure out what happened. Children—even very young children—need to be told about the death in simple, concrete terms that they can understand, including the following elements:

- A clear explanation of how and when the person died, as soon as possible after the death, including the cause, location, and circumstances of the death.
- Help with understanding what death is, in clear, concrete terms.
- A check-in to make sure the child understands what happened.
- An invitation for the child to ask questions about this death in particular and about death in general.

When children are told only part of the story about the death of someone important in their lives, their grief is compounded by confused thinking, unanswered questions, and in many cases, frustration and mistrust. Without a clear explanation, the child has a hard time figuring out, understanding, and accepting the disappearance from the family or the community of the person who died and what it means.

Timing is also important. If parents wait to tell children about the death, children feel both anxious and shut-out during the period when they are left wondering what has happened. Later, when they learn the truth, they often feel hurt and resentful that it was withheld from them. Even very young children need to have the death explained to them in a timely manner.

I have known many parents who have hidden the truth about an important death from their children with the best of intentions. Some parents try to soften the blow by using euphemisms to make the death sound like a good thing or give children figurative or spiritual ways of thinking about the death without giving concrete, physical explanations. These abstract accounts can *really* confuse children. When children are told that the deceased person "fell asleep and didn't wake up," the children may conclude that sleeping is a risky proposition and may resist going to bed or even have night terrors. In another example of why to avoid euphemisms when talking to children about death, one mother relayed to her 7-year-old son that his father had died by saying simply, "Daddy went away. He's in a better place, in heaven with God and the angels and Grandma." One week later, the child stunned his mother when he told her that he wanted to die too, so he could be in "a better place" with his dad. Finally, one young boy was told that Jesus loved his father so much that Jesus came down and took him up to heaven to be with him. One day in his grief support group, the child exclaimed, "If I ever see Jesus, I'm going to kick him in the pee-pee doo-doo!"

To avoid confusing children, use the words "died," "dead," and "death." It is also helpful to explain that when a person dies, their heart stops beating, and they stop breathing; their body does not work anymore. Children's books that explain death and dying as part of a story also help bereaved children understand what has happened to their special person (see the appendix in this book for examples of such literature).

When children are younger than 6 years old, be prepared for the possibility of questions about the death such as, "When will I see Daddy again?" or "Is Mommy coming back?" Sometimes a child repeats these questions no matter how many times an adult answers them, indicating that the child is not so much seeking an explanation as testing what is real and trying to keep hope alive that the beloved person will return. The child may not yet be at a developmental stage where he or she can cognitively grasp the finality of death. A helpful response to such a recurring question is, "You're really missing your mom and wanting to see her again, aren't you?"

It is also a good idea to ask if a child has any questions about the death. Many uncertainties and misunderstandings can be resolved that way. If the child's questions are spiritual or metaphysical, such as "Why do people die when they die?" or "Is he with grandpa now?" a concrete answer is not as important. These are mysteries that children can ponder and have their own processes around. Parents can, of course, share their own beliefs, but it is also okay to say, "I don't know," or to explore possible answers with the child. Asking the child what he or she thinks may help that child deal with his or her own thoughts and feelings about the death.

Acknowledge Their Grief

It is incredibly helpful to grieving children when adults validate that a great loss has occurred in the child's life. Validating the child's loss goes a long way toward legitimizing the child's pain, confusion, shock, and other manifestations of grief. It is even more helpful when adults also acknowledge children's grief, letting them know that their grief is real and normal in this situation. Another great gift we can give bereaved children is to tell them that we see what they are going through and that we care.

An example of a "grief talk" to acknowledge a child's grief appears in the next paragraph, but it is not important to use these or any other exact words. In fact, it is better to find words that feel authentic to you, emphasizing what you witness happening for that child. Try to imagine being a loving mirror, reflecting back the child's experiences. The power of this approach is twofold: First, it allows the child to see herself (Oh! I get what's happening to me now. I'm grieving! And it's okay! It's normal!). Second, it lets the child know that someone sees her. In some Native American spiritual traditions, this reflective listening is called Eagle Medicine. In my experience, reflective listening is one of the most powerful gifts anyone can give a child in distress. For many children, having even just one person who witnesses them can sustain them through tremendous difficulties. Even a brief acknowledgment, such as "I know it's been very hard for you since your brother died. You used to spend so much time together," can help a bereaved sibling. A longer "grief talk" gives the bereaved child a framework to help him understand so many of the confusing things happening in his world:

> What you're experiencing now is something called *grief*. Everyone has grief reactions after someone important to them dies. It's normal. And what *grief* means is all the feelings you have, and all the things you are going through— in your body and even in your life—because someone important to you died. You might feel scared, or mad, or very sad, or different, or alone. You might feel fine or even happy one minute, and then upset the next, and that's normal too. It can be kind of like riding on a roller coaster. And it might be confusing. With all this going on, you might be tired. Sometimes it's hard to think straight, or it might be hard to fall asleep. And you might have times when you feel alone or different from other kids, especially the ones who aren't grieving. Even though that might be hard, it's normal too. Also, other people in your family are going through their own grief. So you

might notice your mom and dad or your brother or sister acting different, like being sad and missing the person who died, but also, they might not have as much energy, or maybe they will get mad at you more easily. This isn't your fault; it's because they are grieving. Everyone lives with his or her grief differently, so you might not feel the same way your mom feels or act the way she's acting, but that's okay.

Later, more information can be added, telling the child, for example, that there is no time limit to grief, that it may go on for a long time and come in waves, or anything else relevant to that child's situation.

Gently Invite the Child to Talk About It

Phrase the invitation in a way that gives the child the option of not answering. For example: "I know a lot of things have changed for you since your father died. Is there anything you want to tell me about what it's been like for you?" Broad or open-ended questions allow children to choose what they want—or need—to talk about, instead of requiring that they discuss something they may not feel comfortable trying to put into words or that may be less helpful to them. Many bereaved children I have known rate "How do you feel?" as the most unhelpful thing people said to them after the death. It is hard for most children to talk about their grief in the first place, but for many children, this particular phrasing is especially unsupportive. Even "How are you?" is hard to answer, partly because it is a social question to which we are conditioned to answer, "Fine." This is why an open-ended invitation to talk, especially when preceded by an acknowledgment of the child's experience, works better for most children.

Do Not Try to Get Them to Open Up

If a child does not say much, or does not accept your invitation to talk at all, that is okay. Most children have a hard time putting their feelings about grief into words, if they even know, and can explain, what they are feeling. When pressured to talk about their grief, children can feel embarrassed, invaded, unsafe, and resentful. Honor their boundaries by telling them it is okay if they don't want to talk about it right now. As adults who care about children, we hope they will open up so that we can be there for them. Sometimes we are so eager to help, we forget for a moment that we are there for the bereaved child, not for the answer or for the profound conversation. It can be very helpful to build trust slowly while giving bereaved children your caring presence, faithfully witnessing their experiences, being a good listener, and letting them go at their own pace.

Listen With Empathy

I have found the need to fill silences and treat bereaved children as patients results from contamination by a medical model of mental health care-giving. This model teaches us to study a body of knowledge, assess patients, and treat them with the hopes of resolving issues and conflicts. In my experience, there is one major problem with this model as it applies to caring for bereaved children—it doesn't work!

—Alan Wolfelt (1996, p. x)

Nothing we adults can say to a grieving child is more helpful than listening when that child speaks. It sounds so simple, but it is a profound form of support. While the child is talking, I suggest resisting the temptation to try to fix or change the child's feelings, to get the child to look on the bright side, or to try to get the child to go deeper into his or her pain. Instead, hear the child. Try to be present and savor the moment of sharing, even if some of what the child is saying is painful. Focus on being with the child. Once you have listened, there are many helpful things you can say, including acknowledging and reflecting what the child has said, empathizing, asking gentle questions to help draw the child out, and normalizing and helping the child understand his or her grief process.

Many children will appreciate your sharing your own experiences of grief and loss, as long as this sharing is offered as a way of relating, and not intended to equate or compare losses. For example, most children object to adults telling them, "I know just how you feel" or "the same exact thing happened to me." When it comes to adults' self-disclosure about our own grief, our vulnerability and authenticity is perhaps what children appreciate the most.

Sharing Experiences of Being Alone and Different

It is common for children who have experienced the death of someone important in their lives to feel very much alone and different from their peers. Such children may not know anyone who has ever been in their current situation. As a result, they may feel that no one else has ever had experiences like this. If that is true, then no one else can understand or appreciate what has happened and is still happening to them.

A parent or other adult can ease the child's experience of feeling alone in grief by helping the child to feel nurtured, witnessed, and loved and thus safe enough to accept experiencing this grief as uniquely his or hers, instead of feeling estranged from others. A caring adult can talk to the child about why feeling alone is a normal part of grief, saying, for example, "As you go through your grief journey, you may feel alone sometimes because no one else will be able to understand exactly how you feel every moment. It's normal to feel different or alone sometimes when you're grieving. You can always come and talk to me, though, and tell me what's going on." A conversation like this is not intended to make the "different" feeling go away but can make it easier to bear. This acknowledgment of the child's emotional world can be especially precious to a child because most children are not adept at sorting out their feelings on their own or making sense of the pain and turmoil they feel.

The same parent or caring adult can acknowledge to the bereaved child that the adult is also encountering difficult grief reactions (if, indeed, that is so), that the adult recognizes that the child may be encountering similar grief reactions, and that the adult is willing to talk with the child about their shared experiences. All of this honest sharing can give the child important permission to have these hard-to-accept feelings and other reactions and to disclose them to someone who cares. Acknowledging that we are feeling alone and different together can be a powerful way of opening lines of communication and building trust in a difficult situation.

Helping Bereaved Children Vent Their Anger

> There is a healthy survival value in being able to temporarily protest the painful reality of the loss. Having the capacity to express anger gives a child the courage to survive during a difficult time.
>
> —Alan Wolfelt (1996, p. 78)

It is wholly understandable for a child who has been hurt by the death of a loved one to become angry and to project that anger on nearby people and objects. Adults who want to help grieving kids can start by normalizing anger as a part of grief and by making a space of acceptance for the child's anger. Most grieving children do not understand that there are valid and natural reasons for their being angry. Instead, they usually think they are being "bad." The parent (or other adult) can say something like, "I've noticed that you get mad more than you used to, like when you yell at me, or when you hit your sister. Some people get mad a lot when someone important to them dies. Also, things have changed a lot in our (or your) family. It's okay for you to be angry. You have a right to be!"

The parent or other adult can then give the child specific anger outlets, saying, "I don't like it when you yell at me or when you hit your sister, and you probably don't like it when we get mad at you for doing these things. So let's try to find ways you can get your anger out without hurting yourself or anyone else." The child can help think of ways to express anger that he or she thinks might work best. For many children, physical outlets are the best—sports and play. Some children like to write angry letters, draw pictures of what they are mad about, or tell you why they are angry.

When an adult can model getting angry in a healthy way without taking it out on anyone, this is helpful for children who struggle with their anger. One way a parent or other adult can do this modeling is by inviting a grieving child to join in getting mad together. At Gerard's House we have a Storm Room, similar to the Dougy Center's Volcano Room. It has padded walls and a punching bag, and is full of big stuffed animals and padded bats. Children use the room two at a time for wild play and anger release. Every so often, we go into the room as a group and yell as loud as we can, thinking about or yelling out things that make us mad. But even without a padded room, an adult can find a place where it is safe to yell and scream together and hit something soft—a bed, pillows, or large stuffed animals. Another safe way to vent anger might be to mix up mud balls with a child and then throw them as hard as possible against an "anger wall."

Give the Child Ways to Work Through His or Her Grief

Adults can help by accepting that the child misses the person who died. Though it is likely to be painful, missing the person is part of the grief process. Acknowledging and validating children's grief can help children with their sadness. It can help them feel loved and safe so that they can cope with the sad feelings instead of holding them in or pushing them away. By surfacing, feeling, and expressing sad feelings, the child will move through them eventually. Keep in mind that the goal of supporting a sad child is not to make the sadness go away, but to support the child in his or her natural grief process.

Formal or informal family rituals can give bereaved children meaningful ways of connecting with the deceased individual. Making art to memorialize the person who died, helping children to imagine what they would like to say to the deceased person and then saying it out loud, writing a letter to that person, or making cards on his or her birthday or other holidays are all ways that a child can feel the bond and remember both the person who died and their relationship. Families can also take time to remember the deceased person with a moment of silence before a meal at family gatherings or on holidays, anniversaries, and other special times. Just by taking time to sit together and share memories, parents and other caring adults validate and honor the grief experience they share with children. Looking at pictures and talking about the person who died is another activity children usually appreciate.

Parents can also help by consciously bringing the family together to talk about all these issues once some time has elapsed after the death: "How did the person who died fit into our family? How are we going to adjust, together, to our special person not being here anymore?" A conversation like this brings these concerns into the consciousness of children who might otherwise be unaware of the pressure to fill the void and how they may be responding to that pressure. Though it may not occur to parents and caregivers who love their children, a sibling-bereaved child may benefit from being told something like the following by his or her parents or caregivers: "We love you just the way you are. And even though we miss your brother, we don't want you to feel that you have to change or fill in his shoes in any way. We want you to keep being you."

As they try to help bereaved children address all the fears and other concerns that these children are likely to have, whether a child has brought them forward or not, parents and other adults can expect to encounter questions that they find uncomfortable. For example, if Daddy died, and Mommy encourages her children to share their worries, she might find herself asked questions like "Are you going to die, too?" It is not enough to dismiss such a question or to promise that she will not die. A false promise is not an adequate response to a child's deep anxieties. It would be far better to say that such a death is neither likely nor expected and then to add that plans have been made to ensure that the children will be cared for by someone they know and love. It is a good idea to discuss with the children where they would live and with whom in the event that both parents should die. But be prepared for the child to ask, "And what if *they* die?"

As a parent or other adult tries to help grieving children find specific ways to express their grief, it is important to create opportunities that let each child find his or her own way without insisting on one particular way or putting some ways off-limits for any reason other than direct harm they might cause. A good example is the question of crying. In some of the families seen at Gerard's House, parents and caregivers reproach their children for not crying. One child's grandmother asked her, "Don't you miss your sister? Why don't you ever cry?" The grandmother told me that she was worried about her grandchild holding it in and was trying to encourage her children to let it out. What the granddaughter revealed was that she did cry about her sister, just not as much as her grandmother thought she should. And even when she did cry, she did not do it around her grandmother because her grandmother was "so weird about it."

In other families, some parents or other caregivers seek to limit the child's grief expression, telling the child, "Come on. That's enough now," or "Don't start crying. It will make me cry," perhaps without thinking of the larger message they are sending to the child. In situations of this type, parents and caregivers can help children by giving them the message—verbally and nonverbally—that crying is okay, and not crying is okay, too. Caring adults can also help a child brainstorm about what he or she finds to be effective ways to cope with loss and grief.

Anticipating the Long Haul

Parents and other adults can be a great help to grieving children by being aware that they may display new manifestations of grief a long time after the death (Schuurman, 2003). Most bereaved children, in fact, are likely to need support, compassion, and understanding many months or even years later—whenever the grief comes up for them. One important lesson learned from the Harvard Child Bereavement Study was that children's grief reactions are often more intermittent in character than those of adults and thus longer in their overall duration (Worden, 1996). A second major lesson was that a significant minority (though not all) of the school-age children in this research were found to be encountering more difficulties at 2 years after the death of a parent than they were at earlier times (4 months and 1 year after the death). Children at Gerard's House often remark that one of the things they like about their grief support group is that no one expects them to get over it, and everyone there understands that grief does not end; it just changes.

Knowing and being able to recognize possible indicators of grief is important too. For instance, a child may experience a year when he is truly not able to live up to his previous level of academic performance. He may not be able to sit still or pay attention in class. If this behavior pattern is seen, understood, and acknowledged as part of his grief process, it will help the child get through the period of intense grief. Parents, caregivers, and teachers who are prepared for this delayed grief response can be compassionate with the child's grief timing and help the child understand what is happening.

GRIEF SUPPORT GROUPS AND GRIEF COUNSELING

Peer grief support groups are ideal for most bereaved children because in peer groups, children can be with other kids who are grieving and listen to other kids talk about their deaths and their grief. This *normalizing* is a powerful antidote to feeling different and alone. In most peer support groups, as well as in individualized grief counseling, bereaved children will also be given many ways to express their grief. Activities may include art, play, memorializing rituals, skits, cards or letters to the person who died, and puppet shows (see, for example, McWhorter, 2003; Webb, 1999). Resources of this type are particularly useful when a child's grief is troubling to the child and to his or her family or when parents and other adult care providers find that their efforts to help such a child are not sufficient, perhaps because these adults do not know what to do or say or because they are so overwhelmed by their own grief that they find it difficult or impossible to help the grieving children in their care.

Children's Grief Support Groups

Support groups for children offer settings in which grieving children can focus on their grief and their needs (Stokes, 2004; see also chapter 18 in this book). In those settings, grief-inhibited children can know they will not upset anyone else, and the people they meet are comfortable hearing and talking about death and grief. Within the group, children can learn to recognize and understand all of their different feelings and grief reactions, and they can find constructive ways to express what they are experiencing. Sharing regrets and guilty feelings with other grieving children is a good example of how a group can be beneficial. Because people tend not to talk about these kinds of feelings in day-to-day conversations, children often feel that they are the only ones suffering with a wish to take back hurtful things they said or did when the person was still alive. That reinforces the belief that if they feel guilty, they must be at fault. Many children have felt that a great weight has been lifted from them when they find out that other children are struggling with similar thoughts.

Peer grief support groups can give significant relief to many bereaved children who assume blame for a death. In activities within the group, children can surface these thoughts, feelings, and beliefs. Group sharing lets children get the guilt off their chest and hear that they are not alone in thinking they could have prevented the death or that it was their fault. It is important to give children an opportunity to express these feelings and to honor how powerfully children are affected emotionally when they blame themselves for a loved one's death.

Above all, a peer grief support group is especially effective at relieving a bereaved child's sense of being "all alone." In evaluations administered to bereaved children in peer grief support groups at Gerard's House in 2008, we asked, "Does being with other kids who have had someone die help you feel that you're not the only one?" and 92% answered "yes." One girl whose father had died said that what helped her most about her group at Gerard's House was "just being with other kids who have had someone die. Even if we're not talking about it, even if we're just playing ball, I know that everyone else is like me and knows how it feels, and that really helps."

Grief Counseling for Bereaved Children

Grief counseling is often helpful when the specific grief reactions or coping processes of an individual child are not being adequately addressed within the family or within a children's grief support group. Sometimes there may be no grief support group available locally, or it may be too general in nature and not sufficiently focused on the child's particular needs. Sometimes the child may not fit in well with the group and may be disruptive or causing difficulties for other members.

Children's grief support centers often offer individual counseling to the children and families they serve, provided either by their own staff or by referrals to counseling resources in the community. In either case, it is important that the counselor be experienced in matters of bereavement and grief, be knowledgeable about the needs of bereaved children, and be skilled in ways of working with such children, such as expressive arts therapies or play therapy (see, e.g., Fiorini & Mullen, 2006; Webb, in press; and chapter 19 in this book). One cannot assume that every individual working as a counselor possesses this background and skill.

TEACHERS AND SCHOOLS

Teachers, schools, and school staff play a major role in the life of a child. For that reason alone, the death of a significant person in the life of a child must be addressed in a meaningful and sensitive way by the schools that all children in the family attend. For example, the school can help by having each teacher tell each class about the death the child has experienced, including the cause of death, when it happened, and other important facts (Klicker, 2000; Lerner, Volpe, & Lindell, 2003; Servaty-Seib, Peterson, & Spang, 2003). Sharing information in this way keeps rumors to a minimum and protects child survivors from being bombarded with questions. It also helps such children to know that everyone knows the truth, instead of having to wonder who has heard what.

In addition, where it is appropriate, grief groups or rituals at the school can give other children ways to interact with the bereaved child and talk about what is really happening instead of avoiding the subject, asking unhelpful questions, or not knowing what to say. A condolence card signed by a child's classmates also helps give the child a sense of belonging. For more information about how to respond to a student's death in the schools, see two booklets published by the Dougy Center (1998, 2000; also available at http://www.dougy.org).

SPECIAL CIRCUMSTANCES THAT INFLUENCE CHILDHOOD BEREAVEMENT

All experiences of bereavement during childhood are not the same, not only because the children involved are different in so many ways, but also because the circumstances of the loss or death may be special in many ways. This section describes some of those differing circumstances that parents and other caring adults will want to take into account when they seek to help bereaved children.

Long Illness Leading Up to the Death

When an important person in a child's life dies of a long-term illness, the adults have usually had some time to anticipate this encounter and adjust to what may occur. Children may not always have this advantage, but most of them will benefit from knowing that death is a possibility, being told what to expect from the dying process and the death, and being encouraged to communicate with each other. The opportunity for each child to say what he or she wanted to say to a beloved grandparent, a dying parent, or a sibling with a life-threatening illness is precious. When children have not been given this chance, they usually later say that they wish they could have said goodbye, made amends, or told the person before death, "I love you." Sometimes children cannot be given advance notice that a death is imminent, perhaps because the adults cannot admit that the death is likely, because the final event arrives suddenly, or because the adults cannot bring themselves to have this conversation with their children, possibly even believing they are sparing the children by not telling them.

Kimmy's story illustrates how being talked to honestly and encouraged to communicate during a sibling's life-threatening illness can help a bereaved child with the grief process. Kimmy's sister Nat was 9 years old when she was diagnosed with cancer. As Nat's disease progressed, their mother told both girls everything she knew. Each time bad news came, they all struggled to accept it together. Kimmy was able to bond with her mother in the shock, helplessness, dread, and anguish they were both feeling as Nat's condition deteriorated. Kimmy felt loved and respected, and she trusted her mother because she was told the truth and all of her thoughts and feelings were welcome.

Still, the timing seemed very sudden for Kimmy when Nat actually died 14 months after her diagnosis. Even though she knew Nat was dying, had gotten to say everything she wanted to say to Nat, and had told her how much she loved her the last time they saw each other, Kimmy still felt unprepared for Nat's death. "She was so sick for a long time," Kimmy remembers, "but she was doing so good right before she died. We thought she might be getting better. When she died, it was a shock."

After Nat's death, Kimmy was able to lean on her mother for support. Though devastated over the loss of her best friend and sister, Kimmy has been able to express her feelings freely throughout her grief process and has not felt as alienated or as pent-up with emotions as many other sibling-bereaved children her age.

A long illness also usually means that the family has been preoccupied with the dying person's sickness for some time, which means that both the family system and the child's life have already been disrupted before the death actually takes place. Kimmy did not feel at all neglected during Nat's illness; her mother was able to give extra quality time and attention to both girls in the months leading up to Nat's death. In many families, however, surviving siblings feel that they have gotten short shrift while so much of the family's attention was focused on the dying child.

Helping a Child During a Family Member's Life-Threatening Illness and Dying Process

When a family member has a life-threatening illness, adults can help children in many of the same ways that they can help children after a death, including by modeling and sharing healthy open grief, as Kimmy's mother did. In addition, adults can help by not placing excessive burdens or responsibilities on the child—for example, not leaning on the child to comfort the dying person or other family members, recognizing instead that the child may need a break from hospital visits or other exposure to the dying person (Saldinger, Cain, & Porterfield, 2003). The child can also be helped by having the difficulty and intensity of his or her experience repeatedly acknowledged: first, how hard it may be to watch the dying family member's body and/or mind break down and to witness the pain and anguish, both physical and emotional, that may be involved; second, the anxiety and distress of anticipating the person's death; third, how upsetting it can be to see and feel how the family and its members, and especially the dying person's primary caretakers, are affected by the long illness; and, fourth, the challenge of managing the normal ambivalence and guilt about both wanting and not wanting to spend time with the dying person. It is also helpful to validate whatever specific issues may be painful or thorny for that particular child.

Finally, adults can help by being aware of—and countering—the widespread misconception that the death of a loved one is always easier for children when it is preceded by a long illness (Saldinger, Cain, Kalter, & Lohnes, 1999). Sometimes children whose loved ones died of long illnesses start their grief groups at Gerard's House with an unusual level of acceptance and equanimity about the death, especially if they feel good about all the time they spent bonding with the person before he or she died, and the person died in a state of peace, surrounded by loved ones. Nevertheless, when children have experienced the primary and secondary effects of the person's long illness and dying process as outlined earlier, they are likely to have special issues to work through that are every bit as challenging and significant as the issues of children whose family members have died suddenly. During the illness (and also after the death), it is often especially difficult for children when their dying loved one is in a great deal of pain, when the person wastes away physically so that he or she looks like a different person, or when he or she enters a state of dementia where the relationship and ability to communicate is altered. For these children, a play medical cart can help them process what they are experiencing and feeling in relation to both the illness and the impending death.

Sudden, Unexpected Death

When a death is unexpected—for example, as a result of an accident, sudden illness, suicide, or murder—the shock is tremendous. Any sudden death is devastating, but some, such as the unexpected death of a young person, constitute an almost unbelievable outrage. Here is a brief inventory of some common themes in children's grief after suicides, accidents, murders, and sudden illnesses.

Suicide

Many prominent elements in children's grief after a suicide include the following:

- Stigma and shame: Embarrassment and a sense of disgrace are common in the aftermath of a suicide.
- Guilt, regrets, and magical thinking: A child may regret things he or she had said to the person who died and believe himself or herself to be somehow responsible for the suicide.
- Blame: Family members often blame each other for a suicide, and people in the community frequently point fingers as everyone tries to make sense of the death.

Other elements of children's grief after suicides may include unanswered questions about why the individual took his or her own life and hurt and angry feelings toward the deceased person for abandoning everyone. The child may also be affected by disputes within the family about whether the death was a suicide or an accident and also by secrets, lies, or rumors surrounding the death and media attention that publicizes the suicide, sometimes in thoughtless or unsavory ways.

Murder

Children who encounter a death by homicide of someone they love often experience the following:

- Anger at the murderer: Extreme anger and hostility toward those who were involved in the death are often experienced by children in these situations and are commonly acted out toward family members, teachers and other authority figures, and their classmates and peers.
- Frustration and powerlessness at the injustice of the murder and at the inability to retaliate: Children typically feel a desire for revenge, even while knowing that revenge is not an appropriate response; this quandary puts them in an emotional double-bind. Adults can help by letting children know that feelings of wanting revenge are normal in such a situation and that feelings are different than actions.
- Family anger at murderer(s): Adult members of a family may be filled with rage after one of their members has been murdered; sadly, in some cases they may take some of that anger out on surviving children, or at least impact the child negatively by being angry all the time. A parent in this situation can help the child by getting help with his or her own anger issues, which are common byproducts of posttraumatic stress.
- Family thrust into intensely emotional relationships with media, the court system, the perpetrator, and his or her family: Families typically resent what many have called the "circus" they find themselves caught up in after a murder; they usually want the media, especially, to leave them alone.
- A prolonged and difficult trial process: Involvement in the legal system after a murder can often drag on for years and be very painful and upsetting for everyone.
- Fear of the murderers: Children who encounter the perpetrator of the murder through the media or at the trial frequently are afraid that that individual might come after them at some point.

Accident or Sudden Illness

Accidental deaths can occur in a wide variety of ways (see chapter 6 in this book), as can sudden illnesses. Their effects on surviving children can include the following:

- Guilt, regrets, and magical thinking: Accidents often seem so freakish and random that it is hard not to think about how they could have been avoided. Children who take on responsibility for many bad things that occur in their lives often feel at fault for what has happened.
- Blame: Children who are angry at what has happened to a loved one frequently feel blame toward someone or something they believe caused the death.

Violent Death and PTSD

Researchers who have examined children's bereavement over antici-pated parental deaths have noted that "few have gone as far as Rando (1997) to argue that all acute grief is, by definition, a form of traumatic stress reaction" (Saldinger, Cain, & Porterfield, 2003, p. 169). Evidence from the best research studies of children's parental grief (e.g., Haine et al., 2006; Sandler, Ayers, Wolchik, 2003; Worden, 1996) makes clear that posttraumatic stress is not the typical response of children to paren-tal death. However, when a child has seen or been present for a suicide, murder, violent accident, or certain kinds of harrowing illnesses or dis-eases (see chapter 13 in this book), the posttraumatic stress can be acute, sometimes even towering over other aspects of grief. Even if the child did not actually witness a horrific scene, hearing the story of a traumatic death can leave a child with unwanted images and thoughts of pain and violence. Because children may not understand what is happening to them, they need a parent or other adult to initiate a conversation about PTSD and its symptoms.

One child's older brother killed himself with a gun. In the shock of their grief, his parents leaned on their surviving child, Johnny, in tragic and inappropriate ways that have had life-changing consequences for him.

> My Dad wanted to see the place where Isaiah died, and I don't know why, but for some reason, somebody asked me to go down there with my Dad.

To this day I still can't get the smell and the sight out of my head. I saw blood and gore splattered everywhere. He was at the top of the stairs when he did it, and broke most of the stairs on the way down.

After witnessing the grisly scene of his brother's death, 9-year-old Johnny experienced unbearable nightmares and night terrors, along with other symptoms of severe posttraumatic stress. Eleven years later, the smell and sight of blood continue to keep him awake at night, along with everything else he saw that day. What made the aftermath of the ordeal so much worse for Johnny is that nobody talked to him about what he had seen that day or comforted him during his nightmares. Perhaps the most harrowing feature of Johnny's PTSD was going through it alone. No one knew. He did not tell his parents or any of his relatives because they were looking to him for support.

If children have been present for a scene of terrible violence, or if they have heard or seen grisly details or evidence related to death, a caring adult can help by acknowledging the horror of what the child saw or heard, inviting the child to talk about his or her experience, expressing concern, offering comfort during distressing symptoms, and getting professional help for the child's PTSD. One of the rules of thumb is to help the child talk about specifics of the trauma (Pynoos et al., 1987).

Even when the death was relatively peaceful and had been anticipated for a long time, an adult can help the bereaved child by recognizing how distressing it may be for the child to lose a parent, sibling, primary caregiver, best friend, or other significant person. One study comparing parentally bereaved children to disaster survivors and non-trauma groups found "parentally bereaved children reporting significantly more [posttraumatic stress disorder] symptoms" than children who had survived fatal tornadoes or other stressors such as academic difficulties (Stoppelbein & Greening, 2000, p. 1116).

SUPPORT FOR PARENTS AND PRIMARY CAREGIVERS

Any parent or other caring adult who is grieving a devastating loss while trying to care for children who are also bereaved is carrying a heavy load. Such parents or caring adults can often benefit from at least trying some kind of grief counseling or support group. This support can benefit both the adults in question and the children in their care. For those willing to try a group, the Compassionate Friends (http://www.compassionatefriends.org) is a national organization of-fering free grief support groups for parents who have experienced the death of a child. Many children's grief centers also provide concurrent support groups for parents and caregivers while children and teenagers are in their groups. For some bereaved parents, one-on-one counseling is more helpful. When everyone in the family is receiving the right kind of grief counseling or support, the benefits are multiplied.

REFERENCES

Chappell, B. J. (2008). *Children helping children with grief: My path to founding the Dougy Center for Grieving Children and Their Families*. Troutdale, OR: NewSage Press.

The Dougy Center: The National Center for Grieving Children and Families. (1998). *Helping the grieving student: A guide for teachers*. Portland, OR: Author.

The Dougy Center: The National Center for Grieving Children and Families. (2000). *When death impacts your school: A guide for school administrators*. Portland, OR: Author.

Fiorini, J. J., & Mullen, J. A. (2006). *Counseling children and adolescents through grief and loss*. Champaign, IL: Research Press.

Fristad, M. A., Cerel, J., Goldman, M., Weller, E. B., & Weller, R. A. (2001). The role of ritual in children's bereavement. *Omega, Journal of Death and Dying, 42*, 321–339.

Haine, R. A., Wolchik, S. A., Sandler, I. N., Millsap, R. M., & Ayers, T. S. (2006). Positive parenting as a protective resource for parentally bereaved children. *Death Studies, 30*, 1–28.

International Work Group on Death, Dying, and Bereavement. (1999). Children, adolescents, and death: Myths, realities, and challenges. *Death Studies, 23*, 443–463.

Klicker, R. L. (2000). *A student dies, a school mourns: Dealing with death and loss in the school community*. Philadelphia: Accelerated Development.

Lerner, M. D., Volpe, J. S., & Lindell, B. (2003). *A practical guide for crisis response in our schools: A comprehensive school crisis response plan* (5th ed.). Commack, NY: American Academy of Experts in Traumatic Stress.

LeShan, E. (1976). *Learning to say good-by: When a parent dies*. New York: Macmillan.

McWhorter, G. (2003). *Helping activities for children in grief: Activities suitable for support groups with grieving children, preteens and teens*. Roanoke, TX: Author.

Pynoos, R. S., Frederick, C., Nader, K., Arroyo, W., Steinberg, A., Eth, S., et al. (1987). Life threat and posttraumatic stress in school-age children. *Archives of General Psychiatry, 44*, 1057–1063.

Rando, T. (1997). Forward. In C. Figley, B. Bride, & N. Mazza (Eds.), *Death and trauma: The traumatology of grieving* (pp. xv–xix). Washington, DC: Taylor & Francis.

Saldinger, A., Cain, A., Kalter, N., & Lohnes, K. (1999). Anticipating parental death in families with young children. *American Journal of Orthopsychiatry, 69*, 39–48.

Saldinger, A., Cain, A., & Porterfield, K. (2003). Managing traumatic stress in children anticipating parental death. *Psychiatry, 66*, 168–181.

Sandler, I. N., Ayers, T. S., Wolchik, S. A., Tein, J.-Y., Kwok, O.-M., Haine, R. A., et al. (2003). The Family Bereavement Program: Efficacy evaluation of a theory-based prevention program for parentally-bereaved children and adolescents. *Journal of Consulting and Clinical Psychology, 71,* 587–600.

Schuurman, D. (2003). *Never the same: Coming to terms with the death of a parent.* New York: St. Martin's Press.

Schuurman, D. (2004). Literature for adults to assist them in helping bereaved children. *Omega, Journal of Death and Dying, 48,* 415–424.

Servaty-Seib, H. L., Peterson, J., & Spang, D. (2003). Notifying individual students of a death loss: Practical recommendations for schools and school counselors. *Death Studies, 27,* 167–186.

Silverman, P. R. (2000). *Never too young to know: Death in children's lives.* New York: Oxford University Press.

Stokes, J. A. (2004). *Then, now and always—Supporting children as they journey through grief: A guide for practitioners.* Cheltenham, England: Winston's Wish.

Stoppelbein, L., & Greening, L. (2000). Posttraumatic stress symptoms in parentally bereaved children and adolescents. *Journal of the American Academy of Child and Adolescent Psychiatry, 39,* 1112–1119.

Webb, N. B. (Ed.). (1999). *Play therapy with children in crisis: Individual, group, and family treatment* (2nd ed.). New York: Guilford.

Webb, N. B. (Ed.). (in press). *Helping bereaved children: A handbook for practitioners* (3rd ed.). New York: Guilford.

Wolfelt, A. (1996). *Healing the bereaved child: Grief gardening, growth through grief and other touchstones for caregivers.* Fort Collins, CO: Companion Press.

Worden, J. W. (1996). *Children and grief: When a parent dies.* New York: Guilford.

17

Supporting Resilience in Bereaved Youth in Sub-Saharan Africa Who Have Lost a Parent to HIV/AIDS

MELISSA J. HAGAN AND IRWIN N. SANDLER

This chapter focuses on the promotion of psychosocial adjustment among children who have experienced the death of a parent as a result of AIDS-related illness, with a focus on the region most affected by the epidemic, sub-Saharan Africa. Utilizing a contextual resilience framework, we explore the multiple potential routes by which AIDS-related bereavement may affect psychological outcomes in youth. We begin with a review of the contextual resilience model articulated by Sandler, Wolchik, and Ayers (2008). We then apply this framework to an exploration of the process of adaptation among youth who have experienced AIDS-related bereavement. We review the efforts currently underway to provide psychosocial support and life skills to parentally bereaved youth and conclude with a fictional case study, depicting the points and strategies that can be used to promote resilient adaptation in an adolescent girl who has lost her mother to HIV/AIDS.

PARENTAL DEATH IN THE CONTEXT OF THE HIV/AIDS EPIDEMIC IN SUB-SAHARAN AFRICA

The death of a caregiver can give rise to a unique set of vulnerabilities among children and adolescents. In addition to the psychological pain associated with the loss itself, bereaved youth face the challenge

337

of adapting to environmental and interpersonal disruptions that accompany parental loss while simultaneously accomplishing the developmental tasks that are necessary for long-term psychosocial adjustment. Research has shown that children's psychosocial functioning following bereavement is best predicted from the accumulation of risk factors and protective resources preceding and/or following the death of a parent. Within a contextual resilience framework, these factors impact multiple interrelated domains of outcomes (e.g., problematic functioning, positive well-being, and grief) by influencing the satisfaction of children's basic needs, such as the need for social relatedness (confidence that one will be taken care of and feeling that others will be responsive and emotionally available), physical safety and security, a sense of control over one's problems, and positive self-worth (Sandler, 2001; Sandler et al., 2008). Further, the ways in which the satisfaction of basic needs are threatened or promoted depend on a host of contextual factors, including the child's age and developmental stage, the circumstances surrounding the illness and death, and the characteristics of the family's community and culture.

The delicate balance between risk and resilience in parentally bereaved youth is no more apparent than in the millions of families affected by the HIV/AIDS epidemic in sub-Saharan Africa (SSA). By the end of 2007, 12 million children and adolescents in this region had lost one or both parents to AIDS, and in some countries as many as 15%–24% of children under the age of 17 have experienced AIDS-related bereavement (UNAIDS, UNICEF, & USAID, 2004; UNAIDS & WHO, 2008). The likelihood of losing both parents is disproportionately high in countries hardest hit by the epidemic (Bicego, Rutstein, & Johnson, 2003). Children may lose both parents to AIDS-related illness or one parent to illness and one to labor migration. The majority of these children are in the care of extended family members, and as many as 60% of orphaned youth in SSA are cared for by grandmothers (UNAIDS & WHO).

There is considerable empirical evidence that parental bereavement in the general population is associated with a variety of mental and physical health problems throughout the life span (Cerel, Fristad, Verducci, Weller, & Weller, 2006; Melhem, Walker, Moritz, & Brent, 2008). Although research on parentally bereaved youth in SSA is limited, there is evidence that children who have experienced the AIDS-related death of a parent have a higher risk of mental health problems. For example, compared to non-orphans, children orphaned by AIDS in Uganda were found to be more likely to experience vegetative symptoms, feelings of hopelessness, and suicidal ideation as well as higher levels of anxiety, depression, and anger (Atwine, Cantor-Graae, & Bajunirwe, 2005; Makame, Ani, & Grantham-McGregor, 2002). In South Africa, children orphaned by AIDS were more likely to experience depression, peer relationship problems, PTSD, delinquency, and conduct problems compared to children orphaned by other causes and non-orphaned children (Cluver, Gardner, & Operario, 2007). Cluver and Gardner (2006) reported finding that in comparison to matched controls, children bereaved by AIDS were more likely to report having no good friends and to experience frequent somatic symptoms and nightmares. In addition, there is evidence that youth orphaned by HIV/AIDS begin sexual activity earlier than non-orphaned peers and are especially vulnerable to infection with HIV (Atwine et al., 2005; Gilborn, 2002).

FACTORS THAT INFLUENCE CHILDREN'S ADAPTATION FOLLOWING AIDS-RELATED BEREAVEMENT

Research conducted in the United States with a sample of children whose parents died from a wide range of causes has shown that resilient adaptation following parental death is influenced by the degree to which children's basic needs are threatened or promoted (Wolchik, Tein, Sandler, & Ayers, 2006). The fatalities associated with the HIV/AIDS epidemic have impacted communities in distinct ways that have substantial consequences for bereaved youth. Given the stigma attached to the disease, the extent to which the disease has affected entire communities, and the socioeconomic climate of many countries in SSA, the challenges faced by children experiencing AIDS-related bereavement are varied and, in some ways, unique (Miller & Murray, 1999; Stein, 2003). Following a review of the threats to children's functioning after the AIDS-related death of a parent, we discuss ways in which families and communities can promote the satisfaction of children's basic needs and resilient adaptation.

Safety and Biological Integrity

Parental illness and/or death often result in a significant decline in standard of living. The loss of income that comes with the death of an adult family member and the costs associated with treatment prior to death and funeral arrangements following the death leave many bereaved children in poverty (Andrews, Skinner, & Zuma, 2006). This situation is exacerbated in countries where economic and political crises have led to rises in unemployment and the breakdown of national and local infrastructure (Madhavan, 2004). As a result, many children experience reduced access to basic necessities such as food, health care, shelter, and clothing (Stein, 2003). Studies have found that caregivers of parentally bereaved children in SSA are having difficulty meeting children's emotional, educational, and physical needs, and there are growing concerns that the extended family system is faltering because of severe economic constraints (Heymann, Earle, Rajaraman, Miller, & Bogen, 2007; Madhavan, 2004). In addition, there are reports that conditions of poverty have resulted in children falling victim to the exploitation of child labor or appropriation of property by the foster family (Ansell & Young, 2004; Bedri, Kebede, & Negassa, 1995; Foster et al., 1995; Stein).

Social Relatedness to One's Primary Caregivers

Sandler (2001) conceptualized a sense of social relatedness as a child's belief that there is an interpersonal bond "marked by stability, affective concern and continuation into the foreseeable future" (Baumeister & Leary, 1995, p. 500). From the time a caregiver becomes ill, the security of the bond between parent and child is threatened by multiple factors. Prior to parental death, children of parents with HIV/AIDS are likely to witness the debilitating illness of their caregiver and must face the emotional impact of the disease on surviving family members as well as the uncertainty that comes with not knowing how they will be cared for (Wood, Chase, & Aggleton, 2006). The unpredictable nature of HIV/AIDS-related illness places stress not only on the child but also on the child–caregiver relationship. Some have suggested that parenting practices are compromised during terminal illness (Armistead & Forehand, 1995). Research conducted in the United States suggests that children's psychosocial functioning improves when they are placed within a stable and supportive home following the death of their parent from AIDS, suggesting that this positive outcome indeed may be the case (Rotheram-Borus, Weiss, Alber, & Lester, 2005). During a parent's illness and following parental death, the stigma and secrecy associated with HIV infection can also result in significant stress on parent–child relationships as well as relationships with extended family (Miller & Murray, 1999). For example, studies have shown that children bereaved by AIDS experience discrimination within their own families as well as in the community and, as a result, may experience social isolation and an absence of emotional support after the death of a parent from HIV/AIDS (Stein, 2003). Finally, the emotional and behavioral problems exhibited by many AIDS-bereaved youth can place considerable strain on the extended family system. Indeed, guardians of AIDS-affected children in Malawi report high levels of frustration as a result of orphaned children's lack of respect, disobedience, and under-appreciation of the difficulties inherent in caring for additional children (Mann, 2003). All of these factors can threaten a child's need for social relatedness by increasing fear of abandonment, one of the strongest predictors of children's mental health problems following parental death (Wolchik et al., 2006).

Positive Self-Worth

There is considerable evidence that parental death and associated stressors have a negative impact on children's self-esteem (Haine, Ayers, Sandler, Wolchik, & Weyer, 2003; Wolchik et al., 2006). This may occur as a result of bereavement-related challenges to the fulfillment of important social roles in the context of school and family (Sandler, 2001). Children bereaved by HIV/AIDS are especially likely to experience interferences with school functioning and positive role functioning in the home. For example, children orphaned by HIV/AIDS are significantly less likely to be in school (Andrews et al., 2006; Bhargava, 2005). Reasons for this include the need for many youth to take on caregiving duties prior to and/or following a parent's death, the priority placed on bringing in additional income, lack of financial support for education, and social discrimination. Many of the bereaved children who remain in school experience considerable social isolation as a result of bullying, shame, and the stigma and secrecy surrounding HIV/AIDS (Cluver & Gardner, 2007; Foster, Makufa, Drew, Mashumba, & Kambeu, 1997), factors that are likely to encourage negative self-evaluation. At home, many older bereaved children must assume caregiving responsibilities for an ailing parent, sibling, or grandparent. Although such "parentification" of children has been linked to psychosocial problems in American youth, children in many non-Western nations are often expected and encouraged to take care of younger siblings regardless of a family's circumstances, which suggests such caregiving roles may be adaptive for bereaved children. However, at least one study found that caregivers in youth-headed households reported high levels of depressive symptoms, social isolation, and poor physical and mental health of their youngest siblings (Boris, Thurman, Snider, Spencer, & Brown, 2006).

A Sense of Control

Children who lack a sense of control in regard to life's problems are less likely to engage in adaptive coping to negative events and are more likely to experience mental health problems (Kim, Sandler, & Tein, 1997; Lin, Sandler, Ayers, Wolchik, & Luecken, 2004). In the absence of a stable and supportive environment, the death of a parent and the stressful events surrounding the loss can threaten a child's sense of control by re-inforcing children's perception that problems are unmanageable or un-controllable (Wolchik et al., 2006). Children of parents with HIV/AIDS are particularly vulnerable to a reduced sense of control. For example, the clinical course of HIV/AIDS is often unpredictable, and many children are uninformed about the disease or the possibility of an infected parent's death from AIDS-related illness. Moreover, during a caregiver's illness, children are likely to experience disruptions in daily routines and frequent periods of informal fostering by other adults (Stein, 2003). Following parental death, many youth experience multiple migrations as a result of feeling ill-treated or because of changes in caregiver cir-cumstances (Ansell & Young, 2004). Given the infectious nature of the disease, children who have experienced AIDS-related bereavement are also likely to suffer multiple losses.

MEETING THE NEEDS OF CHILDREN AND ADOLESCENTS BEREAVED BY HIV/AIDS

Despite the multiple losses, accumulated stressors, and negative out-comes associated with the AIDS-related death of a caregiver, activities to promote parentally bereaved children's psychosocial well-being are reportedly one of the most neglected areas of help to children bereaved by HIV/AIDS in SSA (Stein, 2003). Part of this perception may be due to confusion surrounding the meaning of psychosocial interventions versus psychosocial care and support (Richter, Foster, & Sherr, 2006). Within a contextual resilience framework, resilient adaptation following parental death involves the reorganization of individual and social environmental systems, and there are multiple potential routes by which the strengths of the family or the individual might be mobilized to enable satisfaction of basic needs and developmentally competent role performance (Sandler et al., 2008). Based on this model, psychosocial care and support are the foundation of a family's capacity to enable satisfaction of parentally bereaved children's basic needs, and this capacity is influenced by a multitude of factors. UNICEF established a multilevel approach to protecting and supporting HIV/AIDS-affected youth, including but not limited to ensuring access to essential services; raising awareness to reduce the silence, stigma, and discrimination associated with HIV/AIDS; mobilizing effective community responses to create a supportive environment for vulnerable children; and strengthening the capacity of families to meet the needs of children orphaned by HIV/AIDS (UNICEF & UNAIDS, 2004). We adapt the UNICEF framework for the protection of vulnerable children and explore from a contextual resilience perspective the ways in which families can be supported to ensure resilient adaptation among bereaved youth in the context of the HIV/AIDS epidemic in SSA.

Raising Awareness and Reducing HIV/AIDS and Orphan-Related Stigma

The stigma associated with HIV/AIDS continues to threaten children's adaptation even after the parent has succumbed to the disease. Lessening the influence of factors that contribute to the ostracism of families affected by HIV/AIDS could decrease the social isolation that many experience and strengthen communities in ways that would promote children's sense of social relatedness, sense of self-worth, and achievement of developmental competencies. Nation- and community-wide education and awareness-raising initiatives focused on reducing HIV/AIDS-related stigma and discrimination have the potential to benefit HIV/AIDS-affected youth in a number of realms. For example, decreasing discrimination by teachers and ostracism by peers would result in a wider social support network for AIDS-bereaved youth and decrease the likelihood of withdrawal from school. Given the established link between AIDS-related stigma, AIDS-orphanhood, and psychopathology, stigma reduction strategies may also have a direct affect on children's mental health (Cluver, Gardner, & Operario, 2008). A review of 21 studies that examined the effectiveness of stigma reduction activities indicated that provision of information on HIV/AIDS, counseling, group desensitization to the disease, and contact with HIV-positive individuals can decrease discrimination (Cluver et al., 2008). Atwine and colleagues

(2005) suggested that such awareness-raising efforts be built into village meetings, religious sermons, and community gatherings.

Mobilizing Community-Based Resources and Responses

Nurturing Collective Efficacy

Based on the contextual resilience model, the extent to which families are able to promote children's satisfaction of basic needs is affected by the ecological context within which they live (e.g., children are nested within families, communities, and culture—all of which are subject to economic, social, technological, and political realities). The financial deprivation experienced by many AIDS-affected families increases the likelihood of discrimination by the community and limits the ability of families to support the physical, educational, and psychosocial needs of parentally bereaved youth. Although a number of governmental and nongovernmental agencies offer economic and material support to families, it has been suggested that these externally based resources may undermine community coping mechanisms, whereas community-based efforts could encourage the kinds of social support characteristic of collectivistic communities (Foster, Makufa, Drew, Kambeu, & Saurombe, 1996; Richter et al., 2006). Encouraging collective efficacy, defined as "a normative property of social networks reflecting the potential that members will act accordingly to achieve a common purpose," has the potential to increase the protection of children in the context of the HIV/AIDS epidemic in SSA (Earls, Raviola, & Carlson, 2008, p. 300). Earls and colleagues have suggested that increasing the extent to which adults know children in the community, encouraging the sharing of material and social resources, and fostering the willingness of community members to intervene when HIV/AIDS-affected children are in need of care or discipline has the potential to advance children's physical and emotional health. Thus, nurturing collective efficacy and natural support systems at the community level is likely to have a positive impact on biological and physical integrity, social relatedness, positive self-worth, and a sense of control among AIDS-bereaved children and adolescents.

Financial Assistance to HIV/AIDS-Affected Families

Because of the effects of war, poverty, and other wide-scale threats to social systems, it is likely that many AIDS-affected families will require assistance beyond the support offered by fellow community members. Targeted interventions may be needed to meet the financial and material needs of the most at-risk AIDS-bereaved youth. Economic interventions targeting families who have experienced the AIDS-related death of a caregiver could enhance the capacity of extended families to provide a stable, caring environment for orphaned children. For example, reducing the costs of child care would facilitate the care of children by relatives who are best able to meet their psychosocial needs. This positive financial effect would in turn diminish the occurrence of multiple migrations, changes in caregivers, and withdrawal from school. Lessening the cost of caring for orphaned children to increase the capacity of surviving caregivers might take the form of offering primary schooling free of cost or providing child care so that caregivers can work, or facilitating income-generating projects (e.g., communal gardening, animal-rearing, vocational training) to increase capacity of surviving caregivers (Ansell & Young, 2004). There is also a need to improve working conditions for caregivers of parentally bereaved children. Workplaces could adapt to increased caregiving needs that have resulted from the HIV/AIDS epidemic by providing more paid leave, increasing flexibility of schedules, and/or offering child care to guardians (Heymann et al., 2007).

Strengthening Families' Capacity to Meet Children's Psychosocial Needs

From a contextual resilience perspective, parental death is seen as having long-term effects on development through a cascading process: efforts to adapt to parental loss at one stage of development influence later changes in the individual and environment (Sandler et al., 2008). It is critical to strengthen the capacity of families to promote and sustain orphaned children's growth following AIDS-related bereavement. For the majority of AIDS-bereaved children and adolescents, their psychosocial needs can be sufficiently met by extended family care and community resources (Richter et al., 2006). The care of orphaned children by extended family has been a feature of community life in many SSA countries well-before the onset of the HIV/AIDS epidemic (Madhavan, 2004). Kinship ties with families, clans, and communities "form the foundation of people's sense of connectedness and continuity" and are the basis upon which culturally informed life skills are built (Phiri & Tolfree, 2005, p. 16). The extended family thus represents AIDS-orphaned youth's greatest asset, and strengthening this invaluable resource will go far in ensuring the healthy social and emotional development of parentally bereaved youth.

Increase and/or Sustain a Supportive and Stable Home Environment Prior to and Following the Death of a Parent

Research has shown that warmth and guidance provided by families represent a significant source of resilience for children exposed to adversity (Sandler, Miller, Short, & Wolchik, 1989). High-quality caregiver–child relationships in particular have been identified as a critical resource for parentally bereaved children. Research has shown that caregiver–child relations that are characterized by warmth, acceptance, low rejection, positive dyadic routines, and positive reinforcement lower the risk of mental health problems in parentally bereaved children and adolescents (Haine, Wolchik, Sandler, Millsap, & Ayers, 2006). Moreover, a positive parent–child relationship and parental structure in the home has been found to predict resiliency among children whose mothers are HIV-infected (Dutra et al., 2000).

During the AIDS-related illness of a parent, efforts by extended family and community members could go a long way in helping the household maintain a supportive environment for the children who will be left behind. The presence and participation of other adults in the caring of the child prior to the parent's death are likely to communicate to the child that he or she matters and will be cared for, thereby decreasing fears of abandonment and rejection. The participation of family and community members in the care of children is characteristic of many African societies, and this natural resource should be encouraged. This participation might include monitoring children's activities when the ill parent is unable to (e.g., ensuring the child attends school and completes household chores) or teaching children positive life skills (such as crafting or building). In addition, initiation of home-based care activities and the participation of family in facilitating these activities would offer opportunities for discussions around succession planning, inheritance, and property rights. This planning would decrease the likelihood of family conflict, multiple migrations of the children, and children feeling that they may be abandoned. Indeed, children are able to cope better when guardianship planning takes place prior to parental death (Dane & Levine, 1994).

Increase High-Quality Caregiver–Child Relationships

Research in the United States has shown that the living circumstances of AIDS-bereaved youth actually improve following the death of a parent. One study found that caregivers of bereaved youth had greater financial resources, higher levels of education, and a stable and routinely run household in comparison with the parent who died from AIDS (Rotheram-Borus, Leonard, Lightfoot, Franzke, Tottenham, & Lee, 2002). Unfortunately, this is not the case in many African communities. Caregivers who assume responsibility for children following the AIDS-related death of a parent in SSA do so in the context of very stressful circumstances. For example, extended family members often assume care for multiple children who have lost their parents—children who may or may not be kin. Elderly caregivers have been reported to have as many as six orphaned children under their care (Nemapare & Tang, 2003). Moreover, many of those caring for AIDS-bereaved youth are themselves experiencing multiple losses, mourning the death of a son, daughter, niece, nephew, or other family member, contending with the stress and isolation associated with HIV/AIDS stigma, and struggling to obtain the financial resources necessary to ensure the family's basic needs are met. These challenges limit the time and psychological resources needed to provide a supportive caregiving environment.

Skills training, respite care, and psychosocial support to fostering families can help caregivers positively influence the social and emotional development of parentally bereaved youth. For example, working with family members to understand the unique psychosocial needs of AIDS-bereaved children can increase their ability to respond appropriately to behavioral difficulties, decrease tension in the family, and increase healthy communication, thereby increasing children's sense of social relatedness and decreasing fears of rejection and abandonment.

Increase Opportunities for Parentally Bereaved Children and Their Families to Engage in Meaningful Social Networks

Embedding children in multiple, healthy social support networks can have the added effects of increasing bereaved children's self esteem, sense of control, and feeling of social relatedness. Many families are faced with competing needs, including education of children and generation of income to support survival. As a result, children are often taken out of school and put into the workforce. Alternative strategies are needed to ensure that children and adolescents remain connected to their peers and are able to fulfill developmental competencies associated with their role as student and friend. Youth-headed households are particularly at risk of experiencing social isolation and would benefit immensely from social support. For example, in Rwanda mentors to child-headed households are trained to provide children with needed psychosocial support, and in Mozambique, older female orphans are trained in dressmaking and selling their crafts in the community (Institute of Medicine, 2007). Mentoring programs not only can be effective for increasing the capacity of youth as caregivers, but also may increase sense of social interconnectedness (Boris et al., 2006).

Create Opportunities for Bereaved Youth to Participate in Healthy Grieving

An inability to engage in a healthy, culturally appropriate grieving process may lead to development of unhealthy emotion-regulation strategies and lead children to interpret their situation in ways that demean their self-worth and sense of social connectedness; thus, there is a need to help families respond appropriately to children's reactions to and questions regarding parental death from HIV/AIDS. "Parental response to an HIV diagnosis is affected by cultural mores, economic factors, and religious, personal and social beliefs, perhaps to a greater extent than with other medical conditions" (Miller & Murray, 1999, p. 284). Although some have called for teaching HIV-diagnosed parents and surviving caregivers to encourage children's expression of emotion and communication regarding AIDS-related illness and parental death, doing so may go against cultural and societal norms. In Zimbabwe, disclosure to children that their parent died of an AIDS-related illness is the exception rather than the norm (Wood et al., 2006). In many African communities, discussing death is considered taboo, and talking to children about death is seen as inappropriate. As such, encouraging children to talk about a parent's death may be seen as creating disunity in the family, thereby creating social disconnection and negative self-evaluation rather than increasing children's sense of social relatedness and positive self-worth (Wood et al., 2006).

Alternatively, threats to these self-system beliefs can be mitigated by focusing on the value of continuing bonds and seeking ways to help families sustain a child's connection to his or her deceased parent in culturally appropriate ways (Shapiro, 2008). Research in the United States describes the benefits of caregivers responding positively to children's attempts to discuss their deceased parent, remaining sensitive and open to hearing about the child's feelings, and providing opportunities for children to engage in traditional memorial practices that acknowledge the deceased (Normand, Silverman, & Nickman, 1996). One example of fostering continuing bonds that is currently being used in SSA is the creation of memory books or memory boxes to help families discuss the possibility of parental death, communicate wishes for the future, encourage disclosure about HIV/AIDS status, and talk about changes happening in the family and community (Pillay, 2003).

In many SSA communities, HIV/AIDS is believed to be a punishment for living an immoral lifestyle, and those who succumb to AIDS are seen as having died a "bad death" (Pillay, 2003; Wood et al., 2006); as a result, grieving may be complicated for AIDS-bereaved youth, who may not have adequate opportunities to talk openly about the loss (Bray, 2003; Cluver & Gardner, 2006). Cook, Fritz, and Mwonya (2003) note that in African communities most affected by HIV/AIDS, mourning rituals and funeral practices have been scaled back because of the cost of funeral arrangements and other competing needs. However, offering children and adolescents the opportunity to engage in traditional mourning rituals can help families transform a "bad" death into a "good," socially acceptable death (Abramovitch, 2000).

Offering Psychosocial Interventions to Families Most in Need

Many international aid agencies have called for an increase in interventions to address the risks to positive psychosocial functioning of youth who have experienced the AIDS-related death of a parent (Family Health International, 2001; Stein, 2003; UNAIDS & WHO, 2008). Although there are some organized efforts to support the psychological needs of this vulnerable population, the delivery of these interventions is sporadic. The majority of these efforts started as programs to increase material support to orphans and their families, including financial, nutritional, and housing support (Bauman & Germann, 2005). These interventions have since added components to address the psychosocial needs of the children served. In addition, many residential camps for orphaned youth now include counseling, recreational, and creative activities, offering youth different opportunities to express their feelings (Wood et al., 2006).

Research conducted in the United States suggests that group-based psychosocial interventions can improve outcomes among children who have experienced the AIDS-related death of a parent. For example, Rotheram-Borus and colleagues (1997) designed a group-based, cognitive-behavioral intervention for parents living with HIV/AIDS and their children. The 31-session program focuses on improving coping with illness and related stressors, disclosing HIV status and engaging in custody planning, establishing positive daily routines, and increasing positive communication between family members (Rotheram-Borus, Murphy, Miller, & Draimin, 1997). A randomized controlled trial of the program found that participating parentally bereaved youth exhibited fewer behavior problems and reported fewer sexual partners 2 years following the intervention (Rotheram-Borus, Stein, & Lin, 2001).

There are significant challenges to implementing resource-intensive psychosocial interventions that were designed in the United States in countries that lack adequate resources or infrastructure to meet the basic survival and security needs of children and families. Without adequate shelter, nutrition, and financial resources, it is unlikely that external psychosocial support would be actively sought out or would be very useful. Moreover, depending on the cultural relevance of the program, interventions demonstrated to be effective in Western countries may have limited benefits to AIDS-affected families in non-Western countries. Assuming an intervention is both effective and feasible to implement, there are still likely to be significant barriers to accessing such services: it has been pointed out that the majority of HIV-infected persons in Uganda are "living in family clusters in small villages with few formal organization entry points for interventions" (Rotheram-Borus, Flannery, Rice, & Lester, 2005, p. 979).

HELPING FAMILIES CARE FOR AIDS-BEREAVED CHILDREN AND ADOLESCENTS: "WALKING THE ROAD" FROM A CONTEXTUAL RESILIENCE PERSPECTIVE

Despite the previously noted challenges, there is a recognized need to build the capacity of surviving relatives, new caregivers, and the community to meet the psychosocial needs of children bereaved by HIV/AIDS.

A researcher at the University of KwaZulu-Natal, South Africa, developed a conceptual framework for illustrating the multiple points at which intervention and support can occur when a household is affected by HIV/AIDS (Schoeman, 2000). The "walking the road" model looks at the impact of HIV/AIDS from the time the disease enters the household until after the caregiver has died and "illustrates the multiple loss, multiple risk, and overall complexity" that characterizes the life of a child who is affected by HIV/AIDS (Germann, 2005, p. 64). Utilizing this model in conjunction with a contextual resilience perspective, we explore various ways in which the multiple needs of an adolescent female could be met to promote resilient adaptation following the AIDS-related death of her mother. The following fictional case study is a composite of characteristics prominent in the qualitative research literature on the experiences of Zimbabwean youth affected by AIDS (Foster, Levine, & Williamson, 2005; Germann, 2005; Singhal & Howard, 2003; Wood et al., 2006).

CASE STUDY

Mudiwa, a 14-year-old Shona female living in an urban region of Zimbabwe, became aware that her mother was unwell soon after the disappearance of her father. As her mother's health deteriorated, Mudiwa began to suspect that her mother had contracted "the disease"; however, she was too afraid to ask her mother or her maternal grandmother ("granny"), with whom they lived. Mudiwa's mother eventually became so ill she was unable to work, and a nurse who lived in the community began to visit the family each week to provide home-based care. This was fortunate for Mudiwa because as the oldest of three children, she could have been expected to withdraw from school to assume household duties and assist in the caring of her mother. This responsibility would have been physically and emotionally taxing for Mudiwa and would have separated her from her peers. Like Mudiwa, members of the community and local school suspected that her mother was ill as a result of contracting HIV/AIDS. Mudiwa's school had recently participated in an awareness-raising initiative focused on HIV/AIDS. Part of the initiative included a weekly storytelling hour in which teachers and adolescents explored difficult issues related to HIV/AIDS through the use of stories and metaphor. Mudiwa and her siblings benefited from the structure and predictability offered in the school environment and received social and academic support from their classmates and teachers.

As Mudiwa's mother became increasingly ill, the volunteer worked with Mudiwa's mother to engage in succession planning to ensure that the children would be provided and cared for after her passing. The volunteer also helped the family create a memory book for each of the children. In the memory books, Mudiwa's mother and granny placed photographs, family tree illustrations, descriptions of family traditions, and notes from Mudiwa's mother communicating her wishes for each child's future. Mudiwa's mother used the memory books to talk with her children about what their lives might look like when she was gone. When her mother died, Mudiwa's granny benefited from a solid community support system. The recent acknowledgement of the HIV/AIDS crisis by the national government and the local presence of a community-based orphan visiting program had increased acceptance of HIV/AIDS-affected families and alerted community members to their plight. In addition, an external agency had begun to facilitate local income-generating projects (e.g., communal gardening, animal-rearing, vocational training), thereby decreasing the poverty rate in the community, which increased the capacity of community members to offer material support to one another. Members of granny's church covered the cost of funeral arrangements and offered spiritual and psychosocial support to granny, which enabled her to better support her grandchildren.

Unlike many orphans who are separated from their siblings and forced to relocate throughout the country, Mudiwa and her siblings were able to stay together under their granny's care. Compared to many elderly caregivers, Mudiwa's granny was in a good position to support Mudiwa and her siblings. For example, her granny lived in a large building in an urban region of Zimbabwe and was able to rent out part of the house to lodgers—this income was used to pay school fees and to buy uniforms for the children. In addition, extended family living in a rural part of the country would send the family food (a practice known as "urban-rural interhousehold income transfer"). Mudiwa's granny was also able to provide psychosocial support to her grandchildren and to intervene when it appeared that Mudiwa was having trouble adjusting to the death of her mother. The visiting nurse had continued to visit the family and offered granny information on the kinds of behaviors she could expect grieving grandchildren to exhibit. When Mudiwa complained of stomachaches and nightmares and continued to act withdrawn and preoccupied, her granny recognized that Mudiwa might need extra support.

Granny enrolled Mudiwa in a nearby 10-day camp facilitated by the Salvation Army and designed for children who had been orphaned. At the camp, Mudiwa gained a greater sense of self-efficacy, identity, and purpose as she participated in various outdoor activities and took advantage of leadership activities.

This fictional case study illustrates a system of care that focuses on promoting the well-being of AIDS orphans by providing for their needs for safety, ongoing social connectedness, positive self-worth, and sense of efficacy. The system of care involves building upon and supporting the existing resources of the communities that are strained by the AIDS epidemic. In many ways the system of care described is a composite of programs that are currently being carried out. However, from another perspective, this idealized description points to the urgent need for future work that is needed to promote healthy futures for these children.

REFERENCES

Abramovitch, H. H. (2000). "Good death" and "bad death": Therapeutic implications of cultural conceptions of death and bereavement. In R. Malkinson, S. S. Rubin, & E. Witztum (Eds.), *Traumatic and nontraumatic loss and bereavement: Clinical theory and practice* (pp. 255–272). Madison, CT: Psychosocial Press.

Andrews, G., Skinner, D., & Zuma, K. (2006). Epidemiology of health and vulnerability among children orphaned and made vulnerable by HIV/AIDS in sub-Saharan Africa. *AIDS Care, 18*(3), 269–276.

Ansell, N., & Young, L. (2004). Enabling households to support successful migration of AIDS orphans in southern Africa. *AIDS Care, 16*(1), 3–10.

Armistead, L., & Forehand, R. (1995). For whom the bell tolls: Parenting decisions and challenges faced by mothers who are HIV seropositive. *Clinical Psychology: Science and Practice, 2*(3), 239–250.

Atwine, B., Cantor-Graae, E., & Bajunirwe, F. (2005). Psychological distress among AIDS orphans in rural Uganda. *Social Science & Medicine, 61*(3), 555–564.

Bauman, L. J., & Germann, S. (2005). Psychosocial impact of the HIV/AIDS epidemic on children and youth. In G. Foster, C. Levine, & J. Williamson (Eds.), *A generation at risk: The global impact of HIV/AIDS on orphans and vulnerable children* (pp. 93–133). New York: Cambridge University Press.

Baumeister, R. F., & Leary, M. R. (1995). The need to belong: Desire for interpersonal attachments as a fundamental human motivation. *Psychological Bulletin, 117*(3), 497–529.

Bedri, A., Kebede, S., & Negassa, H. (1995). Sociodemographic profile of children affected by AIDS in Addis Ababa. *Ethiopia Medical Journal, 33*(4), 227–234.

Bhargava, A. (2005). AIDS epidemic and the psychological well-being and school participation of Ethiopian orphans. *Psychology, Health & Medicine, 10*(3), 263–275.

Bicego, G., Rutstein, S., & Johnson, K. (2003). Dimensions of the emerging orphan crisis in sub-Saharan Africa. *Social Science & Medicine, 56*(6), 1235–1247.

Boris, N. W., Thurman, T. R., Snider, L., Spencer, E., & Brown, L. (2006). Infants and young children living in youth-headed households in Rwanda: Implications of emerging data. *Infant Mental Health Journal [Special Issue: Culture and infancy]*, 27(6), 584–602.

Bray, R. (2003). *Predicting the social consequences of orphanhood in South Africa*. Cape Town, South Africa: Centre for Social Science Research, University of Cape Town.

Cerel, J., Fristad, M. A., Verducci, J., Weller, R. A., & Weller, E. B. (2006). Childhood bereavement: Psychopathology in the 2 years postparental death. *Journal of the American Academy of Child & Adolescent Psychiatry*, 45(6), 681–690.

Cluver, L., & Gardner, F. (2006). The psychological well being of children orphaned by AIDS in Cape Town, South Africa. *Annals of General Psychiatry, 5*, 8.

Cluver, L., & Gardner, F. (2007). Risk and protective factors for psychological well-being of children orphaned by AIDS in Cape Town: A qualitative study of children and caregivers' perspectives. *AIDS Care, 19*(3), 318–325.

Cluver, L., Gardner, F., & Operario, D. (2007). Psychological distress amongst AIDS-orphaned children in urban South Africa. *Journal of Child Psychology and Psychiatry, 48*(8), 755–763.

Cluver, L. D., Gardner, F., & Operario, D. (2008). Effects of stigma on the mental health of adolescents orphaned by AIDS. *Journal of Adolescent Health, 42*(4), 410–417.

Cook, A. S., Fritz, J. J., & Mwonya, R. (2003). Understanding the psychological and emotional needs of AIDS orphans in Africa. In A. Singhal & W. S. Howard (Eds.), *The children of Africa confront AIDS* (pp. 85–104). Athens: Center for International Studies, Ohio University.

Dane, B. O., & Levine, C. (Eds.). (1994). *AIDS and the new orphans: Coping with death*. Westport, CT: Auburn House/Greenwood.

Dutra, R., Forehand, R., Armistead, L., Brody, G., Morse, E., Morse, P. S., et al. (2000). Child resiliency in inner-city families affected by HIV: The role of family variables. *Behaviour Research and Therapy, 38*(5), 471–468.

Earls, F., Raviola, G. J., & Carlson, M. (2008). Promoting child and adolescent mental health in the context of the HIV/AIDS pandemic with a focus on sub-Saharan Africa. *Journal of Child Psychology and Psychiatry, 49*(3), 295–312.

Family Health International. (2001). *Care of orphans, children affected by HIV/AIDS and other vulnerable children*. Washington, DC: Author.

Foster, G., Levine, C., & Williamson, J. (Eds.). (2005). *A generation at risk: The global impact of HIV/AIDS on orphans and vulnerable children*. New York: Cambridge University Press.

Foster, G., Makufa, C., Drew, R., Kambeu, S., & Saurombe, K. (1996). Supporting children in need through a community-based orphan visiting programme. *AIDS Care, 8*(4), 389–403.

Foster, G., Makufa, C., Drew, R., Mashumba, S., & Kambeu, S. (1997). Perceptions of children and community members concerning the circumstances of orphans in rural Zimbabwe. *AIDS Care, 9*(4), 391–405.

Foster, G., Shakespeare, R., Chinemana, F., Jackson, H., Gregson, S., & Mashumba, S. (1995). Orphan prevalence and extended family care in a peri-urban community in Zimbabwe. *AIDS Care, 7*(1), 3–17.

Germann, S. (2005). *An exploratory study of quality of life and coping strategies of orphans living in child-headed households in the high HIV/AIDS prevalent city of Bulawayo, Zimbabwe.* Cape Town: University of South Africa Press.

Gilborn, L. Z. (2002). In the public eye—beyond our borders, the effects of HIV infection on children in Africa. *Western Journal of Medicine, 176,* 12–14.

Haine, R. A., Ayers, T. S., Sandler, I. N., Wolchik, S. A., & Weyer, J. L. (2003). Locus of control and self-esteem as stress-moderators or stress-mediators in parentally bereaved children. *Death Studies, 27*(7), 619–640.

Haine, R. A., Wolchik, S. A., Sandler, I. N., Millsap, R. E., & Ayers, T. S. (2006). Positive parenting as a protective resource for parentally bereaved children. *Death Studies, 30*(1), 1–28.

Heymann, J., Earle, A., Rajaraman, D., Miller, C., & Bogen, K. (2007). Extended family caring for children orphaned by AIDS: Balancing essential work and caregiving in a high HIV prevalence nation. *AIDS Care, 19*(3), 337–345.

Institute of Medicine. (2007). *PEPFAR implementation: Progress and promise.* Washington, DC: National Academies Press.

Kim, L. S., Sandler, I. N., & Tein, J. Y. (1997). Locus of control as a stress moderator and mediator in children of divorce. *Journal of Abnormal Child Psychology, 25*(2), 145–155.

Lin, K. K., Sandler, I. N., Ayers, T. S., Wolchik, S. A., & Luecken, L. J. (2004). Resilience in parentally bereaved children and adolescents seeking preventive services. *Journal of Clinical Child and Adolescent Psychology, 33*(4), 673–683.

Madhavan, S. (2004). Fosterage patterns in the age of AIDS: Continuity and change. *Social Science & Medicine, 58*(7), 1443–1454.

Makame, V., Ani, C., & Grantham-McGregor, S. (2002). Psychological well being of orphans in Dar El Salaam, Tanzania. *Acta Paediatrica, 91,* 459–465.

Mann, G. (2003). *Family matters: The care and protection of children affected by HIV/AIDS in Malawi.* Stockholm: Save the Children Sweden.

Melhem, N. M., Walker, M., Moritz, G., & Brent, D. (2008). Antecedents and sequelae of sudden parental death in offspring and surviving caregivers. *Archives of Pediatric Adolescent Medicine, 162,* 403–410.

Miller, R., & Murray, D. (1999). The impact of HIV illness on parents and children, with particular reference to African families. *Journal of Family Therapy [Special issue: Parental illness], 21*(3), 284–302.

Nemapare, P., & Tang, D. D. (2003). The vulnerability of children and orphaned youth in Zimbabwe. In A. Singhal & W. S. Howard (Eds.), *The children of Africa confront AIDS* (pp. 51–58). Athens: Center for International Studies, Ohio University.

Normand, C. L., Silverman, P. R., & Nickman, S. L. (1996). Bereaved children's changing relationships with the deceased. In D. Klass, P. R. Silverman, & S. L. Nickman (Eds.), *Continuing bonds: New understandings of grief* (pp. 87–111). Washington, DC: Taylor & Francis.

Phiri, S. N., & Tolfree, D. (2005). Family- and community-based care for children affected by HIV/AIDS: Strengthening the front line response. In G. Foster, C. Levine, & J. Williamson (Eds.), *A generation at risk: The global impact of HIV/AIDS on orphans and vulnerable children* (pp. 11–36). New York: Cambridge University Press.

Pillay, Y. (2003). Storytelling as a psychological intervention for AIDS orphans in Africa. In A. Singhal & W. S. Howard (Eds.), *The children of Africa confront AIDS* (pp. 105–118). Athens: Center for International Studies, Ohio University.

Richter, L., Foster, G., & Sherr, L. (2006). Where the heart is: Meeting the psychosocial needs of young children in the context of HIV/AIDS. Retrieved April 2, 2009, from http://www.bernardvanleer.org/publication_store/publication_store_publications/where_the_heart_is_meeting_the_psychosocial_needs_of_young_children_in_the_context_of_hivaids/file

Rotheram-Borus, M. J., Flannery, D., Rice, E., & Lester, P. (2005). Families living with HIV. *AIDS Care, 17*(8), 978–987.

Rotheram-Borus, M. J., Leonard, N. R., Lightfoot, M., Franzke, L. H., Tottenham, N., & Lee, S.-J. (2002). Picking up the pieces: Caregivers of adolescents bereaved by parental AIDS. *Clinical Child Psychology and Psychiatry, 7*(1), 115–124.

Rotheram-Borus, M. J., Murphy, D. A., Miller, S., & Draimin, B. H. (1997). An intervention for adolescents whose parents are living with AIDS. *Clinical Child Psychology and Psychiatry, 2*(2), 201–219.

Rotheram-Borus, M. J., Stein, J. A., & Lin, Y.-Y. (2001). Impact of parent death and an intervention on the adjustment of adolescents whose parents have HIV/AIDS. *Journal of Consulting and Clinical Psychology, 69*(5), 763–773.

Rotheram-Borus, M. J., Weiss, R., Alber, S., & Lester, P. (2005). Adolescent adjustment before and after HIV-related parental death. *Journal of Consulting and Clinical Psychology, 73*(2), 221–228.

Sandler, I. (2001). Quality and ecology of adversity as common mechanisms of risk and resilience. *American Journal of Community Psychology, 29*(1), 19–61.

Sandler, I. N., Miller, P. A., Short, J., & Wolchik, S. A. (1989). Social support as a protective factor for children in stress. In D. Belle (Ed.), *Children's social networks and social supports* (pp. 277–307). Oxford, England: John Wiley & Sons.

Sandler, I. N., Wolchik, S. A., & Ayers, T. S. (2008). Resilience rather than recovery: A contextual framework on adaptation following bereavement. *Death Studies, 32*(1), 59–73.

Schoeman, R. (2000). *Walking the road concept.* Unpublished concept paper. Pietermaritzburg, South Africa: University of KwaZulu-Natal.

Shapiro, E. R. (2008). Whose recovery, of what? Relationships and environments promoting grief and growth. *Death Studies [Special issue: Bereavement, outcomes, and recovery], 32*(1), 40–58.

Singhal, A., & Howard, W. S. (Eds.). (2003). *The children of Africa confront AIDS.* Athens: Center for International Studies, Ohio University.

Stein, J. (2003). *Sorrow makes children of us all: A literature review on the psychosocial impact of HIV/AIDS on children.* Cape Town, South Africa: Centre for Social Science Research, University of Cape Town.

UNAIDS, UNICEF, & USAID. (2004). *Children on the brink: Joint report of new orphan estimates and a framework for action.* New York: Authors.

UNAIDS, & WHO. (2008). *2008 Report on the Global AIDS Epidemic.* Retrieved April 2, 2009, from http://www.unaids.org/en/KnowledgeCentre/HIVData/Global Report/2008/2008_Global_report.asp

UNICEF, & UNAIDS (2004). *The framework for the protection, care and support of orphans and vulnerable children living in a world with HIV and AIDS.* Geneva, Switzerland: Authors.

Wolchik, S. A., Tein, J.-Y., Sandler, I. N., & Ayers, T. S. (2006). Stressors, quality of the child–caregiver relationship, and children's mental health problems after parental death: The mediating role of self-system beliefs. *Journal of Abnormal Child Psychology, 34*(2), 221–238.

Wood, K., Chase, E., & Aggleton, P. (2006). "Telling the truth is the best thing": Teenage orphans' experiences of parental AIDS-related illness and bereavement in Zimbabwe. *Social Science & Medicine, 63*(7), 1923–1933.

18

Principles and Practices of Peer Support Groups and Camp-Based Interventions for Grieving Children

DONNA L. SCHUURMAN AND JANA DECRISTOFARO

This chapter provides an overview of principles and practices that guide peer support groups and camp-based interventions designed to help grieving children. The chapter begins with a brief retrospective that outlines the development of these support groups and camps in recent years. It then turns to guidelines for best practices proposed by the Child Bereavement Network in the United Kingdom and four operating principles that underlie the work of the Dougy Center, the National Center for Grieving Children and Families. Next, this chapter offers comments on group structure, format, and effective size; variables involved in grouping children by type of death and developmental factors; issues in determining the suitability of children for grief support groups; and concerns about adult caregivers. The chapter closes with comments on bereavement camps for children and concerns about evaluation of program effectiveness.

A BRIEF RETROSPECTIVE

Support groups and camps for children grieving a death have proliferated in the last quarter century. Since the founding of the first peer support grief groups at the Dougy Center in Portland, Oregon, in 1982, more than 300 programs now exist to serve this population in 47 states

359

throughout North America. The national programs listed on the Dougy Center's Web site (http://www.dougy.org) have volunteer training programs, ranging from 2 to 5 days, as well as ongoing training and supervision. Children's bereavement programs and models have evolved to the degree that an umbrella nonprofit organization, the National Alliance for Grieving Children, was formed in 2004 to provide resources and education for those who are supporting children and teens grieving a death. The National Alliance's Web site (http://www.nationalalliancefor grievingchildren.org) provides links to U.S. programs and information on resources in the field. The National Alliance for Grieving Children lists as its mission "to promote awareness of the needs of children and teens grieving a death and providing education and resources for anyone who wants to support them."

Additionally, population-specific programs and organizations have evolved to serve bereaved children, including Families of September 11, founded in October 2001 (http://www.familiesofseptember11.org); and TAPS, the Tragedy Assistance Program for Survivors, Inc. (http://www. taps.org). TAPS is described on its Web site as "America's only nonprofit Veterans Service Organization chartered solely to assist the surviving families of military members who have died while serving our nation."

Internationally, there are grief support programs for children in Australia, New Zealand, England, Germany, Ireland, Switzerland, Israel, Japan, Mexico, Jamaica, Uganda, and the Congo (e.g., Stokes, 2004). These groups, as well as their North American counterparts, include school-based, faith-based, and non-sectarian groups; programs created through hospitals, hospices, mental health and community social service organizations, and independent nonprofits.

These services have come a long way since 1982, when the Dougy Center's founder, former nurse Beverly Chappell, was told by the chief physician of a local pediatric unit that her plan for a safe place for children to grieve a death sounded like "voodoo medicine" and that he did not want anyone "messing" with his patients' heads (see Chappell, 2008). The Dougy Center's initial group of six children meeting in the basement of the Chappell's home has grown into nearly 50 groups for children, teens, young adults, and their parents or adult caregivers. Many new program models have developed throughout the country, as well as grief camps for children, and interest in conducting research on program efficacy is growing.

Children's grief groups may be characterized as therapy groups, psycho-educational groups, support groups, or some combination of the three. Therapy groups are typically led by professionals with a master's degree or higher and often are geared for children in mental health settings, for residential treatment, or for those whose emotional problems are severely limiting their ability to function. Psycho-educational and support groups, considered therapeutic though not "therapy," may be run by professionals, volunteers, or a combination of both. Regardless of the model used, the therapeutic relationship components of safety and trust are likely to be the foundation of the program. Physician and author Daniel Siegel (see Siegel, 1999), who originated the term "interpersonal neurobiology," which studies how the brain grows and is influenced by personal relationships, has stated that "the most consistent finding in psychotherapy research is that when a relationship of trust and acceptance develops between therapist and client, regardless of clinical method, therapy works" (Wylie & Simon, 2002, p. 34).

PHILOSOPHICAL FRAMEWORK

In determining a philosophical framework and goals for any bereavement service, programs need to assess what their theoretical belief system is and what their program goals encompass. Critical questions to address philosophically include the following, not intended as a comprehensive list:

- Is grief a normal response to loss, something that needs to be "treated," or some combination of the two? If grief requires treatment, under what circumstances, or based on what symptoms?
- Do children need to be *taught* how to grieve, or will they grieve constructively under supportive conditions with encouragement, permission, and safety?
- Is there a normal grief process, and if so, what is an abnormal grief process, and in what ways does it manifest?
- In what ways do parents and other adults influence how children cope following death?
- What are the needs of grieving children and families following a death?
- How is our program intending to address these needs?
- What needs are we not planning to address?

The format and nature of the program will depend on whether the goals are to provide support during a difficult time, change behavior, teach skills, model healthy expression, or some combination of these and other goals.

GUIDELINES FOR BEST PRACTICES

Children's bereavement is a relatively young field with wide-ranging independence. Though it may be on the horizon, North American practitioners have yet to develop a universally accepted set of guidelines for principles and best practices. In the United Kingdom, the Childhood Bereavement Network secured funds in 1999 from the Diana, Princess of Wales Memorial Fund to set up a nationwide network of support services for bereaved children and to develop standards and codes of good practice. Their model serves as a good starting point, stating,

> Any information, guidance and support offered to children should:
>
> - acknowledge the child's grief and experience of loss as a result of death
> - be responsive to the child's needs, views, and opinions
> - respect the child's family and immediate social situation, and their culture, language, beliefs, and religious background
> - seek to promote self-esteem and self-confidence, and develop communication, decision making, and other life skills
> - be viewed as part of a continuous learning process for the child, contributing to the development of the child's knowledge and understanding as they grow into adulthood
> - aim, wherever possible, appropriate, and feasible, to involve family members, other caregivers, and any professionals working with the individual child in a wider social context. (Childhood Bereavement Network, n.d.)

FOUR OPERATING PRINCIPLES

The Dougy Center's four operating principles provide a theoretical basis for program practices and have been widely accepted by and expanded on by other programs.

1. Grief is a natural reaction to loss.

Proponents of grief support groups generally accept that grief is not an illness or disease and therefore not something we should seek to "cure" or "treat." Our society does not always provide a healing environment for grievers, which can lead to their grief being exacerbated by the well-meaning but uninformed responses of others. Grief support groups help to normalize the responses children are experiencing physically, emotionally, intellectually, socially, and spiritually. This normalizing function does not mean that reactions or symptoms brought about by a death can always be handled effectively solely through support groups or that individual therapy or group therapy may not be warranted. It simply means that for some children, helping them know that they are not alone and providing avenues for expression and understanding may support their healthy resilience following a death.

2. Within each child is the natural capacity to heal.

Although it is recognized that children have within them the ability and capacity to heal, resilience does not happen in a vacuum. The capacity to heal is fostered through an environment of healing. The view that each child has the natural capacity to heal gives the message that children need both choice and a sense of control when it comes to their grief. Peer support groups enable children to move at their own pace in the company of other children who are also navigating life after a death. Because children do not have any say in whether or when someone dies, it is invaluable for them to have opportunities to reestablish a sense of personal agency in their lives. Allowing them to have a say in their grief journey is one way to help make the world feel less unpredictable.

3. The duration and intensity of grief are unique for each child.

Children who have experienced a loss through death are thrust into a frightening and unpredictable reality, including the knowledge that those they love (or hate, for that matter) may be taken away in an instant, or through a long period of intense suffering. Although common developmental issues for preadolescents impact their understanding of and reactions to loss, children have individual and unique experiences of grief. Peer support groups and camps allow children to articulate and express their intensely personal reactions to loss. Ideally, these programs and groups create a sense of safety that enables children to feel able to chart their own course through grief, rather than only accommodating the wishes of others.

4.   Caring and acceptance assist in the healing process.

Too often, society is not accepting of death or the grief process. Families hear many unsupportive comments, such as "Don't you think it's time to move on?" or "It's been 3 months; aren't you over it yet?" These comments usually stem from a collective discomfort with the concept of death and a wish to downplay the reactions of grieving people. It is not uncommon for schools to pressure students to perform at the same level as before the death, without acknowledging the toll grief takes on their ability to concentrate and complete tasks. Families find that after a brief wave of care and concern, the outside support starts to diminish. Peer support groups and camps work to provide this missing care and support in an environment that welcomes sharing about the challenges of living, learning, and connecting after the death. Children are able to tell their stories as often as they need to without fear that they will be criticized for continuing to process the impact the death has on their lives. "The common ground of group support helps to decrease feelings of embarrassment or being different that might otherwise lead the child to withdraw while grieving" (Mitchell et al., 2007, p. 4).

Although these four principles provide a basis for a theoretical orientation to working with children and grief, there are numerous practical and logistical factors that require consideration. Depending on the setting, resources, and intent, grief support programs need to make decisions about group size, demographics, and time length. What follows are some of the practice issues that bereavement programs and camps should consider.

GROUP STRUCTURE

Among the decisions for running grief support groups are those related to structure. Will the group be time-limited or ongoing? Will it contain the same members for the duration of the group or allow members to join and leave as they wish? Deciding whether to hold ongoing groups or time-limited groups depends on a combination of factors, not the least of which are available time and resources. Many school-based groups elect to run time-limited groups, most frequently in the 6-, 8-, or 10-week range. These groups usually are closed groups, not permitting new members to participate after the group has started. Frequently these groups originate in the school setting because of an identified incident or need, such as the death of a member of the school community or the prevalence of students dealing with grief in their personal lives.

Both time-limited and ongoing grief support groups have strengths and challenges, as well as situations where one or the other might be most practical. Most often time-limited groups include specific themes or activities for each session. These session themes are typically determined by the adults running the groups, much like a school classroom setting. Time-limited groups often focus on teaching particular skills and coping methods that can unintentionally imply that a child should be "better" after 6 or 8 weeks.

Advocates of open-ended groups favor the individuality offered to children who choose when they are ready to end their participation. Ongoing groups allow for new members and have the benefit of existing members extending help to new members, often resulting in the former acknowledging how much they have grown.

By contrast, open-ended groups may face criticism for prolonging the child's focus on his or her grief journey. They may also be impractical from a cost perspective or in rural areas with small populations. Sometimes time-limited groups are necessary because of resource restraints imposed by an umbrella agency, and they offer a way for a program to provide services to the largest number of children. Advocates of open-ended groups counter that offering ongoing support is beneficial in terms of allowing children an element of choice and control when it comes to reaching out for assistance (Schuurman, 2008). After a death, children often experience an overwhelming sense of helplessness; resilience studies have found that "mastery, or having a strong sense of control over one's life, was significantly associated with recovered status" following trauma (Cassels, 2008).

GROUP FORMAT

Another question to be addressed is whether to run non-directive or curriculum-based groups. Curriculum-driven groups select topics for each of the allotted sessions and tend to be educationally based. Topics may include identifying and coping with feelings, exploring the participant's experiences, and practicing new skills through the use of activities. A growing number of curriculum materials for grief groups may be found through resources such as the Association for Death Education and Counseling (http://www.adec.org), Compassion Books (http://www.compassionbooks.com), and Centering Corporation (http://www.centering.org). The Arizona State University's Family Bereavement Program, a 12-week psycho-educational program, focuses on teaching and practicing parenting skills in a close-ended setting.

Non-directive groups allow participants to make choices about how their time will be spent. Non-directive does not necessarily mean non-structured. At the Dougy Center, each group has an opening circle to share names and whatever the participants would like to share about who died. As the group becomes more self-directed, the children make suggestions for the opening circle questions or content, rather than relying on an adult leader to tell them what to talk about. Sometimes an activity is proposed by the group's facilitators; other times discussions evolve naturally from anniversary or holiday times, or topics shared in the circle. An unstructured play time follows where children select from a range of activities throughout the center's grounds, including art rooms; "big energy" rooms such as the Volcano Room or air hockey and foosball game areas; and dress-up, sand tray, puppet, or other play areas. Part of the philosophy that guides non-directive groups is that allowing children to decide what they want to do empowers them, and they may begin to regain a lost or threatened sense of control.

Play is the tool children use to learn about and understand their world. As Bettelheim wrote, "The child's play is motivated by inner processes, desires, problems, and anxieties...play is the royal road to the child's conscious and unconscious inner world; if we want to understand his inner world and help him with it, we must learn to walk this road" (1987, p. 35). Children will often repeat a play scenario in an attempt to make sense of something in their world. Shelby wrote, "Children use play to move from crisis to confidence as they learn to manage their distress" (1997, p. 144). A 7-year-old participant in the Dougy Center's program, Meghan, whose mother died from cancer, demonstrated this principle in dress-up play. Each time she came to group, Meghan dressed up as a doctor and "cured" her patient. She repeated this activity for several sessions until one day, dressed in her doctor's uniform, she declared that she was unable to "fix" the patient that day. Meghan covered the face and body of the volunteer who was playing the role of the patient with a blanket, and then took off her doctor's clothes. That was her last medical play session. Through her play she gained an understanding of the issue and was able to move on to something different. As is evidenced by the long-standing tradition of play therapy, directed and non-directed, the opportunities that bereavement support programs and camps provide grieving children help them make sense of their circumstances.

EFFECTIVE GROUP SIZE

The size of a group is determined by the age of the children, the number of facilitators available, and how much individual attention the program intends to provide within the group format. In general, the younger the child, the more adult assistance required. The 3- to 5-year-old groups at the Dougy Center have a child-to-adult ratio of two-to-one, whereas the ratio for 6- to 12-year-olds is one adult for every three children. The group size ranges from 10 to 15 child members.

TYPE OF DEATH AND DEVELOPMENTAL FACTORS

Other practical considerations for running grief support programs and camps relate to how to group children by age and cause of death. The Dougy Center runs groups for 3- to 5-year-olds who have had a parent or sibling die. Groups for 6- to 12-year-olds are divided by either the cause of death or whether the death was that of a parent or sibling. These groups include "Parent Death," "Sibling Death," "Healing From a Suicide Death," and "Healing From a Homicide or Violent Death." The demographics and size of the targeted population will determine, in part, whether groups include mixed losses. At the Dougy Center, a family who has experienced the suicide death of a father, for example, would be given the choice of participating in a parent death group or a suicide-specific group. Either grouping can be effective. More important than the specifics of splitting children up by type of death is ensuring that the group helps children to feel safe and accepted, regardless of the specific circumstances of the death in their lives.

WHICH CHILDREN ARE SUITABLE FOR GRIEF SUPPORT GROUPS, AND SHOULD THEY BE SCREENED?

The screening process for any type of group will be determined by the structure of the program. At the Dougy Center, we have chosen to do a group orientation instead of individual intakes. A group orientation is an effective way to assess whether the child will feel comfortable in a group setting. Also, because an average of 30 new families inquire about our services every month, a group intake allows the families to explore what the program offers without having to wait a long time for an intake.

The orientation serves a screening-like role for the child. Some children will fare better with the addition of either individual or family counseling, whereas others decide that the peer support setting is not right for them. We have found that many children who have been labeled as "inappropriate" for a group setting are able to function well in our program when they have clear safety rules, structure, and a degree of choice in their participation.

One of the primary goals of a peer support group is for children to experience the normalization that comes from being with others who are dealing with grief. It is important for children to feel as though they "fit in" with the other members. In the Dougy Center's setting, children participate with others who have had a parent die or a sibling die. Although groups with mixed losses may be effective as well, the similarity of stories helps to promote a sense of acceptance and being with others who "get it."

When determining whether a child would benefit more from individual therapy than a support group, it is important to consider the child's preference and preexisting mental health, behavioral, or family system challenges. Some children at the Dougy Center work with an individual therapist and also attend peer support groups.

WHAT ABOUT THE ADULT CAREGIVERS?

Numerous research studies support that adult influence, particularly that of a surviving parent, is one of the biggest predictors of how children will cope following a loss through death (Kalter et al., 2002; Lutzke, Ayers, Sandler, & Barr, 1997; Silverman, 2000; Worden, 1996). Concurrent adult groups allow parents and caregivers to have time off from parenting, enable them to discuss with other adults in similar situations the challenges of raising grieving children, and provide opportunities for them to give and receive support and advice as requested.

BEREAVEMENT CAMPS

Bereavement camps offer children an opportunity to come together with others who are grieving to talk and express their grief through a variety of activities in an intensive time period. As Nabors and colleagues have said, "The opportunity to share feelings of grief in a supportive environment among peers who have endured the death of a loved one may be one of the most powerful aspects of the camp experience" (2004, p. 404).

There are many models for bereavement camps in existence. From weeklong day camps to overnight weekends, camps combine play with grief-focused activities in order to provide children with a unique chance to process their experiences in ways that are both fun and meaningful. Camps also provide a normative social experience for children who may feel different or isolated from their non-bereaved peers. As opposed to adults or sometimes even teens, children grieve in short bursts, so camps and retreats facilitate an ability to "take breaks from their painful feelings and experience a balance of fun and grief work" (Schachter & Georgopoulos, 2008, p. 247).

Bereavement camps take children out of their normal daily environments and invite them to express their grief in new and different ways. There is something about the camp environment that lends intensity to the activities and expression opportunities in which the children participate. Bereavement camps fit well with the rhythm of children's grief as they mix opportunities for processing with regular camp-like activities such as swimming, archery, hiking, and tag.

As with the majority of interventions aimed at bereavement and children, camps focus on creating a safe environment for children to grieve in their own ways and at their own pace. Most camps have volunteers and clinical staff members who work to facilitate the camp experience in a way that helps children to feel accepted and free to engage in life while in the midst of grieving.

Although there are many bereavement camps and retreats offered by different programs throughout the country, three of the largest include Comfort Zone Camp, Camp Erin, and TAPS. Comfort Zone camps "offer bereaved children the opportunity to remember their loved ones in a safe and healing camp environment" (http://www.comfortzone.org) and are offered free of charge for 7-year-olds through teens. Camp Erin was initiated by the Moyer Foundation's Jamie Moyer, a professional baseball player, with the goal of having a camp in every city with a major league baseball team (http://www.moyerfoundation.org). TAPS, the Tragedy Assistance Program (www.taps.org), runs grief camps for children and teens who have lost a parent in military service. The Moyer Foundation's listing of Camp Erin's benefits sums up what most children's grief support programs and camps offer to their participants: Grieving children learn that they are not alone; that their feelings are perfectly normal; and that they have an opportunity to address their feelings and memorialize their loved ones.

EVALUATING PROGRAM EFFECTIVENESS

The increased supply of services for bereaved children and adolescents leads to the important questions of whether they work and, if so, what makes them work. Although some progress has been made in the area of research, program effectiveness has not received the quantity or quality of research the subject warrants.

Curtis and Newman (2001) reviewed nine studies of programs for bereaved children, concluding that the programs produced moderate positive effects. They underscored that methodological weaknesses hampered most of the studies, including small sample sizes, lack of control groups, high attrition rates, and short-term evaluation, among other issues. Currier, Holland, and Neimeyer (2007) conducted a meta-analytic review of controlled outcome research on the effectiveness of bereavement interventions with children, analyzing the paucity of studies. "Unfortunately, the fact that the total controlled outcome literature on bereavement interventions with children appears to consist of a mere 13 studies restricted the number of questions that could be legitimately examined in this review and reduced the level of confidence that could be placed in the results" (p. 258).

Although there is minimal research on the efficacy of bereavement camps for children, Nabors and colleagues (2004) conducted a pilot study of a weekend-long camp for grieving children. Their research indicated that children reported the art activities to be helpful avenues for expression and reported that being with other grieving children assisted them to feel less alone in their experiences. Searles McClatchey, Vonk, and Palardy (2008) researched a short-term, camp-based, trauma-focused intervention and found that it reduced the symptoms of trauma and PTSD in parentally bereaved children.

Clearly more research is needed. Currier and his colleagues have concluded that "as for future research, the first priority is to develop well-validated and clinically relevant measures of child grief. Second, researchers need to flesh out the theoretical underpinnings and the operational implementation of their interventions" (2007, p. 258). Although their meta-analysis does not "support the assumption that the bereavement interventions with children have a significant influence on adjustment" (p. 257), the paucity of research makes it difficult to formulate conclusions on this topic.

This assessment ought not discourage those of us engaged in bereavement services for children, adolescents, and families. Rather, it may serve as a springboard to encourage more research, collaboration, evaluation, and interest in our work. After all, the entire field of psychology is a young phenomenon, hotly contested since Freud's bold assertions and controversy-fueled in the current air of managed care and evidence-based practice.

REFERENCES

Bettelheim, B. (1987, March). The importance of play. *The Atlantic Monthly, 35–46.*

Cassels, C. (2008, November 24). Sense of purpose predicts mental health outcomes following severe trauma. *Medscape Medical News.* Retrieved March 30, 2009, from http://www.medscape.com/viewarticle/584181

Chappell, B. J. (2008). *Children helping children with grief: My path to founding the Dougy Center for Grieving Children and Their Families.* Troutdale, OR: NewSage Press.

Childhood Bereavement Network. (n.d.). About us: What we believe. Retrieved September 10, 2009, from http://www.childhoodbereavementnetwork.org.uk/aboutUs_whatWeBelieve.htm

Currier, J. M., Holland, J. M., & Neimeyer, R. A. (2007). The effectiveness of bereavement interventions with children: A meta-analytic review of controlled outcome research. *Journal of Clinical Child and Adolescent Psychology, 36*(2), 253–259.

Curtis, K., & Newman, T. (2001). Do community-based support services benefit bereaved children? A review of empirical evidence. *Child: Care, Health, and Development, 27*(6), 487–495.

Kalter, N., Lohnes, K. L., Chasin, J., Cain, A. C., Dunning, S., & Rowan, J. (2002). The adjustment of parentally bereaved children: Factors associated with short-term adjustment. *Omega, Journal of Death and Dying, 46,* 15–34.

Lutzke, J. R., Ayers, T. S., Sandler, I. N., & Barr, A. (1997). Risks and interventions for the parentally bereaved child. In S. A. Wolchik & I. N. Sandler (Eds.), *Handbook of children's coping with common life stressors: Linking theory, research and interventions* (pp. 213–243). New York: Plenum.

Mitchell, A. M., Wesner, S., Garand, L., Dysart Gale, D., Havill, A., & Brownson, L. (2007). A support group intervention for children bereaved by parental suicide. *Journal of Child and Adolescent Psychiatric Nursing, 20*(1), 3–13.

Nabors, L., Ohms, M., Buchanan, N., Kirsh, K. L., Nash, T., Passik, S. D., Johnson, J. L., Snapp, J., & Brown, G. (2004). A pilot study of the impact of a grief camp for children. *Palliative and Supportive Care, 2,* 403–408.

Schachter, S., & Georgopoulos, M. (2008). Camps for grieving children: Lessons from the field. In K. J. Doka & A. S. Tucci (Eds.), *Living with grief: Children and adolescents* (pp. 233–251). Washington, DC: Hospice Foundation of America.

Schuurman, D. (2008). Grief groups for grieving children and adolescents. In K. J. Doka & A. S. Tucci (Eds.), *Living with grief: Children and adolescents* (pp. 255–269). Washington, DC: Hospice Foundation of America.

Searles McClatchey, I., Vonk, M. E., & Palardy, G. (2008). Efficacy of a camp-based intervention for childhood traumatic grief. *Research on Social Work Practice, 19*(1), 19–30.

Shelby, J. S. (1997). Rubble, disruption, and tears: Helping young survivors of natural disaster. In H. G. Kaduson, D. Congelosi, & C. E. Schaefer (Eds.), *The playing cure: Individualized play therapy for specific childhood problems* (pp. 143–169). Northvale, NJ: Jason Aronson.

Siegel, D. (1999). *The developing mind.* New York: Guilford.

Silverman, P. (2000). *Never too young to know.* New York: Oxford University Press.

Stokes, J. A. (2004). *Then, now and always—Supporting children as they journey through grief: A guide for practitioners.* Cheltenham, England: Winston's Wish.

Worden, J. W. (1996). *Children and grief: When a parent dies.* New York: Guilford Press.

Wylie, M. S., & Simon, R. (2002, September/October). Discoveries from the black box: How the neuron-science revolution can change your practice. *Psychotherapy Networker, 26*–37, 68.

Using Expressive Arts When Counseling Bereaved Children

19

DAYNA D. WOOD AND REBEKAH LANCTO NEAR

There are few statistics available to determine how many children are directly affected by the death of a family member or other significant person. Schachter and Georgopoulos (2008) reported that "approximately 4% of children in the United States under the age of 18 years have experienced the death of a parent" (p. 233). When other deaths are considered, the number of bereaved children becomes quite considerable. Evidence suggests that the death of a significant person in a child's life can have detrimental consequences. For 50%–66% of parentally bereaved young people, crying, distress, and depressive symptoms are widespread, and 20%–30% are regarded as "at risk" to an extent that could call for direct intervention (McCarthy, 2006). Research on sibling and peer bereavement suggests similar findings. The Harvard Child Bereavement Study of parentally bereaved children found that approximately 30% of the children were "at some degree of risk for high levels of emotional and behavioral problems" (Worden, 1996, p. 16). Worden also found higher levels of aggression among bereaved children and associations between bereavement and delinquent behavior. Furthermore, he reported that the "risk" status increased between the first and second years after the death and that children might experience more signs of negative consequences at 2 years than at 4 months or 1 year. Mack (2001) investigated depression among adults in the United States. Results indicated higher levels of depression among adults who had experienced parental death during childhood. It appears that the effects of bereavement are not a short-term matter of concern.

How can counselors and institutions best address the possible needs of bereaved children and families? One method is for clinicians to align themselves with theories that arise from a child's perspective. It has been recognized that talk and individual counseling are not always the most appropriate forms of intervention for bereaved children (Silverman, 2000). Art and creative expression are natural ways children communicate, learn, and participate in life. A therapeutic framework that originates from this perspective can have positive influences for children who are experiencing pain and distress, including death, dying, and bereavement. This chapter examines the use of the arts with dying and bereaved children. An illustrative case study and a description of an arts-based family program and children's bereavement groups depict various ways in which the arts can help transform childhood grief.

HISTORY OF THE ARTS AS HEALING

The arts have been used throughout history to assist in the treatment of physical and emotional ailments. In fact, in early human cultures the creative arts were inseparable from the healing arts. In animistic cultures where people believed individual spirits inhabited natural objects and influenced phenomena, shamans were considered the healers for the community. Shamans used the arts, including drumming, chanting, and dancing, to be "transported" to the spirit world, where they would journey to find the cure for sickness in an individual or tribe (Brandman & Sonke-Henderson, 2005). In Greece theater was used prescriptively. Comedy or satire was prescribed for depressive patients, and tragedy was encouraged for manic patients (Brandman & Sonke-Henderson). During the 10th through 12th centuries, Islam led the development of scientific medical practices. Sufis, or Islamic mystics, who maintain that a person can experience God directly, still practice today a type of dancing, or whirling, in order to create an altered consciousness in which they directly experience God (Brandman & Sonke-Henderson). In the 13th century, shatkhs healers (Sufi orders in the Asian subcontinent of India) used the healing properties of words. They would inscribe healing amulets to be worn around the patient's neck (Brandman & Sonke-Henderson).

A paradigm shift took place during the "Age of Enlightenment" in the 18th century. The establishment of hospitals, and therefore the role of the passive patient, made a distinct separation between body, mind, and spirit (Brandman & Sonke-Henderson, 2005). Hospitals became places for the facilitation of Western medical science and experimentation. Respite and comfort while healing were not the goals of these facilities. The 1930s marked the reintegration of the arts into health care with the forming of music therapy as a formal discipline (Brandman & Sonke-Henderson).

CREATIVE ARTS THERAPIES AND GRIEF

Creative arts therapies have widely been used when working with children who are faced with death and bereavement needs. Creative arts therapies are loosely defined as art therapy, music therapy, dance/movement therapy, drama therapy, poetry therapy, psychodrama, and expressive arts therapy. At times among these therapies there are subsets. For example, in art therapy there is photo therapy and coloring therapy.

Creative arts therapists are professionals who use arts modalities and creative processes when providing intentional interventions in various settings (see the National Coalition of Creative Arts Therapies Associations at http://www.nccata.org). Each field has its own association and established standards for professional training, including an approval and monitoring procedure, a code of ethics, standards of clinical practice, and a credentialing process. Creative and expressive arts counselors receive graduate training and supervised practice before they are qualified to practice independently. Many also obtain board certification by taking a national exam and have additional training in a specific modality.

Goals of creative arts therapies include "improving communication and expression, and increasing physical, emotional, cognitive and/or social functioning" (http://www.nccata.org). There are basic shared assumptions of how and why the arts (which can be used to describe all the creative modalities) promote wellness. The act of creating accesses both the right and left hemispheres of the brain, encouraging an integration of feeling, cognition, and sensation that can lead to new understanding. Furthermore, symbolic imagery and metaphor emerge during the creative process. Investigating possible meanings of the imagery promotes increased options and cognitive restructuring. The image can also act as a bridge between conscious and unconscious processes and often bypasses our defenses. Through the activation of neural pathways, which affect the autonomic nervous system, the human body reacts to images as if they are real (Brandman & Sonke-Henderson, 2005). Therefore, images have a direct influence on body functions. The creative modalities can also serve as relatively nonthreatening means to promote spontaneity, feelings of self-worth, and autonomy. Moreover, if a product is created, it can act as a way to archive, or concretize, client awareness and understanding.

These assumptions have specific relevance when working with the bereaved. Few words are readily available to communicate the depth, confusion, and often-conflicting emotions related to grief. The act of creating, however, can lend itself to express through image, symbol, sound, metaphor, enactment, and/or movement that which cannot be easily "talked through" (Borden, 1992; Irwin, 1991; Mayo, 1996; Raymer & McIntyre, 1987; Simon, 1981; Tate, 1989). Using the arts in grief and bereavement work provides methods for people who have experienced the pain of loss to help identify, cope, and heal from that pain (Carbone, 2003; Forrest & Thomas, 1991; Graves, 1994; Orton, 1994). The arts promote healing during the grief process in a variety of ways.

Grief can often make a person feel out of control. Art allows the bereaved to express their grief at their own rate and can often be less threatening than words alone (Schimmel & Kornreich, 1993). It facilitates a safe container to express intense, and sometimes contradictory, thoughts and feelings by offering containment and help in organizing these feelings, thoughts, and sensations (Aldridge, 1993; Graves, 1994; Irwin, 1991; Junge, 1985). The arts allow for catharsis and kinesthetic release, and if a final product of art is produced, it can act as a record of the person's grief process and progress (Irwin; Schimmel & Kornreich). Additionally, the creative arts have a unique way of commemorating (Graves). Memory boxes and books of stories, pictures, poems, and drawings can help the bereaved reminisce and maintain a relationship with the deceased (Junge). Furthermore, the simple act of creating can be pleasurable and has the ability to increase a person's sense of joy, peace, and relaxation (Rogers, 1993). This chapter offers an intensive look at expressive arts therapy and how it can be integrated in working with dying and bereaved children.

THE CREATIVE ARTS AND OTHER DISCIPLINES

Overlap exists between creative arts therapies and other disciplines. For instance, art and play are closely related. "Playfulness is a part of any creative process and there is artistry in play therapy" (Rubin, 1999, p. 70). In both, the goals may be similar, but the modality (art vs. play) is different. Similarly, in other disciplines such as counseling, psychology, social work, child life, therapeutic recreation, and art education, art is incorporated, but generally during structured activities designed for a specific purpose. For instance, "counseling at its best employs an artistic quality that enables individuals to express themselves in a creative and unique manner" (Gladding & Newsome, 2002, p. 251). Counseling can even be enhanced by encouraging some clients to participate in creative experiences, including painting, writing, dancing, drumming, drama, or playing (Gladding, 2005). Creative arts therapies, however, use art as the "central modality" in therapy, often foster free self-expression, and use a greater variety of art materials (Rubin). Elinor Ulman, founder, editor, and publisher of the first art therapy journal, wisely stated, "The boundaries between art therapy and other disciplines are inevitably blurred ... [Those] who use art in their practice must live with the task of sharing their common ground as peacefully as possible and must learn to respect each other for the special knowledge and skills that are unique to each professional group" (1977, pp. 7, 39).

Clinicians who have an attraction toward artistic expression and integrate the arts into their work, but who do not have specific training in the creative arts therapies, must be cautious that they use the arts in ways that are "not mechanical, gimmicky, or otherwise nontherapeutic" (Gladding & Newsome, 2002, p. 251). It is important for clinicians to remember that ethically no mental health professional should practice beyond the scope in which he or she has been trained (American Counseling Association, 2005). According to Hammond and Gantt (1998), counselors should be able to talk about a piece of art brought in by a client and prompt him or her to create when talking becomes difficult and clarification is needed. However, most counselors do not have adequate training to interpret a client's art or make generalizations about its meaning to others. It is imperative that mental health professionals be cognizant of the limits of their abilities and recognize when consultation or referral is appropriate (Gladding & Newsome). Clinicians and students who are interested in incorporating the arts into their work are encouraged to take courses, participate in a creative art therapies group, or work individually with a creative arts therapist.

EXPRESSIVE ARTS THERAPY

> Art heals by accepting the pain and doing something with it.
> —Shaun McNiff (2004, p. v)

So often it is hard to find the "right words" when working with children who are faced with death, dying, and their personal grief. We struggle to find the answers, as though there was one perfect response to all their questions. The use of expressive arts can act as another forum to relate to children, their families, and their needs. The expressive arts incorporate a variety of creative processes to foster personal growth. This model integrates the many creative art therapies into an interdisciplinary framework with an emphasis on the creative process. Within expressive arts therapy, the process of creation is itself valued instead of the main focus being on the technical skill or artistic merit of the product (Knill, Levine, & Levine, 2005). Expressive arts therapy distinguishes itself from its closely associated disciplines of art, music, drama, dance/movement, poetry therapy, and psychodrama by being grounded in the interrelatedness of the arts (see the International Expressive Arts Therapy Association at http://www.ieata.org). It allows the inner imagery of a person's thoughts to become concrete through the use of sound, words, movement, and images. Expressive arts therapy is a field that is grounded in philosophy, psychology, and the intermodal use of the arts (Knill et al., 2005). The application of expressive arts therapy fosters awareness, builds connections within relationships, and encourages emotional growth.

The expressive arts in bereavement counseling have been beneficial for children and adults alike. Just as the grieving process is not a linear path, expressive arts therapy also follows a fluid course, like water ebbing and flowing. Through creative expression and tapping into one's imagination, intermodal expressive arts therapy invites a child to move flexibly among media, following that person's intuitive instincts and interests. The use of a multiple approach of the arts allows a child to see, hear, move, and verbalize his or her grief in ways that may never have been experienced before. Children manifest their grief in a multitude of ways. They may be sullen and withdrawn or argumentative and aggressive. The benefits of expressive arts therapy interventions are that they directly

Table 19.1

A FRAMEWORK FOR AN EXPRESSIVE ARTS GRIEF COUNSELING SESSION		
Life of client	Habitual world experience before the session	
Opening of session	Connecting to the daily reality	D
Bridge	Guidance toward art-making or play	E
		C
Art-making or play	Alternative world experience	E
	Decentering techniques	N
	Work-oriented, play- or ritual-oriented	T
	Far from or close to the theme	E
Aesthetic analyses	Recognizing the imaginary reality	R
		I
Bridge or "harvesting"	Recollecting the effective reality	N
Closing of session	Connecting back to the opening of the session	G
	Homework	
Life of client	Habitual world experience is challenged	

engage auditory, visual, and kinesthetic senses, as well as facilitate a full range of emotions. The arts allow a clinician to meet the child where that individual is in his or her grief process. For example, when working with a client, one might start out creating a visual piece and then allow that piece to be experienced through movement and reflected with a poetic verse. This pattern is not the same in every session. As a clinician, one should pay attention to nonverbal cues and facilitate expression through a variety of arts. This exploration can evoke different senses, and new dimensions of experiences can arise that are aesthetically rewarding, as well as an effective means of conversation with clients/artists. This practice allows the child to examine his or her body, feelings, emotions, and thought processes. Each clinician has his or her way of introducing the expressive arts into a session with grieving children. An expressive arts grief-counseling session may proceed according to the framework outlined in Table 19.1 (Knill et al., 2005, p. 95).

Case Study: The Torres Family

The case study of the Torres family illustrates the "architecture" of a session using expressive arts therapy (Knill et al., 2005, p. 94). Terminology used in the preceding chart will be highlighted throughout the case study, which will offer further explanation into the application of expressive arts therapy. The arts are beneficial in journeying through the grief process. Expressive arts therapy enabled Ryan, a young boy with a brain tumor, and his entire family to deal with the pain as they mourned their mother's death and prepared for Ryan's impending death. Consent was given by the family to share their story.

The Torres family members are immigrants from the Dominican Republic. Juan and Silvia came to America with hopes of building a family and providing them with a better life. Two years prior to when the expressive arts therapist met the Torres family, they had experienced a devastating loss. Silvia Torres, Juan's wife, and mother to Maria, age 12, Ryan, age 10, and Kyle, age 8, had died from brain cancer. In the past 2 years, the family had experienced many changes and adjustments. Juan had remarried Angela, who had a daughter, Anna, age 6. They had blended their families together in anticipation of a new start for everyone. But these dreams were soon overshadowed, with Ryan being diagnosed with a brain tumor. The doctors speculated that he would be dead within 6 months. Haine, Wolchik, Sandler, Millsap, and Ayers (2006) have suggested that pre-bereavement interventions, such as the following, are appropriate when working with children who have a family member with a life-threatening illnesses.

It was mid-fall when the licensed expressive arts therapist was invited to visit the Torres family. Maria, now age 14, answered the door. She eagerly brought the therapist to her brother Ryan's bedside. They walked through the living room where Angela, Juan's new wife, was preoccupied with watching TV. Although Angela took care of household duties, the care of the children was left to Maria. Juan worked two jobs to make adequate money, and his daughter, Maria, took on the responsibilities of primary caregiver to Ryan. Fourteen-year-old Maria was in charge of giving her dying brother his medicine and administering to his sickbed.

Shortly after the therapist arrived at the house, Kyle and Anna rushed in from school. The now 10- and 8-year-old children came into the small room, which was filled with Ryan's hospital bed and a bunk bed. Maria and Anna shared the bottom bunk while Kyle was on top. The cramped room offered just enough space to walk by the beds. A small chair in which the therapist sat fit next to Ryan. Ryan lay in the hospital bed while his siblings climbed onto their bed.

The children looked at the therapist with curious eyes. She asked them if they knew why she was there. This was the beginning of the opening of the session. They shyly shook their heads no and waited for the therapist to respond. It was important to convey to the children that she was there to help them cope with the illness and changes their brother was going through. The other service providers—nurses, social workers, chaplain, and home health aides—came primarily to support Ryan. The children needed to know that the therapist was part of the team responsible for supporting them and their needs. The therapist was making a connection to the reality of their situation.

As the sessions continued, the therapist would make a link from where they were to where they were heading. She made it clear to the children that they could ask her any questions and that she would always be honest with her answers. The therapist told the children how she worked with the arts and explained that when they were together, they would explore various types of the arts. Their eyes lit up, and quickly they began to let the therapist into their world.

The therapist was unsure where to begin because she had been informed that no one had told the children that Ryan was dying. She needed to respect the family in their level of comfort and acceptance regarding Ryan's progressive illness. She wanted to create a space that could hold all the questions the children might have, while still allowing hope and reality a place to dance together.

The therapist wondered what it was like for the children to see Ryan change physically. Without delay, she began to assess the children's understanding of the situation while also building trust with them. The therapist began to decenter into the art-making experience. *Decentering* is the act of moving from present reality into the creative process. "Being present is understood as being courageous enough to 'step forth' into decentering" (Knill et al., 2005, p. 168). We continue forward even though "we are ourselves helpless to fix the problematic, helpless situation of the client, while still trusting in the process of facilitation through the arts" (p. 168).

The therapist and children played a game called "one up, one down." This soon became the greeting ritual every session. The therapist gave the children wipe boards and told them that they would be making just a quick sketch or representation of what was going on. They were asked to convey one good thing that had happened to them, and one not so good thing that had happened to them. This became a way that the therapist was able to get a sense of their emotional well-being at the time. Each child took to this game in a different way. The therapist encouraged them to express their one up and one down in any avenue they felt comfortable. Maria typically would draw a little something but preferred to write hers out. Kyle loved drawing with precise detail. Anna struggled at times in what to put down, and Ryan always liked to talk about his one up and one down. This game became the lifeline that let the therapist know when the children had matters on their minds. It was also a great way to honor the good things that were happening among all the difficulties. Much to the therapist's surprise, the children believed that Ryan was just sick, but he would be getting better soon. Ryan believed this as well.

As Ryan's tumor got bigger, and his behaviors started to change, the therapist encouraged Juan to be open with the children about Ryan's advancing illness. He said, "I don't know how to tell my children their brother is dying. I can't look at them and see that pain in their eyes without crying." With a lot of encouragement and educating, Juan finally agreed that his family should know Ryan's prognosis. Juan asked if the therapist would tell the children in her next session. Juan agreed to join the session after the children were told. By this time, Ryan knew he was dying, and often in his private sessions, he would let the therapist know that he had a secret. "Shhh, I am dying, but please don't tell my father or brother and sisters because they will be sad." Through the use of puppets and imagination, Ryan created scenes of characters dying and everyone else being sad. The therapist would often prompt questions or create new characters to allow Ryan to think of stories in different ways. By being in the imaginative play, he was able to bridge the stories he created to his real life story. Ryan eventually was able to talk with his father and siblings about his fear of dying and saying goodbye to them.

Throughout the sessions other forms of art-making and play were incorporated. When the therapist talked to the children about Ryan's impending death, she employed these other forms. She started their time together as usual with the one up, one down game. She found in her work that children typically know what is going on, no matter how much the adults in their lives try to keep it from them. This fact seemed to have been the case with the Torres siblings. While Ryan was sleeping in a different room, Kyle had drawn his one down of Ryan yelling and being nasty to him. When they explored the picture, Kyle talked about how much his brother's behaviors were changing. Sometimes he was nice, and other times he was not. The therapist explained to the children about Ryan's disease and what was happening to him physically. She explained that the tumor was making him act out, and that was not really the brother they had known. She then prompted them to create a story or visual form of what they thought was going to happen to Ryan. They paused for a while and looked at each other for support. No one wanted to be first, but Maria, the eldest, began. Kyle and Anna followed. Anna created a picture of the whole family outside in the park. Kyle drew a picture of him and his brother playing together. And then, there, in Maria's picture, was what no one wanted to name. She drew an image split in half. On one side was a picture of her brother "hanging out," telling jokes. The other side was Ryan as an angel. At this time they simply looked at the aesthetics of the images, such as the color, line quality, form, and whether they would change something about it. As outlined earlier, in the structure of an art-based session, we observe that the alternative world experience, or decentering with the arts, includes aesthetic analyses. The purpose of aesthetic analysis is to validate the work (Knill et al., 2005). From this aesthetic analysis they began to harvest the images, or rather process the artwork with the therapist. The children and therapist bridged connections from the pictures to the actuality of the situation. Harvesting is important because it can aid changes in the "helpless situation and justifies restoration" (Knill et al., 2005, p. 151). Even in the somber situation of death, a person can find solace in the arts.

The floodgates had been opened, and the children started voicing their many questions and concerns. "What would death look like?" "When would it happen?" "Couldn't there still be a miracle?" These were questions to which the therapist could not give definitive answers. She spoke with them about the physical aspects of death, the possibilities of what death might look like, and when it could happen. The other questions she brought back to the arts. The therapist realized she did not need to answer all their questions; she just needed to create a place where they could continue to explore their hopes and fears.

Weeks flowed into months, during which the therapist made weekly visits. By this point, Ryan was sleeping much of the time. He would engage as much as he could and then resume resting. The therapist walked into the room with the children eagerly waiting for her to arrive. They proceeded with their one up, one down, as they had always done. The therapist then continued to offer the children a variety of art media to begin the decentering. Once, they all meekly looked at each other and then looked to the therapist. Kyle softly whispered to Maria, "You ask the question." Maria sharply answered back, "No, you ask." The therapist reassured them that they could ask her anything, and together they would figure it out. Then Ryan blurted out, "What does heaven look like?" "Is that what you all were wondering?" the therapist replied. They all shook their heads yes. Using the language of their psyche, the therapist took this as an opportunity to facilitate creating what heaven looks like.

She opened up her magic bag filled with all sorts of materials. There were markers, colored pencils, pastels (oil and chalk), crayons, colored paper, glue, scissors, and various miscellaneous objects that could be used to create. Each child dove into the materials with delight. Ryan began to create an image of a ship. He talked about how the ship was coming to take him to heaven and said his mother was on it. As the session continued, Ryan became very tired and asked his brother Kyle to finish his drawing for him. Ryan instructed his brother to draw himself on a bike and to make sure that there were birds in the sky. (See Figure 19.1.)

When Kyle finished his brother's heaven, he completed working on his representation. Kyle depicted a road that was paved with gold and lions that you could pet and talk to. Anna had angels lining the path to heaven. Maria's image included God and her family as angels in heaven. (See Figures 19.2, 19.3, and 19.4.)

While the children worked, the song "Shout" by Tears for Fears was playing in the background. Ryan and Maria were singing along to the

Figure 19.1 Ryan's drawing of heaven.

Figure 19.2 Kyle's drawing of heaven.

Figure 19.3 Anna's drawing of heaven.

Figure 19.4 Maria's drawing of heaven.

song. The song they were singing provided the opportunity to shift from one art modality to another, labeled "intermodal transfer" (Knill et al., 2005, p. 125). This intermodal transfer brought the children to a deepening of their creative reality. Together the therapist and children began to play with sounds and words. As the decentering continued, these are the improvised lyrics that emerged:

> NO PAIN
> NO MORE BAD RELATIONSHIPS
> NO MORE SICKNESS
> NO MORE BEING IN THIS BED
> I JUST WANT TO LET GO

The children each shouted what he or she could do without. Anna shouted "NO PAIN," Maria shouted "NO MORE BAD RELATIONSHIPS," Kyle shouted "NO MORE SICKNESS," and Ryan shouted "NO MORE BEING IN THIS BED. I JUST WANT TO LET GO."

When they harvested the images and music, the children discovered that they believed Ryan would not go to heaven because he was not baptized. Ryan believed this to be true as well. The arts allowed the children to explore this imaginary reality and then bring it back to their everyday circumstances. In closing the session, the children gave the therapist permission to share with Juan and the team about their concern. The chaplain went out a few days later and baptized Ryan. A week later, Ryan died.

The therapist was called when Ryan was actively dying. The family requested her presence. When she arrived, the small house was filled with family, friends, and church members. The children were huddled in the living room just observing the chaos around them. She asked them if they wanted to go be with Ryan. They said they were scared because everyone was around Ryan wailing, with tears streaming down their faces. As the therapist took the first step into the room with the children following, the sea of people parted and made room for them to be by Ryan's bedside. A hush fell over the crowd. The therapist let the children know that Ryan could still hear them, and it was okay to talk to him. The crowd created a circle around the children and therapist as they began to create a dying ritual. The parallels of the uncertainty of death mirror those of the arts. What would happen, what would emerge, was undefined to everyone. Once again, the therapist looked to the arts to hold this space of such vagueness. Through her interaction with Ryan, she showed everyone that they could still touch him and communicate to him. Kyle and Anna sat in his bed, while Maria and the therapist were next to it. They held hands and began to hum. The humming turned into chants, the chants into words, and words into tears. Their bodies moved to the rhythms of the sounds their voices were making. This cycled over and over. The crowd, filled with familiar onlookers, took cues from the children and participated in the sounds, rhythms, and movement. The therapist spread visual art media around the room for individuals to create an intermodal transfer. Some of the youngest children (nieces and nephews) whom the therapist had never met drew pictures saying, "I love you." and "I miss you." The adults also took to the arts. They wrote messages to Ryan. Together with the children, they placed them around his head and the bed. These activities lasted for several hours until Ryan took his last breath.

The therapist continued working with the Torres family for over a year. She journeyed with them as they began to face their grief and as old pains of their mother's death reemerged. This poetic rap was one of the first artistic expressions that materialized after Ryan's death.

The Truth

face the truth
even though you don't want to
face the truth
even though it hurts
face the truth
cause you are going to have to
face the truth

Over the year, as the therapist listened to the children's explanation of their imagery, she poignantly began to see the world as they viewed it. The arts became a container for their pain as well as an avenue to celebrate life. "When dealing with devastating losses, traumas, and crises…people need to have access to a full range of human communications and creative outlets" (McNiff, 2004, p. 292). For the Torres family, the use of expressive arts acted as a concrete reminder of where they had been and where they were going.

FAMILY ARTS PROGRAMMING AND CHILDREN'S BEREAVEMENT GROUPS

Children live within multiple socio/familial systems including the family, school, and health care. Services should be geared toward delivery on these many levels. Using multiple modalities of expression and healing, bereavement professionals can assist children in transforming their grief.

Bereavement camps that incorporate the arts and play have become a popular method of reaching grieving children (e.g., Schachter & Georgopoulos, 2008). Helping Each Other After Loss (H.E.A.L.) is a one-day event devoted to bereaved children and their families. It is a family arts program that accommodates several families and provides the opportunity for various forms of expression through the arts. The focus is on the family unit rather than any one individual participant. The day is interactive and involves art-based activities for members of the family of all ages (Brandoff, McIntosh, Rangel, & Wood, 2008). Families work together as a unit for a portion of the day and also within the larger group. The goal of the annual event is to assist families in the facilitation of children's four tasks of mourning: (1) accepting the reality of loss, (2) experiencing the pain or emotional aspects of loss, (3) adjusting to an environment without the deceased person, and (4) relocating the deceased person within one's life and finding ways to memorialize that person (Worden, 1996, pp. 13–15).

The occasion makes available a place and time when families are able to acknowledge their grief, honor their deceased, renew their strength as a family, learn new ways to cope, and reduce isolation through an opportunity to connect with others. H.E.A.L. allows families to share their feelings, thoughts, experiences, and memories with each other by working together on commemorative art projects. Examples of projects that have been used during H.E.A.L. days include families creating a "Plate of Honor" made out of malleable and self-hardening clay, dedicated to the deceased. Another example is the "Grief Tool Box" containing a self-decorated personal journal, picture frame, and family emblem. Family mobiles, with dangling reflective CDs, were also created to demonstrate family systems and balance. Part of the day is used to present education about the grief process. Also, always included is an opportunity for the families to laugh together through the prompting of a magician, clown, or interactive music and movement. Events such as H.E.A.L. provide an alternative setting and method for reaching multiple bereaved families. (See Figure 19.5.)

Crenshaw (2008) has suggested that school-based programs present additional opportunities to make bereavement services available to children. Many hospices are now assisting in the facilitation of children's grief groups within schools. Tonkins and Lambert's (1996) research supports the notion that peer support groups can be useful for children. They can provide coping resources and reduce feelings of isolation. Moreover, bereavement professionals co-facilitating and collaborating with school counselors and social workers can increase the knowledge base of these professionals and their confidence in the areas of grief and bereavement.

One hospice in a large metropolitan area has taken the initiative to collaborate with local schools to offer bereavement support groups to at-need children within those settings. The groups are offered in either a 6- or 8-week format and are held for one full class period. At the beginning of each group, there is a brief check-in period, normally when each student has the opportunity to provide a "weather report" of how he or she is feeling. Students are always allowed to "pass" if they do not want to share. This rule allows them to express their grief at their own pace and level. Information is given about the topic for the day, and directions on how to create the project are provided. The majority of the

Figure 19.5 Children and adults at a H.E.A.L. event.

group time is spent creating, with time at the end to draw a picture of the experience. This activity provides an opportunity to process the day's activities and gives the counselor the chance to answer any questions.

The last portion of the group is reserved for every child to share, if he or she chooses to, what has been created. Often children are more comfortable talking about their project than speaking directly about their painful thoughts and feelings. The creative process allows distance and containment, so powerful emotions can be expressed. Discussion can then be introduced generally around the topics, questions, and/or misconceptions that were brought up in the children's art pieces. The students also see that their feelings are not unusual and that they are not alone in their grief. In addition, children learn more about their individual strengths and can experiment with new coping skills through the art-making process (Graves, 1994).

A variety of art modalities and projects, which correlate with grief topics, are presented during the course of a group. In her chapter "Using the Arts in a Bereavement Group for Children," Carbone (2003) outlined creative multimodal projects used in bereavement groups for children. An example of one such activity is "The Yes, No, Sometimes" game. The game is simple, interactive, and fun. Every student is given a colored card that states *yes, no,* or *sometimes.* The counselor begins with safe or silly questions to warm-up, such as "I like ice cream" or "I eat bugs in the morning." The children respond by putting down the card that matches their response. More sensitive grief-related statements are then introduced. The children are encouraged to make their own statements as well, which the group can then answer. This activity in particular lets the students know they are not alone in their feelings. The group is given time to draw a picture of something that was said that was meaningful for each participant. Other activities include "Musical Emotions," where the concepts of change and before and after are introduced through musical instruments, and "Move to the Music," "Clay Creations," and drawing pictures with oil pastels allow access to deeper emotional states (Carbone, 2003). Making memory collages is often part of the last group and serves as a way to memorialize the person who died.

CONCLUDING THOUGHTS

The arts can be used to transform grief. The expressive arts incorporate the visual arts, movement, drama, music, writing, play, and other creative processes in an interrelatedness to foster personal growth. Expressive arts provide an opportunity for children and families to relate to their grief on an individual and group level. People can learn to channel their grief in a multitude of ways by employing the expressive arts as a tool. The expressive arts are about connecting creatively, allowing oneself to be moved by the practice of creating within the arts. Expressive arts therapy is a creative process of art-making that enhances the physical, mental, and emotional well-being of individuals of all ages.

REFERENCES

Aldridge, D. (1993). Hope, meaning and the creative arts therapies in the treatment of grief. *The Arts in Psychotherapy, 20,* 285–297.

American Counseling Association. (2005). *ACA Code of Ethics.* Alexandria, VA: Author.

Borden, G. (1992). Metaphor: Visual aid in grief work. *Omega, Journal of Death and Dying, 25*(3), 239–248.

Brandman, R., & Sonke-Henderson, J. (2005). *Introduction to the arts in medicine handbook.* Gainesville: University of Florida Center for the Arts in Healthcare.

Brandoff, R., McIntosh, K., Rangel, R., & Wood, D. (2008, November 21). *Family art therapy: Case study of a community art program for families.* Paper presented at the American Art Therapy Association (AATA) 39th Annual International Conference, Cleveland, OH.

Carbone, L. M. (2003). Using the arts in a bereavement group for children. In D. Capuzzi (Ed.), *Approaches to group work: A handbook for practitioners.* Upper Saddle River, NJ: Pearson Education.

Crenshaw, D. A. (2008). Grief therapy with children and adolescents: An overview. In K. J. Doka & A. S. Tucci (Eds.), *Living with grief: Children and adolescents* (pp. 217–231). Washington, DC: Hospice Foundation of America.

Forrest, M., & Thomas G. V. (1991). An exploratory study of drawings by bereaved children. *British Journal of Clinical Psychology, 30*(4), 373–374.

Gladding, S. (2005). *Counseling as an art: The creative arts in counseling* (3rd ed.). Englewood Cliffs, NJ: Prentice Hall.

Gladding, S., & Newsome, D. W. (2002). Art in counseling. In C. A. Malchiodi (Ed.), *Handbook of art therapy* (pp. 243–253). New York: Guilford.

Graves, S. (1994). *Expressions of healing.* Van Nuys, CA: New Castle.

Haine, R. A., Wolchik, S. A., Sandler, I. N., Millsap, R. E., & Ayers, T. S. (2006). Positive parenting as a protective resource for parentally bereaved children. *Death Studies, 30,* 1–28.

Hammond, L. C., & Gantt, L. (1998). Using art in counseling: Ethical considerations. *Journal of Counseling and Development, 76*(3), 271–276.

International Expressive Arts Therapy Association. Retrieved March 14, 2009, from http://www.ieata.org

Irwin, H. J. (1991). The depiction of loss: Use of clients' drawings in bereavement counseling. *Death Studies, 15,* 481–497.

Junge, M. (1985). The book about Daddy dying: A preventive art therapy technique to help families deal with the death of a family member. *Art Therapy: Journal of the American Art Therapy Association, 2*(1), 410–419.

Knill, P. J., Levine, E. G., & Levine, S. K. (2005). *Principles and practice of expressive arts therapy: Towards a therapeutic aesthetic.* Philadelphia: Jessica Kingsley.

Mack, K. Y. (2001). Childhood family disruptions and adult well-being: The differential effects of divorce and parental death. *Death Studies, 25,* 419–443.

Mayo, S. (1996). Symbol, metaphor and story. The function of group art therapy in palliative care. *Palliative Medicine, 10*(3), 209–216.

McCarthy, J. R. (2006). *Young people's experience of loss and bereavement: Towards an interdisciplinary approach.* New York: Open University Press.

McNiff, S. (2004). *Art heals: How creativity cures the soul.* Boston: Shambhala.

National Coalition of Creative Arts Therapies Associations. Retrieved March 14, 2009, from http://www.nccata.org

Orton, M. (1994). A case study of an adolescent mother grieving the death of her child due to Sudden Infant Death Syndrome. *American Journal of Art Therapy, 33*(2), 37–44.

Raymer, M., & McIntyre, B. B. (1987). An art support group for bereaved children and adolescents. *Art Therapy: Journal of the American Art Therapy Association, 4,* 27–35.

Rogers, N. (1993). *The creative connection: Expressive arts as healing.* Palo Alto, CA: Science and Behavior Books.

Rubin, J. A. (1999). *Art therapy: An introduction.* New York: Psychology Press.

Schachter, S. R., & Georgopoulos, M. (2008). Camps for grieving children: Lessons from the field. In K. J. Doka & A. S. Tucci (Eds.), *Living with grief: Children and adolescents* (pp. 233–251). Washington, DC: Hospice Foundation of America.

Schimmel, B. F., & Kornreich, T. Z. (1993). The use of art and verbal process with recently widowed individuals. *American Journal of Art Therapy, 31,* 91–97.

Silverman, P. R. (2000). *Never too young to know: Death in children's lives.* New York: Oxford University Press.

Simon, R. (1981). Bereavement art. *American Journal of Art Therapy, 20,* 135–143.

Tate, F. B. (1989). Symbols in the graphic art of the dying. *The Arts in Psychotherapy, 16,* 115–120.

Tonkins, S. A. M., & Lambert, M. J. (1996). A treatment outcome study of bereavement groups for children. *Child and Adolescent Social Work Journal, 13*(1), 3–21.

Ulman, E. (1977). *Art therapy in theory and practice.* New York: Schocken.

Worden, J. W. (1996). *Children and grief: When a parent dies.* New York: Guilford.

.

Children With Developmental Disabilities, Death, and Grief

20

MARC A. MARKELL AND JOHN H. HOOVER

Even starting from the position that individuals with disabilities enjoy the legal and moral right to take their normative place in society, the existence of physical, emotional, or intellectual differences engenders disadvantage (Wolfensberger, 2000). Disability complicates the lives of affected children and those of immediate family members. These individuals must navigate the complexities of service providers, participate in school services through the vehicle of interdisciplinary teams, and confront the complexities associated with the disability itself.

Theologians, philosophers, and grief experts agree that the end of life is a deeply complex experience. Consider the existential questions of young children about death that have no good answer: "What is death?" "Where do we go when we die?" Add to these the theological implications of afterlife issues, and children confront an endless array of complexities regarding death—many of which make adjustment to loss particularly difficult for children and, as we will explore in this chapter, the developmentally young (see comprehensive reviews by Oltjenbruns, 2001; Stevenson, 2009).

Although physical, emotional, and learning disabilities (e.g., in reading) certainly challenge individuals and families in their ability to deal with bereavement, it is cognitive impairment that most directly and severely affects the grief process. In this chapter, we explore the connections between issues surrounding death and dying on the one hand and developmental disabilities on the other. Our primary goal is to provide a resource that will support parents and caregivers as they help persons with developmental disabilities understand bereavement and mourn adaptively (Hunter & Smith, 2008).

We begin by laying out the overall characteristics of developmental disabilities (DD) before turning to a description of how characteristics in DD likely intersect with end-of-life issues. An important consideration in dealing with the grieving process is the many transitions experienced by children and adolescents with cognitive disabilities. It does not always occur to caregivers that grieving may be invoked by movement from home to a group home or the loss of a favorite care worker through normal job attrition.

A third section of this chapter deals specifically with Doka's (1989, 2002) concept of disenfranchised grief, certainly a significant issue for persons with developmental disabilities, their parents, and their care providers (Hoover, Markell, & Wagner, 2005). In this section, we address complex grief and factors producing difficulties in adjustment to the death of a loved one (or to disruptive change), including, most importantly, disenfranchised grief. Disenfranchised grief refers to situations where individuals' ability to grieve is curtailed by social factors (e.g., age, status as disabled), often with resultant wellness difficulties; in essence, the term *disenfranchised grief* is employed in reference to situations where directly or indirectly a person is not allowed to grieve effectively.

Persons with developmental disabilities die at earlier ages than do age-matched individuals who do not manifest such disabilities (Doka, 2002). With this mortality issue in mind, a fourth section of the chapter deals with parental grief over the death of a child with disabilities, perhaps best conceptualized as a specific subset of disenfranchised grief.

Finally, we examine programs and treatment modalities of two types. First, we attend to death education programs and practices in general that have a track record of effectiveness with children who are developmentally disabled. Steps to facilitate the grieving process are also addressed.

DEVELOPMENTAL DISABILITIES

Generic Definition

Developmental disabilities refer broadly to conditions that manifest during the developmental period. In a sense, the designation distinguishes diseases and syndromes affecting cognition and learning that exist at birth, develop during early childhood, or unfold with development from those that occur adventitiously (e.g., mental disability versus acquired brain damage). Though causation differs widely, the two most prominent categories in most taxonomies are mental disability and disorders in the autism spectrum. In texts dealing with developmental disabilities, causal factors tend to be divided into the following categories:

- Structural chromosomal abnormalities (e.g., Down syndrome; see Batshaw, 2002).
- Standard genetic mechanisms (e.g., autosomal recessive inheritance, phenylketunoria).
- Maternal diseases and conditions affecting fetal development (toxoplasmosis gondii, maternal-fetal rh incompatibility).
- Teratogens, defined as toxins affecting fetal development (e.g., alcohol-related neurological disorders such as fetal alcohol syndrome).

Cognitive Disabilities (Mental Retardation)

Developmental cognitive disabilities, more widely identified in years past as mental retardation, refer to a constellation of three diagnostic criteria (American Association on Mental Retardation [AAMR], 1992). First, some indication must exist that the individual demonstrates global deficits in cognitive abilities. Though difficult to measure in young children, the first criterion is typically established via scores on general intelligence measures that are two standard deviations or more below the mean. Conventionally, because so-called intelligence tests are set with a mean of 100 and a standard deviation of 15, scores below 70 indicate the existence of a cognitive disability. For the case of infants and young children, the determination is made either via invoking biological conditions that *typically* manifest in global cognitive deficits or through careful observation of the developmental process (McLean, Wolery, & Bailey, 2004).

A second criterion established for cognitive disabilities refers to adaptive behavior. Though measures of general intelligence are moderately correlated with learning indices, these correlations are less than perfect (AAMR, 1992). As a result, parents and professionals in the field have set a standard that children must show not just a decrement in test scores, but real deficits in everyday life skills, so-called adaptive behaviors. Adaptive behaviors are divided typically into such domains as communication, functional academics, daily/independent living (e.g., toileting/feeding), social/interpersonal skills, community participation (for example, age-appropriate mobility in the community), and leisure/recreation skills (AAMR).

Finally, to identify a child with a cognitive disability, the diagnostician must believe that the condition is associated with a slowed unfolding of the developmental sequence or that low cognitive skills exist as a function of a condition extant at birth or in early childhood. For obvious reasons, this final criterion is a difficult case to make and thus tends to be based on the judgment of the diagnostician.

Pervasive Developmental Disabilities/ the Autism Spectrum

A second broad division within developmental disabilities with implications for the grieving process is made up of conditions in the autism spectrum. For this discussion, we have divided autism spectrum disorders (ASD) into two rough categories, early infantile autism and Asperger syndrome, both considered to lie within the more global category of pervasive developmental disabilities (Volkmar & Klin, 2005).

Diagnosis within the autism spectrum is based on a constellation of three sets of indicators, including, first, impairments in social reciprocity. Persons identified in the autism spectrum tend to find it problematic to engage in interactive social exchanges. For example, it has frequently been noted that persons with ASD find it difficult to interpret visual social cues (e.g., social distance, facial expressions) and thus to modulate behaviors based on accurately reading these signals. Difficulties managing social relationships and communication should probably be considered *the* defining characteristics across ASD conditions (Carter, Davis, Klin, & Volkmar, 2005; Mundy & Sigman, 1989).

A second category of difficulty associated with ASD is impairment in communication, including both receptive and expressive aspects of language. Persons with autism often find it particularly difficult to manage pragmatics, the aspect of language referring to communication's purpose-driven features. For example, turn-taking is one defining characteristic of conversation. A person identified with ASD might not understand conversation's complex pragmatics and thus carry on a monologue when a communication partner desires more give-and-take. To further complicate this issue, a person with autism or Asperger syndrome might fail to recognize or act on the facial and body posture cues that indicate frustration with the way a communication episode is unfolding. Overall language ability in autism may run from near normal levels to severe impairment. Obviously, receptive language skills hold great implications for explaining death-related phenomena, and expressive language deficits will likely affect the ability of the person with ASD to grieve or to garner assistance with symptoms of incomplete grieving from helpers or counselors.

Behavioral idiosyncrasies or abnormalities make up a third class of autism characteristics. Children with ASD might engage in odd or nonfunctional toy play, such as twirling objects, or engage in such responses as self injury, routines, rituals, preoccupations, or temper tantrums. Extraordinary and often dysfunctional responses to sensory stimuli are other commonly observed behavioral idiosyncrasies. For example, we are aware of an individual with ASD who touched young children's heads, much to their parents' consternation, because he liked the smell of children's shampoo. Self-injurious behaviors are associated with disorders in the autism spectrum (Oswald, Ellis, Singh, & Singh, 1994). Impairments in general intelligence are associated with autism, less so with Asperger syndrome (Volkmar & Klin, 2005).

Though perhaps an oversimplification, the diagnostic distinction between autism (early infantile autism) and Asperger syndrome is related to (a) severity and (b) time of diagnosis. Typically, for classical autism, the symptoms are severe, and the functioning level is quite low. In addition, it can usually be established that two specific characteristics in area one (impaired social interactions) and one each in the remaining two domains are observed before an age of 36 months. In contrast, children might be identified as meeting the criteria for Asperger syndrome if they clearly demonstrate impairments in social reciprocity, but show fewer and less severe behavioral, linguistic, and cognitive decrements.

Parents and caregivers may be concerned about the attendance of persons with ASD at end-of-life events because of worries about behavioral excesses—either those directly related to the condition or behaviors that may result from feelings of loss. Otherwise, all of the implications discussed as this chapter continues apply to persons with autism, perhaps less so to those identified with Asperger syndrome. The mean intelligence measure in full-blown autism lies in the moderate range (scores from about 40 to about 55; further on in this chapter for a discussion; Rimland, 1994). Though this is controversial because it is often thought that autism's communication deficits "hide" higher intelligence, general intelligence scores predict functioning levels of individuals with autism as well as they do for members of other groups (Rutter & Bartak, 1973).

DEVELOPMENTAL DISABILITIES AND END-OF-LIFE CONCEPTS

The idea of mental age, though justifiably in disfavor, nonetheless emerges as a useful metaphor for dealing with cognitive issues surrounding death and dying. Although a person with cognitive disabilities would not "think like" a younger child, the mental age will probably suggest to a caregiver or helping professional reasonable approaches to employ in helping a child with developmental disabilities deal with the loss of a loved one—or other life transition that may produce the need to mourn (see Table 20.1).

Mental age is not a perfect predictor of what a child will understand. A 10-year-old, for example, will have encountered many more

Table 20.1

LEVELS OF GLOBAL COGNITIVE DISABILITY AND THE ATTAINMENT OF THE UNDERSTANDING OF DEATH CONCEPTS (MENTAL AGE 7–11)

LEVEL	STANDARD DEVIATIONS BELOW THE MEAN	APPROXIMATE GLOBAL INTELLIGENCE TEST SCORES ($M = 100$, $SD = 15$)	CHRONOLOGICAL AGE EXPECTATION FOR UNDERSTANDING DEATH PRIMARY CONCEPTS
Not cognitively disabled	NA	100 (85 to115)	6 to 7
Mild mental disability	−2 to −3	55 to 70	10 (9 to 11)
Moderate mental disability	−3 to −4	40 to 55	13.5 (11 to 15)
Severe/profound	−4 to −5	Undetermined	At adulthood

Mental-age estimates do not often extend beyond age 17 or 18, so the scale flattens out after age 16. Many students with moderate to severe cognitive disabilities do not, strictly speaking, attain the concrete operations stage.

life experiences than will have a 5-year-old. Independently of mental age, these experiences (certainly including formal education) provide more opportunities for dealing with life's issues. In addition, some experts believe that in dealing with extremely abstract constructs (those that cannot readily be represented with objects and actions), students with global cognitive disabilities operate at slightly lower levels than do their normal-IQ mental age peers (Baroff, 1986). It is probably most defensible to predict, though not to assume, that a person with global cognitive disabilities will perform below age expectations cognitively when dealing with the complexities of death. This likelihood means that caregivers will most likely need to adjust expectations for concept development for the child's functional capacity. As a result, explanations, death education sequences, and counseling methods will also need to be modified.

A caveat needs to be introduced at this point. Experts in the field of education in developmental disabilities point out, quite correctly, that programs for and generic treatment of persons with developmental disabilities should be age-appropriate. Wolfensberger (2000) argued this point persuasively when he pointed out that surrounding persons with disabilities with symbols (pictures, posters, modes of address, curriculum materials) designed for young(er) children tends to unfairly label such individuals as less able than is objectively the case. Thus, parents and death educators are faced with the dual challenge of balancing their approach between age appropriateness (especially of educational materials and explanations of concepts related to death) and cognitive accessibility. Attaining the delicate balance between age appropriateness and cognitive understanding lies at the core of best practices in working with children manifesting cognitive disabilities.

Cognitive Conceptualizations of Death

This section is largely adopted from a chapter regarding the developmental aspects of dealing with end-of-life issues penned by Oltjenbruns (2001; see also Hunter & Smith, 2008); we have organized these materials for the special case of developmental disabilities. As argued earlier regarding mental age in DD, Oltjenbruns has noted that approaches to dealing with death and grief must be tuned to the child's developmental age in terms of cognition, language, and psychosocial adjustment. This necessity is no less the case in dealing with a child identified with a developmental disability.

The Nature of Death

At least three concepts are essential for understanding death and probably underpin communication required to support the grieving process. First, a child must understand that "dead people are nonfunctional" (Oltjenbruns, 2001; see also chapter 2 in this book). Although this concept seems straightforward to adults and cognitively older youngsters, it may not be apparent to young children and children with cognitive disabilities. At a fundamental level, this lack of biological functioning implies that the decedent can no longer visit the child, bring presents, read stories, or talk to the youngster. Many adults express surprise over such confusion.

> A teacher told a 10-year-old child with a mild cognitive disability about events to be expected at his aunt's funeral. As a comprehension check, the teacher asked the youngster to paraphrase these funereal events. "OK," he responded, "I will go to the funeral home. There will be a lot of people around. I will walk up to and look in a box called a casket where my aunt's body will be. Then," he argued, "my aunt will get up and make dinner." The teacher carefully, but gently, explained that this would *not* happen because the aunt's body "no longer worked." The child retorted indignantly, "You do not know my aunt! She always makes dinner when I visit."

A second concept about death that may not be readily accessible to persons with developmental disabilities is the notion of irreversibility. In our experience, children with developmental disabilities often express confusion about irreversibility, most commonly conflating death with illness. Perhaps they expect the decedent to return once that person "feels better." A failure to understand irreversibility probably underpins such questions as the following: "When can mom come home from the hospital?" "When will grandpa take me fishing again?" "When will Sally wake up?"

> The father of an 11-year-old boy with a developmental disability enrolled him in a grief support group following the mother's death. The boy told the facilitator that his mom would come back on his birthday. The facilitator reemphasized that the boy's mother was dead and would not return. The boy paused momentarily before continuing, "Oh, I know—the gates of heaven must be locked. When mom finds a way to open them, she will come back."

Another complexity regarding irreversibility that produces confusion in children is engendered by faith traditions invoking an afterlife.

Youngsters might have picked up from discussions at home and during religious education the expectation of life after death. It is an understandable, straightforward misunderstanding to move from resurrection theology, well represented in Christian tradition by Jesus's post-crucifixion return, to the notion that death is reversible in real—as opposed to spiritual—time. Sensitive helpers will understand and commiserate with a young child or a slightly older youngster with developmental disabilities who evidences this misconception by hearkening to the very real complexities engendered by spiritual questions—especially those surrounding death. Most adults who are honest with themselves will admit that, although they may not struggle with belief in an afterlife, they do wrestle with understanding it.

Oltjenbruns (2001; see also chapter 2 in this book) identified a third concept related to death that might prove confusing to the developmentally young, the notion of death's universality. Clearly, grounds for confusion and hurt exist in what must seem like cosmic unfairness to a child whose father dies while those of other children remain alive. Grief helpers must understand that misconceptions about universality may complicate the grieving process.

A fourth concept, closely related to universality, has often been invoked in the literature: the notion of inevitability. Children must come to understand that all living beings must eventually die (Candy-Gibbs, Sharp, & Petrun, 1985); once more, this concept may not seem apparent to children under the age of 6 or who manifest mental ages below that figure.

According to Oltjenbruns (2001), children must attain what Piaget (1976) refers to as the concrete operations stage of development before they can understand the three main death-related concepts. We contend that misunderstanding one or more of the previously noted concepts will likely complicate grieving. Because conceptual development is related to mental age, it is essential to think about how this issue plays out if caregivers are to assist with healthy grieving. Oltjenbruns has pointed out that the ability to mentally reverse processes is related to the capability of understanding the essential death concepts. Despite some recent criticism of this truism, Piaget argued that a mental age of about 9 is required (the range being 7 to 11; see also Baroff, 1986) for students to confidently perform concrete mental operations, such as reversibility. Before this age, children often demonstrate problems of conservation, tend to be egocentric in their thinking, and are "indifferent to logic and consistency" (Baroff, p. 6). This earlier stage is known as the preoperational period.

Though no absolutes exist as to how children understand end-of-life phenomena, there are some general guidelines as to understanding of death at different ages and cognitive levels (Slaughter, 2005). Hunter and Smith (2008) detected a significant relationship between the age of a child and the understanding of death, between seriation ability (a way of positioning an item within a series, another concrete operations task) and the understanding of death, and between children's experience of death and their understanding of the concept. Hunter and Smith found that children attained a clear understanding of the four components at a mental age slightly lower than typically assigned to the concrete operations stage, at an average (mental) age of between 6 years, 3 months and 6 years, 4 months.

According to Kauffman (2005), people with mild to moderate developmental disabilities are able to understand the key concepts that are used to define a person's ability to understand death—those being irreversibility of death and nonfunctionality of the person who has died. Both people with developmental disabilities and people without may have difficulty understanding death and loss, but ultimately do understand that death is irreversible and that the body of the person who died no longer works. People with severe developmental disabilities are also able to grieve the absence of a significant person, though some may argue that what a person with a severe disability experiences cannot be considered grief resulting from the death of a person. People with severe disabilities may not have the communication skills necessary to "tell" others of their pain or how they understand the death, but they often "show" how they are experiencing the loss through actions. Table 20.1 serves as a general guide for helpers as they think about the level of vocabulary to employ in counseling a child about death.

As can be seen from Table 20.1, the understanding of death and the cognitive load based on its complexities introduces complications into the grieving process. At least three implications are to be drawn from this observation:

1. As established, those helping with the grieving process must account for cognitive disabilities in their discourse with affected individuals.
2. Because half-truths about the nature of death have the potential to further complicate accessing matters such as irreversibility, the best policy is to answer children's questions with the utmost honesty—while, of course, tuning comments to the child's

developmental age. Consider adjusting the vocabulary based on the accessibility of each concept. For example, one might describe a coffin as, "a box that a dead person's body is put into before it is buried." (See chapter 14 in this book for other concrete ways to talk about death-related issues with children.)

3. Perhaps the strongest implication of the conceptual issues raised here is that death education should be offered to all students with cognitive disabilities. We can think of few instances where this education would not be recommended. Because of their difficulties understanding the phenomena, parents and educators cannot wait until faced with the death of a loved one to start this process. Recommendations for death education curriculum will be addressed in a special section of this chapter, but it certainly should include methods for teaching clearly (meaning concretely) about the meaning of death.

DISENFRANCHISED AND COMPLICATED GRIEF

The death of a significant person may bring about one of the most intense, difficult, and painful experiences of a person's life. As is true of people without disabilities, persons with developmental disabilities experiencing the death of a significant other may require considerable support (Bonnell-Pascual et al., 1999; Lavin, 1989).

Grief is paradoxically universal and unique. Everyone grieves, but how each person grieves is unique. A person's beliefs, social condition, family situation, and relationship with the person who died are all significant in how intensely one experiences the feelings associated with loss (Hollins, 1995; Myreddi & Naryan, 1993). For some, the death of a significant person may bring about feelings of sadness, fear, and confusion (Lavin, 1989). Others may feel indifference or relief (Yanok & Beifus, 1993). Yet for some there may be a combination of intense sadness and a strong sense of relief.

People who are grieving a loss require support, so that they are able to progress through the grief process in a healthy manner. People who provide care for individuals with developmental disabilities (parents, group home staff, teachers) need to recognize that the grief is a primary and significant life event for the people in their care (Hollins, 1995; Lipe-Goodson & Goebel, 1983). Care providers may overlook the grief of people with developmental disabilities who are mourning because care providers may see their role as teaching skills and managing behavior, not as supporting people as they mourn (Hoover et al., 2005; Kauffman, 2005).

Support for a person in mourning can be expressed in a variety of ways. Attending death rituals, such as funerals or memorial services, is something that many people choose to do when a central person in their lives dies. Death rites not only help people understand and accept the reality of death, but also enable mourners to mutually support one another. End-of-life formalities also provide opportunities for mourners to talk about the life and death of the person who died. Many mourners, both people with and without developmental disabilities, find funeral and memorial services to be healing (Luchterhand & Murphy, 1998; National Funeral Directors Association, 1997; Worden, 1996). Mourning the death of a significant person is so important that Huston (1992) wrote, "Grieving without mourning is unhealthy and can lead to emotional or physical complications—even death" (p. 9).

According to Wolfelt (1991), anyone who is able to love is able to grieve; unfortunately, some feel this contingency does not apply to people with developmental disabilities. In fact, some may even believe that people with severe DD are unable to love. Therefore, people with DD are often not given the same level of support in their grief as people without disabilities. As noted earlier, although the cognitive complexities engendered by death render mourning more intricate, this complexity does not mean that mourning lacks meaning in the lives of persons with cognitive disabilities.

Anyone who experiences a significant loss and receives little or no support, is, as Doka (2002) has noted, disenfranchised in their grief. Doka (1989, p. 4) defined disenfranchised grief as "the grief that persons experience when they incur a loss that is not or cannot be openly acknowledged, publicly mourned or socially supported" and suggested that grief can be disenfranchised in three primary ways: (1) the relationship is not recognized, (2) the loss is not recognized, and/or (3) the griever is not recognized and thus not perceived as one with permission to grieve. Another way that grief or the griever may be disenfranchised is that society often disenfranchises some types of deaths, such as death by suicide, AIDS, driving while impaired, or execution (Doka, 1989, 2002). As with people without disabilities, people with developmental disabilities can be disenfranchised for any or all of the reasons Doka suggests. However, the primary reason persons with disabilities are disenfranchised in their grief is that others fail to acknowledge them as grievers. Persons with disabilities may also need to grieve significant life transitions, such as the natural movement of care workers from their current support position to another job or a change in residential placement (home to residential facility, one placement to another). Caregivers may disenfranchise very real grief over such life transitions simply because caregivers do not recognize behavioral manifestations as mourning.

Some care providers believe that if persons with DD are "allowed" to mourn openly, their behaviors could become problematic (acting out their grief, ruminating on the loss, or misbehaving at events). If this acting-out occurs, the behavior should be addressed, no matter how challenging the situation. Much time may be spent supporting people in the process, and care providers may not want or be able to effectively manage the situation. They may also feel that the person with a developmental disability needs to be protected from the pain brought on by a loss (Hoover et al., 2005). Rather than showing support for the loss, the loss is ignored or downplayed. Caregivers might fabricate a "story" about the death or loss (the person who dies is sleeping—see the concept of functionality mentioned earlier—or the dog who was euthanized was given to a good home).

If children with developmental disabilities do not receive necessary grief support, they may experience complicated grief or what has recently come to be called "prolonged grief disorder" (Prigerson, Vanderwerker, & Maciejewski, 2008). Many people who are grieving a loss may feel a sense of sadness, disturbed sleep, and difficulty functioning in daily tasks. These feelings and behaviors generally subside within 2 to 4 months. Prolonged grief disorder, however, is characterized by symptoms of grief lasting longer in duration than what may be expected, by grief symptoms interfering with the normal functioning of the mourner, or by grief being more intense than what others may experience (for example, suicidal thoughts or acts).

It is very important for children to find effective ways to cope with loss and grief because if grief is not addressed effectively, it can negatively affect later relationships and also increase the possibility of adult psychopathology (Edmans & Marcellino-Boisvert, 2002). O'Gorman (1998) has suggested that lack of ritual and death education in childhood is destructive and undermines a child's future development of an optimistic view of life. When individuals are not involved with death rituals, grieving may become extremely difficult. Consider the situation of a nonverbal individual with cognitive disabilities or autism who experiences a significant loss or transition: It is quite possible that language difficulties may render grief complicated because it is objectively more difficult to provide support. The end result may include sleep problems, stereotypical (e.g., repetitive nonfunctional) behaviors, or even the onset of or increases in the frequency and intensity of self injury. Thus, despite the difficulty of involving such individuals in end-of-life rituals, every effort must be made to do so (Hoover et al., 2005).

PARENTAL GRIEF IN DEVELOPMENTAL DISABILITIES

One type of grief, recognized more now than in the past, is the grief that parents of children with disabilities experience. Parental grief is experienced at the time of diagnosis and throughout life (Blaska, 1998; Olshansky, 1962). Grief might be particularly intensely felt by some parents because mortality estimates suggest that many of the same conditions that produce developmental disabilities also result in death during infancy, childhood, or the teen years (Batshaw, 2002). Olshansky referred to the grief that parents of children with cognitive disabilities experience and that does not end as *chronic grief*. He contended that the intensity of the grief changes over time but is constantly present throughout a parent's life. The intensity of the pain depends largely on the circumstances and a parent's personality.

Blaska (1998) contended that parents' unceasing grief manifests not just chronically, but cyclically. Via interviews, Blaska determined that parents of children with disabilities do not continually grieve; rather they experience sadness that comes and goes throughout life.

Some of the events that may generate grief for the parents of children with disabilities are developmental milestones, society's lack of understanding about this specific type of grief, health and behavior issues that their children may experience, and also seemingly insignificant events, such as watching healthy children enjoying themselves playing baseball (Blaska, 1998). Cyclical grief is much like grief that people experience from any significant loss. Though the grief is not always present, grief "bursts" may occur throughout life. These eruptions may be mild or very intense and often occur unexpectedly. Todd (2007) referred to parental grief over the loss of a child with developmental disabilities as "silenced"; the implication is that these parents are often disenfranchised from grieving effectively because of the devaluation of persons with disabilities. Statements such as "perhaps both you and the child are better off" potentially freeze a loving parent's mourning at an incomplete stage in the process.

RECOMMENDED PROGRAMS AND TREATMENT MODALITIES

Death education is essential and can benefit people with developmental disabilities (Yanok & Beifus, 1993). Some curricula are available for people with developmental disabilities, but most of these curricula are intended for adults rather than children. Some curricula used for children without disabilities can be used and modified for children with developmental disabilities.

There are also workbooks about the death of a specific person for children without disabilities that can be used for children with developmental disabilities. For example, Deaton and Johnson (2002) authored a workbook with pages asking different questions about how the child felt about the death of a significant person such as why the person died, what the child feels happens after death, and how the child feels when he or she thinks about the person who died. In particular, Deaton and Johnson ask children to write about their feelings. For children with developmental disabilities who are unable to write proficiently enough to complete the activity, a parent, teacher, or other care provider could write while the child dictates. Other pages ask the child to draw a picture about how he or she is feeling. Some modification may need to be made with materials such as these, but modifications may be fairly easy to make once care providers know the abilities of the child with whom they are working.

Specialists have developed activity-based books that use activities and stories to help children with their grief (e.g., Sorensen, 2008). This type of material can be modified to meet the needs of children with developmental disabilities by rendering the vocabulary mental age–appropriate and via finding concrete ways to illustrate concepts (i.e., using real objects, visits to funeral parlors, and pictures).

Grief support groups for children with developmental disabilities are not common. If the child with a developmental disability is able to find a support group, it is likely to be with children without disabilities. However, some, if not many, children's grief groups will not accept children with developmental disabilities into their groups because of lack of knowledge or experience on the facilitator's part about what to expect from a child with a developmental disability. It may be necessary for agencies working with children with developmental disabilities to organize grief groups specifically for these children.

REFERENCES

American Association on Mental Retardation. (1992). *Mental retardation: Definition, classification, and systems of support*. Washington, DC: Author.

Baroff, G. S. (1986). *Mental retardation: Nature, causes, and management*. New York: Hemisphere.

Batshaw, M. L. (2002). *Children with disabilities* (5th ed.). Baltimore: Paul H. Brookes.

Blaska, J. (1998). *Cyclical grieving: Reoccurring emotions experienced by parents who have children with disabilities*. Eugene, OR: ERIC Clearinghouse on Educational Management. (ERIC Document Reproduction Service No. ED 419 349)

Bonnell-Pascual, E., Huline-Dickens, S., Hollins, S., Esterhuyzen, A., Sedgwick, P., Abdelnoor, A., & Hubert, J. (1999). Bereavement and grief in adults with learning disabilities: A follow-up study. *British Journal of Psychiatry, 175*, 348–351.

Candy-Gibbs, S. E., Sharp, K. C., & Petrun, C. J. (1985). The effects of age, object, and cultural-religious background on children's concepts of death. *Omega, Journal of Death and Dying, 15*, 329–346.

Carter, A. S., Davis, N. O., Klin, A., & Volkmar, F. R. (2005). Social development in autism. In F. R. Volkmar, R. Paul, A. Klin, & D. Cohen (Eds.), *Handbook of autism and pervasive developmental disorders* (3rd ed., pp. 288–311). Hoboken, NJ: Wiley.

Deaton, W., & Johnson, K. (2002). *Someone I love died: A child's workbook about loss and grieving*. Alameda, CA: Hunter House.

Doka, K. J. (1989). Disenfranchised grief. In K. J. Doka (Ed.), *Disenfranchised grief: Recognizing hidden sorrow* (pp. 3–11). Lexington, MA: Lexington Books.

Doka, K. J. (Ed.). (2002). *Disenfranchised grief: New directions, challenges and strategies for practice*. Champaign, IL: Research Press.

Edmans, M. S., & Marcellino-Boisvert, D. (2002). Reflections on a rose: A story of loss and longing. *Issues in Mental Health Nursing, 23*(2), 107–119.

Hollins, S. (1995). Managing grief better: People with developmental disabilities. *The Holistic Healthcare Newsletter, 14*(3), 1–3.

Hoover, J. H., Markell, M. A., & Wagner, P. (2005). Death and grief as experienced by adults with developmental disabilities: Initial exploration. *Omega, Journal of Death and Dying, 50*, 181–196.

Hunter, S. B., & Smith, D. E. (2008). Predictors of children's understandings of death: Age, cognitive ability, death experience and maternal communicative competence. *Omega, Journal of Death & Dying, 57*, 143–162.

Huston, L. (1992, Fall). Helping people with developmental delays to grieve and mourn. *NAPMR Quarterly*, 6–11.

Kauffman, J. (2005). *Guidebook on helping persons with mental retardation mourn*. Amityville, NY: Baywood.

Lavin, C. (1989). Disenfranchised grief and the developmentally disabled. In K. J. Doka (Ed.), *Disenfranchised grief: Recognizing hidden sorrow* (pp. 229–238). Lexington, MA: Lexington Books.

Lipe-Goodson, P. S., & Goebel, B. L. (1983). Perception of age and death in people with mental handicap. *Mental Retardation, 21,* 68–75.

Luchterhand, C., & Murphy, N. E. (1998). *Helping adults with mental retardation grieve a death loss.* Philadelphia: Taylor & Francis.

McLean, M., Wolery, M., & Bailey, D. B. (2004). *Assessing infants and preschoolers with special needs* (3rd ed.). Upper Saddle River, NJ: Pearson.

Mundy, P., & Sigman, M. (1989). Specifying the nature of the social impairment in autism. In G. Dawson (Ed.), *Autism: nature, diagnosis, and treatment* (pp. 3–21). New York: Guilford.

Myreddi, V., & Naryan, J. (1993). The concept of death among people with mental handicap. *International Journal of Rehabilitation Research, 16,* 328–330.

National Funeral Directors Association (NFDA). (1997). *Grief: A time to heal.* Milwaukee, WI: Author.

O'Gorman, S. M. (1998). Death and dying in contemporary society: An evaluation of current attitudes and the rituals associated with death and dying and their relevance to recent understandings of health and healing. *Journal of Advanced Nursing, 27,* 1127–1135.

Olshansky, S. (1962). Chronic sorrow: A response to having a mentally defective child. *Social Casework, 43,* 190–193.

Oltjenbruns, K. A. (2001). Developmental context of childhood: Grief and regrief phenomena. In M. S. Stroebe, R. O. Hansson, W. Stroebe, & H. Schut (Eds.), *Handbook of bereavement research: Consequences, coping, and care* (pp. 169–197). Washington, DC: American Psychological Association.

Oswald, D. P., Ellis, C. R., Singh, N. N., & Singh, Y. N. (1994). Self injury. In J. L. Matson (Ed.), *Autism in children and adults: Etiology, assessment, and intervention* (pp. 147–164). Pacific Grove, CA: Brooks/Cole.

Piaget, J. (1976). *The child and reality.* New York: Penguin Books.

Prigerson, H. G., Vanderwerker, L. C., & Maciejewski, P. K. (2008). A case for inclusion of prolonged grief disorder in *DSM-V.* In M. S. Stroebe, R. O. Hansson, H. Schut, & W. Stroebe (Eds.), *Handbook of bereavement research and practice: Advances in theory and intervention* (pp. 165–186). Washington, DC: American Psychological Association Press.

Rimland, B. (1994). The modern history of autism: A personal perspective. In J. L. Matson (Ed.), *Autism in children and adults: Etiology, assessment, and intervention* (pp. 1–12). Pacific Grove, CA: Brooks/Cole.

Rutter, M., & Bartak, I. (1973). Special education treatment of autistic children: A comparative study, II: Follow up findings and implications for services. *Journal of Child Psychology and Psychiatry, 14,* 241–270.

Slaughter, V. (2005). Young children's understanding of death. *Australian Psychologist, 40*(3), 179–186.

Sorensen, J. (2008). *Overcoming loss: Activities and stories to help transform children's grief and loss.* Philadelphia: Jessica Kingsley.

Stevenson, R. (2009). Children and death around the world. In J. D. Morgan, P. Laungani, & S. Palmer (Eds.), *Death and bereavement around the world: Vol. 5, Reflective essays* (pp. 144–162). Amityville, NY: Baywood.

Todd, S. (2007). Silenced grief: Living with the death of a child with intellectual disabilities. *Journal of Intellectual Disability Research, 51*(8), 637–648.

Volkmar, F. R., & Klin, A. (2005). Issues in the classification of autism and related conditions. In F. R. Volkmar, R. Paul, A. Klin, & D. Cohen (Eds.), *Handbook of autism and pervasive developmental disorders* (3rd ed., pp. 5–41). Hoboken, NJ: Wiley.

Wolfelt, A. (1991). *A child's view of grief* [video]. Fort Collins, CO: Center for Loss and Life Transition.

Wolfensberger, W. (2000). A brief overview of social role valorization. *Mental Retardation, 38*(2), 105–124.

Worden, J. W. (1996). *Children and grief: When a parent dies.* New York: Guilford.

Yanok, J., & Beifus, J. A. (1993). Communicating about loss and mourning: Death education for individuals with mental retardation. *Mental Retardation, 31*, 144–147.

21

Pediatric Palliative and Hospice Care

STACY F. ORLOFF AND SUSAN M. HUFF

Children are precious gifts. We expect to watch them grow, and we look forward to those moments and memories that define parenthood. Experiencing the death of one's child is not on the list of those anticipated moments. In our scientifically advanced society, despite modern medicine and state-of-the-art technology aimed at prolonging life, children die. As a society, we neither acknowledge nor cope well with this loss. Most children die from conditions related to development and birth, some tragically from accidents or trauma, and others from chronic illness that leads to premature death. The stresses associated with caring for children with chronic illness and their impending death often result in needless suffering and devastating consequences for both the affected child and his or her family. When tragedy strikes, pediatric palliative and hospice care can minimize the suffering and harm that children and families incur associated with the death of a child (Children's International Project on Palliative/Hospice Services [ChiPPS], 2001).

In 2003 the Institute of Medicine (IOM) published a landmark report titled *When Children Die: Improving Palliative and End-of-Life Care for Children and Their Families* (Field & Behrman, 2003). Written with expert testimony from both professionals and parents, this seminal report served as the impetus for many sweeping organizational changes throughout the country. Policy advocates across the United States used

413

the findings to propose legislative and policy changes aimed at enhancing care for children and their families.

The IOM report acknowledged that a child's death has devastating and enduring impact on the family and larger community. The report further states that improved care is possible, but current methods of organizing and financing palliative, end-of-life, and bereavement care make providing services difficult. Palliative care programs should be integrated in the care continuum and should be available to families during the diagnostic process. Palliative care staff must communicate with families in a timely fashion and in a way that reflects the family's values and background. This approach allows parents to consider all available care options when making decisions regarding their child's plan of care (Field & Behrman, 2003).

Suggesting the integration of palliative care at diagnosis presents challenges to the traditional way of thinking about how and when hospice care is offered. Pediatric palliative and hospice care are two distinct methods of delivering care that can be provided at home, in the community where one lives, surrounded by family and friends. In communities or homes that are not safe and do not provide a source of comfort, care at home may not be an option and alternative settings are available.

This chapter presents an overview of pediatric palliative and hospice care, including unique challenges in identifying and serving this vulnerable population, when to make a referral, and models of care. Throughout the chapter, the term "children" refers to the perinatal period before birth, infants, children, and adolescents.

BACKGROUND

Approximately 53,500 children die annually in the United States, with infants under a year old accounting for almost half of this number (Centers for Disease Control and Prevention, 2008). Deaths resulting from congenital anomalies and chronic conditions are escalating, with accidents, trauma, cancer, suicide, and homicide accounting for the remainder. There are many more children living with the possibility of a premature death. Approximately 400,000 children in the United States struggle every day with chronic life-threatening conditions, and most of these children will not live to adulthood. This number will continue to rise as treatment modalities improve, increasing the odds of survival.

Where do childhood deaths take place? Almost 85% occur in a hospital, most in an intensive care unit or in the emergency room (Carter, Hubble, & Weise, 2006). Less than 20% of dying children in the United States are even referred to a hospice program (National Hospice and Palliative Care Organization [NHPCO], 2009). We know less about the death rate of children enrolled in a palliative care program because of the limited existence of programs and the lack of published data. However, there is recent evidence to show deaths at home are increasing in children with chronic conditions (Feudtner, Feinstein, Satchell, Zhao, & Kang, 2007). This report has been the first hint of a change in the place of death for children in decades. The review of deaths between 1989 and 2003 by Feudtner and his colleagues found that 22.1% were attributed to complex chronic conditions. Of those, the percentage of individuals dying at home increased significantly. Infant deaths at home increased by 2.5%; 1- to 9-year-old home deaths increased by 13%, and 10- to 19-year-old home deaths by 14%. National educational efforts supporting the need for quality pediatric palliative and hospice care services and the development of new technology used at home to care for children with complex conditions may be factors influencing these changes.

The number of deaths attributed to children pales in comparison to the vast number of adult deaths; however, the impact on families left behind and on the future of society is profound. We have a responsibility to protect our children and advocate for the health of siblings and families of the future. An increasing body of evidence demonstrates that delayed implementation of hospice and palliative care interferes with the treatment of pain and symptoms, coordination of care, effective communication, preparation for death, and ability to achieve the child's and family's goals related to quality of life (Freibert & Huff, 2009).

DEFINING PALLIATIVE AND HOSPICE CARE

Palliative care aims to improve the quality of life of patients facing life-threatening illness and their families through the prevention and relief of suffering by early identification of pain and accompanying symptoms, whether physical, psychosocial, or spiritual (World Health Organization, 1990). It is a concept of care that is not yet regulated, is provided in various settings, is not yet clearly defined, and has limited reimbursement potential within our current system of health care. Pediatric palliative care is often described as both a holistic philosophy of care and an organized method for delivering care to any infant, child, or adolescent diagnosed with a life-limiting condition. Services provided to children and families focus on enhancing quality of life, preventing and/or minimizing suffering, managing pain and symptoms, optimizing function, and providing opportunities for personal and spiritual growth. As such, care can be provided concurrently with life-prolonging treatment and curative care, or with care in advanced disease at the end of life. Anticipatory grief and bereavement services are offered to siblings, family, and significant others. Embracing a holistic approach, therapies should assist children and families in fulfilling their physical, social, developmental, educational, and spiritual goals while remaining sensitive to personal, cultural, and religious values, beliefs, and practices.

Pediatric palliative care is planned and delivered through the collaborative efforts of an interdisciplinary team (IDT) including the child, family, and caregivers. Effective palliative care also recognizes the need to support the caregivers and team who do this special work (NHPCO, 2009).

In contrast, hospice has been clearly defined and federally regulated since the early 1980s in the United States. Hospice care requires a license under which each hospice provider must offer services administered by these core disciplines: nursing, social work, pastoral care, volunteers, and bereavement. Traditionally, hospice care is offered when a decline is evident, curative treatments become questioned, and life expectancy is usually measured in months. The origins of hospice care are rooted in the holistic approach to care. Services are aimed at optimizing quality of life, reducing pain and symptoms, and providing spiritual support and bereavement care for the family. Hospice offers individuals a voice and supports their decisions to die with dignity, in comfort, while respecting values, cultures, religious desires and while the person is surrounded by family and friends, in a setting that supports his or her needs.

Interdisciplinary teams in both hospice and palliative care work in tandem to meet goals of care set forth by the child, family, and the medical team. Each member of the team may address different aspects of care with respect to his or her specialty; however, they all communicate and work together toward common goals. The IDT consists of disciplines trained to deliver support to children of all ages and their families in the physical, psychosocial, and spiritual domains. A team may consist of physicians, nurses, social workers, chaplains, physical therapists, occupational therapists, child life specialists, art or music therapists, psychologists, and pharmacists. Any discipline that is truly involved in providing care to the child and family should be a part of the team meetings. The frequency of IDT meetings should reflect the individual nature of the care, the child's and family's needs, and any regulatory requirements. A particular challenge is communication between settings. Preserving communication between the children's hospital and the palliative care or hospice team is vital. All teams must ensure that care is well coordinated and integrates the child's and family's decisions with their family's values and beliefs, their culture, and their communication systems. Table 21.1 compares and contrasts palliative care and hospice care.

There are several differences between adult and pediatric hospice and palliative care (Carter & Levetown, 2004). Children die from different diseases and conditions than adults do; therefore, the preparation, the care, and the trajectory of the illnesses are not the same. Children's general physiologic resiliency complicates predictions about their future. Many children who die early in life are born with rare medical conditions, with associated uncertainty in diagnosis, prognosis, and medical management. Children are not small adults, and their care should not mimic adult care. Many practitioners who care for adults often want to focus on the similarities in care, not understanding that the unique differences drive the important components of care delivery. Developmental differences among infants, children, and adolescents affect diagnosis, prognosis, treatment strategies, communication, and the decision-making processes. All of these areas present challenges to providers who do not have training or experience in caring for children.

Gaining experience caring for various age groups is often difficult in settings where there is not a concentrated population of children. Often rural areas and suburbs do not have access to major pediatric health centers. When expertise is not established, assessment and evaluation prove challenging, resulting in seriously ill children and their families traveling far from home for treatment. This approach fragments care and removes children from their logistical, emotional, and spiritual sources of support, frequently disrupting parents' employment and straining family relationships and finances.

Another critical difference between the care of adults and children is that children do not have a legal voice. They are represented by their parent or legal guardian, unless considered an emancipated adult. In the majority of situations, parents or guardians have the legal authority to make decisions about medical treatments for their child. Most states will not recognize a formal advance directive signed by a minor, even a minor who is living independently. Hospice and palliative care principles

Table 21.1

DIFFERENCES BETWEEN PALLIATIVE AND HOSPICE CARE

QUESTION	PALLIATIVE CARE	HOSPICE CARE
Eligibility	Varies between programs Life expectancy may be measured in years	Life expectancy measured in months
Treatment goals	Adjustment to illness Coping with changes Relief of pain/symptoms Retain quality of life Treatment focus is cure Return function	Quality of life Treatment focused on comfort, relief of pain, and symptoms Supportive care Dignity in death Bereavement for family
Providers	Hospitals Home health care agencies State waiver programs Community programs	Hospice certified agency
Where services are available	Hospital Home Hospice facility	Home Special hospital beds Short-term stay facilities Long-term facilities Hospice facilities
Services	Varies Nursing Social work Chaplain/pastoral care Child life Art/music therapy Volunteers Respite Bereavement	Nursing Social work Chaplain/pastoral care Bereavement Volunteers Home health aide Child life Art/music therapy Respite Pharmacy, DME, IV
How it is paid for	Philanthropic donations Grants, special state or federal funding (Medicaid waivers) Home health benefits (limited services)	Hospice benefit (accessed through most insurances, Medicaid, Medicare) Philanthropic donations

address this issue and recommend respecting parents' or guardians' decisions while encouraging assent from children who are able to comprehend and participate in decisions regarding their care.

Children are members of many communities, including neighborhoods, places of worship, and schools. Their roles within these communities should be incorporated into their plan of care. School is an integral part of children's lives at all ages, and it is essential that they have ongoing opportunities for education and peer interactions. Relationships with siblings are also unique and an important aspect of the developmental process for the sick child and siblings. Consideration of siblings' needs and the relationship the sick child has with siblings adds to the complexity of caring for children and their families. The needs of divorced families, stepfamilies, and other nontraditional families must also be met. Children are dependent on the adults who care for them and the relationship they have within their family unit. All these families bring both blessings and challenges for the pediatric hospice and palliative care team.

CHILDREN WHO MAY BENEFIT FROM PALLIATIVE CARE

All children with life-limiting conditions and their families deserve access to palliative care, either as the primary goal of treatment or concurrent with disease-modifying or curative therapies. Delays in the inclusion of pediatric palliative care services are associated with increased physical, emotional, and spiritual suffering of children and their families.

Many health care professionals struggle with the delivery of bad news, including when and how to discuss hospice care with children and their families. In reality, many of these same health care professionals also struggle to discuss palliative care even when it can be helpful early on in the diagnosis. Preliminary research shows that professional education regarding communication may help to increase clinician comfort and proficiency (Browning & Solomon, 2005). Practitioners should ask themselves the following questions when considering a palliative care referral: "What are the chances this child will live to adulthood?" "Could this family use supportive resources to help them cope and adjust to caring for this child?" "Do siblings need support?"

Table 21.2 describes four groups of diagnostic categories, with examples of what types of patients should be afforded hospice or palliative care services with or without continuing curative or disease-modifying treatments. Below is a case example of palliative care initiated at diagnosis.

Table 21.2

REFERRAL CONSIDERATIONS

GROUP	EXAMPLE DIAGNOSES	PALLIATIVE CARE	HOSPICE CARE
I. Conditions where curative treatment is attempted, but there is risk of failure	Cancer Severe congenital or acquired heart disease	Consider referral at diagnosis with high-risk cancers or presence of metastatic disease Following a relapse Multiple acute-care admissions during treatment; wanting to be home, back to school	Unresponsive to standard therapies; when offered Phase I studies No longer a candidate for surgical intervention Desire for care at home
II. Conditions for which premature death is inevitable; faces long periods of treatment, stable periods, relapse, and complications	Cystic fibrosis Chronic renal failure Duchene's muscular dystrophy	May be difficult to offer referral at diagnosis; usually is years before decline is experienced Consider referral with trend of multiple acute-care admissions Psychosocial support would benefit family functioning, coping with needs related to illness	When acute-care stay or treatment no longer presents a benefit; care at home or in long-term care facility is desired Respite care is needed
III. Progressive conditions with no curative treatment options	Leukodystrophies Tay-Sachs Trysomy 13, 18	Consider referral at diagnosis	Consider referral at diagnosis
IV. Irreversible non-progressive conditions, with complex health care needs leading to multiple complications and high likelihood of premature death	Birth asphyxia Micro anencephaly Severe seizure disorder	Consider referral at diagnosis to set the stage for long-term support; may graduate and pick up later in disease trajectory	Consider referral at diagnosis especially with serious complications Respite care is needed

David was 15, a sophomore in high school studying art and design, when he was tragically diagnosed with a rare cancer in his abdomen. Since his parents' divorce, David had been living with his mother and brother Joshua, age 17. David's father had recently remarried and had a newborn son. David had been estranged from his father since the birth of the new baby. David loved school and skateboarding. After surgery to remove his tumor, the palliative care team was introduced to David prior to hospital discharge. David had a central line placed and was in need of home nursing to manage wound care, central line care, side effects from chemotherapy, and blood work. David received chemotherapy for almost a year after recovering from surgery. He went in and out of the hospital during this time while receiving care at home from the palliative care team. His team at home consisted of a nurse, social worker, and a child life specialist. Goals of care were individualized and included the following: (1) David—returning to school, keeping up with schoolwork and peer relationships, adjusting to the illness, and managing physical changes; (2) Joshua—addressing guilt related to not being the one sick, working on communication with peers about David's status, coping with depression related to watching David physically deteriorate and suffer during chemotherapy treatments; (3) David's mother—addressing communication issues with David's father, managing feelings of helplessness related to David's condition, dealing with worry over attention and care of Joshua; (4) David's father—wanting to improve the relationship with his sons and remain central in decision making.

The palliative care team made visits at home to David and his family weekly to monthly for 1 year before David suffered a relapse, including metastatic disease to the lungs. His second round of chemotherapy was unsuccessful. During a discussion with his oncologist, home care nurse, and mother, David asked to stop all chemotherapy and go home. He worked with the child life specialist for 2 weeks on how to get up enough nerve to actually say the words out loud to his mother and his doctor. He wanted to stop his experimental chemo because it was not working. In David's words, "Everyone is going to die sometime. I don't want to be sick and not be able to see my friends or go to school in the next few months." His mother and father argued with David, but through counseling and support of the social worker, their parish priest, and the palliative care chaplain, they agreed to honor his wishes.

David lived another 4 months with supportive care at home. He and his family went on a Make-A-Wish trip to Cancun. He healed the relationship with his father, became a big brother to the newest member of his family, and went away on a weekend trip with his brother and friends 2 weeks before he died, with his pain management pump and meds in tow, despite his mother's trepidation. He designed a tee shirt distributed to all his friends at his funeral and completed a skateboard instruction video with his friends and the child life specialist. When it came to the end, his mother was fearful of his dying in their small apartment. She was afraid of being alone, and David's pain was severe, his tumor burden extreme. The family persevered with support from their palliative care team at home and their oncology team at the hospital. Communication between settings was key to respect David's desires and fulfill his needs. He died on his couch, surrounded by his family.

On a bereavement visit at home 2 weeks after David's death, his mother said to the nurse and social worker, "Almost 2 years ago, we were a different family until this cancer invaded David, and I would never have thought we would need you. I didn't even understand what this team was when we first met you. David lived the last year of his life better than any of us had before the cancer. You all have become an intimate part of our lives, and I thank you for helping our family." David was enrolled in a palliative care program at diagnosis. He died 18 months later. He would not have been eligible for hospice until 4 months prior to his death.

MODELS OF CARE

There are many different models of pediatric palliative care and pediatric hospice care. Special consideration must be given to regulatory compliance and meeting the needs of specific populations served, such as the adolescent patient, diverse cultures and religious/spiritual beliefs, and perinatal loss. Regulatory requirements and rules for payment are an integral consideration in developing programs. Program administrators must consider reimbursement regulations as well as grant funding and charitable dollars when designing programs (Knapp, Thompson, Vogel, Madden, & Shenkman, 2009). Program administrators must also consider the needs of the population being served. Caring for an adolescent with a life-limiting illness/condition is very different from caring for a 2-year-old. The bereavement needs of a family whose child died suddenly may vary from a family whose child died after a long illness. A pregnant woman informed that her pregnancy is not going to result in the birth of a live healthy child has different needs than does a mother whose child died of a chronic illness after 15 years. Cultural, religious, and spiritual beliefs will impact access to palliative care and hospice care. Successful programs design services with this level of understanding.

The United States has several different care models in which children and their families may access both palliative care and hospice care. The following program models will be described here: home health care, home- and community-based waiver programs (typically offered through a Medicaid-certified home health agency), home-based hospice care, and hospital-based palliative care and hospice care.

There are distinct advantages to each care model. Some, such as home health care and Medicaid waiver programs, offered early in the diagnostic process are less fearful to parents who are often afraid of giving up hope or hearing a "death sentence."

Home Health Care

Home health care is part of a medical benefit that approves short-term care provided to patients in their home when they are recovering from an illness, do not need hospital care to complete their recovery, and are considered to be "homebound." Homebound is a term insurance providers use to determine whether "home health care" is approved. It is a strict requirement used in determining care for adults at home; however, insurers are less strict with this requirement with children needing medical care at home. This requirement varies between states and insurance providers.

Home care services must be prescribed by the child's physician. The child's safety is important, and the home environment is assessed to ensure it is adequate for ordered treatment or therapies to be administered at home. Services offered in the home include nursing; social work; physical, occupational, speech, and respiratory therapy; medical supplies; and equipment. These services assist the parent or guardian to take care of the child with a goal of returning the child to his or her normal level of functioning. Home care is not meant to provide total care for the ill child; it supplements the care that family members or friends provide. Many children receiving home health care will also actively participate in providing their own self-care.

In some states pediatric palliative care programs have been developed within home health programs. There are advantages and disadvantages to providing palliative care to children through a home health program. Home health care in the United States is highly regulated and as such has very clear rules about the scope and frequency of services. This scope and frequency are identified by the medical skill needed that dictates the visit type and the reimbursement of services. The challenge in providing palliative care within a home health program is that not all palliative care services are reimbursed, and typical reimbursement is for a limited amount of visits. Most services are reimbursed as a fee for service, so non-reimbursable services must be funded by other sources. A home health agency may choose to provide services that are beyond third-party payment; however, many free-standing home health agencies cannot afford to provide non-reimbursable care. This constraint often leads to home health agencies providing primarily medical or nursing-based palliative care. Social work services may be reimbursable; it depends on the payer and the reason for social work assistance. Often, the scope and frequency of social work care is limited. Spiritual care support is rarely offered from a traditional home health agency because it is not a reimbursable service. Home health agencies providing additional services outside of nursing such as social work, spiritual care, or child life specialists must do so with much creativity and private funding sources.

Children who are home health patients typically receive curative, life-sustaining care for their illnesses/conditions. In active treatment, many of these children have uncontrolled pain and may benefit from pain management from a palliative care physician, nurse, or nurse practitioner with advanced training and expertise in pain management. Parents do not want their children to be in pain, and a pain consult is often an "easy" way to introduce palliative care to parents and the child. Once the practitioners have successfully managed the child's pain, the parents are often more willing to consider accessing additional palliative care services.

Essential Care Program is an example of a pediatric palliative care program. Established in 1988 in Buffalo, New York, it has an active census of 30 patients a day. It was developed within a home health care company, with services supported by the community, private funds, donations, and grants. Services provided at home include nursing, social work, child life, music/art therapy, pastoral care, psychology, and volunteers. The greater Buffalo community identified unmet needs for the pediatric patient population and collaborated with a local hospice organization that holds a home health license, a university-based hospital system, and the greater pediatric community to develop a model where children and families could experience a seamless transition from diagnosis through end-stage care and into bereavement.

Reimbursement and funding are the primary barriers that prevent this program from growing. In fact, at one point in time, the active daily census averaged 50 pediatric patients a day. However, this census required fundraising close to $500,000 annually to keep services going. That factor and others led to the decision to decrease census in the last few years.

Essential Care works directly with the acute care hospitals to provide consultation and visits by the palliative care team before patients go home and then again if patients are readmitted. Approximately 60% of all oncology patients are referred upon diagnosis. Patients and families are introduced to their home care team by the oncology team in the hospital. Relationships built at the beginning of the diagnosis foster trust and rapport between the palliative care team, the child and family, and the acute care team. Eighty-five percent of patients cared for in Essential Care choose to die at home.

Medicaid Waiver Programs: Home- and Community-Based Waivers

Since the Institute of Medicine report was published in 2003, many states have begun initiatives to develop new programs and services to serve children with life-limiting illnesses/conditions. Policy initiatives and advocacy efforts for pediatric hospice and palliative care are at an all-time high. Among these policy and advocacy changes are various Medicaid pediatric palliative care demonstration programs. To date, three states have currently received federal approval for Medicaid demonstration programs (Florida in 2005, Colorado in 2007, and California in 2008). Many other states are considering applying for a Medicaid waiver or finding other ways to authorize payment for palliative care services while the ill child is continuing to receive care for his or her life-limiting illness/condition. Prior to these Medicaid waiver programs, children and families had little opportunity to access such care. Additionally, providers were limited in what they could offer children and families because of regulatory requirements and lack of reimbursement.

Section 1915(c) of the Social Security Act allows states to request a waiver of federal Medicaid requirements to offer additional community support services to Medicaid beneficiaries who would otherwise require institutional care. These programs can be used to fund services not normally provided, such as respite care, home modifications, and non-medical transportation. These waivers can also be used to provide additional Medicaid services such as case-management and personal assistance services (O'Connell & Watson, 2001).

Home- and community-based waiver programs provide flexibility so that waiver programs can offer a variety of services that meet the needs of the population to be served. Federal regulations allow programs to serve the elderly and people with physical disabilities, developmental disabilities, mental retardation, or mental illness. States may also choose to develop programs by focusing on specific illness or conditions, such as technology-assisted children or individuals with AIDS (O'Connell & Watson, 2001).

Children who are Medicaid recipients may access palliative care services through such a home- and community-based waiver provider. It is possible for a licensed home health care agency to apply for provider status and offer palliative care services. It is believed that many pediatric home health agencies are underutilizing this opportunity. Many of them are unaware of these different Medicaid waivers and have not applied for provider status.

Perhaps the most well-known home- and community-based waiver in the pediatric hospice and palliative care community is the Children's Hospice International Program for All-Inclusive Care for Children and Their Families (CHI PACC). In 1996 Children's Hospice International (CHI) began a series of conversations with members of the U.S. Congress and pediatric hospice and palliative care leaders across the country. What came from those early conversations was a new model of care known as CHI PACC (Lowe et al., 2009).

The CHI PACC model offers palliative care services from the time of diagnosis of a life-limiting illness/condition with hope for cure through bereavement if the child dies. All CHI PACC programs must establish and implement consistent goals of care across the care continuum. These goals reflect the values, hopes, and beliefs of each individual child and his or her family. Care is interdisciplinary and reflects the child's developmental stage, spiritual beliefs, and choices.

In 2005 the Center for Medicare and Medicaid Services approved Florida's 1915(b)(3) waiver to implement a CHI PACC program called Partners in Care: Together for Kids. This demonstration program is a public/private partnership with the Agency for Health Care Administration (Medicaid), the Department of Health's Children's Medical Services Network (CMSN, Title V Children with Special Health Care Needs), and Florida Hospices and Palliative Care, Inc. Children must meet the

CMSN medical eligibility criteria and be diagnosed with a life-limiting condition.

Partners in Care: Together for Kids services include counseling (individual, family, group), music, art, play therapy, inpatient respite, in-home respite, hospice nursing care, personal care, and pain and symptom management. All these services are available to children and their families, all while the ill child continues to receive curative or life-prolonging care for his or her life-limiting illness/condition. What is remarkable about this waiver program is that Medicaid will pay for the counseling services for any immediate family member of the child, even if the child is not present for the counseling. Traditional Medicaid payment is typically only for the Medicaid recipient; services are not generally offered to the extended family (Lowe et al., 2009).

After two statewide trainings, the initial seven pilot sites were able to enroll children. Children may be enrolled at any point during their treatment process. As the program has progressed, additional sites have been added. To date over 600 children and their families have been cared for in this waiver program. Research has shown that service utilization has increased, patients and families are satisfied with the services, and patients and families report better understanding of the impact of the illness/condition on the larger family (Knapp et al., 2008).

Pediatric Hospice and Palliative Care Programs

In spite of the best care possible, some children will die. Many children who received palliative care and life-saving care will at some point qualify for hospice care. Hospice care is a benefit for Medicare, Medicaid, and private insurance recipients whose physician has certified they have a life-limiting illness or condition with a life expectancy of 6 months or less.

In order to qualify for hospice care, a patient must forego further curative life-prolonging care and accept comfort care. As one might imagine, the decision to forego curative care is very difficult for parents of seriously ill children. It may only be after they have exhausted all of their palliative care options previously described in this chapter that the family is willing to accept hospice care.

According to NHPCO (2009), a goal of hospice care is to ensure that all people have access to a pain-free and dignified end of life. Hospice services are offered through the interdisciplinary team, with each child and family at the center of care directing what services they would like. The hospice patient and family have access to nursing, medical, psychosocial, home-health aide care, and spiritual support. Additional services include hospice volunteers and inpatient residence.

Children admitted into hospice care are offered a full spectrum of services in their home or wherever the child resides. In the United States, the majority of hospice care for children is provided by community-based hospices in the child's home (NHPCO, 2004). This arrangement, however, is not the only model of pediatric hospice care. There are hospital-based pediatric hospice and palliative care programs and community-based pediatric hospice programs that are partnered with a local children's hospitals to provide both inpatient and home-based hospice care.

There are many hospice programs across the United States that provide care to children with life-limiting illnesses/conditions. An NHPCO (2008) survey of its member hospices conducted in order to better understand the scope of care currently offered elicited responses from approximately 400 out of over 2,500 hospices. One-third of the hospices who identified themselves as serving pediatric patients have a formal pediatric hospice/palliative care program that includes specially trained staff. Most of these same hospice programs provide care in the child's home. One-third offer palliative care consults. Far fewer provide in-patient palliative care. Hospices that do not provide care to children identified limited access to trained pediatric staff during the day and "after hours" as a major barrier to providing care. Many hospices also identified having other established programs in the area as a barrier. What is interesting is that these other established programs are primarily acute care providers—not other hospice or palliative care programs. Competing programs minimize patient base and affect referral patterns.

Recently, NHPCO (2009) approved the first national pediatric standards for hospices that currently provide care to children or want to develop pediatric programs. The standards define state-of-the-art pediatric practice for hospice and palliative care and revolve around 10 components of quality care. Organizations should use these best practice standards to assure the delivery of safe, effective, and quality care to children and families. The standards are available free to any member of NHPCO and can be accessed on their Web site at http://www.nhpco.org/pediatrics. Readers may also access this Web site for archived issues of NHPCO's ChiPPS e-newsletters. These newsletters contain additional information related to pediatric palliative and hospice care.

Hospice houses have existed for many years in European countries, with 34 currently opened and directly serving children and their families (EAPC Task Force on the Development of Palliative Care in Europe, 2005). Still, it was not until 1995 that Canuck Place in Vancouver, Canada, opened its doors as the first hospice house in North America, serving children with life-limiting illnesses in British Columbia (http://www.canuckplace.org). In 2004, the George Mark Children's House (GMCH) opened in San Leandro, California. A large 15,000-square-foot home, GMCH offers three different types of services: respite care, transitional services, and end-of-life care. There is no time limit to any of these services, so children and their families may access care in the home from diagnosis through bereavement (http://www.georgemark.org). Other pediatric hospice houses have been developed in Canada and are in development in the United States.

The following examples of hospice programs highlight different care models. Each is a unique example of how creative program development creates important partnerships and provides seamless care to children and families, regardless of care setting. These programs have met the needs of their unique populations including diverse cultures, pregnancy loss, and sudden loss. These programs and partnerships include freestanding community-based hospice programs that offer palliative care and hospice care, hospital-based palliative care programs, and hospital- and home-based palliative care and hospice care programs. They all exemplify the different care models described in this chapter.

The palliative care program at Lucile Packard Children's Hospital at Stanford in Palo Alto, California, was launched in 2001. It evolved out of two major needs assessments (Contro, Larson, Scofield, Sourkes, & Cohen, 2002, 2004) that documented the needs from bereaved families and interdisciplinary staff. The program was conceptualized as a full academic program: The clinical service is at the hub, with components of education, research, and advocacy. The interdisciplinary consultation team meets twice monthly. A newly established clinical meeting addresses the needs of children and families that have been referred. Anyone—family members or staff—may request consultation from the palliative care team. The palliative care team works collaboratively with others in the hospital, including the pain and symptom management team. A nurse and physician from that team overlap with the palliative care team to specifically address palliative referrals. Over the last few years, the palliative care team has received between 200 and 250 referrals.

The palliative care team ensures collaboration with all care partners (including community partners) so that children and families have
one consistent care plan. Primary services include managing distressing
symptoms, both physical and emotional; facilitating communication between and among children, families, and professionals; consulting on the
care of healthy siblings; and planning for present and future choices and
decisions in patient care. Transition to hospice home care upon hospital
discharge is coordinated as part of discharge planning.

The palliative care team is very involved in research. Ongoing research areas include a focus on multiculturalism given that over 45%
of the population served are Spanish-speaking families, many of whom
are impoverished migrant workers and do not speak English. Additional
research focuses on bereavement needs.

Children's Hospitals and Clinics of Minnesota in Minneapolis, Minnesota, offers an extensive care continuum for children with life-limiting
illnesses/conditions and their families. Hospital-based care includes the
pain and palliative care interdisciplinary consultation team. Pain services
include an inpatient rounding team, as well as the chronic pain clinic and
consultations. Palliative care focuses on aggressive pain and symptom
management, holistic, supportive care for the child and family, and improved linkages and coordination among all sites of care: home, hospital,
clinics, and school.

Home-based care includes the Karuna palliative care program. This
program provides interdisciplinary team support for children who are
not expected to live to adulthood and their families. The focus of the
care is families, emphasizing symptom management, comfort, and continuity of care.

The hospital also offers hospice care. The focus of the hospice program is to help each child live as fully as possible even when death is expected. Holistic care is available for the dying child and family through
an interdisciplinary team, which provides a broad array of services
within the home setting and in the hospital. Support is also available
for the broader community, including extended family and the school
community.

The Deeva perinatal hospice program is another home-based program. This program provides support for families who choose to continue a pregnancy when informed the fetus has fatal anomalies. It offers
support in pregnancy, at the time of the birth, and in follow-up after
delivery. If families choose to go home with their child, they can become
part of the hospice or Karuna programs.

The hospital also provides education and support to the community through the Children's Institute for Pain and Palliative Care, a lending library called The Caring Place, and grief and bereavement support through home visits to bereaved families and bereavement support groups for families and the community, including schools.

Suncoast Hospice in Clearwater, Florida, provides an extensive array of services to children with life-limiting illnesses/conditions and their families. Their specialized children's program began in 1983 and includes a wide continuum of care programs. Care programs include counseling for families during the course of life-sustaining treatment, perinatal support for pregnancy loss, Partners in Care: Together for Kids (a Medicaid demonstration program), palliative care home health (and access to different home- and community-based Medicaid waivers), hospice care, and bereavement counseling for families impacted by the sudden death of a child.

Families may refer themselves for palliative care counseling assistance, including individual, family, and group support. Families may also request spiritual care support. Trained adult and teen volunteers are able to provide help with child care, homework assistance, "buddy support," transportation, and lifetime legacy and creative memories (scrapbooking and video life review). The child's physician may request a palliative care consult with the hospice's pediatric medical director. Suncoast Hospice also has an extensive perinatal loss program. Staff includes volunteer doulas trained in perinatal loss and pediatric social workers and nurses. The doula advocates for the mother to ensure that her individual needs are met and that she has an opportunity to acknowledge the pregnancy by saying hello and goodbye. The doula service also provides "care kits" that include a special baby book for loss and books on bereavement for fathers, mothers, siblings, and grandparents. If the pregnancy results in a live birth, the team will work with the family to arrange for hospice support.

The Partners in Care Program has been described in a previous section of this chapter. Suncoast Hospice has been a participant in this demonstration program since its inception in 2004.

Suncoast Hospice is also certified as a home health provider, and many children are patients in the home health program. In addition to traditional home health services, all children and their families are offered the same services as the palliative care program and traditional hospice patients (full range of psychosocial, spiritual care, and volunteer assistance). The hospice is a provider for several different home- and community-based waivers described previously in this chapter.

Specially trained pediatric nurses and social workers coordinate hospice care for children who meet medical eligibility for the hospice benefit. Children and their families have access to the full range of hospice services. Additional services are customized for the pediatric patient, such as pharmacy and durable medical equipment needs.

Bereavement counseling (individual, group, family) is available for families whose children may have died suddenly (whether from trauma or illness) or without benefit of hospice or home care services.

Additional services include annual specialized events for families. These social gatherings provide opportunities for families to meet each other in a nonthreatening way. The program has also offered a weekend bereavement camp for children for over 25 years, a weekend retreat for bereaved families, and a day retreat for bereaved adolescents.

CONCLUSION

The different program models discussed in this chapter show the variability in pediatric palliative and hospice care development. Communities have been forced to think outside the realm of hospice regulation to create innovative models to meet needs. Both hospice and palliative care embrace a family-centered holistic approach to care. Palliative care can be offered early in the disease process, but access is affected by lack of a consistent reimbursement mechanism that allows for program growth. Few programs exist beyond the hospital setting, and children want to be home. More research is needed to determine program efficacy and measure patient and family satisfaction. We also need to better understand the long-term bereavement needs of families: those who received palliative and/or hospice care and those who did not. The newly developed program standards are the first step in ensuring quality and consistency in care. Current providers of services should unite and work together to gather data for the support of evidence-based practice in this growing field.

REFERENCES

Browning, D., & Solomon, M. (2005). The Initiative for Pediatric Palliative Care: An interdisciplinary educational approach for healthcare professionals. *Journal of Pediatric Nursing, 20*(5), 326–334.

Carter, B., & Levetown, M. (Eds.). (2004). *Palliative care for infants, children, and adolescents.* Baltimore, MD: Johns Hopkins University Press.

Carter, B. S., Hubble, C., & Weise, K. L. (2006). Palliative medicine in the neonatal and pediatric intensive care unit. *Child and Adolescent Psychiatric Clinics of North America, 15,* 759–777.

Centers for Disease Control and Prevention. (2008). *United States death statistics.* Retrieved January 22, 2009, from http://www.disastercenter.com/cdc

Children's International Project on Palliative/Hospice Services (ChiPPS) (2001). *A call for change: Recommendations to improve the care of children living with life threatening illnesses.* Alexandria, VA: National Hospice and Palliative Care Organization. Retrieved January 15, 2009, from http://www.nhpco.org/pediatrics

Contro, N., Larson, J., Scofield, S., Sourkes, B., & Cohen, H. (2002). Family perspectives on the quality of pediatric palliative care. *Archives of Pediatric and Adolescent Medicine, 156,* 14–19.

Contro, N., Larson, J., Scofield, S., Sourkes, B., & Cohen, H. (2004). Hospital staff and family perspectives regarding the quality of pediatric palliative care. *Pediatrics, 114,* 1248–1252.

EAPC Task Force on the Development of Palliative Care in Europe. (2005). *Hospice and palliative care directory UK and Ireland 2005.* Retrieved February 20, 2009, from http://www.eapcnet.org/download/forPolicy/CountriesRep/UnitedKingdom.pdf

Feudtner, C., Feinstein, J. A., Satchell, M., Zhao, H., & Kang, T. I. (2007). Shifting place of death among children with complex chronic conditions in the United States, 1989–2003. *Journal of the American Medical Association, 297,* 2725–2732.

Field, M. J., & Behrman, R.E. (2003). *When children die: Improving palliative and end-of-life-care for children and their families.* Washington, DC: National Academies Press.

Freibert, S., & Huff, S. (2009, February). NHPCO's pediatric standards: A key step in advancing care for America's children. *Newsline,* 8–13.

Knapp, C., Madden, V., Curtis, C., Soyer, P., Huang, I., Thompson, L., et al. (2008). Partners in care: Together for kids: Florida's model of pediatric palliative care. *Journal of Palliative Medicine, 11,* 1212–1220.

Knapp, C., Thompson, L., Vogel, W., Madden, V., & Shenkman, E. (2009). Developing a pediatric palliative care program: Addressing the lack of baseline expenditure information. *American Journal of Hospice and Palliative Medicine, 26,* 40–46.

Lowe, P. A., Curtis, C. M., Greffe, B., Knapp, C., Shenkman, E., & Soyer, P. J. (2009). Children's hospice international program for all-inclusive care for children and their families (CHI PACC). In A. Armstrong-Dailey & S. Zarbock (Eds.), *Hospice care for children* (3rd ed., pp. 398–438). New York: Oxford University Press.

National Hospice and Palliative Care Organization (NHPCO). (2004). *Caring for kids: How to develop a home-based support program.* Alexandria, VA: Author.

National Hospice and Palliative Care Organization (NHPCO). (2008). *2007 Pediatric Services Survey.* Unpublished report. Alexandria, VA: Author.

National Hospice and Palliative Care Organization (NHPCO). (2009). *Pediatric palliative care standards.* Alexandria, VA: Author.

O'Connell, M., & Watson, S. (2001, March). *Home and community based waiver programs.* Retrieved January 17, 2009, from http://www.nls.org/conf/waiver.htm

World Health Organization. (1990). *Definition of palliative care.* Retrieved February 16, 2009, from http://www.who.int/cancer/palliative/definition/en

Psychotherapeutic Approaches for Children With Life-Threatening Illnesses

22

MICHELLE R. BROWN AND BARBARA SOURKES

Psychotherapy is a treatment modality unique to mental health clinicians, and within its framework, the child seeks to integrate the facets of his or her life (Sourkes, 2000). For the child with a life-threatening illness, psychotherapy can provide the opportunity for the expression of profound grief and for the synthesis of all that he or she has lived in an abbreviated life span. Through words, art, and play, the child conveys his or her experience of living with the threat of loss. Typically, these children are well-adjusted individuals dealing with tremendous stress. Psychopathology is the exception rather than the rule. As such, the goal of psychotherapy is not only symptom reduction, but also to bear witness to and respond within the context of the child's extraordinary situation (Sourkes, 1995). As Erich Lindemann explained in reference to his work with children during the polio epidemic of the 1950s,

> These are young people who suddenly have become quite a bit older; they are facing possible death, or serious limitation of their lives; and they will naturally stop and think about life, rather than just live it from day to day. A lot of what they say will be reflective—and you might respond in kind. It would be a mistake, I think, to emphasize unduly a psychiatric point of view. If there is serious psychopathology, you will respond to it, of course; but if those children want to cry with you, and be disappointed with you,

and wonder with you where their God is, then you can be there for them. (as quoted in Coles, 1990, p. 101)

When is a referral for psychotherapy indicated? Sadness and anxiety are typical and expected reactions to prolonged illness and treatment. As such, psychotherapy is not universally necessary for all children facing life-threatening illnesses. Yet under sustained stress, such responses may progress to disabling clinical disorders that may ultimately necessitate psychotherapy and/or psychotropic medication. This need is especially true in the child with preexistent vulnerabilities, or when there is a prior psychiatric history in the child or a family member. Differential diagnosis can be challenging even for mental health providers given that normal emotions of sadness and grief overlap with the symptoms of a clinical depression (e.g., crying, decreased appetite, difficulty sleeping, and decreased attention and concentration) (Kersun & Shemesh, 2007; Shemesh et al., 2005). By assessing the severity of symptoms, particularly in terms of intensity and duration relative to the child's current reality, the mental health clinician can determine if psychotherapy is necessary, or whether existing supportive services (e.g., child life, chaplaincy, ongoing relationships with physicians and nurses) would suffice.

INDIVIDUAL PSYCHOTHERAPY

The therapeutic approaches employed in individual psychotherapy are determined in part by the child's age and developmental level. Thus, knowledge of normal psychological development is essential to evaluate the impact of illness, to provide developmentally appropriate explanations, and to identify appropriate psychotherapeutic interventions. Conceptions of death have been thought to generally correspond with the progression through four sequential stages of cognitive development (Poltorak & Glazer, 2006). It is important to note, however, that there is considerable variability in how children think about death at any age or level of cognitive development and that children with a life-threatening illness often possess an advanced understanding of death relative to their healthy, same-age peers (Bluebond-Langner, 1996; see also chapters 2 and 8 in this book).

During infancy and toddlerhood, children hold little, if any, understanding of death. Rather, death is equated with separation from caregivers. By preschool, most children develop an awareness of death.

However, they are less likely to recognize that death is universal, an inevitable outcome for all living things including themselves and loved ones (Poltorak & Glazer, 2006). Lacking the concept of irreversibility, young children are also unlikely to understand the permanence of death. Thus, a young child of a deceased sibling may continue to ask days after his passing when her brother will be returning home. Additionally, preschoolers' limited understanding of cause and effect may lead them to wrongly infer causality when such events have coincided closely in time with their own actions or thoughts, referred to as magical thinking. For example, a 4-year-old may perceive herself as responsible for "catching cancer" after refusing her mother's request to wear a coat earlier that morning. Even older children may demonstrate such magical thinking despite their simultaneous ability to recognize the irrationality associated with such reasoning. Within the context of psychotherapy, such beliefs can be explored, and misconceptions can be clarified.

Through ages 6 to 12, children typically develop logical reasoning skills and are able to understand more objective causes of death. In general, they also grasp that all functions of the living physical body cease to exist at the time of death. Yet children's fears of death remain primarily centered on the concrete fear of being separated from parents and other loved ones. By adolescence, abstract reasoning enables them to anticipate the future in a way that younger children often cannot. The experience of death for the adolescent becomes more focused on existential issues related to an afterlife, similar to that seen in adults.

For younger children in psychotherapy, play can be a crucial vehicle of communication. The fantasy afforded by play is what allows reality to be integrated. Through play, children can advance and retreat from the intensity of their illness at will, thereby allowing a sense of command over their emotional experience. Furthermore, the fantasy expressed through play is often thinly veiled and thus reveals the child's experience even when not directly addressed. The clinician's willingness and ability to enter into the play are of utmost importance because shared imaginative play enables the child to confront the realities of life and death (Sourkes, 1995).

For older children, psychotherapy can facilitate psychological adjustment by enabling discussions around their illness and prognosis, sensitive topics that may be avoided by family and friends (Brown & Sourkes, 2006). Responding to questions about their illness and prognosis, or about the possibility of their death, requires careful exploration of what is already known by the child, what is really being asked (the question behind the question), and why these questions are being asked at this particular time (Brown & Sourkes, 2006; Sourkes, 1992). At times, clinicians may find themselves caught "off guard" by difficult questions, leaving them unsure how to respond. In such instances, responses can be deferred by reframing the question (e.g., "Is that something you've been thinking about?"), postponing an answer (e.g., "I'm not sure about that. Let me think about it, and I will get back to you"), or redirecting the question to the appropriate individual ("I don't know the answer to that. Perhaps we can ask your [doctor, parent, teacher] that question"). In this way, the clinician communicates a sense of openness to such questions while ensuring a measured response.

The therapeutic relationship in and of itself may be a profound intervention, even when issues of death and loss are not explicitly addressed, for it can provide a sense of stability and continuity during a time that may otherwise feel chaotic and unanchored. Often, mental health providers working with children facing a life-threatening illness feel pressured to elicit the child's emotions around his or her illness and prognosis, perhaps erroneously perceiving this task to be a requisite component of a therapeutic intervention. However, such therapist-driven goals are not necessarily therapeutically indicated. Rather, mental health clinicians should follow and respect children's cues to ensure that they are not overtaxing their defenses or diminishing their sense of control.

Because some children may not understand the clinician's role or the process of psychotherapy, it is important that simple, nonthreatening explanations be offered to the child. Terms such as "the talking doctor" provide a functional description that clearly distinguishes the therapist from other professionals on the medical team (Sourkes, 1995). Anxiety about seeing a therapist is often reduced when children are told that their feelings are common to all children and that therapy can help them feel less distressed. When the concept of confidentiality, or privacy, is introduced early on, children may feel relieved to disclose thoughts or feelings that they have been reluctant to share with others.

THEMES OF LOSS THAT OFTEN ARISE IN PSYCHOTHERAPY WITH CHILDREN

Themes of loss are central to the psychotherapeutic work with the ill child. Actual and/or feared losses include the child's sense of identity, control, and overwhelmingly, relationships. From an early age, children define themselves according to physical attributes (e.g., "I am a girl because I have long hair"), participation in activities (e.g., "I am an honor student, a soccer player"), and their relationships to others (e.g., "I am a daughter, a best friend"). Thus, manifestations of illness often have a major impact on a child's sense of personal identity. The visible markers of illness, whether temporary or permanent (e.g., hair loss, drastic changes in weight, stunted growth, wheelchair dependence, amputation), can lead to feelings of inferiority and low self-esteem. Compounding the child's own difficulty in adjusting to an altered body image is the fear of others' shock and revulsion at his or her appearance. Such shame and embarrassment can lead to children refusing to return to school and withdrawing from other activities. In turn, the maintenance of preexisting relationships and the development of new peer relationships are hindered (Easson, 1985).

Restrictions imposed by illness and treatments interfere with experiences through which children ordinarily develop their sense of competence, self-worth, and positive self-esteem (McSherry, Kehoe, Carroll, Kang, & Rourke, 2007). School is the defining structure of normal life for all children and affords opportunities for achievement in both academic and extracurricular/social domains. Yet school attendance for children with a life-threatening illness is often sacrificed to hours spent at clinic visits, in outpatient treatment, in hospitals, and at home. Less visible effects of the disease process and its treatment, including neurocognitive deficits and altered mental status, can significantly impair academic and social functioning. Overwhelming fatigue commonly limits children's ability to remain in school full-time and thereby reduces opportunities for learning as well as socialization.

Often, children are labeled as "difficult" or "noncompliant" by caregivers when their behavior is notable for anger and/or resistance to their treatment regimen. Yet in most instances, these children are merely acting out their inordinate difficulty in coping with a sense of total powerlessness. Once the meaning of this anger is acknowledged, and the caregiving environment is structured to allow for as much control as feasible, the child's behavior usually changes dramatically.

A six-year-old boy refused his oral medications, required physical restraint for daily blood draws, and prohibited the medical team from examining him. The psychologist determined that several factors contributed to his difficulties: multiple, unexpected visits by staff he did not know; procedures done without any explanation of their purpose or forewarning before touching him; and no opportunity for him to make any decisions in his care. A plan was created such that the number of visits by treatment team members was limited and scheduled; his physicians and the child life specialist provided him with age-appropriate explanations of his illness and related treatment; and the boy was also given the choice of which arm to use for taking his blood pressure, as well as which stickers he wanted after taking his medications. Within a few days, the child was entirely cooperative with his treatment regimen and demonstrated a remarkable decrease in anger, frustration, and anxiety. (Sourkes et al., 2005, p. 370)

Typically, children also have very little control over the decisions that are made regarding their treatment plan. Decisions during the end-phase of life are particularly difficult: The parents do not want their child to suffer more, yet they often cannot tolerate the thought of ending life-prolonging or curative treatment, of "leaving any stone unturned." The child's quality of life is often central to parents in finding the balance between aggressive interventions and the cessation of life-prolonging treatment. In most instances, the parents make the decisions; however, to varying degrees, the child may be involved in such discussions. Because children often express their understanding, awareness, and thoughts about treatment options, as well as living/dying, to individuals other than their parents or primary physician, the psychotherapist can be an important liaison during various junctures in treatment.

A ten-year-old child with medulloblastoma deliberated with her therapist the pros and cons of continuing chemotherapy after a second relapse. She noted, "…I had two choices and I didn't want to take either of them. One of the choices was to get needles and pokes and all that stuff to make the tumor go away. My other choice was letting my tumor get bigger and bigger and I would just go away up to heaven…My mom wanted me to get needles and pokes. But I felt like I just had had too much—too much for my body—too much for me…So I kind of wanted to go up to heaven that time…But then I thought about how much my whole entire family would miss me and so just then I was kind of like stuck." (Sourkes et al., 2005, p. 368)

Parents and/or treatment providers may hold differing opinions regarding the treatment goals. Physicians may encourage a family to continue an aggressive course of treatment when the parents are concerned about the pain and suffering associated with such a treatment approach. Alternatively, physicians may hold little hope for cure and encourage a transition to comfort care while the family wishes to exhaust every possible treatment option. Differing priorities may also lead to misunderstandings between the child/family and provider. These failures in communication are especially likely when curative and comfort care are perceived as mutually exclusive. For example, a child's behavior might be perceived as nonadherent when medications or procedures that are time-consuming or painful are missed. However, the child may simply value quality of life and comfort above curative efforts. Physicians may be reluctant to negotiate terms of a prescribed treatment regimen knowing that such changes could reduce the treatment effectiveness or jeopardize a child's long-term prognosis. In this vein, the psychologist plays a vital role as liaison between the child, family, and treatment team in order to facilitate communication and reduce the risk of misunderstandings around the treatment plan.

> A twelve-year-old girl being treated for relapsed leukemia asked her physician to delay her scheduled chemotherapy in order to participate in her school play in which she had a leading role. Both she and her mother recognized the potential risks associated with postponing treatment but felt that such risks were worth taking given the uncertainty of her prognosis. Although the physician was initially reticent to provide less than optimal medical care, he acknowledged their wish and agreed to the family's request.

PSYCHOTHERAPEUTIC TECHNIQUES

Within psychotherapy, self-help techniques, including relaxation, guided imagery, and hypnosis, are integral in providing children with a sense of control over symptoms such as anxiety, nausea, and pain. Children and caregivers alike have reported dramatic reductions in both physical and emotional distress as a result of these strategies (Kazak, 2005; Kazak et al., 1996; Kersun & Shemesh, 2007; Steif & Heiligenstein, 1989). Furthermore, regardless of the actual impact of such techniques on symptoms, most children report an increased sense of well-being resulting simply from their perception of exerting control.

> An eight-year-old girl complained of phantom limb pain following leg amputation. During hypnosis, she was instructed to identify the switch in her head that could turn off incoming pain messages from various parts of her body. After one session, she reported a greater sense of control over

her pain and her discomfort appeared significantly reduced. (Brown & Sourkes, 2006, p. 592)

Psychotherapeutic techniques can also assist children in restoring a sense of control over emotions that are often experienced as overwhelming. Specific play-therapy techniques allow unstructured associative communication to be combined with a highly focused intervention. For a detailed review of play and art therapy techniques, please refer to Sourkes (1995).

Use of Stuffed Animals, Puppets, and Dolls

Therapeutic toys can be valuable tools in exploring concerns that may be too threatening or overwhelming for a child to discuss directly. By integrating a stuffed animal, puppet, or doll in a sustained way over time, it can function as a bridge between the child's internal emotional experience and the outside world. The toy can be brought into the psychotherapeutic process by introducing it simply as one of the clinician's toys, or the toy may be presented with a more focused agenda. In the latter instance, the clinician may draw attention to the toy and disclose that it is being treated for the same illness as the child. Most children are intrigued by this connection (even if skeptical) and question the clinician about the toy's experiences. Through this commonality, an alliance is formed between the child and the toy. For a child who is receptive to this form of play, the identification with the toy and the projective process do not take long to establish. Once this identification has occurred, the clinician can utilize the toy as a means of indirectly assessing the child's fears and anxieties as well as validating the child's experience by attributing similar feelings to the toy. The toy may be useful in preparing a child for a new medical procedure or practicing a new coping technique by modeling it first on the toy. This strategy also provides the child with an opportunity to experience some mastery over events that previously have been out of his or her control.

> Jessie, an 8-year-old girl, was referred to psychotherapy for treatment of procedural anxiety around blood draws. The medical team noted that Jessie would become aggressive (e.g., hitting, spitting, screaming) during her weekly procedure. Because her behavior was so difficult to control, additional staffing was required. Upon her first therapy session, Jessie was introduced to Penny, a porcupine puppet, who also required weekly blood

draws. Through her discussions with Penny, Jessie was able to express her fear and anger around the procedure and her illness, and Penny was able to teach Jessie skills that she used to manage similar feelings. Within a few sessions, Jessie was able to tolerate her blood draws without any disruptive behavior.

Creation of a Book

Children are often intrigued by the idea of writing (or dictating) and illustrating a book about their experience of illness. As with the therapeutic stuffed animal, the book becomes an intermediary between the child and the therapist, allowing more threatening material to be presented than what might be discussed directly. Themes of illness can be clearly stated or may be embedded within some other storyline. Such books may be composed in one session or over an extended period of time.

The Therapist's Monologue

In this technique, the therapist articulates what the child is believed to be thinking or feeling, without any expectation of reaction from the child. The monologue should be used extremely selectively, reserved for those situations where the therapist judges that the child simply cannot form the words independently but is longing to be understood. These are times when the child is withdrawn, either too exhausted physically to talk or paralyzed by intense vulnerability. However, through the therapist's monologue, the child hears the actual "unsayable" words framed in a context, feels understood, and thus experiences reconnection and relief. These therapeutic effects are often manifested dramatically through words, body language, or behavior.

The therapist may talk about the child directly, allude in more general terms to how "some children feel," or use a therapeutic stuffed animal as the subject. The therapist should speak slowly, calmly, and repetitively, not emphasizing any one point over another. The therapist should proceed from peripheral to more central issues in a gradual stepwise approach, allowing the child time to absorb what is described at each level. The child need only listen, or answer yes or no to questions. Often the yes is signaled simply through sustained attention.

A four-year-old boy had refused to speak to anyone for days during a difficult hospitalization. Prior to the onset of the silence, he had cried about having to leave his new puppy at home. After greeting the boy and receiving no response, the therapist began talking about "kids being angry and sad." The child listened intently as the therapist said, "Kids are angry that they have so many things done to them when they are in the hospital...They are mad because needles hurt...Kids hate to be bothered all the time when they are trying to sleep...They are sad that they can't be home with their families...and they can really miss their puppies too." The therapist continued, now involving a nurse who had just come into the room:

> *Therapist:* I bet that he misses his puppy. Do you know his puppy's name?
> *Specialist:* No, I don't know its name.
> *Therapist:* Me neither.
> *Child:* [whispering] It's Chance.

The child became teary at this point and allowed the therapist to sit closer to him and play with some of his toys.

Art therapy can also be a powerful tool to facilitate the child's expression and integration of complex experiences. Structured art techniques allow the therapist to pose questions earlier in the process and with more specificity than might be done through verbal means alone. Further, children who have been unable or unwilling to articulate their feelings verbally often communicate their experience through drawings.

Feelings Circle

The feelings circle is a tool for facilitating expression of emotion either generally or more specifically around a particular topic (e.g., "how I felt when I heard that I had cancer"). In this activity, children are presented with a number of feelings written on separate cards that might include shocked, scared, sad, angry, or hopeful. With markers or crayons, the child is then asked to match a different color to each feeling. Next, the child is given a piece of paper with an outline of a circle drawn in the center and is instructed to color in the circle such that the amount of space used by each color is proportional to the size of the feeling it represents. If the feeling was big, then it becomes a big part of the circle; if it was small, a smaller area is colored in. When the circle is complete, the clinician and child can discuss the feelings and colors that were chosen. Because the feelings circle requires little time and minimal exertion or coordination, it can be used even with a child who is very ill. Most children find the technique nonthreatening and enjoyable, and they often express relief at having an array of feelings already articulated for them.

Change-in-Family Drawing

The kinetic family drawing is a widely used art therapy technique. The child is asked to draw a picture of the entire family engaged in an activity together. The drawing is then analyzed for the child's perception of his or her position within the family and the nature of the family relationships. Sourkes (1995) has added another step to this technique to explore the child's perceptions of the impact of his or her illness on the family. After the child has completed the basic family portrait, the therapist asks, "What changed in your family after you got sick? Show the change in your drawing either in picture or in words." The responses to this simple question are often dramatic and can be used for any before-and-after situation.

Life Map

A life map can be used in the early stages of therapy as a way of getting to know the child and all that he or she has been through or can be organized around a more specific time period. In general, the therapist draws a winding road on a blank piece of paper. If birth is the starting point, the therapist or child may draw a building at the beginning of the road to represent a hospital or their first home. Often, more typical milestones are then added along the road such as the start of school, any changes in residence, significant life events, or even fond memories such as family vacations. With that framework established, the therapist can then inquire about events specifically related to the child's illness such as age at diagnosis and treatment course. The life map also offers the opportunity to incorporate plans for the future as a way of discussing the child's hopes as well as fears.

Children's picture books are a useful tool to introduce the subject of illness and the concept of death. By reading the book aloud, the clinician is able to query about the child's thoughts and feelings indirectly through the characters in the story. Furthermore, it allows the child to project his or her own experience onto the characters or may even incite the child to discuss related topics directly. Activity books can also be used as a way to structure a discussion around the topic of illness or death. These books can be useful when a child is uncomfortable disclosing information through less structured activities or when a therapist is less certain how to guide a discussion around such sensitive topics. Corr (2004; see also the appendix in this book) has provided an extensive review of death-related literature for children.

ANTICIPATORY GRIEF

Although issues of identity and control belong primarily to the child, the loss of relationships is shared by both child and family. Anticipatory grief (i.e., grief associated with the threat of loss) is often profound. Commencing at the time of diagnosis, its manifestation throughout the illness trajectory will differ depending on whether the child is living with a life-threatening diagnosis, but doing well; the child is going to die, but not imminently; or the child is actually dying (Aldrich, 1974).

Anticipatory grief may show itself in various ways. Most often, a child will demonstrate increased sensitivity to separation, without any specific reference to death. Examples include insistence on sleeping with parents, refusal to attend school without a parent present, and declining invitations to social activities in order to stay home with family. The child might also project concern about himself or herself onto a significant adult, usually a parent or the therapist (Sourkes, 1995). On one level, the child recognizes his or her extreme dependence on the adult and is terrified at the thought of something happening to that person. On another level, the child is expressing fear about his or her own situation through this mirror image. At least initially, the projection is best left untouched because the child is clearly communicating extreme vulnerability.

> An 8-year-old girl had only recently immigrated to the United States when she was diagnosed with cancer. When hospitalized, she spent many hours alone because her mother was home caring for her younger sibling. During an early session with her therapist, she began to sob and through her tears exclaimed, "I'm so worried about my mom. She works so hard, and I don't think that she gets enough food to eat. I don't want her to get sick. She has no one here to help her."

The child's grief related to the possibility of his or her own dying may also be veiled in questions about others. Often, the child will make an isolated statement or pose one question and then, without further comment, turn to other subjects. As in all other communications, the therapist must stay close to the immediate concern, leaving the child in control of how far to pursue the topic. In addition, as the child confronts death, signs of preparation can be quite matter-of-fact with no elaboration.

> A 6-year-old boy approaching end-of-life focused intently on his video game while his mother read silently at his bedside. Suddenly, as if to no one in particular, he questioned aloud, "I wonder what grandma looks like up in heaven," and then returned his attention back to his game.

> Upon learning that curative treatments had been exhausted, a 9-year-old boy without explanation offered his treasured baseball card collection to a best friend.

An upsurge of jealousy or resentment toward well siblings may manifest in the sick child as the end of life approaches, often reflecting the sick child's fear of replacement (Brown & Sourkes, 2006). This fear may find expression either directly or through play. Although the child's fear of replacement cannot be eliminated entirely, it certainly can be worked through in psychotherapy and assuaged by the parents' reassurance. A preoccupation with being replaced usually signifies the child's need to talk about his or her life-threatening situation, with particular focus on the fear of death. In addition, the child is often speaking for the family's difficulty in negotiating the possibility of loss.

> The mother of a seven-year-old boy who had recently relapsed noted that he had become unusually hostile to his younger brother. Although they previously had been close playmates, the child had become bossy, argumentative, and even physically assaultive towards his sibling. He also became extremely protective of his mother's time, limiting the individual attention she could provide her youngest son. (Brown & Sourkes, 2006, p. 595)

Anticipatory grief is not static but fluctuates with periods of lesser and greater presence. Families may panic over separation when a condition is stable and death is not imminent. Or in contrast, a denial of impending loss may occur when time is short. These seeming inconsistencies arise from the fact that the child and family can simultaneously live within two distinct realities: one based on logic and finite time and the other based on hope and belief in endless time. Members of the treatment team who are unaware of children's ability to fluidly shift between these two realities often mistake the child's fantasy life for ignorance or denial (Brown & Sourkes, 2006). When a child facing death refers to future dreams, those individuals who struggle to balance the reality of prognosis with hope may rigidly comment, "Doesn't that child know he is going to die? Someone needs to tell him." Adherence to magical beliefs to the exclusion of impinging reality may signify fear and dysfunction. However, most children and families flow between the two worlds in a normal adaptive process. Psychotherapy can play a vital role in supporting this process.

FAMILY PSYCHOTHERAPY

Family therapy can play a pivotal role in sustaining, strengthening, and repairing family resources. The profound and enduring impact of the child's illness on the family is addressed within this context. Family therapy does not in any way preclude individual psychotherapy with the child; rather it affirms the family unit as a whole (Sourkes, 1995). Family therapy is often provided in combination with individual psychotherapy to help open the lines of communication between children and their family about topics that parents are uncertain how to approach.

Over the past two decades, a shift toward open communication has become more evident. Although the protective stance of the past maintained that disclosure to children of their prognosis (and even, in some instances, the diagnosis) would increase anxiety and fear, it is now generally believed that shielding children from the truth only serves to heighten anxiety and leave them feeling isolated, lonely, and unsure of whom to trust (Sourkes, 1995). A recent study (Kreicbergs, Valdimarsdóttir, Onelöv, Henter, & Steineck, 2004) supporting this notion found that bereaved parents who had discussed impending death with their child had no regrets about doing so. This report was in sharp contrast to regrets expressed by some of the parents who had avoided such openness.

When facing the death of their child, many parents attempt to keep the possibility of death hidden from their children, with the hope of shielding them from unnecessary anguish. They may discourage questions from the child (e.g., "You don't need to worry about that") or provide overly optimistic responses (e.g., "You are going to be just fine"). In essence, their efforts to limit information are aimed at gaining control over the pain and suffering that their child must endure. Some parents fear that discussion of death may impede their child's ability to maintain hope or lead care providers to "give up" rather than provide the maximum care possible. Parents may also be reluctant to discuss impending death with their child because they personally feel overwhelmed by the reality of the prognosis and feel unable to provide requisite emotional support to their child as they are struggling to cope with their own distress.

While respecting parental wishes, team members can help parents talk through their own terror and can share their professional knowledge from work with other families caught in this same excruciating situation. Through these discussions, parents may begin to understand that many young children already know what is happening to them, even when it has been purposely left unspoken by the adults. Specific examples of a child's own awareness may even be provided to the parent through a drawing or a comment made by their child in therapy. Thus, parents come to appreciate how shielding children from the truth may inadvertently heighten their anxiety and cause them to feel isolated, lonely, and unsure of whom to trust. Because the most basic tenet of parenthood is absolute trust, most parents can realize the need for responding honestly to their child's questions or fears. Perpetuating the myth that "everything is going to be all right" takes away the chance to explore fears and provide reassurance. For example, children may blame themselves for their illness and the hardships that it causes for their loved ones. Their guilt can be addressed and resolved only by open, honest communication, requiring a sensitive response that takes into account the child's developmental stage and unique lived experience. As a caveat, overriding all of these factors must be a sensitivity to cultural beliefs and traditions.

In general, the individual child's competence and vulnerability serve as the context for decisions regarding disclosure at any point in the illness trajectory. Considerations about what to tell or how much include the child's age, cognitive and emotional maturity, family structure and functioning, cultural background, and history of loss. These same factors apply at end-of-life, with extreme sensitivity to how the parents have chosen to inform the child throughout the illness experience, how the child has understood and processed information up to this time, and what the child is not asking—both implicitly and explicitly—about his or her situation (Abrahm & Sourkes, 2004; Sourkes, 1995).

Beyond issues of disclosure, the therapist can also enhance the parents' understanding of and competence with their child. By sharpening their observation and listening skills, they become partners in the therapeutic process (Sourkes, 1995). When parents are kept informed about the direction of the child's therapy, their grasp of the child's emotional experience is further deepened. In this context, it is important that the therapist explain the importance of any object to which the child has become attached during the psychotherapy. For example, once the parents understand the role of the therapeutic stuffed animal or doll as "alter ego," that object can be incorporated into their conversations with the child. This inclusion provides the child and parents an additional route of communication with one another and extends the therapy into daily life. Relaxation techniques are valuable for the parents to learn with the child, so that eventually they can help him or her through medical procedures or at home. Any means of intervention that the therapist can provide for the parents to use with the child is an antidote to their helplessness.

SIBLINGS

A focus on the well siblings must be an aspect of the family work. Too often, the siblings stand outside the spotlight of attention, even though they have lived through the illness experience with the same intensity as the child and parents (Sourkes, 1987). Healthy siblings experience many of the same issues as the ill child: loss of control and predictability over their schedules, loss of a personal identity (e.g., being identified exclusively as the sibling of a dying child), and loss of interpersonal relationships (because of changes in routine that exclude them from their normal social opportunities) (McSherry et al., 2007). The healthy siblings share common questions and concerns; some they raise with parents, professionals, or another trusted adult; others they harbor silently.

Typical sibling concerns may include the fear of becoming ill, guilt about escaping the disease, and anxiety resulting from a lack of information or misinformation (Sourkes, 1987). Rarely mentioned but often present is the unacceptable feeling of shame at having a "different" family, marked by an ill sibling who is disfigured or dying. Siblings may harbor anger around diminished attention and nurturance from their parents, especially when the child is in the hospital. Siblings who themselves are feeling deprived may also resent stepping in as surrogate parents for younger brothers and sisters. Once the ill sibling is home, well siblings may resent the extra attention and privileges accorded to the ill child, shifting their complaint from that of "too little attention" to "preferential treatment." Parents, meanwhile, struggle to maintain equality and normality when, in fact, a distinctly "abnormal" factor in the family constellation exists (Sourkes et al., 2005). Another common issue is that of siblings' anger at parents for not having been able to protect the patient, or even their perception that the parents (by commission or omission) played a role in the cause of the illness.

Siblings' academic performance may suffer because of their preoccupation, or they may focus on school to assert a sense of competence in the face of stress and helplessness. Similarly, siblings may restrict contact with peers in their need to focus on family, or they may turn increasingly to their friends for support or to flee the pain at home. Commonly, physical symptoms and sleep problems are experienced by healthy siblings. In some instances, psychosomatic symptoms symbolically represent a sibling's concerns or fears (e.g., the sibling of a child with a brain tumor who develops intense headaches).

CULTURAL CONSIDERATIONS

In geographic areas with a complex mix of ethnicities and cultures, care providers cannot be expected to be experts in the background of all of the families they serve. However, through sensitive and thorough inquiry, important information can be gleaned that promotes therapeutic relationships based on mutual understanding and respect. Some important areas to explore in this regard include the following: (1) how the family's ethnic, cultural, or national background impacts their experience in the hospital and with caregivers; (2) whether the family is a member of the dominant ethnicity in the medical environment or is in the minority (special attention should be directed to immigrant and minority families); (3) the presence of cultural or linguistic barriers, overt or covert, that may affect their experience; (4) the beliefs and values related to childhood illness, death, medical care, and family involvement; and (5) the unique roles that the patient/family and extended community play in their culture.

It remains questionable whether the prevailing principles of Western culture are relevant to children and families of different cultural origins. For example, although open communication is emphasized in Western medical practice, other cultures exclude children from discussion of disease diagnosis and death (Liben, Papadatou, & Wolfe, 2008). For instance, in Chinese culture, discussion around the possibility of death in the presence of a sick person can be perceived as a curse or effort to hasten death. Some cultures perceive that honest discussions about dying deprive children of the sense of safety and security associated with the innocence of childhood and rob parents of their role as protector from harm.

Culturally defined health beliefs and practices can significantly influence acceptance of and adherence to prescribed therapies, the degree and quality of parental involvement in patient care, and the family's relationship with health care staff. Behavior that is viewed in isolation without consideration of the cultural context is often misinterpreted by treatment providers. For example, "resistances" observed among many Asian Americans (hesitancy to open up, tendency to give limited information) may be mislabeled (Lee, 1982). Whereas openness may be embraced by European Americans, many Asian Americans have been taught that premature disclosure of emotions to a stranger is an indication of lack of self-control and immaturity and is a cause for shame. Similarly, a mother from a patriarchal sociocultural system may be regarded by a medical team as passive or uninvolved because of her silence during discussions about medical treatment or her refusal to consent to procedures in the absence of her husband. Yet according to her cultural norms, acting otherwise may be considered reprehensible. As a cultural broker, the therapist can raise awareness of cultural influences, thereby facilitating understanding, communication, and the development of a treatment plan that is congruent with a family's cultural heritage (Trill & Kovalcik, 1997).

FUTURE DIRECTIONS

The advancement of medicine and technology has enabled children with life-limiting illnesses to live longer than ever before. Yet the goal of medicine is not simply to extend the days of a child's life, but also to add life to their remaining days (American Academy of Pediatrics, 2000). The newly emerging field of pediatric palliative care offers unique opportunities for mental health clinicians to participate in enhancing the quality of life of our most vulnerable children and families. Historically, mental health clinicians have remained on the periphery in the care of children with life-limiting illnesses rather than serving as core members of the interdisciplinary treatment team (Bearison et al., 2005; Haley et al., 2003; Nydegger, 2008). Whereas mental health clinicians are trained in the assessment and treatment of psychiatric disorders, limited educational curricula exist around translating such clinical skills to this specific population of children and families. Interdisciplinary trainings (see, e.g., Children's Project on Palliative/Hospice Services, National Hospice and Palliative Care Organization, http://www.nhpco.org/pediatrics; and the Initiative for Pediatric Palliative Care, http://www.ippcweb.org) are inclusive of psychosocial issues and provide a cohesive framework for understanding the complexity of the field. Additional efforts aimed at expanding awareness in mental health professions are needed to increase their integration as the field continues to evolve.

Children with life-threatening conditions live in two worlds: the world of medicine (with all the attendant physical and emotional stressors) and the wider world of family, school, and community. Negotiating each of these individual orbits—and the interface between them—is an ongoing challenge, even for the most resilient children. Psychotherapy can facilitate children's optimal coping and adaptation and, in so doing, enhance their quality of life.

REFERENCES

Abrahm, J., & Sourkes, B. (2004). Palliative care. In R. Hoffman, E. Benz, & S. Shattil (Eds.), *Hematology: Basic principles and practice* (pp. 1639–1645). Philadelphia: Elsevier Science.

Aldrich, C. (1974). Some dynamics of anticipatory grief. In B. Schoenberg, A. Carr, & A. Kutscher (Eds.), *Anticipatory grief* (pp. 3–9). New York: Columbia University Press.

American Academy of Pediatrics, Committee on Bioethics and Committee on Hospital Care. (2000). Palliative care for children. *Pediatrics, 106,* 351–357.

Bearison, D., Cohen, I., Kazak, A., et al. (2005). *Report of the Children and Adolescents Task Force of the Ad Hoc Committee on End-of-Life Issues.* Retrieved March 15, 2009, from http://www.apa.org/pi/eol/final_pediatric_eol_report.pdf

Bluebond-Langner, M. (1996). *In the shadow of illness: Parents and siblings of the chronically ill child.* Princeton, NJ: Princeton University Press.

Brown, M. R., & Sourkes, B. (2006). Psychotherapy in pediatric palliative care. *Child and Adolescent Psychiatric Clinics of North America, 15*(3), 585–596.

Coles, R. (1990). *The spiritual life of children.* Boston: Houghton Mifflin.

Corr, C. A. (Ed.). (2004). Death-related literature for children [Special issue]. *Omega, Journal of Death and Dying, 48*(4).

Easson, W. M. (1985). The seriously ill or dying adolescent. Special needs and challenges. *Postgraduate Medicine, 78*(1), 183–184, 187–189.

Haley, W., Larson, D., Kasl-Godley, J., et al. (2003). Roles for psychologists in end-of-life care: Emerging models of practice. *Professional Psychology: Research and Practice, 14,* 626–633.

Kazak, A. E. (2005). Evidence-based interventions for survivors of childhood cancer and their families. *Journal of Pediatric Psychology, 30*(1), 29–39.

Kazak, A. E., Penati, B., Boyer, B. A., Himelstein, B., Brophy, P., Waibel, M. K., et al. (1996). A randomized controlled prospective outcome study of a psychological and pharmacological intervention protocol for procedural distress in pediatric leukemia. *Journal of Pediatric Psychology, 21*(5), 615–631.

Kersun, L. S., & Shemesh, E. (2007). Depression and anxiety in children at the end of life. *Pediatric Clinics of North America, 54*(5), 691–708.

Kreicbergs, U., Valdimarsdóttir, U., Onelöv, E., Henter, J. I., & Steineck, G. (2004). Talking about death with children who have severe malignant disease. *New England Journal of Medicine, 351*(12), 1175–1186.

Lee, E. (1982). A social systems approach to assessment and treatment for Chinese American families. In M. McGoldrick, J. Pearce, & J. Giordano (Eds.), *Ethnicity and family therapy* (pp. 527–551). New York: Guilford.

Liben, S., Papadatou, D., & Wolfe, J. (2008). Paediatric palliative care: Challenges and emerging ideas. *Lancet, 371,* 852–864.

McSherry, M., Kehoe, K., Carroll, J. M., Kang, T. I., & Rourke, M. T. (2007). Psychosocial and spiritual needs of children living with a life-limiting illness. *Pediatric Clinics of North America, 54*(5), 609–629.

Nydegger, R. (2008). Psychologists and hospice: Where we are and where we can be. *Professional Psychology: Research and Practice, 39,* 459–463.

Poltorak, D. Y., & Glazer, J. P. (2006). The development of children's understanding of death: Cognitive and psychodynamic considerations. *Child and Adolescent Psychiatric Clinics of North America, 15,* 567–573.

Shemesh, E., Annunziato, R. A., Shneider, B. L., Newcorn, J. H., Warshaw, J. K., Dugan, C. A., et al. (2005). Parents and clinicians underestimate distress and depression in children who had a transplant. *Pediatric Transplantation, 9*(5), 673–679.

Sourkes, B. (1987). Siblings of the pediatric cancer patient. In J. Kellerman (Ed.), *Psychological aspects of childhood cancer* (pp. 47–69). Springfield, IL: Charles C Thomas.

Sourkes, B. (1992). The child with a life-threatening illness. In J. Brandell (Ed.), *Countertransference in child and adolescent psychotherapy* (pp. 267–284). New York: Jason Aronson.

Sourkes, B. (1995). *Armfuls of time: The psychological experience of the child with a life-threatening illness.* Pittsburgh, PA: University of Pittsburgh Press.

Sourkes, B. (2000). Psychotherapy with the dying child. In H. Chochinov & W. Breitbart (Eds.), *Handbook of psychiatry in palliative care* (pp. 265–274). New York: Oxford University Press.

Sourkes, B., Frankel, L., Brown, M., Contro, N., Benitz, W., Case, C., et al. (2005). Food, toys, and love: Pediatric palliative care. *Current Problems in Pediatric and Adolescent Health Care, 35*(9), 350–386.

Steif, B. L., & Heiligenstein, E. L. (1989). Psychiatric symptoms of pediatric cancer pain. *Journal of Pain and Symptom Management, 4*(4), 191–196.

Trill, M. D., & Kovalcik, R. (1997). The child with cancer: Influence of culture on truth-telling and patient care. *Annals of the New York Academy of Sciences, 809,* 197–210.

Appendix: Selected Books to Be Read by or With Children

CHARLES A. CORR

COLORING AND ACTIVITY BOOKS

Anonymous. (2004). *My Always Sister Coloring Book.* St. Paul, MN: A Place to Remember (1885 University Ave., Suite 110, St. Paul, MN 55104; www.aplacetoremember.com; tel. 800-631-0973 or 651-645-7045). A bunny learns that his new baby sister is sick and has to stay in the hospital. After the baby dies, they have a funeral. Callie experiences many emotions and draws a picture of how he feels.

Arenella, B. B. (2007). *Isabelle's Dream: A Story and Activity Book for a Child's Grief Journey.* Naples, FL: Quality of Life Publishing. (P.O. Box 112050, Naples, FL 34108; 877-513-0099; www.QoLpublishing. com). When Sophia died unexpectedly a week after her first birthday, her sister had many questions. Here, Isabelle dreams about visiting Sophia in heaven. But Sophia tells Isabelle she cannot stay because "You still have a lot of things to do on Earth." However, Sophia says they will be sisters forever, and Isabelle can always find Sophia in her dreams. Activity pages and tips for parents of bereaved children round out the book.

Boulden, J. (1989). *Saying Goodbye.* Weaverville, CA: Boulden (P.O. Box 1186, Weaverville, CA 96093-1186; 800-238-8433). Depicting death as a natural part of life, this book identifies feelings involved in saying goodbye, affirms that love is forever, and allows a child to draw, color, or insert thoughts on its pages.

Carney, K. L. (1997–2001). *Barklay and Eve Activity and Coloring Book Series.* Wethersfield, CT: Dragonfly (277 Folly Brook Blvd.,

Wethersfield, CT 06109; tel. 860-257-7635; www.barklayandeve.com). The eight titles in this series include: #1, *Together We'll Get Through This!*; #2, *Honoring Our Loved Ones: Going to a Funeral*; #3, *What Is the Meaning of Shiva?*; #4, *Our Special Garden: Understanding Cremation*; #5, *What IS Cancer, Anyway?*; #6, *Everything Changes, But Love Endures: Explaining Hospice to Children*; #7, *Precious Gifts: Katie Coolican's Story*; #8, *They're Part of the Family: Barklay and Eve Talk to Children About Pet Loss*. Each book tells stories and offers sketches to color or blank spaces to draw pictures about a loss-related topic that adults may find difficult to discuss with children. Also, two curious Portuguese water dogs learn lessons such as the following: Loss and sadness do happen; those events are not their fault; it is okay to have strong feelings as long as they are expressed in constructive ways; and "we can get through anything with the love and support of family and friends" (#1, p. 5).

Keough, P. (2001). *Remembering Our Baby: A Workbook for Children Whose Brother or Sister Dies Before Birth.* Omaha, NE: Centering Corporation. This workbook encourages writing, drawing, and asking questions about a new baby who was to come but then died. It also offers suggestions about things to do to remember the baby.

Leeuwenburgh, E., & Goldring, E. (2008). *Why Did You Die? Activities to Help Children Cope With Grief and Loss.* Oakland, CA: Instant Help Books (5674 Shattuck Ave., Oakland, CA 94609; www.newharbinger.com). This book offers 40 activities to children who can follow directions, draw pictures, and answer questions about loss and grief experiences. The goal is to help children express difficult feelings, separate myths from facts, and thrive despite their losses.

Mundy, M. (1998). *Sad Isn't Bad: A Good-Grief Guidebook for Kids Dealing With Loss.* St. Meinrad, IN: Abbey Press. Colorful "Elf-help" drawings alternate with pages of text in this guidebook for grieving children. The text confirms it is okay to cry, ask questions, and ask for help, along with other positive, life-affirming messages.

Parga, E. (2009). *Kids Can Cope: An Activity Book From Children for Children Who Are Living With Change and Loss.* Omaha, NE: Centering Corporation. Over 60 pages of text offer many opportunities and cues for children to address what is happening when they encounter life-threatening illnesses—their own or those of loved ones. Children can write out questions, draw pictures, identify sources of help, and engage in other activities to help them cope. A four-page glossary explains terms that may puzzle children.

Stillwell, E. (1998). *Sweet Memories.* Omaha, NE: Centering Corporation. Here are a dozen different hands-on craft activities through which children can preserve memories of loved ones who have died.

Traisman, E. S. (2003). *A Child Remembers: A Write-In Memory Book for Grieving Children* (rev. ed.). Omaha, NE: Centering Corporation. This book permits its owner to describe a special person who has died and their relationship. Issues mentioned include getting the news, the funeral or memorial service, going back to school, coping with feelings, honoring the life, unfinished business, and living without the person who died.

Zotovich, K. D. (2000). *Good Grief for Kids: A Journal to Help Children Cope With Their Grief During Times of Loss.* Los Osos, CA: Journal Keepers (P.O. Box 6173, Los Osos, CA 93412; www.Journalkeepers.com). This book seeks to help children 6–12 years of age write, color, and draw about losses they have experienced, as well as providing guidelines and resources for caring adults.

CONFRONTING DIFFICULT FEELINGS

Blackburn, L. B. (1991). *I Know I Made It Happen: A Gentle Book About Feelings.* Omaha, NE: Centering Corporation. Many children believe they are responsible when bad things happen. Here, adults explain that bad things do not happen because of a child's words or wishes. It helps to share bad feelings and to know you are not at fault. The adults also suggest positive things children can do when someone becomes ill or after an accident, a death, or a divorce.

Doleski, T. (1983). *The Hurt.* Mahwah, NJ: Paulist Press. Justin is hurt by a friend's angry insult, but he does not share his feelings with anyone. He takes The Hurt into his room, like a big, round, cold, hard stone, but it just gets bigger and bigger. It is ruining everything until he finally tells Daddy. As he gradually lets it go, The Hurt gets smaller until at last it goes away.

Holmes, M. M. (2000). *A Terrible Thing Happened.* Washington, DC: Magination Press. A raccoon named Sherman Smith saw a terrible thing happen. He is afraid and tries not to think about it but is still troubled. His stomach and head ache, he feels sad and nervous, he isn't hungry, he can't sleep, and he has bad dreams. Often angry, he gets into trouble at school. Ms. Maple listens to Sherman and helps him understand his feelings. Talking to her and drawing pictures help Sherman vent his feelings.

Johnson, J. (2001). *The Very Beautiful Dragon*. Omaha, NE: Centering Corporation. Two young boys are scared when they first see a dragon and become even more frightened when they encounter it again. It is not enough to be shown there actually is no dragon present. What helps is a neighbor who teaches the boys to face their fears and get to know what scares them. That is how to face down terrors and recognize one's own strengths and power. The *Beautiful Dragons and Other Fears Workbook* accompanies this title.

DEATHS OF PETS

Fontaine, A. (2007). *Ocho Loved Flowers*. Seattle, WA: Stoneleigh Press (P.O. Box 9673, Seattle, WA 98109-9673). Vibrant illustrations depict the activities of Annie's cat. When Ocho gets sick, the vet says he has only about a month to live. Mom explains to Annie what is happening and they agree to take good care of Ocho. He does not like his medicine but loves to chew flowers; when he dies, they get some flowers in his memory.

Harris, R. H. (2001). *Goodbye Mousie*. New York: Margaret K. McElderry Books (Simon & Schuster). A boy finds it hard to believe his pet Mousie has died. Over time, he comes to understand that Mousie is dead and will not be coming back. The boy shares his grief with his parents, and they prepare a shoebox together in which they bury Mousie.

Hemery, K. M. (2000). *Not Just a Fish*. Omaha, NE: Centering Corporation. Marybeth loves her pet goldfish because he always listens to her. Watching him makes her feel calm and peaceful. So Marybeth is shocked when she finds Puffer floating upside down in his bowl. People tell Marybeth they are sorry Puffer died, but they also say he was "just a fish," and that makes her angry. Then her father flushes Puffer down the toilet before Marybeth can bury him! Only Aunt Lizzie understands Marybeth's loss and helps by arranging a memorial service with music, a few words from Marybeth about Puffer, and a heart-shaped pin with a fish painted on it.

Johnson, J. (1998). *Remember Rafferty: A Book About the Death of a Pet...for Children of All Ages* (rev. ed.). Omaha, NE: Centering Corporation. When a sheepdog becomes ill and has to be euthanized, a neighbor, Miss Bertie, who lives with Rafferty's friend, a cat named Four-Eyes, helps by sharing stories of the deaths of other pets and the importance of such losses. Mom encourages the child to write down memories of Rafferty. The book also offers two pages of suggestions for adults and eight pages for a memorial scrapbook.

Meagher, D. K. (2009). *Zach and His Dog: A Story of Bonding, Love, and Loss for Children and Adults to Share Together.* Bloomington, IN: AuthorHouse (1663 Liberty Dr., Suite 200, Bloomington, IN 47403; 800-839-8640; www.authorhouse.com). Nine brief chapters describe a boy's desire to get a dog for his fifth birthday, their adventures together, Freckles's involvement in an accident, his death, and Zach's experiences of loss. Each chapter ends with discussion questions for the child reader; the book concludes with materials to guide adult discussion of the chapters and a brief list of suggested resources

Parker, M. B. (2002). *Jasper's Day.* New York & Toronto: Kids Can Press (2250 Military Rd., Tonawanda, NY 14150; www.kidscanpress.com). On Jasper's day, Riley and his parents let their dog sleep late, feed him favorite foods, take him for a ride, get him ice cream, and bring him to visit Grandma. But this is not a birthday. Jasper is arthritic and ill with cancer, and he sleeps a lot. This is the day Jasper will go to the clinic before his pain pills wear off. There the veterinarian gives him a shot, and his death is quick and gentle. Afterward, the family buries Jasper's body in the backyard, and Riley plans a memory book of Jasper's life.

Tamberrino, S. S. (2001). *Grunt.* Omaha, NE: Centering Corporation. Grunt is an old dog, now blind, in pain, and sick with both cancer and arthritis. A boy and Dad agree it will be best for Grunt to be euthanized. Still, it is not easy to take Grunt to the vet's office and hold him while the shot takes effect. They bury Grunt in a box in the back yard and then sit together and talk about happy times with Grunt and memories of a good dog.

Viorst, J. (1971). *The Tenth Good Thing About Barney.* New York: Atheneum. When a pet cat dies, a boy tries to think of 10 good things to say at the funeral. At first, he can only think of nine: Barney was brave and smart and funny and clean; he was cuddly and handsome and he only once ate a bird; it was sweet to hear him purr in my ear; and sometimes he slept on my belly and kept it warm. Out in the garden, he realizes the tenth good thing: "Barney is in the ground and he's helping grow flowers" (p. 24).

Wilhelm, H. (1985). *I'll Always Love You.* New York: Crown. A boy and his dog grow up together, but Elfie grows old and dies while the boy is still young. Afterward, family members regret not telling Elfie they loved her. But the boy did so every night, and he realizes that his love for her will continue even after her death. He does not want a new puppy right away, even though he knows Elfie will not come back. But he knows there will be a time when he is ready for a new pet.

COPING WITH ILLNESS AND APPROACHING DEATH

Barreras, C. (1998). *Hope in Heaven.* Folsom, CA: Hope in Heaven (P.O. Box 874, Folsom, CA 95763). This book's goal is to show how to talk to a child with a life-threatening illness about the possibility of death. It insists the child is important and is loved and promises that no one will give up the fight, even while admitting that things do not always turn out as we might wish. God's presence and the expectation of heaven are affirmed.

Copeland, K. M. (2005). *Mama's Going to Heaven Soon.* Minncapolis, MN: Augsburg Fortress. Vivid colors and minimal text in this storybook for young readers describe reactions of two children when their Mama becomes ill, and Daddy says she will soon go to heaven to live with God and the angels. Mama will be gone forever, but she will always love her children. Remembering her love and talking about feelings with Daddy can help.

McNamara, J. W. (1994). *My Mom Is Dying: A Child's Diary.* Minneapolis, MN: Augsburg Fortress. The illustrated diary format of this book offers an imaginary record of Kristine's conversations with God while her mother is dying. Author's notes identify Kristine's reactions and suggest how they could become a basis for talking with children.

Miles, M. (1971). *Annie and the Old One.* Boston: Little, Brown. A 10-year-old Navajo girl is told it will be time for her grandmother "to go to Mother Earth" when her mother finishes weaving a rug. Annie secretly tries to delay the weaving, until the adults realize what is going on, and her grandmother explains that we are all part of a natural cycle. When Annie realizes she cannot hold back time, she is ready herself to learn to weave.

Mills, J. C. (2004). *Gentle Willow: A Story for Children About Dying* (2nd ed.). Washington, DC: Magination Press. A squirrel named Amanda is upset to learn her tree-friend, Gentle Willow, is dying. The Tree Wizards explain that they can give Gentle Willow their love and some medicines to help her feel more comfortable, but they cannot make her all better. Even so, they point out many gifts Gentle Willow has given to Amanda over the years—gifts that are now memories in Amanda's mind. One day, Gentle Willow cries and tells Amanda she is afraid to face this change. Amanda listens, stays close, and tells Gentle Willow the comforting story of a caterpillar that changed into Yellow Butterfly.

Mills, J. C. (2003). *Little Tree: A Story for Children With Serious Medical Problems* (2nd ed.). Washington, DC: Magination Press. Little Tree lives happily at the edge of the forest until a storm causes her to lose some branches and makes her sad. Two tree wizards remove some dead branches and point out that Little Tree still has a strong trunk, deep roots, and a beautiful heart. Wizardly care helps Little Tree cope with her fears.

Newman, L. (1995). *Too Far Away to Touch.* New York: Clarion. Uncle Leonard is Zoe's favorite relative. He takes her to special places, tells her jokes, and makes her laugh, but now he is sick and has less energy (gradually, we learn he has AIDS). One day at a planetarium and another evening at the seashore watching the sky, Uncle Leonard says he will be like the stars after he dies, "too far away to touch, but close enough to see."

Peterkin, A. (1992). *What About Me?* Washington, DC: Magination Press. Laura likes to play with her younger brother, Tom. When Tom gets sick and is hospitalized, Laura misses him, feels responsible for his illness, and worries he might die. Their parents and other adults focus mostly on Tom, ignoring Laura's needs. Finally, the adults explain Tom's illness to her, let them play together, and take her out for a special treat.

Powell, E. S. (1990). *Geranium Morning.* Minneapolis, MN: Carol-Rhoda Books. Two children—Timothy, whose father died suddenly in an accident, and Frannie, whose mother is dying—struggle with strong feelings, memories, guilt ("if onlys"), and some unhelpful adult actions. In sharing their losses, the children help each other; Frannie's father and her mother (before she dies) are also helpful.

Raschka, C. (2007). *The Purple Balloon.* New York: Schwartz & Wade (Random House). The author writes that children who become aware of their impending deaths often draw their feelings as blue or purple balloons, released and floating free. Here balloon images first depict the death of an elderly person before turning to a dying youngster. The text says, "Good help makes leaving easier" and offers suggestions for those who want to help make dying not so hard.

PICTURE BOOKS ABOUT LOSS AND GRIEF

Brown, M. W. (1958). *The Dead Bird.* Reading, MA: Addison-Wesley. Some children find a dead bird in the woods, touch its body, bury it in a simple ceremony, and return to the site each day to mourn ("until they forgot"). Sadness need not last forever; life can go on again.

Clardy, A. F. (1984). *Dusty Was My Friend: Coming to Terms With Loss*. New York: Human Sciences. When his friend is killed in an automobile accident, Benjamin struggles to understand his reactions. His parents let him express his thoughts and feelings, mourn his loss, remember the good times shared with Dusty, and go on with his own life.

Cohn, J. (1987). *I Had a Friend Named Peter: Talking to Children About the Death of a Friend*. New York: Morrow. This book describes Beth's reactions when a car kills her friend, along with helpful ways her parents and teacher respond to Beth, her classmates, and Peter's parents. It also suggests ways for adults to help children cope with death.

Connolly, M. (1997). *It Isn't Easy*. New York: Oxford University Press. When his 9-year-old brother is killed in a car accident, a little boy is sad, lonely, and angry. Recalling good memories of his brother, he gradually gets used to being an only child—but it isn't easy.

Czech, J. (2000). *The Garden Angel: A Young Child Discovers a Grandparent's Love Grows Even After Death*. Omaha, NE: Centering Corporation. After her grandpa dies, 8-year-old Camilla remembers his many gardening activities. This year she plants the new garden herself, dresses a scarecrow with his old clothes, and spreads his old quilt behind it like an angel's wings.

Dean, A. (1992). *Meggie's Magic*. New York: Viking Penguin. After 8-year-old Meggie's illness and death, her parents and sister are sad and lonely. Then one day, Meggie's sister goes to their special place and finds it still filled with magical qualities of the games they used to play. The girl realizes that Meggie's magic still remains inside each of them.

De Paola, T. (1998). *Nana Upstairs and Nana Downstairs*. New York: Putnam's (rev. ed.). Tommy loves to visit his great-grandmother ("Nana Upstairs"). When told she has died, he does not believe it until he sees her empty bed. A few nights later, when Tommy sees a falling star, his mother suggests it might represent a kiss from Nana who is now "upstairs" in a new way. Later, an older Tommy has a similar experience after the death of "Nana Downstairs" (his grandmother).

Ewart, C. (2003). *The Giant*. New York: Walker & Co. Before she died, a young girl's mother said that a giant would look after her. As the seasons pass on the family farm, the girl misses her mother and searches for the giant. Her Pa says there is no such thing as a giant, but the girl keeps searching everywhere until she realizes that her tall, strong Pa is, in fact, the giant looking after her.

Fassler, J. (1971). *My Grandpa Died Today.* New York: Human Sciences. Although his grandfather tried to prepare David for his impending death, when it happens, David still needs to mourn his loss. He finds comfort in good memories and knowing that his grandfather does not want him to be afraid to live and enjoy life.

Fox, M. (1994). *Tough Boris.* New York: Harcourt Brace. Boris von der Borch is a huge, tough, scruffy, greedy, fearless, and scary pirate—just like all pirates. But when his parrot dies, Boris cries and cries—just like all pirates and everyone else.

Gryte, M. (1988). *No New Baby: For Siblings Who Have a Brother or Sister Die Before Birth.* Omaha, NE: Centering Corporation. Also available in Spanish as *No Tenremos Un Nuevo Bebé.* Grandma uses a young bud to explain that although most buds keep growing and become flowers, some do not, like this one. The girl realizes that something like this happened to the new baby their family had expected. Grandma says no one is to blame, and we do not always have answers.

Hemery, K. M. (1998). *The Brightest Star.* Omaha, NE: Centering Corporation. Molly and her parents often went to the beach at night to look at the stars. After Mommy dies, Molly is troubled when Ms. Baylor asks her class to draw pictures of their families for the school's open house. Daddy helps by taking Molly to the beach and pointing out the brightest star, which reminds her of her mother's love.

Hodge, J. (1999). *Finding Grandpa Everywhere: A Young Child Discovers Memories of a Grandparent.* Omaha, NE: Centering Corporation. A little boy realizes that Grandpa is dead, not "lost" as the adults keep saying. He consoles himself and his grandma with this thought: Grandpa always said "to do something for someone you have to put a little of yourself into it." So memories of Grandpa and his love live on everywhere the boy looks.

Horn, G. (White Deer of Autumn). (1992). *The Great Change.* Hillsboro, OR: Beyond Words Publishing. (20827 NW Cornell Rd., Suite 500, Hillsboro, OR 97124-9808; 800-284-9673). A Native American woman explains to her 9-year-old granddaughter that death is not the end, but the Great Change—a part of the unbreakable Circle of Life in which our bodies become one with Mother Earth while our souls or spirits endure.

Jordan, M. K. (1989). *Losing Uncle Tim.* Morton Grove, IL: Albert Whitman. After Uncle Tim develops AIDS and dies, his nephew finds solace in an idea they once had discussed: "Maybe Uncle Tim is like the sun, just shining somewhere else."

Joslin, M. (1998). *The Goodbye Boat.* Grand Rapids, MI: Eerdmans. Unadorned pictures and just a few words describe friendships, loving, loss and grief, and the view that when a boat is gone from view, it is surely sailing somewhere new.

Muñoz-Kiehne, M. (2000). *Since My Brother Died/Desde Que Murió Mi Hermano.* Omaha, NE: Centering Corporation. With text in both English and Spanish, a child wonders if a brother's death is only a dream or if anything could have been done to keep him from dying. The child reports sadness in the family as well as the child's own physical reactions (headaches and stomachaches). Afraid of forgetting this brother, the child begins to paint, with simple watercolor illustrations gradually turning into rainbows and the confidence that life can go forward.

Schlitt, R. S. (1992). *Robert Nathaniel's Tree.* Maryville, TN: Light-bearers Publishers (P.O. Box 5895, Maryville, TN 37802-5895). A child describes the things he likes in getting ready for a new baby. But when the baby dies, there is much that he does not like. Later, he likes caring for Robert Nathaniel's memorial tree and being his big brother—"even if he didn't come home."

Schwiebert, P. (2003). *We Were Gonna Have a Baby, But We Had an Angel Instead.* Portland, OR: Grief Watch (2116 NE 18th Ave., Portland, OR 97212; 503-284-7426; www.griefwatch.com). Bright, colored drawings and a single sentence on each page let a young boy tell how excited he was as he anticipated the birth of the new baby. But something happened; the baby died, and everyone is sad. Having the baby would have been more fun than missing him.

Schwiebert, P. (2007). *Someone Came Before You.* Portland, OR: Grief Watch. Vivid artwork and simple text describe a couple who desperately want to have a child with whom to share their love. They are excited during the pregnancy but saddened when the baby dies. In time, their hearts stretch enough to enable them to have a new baby—YOU! Through this book and in other ways, they share the memory of that prior baby with you.

Shriver, M. (1999). *What's Heaven?* New York: Golden Books. This book reflects the author's discussions with her 5- and 6-year-old daughters when their great-grandmother, Rose Fitzgerald Kennedy, died. It depicts heaven as a place without hurts where your soul goes when you die.

Simon, J. (2001). *This Book Is for All Kids, But Especially My Sister Libby. Libby Died.* Austin, TX: Idea University Press. After the death of his young sister, 5-year-old Jack struggled to understand what happened and its consequences. This book shares his questions and comments, along with dramatic, colorful illustrations.

Woodson, J. (2000). *Sweet, Sweet Memory.* New York: Hyperion Books for Children. When Grandpa dies, a young African American girl named Sarah and her grandmother find solace in stories and funny memories of him and by recalling him saying, "The earth changes... Like us it lives, it grows. Like us... a part of it never dies. Everything and everyone goes on and on."

Yeomans, E. (2000). *Lost and Found: Remembering a Sister.* Omaha, NE: Centering Corporation. A girl reports confusing experiences that she and her parents have after her sister dies, but also realizes many ways in which she still feels her sister's love. So Paige is not "lost" forever; she is right there in their hearts, and the girl knows where to find her.

Zolotow, C. (1974). *My Grandson Lew.* New York: Harper & Row. When 6-year-old Lewis wonders why his grandfather has not visited lately, his mother says she did not tell him his grandfather had died because he never asked. The boy says he had not needed to ask; his grandfather just appeared to be with him when his parents were away. Son and mother share warm memories of someone they both miss: Lewis says, "He gave me eye hugs"; his mother concludes, "Now we will remember him together and neither of us will be so lonely as we would be if we had to remember him alone."

PICTURE BOOKS WITH ANIMALS TELLING ABOUT LOSS AND GRIEF

Duckworth, L. (2003). *Ragtail Remembers: A Story That Helps Children Understand Feelings of Grief.* Omaha, NE: Centering Corporation. A mouse is sad, lonely, and angry when he learns his friend, Old Tim the cat, is dead. Ragtail wishes Old Tim would come back, but as he learns what dead means, he begins to come to terms with his loss, and he makes a new friend.

Gant, L. G. (2003). *Never Say Goodbye.* Nashville, TN: Tommy Nelson. An older rabbit tells a beloved younger rabbit that she has to "go away." Netta's replies to Hannah's questions convey two convictions: "God has made me a new home," and even in death, they will always be connected.

Goldman, L. (1997). *Bart Speaks Out: An Interactive Storybook for Young Children About Suicide.* Los Angeles: Western Psychological

Services. A family dog describes confusion, hurt, and grief after the suicide of his owner, thereby providing words for children to use to discuss the sensitive topic of suicide.

Krasny Brown, L., & Brown, M. (1998). *When Dinosaurs Die: A Guide to Understanding Death.* Boston: Little, Brown. Young children are introduced to issues of death and loss through a cartoon format in this book.

London, J. (1994). *Liplap's Wish.* San Francisco: Chronicle Books. As a rabbit builds the winter's first snow bunny, he remembers his grandma and misses her. He finds comfort in an old Rabbit's tale his grandmother used to tell about how, long ago, when the First Rabbits died, they became stars in the sky that even now come out at night, watch over us, and shine forever in our hearts.

Mellonie, B., & Ingpen, R. (1983). *Lifetimes: A Beautiful Way to Explain Death to Children.* New York: Bantam. Multiple examples affirm that "there is a beginning and an ending for everything that is alive. In between is living. . . . So, no matter how long they are, or how short, lifetimes are really all the same. They have beginnings, and endings, and there is living in between."

O'Toole, D. (1988). *Aarvy Aardvark Finds Hope.* Burnsville, NC: Compassion Books (477 Hannah Branch Rd., Burnsville, NC 28714). Many animals offer unhelpful advice to Aarvy Aardvark as he tries to come to terms with the deaths of his mother and brother. Only one friend, Ralphy Rabbit, really listens to Aarvy as the two of them share their losses and is truly helpful.

Puttock, S., & Bartlett, A. (2001). *A Story for Hippo: A Book About Loss.* New York: Scholastic Press. Bright artwork depicts the friendship between Hippo and Monkey. They share many activities until one day Hippo tells Monkey it is time for her to die. Monkey is sad: Who will tell wonderful stories, play games, and laugh at his jokes? When Monkey promises not to forget her, Hippo says "that will be part of my happily ever after." After Hippo dies, Little Chameleon persuades Monkey that Hippo's stories still need to be told—and a new friendship begins.

Varley, S. (1992). *Badger's Parting Gifts.* New York: Mulberry Books. Badger is old and knows he must die but is mainly worried about his friends. They are sad when he dies but find comfort in the special memories he left with each of them and in sharing those memories with others.

Weigelt, U. (2003). *Bear's Last Journey.* New York: North-South Books. All the forest animals are upset when they learn that Bear is sick. Bear explains he has to say goodbye to his friends because he is dying.

He says no one really knows what it means to be dead; some say one simply sleeps, and Bear and others believe one goes to heaven. The little fox is frustrated: He wants to know what will happen now, and he is angry when Bear dies. Sharing memories of Bear and some of his things helps the little fox and other animals.

BOOKS DESIGNED TO EDUCATE OR GUIDE CHILDREN

Adams, G. (2006). *Lessons From Lions: Using Children's Media to Teach About Grief and Mourning* + CD. Little Rock, AR: Center for Good Mourning, Arkansas Children's Hospital (800 Marshall St., Slot 690, Little Rock, AR 72202; www.goodmourningcenter.org). This booklet explains how to use 10 slides from Disney's *The Lion King* (1994) with children to encourage discussions about grief and mourning. The text and slides illustrate three common but unhelpful reactions following a loss: (1) running away from the problem, the pain, and those who know and love you best; (2) pretending the bad thing never happened—living as if the past does not matter; and (3) treating your feelings, experiences, and story as a big secret—never telling anyone about them. The positive lesson is that by not making these mistakes, we can keep the person with us in our hearts.

Goldman, L. (2006). *Children Also Grieve: Talking About Death and Healing.* Philadelphia: Jessica Kingsley. Here we find a story told by a dog named Henry and his questions to readers; a section for making a memory book; a two-page glossary of grief words; and advice for caring adults. Henry's story uses photographs and text to tell about the sadness following the death of Grandfather. He explains what death means, what grief is like, things to do when you are sad or scared, and ways to feel a bit better, while offering blank spaces in which readers can respond to questions.

Grollman, E., & Johnson, J. (2006). *A Complete Book About Death for Kids.* Omaha, NE: Centering Corporation. This book discusses three main topics: death and feelings, funerals and cemeteries, and cremation. Photos and a few simple sentences on each page address child readers and adults involved with those children. The authors are experts in this field, sensitive to the needs of children, and insightful in how to address those needs.

Johnson, J., & Johnson, M. (2004). *Where's Jess?* (rev. ed.) Omaha, NE: Centering Corporation. To help young children cope with infant sibling death, this book explores topics such as what "death" means, re-membering the dead child, and the value of tears.

Tesh, M., & Schleich, E. (2009). *Are You Like Me?: Helping Children Cope With Suicide.* Clearwater, FL: The Hospice of the Florida Suncoast (5771 Roosevelt Blvd., Clearwater, FL 33760; 727-586-4432; www.thehospice.org). This colorful book responds to difficult questions children often have about the meaning and causes of suicide. It seeks to validate children's responses after a loved one dies from suicide, encourage discussion with trusted adults, and guide conversations.

STORYBOOKS ABOUT DEATH, LOSS, AND GRIEF

Alexander, A. K. (2002). *A Mural for Mamita/Un Mural Para Mamita.* Omaha, NE: Centering Corporation. Text in both English and Spanish. A young girl, her family, and her neighbors plan a fiesta to celebrate the life of her grandmother, who recently died after a long illness. Mamita was well-known and greatly loved as the proprietor of the local bodega. The girl paints a brilliant mural on the side of Mamita's store.

Alexander, S. (1983). *Nadia the Willful.* New York: Pantheon Books. After Nadia's older brother dies, her father in his grief decrees that no one may speak of this death. Nadia helps her father and others cope with their grief by willfully talking about her brother.

Alexander-Greene, A. (1999). *Sunflowers and Rainbows for Tia: Saying Goodbye to Daddy.* Omaha, NE: Centering Corporation. A 10-year-old African American girl tells about her sadness and grief when Daddy dies suddenly, along with her fears that Mama might also die and leave the children alone. She explains how people came to the house to share their love for Daddy, support her family, and bring food. It helps Tia to be involved in preparations and participate in the funeral, especially when she is allowed to bring Daddy's favorite sunflowers to the ceremony and sees a big, shining rainbow.

Barron, T. A. (2000). *Where Is Grandpa?* New York: Philomel Books. Family members share memories after Grandpa dies. When a boy asks where Grandpa is now, they decide Grandpa is in heaven and say, "Heaven is any place where people who love each other have shared some time together." It comforts the boy to think of Grandpa as way off in the Never Summer range of the Rockies that they used to look at from the tree house they built together.

Bunting, E. (1982). *The Happy Funeral.* New York: Harper & Row. Mother's promise of a "happy funeral" for their grandfather puzzles two young Chinese American girls. At the funeral, food is given for the journey to the other side, paper play money is burned, people cry and give speeches, a marching band plays, and a small candy is provided after the ceremony to "sweeten the sorrow" of the mourners. In the end, the children realize that although no one was happy that grandfather died, his good life and everyone's fond memories did make for a happy funeral.

Bunting, E. (1999). *Rudi's Pond.* New York: Clarion. While Rudi is sick, his classmates send cards and make a big "GET WELL RUDI" banner for his hospital room. After Rudi dies, the children write poems and make a memorial pond in the schoolyard that attracts a beautiful hummingbird.

Bunting, E. (2000). *The Memory String.* New York: Clarion. Laura is still grieving after her mother's death 3 years earlier and is having trouble accepting her new stepmother, Jane. Laura consoles herself with a string of buttons going back three generations in her family, but especially with the buttons from Mom's prom and wedding dresses and from the nightgown she was wearing when she died. When the string breaks, the 43 buttons are scattered all over the yard. Laura, Dad, and Jane find all but one button. Dad suggests that they substitute a twin for the missing button, but Laura overhears Jane wisely saying, "It's like a mother. No substitute allowed" (p. 25). When Jane finds the missing button, Laura asks her to help restring the buttons.

Coerr, E. (1977). *Sadako and the Thousand Paper Cranes.* New York: Putnam's. This book is based on a true story about a Japanese girl who died of leukemia in 1955 as one of the long-term results of the atomic bombing of Hiroshima. In the hospital, a friend reminds Sadako of the legend that the crane is supposed to live for a thousand years, and good health will be granted to a person who folds 1,000 origami paper cranes. With family members and friends, they begin folding. Sadako died before the project was finished, but her classmates completed the work, and children all over Japan have since contributed money to erect a statue in her memory.

Cohn, J. (1994). *Molly's Rosebush.* Morton Grove, IL: Albert Whitman. Molly was eagerly waiting for the birth of her new baby when her mother experienced a miscarriage. Her father explained to her that not all babies are strong enough to be born. And her grandma helped by comparing this death to a flower bud that does not blossom.

Coutant, H. (1974). *First Snow*. New York: Knopf. A Vietnamese American girl is eager to encounter snow for the first time, but puzzled when her parents say, "Grandmother is dying." No one explains to Liên what it means to be dying until she is told to catch a snowflake on her finger. The snowflake is a tiny, fleeting thing, beautiful and delicate. When the sun causes the edges of the snowflake to burst into a thousand tiny rainbows, it changes to a drop of water and falls on the ground, where it nourishes a tiny pine tree. This affirms Liên's Buddhist beliefs: Life and death are but two parts of the same thing.

Dickerson, J. G. (1995). *Grandpa's Berries: A Story to Help Children Understand Grief and Loss*. Johnstown, PA: Cherubic Press (P.O. Box 5306, Johnstown, PA 15904). When Alice visits her grandparents, she likes gathering vegetables and berries from the garden. One day she spies a single, orange-gold berry on a golden raspberry bush that Grandma says had never done well. The berry tastes wonderful, and Grandpa says she can have the bush all for her own. Many summers later, after Grandpa has died, Alice discovers the little bush is also dead. As they share their grief, Alice's mother says she will never forget the special taste of those berries even though now they are gone. The same will be true for Grandpa: "The remembering will become easier until one day you'll notice that all that's left is the sweetness that you remember. Just like the berries."

DiSunno, R., Zimmerman, S., & Ruffin, P. (2004). *Jeremy Goes to Camp Good Grief*. Westhampton Beach, NY: East End Hospice (481 Westhampton-Riverhead Rd., P.O. Box 1048, Westhampton Beach, NY 11978; www.eeh.org). This story describes a weeklong summer day camp for children who have experienced the death of someone they love. During the week, Jeremy learns how to give words to his grief and begins to realize how loss has changed his family. With new friends, he realizes he is not alone in his grief.

Douglas, E. (1990). *Rachel and the Upside Down Heart*. Los Angeles: Price Stern Sloan. After Rachel's daddy died when she was 4 years old, she is sad and has to move from a house with a yard, green grass, and two dogs in Kentucky to a noisy apartment in New York City. Mommy says Daddy will always be in Rachel's heart, so she begins to draw hearts but can only make them upside down. Later, Rachel finds some new friends, and some of her hearts are upside up. Finally, when a new friend's father dies, Rachel is able to talk to him and help him with his loss.

Evarts, D. M. (1998). *The Butterfly Bush: A Story About Love*. Omaha, NE: Centering Corporation. For her birthday, Grandma gave Lindsay some sticks they planted in a clearing by the woods. But nothing happened, and Lindsay soon forgot the developing butterfly bush. Each year after that, Grandma gave Lindsay expensive birthday gifts. Lindsay always thanked Grandma for these gifts but then ran off to open other presents while Grandma visited the butterfly bush. One year, Grandma died before Lindsay's birthday, but not before mailing her a small package containing a locket with two pictures inside; one of Grandma holding Lindsay as a small child, the other of a mass of beautiful purple flowers. In the woods, Lindsay found the butterfly bush was now over 15 feet tall and covered with lovely flowers and butterflies. Years later, Grandma Lindsay gave her granddaughter a pot of sticks on her birthday.

Frantz, I. (2007). *Sargeant's Heaven* (www.sargeantsheaven.org). Family members developed this tribute to a boy born with an illness that took his life shortly before his second birthday. The book describes the place where Sargeant is now. It is a place filled with happy activities where Sargeant is busy all day and can look down at Earth, celebrate holidays, and remember his family.

Goble, P. (1993). *Beyond the Ridge.* New York: Aladdin/Simon & Schuster. At her death, while her family members prepare her body according to their custom, an elderly Plains Indian woman experiences the afterlife believed in by her people. She makes the long climb up a difficult slope to see the Spirit World beyond the ridge.

Godfrey, J. (1996). *The Cherry Blossom Tree: A Grandfather Talks About Life and Death.* Minneapolis: Augsburg Fortress. A cherry tree planted by Grandpa and 5-year-old Harriet is covered with pink blossoms each year on his birthday. One year, when the tree has fallen down, Grandpa says, "It was very, very old, and time for it to die." He explains, "Everything that is born has to die sometime.... And that makes us sad. But death is a new beginning, like waking up after a long sleep." Grandpa adds that everyone who loves God can go and be with him when they die in a new and different place called heaven.

Hanks, B. H. (1996). *Green Mittens From Grandma: A Gentle Story About a Child's Grief.* Omaha, NE: Centering Corporation. While Grandma made green mittens for a young girl, she told stories about when she was a little girl and the girl's mother was small. After Grandma died, the girl missed Grandma, recalled things she had said and done, and held tight to her green mittens. She knew her memories of Grandma and the green mittens would stay with her always.

Hanson, R. (2005). *A Season for Mangoes.* New York: Clarion. In Jamaica, Sareen is concerned about participating in her first sit-up, a ritual in which villagers share food and tell stories to celebrate the life of her recently deceased grandmother. Sareen discovers that sharing her stories of Nana's passion for mangoes helps ease her sadness.

Hemery, K. M. (2001). *The Healing Tree*. Omaha, NE: Centering Corporation. One day Baba Marta tells Sammy a story about the oak tree in her backyard with a long bare strip on its trunk where there is no bark. Baba says that when she was a little girl, her mamma became very sick and died. Baba just wanted to be alone, so she went to the swing under the tree where she had shared many good times with her mother. When a storm came up, Baba did not want to leave that special place. Her Papa rushed out and took Baba into the house just before lightning struck the tree and tore off one of its massive branches. The next day, Papa said they were all just like the tree: in pain from losing a big part of their family. Like the tree, he said, we will heal and go on living, but life will be different and forever changed. After telling her story, Baba explains to Sammy that her Papa was right; she did go on to enjoy love, laughter, and a good life.

Holmes, M. M. (1999). *Molly's Mom Died* and *Sam's Dad Died*. Omaha, NE: Centering Corporation. In these two brief books, Molly and Sam tell about how things are different after a parent has died, how they feel now, and what they can do to feel better.

Hopkinson, D. (2001). *Bluebird Summer*. New York: Greenwillow Books/HarperCollins. Every summer, Meg and her little brother Cody visit Grandpa's farm. Now that Grandma has died, they miss her great garden of flowers and vegetables, along with the bluebirds that used to visit regularly to enjoy their favorite plants. Then the children decide to pull out the tangle of weeds and grass that has sprung up and replace it with a new garden in memory of Grandma and a new birdhouse to encourage the bluebirds to return.

Hucek, M. W. (2002). *Lilacs for Grandma*. Omaha, NE: Centering Corporation. Megan shared a special hiding place with Grandmother under an old lilac bush in the yard. So, as Grandmother is dying, she asks Megan to bring her some lilacs each morning when they bloom and promises to enjoy them even when she no longer can talk. After Grandmother dies, Megan brings a big bouquet to put on her grave as "a kiss for you Grandma, to send you on your way" (p. 20).

Kadono, E. (1999). *Grandpa's Soup*. Grand Rapids, MI: Eerdmans. After his wife's death, an old man gradually realizes that making her meatball soup and sharing it with friends eases his loneliness. While singing the song his wife used to guide her soup making, the old man progressively adds more ingredients as he advances from smaller to larger pots and better and better tasting soup to share with his newfound friends (three mice, a cat, a dog, and some children).

Klein, L. (1995). *The Best Gift for Mom.* New York: Paulist Press. Jonathan's dad died when he was just a baby, so he feels bad when classmates talk about their two parents, and he can only mention his mom. After Mom shares stories about his dad, plus the only two songs Dad knew to sing when he put Jonathan to bed ("Taps" and "Silent Night"), Jonathan joins a glee club. At a school concert, Jonathan sings a solo rendition of "Silent Night" as a surprise present for Mom and then writes a letter to his father.

Lowden, S. G. (1993). *Emily's Sadhappy Season.* Omaha, NE: Centering Corporation. Emily's daddy taught her to play baseball. After he dies, her grief is confusing and complicated. She fears playing baseball might have caused Daddy's death and worries that Mom might now die. In time, Mom encourages Emily to teach her to play baseball. Mom says they will feel "sadhappy": happy remembering fun times they had with Daddy, but sad because he is not with them.

McLaughlin, K. (2001). *The Memory Box.* Omaha, NE: Centering Corporation. A boy is mad at Grandpa for dying when he promised they would go fishing. Mommy says the boy will miss doing things with Grandpa but asks him to hold onto good memories of all they shared. She tells him to make a memory box and put into it objects to help remember this special relationship.

Miller, M. (1987). *My Grandmother's Cookie Jar.* Los Angeles: Price Stern Sloan. Grandma's cookie jar is shaped like an Indian head. It is a little scary to her granddaughter, but not when Grandma takes off the headdress and takes out a cookie. As they share cookies each evening, Grandma tells stories of her Indian people of long ago. The stories make Indian ways, pride, and honor come alive for the girl. One day, after Grandmother is gone, Grandfather gives the jar to the girl and tells her it is full of Grandma's love and her Indian spirit heritage. The girl knows that when she has her own children and tells Grandma's stories with each cookie, she will be keeping Grandma's spirit alive and the spirit of those who went before her.

Mills, L. (1991). *The Rag Coat.* Boston: Little, Brown. After Papa died, Minna could not start school because she had to help Mama make quilts to support the family. Later, Minna wanted to go to school, but did not have a winter coat. Happily, the "Quilting Mothers" volunteered to piece together a coat out of scraps of old materials and get it ready for

Sharing Day. Some children teased her about her rag coat, but not after she told the stories about each scrap she had selected.

Morning, B. (1994). *Grandfather's Shirt.* Omaha, NE: Centering Corporation. Peter enjoyed working with Grandfather in his garden. When Grandfather got sick and was hospitalized, Peter and his parents shared special memories of Grandfather. After Grandfather's death, Peter's dad told him they were "the seeds Grandfather left behind when he died. Grandfather lives forever through us and our memory of him." Peter found comfort in Grandfather's old baseball cap and especially in his musty old gardening shirt.

Old, W. (1995). *Stacy Had a Baby Sister.* Morton Grove, IL: Albert Whitman. Stacy liked her baby sister but was jealous because she took up a lot of their parents' time. Then one night, Stacy woke to find the baby had died from SIDS. Stacy wondered if she had caused the baby to die and if she would get SIDS. She also had trouble sleeping until she talked with her parents about it.

Plourde, L. (2003). *Thank You, Grandpa.* New York: Dutton Children's Books. Over the years, a girl and her grandfather enjoyed walking in the woods together. They shared many discoveries, including finding a dead grasshopper one day. The girl asked, "What can we do?" Grandpa replied, "We can say thank you and good-bye." Over time, Grandpa became too old to walk, and eventually the girl had to walk alone. As she walked, she thought, "Thank you, Grandpa, for our walks. You kept me steady when I wasn't so steady. You let me run ahead when I was ready to run ahead. Thank you for sharing spiderweb tears and firefly flashes. But most of all, thank you for teaching me the words I need to say.... Grandpa, I love you and I'll miss you. But I will never forget you. Thank you and good-bye."

Roper, J. (2001). *Dancing on the Moon.* Cheverly, MD: SIDS Educational Services (2905 64th Ave., Cheverly, MD 20785; tel. 877-935-6839). Five-year-old Carly is jealous over all the attention paid to the new baby. But when Nigel dies suddenly, she is sad and wants very much to bring him back home. In a dream, she imagines flying to the moon to find him. Carly knows she cannot bring Nigel back but realizes he is inside her heart, and they will never again be apart.

Rosen, M. (2004). *Michael Rosen's Sad Book.* Cambridge, MA: Candlewick Press. Michael Rosen pretends to be happy when he is sad "because I think people won't like me if I look sad." Michael is sad because his son died. Sometimes he wants to talk about this and sometimes not. Sometimes he does crazy things because life just is not the same as it used to be. Michael knows being sad is not the same as being bad, so he tries to figure out ways of being sad that do not hurt so much. He also tries to do one thing each day that involves a good time—it can be anything so long as it does not make anyone else unhappy. Memories of Eddie and good times seem to help.

Russo, M. (1996). *Grandpa Abe.* New York: Greenwillow Books. Soon after Sarah's first birthday, her grandmother marries Abe, and she gets a new grandfather. Through the years, Sarah and Abe share many happy times together, but after Abe dies when she is 9, Sarah knows that he enriched her life in many ways.

Santucci, B. (2002). *Anna's Corn.* Grand Rapids, MI: Eerdmans. Grandpa taught Anna to hear the music of the wind breathing through dry corn stalks and gave her a few kernels of corn to keep for her own. After his death, Anna is reluctant to plant her seeds next spring as promised because she fears they will then be gone forever. Mama explains that the seeds will not be gone; they will just be different. In the fall, after Anna planted the seeds, and the corn has grown, Anna again hears the song she had shared with Grandpa, and she takes some new seeds to plant next spring.

Schwiebert, P., & DeKlyen, C. (1999). *Tear Soup: A Recipe for Healing After Loss.* Portland, OR: Grief Watch (2116 NE 18th Ave., Portland, OR 97212; 503-284-7426; www.tearsoup.com). "An old and somewhat wise woman" called Grandy who has just suffered a big loss in her life makes tear soup by filling a large pot over and over again with tears, feelings, memories, and misgivings. Rejecting foolish advice, *Tear Soup* affirms all of the feelings and experiences that bereaved persons encounter, while encouraging them as they cope with loss and grief.

Simon, N. (1979). *We Remember Philip.* Chicago: Whitman. When the adult son of a primary school teacher dies in a mountain climbing accident, Sam and other members of his class observe how Mr. Hall is affected by his grief. In time, the children persuade Mr. Hall to share with them a scrapbook and other memories of his son, and they plant a tree as a class memorial.

Vogel, R. H. (2002). *The Snowman* (rev. ed.). Omaha, NE: Centering Corporation. Two brothers are building their first snowman since their dad died. Talking about Dad's illness and how he died helps answer some of 8-year-old Buddy's questions. It also lets 12-year-old Tommy release some of his internal anger and guilt. Using Dad's old pipe, hat, and favorite scarf, the boys finish the snowman and share good memories of Dad.

Wrenn, E. (2001). *The Christmas Cactus.* Omaha, NE: Centering Corporation. As Christmas nears, Nana is in the hospital, and Megan cannot feel joy. When they prepare to visit, Megan asks her father if Nana is dying. He says, "We never know for sure when someone will die....So what we need to do is tell the people we love just how much we love them, every chance we get." Megan brings a Christmas cactus as a present, and Nana explains that this plant waits all year for the one season when it blooms. "Well, I think our lives are like that. We live and grow for a whole lifetime. And then at the end of our lives, we bloom. We become something very different and wonderful." Nana asks Megan to take care of the plant and to think of her when it blooms.

Zebrowski, M. (2002). *Babka's Serenade.* Omaha, NE: Centering Corporation. Babka shared magical stories with her granddaughter in her garden. After Babka dies, Pipkin cannot imagine not seeing her anymore and finds it hard when Mama and Daddy sell her house. In the spring, Pipkin decides to build Babka's garden in their backyard so that she can visit that special place anytime she wishes. There she smells the flowers and thinks of Babka and her stories.

Name Index

Subject Index

Lightning Source UK Ltd.
Milton Keynes UK
UKHW022132260819
348667UK00005B/15/P